Handbook of Radar Signal Analysis

Advances in Applied Mathematics
Series Editors:
Daniel Zwillinger, H. T. Banks

CRC Standard Curves and Surfaces with Mathematica
David H. von Seggern

Handbook of Peridynamic Modeling
Edited by Florin Bobaru, John T. Foster, Philippe H Geubelle, Stewart A. Silling

Linear and Complex Analysis for Applications
John P. D'Angelo

Advanced Engineering Mathematics with MATLAB, 4th Edition
Dean G. Duffy

Quadratic Programming with Computer Programs
Michael J. Best

Introduction to Radar Analysis
Bassem R. Mahafza

CRC Standard Mathematical Tables and Formulas, 33rd Edition
Edited by Daniel Zwillinger

The Second-Order Adjoint Sensitivity Analysis Methodology
Dan Gabriel Cacuci

Operations Research
A Practical Introduction, 2nd Edition
Michael Carter, Camille C. Price, Ghaith Rabadi

Handbook of Mellin Transforms
Yu. A. Brychkov, O. I. Marichev, N. V. Savischenko

Advanced Mathematical Modeling with Technology
William P. Fox, Robert E. Burks

Handbook of Radar Signal Analysis
Bassem R. Mahafza, Scott C. Winton, Atef Z. Elsherbeni

The Geometry of Special Relativity, Second Edition
Tevian Dray

https://www.routledge.com/Advances-in-Applied-Mathematics/book-series/CRCADVAPPMTH?pd=published,f orthcoming&pg=1&pp=12&so=pub&view=list

Handbook of Radar Signal Analysis

Edited By
Bassem R. Mahafza
Scott C. Winton
Atef Z. Elsherbeni

CRC Press
Taylor & Francis Group
Boca Raton London New York

CRC Press is an imprint of the
Taylor & Francis Group, an **informa** business

A CHAPMAN & HALL BOOK

First edition published 2022
by CRC Press
6000 Broken Sound Parkway NW, Suite 300, Boca Raton, FL 33487-2742

and by CRC Press
2 Park Square, Milton Park, Abingdon, Oxon, OX14 4RN

Library of Congress Cataloging-in-Publication Data

Names: Mahafza, Bassem R., editor. | Winton, Scott C., editor. |
Elsherbeni, Atef Z., editor.
Title: Handbook of radar signal analysis / edited by Bassem R. Mahafza,
Scott C. Winton, Atef Z. Elsherbeni.
Description: First edition. | Boca Raton : C&H\CRC Press, 2021. | Series:
Advances in applied mathematics | Includes bibliographical references
and index.
Identifiers: LCCN 2021000972 (print) | LCCN 2021000973 (ebook) | ISBN
9781138062863 (hardback) | ISBN 9781315161402 (ebook)
Subjects: LCSH: Radar. | Signal processing.
Classification: LCC TK6575 .H3185 2021 (print) | LCC TK6575 (ebook) | DDC
621.3848--dc23
LC record available at https://lccn.loc.gov/2021000972
LC ebook record available at https://lccn.loc.gov/2021000973

ISBN: 9781138062863 (hbk)
ISBN: 9781032003559 (pbk)
ISBN: 9781315161402 (ebk)

DOI: 10.1201/9781315161402

Table of Contents

Preface

In recent years, the radar book market has been flooded with many publications on the subject matter. A small portion of these publications were written to serve as college-level textbooks. Many others are solely focused on recent hardware developments and they cater to a very specific and narrowly defined segment of readers. Alternatively, a small percentage of these publications took aim at being a single comprehensive source on the subject; accordingly, the depth and breadth of the presented material in more cases than not lacked the necessary rigor and ease of presentation. A limited number of these publications have been very successful, however. Nonetheless, it is our contention that the need and demand for a comprehensive reference book focused on radar signal analysis remains very strong. Therefore, our desire to write this new handbook has materialized into this product.

This new handbook on radar signal analysis adopts a deliberate and systematic approach for presentation of the subject matter. It uses a clear and consistent level of delivery while maintaining strong and easy to follow mathematical details. The emphasis of this book is on radar signal types and their relevant signal processing, and not on radar systems hardware or components. Because of the nature of the topics found in this publication along with the associated level of presentation, it is our belief that this handbook will serve as a valuable reference to a wide range of audience. More specifically, college-level students, practicing radar engineers, as well as casual readers of the subject are the intended target audience of the first few chapters of this book. The level of advancement, as the book chapters progress, grows in complexity and specificity. Accordingly, later chapters are intended for practicing engineers, graduate college students, and advanced readers. Finally, the last few chapters contain several special topics on radar systems that are both educational and scientifically entertaining to all readers.

The word, radar, is an abbreviation for *ra*dio *d*etection *a*nd *r*anging. Radar systems use modulated bandpass radio frequency (RF) signals and directive antennas to search for targets within the radar field of view. When this RF signal is incident on a target, it interacts with the target in accordance with Maxwell's equations, and RF energy is scattered out in all directions from the target. Some portion of the scattered energy (target return or echo) is in the direction of the radar. The radar, through its antenna, captures the echo signal and through signal processing (using specialized hardware along with signal / data processing algorithms), the radar extracts target information such as target range, target velocity, target angular position, etc. More specifically, the radar system emits a completely known waveform (signal) into free space with the expectation that a modified version of this transmitted signal scattered from the target will return to the radar. Accordingly, understanding the radar signal types and their associated radar signal processing techniques are key to understating how radars function. In this context, the radar system hardware becomes an enabler that generates the desired transmitted signals and facilitates the extraction of target information from the returned echoes.

The presentation of topics in this handbook takes the reader on a scientific journey whose major landmarks comprise the different radar subsystems and components. In this context, the chapters of this book follow the radar signal along this journey from its birth to the end of its life. Along the way, the different relevant radar subsystems are analyzed and discussed in a great level of detail. First, the waveform generator produces a lowpass waveform (signal), then through modulation this lowpass signal is up-converted in frequency into a bandpass signal inside the transmitter. The bandpass signal goes through the radar directive antenna and is transformed into an electromagnetic (EM) wave that propagates through space (or medium of propagation). This signal is modified in both amplitude and phase as it travels through the propagation medium, and it experiences significant changes as it interacts with the target. The target acts as an RF source and scatters the incident EM energy in many directions. Portions of this scattered energy usually returns to the radar and enters its receiver through its antenna. The radar receiver's main purpose is to process received signals that resemble the original transmitted ones to extract the basic target attributes (range, size, range rate, angles, etc). The signal processor reshapes the noisy received bandpass signal into a noisy copy of the originally transmitted lowpass signal. Finally, through sampling and quadrature components processing, the signal is transformed into data that is input into the radar data processor whereby using different algorithms the radar estimates the target kinematics such as its track information, classification and type.

Chapter 1 presents a top-level overview of signal theory relevant to radar signal processing. The material in this chapter is not intended to serve as a course on signal design and analysis. It instead presents a quick refresher to many of the relevant concepts of signal analysis in order to facilitate better understanding of radar systems. The motivation behind introducing this chapter is derived from the fact that better knowledge of the time and frequency domain characteristics of radar signals is key to understanding how radar systems operate.

The main thrust of Chapters 2 and 3 is radar fundamentals. Chapter 2 presents a bird's eye view of radar systems operation and introduces radar systems basic concepts. It discusses the functional subsystems of radar systems. Chapter 3 dives into the derivation of the radar range equation in its many forms and variants. It also talks in depth about system noise and the different sources of radar losses. Pulsed radars as well as continuous wave radars are presented.

Chapter 4 talks about radar wave. Environmental effects like refraction, diffraction, multipath, and diffraction are discussed. Chapter 5 is concerned with an overview of electronic warfare techniques. The presentation covers three major classes of EW: electronic support measures (ESM), electronic counter-measures (ECM) (also called electronic attack (EA)), and electronic counter-counter measures (ECCM) (also called electronic protection (EP)). Common jamming techniques along with common electronic protection techniques are discussed. Hypothetical case studies are introduced to enhance the understating of the material presented.

Chapter 6 introduces the concept of the matched filter. It presents the unique characteristic of the matched filter and develops a general formula for the output of the matched filter that is valid for any waveform. Stationary and moving target cases are analyzed. Pulse compression is then introduced. The correlation processor and stretch processor are presented. High range resolution processing using stepped frequency waveforms is also analyzed.

Chapter 7 takes the reader into the world of most common radar signal types, both analog and discrete. The ambiguity functions for both types of waveforms are analyzed. The analog waveforms discussed include the single unmodulated pulse, linear frequency modulation (LFM) pulse, unmodulated pulse train, LFM pulse train, stepped frequency waveforms, and nonlinear FM waveforms. The rest of the chapter is concerned with common discrete radar waveform types. Unmodulated pulse-train codes as well as binary codes, polyphase codes, and frequency codes are analyzed.

Chapter 8 starts by presenting a single pulse detection with known and unknown signal parameters. Then detection of fluctuating targets is introduced. The analysis is extended to include target fluctuation based on the Swerling target models. Detailed discussion is included of coherent and noncoherent integration in the context of a square law detector. An overview of CFAR, cumulative probability of detection, and M-out-of-N detection are also discussed.

Chapter 9 is concerned with pulse Doppler radars and radar clutter. Area clutter as well as volume clutter are defined and the radar equation is re-derived to reflect the importance of clutter, where in this case, the signal-to-interference ratio becomes more critical than the signal-to-noise ratio. A step-by-step mathematical derivation of clutter RCS, and the statistical models for the clutter backscatter coefficient is also presented. Analyses of the moving target inductor (MTI) and pulse Doppler radars are then presented. Delay line cancelers and how they are used to mitigate the impact of clutter within the radar signal processor are also presented.

Chapter 10 focuses on the two major building blocks of modern tracking approaches: track filtering and data association. This chapter provides an introductory examination of radar tracking while highlighting important concepts and explaining mature techniques. It is intended to provide the reader a foundation on which additional learning can be applied. Radar tracking is the estimation and maintenance of target parameters that can be measured or derived by the radar, such as range and angle. The accuracy of the measurements themselves can be improved by combining received signals as to drive out systemic errors. Monopulse is one of these well-known techniques. The two main functions to be performed in radar tracking are data association and filtering. The first is an attempt to assign incoming detections to established tracks create new ones. Data association techniques range from the simple, such as nearest neighbor, to extremely complicated, such as multiple hypothesis tracking. Track filtering is an attempt to improve the estimate by removing measurement noise. The workhorse of track filtering is the Kalman filter, which has its roots in least squares estimation. The Kalman filter is extremely versatile, can be adapted to nonlinear target dynamics or measurements, and can be included in multiple filter implementations.

Chapters 11 presents the phenomenon of target scattering, and methods of computing the radar cross-section (RCS) are introduced. Target RCS fluctuations due to aspect angle, frequency, and polarization are also investigated. Analytical expressions for RCS characteristics of canonical objects like spheres, cylinders and wedges are derived. Approximate expressions for RCS of simple shapes like finite length cylinders, circular, rectangular, and triangular flat plates, and truncated cones (frustums) are also presented. For more complex-shaped targets like rockets and airplanes, the FDTD method is used to compute their RCS characteristics. Numerical examples are provided to show the salient RCS features of these targets and their combinations. Chapter 12 considers RCS prediction methods, commonly found in predictive codes, common types of RCS data products, and the RCS of complex objects. The radiation and scattering effects are discussed at a high level and several numerical solution methods are presented. RCS computation methods of complex objects are discussed in this chapter. This chapter provides an overview of integral equation techniques, which are most commonly used in electromagnetic scattering analysis. It then discusses the most commonly encountered numerical methods used to solve these equations. Several examples are then considered, comparing the accuracy of different methods for the same problem.

Radar antennas and phased array radars are discussed in Chapter 13. This chapter presents different types of antennas and antenna array in 1-D, 2-D and 3-D configurations commonly used in radar systems. Different methods for tapering the antenna radiation characteristics are illustrated through expressions and numerical examples. Feeding networks (transmission lines) and beamforming networks are also addressed in order to improve the radiation efficiency of these antennas. This chapter starts by developing the general array formulation. Linear arrays and several planar array configurations such as rectangular, circular, rectangular with circular boundaries, and concentric circular arrays are discussed. Beam steering with and without using a finite number of bits is analyzed. Scan loss is also presented.

Chapter 14 discusses tactical synthetic aperture radars (SAR). This chapter presents the key concepts required for high-resolution SAR image formation. Radar system requirements for down range (fast time) and cross-range (slow time) resolution are presented along with array focusing requirements and pulse repetition frequency considerations. Motion compensation required to correct for nonideal platform motion and auto-focus processing to remove residual image formation errors are presented. The use of the polar reformat algorithm of radar returns to compensate for motion through resolution cells is covered with application to high-resolution image formation. The definition of image resolution and the image quality metrics of Peak Sidelobe Level and Integrated Sidelobe Level are presented. Spotlight Synthetic Aperture Radar, Interferometric Synthetic Aperture Radar and Inverse Synthetic Aperture Radar imaging modalities are discussed. Examples for the various key concepts are presented.

Chapter 15 is concerned with wideband radar applications. First, the operational bands are defined using the different standards. This chapter discusses the definitions of various bandwidths, highlights the differences between radar bands and bandwidths, defines narrow band, medium band and wideband radar waveforms, and other wideband radar applications and analyses. Finally Chapter 16, focuses on less commonly covered material regarding phased array antennas, particularly as applied to radar. The chapter begins by describing the various types of electronic steering and various architectures including passive electronically steered array (PESA) and active electronically steered array (AESA). Also discussed are arrays using analog beamforming, digital beamforming, and hybrid beamforming, including use of sub-arrays. The chapter emphasizes modern digital arrays, and the performance advantages of digital versus analog beamforming are discussed. Along the way, digital receiver-exciter (DREX) and direct RF sampling and synthesis (contrasted with superheterodyne and homodyne systems) are discussed including digital down-conversion (DDC), digital up-conversion (DUC), finite impulse response (FIR) filters, analog-to-digital converter (ADC) and digital-to-analog converter (DAC). Also discussed are performance metrics such as signal-to-noise ratio (SNR), spur-free dynamic range (SFDR), noise figure (NF), and third order intercept (TOI), and challenges associated with all-digital array required data rates. Software defined radio (SDR) concepts are described enabling the maximum flexibility in array antenna utilization. Array antenna patterns, their predictions using array factor (AF) and the Huygens-Fresnel principle, and electronic scan loss and bandwidth limitations are described. Finally, grating lobes and simultaneous receive beams are discussed. Extensive examples are presented throughout.

The chapter contributors of this handbook comprise experienced academia members and practicing radar engineers. Their combined years of academic and real-world experiences are in excess of 175 years. Together, they bring a unique, easy-to-follow mix of mathematical and practical presentations of the topics discussed in this book. Two of those contributors have served or still serve as college professors at different academic institutions around the United States. Two more have been, for many years, affiliated with very prestigious research institutes and/or centers. Two have served or still serve the Department of Defense (DoD) specializing in radar systems and associated advanced technologies. The remaining contributors are pillars in the field who have worked on, or are working on, some of the most advanced radar systems in the world. See the "Chapter Contributors" section of this book to learn more about these individuals.

Finally, due to the chapter contributors' professional and employment affiliations, the Editors of this handbook obtained, and have on file, the applicable public release statements as required by their respective affiliates. Additionally, Scott Winton's affiliation with The MITRE Corporation (see "Chapter Contributors") is provided for identification purposes only, and is not intended to convey or imply MITRE's concurrence with, or support for, the positions, opinions, or viewpoints expressed by Scott Winton. Accordingly, the following specific MITRE Corporation release statement is included: "Approved for Public Release; Distribution Unlimited. Public Release Case Number 20-2887."

Bassem R. Mahafza
bmahafza@phasedn.com
Huntsville, Alabama, USA
United States of America
September, 2020

***

Scott C. Winton
Huntsville, Alabama, USA
United States of America
September, 2020

***

Atef Z. Elsherbeni
Golden, Colorado, USA
United States of America
September, 2020

Editors

Mahafza, Bassem R.

Bassem R. Mahafza is the President and Founder of Phased n Research. Dr. Mahafza is recognized as a radar subject matter expert and is widely known for authoring several leading reference and textbooks on Radar Systems. Dr. Mahafza has been a member of the IEEE (Institute of Electrical and Electronics Engineers) since 1984, he has been awarded a Senior IEEE member in 1994, and has been recently nominated for an IEEE Fellow. Dr. Mahafza's over 30 years of experience includes extensive work in radar technology, radar design and analysis (including all sensor subcomponents), radar simulation and model design, radar signatures and radar algorithm development. Through his industry career, he has supported numerous government organizations. Dr. Mahafza's academic experience includes developing and teaching several graduate- and undergraduate-level courses, such as random signal and noise, introduction to radar systems, advanced radar techniques, and signal processing. He supervised many Master's degree student and several PhD candidates. During his academic tenure, his research was mainly focused on advancements in radar and sensor technology. Furthermore, Dr. Mahafza has conducted detailed research in Phased Array Radars, Advanced Radar Signal Processing, Electronic Counter-Measures, and Counter-Counter Measure Techniques.

Winton, Scott C.

Scott C. Winton is a Senior Principal Sensors Engineer with the MITRE Corporation with over 30 years of technical experience in computational electromagnetics, electromagnetic compatibility, and radar systems. He currently leads a team of engineers supporting the Ground Sensors Directorate of the Missile Defense Agency at Redstone Arsenal. Dr. Winton received his PhD from Northeastern University. During his academic tenure, Dr. Winton's research encompassed ground penetrating radar and electromagnetic propagation in inhomogeneous and turbid media. Throughout his career, Dr. Winton has supported numerous Department of Defense (DOD) service components and agencies by developing, testing, and integrating electromagnetic systems. He also has considerable experience in high-powered microwave (HPM), electronic warfare, and wireless communications. Dr. Winton has published numerous papers in several technical journals and has served as a reviewer for IEEE Antennas and Propagation Society.

Elsherbeni, Atef Z.

Atef Z. Elsherbeni earned a Ph.D. degree in Electrical Engineering from Manitoba University, Winnipeg, Manitoba, Canada, in 1987. He started his engineering career as a part-time Software and System Design Engineer at the Data System Center, Cairo, Egypt. Dr. Elsherbeni has been Professor and Associate Dean for Research and Graduate Programs at the University of Mississippi, Dobelman Distinguished Professor and Interim Department Head of the EECS Department at Colorado School of Mines, and the EE Department Head. He was selected as Finland Distinguished Professor by the Academy of Finland and TEKES. Dr. Elsherbeni is the Editor-in-Chief of *ACES Journal*, past Associate Editor of *Radio Science Journal*, past Chair of the Engineering and Physics Division of Mississippi Academy of Science, past Chair of Educational Activity Committee for IEEE Region 3 Section, and the general Chair for the APS-URSI Symposium, President of ACES Society, and IEEE Antennas and Propagation Society Distinguished Lecturer. Dr. Elsherbeni is a Fellow member of IEEE and ACES.

Contributors

Listed in Alphabetic Order

Balla, Robert J.

Robert J. Balla is the Vice President of Systems Engineering at Phased n Research, Inc. He previously served in numerous senior positions at the Aviation and Missile Research Development Center (AMRDEC) and Space and Missile Defense Center (SMDC) in Huntsville, AL, including Missile Defense Agency Sensors Directorate Chief Engineer, AN/TPY-2 Deputy Product Manager, THAAD Systems Integration and Advanced Technology Division Chief, NATO Medium Extended Air Defense System (MEADS) Fire Control and Surveillance Radar Section Lead and Chief Engineer, U.S. Army Cruise Missile Defense System (CMDS) Radar Division Chief, and JLENS Chief Engineer. His experience includes concept development, advanced technology, research and development, countermeasure algorithm development, signal processing, program management and acquisition, hardware and software development, modeling and simulation, system integration and verification, and range testing for radar and missile defense systems. He received a Commanders Award for Civil Service, an Achievement Medal for Civilian Service, and is a member of the Honorable Order of Saint Barbara. He has authored or coauthored numerous published technical papers. Bob Balla earned a BSEE from Virginia Tech, Master of Science in Program Management from the Naval Postgraduate School, and an MBA from the Florida Institute of Technology.

Barnes, Mark A.

Mark A. Barnes is a Principal Engineer at Phased n Research, Inc. He earned his Master of Science Electrical Engineering from The Ohio State University and has over 30 years of experience with commercial and defense systems. He is an expert in electromagnetics, radio frequency systems, algorithms, and project management with significant experience in electronic warfare, radar, wireless communications, and self-locating systems for defense and commercial applications. His efforts span from research in ground penetrating radar for remediation to validation of high-fidelity simulation of missile defense discrimination radars, with emphasis on wideband and ultra-wideband radars.

During his career, he authored a dozen published technical papers and nine patents. Barnes couples his radar expertise with his innate ability to facilitate communications and foster collaboration across multiple design teams to jointly meet larger system of systems objectives. Barnes' radar work is a continuing legacy with respect to his radar engineer father, Walter Barnes, and his mathematics educator grandmother, Anne Barnes who, according to family lore, learned and taught radar shortly after its introduction to the United States.

Fluhler, Herbert U.

Herbert U. Fluhler is President of FreEnt Technologies, Inc., a veteran-owned small business providing technology research and development support services primarily in the defense sector. He holds a MS in Physics with additional post-graduate work from the University of Alabama in Huntsville focused in Optics, and a BS in Physics from Virginia Military Institute. He has studied and worked on military radars of different types for over 40 years, starting with the venerable Nike Hercules and FAAR radars in the U.S. Army as a Captain in Missile Material Management. He has performed studies, simulations, and technology assessments on both domestic and foreign Theater Missile Defense (TMD), and Strategic Missile Defense (SMD) radars along with associated interceptors and fire units. He was a key radar systems engineer in the design of arguably the first commercially available Ultra-Wide Band (UWB) RadarVision and SoldierVision through wall interferometric imaging radars offered by Time Domain Corporation. He has worked on the design and build of a variety of UWB antennas and arrays primarily using the Finite Difference Time Domain (FDTD) and Connected Array technology for Ground Penetrating Radar (GPR) and Over The Horizon (OTH) radar applications. In 1994 he helped birth the U.S. Army's AN/TPQ-64 "Sentinel" Short Range Air Defense (SHORAD) radar, and continues to support the Sentinel Product Office (SPO), continually devising new ways to further improve the capabilities and performance of this now classic radar. He holds two dozen U.S. patents, primarily in antenna and radar technology. He also works on Small Business Innovative Research (SBIR) projects and reading books from his ever growing technical library. Between work he enjoys biking, MATLAB® and FileMaker Pro programming, shop projects and spending time with his 3 children and 5 grandchildren.

Gibson, Walton C.

Walton C. Gibson was born in Birmingham, Alabama, USA on December 9, 1975. He received a B.S. degree in electrical engineering from Auburn University in 1996, and an M.S. degree in electrical engineering from the University of Illinois Urbana-Champaign in 1998. He is a recognized authority in the area of computational electromagnetics (CEM), and has authored *The Method of Moments* in Electromagnetics, a textbook geared to graduate-level courses in CEM, as well as the research community and practicing professionals. He is the owner and President of Tripoint Industries, Inc., through which he has authored *lucernhammer*, an industry-standard suite of radar cross-section solver codes implementing low- and high-frequency numerical techniques. His professional interests include electromagnetic theory, computational electromagnetics, moment methods, numerical algorithms and parallel computing.

Shrider, Kenny D.

Kenny D. Shrider is currently the Chief Scientist at Phased n Research. Through his work, he has accumulated nearly 30 years of experience with radar and electronic warfare related phenomenology. He received his BSEE in 1992 and MSEE in 1997 from the University of Alabama in Huntsville. His work experience includes efforts related to the study, development, and analysis of strategic and tactical US missile and air defense radars and of US air strike aircraft, which included evaluation and analysis of threat air defense systems.

From an early age, Shrider learned many physics-based concepts from his father Kenneth R. Shrider, a 40-year employee of Lockheed Missiles and Space. After receiving his bachelor's degree, he worked at various aerospace technology companies, including Teledyne Brown Engineering, XonTech Inc., Northrop Grumman Mission, Lockheed Martin Aeronautics Advanced Development Programs (SkunkWorks), deciBel, and Phased n Research. He was a fellow at both Lockheed Martin and deciBel. Throughout his career, radar and RF systems technology have been a primary focus with phased array antenna technology being at the center of Shrider's efforts. He has worked on phased array radar programs including Aegis SPY-1, SPY-6, GBR-P, AN/TPY-2, SBX, UEWR, LRDR, HDR-H, AN/TPQ-53, AN/MPQ-64 (A4), and other US radars. He has also extensively studied US adversarial radars, including phased array.

Smith, Brian J.

Brian J. Smith is the Senior Research Scientist (ST) - Radio Frequency Sensors at The U.S. Combat Capabilities Development Command, Aviation & Missile Center. Dr. Smith was selected as a Senior Research Scientist (ST) in July 2017. He serves at the U.S. Army Combat Capabilities Development Command, Aviation & Missile Center (AvMC), Redstone Arsenal, AL. He conducts applied research for advanced ground based radar and millimeter wave seeker systems for the United States Army. Dr. Smith is a nationally and internationally recognized expert in the research and development of radars, Millimeter Wave (MMW) seekers and passive Radio Frequency (RF) sensors for use in Army land combat, Air Defense weapons, and Aviation systems with 60 publications, 6 US Patents, and citations in national and international journals. He provides mentoring for ~2000 technical employees as the Deputy Activity Career Program Manager for Career Program 16 (DAPCM CP-16) at the AvMC. Dr. Smith holds a PhD, a Master of Science, and a Bachelor of Science; all degrees are in Electrical and Computer Engineering. All degrees are from the University of Alabama in Huntsville. Dr. Smith is a certified Professional Engineer in the State of Alabama.

Acknowledgments

We want to thank all of the chapter authors for their contributions and for their reviews of other chapters. We would like to acknowledge the following individuals for their reviews of the book chapters and for their invaluable feedback and comments: Scott MacDonald, Wes Wells, Bill Audenaert, Grace Barnes, and Rama Inguva. A special thanks to Veysel Demir, Matthew Inman, Joshua Kast, Yiming Chen, Andres Velasco, and Yasushi Kanai for their reviews and partial contributions to Chapters 11 and 13.

Chapter 1

Signals and Systems - Refresher

Bassem R. Mahafza

In this chapter a top-level overview of signal theory relevant to radar signal processing is presented. The material in this chapter is not intended to serve as a course on signal design and analysis. It presents a quick refresher to many of the relevant concepts of signal analysis in order to facilitate better understanding of radar systems. Generally speaking, most electrical systems deal with complicated time domain and / or frequency domain signals (or waveforms); to this end, radar systems are no exception. Understanding the time and frequency domains characteristics of radar signals is key to understanding how radar systems operate. In this book, the terms "signal" and "waveform" will be used interchangeably to mean the same thing.

1.1. Signal Classification

In general, electrical signals (waveforms) can represent either current or voltage and may be classified into two main categories: energy signals and power signals. Energy signals can be deterministic or random, while power signals can be periodic or random. A signal is said to be random if it is a function of a random parameter. Additionally, signals may be divided into lowpass or bandpass signals. Signals that contain very low frequencies (close to *0Hz*; i.e., dc) are called lowpass signals; otherwise they are referred to as bandpass signals. Through modulation, lowpass signals can be converted into bandpass signals.

The average power P for the current or voltage signal $x(t)$ over the interval (t_1, t_2) across a 1Ω resistor is

$$P = \frac{1}{t_2 - t_1}\int_{t_1}^{t_2} |x(t)|^2 \ dt.$$

Eq. (1.1)

The signal $x(t)$ is said to be a power signal over a very large interval $T = t_2 - t_1$, if and only if it has finite power and satisfies the relation:

$$0 < \lim_{T \to \infty} \frac{1}{T}\int_{t_1}^{t_2} |x(t)|^2 \ dt \ < \infty.$$

Eq. (1.2)

Using Parseval's theorem, the energy E dissipated by the current or voltage signal $x(t)$ across a 1Ω resistor, over the interval (t_1, t_2), is

$$E = \int_{t_1}^{t_2} |x(t)|^2 \ dt.$$

Eq. (1.3)

The signal $x(t)$ is said to be an energy signal if and only if it has finite energy,

$$E = \int_{-\infty}^{\infty} |x(t)|^2 \, dt \; < \infty.$$
Eq. (1.4)

A signal $x(t)$ is said to be periodic with period T if and only if

$$x(t) = x(t + nT) \qquad for \; all \; t$$
Eq. (1.5)

where n is an integer. By definition, a time limited signal over the period (t_1, t_2) will be non-zero over this interval and zero elsewhere. Clearly, this signal will have finite energy, but will have zero average power over all time. Alternatively, a periodic signal that comprises a periodic sum of finite energy signals (time limited) will have finite average power and infinite total energy when evaluated over all time.

1.2. Signal Expansion Functions

It is often desirable to express complicated signals as a function of much simpler orthogonal functions, referred to as the basis functions. A basis functions set $S = \{\varphi_n(t) \; ; \; n = 1, 2, ...\}$ is said to be orthogonal over the interval (t_1, t_2) if and only if

$$\int_{t_1}^{t_2} \varphi_i^*(t)\varphi_j(t)dt = \int_{t_1}^{t_2} \varphi_i(t)\varphi_j^*(t)dt = \begin{Bmatrix} 0 & i \neq j \\ \lambda_i & i = j \end{Bmatrix}$$
Eq. (1.6)

where the asterisk indicates complex conjugation and λ_i are constants. If $\lambda_i = 1$ for all i, then the set S is said to be an orthonormal set. Accordingly, one may express a certain time domain signal $x(t)$ as an expansion of the orthogonal basis functions $\{\varphi_n(t) \; ; \; n = 1, 2, ...\}$ as follows

$$x(t) = C_1\varphi_1(t) + C_2\varphi_2(t) + C_3\varphi_3(t) + ... + C_N\varphi_N(t) + ...$$
Eq. (1.7)

where $\{C_n \; ; \; n = 1, 2, ...\}$ are complex constants that are yet to be determined. Multiply both sides of Eq. (1.7) by $\varphi_N^*(t)$ and integrate over the interval (t_1, t_2). More specifically,

$$\int_{t_1}^{t_2} x(t)\varphi_N^*(t)dt = \int_{t_1}^{t_2} [C_1\varphi_1(t) + C_2\varphi_2(t) + ... + C_N\varphi_N(t) + ...]\varphi_N^*(t)dt.$$
Eq. (1.8)

By using the orthogonality definition in Eq. (1.6), the right-hand side of Eq. (1.8) is zero except for the Nth term which is equal to $C_N\lambda_N$. It follows that Eq. (1.8) can be rewritten as,

$$\int_{t_1}^{t_2} x(t)\varphi_N^*(t)dt = \int_{t_1}^{t_2} C_N\varphi_N(t)\varphi_N^*(t)dt = C_N\lambda_N.$$
Eq. (1.9)

Therefore, the constant C_N is

$$C_N = \frac{1}{\lambda_N} \int_{t_1}^{t_2} x(t)\varphi_N^*(t)dt,$$
Eq. (1.10)

and if the basis functions set $\{\varphi_n(t) \; ; \; n = 1, 2, ...\}$ is orthonormal, then Eq. (1.10) becomes

$$C_N = \int_{t_1}^{t_2} x(t)\varphi_N^*(t)dt.$$
Eq. (1.11)

There are many possible orthogonal / orthonormal sets that can be used for the expansion, amongst the most common are the Bessel functions, Legendre polynomials, and Tschebyscheff polynomials. For radar systems, the most common and relevant expansion is the Fourier series expansion.

Equation (1.7) may be approximated as

$$x(t) \approx \sum_{n=1}^{N} C_n \varphi_n(t)$$

Eq. (1.12)

where $\{C_n \; ; \; n = 1, 2, ..., N\}$ are complex constants and $\{\varphi_n(t) \; ; \; n = 1, 2, ..., N\}$ is now a finite set of basis functions. If the integral-square error over the interval (t_1, t_2) is equal to zero as N approaches infinity, i.e.,

$$\lim_{N \to \infty} \int_{t_1}^{t_2} \left| x(t) - \sum_{n=1}^{N} C_n \varphi_n(t) \right|^2 dt = 0$$

Eq. (1.13)

then the set $\{\varphi_n(t) \; ; \; n = 1, 2, ..., N\}$ is said to be a complete set, and Eq. (1.12) becomes an equality, and the general form for the constants C_n is given by

$$C_n = \frac{\int_{t_1}^{t_2} x(t) \varphi_n^*(t) dt}{\int_{t_1}^{t_2} |\varphi_n(t)|^2 dt} ; \; ' \; n = 1, 2, ..., N .$$

Eq. (1.14)

1.2.1. Fourier Series Expansion

Trigonometric Fourier Series

Many of the signals used in radar systems are periodic power signals. If one is to expand a periodic function, then it makes sense to also use a periodic set of basis functions in the expansion. Recall the following relationships

$$\int_{-T/2}^{T/2} \cos(n\omega_0 t) \cos(m\omega_0 t) dt = \begin{cases} 0 & n \neq m \\ T/2 & n = m \neq 0 \\ T & n = m = 0 \end{cases}$$

Eq. (1.15)

where T is the period, $\omega_0 = 2\pi/T$, n and m are positive integers. Similarly,

$$\int_{-T/2}^{T/2} \sin(n\omega_0 t) \sin(m\omega_0 t) dt = \begin{cases} 0 & n \neq m \\ T/2 & n = m \neq 0 , \\ 0 & n = m = 0 \end{cases}$$

Eq. (1.16)

finally,

$$\int_{-T/2}^{T/2} \sin(n\omega_0 t) \cos(m\omega_0 t) dt = 0 \qquad \textit{for all } n \textit{ and } m .$$

Eq. (1.17)

It follows that the trigonometric sinusoidal functions are orthogonal over the period T.

The trigonometric Fourier series expansion uses the following orthogonal set of basis functions

$$\{\varphi_n(t) \; ; \; n = 0, 1, 2, \ldots\} = \{\cos(n\omega_0 t); \; n = 0, 1, 2, \ldots\} \qquad \text{Eq. (1.18)}$$

and one can expand the periodic time domain function $x(t)$ as

$$x(t) = C_0 + C_1\cos(\omega_0 t) + C_2\cos(2\omega_0 t) + \ldots + C_N\cos(N\omega_0 t) + \ldots \qquad \text{Eq. (1.19)}$$

which can be written as

$$x(t) = \sum_{n=0}^{\infty} C_n\cos(n\omega_0 t). \qquad \text{Eq. (1.20)}$$

To simplify Eq. (1.20) make the substitution

$$C_n\cos(n\omega_0 t) = a_n\cos(n\omega_0 t) + b_n\sin(n\omega_0 t) \qquad \text{Eq. (1.21)}$$

where

$$C_n = \sqrt{a_n^2 + b_n^2} \qquad ;(n \neq 0) \qquad \text{Eq. (1.22)}$$

and a_n, b_n are real constants. Accordingly $x(t)$ can be written as the sum of its even and odd parts, as

$$x(t) = C_0 + \sum_{n=1}^{\infty} a_n\cos(n\omega_0 t) + \sum_{n=1}^{\infty} b_n\sin(n\omega_0 t) \qquad \text{Eq. (1.23)}$$

and by using the orthogonality property defined in Eq. (1.6) we get

$$a_n = \frac{2}{T}\int_{-T/2}^{T/2} x(t)\cos(n\omega_0 t)dt \qquad \text{Eq. (1.24)}$$

$$b_n = \frac{2}{T}\int_{-T/2}^{T/2} x(t)\sin(n\omega_0 t)dt. \qquad \text{Eq. (1.25)}$$

Finally using the relation $\omega_0 = 2\pi/T$, the trigonometric Fourier series can be written as

$$x(t) = C_0 + \sum_{n=1}^{\infty} a_n\cos\left(\frac{2\pi n t}{T}\right) + \sum_{n=1}^{\infty} b_n\sin\left(\frac{2\pi n t}{T}\right). \qquad \text{Eq. (1.26)}$$

In general, the coefficients a_n are all zeros when the signal $x(t)$ is an odd function of time (i.e., $x(t) = -x(-t)$). Alternatively, when the signal is an even function of time (i.e., $x(t) = x(-t)$) then all b_n are equal to zero. Also, for $n = 0$ the coefficient b_0 is 0.

Complex Exponential Fourier Series

Recall the following two trigonometric identities,

$$\cos(n\omega_0 t) = \frac{e^{jn\omega_0 t} + e^{-jn\omega_0 t}}{2} \qquad \text{Eq. (1.27)}$$

$$\sin(n\omega_0 t) = \frac{e^{jn\omega_0 t} - e^{-jn\omega_0 t}}{2j}, \qquad \text{Eq. (1.28)}$$

where $j = \sqrt{-1}$. Next, rewrite Eq. (1.23) in the form,

$$x(t) = \sum_{n=-\infty}^{\infty} \frac{a_n}{2} \cos(n\omega_0 t) + \sum_{n=-\infty}^{\infty} \frac{b_n}{2} \sin(n\omega_0 t).$$

Eq. (1.29)

Substituting Eqs. (1.27) and (1.28) into Eq. (1.29) and collecting terms yield,

$$x(t) = \frac{1}{2}\left[\sum_{n=-\infty}^{\infty} \frac{a_n - jb_n}{2} e^{jn\omega_0 t} + \sum_{n=-\infty}^{\infty} \frac{a_n + jb_n}{2} e^{-jn\omega_0 t} \right].$$

Eq. (1.30)

As clearly indicated in Eq. (1.30), for each positive n in the first summation there is an equal term for each negative n in the second summation. It follows that,

$$x(t) = \sum_{n=-\infty}^{\infty} \frac{a_n - jb_n}{2} e^{jn\omega_0 t}$$

Eq. (1.31)

which can be rewritten as

$$x(t) = \sum_{n=-\infty}^{\infty} C_n e^{jn\frac{2\pi}{T}t}$$

Eq. (1.32)

where

$$C_n = \left\{ \frac{a_0}{2} \ for \ n = 0; \ \frac{a_n - jb_n}{2}; \ for \ n \neq 0 \right\}.$$

Eq. (1.33)

Equation (1.32) is known as the exponential Fourier series. Applying the relationship in Eq. (1.14) and assuming a basis function $S = \{\exp(j2n\pi t/T)\}$ yields,

$$C_n = \frac{1}{T} \int_{-T/2}^{T/2} x(t) e^{\frac{-j2\pi nt}{T}} dt.$$

Eq. (1.34)

The coefficients C_n are $(-jb_n)/2$ if the signal $x(t)$ is an odd function of time. Alternatively, when the signal is an even function of time, then all C_n are equal to $(a_n/2)$. Finally, one can easily show that $a_n = a_{-n}$, $b_n = b_{-n}$, and $C_n = C_{-n}^*$.

1.2.2. Properties of the Fourier Series

Let the function $x(t)$ be a periodic function with period T_1 and the function $g(t)$ be another periodic function with period T_2. The two functions can be represented using the Fourier series expansion, respectively, as,

$$x(t) = \sum_{n=-\infty}^{\infty} C_n e^{jn\frac{2\pi}{T_1}t}$$

Eq. (1.35)

$$g(t) = \sum_{n=-\infty}^{\infty} G_n e^{jn\frac{2\pi}{T_2}t}.$$

Eq. (1.36)

Addition and Subtraction

The sum or the difference of the functions $x(t)$ and $g(t)$ is identically equal to the sum or difference of their respective Fourier series expansions. More precisely,

$$x(t) \pm g(t) = \sum_{n=-\infty}^{\infty} C_n e^{jn\frac{2\pi}{T_1}t} \pm \sum_{n=-\infty}^{\infty} G_n e^{jn\frac{2\pi}{T_2}t} = \sum_{n=-\infty}^{\infty} \left\{ G_n e^{jn\frac{2\pi}{T_2}t} \pm C_n e^{jn\frac{2\pi}{T_1}t} \right\}$$ **Eq. (1.37)**

and if $T_2 = T_1 = T$, then

$$x(t) \pm g(t) = \sum_{n=-\infty}^{\infty} \left\{ (C_n \pm G_n) e^{jn\frac{2\pi}{T}t} \right\}.$$ **Eq. (1.38)**

Multiplication

The multiplication of the two functions $x(t)$ and $g(t)$ is equivalent to the multiplication of their Fourier series expansions,

$$x(t) \times g(t) = \left\{ \sum_{n=-\infty}^{\infty} C_n e^{jn\frac{2\pi}{T_1}t} \right\} \times \left\{ \sum_{n=-\infty}^{\infty} G_n e^{jn\frac{2\pi}{T_2}t} \right\}.$$ **Eq. (1.39)**

Average Power

The average power for a signal $x(t)$ is

$$P = \frac{1}{T} \int_{-T/2}^{T/2} |x(t)|^2 \, dt.$$ **Eq. (1.40)**

If $x(t)$ is periodic, then its Fourier series expansion is

$$x(t) = \sum_{n=-\infty}^{\infty} \frac{a_n}{2} \cos(n\omega_0 t) + \sum_{n=-\infty}^{\infty} \frac{b_n}{2} \sin(n\omega_0 t).$$ **Eq. (1.41)**

The modulus square of the even part of Eq. (1.41) is

$$|x(t)|_{even}^2 = \frac{1}{4} \sum_{n=-\infty}^{\infty} \sum_{m=-\infty}^{\infty} a_n \cos(n\omega_0 t) \, a_m \cos(m\omega_0 t)$$ **Eq. (1.42)**

while the modulus square of the odd part is

$$|x(t)|_{odd}^2 = \frac{1}{4} \sum_{n=-\infty}^{\infty} \sum_{m=-\infty}^{\infty} b_n \sin(n\omega_0 t) \, b_m \sin(m\omega_0 t)$$ **Eq. (1.43)**

Using Eqs. (1.42) and (1.43) in Eq. (1.40) and performing the integration for the even and odd parts, respectively, yield

$$P_{even} = \frac{1}{T} \int_{-T/2}^{T/2} \frac{1}{4} \sum_{n=-\infty}^{\infty} \sum_{m=-\infty}^{\infty} a_n \cos(n\omega_0 t) \, a_m \cos(m\omega_0 t) = \frac{1}{4} \sum_{n=-\infty}^{\infty} a_n^2$$ **Eq. (1.44)**

$$P_{odd} = \frac{1}{T}\int_{-T/2}^{T/2} \frac{1}{4} \sum_{n=-\infty}^{\infty} \sum_{m=-\infty}^{\infty} b_n \sin(n\omega_0 t)\; b_m \sin(m\omega_0 t) = \frac{1}{4}\sum_{n=-\infty}^{\infty} b_n^2. \qquad \text{Eq. (1.45)}$$

Recall that since $b_0 = 0$, then the total average power for the periodic power signal is

$$P = \frac{1}{T}\int_{-T/2}^{T/2} |x(t)|^2\; dt = \frac{a_0^2}{4} + \sum_{n=1}^{\infty}\left(\frac{a_n^2}{2} + \frac{b_n^2}{2}\right). \qquad \text{Eq. (1.46)}$$

Note that the summation in Eq. (1.46) is from 1 to ∞, and hence the factor of 2 is used when compared to either Eqs. (1.44) or (1.45). Using the exponential Fourier series expansion coefficients, Eq. (1.46) is given by

$$P = \frac{1}{T}\int_{-T/2}^{T/2} |x(t)|^2\; dt = \sum_{n=1}^{\infty} |C_n|^2 = \frac{1}{2}\sum_{n=-\infty}^{\infty} |C_n|^2. \qquad \text{Eq. (1.47)}$$

1.3. Fourier Transform

Consider a time-limited time domain signal $x(t)$ over the interval (t_1, t_2). Using the Fourier series expansion, this function may be expanded over an interval $T \geq (t_2 - t_1)$, as follows

$$x(t)|_T = \sum_{n=-\infty}^{\infty} C_n e^{jn\omega_0 t} \qquad \text{Eq. (1.48)}$$

where $\omega_0 = 2\pi/T$, it follows that as $T \to \infty$ then $\omega_0 \to 0$. Make the change $n \Rightarrow n\omega_0$ so that the coefficients C_n are now denoted by $C_{n\omega_0}$. More specifically,

$$C_{n\omega_0} = \frac{\omega_0}{2\pi}\int_{-\pi/\omega_0}^{\pi/\omega_0} x(t)e^{-jn\omega_0 t} dt. \qquad \text{Eq. (1.49)}$$

Substituting Eq. (1.49) in Eq. (1.48) and rearranging the terms, yield

$$x(t) = \frac{1}{2\pi}\sum_{n\omega_0=-\infty}^{\infty}\left[\int_{-\pi/\omega_0}^{\pi/\omega_0} x(t)e^{-jn\omega_0 t} dt\right] e^{jn\omega_0 t}\omega_0. \qquad \text{Eq. (1.50)}$$

As T becomes very large, the variable $n\omega_0$ approaches a continuous variable, which may be denoted as ω; hence, at the limit $\pi/\omega_0 \to \infty$ and $\omega_0 \to d\omega$. Therefore, Eq. (1.50) can be expressed as

$$x(t) = \frac{1}{2\pi}\int_{-\infty}^{\infty}\left[\int_{-\infty}^{\infty} x(t)e^{-j\omega t} dt\right] e^{j\omega t} d\omega \qquad \text{Eq. (1.51)}$$

and by using the relationship $\omega = 2\pi f$,

$$x(t) = \int_{-\infty}^{\infty}\left[\int_{-\infty}^{\infty} x(t)e^{-j2\pi ft} dt\right] e^{j2\pi ft} df. \qquad \text{Eq. (1.52)}$$

Define the frequency domain function $X(f)$ as

$$X(f) = \mathcal{F}\{x(t)\} = \int_{-\infty}^{\infty} x(t)e^{-j2\pi ft}dt \Leftrightarrow X(\omega) = \mathcal{F}\{x(t)\} = \int_{-\infty}^{\infty} x(t)e^{-j\omega t}dt. \quad \textbf{Eq. (1.53)}$$

The integral in Eq. (1.53) is known as the Fourier transform (FT) integral, the symbol $\mathcal{F}$ denotes Fourier transform integral operation. The integral

$$x(t) = \mathcal{F}^{-1}\{X(f)\} = \int_{-\infty}^{\infty} X(f)e^{j2\pi ft}df \Leftrightarrow \mathcal{F}^{-1}\{X(\omega)\} = \frac{1}{2\pi}\int_{-\infty}^{\infty} X(\omega)e^{j\omega t}d\omega \quad \textbf{Eq. (1.54)}$$

is the inverse Fourier transform (IFT), and the symbol $\mathcal{F}^{-1}$ denotes inverse Fourier transform integral operation.

1.3.1. Fourier Transform Pairs and Properties Tables

Table 1.1 contains some of the most common Fourier transform pairs, while Table 1.2 contains some of the relevant Fourier transform properties.

Table 1.1. Fourier Transform Pairs.

$x(t)$	$X(\omega)$
$A Rect(t/\tau)$; rectangular pulse	$A\tau Sinc(\omega\tau/2)$
$A\Delta(t/\tau)$; triangular pulse	$A\left(\dfrac{\tau}{2}\right)Sinc^2\left(\dfrac{\tau\omega}{4}\right)$
$(1/\sqrt{2\pi}\sigma)\exp(-t^2/2\sigma^2)$; Gaussian pulse	$\exp\left\{\dfrac{(-\sigma^2\omega^2)}{2}\right\}$
$e^{-at}u(t)$; $u(t)$ is step function	$\dfrac{1}{(a+j\omega)}$
$e^{-a|t|}$	$(2a)/(a^2+\omega^2)$
$e^{-at}\sin\omega_0 t \ u(t)$	$\dfrac{\omega_0}{(\omega_0^2+(a+j\omega)^2)}$
$e^{-at}\cos\omega_0 t \ u(t)$	$\dfrac{(a+j\omega)}{\omega_0^2+(a+j\omega)^2}$
$\delta(t)$	1
1	$2\pi\delta(\omega)$
$u(t)$	$\pi\delta(\omega)+\dfrac{1}{j\omega}$
$sgn(t)$	$\dfrac{2}{j\omega}$
$\cos\omega_0 t$	$\pi[\delta(\omega-\omega_0)+\delta(\omega+\omega_0)]$
$\sin\omega_0 t$	$j\pi[\delta(\omega+\omega_0)-\delta(\omega-\omega_0)]$

Table 1.2. Fourier Transform Properties.

Name	Time Domain	Frequency Domain
Linearity	$ax_1(t) + bx_2(t)$	$aX_1(\omega) + bX_2(\omega)$
Time scaling	$x(t/a)$	$aX(a\omega)$
Time shift	$x(t \pm t_0)$	$X(\omega)e^{\pm j\omega t_0}$
Complex shift	$x(t)e^{j\omega_0 t}$	$X(\omega - \omega_0)$
Time reversal	$x(-t)$	$X(-\omega)$
Convolution	$x_1(t) \otimes x_2(t)$	$X_1(\omega)X_2(\omega)$
Multiplication	$x_1(t) \times x_2(t)$	$(1/2\pi)X_1(\omega) \otimes X_2(\omega)$
Differentiation	$\dfrac{d^n}{dt^n}x(t)$	$(j\omega)^n X(\omega)$
Integration	$\displaystyle\int_{-\infty}^{t} x(u)\ du$	$\dfrac{X(\omega)}{j\omega} + \pi X(0)\delta(\omega)$
Time multiplication	$t^n x(t)$	$j^n \dfrac{d}{d\omega^n}X(\omega)$
Energy; Parseval's theorem	$\displaystyle\int_{-\infty}^{\infty} |x(t)|^2 dt$	$\dfrac{1}{2\pi}\displaystyle\int_{-\infty}^{\infty} |X(\omega)|^2 d\omega$
Duality	$X(t)$; $(1/2\pi)X(-t)$	$2\pi X(-\omega)$; $X(\omega)$

1.4. Systems Classification

Any system can mathematically be represented as a transformation (mapping) of an input signal into an output signal. This transformation or mapping relationship between the input signal $x(t)$ and the corresponding output signal $y(t)$ can be written as

$$y(t) = f[x(t); \ (-\infty < t < \infty)].$$ **Eq. (1.55)**

The relationship described in Eq. (1.55) can be linear or nonlinear, time invariant or time varying, causal or noncausal, and stable or nonstable. When the input signal is a unit impulse (Dirac delta function, $\delta(t)$) the output signal is referred to as the system's impulse response $h(t)$.

1.4.1. Linear and Nonlinear Systems

A system is said to be linear if superposition holds true. More specifically, if

$$y_1(t) = f[x_1(t)]$$
$$y_2(t) = f[x_2(t)]$$ **Eq. (1.56)**

then for a linear system

$$f[ax_1(t) + bx_2(t)] = ay_1(t) + by_2(t)$$ **Eq. (1.57)**

for any constants (a, b). If the relationship in Eq. (1.57) is not true, the system is said to be nonlinear.

1.4.2. Time Invariant and Time Varying Systems

A system is said to be time invariant (or shift invariant) if a time shift at its input produces the same time shift at its output. That is if

$$y(t) = f[x(t)]$$ **Eq. (1.58)**

then

$$y(t - t_0) = f[x(t - t_0)]; \quad -\infty < t_0 < \infty,$$ **Eq. (1.59)**

If the above relationship is not true, the system is called a time varying system.

Any linear time invariant (LTI) system can be described using the convolution integral between the input signal and the system's impulse response, as

$$y(t) = \int_{-\infty}^{\infty} x(t - u)h(u) \ du = x(u) \otimes h(u)$$ **Eq. (1.60)**

where the operator $\otimes$ is used to symbolically describe the convolution integral. In the frequency domain, convolution translates into multiplication. That is

$$Y(f) = X(f)H(f)$$ **Eq. (1.61)**

where $H(f)$ is the Fourier transform for $h(t)$ and it is referred to as the system transfer function.

1.4.3. Stable and Nonstable Systems

A system is said to be stable if every bounded input signal produces a bounded output signal. From Eq. (1.60)

$$|y(t)| = \left| \int_{-\infty}^{\infty} x(t - u)h(u) \ du \right| \leq \int_{-\infty}^{\infty} |x(t - u)||h(u)| \ du.$$ **Eq. (1.62)**

If the input signal is bounded, then there is some finite constant K such that

$$|x(t)| \leq K < \infty.$$ **Eq. (1.63)**

Therefore,

$$y(t) \leq K \int_{-\infty}^{\infty} |h(u)| \ du$$ **Eq. (1.64)**

which can be finite if and only if

$$\int_{-\infty}^{\infty} |h(u)| \ du < \infty.$$ **Eq. (1.65)**

Thus, the requirement for stability is that the impulse response must be absolutely integrable. Otherwise, the system is said to be unstable.

1.4.4. Causal and Noncausal Systems

A causal (or physically realizable) system is one whose output signal does not begin before the input signal is applied. Thus, the following relationship is true when the system is causal:

$$y(t_0) = f[x(t); t \leq t_0]; -\infty < t, t_0 < \infty.$$ **Eq. (1.66)**

A system that does not satisfy Eq. (1.66) is said to be noncausal which means it cannot exist in the real-world.

1.5. Spectra of Common Radar Signals

The spectrum of a given signal describes the spread of its energy in the frequency domain. An energy signal (finite energy) can be characterized in the frequency domain by its energy spectrum density (ESD) function, while a power signal (finite power) is characterized in the frequency domain by the power spectrum density (PSD) function. The units of the ESD are *Joules/Hertz* and the PSD has units *Watts/Hertz*.

1.5.1. Continuous Wave Signal

Consider a continuous wave (CW) waveform given by

$$x_1(t) = \cos 2\pi f_0 t.$$ **Eq. (1.67)**

The Fourier transform of $x_1(t)$ is

$$X_1(f) = \frac{1}{2}[\delta(f - f_0) + \delta(f + f_0)]$$ **Eq. (1.68)**

where δ is the Dirac delta function. As indicated by the amplitude spectrum shown in Fig. 1.1, the signal $x_1(t)$ has infinitesimal bandwidth, located at $\pm f_0$.

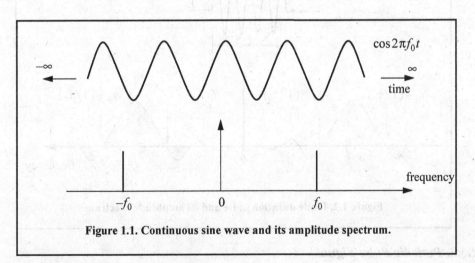

Figure 1.1. Continuous sine wave and its amplitude spectrum.

1.5.2. Finite Duration Pulse Signal

Consider the time-domain signal $x_2(t)$ given by

$$x_2(t) = x_1(t) Rect\left(\frac{t}{\tau_0}\right) = Rect\left(\frac{t}{\tau_0}\right) \cos 2\pi f_0 t$$ **Eq. (1.69)**

$$Rect\left(\frac{t}{\tau_0}\right) = \begin{cases} 1 & |t| \le \frac{\tau_0}{2} \\ 0 & otherwise \end{cases}$$ Eq. (1.70)

and $x_1(t)$ is Eq. (1.67). The Fourier transform of the *Rect* function is

$$\mathcal{F}\left\{Rect\left(\frac{t}{\tau_0}\right)\right\} = \tau_0 Sinc(f\tau_0)$$ Eq. (1.71)

where

$$Sinc(u) = \frac{\sin(\pi u)}{\pi u}.$$ Eq. (1.72)

It follows that the Fourier transform for the signal $x_2(t)$ is

$$X_2(f) = X_1(f) \otimes \tau_0 Sinc(f\tau_0) = \frac{1}{2}[\delta(f-f_0) + \delta(f+f_0)] \otimes \tau_0 Sinc(f\tau_0),$$ Eq. (1.73)

which can be written as

$$X_2(f) = \frac{\tau_0}{2}\{Sinc[(f-f_0)\tau_0] + Sinc[(f+f_0)\tau_0]\}.$$ Eq. (1.74)

The amplitude spectrum of $x_2(t)$ is shown in Fig. 1.2. It is made up of two *Sinc* functions, as defined in Eq. (1.74), centered at $\pm f_0$.

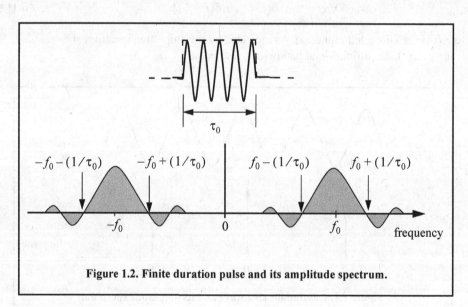

Figure 1.2. Finite duration pulse and its amplitude spectrum.

1.5.3. Periodic Pulse Signal

In this case, consider the coherent gated CW waveform $x_3(t)$ given by

$$x_3(t) = \sum_{n=-\infty}^{\infty} x_1(t)Rect\left(\frac{t-nT}{\tau_0}\right) = \cos 2\pi f_0 t \sum_{n=-\infty}^{\infty} Rect\left(\frac{t-nT}{\tau_0}\right).$$ Eq. (1.75)

The signal $x_3(t)$ is periodic, with period T; let $f_r = 1/T$ be the pulse repetition frequency (PRF) where the condition $f_r \ll f_0$ is assumed. The Fourier transform for the signal $x_3(t)$ is

$$X_3(f) = X_1(f) \otimes \mathcal{F}\left\{ \sum_{n=-\infty}^{\infty} Rect\left(\frac{t-nT}{\tau_0}\right) \right\} = \qquad \text{Eq. (1.76)}$$

$$\frac{1}{2}[\delta(f-f_0) + \delta(f+f_0)] \otimes \mathcal{F}\left\{ \sum_{n=-\infty}^{\infty} Rect\left(\frac{t-nT}{\tau_0}\right) \right\}.$$

The complex exponential Fourier series of the summation inside Eq. (1.76) is

$$\sum_{n=-\infty}^{\infty} Rect\left(\frac{t-nT}{\tau_0}\right) = \sum_{n=-\infty}^{\infty} C_n e^{j\frac{nt}{T}} \qquad \text{Eq. (1.77)}$$

where the Fourier series coefficients C_n are given by

$$C_n = \frac{1}{T}\mathcal{F}\left\{ Rect\left(\frac{t}{\tau_0}\right) \right\}\bigg|_{f=\frac{n}{T}} = \frac{\tau_0}{T}Sinc(f\tau_0)\bigg|_{f=\frac{n}{T}} = \frac{\tau_0}{T}Sinc\left(\frac{n\tau_0}{T}\right). \qquad \text{Eq. (1.78)}$$

It follows that

$$\mathcal{F}\left\{ \sum_{n=-\infty}^{\infty} C_n e^{j\frac{nt}{T}} \right\} = \left(\frac{\tau_0}{T}\right) \sum_{n=-\infty}^{\infty} Sinc(nf_r\tau_0)\delta(f-nf_r) \qquad \text{Eq. (1.79)}$$

where the relation $f_r = 1/T$ was used. Substituting Eq. (1.79) into Eq. (1.76) yields the Fourier transform of $x_3(t)$. That is

$$X_3(f) = \frac{\tau_0}{2T}[\delta(f-f_0) + \delta(f+f_0)] \otimes \sum_{n=-\infty}^{\infty} Sinc(nf_r\tau_0)\delta(f-nf_r). \qquad \text{Eq. (1.80)}$$

The amplitude spectrum of $x_3(t)$ has two parts centered at $\pm f_0$. The spectrum of the summation part is an infinite number of delta functions repeated every f_r, where the nth line is modulated in amplitude with the value corresponding to $Sinc(nf_r\tau_0)$. Therefore, the overall spectrum consists of an infinite number of lines separated by f_r and have $\sin(u)/u$ envelope that corresponds to C_n. This is illustrated in Fig. 1.3, for the positive portion of the spectrum only.

1.5.4. Finite Duration Pulse Train Signal

Define the function $x_4(t)$ as

$$x_4(t) = \cos(2\pi f_0 t) \sum_{n=0}^{N-1} Rect\left(\frac{t-nT}{\tau_0}\right) = \cos 2\pi f_0 t \times g(t) \qquad \text{Eq. (1.81)}$$

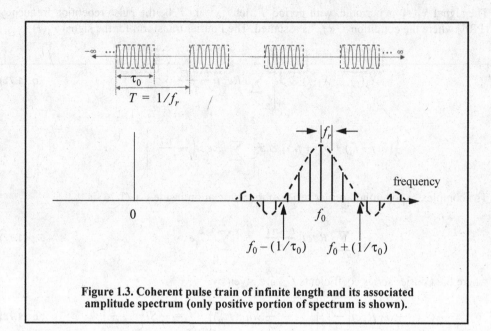

Figure 1.3. Coherent pulse train of infinite length and its associated amplitude spectrum (only positive portion of spectrum is shown).

where

$$g(t) = \sum_{n=0}^{N-1} Rect\left(\frac{t-nT}{\tau_0}\right).$$

Eq. (1.82)

The amplitude spectrum of the signal $x_4(t)$ is

$$X_4(f) = \frac{1}{2}G(f) \otimes [\delta(f-f_0) + \delta(f+f_0)]$$

Eq. (1.83)

where $G(f)$ is the Fourier transform of $g(t)$. This means that the amplitude spectrum of the signal $x_4(t)$ is equal to replicas of $G(f)$ centered at $\pm f_0$, respectively. Given this conclusion, one can then focus on computing $G(f)$.

The signal $g(t)$ can be written as (see top portion of Fig. 1.4)

$$g(t) = \sum_{n=-\infty}^{\infty} g_1(t)Rect\left(\frac{t-nT}{\tau_0}\right)$$

Eq. (1.84)

where

$$g_1(t) = Rect\left(\frac{t}{NT}\right).$$

Eq. (1.85)

It follows that the Fourier transform of Eq. (1.84) can be computed using analysis similar to that which led to Eq. (1.80). More precisely,

$$G(f) = \frac{\tau_0}{T}G_1(f) \otimes \sum_{n=-\infty}^{\infty} Sinc(nf_r\tau_0)\delta(f-nf_r).$$

Eq. (1.86)

The Fourier transform of $g_1(t)$ is

$$G_1(f) = \mathcal{F}\left\{Rect\left(\frac{t}{T_t}\right)\right\} = T_t Sinc(fT_t) \ .$$ **Eq. (1.87)**

Using these results, the Fourier transform of $x_4(t)$ can be written as

$$X_4(f) = \frac{T_t \tau_0}{2T}\left(Sinc(fT_t) \otimes \sum_{n=-\infty}^{\infty} Sinc(nf_r\tau_0)\delta(f-nf_r)\right) \otimes [\delta(f-f_0) + \delta(f+f_0)] \ .$$ **Eq. (1.88)**

Therefore, the overall spectrum of $x_4(t)$ consists of two equal positive and negative portions, centered at $\pm f_0$. Each portion is made up of N $Sinc(fT_t)$ functions repeated every f_r with an envelope corresponding to $Sinc(nf_r\tau_0)$. This is illustrated in Fig. 1.4; only the positive portion of the spectrum is shown.

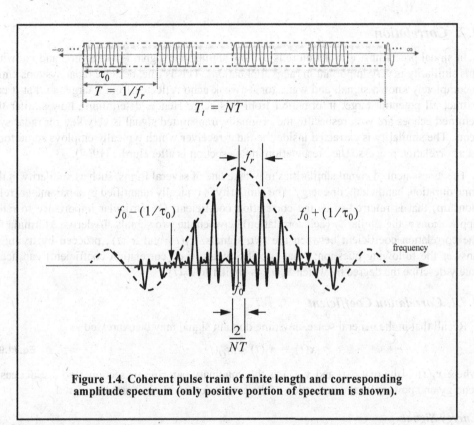

Figure 1.4. Coherent pulse train of finite length and corresponding amplitude spectrum (only positive portion of spectrum is shown).

1.6. Convolution Integral

The convolution integral $\rho_{xh}(t)$ between the signals $x(t)$ and $h(t)$ is defined by

$$\rho_{xh}(t) = x(t) \otimes h(t) = \int_{-\infty}^{\infty} x(\tau)h(t-\tau)d\tau$$ **Eq. (1.89)**

where τ is a dummy variable. Convolution is commutative, associative, and distributive. More precisely,

$$x(t) \otimes h(t) = h(t) \otimes x(t)$$
$$x(t) \otimes (h(t) \otimes g(t)) = (x(t) \otimes h(t)) \otimes g(t) = (x(t) \otimes g(t)) \otimes h(t)$$

Eq. (1.90)

For the convolution integral to be finite at least one of the two signals must be an energy signal. The convolution between two signals can be computed using the Fourier transform:

$$\rho_{xh}(t) = \mathcal{F}^{-1}\{X(\omega)H(\omega)\}.$$

Eq. (1.91)

Consider an LTI system with impulse response $h(t)$ and input signal $x(t)$. It follows that the output signal $y(t)$ is equal to the convolution between the input signal and the system impulse response,

$$y(t) = \int_{-\infty}^{\infty} x(\tau)h(t-\tau)d\tau = \int_{-\infty}^{\infty} h(\tau)x(t-\tau)d\tau.$$

Eq. (1.92)

1.7. Correlation

In signal processing, correlation tells us how similar one signal is to another, and knowing this similarity is very important in radar applications. This is true, because radar systems emits a completely known signal, and waits for its weak echo reflected from a target so that it can extract all potential target information from this echo. Hence, determining how similar the returned echoes are with respect to the originally transmitted signal is very key for radar systems. The similarity is extracted inside the radar receiver which typically employs some form of a correlation process. The presentation in this section is after Burdic (1968).

The assessment of signal similarities may take one of several forms, such as similarity in the time duration, bandwidth, or energy. The similarity is typically quantified by a parameter (relationship) that is referred to as the correlation coefficient. Of particular importance to radar applications is the similarity (i.e., correlation) between the two signals. To derive a formula for the correlation coefficient between the two signals, $x_1(t)$ and $x_2(t)$, proceed by trying to answer the following question: what specific metric (i.e., correlation coefficient) can accurately describe the degree by which $x_1(t)$ is similar to $x_2(t)$.

1.7.1. Correlation Coefficient

Recall that in the general sense, any time domain signal may be expressed as

$$x(t) = x_I(t) + jx_Q(t),$$

Eq. (1.93)

where $x_I(t)$ is the real part and $x_Q(t)$ is the imaginary part. In this section, two distinct cases (energy and power) for the derivation of the correlation coefficient are considered.

Energy Signals

The total energy in the signal $x(t)$ (as defined in Eq. (1.93)) was given in Eq. (1.4). More precisely,

$$E_x = \int_{-\infty}^{\infty} |x(t)|^2 \, dt,$$

Eq. (1.94)

and from Eq. (1.93) the quantity $|x(t)|^2$ is

$$|x(t)|^2 = x(t) \cdot x^*(t) = [x_I(t) + jx_Q(t)][x_I(t) - jx_Q(t)] = x_I^2(t) + x_Q^2(t),$$

Eq. (1.95)

it follows that Eq. (1.94) can be rewritten as

$$E_x = \int_{-\infty}^{\infty} [x_I^2(t) + x_Q^2(t)] \ dt.$$ **Eq. (1.96)**

Next, take the derivative of Eq. (1.96) with respect to time (i.e., the instantaneous power)

$$\frac{\Delta E_x}{\Delta t} = x_I^2(t) + x_Q^2(t) \Rightarrow \Delta E_x = \{x_I^2(t) + x_Q^2(t)\}\Delta t.$$ **Eq. (1.97)**

Consider two signals $x_1(t)$ and $x_2(t)$; the similarity between these signals can be expressed as

$$x_\delta(t) = x_1(t) - c_{12}x_2(t).$$ **Eq. (1.98)**

where $x_\delta(t)$ is the difference signal and c_{12} is a scaling constant. The energy associated with the difference signal $x_\delta(t)$ can be determined from Eq. (1.97) as,

$$\Delta E_{x_\delta} = \{x_{\delta I}^2(t) + x_{\delta Q}^2(t)\}\Delta t.$$ **Eq. (1.99)**

where $x_{\delta I}(t)$ is the real part for the signal $x_\delta(t)$ and $x_{\delta Q}(t)$ is its imaginary part. One can easily show that

$$\begin{Bmatrix} x_{\delta I}^2(t) \\ x_{\delta Q}^2(t) \end{Bmatrix} = \begin{Bmatrix} x_{1I}^2(t) - 2c_{12} \ x_{1I}(t) \ x_{2I}(t) + c_{12}^2 \ x_{2I}^2(t) \\ x_{1Q}^2(t) - 2c_{12} \ x_{1Q}(t) \ x_{2Q}(t) + c_{12}^2 \ x_{2Q}^2(t) \end{Bmatrix}.$$ **Eq. (1.100)**

Using Eq. (1.100) into Eq. (1.99) yields

$$\Delta E_{x_\delta} = \{[x_{1I}^2 - 2c_{12} \ x_{1I}x_{2I} + c_{12}^2 \ x_{2I}^2] + [x_{1Q}^2 - 2c_{12} \ x_{1Q}x_{2Q} + c_{12}^2 \ x_{2Q}^2]\}\Delta t.$$ **Eq. (1.101)**

Note that for notation simplicity the variable (t) was dropped from Eq. (1.101). Next take the derivative of ΔE_{x_δ} with respect to c_{12}, it follows

$$\frac{\partial}{\partial c_{12}}[\Delta E_{x_\delta}] = \{[-2x_{1I}x_{2I} + 2c_{12}x_{2I}^2] + [-2x_{1Q}x_{2Q} + 2c_{12}x_{2Q}^2]\}\Delta t.$$ **Eq. (1.102)**

In order to compute the constant c_{12} that maximizes / minimizes ΔE_{x_δ}, regroup the terms on the right-hand side of Eq. (1.102) and set it equal to zero, it follows

$$0 = -2(x_{1I}x_{2I} + x_{1Q}x_{2Q})\Delta t + 2c_{12}(x_{2I}^2 + x_{2Q}^2)\Delta t.$$ **Eq. (1.103)**

Equation (1.103) can then be rewritten in the form

$$c_{12} = \frac{(x_{1I}x_{2I} + x_{1Q}x_{2Q})\Delta t}{(x_{2I}^2 + x_{2Q}^2)\Delta t},$$ **Eq. (1.104)**

which by using Eq. (1.93) it can be expressed in the form,

$$c_{12} = \frac{(x_{1I}x_{2I} + x_{1Q}x_{2Q})\Delta t}{(x_{2I}^2 + x_{2Q}^2)\Delta t} = \frac{\left(\displaystyle\sum_{k=a}^{b} x_{1k}x_{2k} \ \Delta t\right)}{\left(\displaystyle\sum_{k=a}^{b} x_{2k}^2 \ \Delta t\right)},$$ **Eq. (1.105)**

as $\Delta t \to 0$ the summations in Eq.(1.105) can be replaced with integrals; hence,

$$c_{12} = \frac{\int_{-\infty}^{\infty} (x_{1I}x_{2I} + x_{1Q}x_{2Q})\,dt}{\int_{-\infty}^{\infty} (x_{2I}^2 + x_{2Q}^2)\,dt}. \qquad \text{Eq. (1.106)}$$

Which by using the relationship in Eq. (1.93), one can now write c_{12} as

$$c_{12} = \frac{\int_{-\infty}^{\infty} x_1(t)x_2^*(t)\,dt}{\int_{-\infty}^{\infty} |x_2(t)|^2\,dt}, \qquad \text{Eq. (1.107)}$$

similarly,

$$c_{21} = \frac{\int_{-\infty}^{\infty} x_2(t)x_1^*(t)\,dt}{\int_{-\infty}^{\infty} |x_1(t)|^2\,dt}. \qquad \text{Eq. (1.108)}$$

The correlation coefficient given in either Eq. (1.107) or (1.108) is insensitive to the energy content of the two signals. More specifically, and for example if the amplitude of one signal is one-tenth of the other, then $c_{12} = 100 \times c_{21}$. Although, this constant can be viewed as being the correlation coefficient; it is, however, more meaningful to define a value normalized (with respect to the total energy of the original signal) correlation coefficient, C_{12}. More precisely, define the normalized correlation coefficient C_{12} as,

$$C_{12} = \frac{\int_{-\infty}^{\infty} |c_{12}x_2(t)|^2 \, dt}{\int_{-\infty}^{\infty} |x_1(t)|^2\,dt}. \qquad \text{Eq. (1.109)}$$

which provides a more exact measure of the two signals similarities, than c_{12}. Substituting Eq. (1.107) into Eq. (1.109) yields,

$$C_{12} = \frac{|c_{12}|^2 \int_{-\infty}^{\infty} |x_2(t)|^2 \, dt}{\int_{-\infty}^{\infty} |x_1(t)|^2\,dt} = \left| \frac{\int_{-\infty}^{\infty} x_1(t)x_2^*(t)\,dt}{\int_{-\infty}^{\infty} |x_2(t)|^2\,dt} \right|^2 \frac{\int_{-\infty}^{\infty} |x_2(t)|^2\,dt}{\int_{-\infty}^{\infty} |x_1(t)|^2\,dt}, \qquad \text{Eq. (1.110)}$$

which can be simplified to

$$C_{12} = \frac{\left| \int_{-\infty}^{\infty} x_1(t)x_2^*(t)\,dt \right|^2}{\int_{-\infty}^{\infty} |x_1(t)|^2\,dt \int_{-\infty}^{\infty} |x_2(t)|^2\,dt}. \qquad \text{Eq. (1.111)}$$

It can be easily shown using similar analysis that $C_{21} = C_{12}$. Additionally,

$$C_{12} = c_{12}c_{21}$$
$$0 \le C_{12} \le 1 .$$

Eq. (1.112)

In conclusion, the correlation coefficient C_{12} simply gives us the portion of the energy in $x_1(t)$ contained in $x_2(t)$. Conversely, the value $(1 - C_{12})$ represents the fraction of energy remaining in $x_1(t)$ after removing $x_2(t)$ from it.

Power Signals

The computation of the correlation coefficient for power signals is similar to that of energy signals, expect in this case, one must replace the signals by their time average representations. More specifically replace $x_i(t)$ by $\langle x_i(t) \rangle$, where $\langle x_i(t) \rangle$ is the time average given by

$$\langle x_i(t) \rangle = \lim_{T \to \infty} \frac{1}{T} \int_{-T/2}^{T/2} x_i(t) \ dt \qquad i = 1, 2 .$$

Eq. (1.113)

It follows that the power signal correlation coefficient is given by

$$\overline{C}_{12} = \frac{\langle |x_1(t) \ x_2^*(t)|^2 \rangle}{\langle |x_1(t)|^2 \rangle \ \langle |x_2(t)|^2 \rangle} .$$

Eq. (1.114)

where the over-bar over $\overline{C}_{12}$ indicates normalized correlation coefficient for power signals.

1.7.2. Correlation Integral - Energy Signals

When developing an expression for the correlation coefficient, we assumed that there is no time displacement between the two signals $x_1(t)$ and $x_2(t)$. This is certainly not the case in radar applications, where the radar receiver compares a delayed (time shifted) version (echoes from the target) of the transmitted signal to itself. Accordingly, and in reference to Eq. (1.107), if the signal $x_2(t)$ is delayed by some time value τ (in radar applications, this delay is used to extract the target's range), then we get

$$c_{12} = \frac{\int_{-\infty}^{\infty} x_1(t) \ x_2^*(t - \tau)dt}{\int_{-\infty}^{\infty} |x_2(t - \tau)|^2 dt} ,$$

Eq. (1.115)

and since the denominator is computed over all time, then it is independent of the delay; hence,

$$c_{12} = \frac{\int_{-\infty}^{\infty} x_1(t) \ x_2^*(t - \tau)dt}{\int_{-\infty}^{\infty} |x_2(t)|^2 dt} = \frac{1}{K_1} \int_{-\infty}^{\infty} x_1(t) \ x_2^*(t - \tau)dt ,$$

Eq. (1.116)

and

$$c_{21} = \frac{\int_{-\infty}^{\infty} x_2(t) \ x_1^*(t - \tau)dt}{\int_{-\infty}^{\infty} |x_1(t)|^2 dt} = \frac{1}{K_2} \int_{-\infty}^{\infty} x_2(t) \ x_1^*(t - \tau)dt ,$$

Eq. (1.117)

where K_1 and K_2 are equal to the energy of the signals $x_1(t)$ and $x_2(t)$, respectively.

Define the cross-correlation function between the signals $x_1(t)$ and $x_2(t)$ as

$$\mathcal{R}_{x_1 x_2}(\tau) = \int_{-\infty}^{\infty} x_1(t) \, x_2^*(t-\tau) dt = \int_{-\infty}^{\infty} x_1(t+\tau) \, x_2^*(t) dt \qquad \text{Eq. (1.118)}$$

and

$$\mathcal{R}_{x_2 x_1}(\tau) = \int_{-\infty}^{\infty} x_1^*(t-\tau) x_2(t) dt = \int_{-\infty}^{\infty} x_1^*(t) x_2(t+\tau) dt \ . \qquad \text{Eq. (1.119)}$$

If the two signals are the same, then the correlation function is referred to as the autocorrelation function, as compared to the term cross-correlation function, and it will be given by

$$\mathcal{R}_x(\tau) = \int_{-\infty}^{\infty} x(t) x^*(t-\tau) dt = \int_{-\infty}^{\infty} x(t+\tau) x^*(t) dt \ . \qquad \text{Eq. (1.120)}$$

1.7.3. Relationship between Convolution and Correlation Integrals

Consider two signals $x_1(t)$ and $x_2(t)$, the corresponding convolution integral is given by (see Eq. (1.89))

$$x_1(t) \otimes x_2(t) = \int_{-\infty}^{\infty} x_1(t) x_2(\tau - t) d\tau \qquad \text{Eq. (1.121)}$$

and their cross-correlation is

$$\mathcal{R}_{x_1 x_2}(\tau) = \int_{-\infty}^{\infty} x_1(t) x_2^*(t-\tau) dt \qquad \text{Eq. (1.122)}$$

by making the change of variable $u = t - \tau$, one can easily show that

$$\mathcal{R}_{x_1 x_2}(\tau) = x_1(\tau) \otimes x_2^*(-\tau) \qquad \text{Eq. (1.123)}$$

and

$$\mathcal{R}_{x_2 x_1}(\tau) = x_1^*(-\tau) \otimes x_2(\tau) \ . \qquad \text{Eq. (1.124)}$$

Finally, for the case of an autocorrelation,

$$\mathcal{R}_{x_1}(\tau) = x_1(\tau) \otimes x_1^*(-\tau) \ . \qquad \text{Eq. (1.125)}$$

1.7.4. Effect of Time Translation on the Correlation Function

The autocorrelation function for the signal $x(t)$ is $\mathcal{R}_x(\tau)$, which can be written in terms of the convolution integral as

$$\mathcal{R}_x(\tau) = x(\tau) \otimes x^*(-\tau) \ . \qquad \text{Eq. (1.126)}$$

Now consider the cross-correlation between the signal $x(t)$ and delayed (translated) version of itself, $x_d(t) = x(t - t_0)$, where t_0 is the amount of delay and is positive. It follows that the cross-correlation function between the signal and its delayed version is

$$\mathcal{R}_{xx_d}(\tau) = x(\tau) \otimes x_d^*(-\tau) \ . \qquad \text{Eq. (1.127)}$$

which can be rewritten using the delta function as

$$\mathcal{R}_{xx_d}(\tau) = [x(\tau) \otimes \delta(t)] \otimes [x^*(-\tau) \otimes \delta(-t_0 + \tau)]. \qquad \textbf{Eq. (1.128)}$$

where $\delta(t)$ is the delta function. Rearranging the right-hand side of Eq. (1.128) yields,

$$\mathcal{R}_{xx_d}(\tau) = [x(\tau) \otimes x^*(-\tau)] \otimes [\delta(t) \otimes \delta(-t_0 + \tau)] \qquad \textbf{Eq. (1.129)}$$

and by using Eq. (1.125) along with the convolution properties presented earlier, one can write Eq. (1.129) as

$$\mathcal{R}_{xx_d}(\tau) = [\mathcal{R}_x(\tau)] \otimes [\delta(\tau - t_0)] = \mathcal{R}_x(\tau - t_0). \qquad \textbf{Eq. (1.130)}$$

This means that the cross-correlation between a signal $x(t)$ and delayed version of itself, is a delayed version of its autocorrelation function without any delay.

The result found in Eq. (1.130) is extremely important in radar applications. This is true because, the output of the radar receiver is typically defined by the cross-correlation between the target echoes and a replica of the transmitted signal in order to maximize the signal-to-noise ratio. Outside of the reduction in amplitude of the returned echoes, the delay (i.e., time shift) in this echo signal becomes a measure of the target range R_0. More specifically,

$$R_0 = \frac{ct_0}{2}, \qquad \textbf{Eq. (1.131)}$$

where c is the speed of light, and t_0 is the two-way time it takes a radar signal to travel from the radar to the target and back to the radar; thus, the factor of $(1/2)$ is explained. It follows that a target located at range R_0 will produce a peak at t_0 (as defined in Eq. (1.130)) at the output of the radar receiver, and from which the radar signal processor will determine the target range using Eq. (1.131).

For example, consider two targets located at *200m* and *500m* (i.e., with the help of Eq. (1.131) they are located at $1.33\mu s$ and $3.33\mu s$ within the radar receive window). Figure 1.5 shows the corresponding output of the radar receiver for this case.

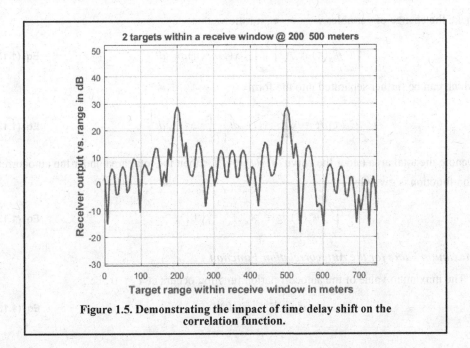

Figure 1.5. Demonstrating the impact of time delay shift on the correlation function.

1.7.5. Correlation Function Properties

The following includes some useful properties of the correlation function:

Conjugate Symmetry

With the help of Eqs. (1.118) and (1.119), one can show

$$\mathcal{R}_{x_1 x_2}(\tau) = \mathcal{R}^*_{x_2 x_1}(-\tau) \qquad \text{Eq. (1.132)}$$

and if both signals are real, then

$$\mathcal{R}_{x_1 x_2}(\tau) = \mathcal{R}_{x_2 x_1}(-\tau) \qquad \text{Eq. (1.133)}$$

which implies that the cross-correlation function is an even function (i.e., symmetrical around $\tau = 0$) if both signals are real.

Total Signal Energy

The total signal energy is equal to $\mathcal{R}_x(0)$. To prove this, start with Eq. (1.120) and set $\tau = 0$, it follows that

$$\mathcal{R}_x(\tau)\Big|_{\tau = 0} = \int_{-\infty}^{\infty} x(t)x^*(t-\tau)dt \Big|_{\tau = 0} \Rightarrow \mathcal{R}_x(0) = \int_{-\infty}^{\infty} |x(t)|^2 dt \qquad \text{Eq. (1.134)}$$

which from Parseval's theorem is the total signal energy.

Total Area under the Autocorrelation Function

Consider the autocorrelation function $\mathcal{R}_x(\tau)$, the total area under the curve is equal to

$$\int_{-\infty}^{\infty} \mathcal{R}_x(\tau)d\tau = \int_{-\infty}^{\infty} \left\{ \int_{-\infty}^{\infty} x(t)x^*(t-\tau)dt \right\} d\tau \qquad \text{Eq. (1.135)}$$

make the change of variables $u = t - \tau$, it follows that

$$\int_{-\infty}^{\infty} \mathcal{R}_x(\tau)d\tau = \int_{-\infty}^{\infty} \int_{-\infty}^{\infty} x(t)x^*(u)du \ dt \qquad \text{Eq. (1.136)}$$

which can be further separated into the form

$$\int_{-\infty}^{\infty} \mathcal{R}_x(\tau)d\tau = \left\{ \int_{-\infty}^{\infty} x(t) \ dt \right\} \left\{ \int_{-\infty}^{\infty} x(t) \ dt \right\}^* . \qquad \text{Eq. (1.137)}$$

Denote the total area under the curve of $x(t)$ by A_x; then the total area under the autocorrelation function is given by

$$\int_{-\infty}^{\infty} \mathcal{R}_x(\tau)d\tau = A_x A_x^* = |A_x|^2 . \qquad \text{Eq. (1.138)}$$

Maximum Value for the Autocorrelation Function

The maximum value of the autocorrelation function occurs at $\tau = 0$, i.e.,

$$|\mathcal{R}_x(\tau)|^2 \leq |\mathcal{R}_x(0)|^2 . \qquad \text{Eq. (1.139)}$$

Fourier Transform for the Correlation Function

It is often desirable to work with the cross-correlation of a time function in the frequency domain. Denote the Fourier transform for the cross-correlation function as $S_{x_1 x_2}(\omega)$, and for the autocorrelation function as $S_x(\omega)$. The cross-correlation function is expressed in terms of the convolution function as

$$\mathcal{R}_{x_1 x_2}(\tau) = x_1(\tau) \otimes x_2^*(-\tau) .$$ **Eq. (1.140)**

Taking the Fourier transform of both sides of Eq. (1.140) yields

$$\mathcal{F}\{\mathcal{R}_{x_1 x_2}(\tau)\} = S_{x_1 x_2}(\omega) = \mathcal{F}\{x_1(\tau) \otimes x_2^*(-\tau)\} ,$$ **Eq. (1.141)**

then by applying the convolution property of the Fourier transform, one can write the Fourier transform for the cross-correlation function as,

$$S_{x_1 x_2}(\omega) = X_1(\omega) \, X_2^*(\omega) ,$$ **Eq. (1.142)**

similarly, the Fourier transform for the autocorrelation function is

$$S_{x_1}(\omega) = X_1(\omega) \, X_1^*(\omega) = |X_1(\omega)|^2 .$$ **Eq. (1.143)**

1.7.6. Correlation Integral - Power Signals

The autocorrelation and cross-correlation formulas for energy signals were derived earlier. Now if the signals $x_1(t)$ and $x_2(t)$ are power signals, then the auto- and cross-correlation functions are, respectively, denoted by $\overline{\mathcal{R}}_{x_1}(\tau)$ and $\overline{\mathcal{R}}_{x_1 x_2}(\tau)$ or $\overline{\mathcal{R}}_{x_2 x_1}(\tau)$, where as before the over-bar indicates power signals. Note that for power signals integrated over infinite time, the correlation integral becomes infinite, thus time averaging must be included. More precisely,

$$\overline{\mathcal{R}}_{x_1 x_2}(\tau) = \lim_{T \to \infty} \frac{1}{T} \int_{-T/2}^{T/2} x_1(t) \, x_2^*(t - \tau) dt .$$ **Eq. (1.144)**

Power signals can be split into two components, the steady state (i.e., dc-component) and varying component (i.e., ac-component). In this context, the autocorrelation function evaluated at $\tau = 0$ represents the total power, while the value at $\tau = \infty$ is the dc-power; hence,

$$\overline{\mathcal{R}}_x(0) \Leftrightarrow total \ power \ (ac + dc)$$
$$\overline{\mathcal{R}}_x(\infty) \Leftrightarrow dc \ power$$ **Eq. (1.145)**
$$\overline{\mathcal{R}}_x(0) - \overline{\mathcal{R}}_x(\infty) \Leftrightarrow ac \ power$$

1.7.7. Energy and Power Spectrum Densities

Consider an energy signal $x(t)$. From Parseval's theorem, the total energy associated with this signal is

$$E = \int_{-\infty}^{\infty} |x(t)|^2 dt = \frac{1}{2\pi} \int_{-\infty}^{\infty} |X(\omega)|^2 d\omega ,$$ **Eq. (1.146)**

when $x(t)$ is a voltage signal, the amount of energy dissipated by this signal when applied across a network of resistance R is

$$E = \frac{1}{R} \int_{-\infty}^{\infty} |x(t)|^2 dt = \frac{1}{2\pi R} \int_{-\infty}^{\infty} |X(\omega)|^2 d\omega .$$ **Eq. (1.147)**

Alternatively, when $x(t)$ is a current signal, we get

$$E = R \int_{-\infty}^{\infty} |x(t)|^2 dt = \frac{R}{2\pi} \int_{-\infty}^{\infty} |X(\omega)|^2 d\omega.$$

Eq. (1.148)

The integral of $|X(\omega)|^2$ represents the amount of energy spread per unit frequency across a 1Ω resistor; therefore, the energy spectrum density (ESD) function for the energy signal $x(t)$ is defined as

$$ESD = |X(\omega)|^2.$$

Eq. (1.149)

The *ESD* at the output of an LTI system is when $x(t)$ is at its input

$$|Y(\omega)|^2 = |X(\omega)|^2 |H(\omega)|^2$$

Eq. (1.150)

where $H(\omega)$ is the Fourier transform of the system impulse response, $h(t)$. It follows that the energy present at the output of the system is

$$E_y = \frac{1}{2\pi} \int_{-\infty}^{\infty} |X(\omega)|^2 |H(\omega)|^2 d\omega.$$

Eq. (1.151)

The total power associated with a power signal $x(t)$ is

$$P = \lim_{T \to \infty} \frac{1}{T} \int_{-T/2}^{T/2} |x(t)|^2 dt.$$

Eq. (1.152)

The power spectrum density (PSD) function for the signal $x(t)$ is the Fourier transform of its autocorrelation function, $S_x(\omega)$. It follows that the signal power in Eq. (1.152) can now be written as,

$$P = \lim_{T \to \infty} \frac{1}{T} \int_{-T/2}^{T/2} |x(t)|^2 dt = \overline{\mathcal{R}}_x(0),$$

Eq. (1.153)

where $\overline{\mathcal{R}}_x(0)$ is the maximum of $\overline{\mathcal{R}}_x(\tau)$, then by applying Parseval's theorem the total power in Eq. (1.153) can be expressed as

$$P = \frac{1}{2\pi} \int_{-\infty}^{\infty} S_x(\omega) d\omega.$$

Eq. (1.154)

1.7.8. Correlation Function for Periodic Signals

Let the signals $x(t)$ and $g(t)$ be two periodic signals with period T. The complex exponential Fourier series expansions for those signals are, respectively, given by

$$x(t) = \sum_{n=-\infty}^{\infty} C_n e^{j\frac{2\pi n t}{T}}$$

Eq. (1.155)

$$g(t) = \sum_{m=-\infty}^{\infty} G_m e^{j\frac{2\pi m t}{T}}.$$

Eq. (1.156)

The power cross-correlation function $\overline{\mathcal{R}}_{gx}(\tau)$ was given in Eq. (1.144) and is repeated here as Eq. (1.157),

$$\overline{\mathcal{R}}_{gx}(\tau) = \lim_{T \to \infty} \frac{1}{T} \int_{-T/2}^{T/2} g(t) x^*(t - \tau) dt.$$

Eq. (1.157)

Note that since both signals are periodic, then the limit is no longer necessary in Eq. (1.157). Substituting Eqs. (1.155) and (1.156) into Eq. (1.157), collecting terms, and using the definition of orthogonality, yields

$$\overline{\mathcal{R}}_{gx}(\tau) = \sum_{n=-\infty}^{\infty} G_n^* X_n e^{j\frac{2n\pi t}{T}}.$$

Eq. (1.158)

When $x(t) = g(t)$, Eq. (1.158) becomes the power autocorrelation function,

$$\overline{\mathcal{R}}_x(\tau) = \sum_{n=-\infty}^{\infty} |C_n|^2 e^{j\frac{2n\pi t}{T}} = |C_0|^2 + 2\sum_{n=1}^{\infty} |C_n|^2 e^{j\frac{2n\pi t}{T}}.$$

Eq. (1.159)

The power spectrum and cross-power spectrum density functions are then computed as the Fourier transform of Eqs. (1.159) and (1.158), respectively. More precisely,

$$\overline{S}_x(\omega) = 2\pi \sum_{n=-\infty}^{\infty} |C_n|^2 \delta\left(\omega - \frac{2n\pi}{T}\right)$$

Eq. (1.160)

$$\overline{S}_{gx}(\omega) = 2\pi \sum_{n=-\infty}^{\infty} G_n^* C_n \delta\left(\omega - \frac{2n\pi}{T}\right).$$

Eq. (1.161)

The line (or discrete) power spectrum is defined as the plot of $|C_n|^2$ versus n, where the lines are $\Delta f = 1/T$ apart. The dc-power is $|C_0|^2$, and the total power is $\sum |C_n|^2$.

1.8. Bandpass Signals

Signals that contain significant frequency composition at a low frequency band including dc-component are called lowpass (LP) signals. Signals that have significant frequency composition around some frequency away from the origin are called bandpass (BP) signals. A real-valued narrow band BP signal $x(t)$ can be represented mathematically by

$$x_{BP}(t) = r(t)\cos(2\pi f_0 t + \phi_x(t))$$

Eq. (1.162)

where the subscript BP indicates a bandpass signal, $r(t)$ is the amplitude modulation or envelope, $\phi_x(t)$ is the phase modulation, f_0 is the carrier frequency, and both $r(t)$ and $\phi_x(t)$ have frequency contents significantly smaller than f_0. The frequency modulation is given as the time derivative of the phase. More specifically,

$$f_m(t) = \frac{1}{2\pi} \frac{d}{dt}\phi_x(t)$$

Eq. (1.163)

and the instantaneous frequency of the time signal $x(t)$ is

$$f_i(t) = \frac{1}{2\pi} \frac{d}{dt}(2\pi f_0 t + \phi_x(t)) = f_0 + f_m(t).$$

Eq. (1.164)

Let B be the signal bandwidth, if f_0 is very large compared to B, the signal $x(t)$ is referred to as a narrow bandpass signal. Bandpass signals can also be represented by two lowpass signals known as the quadrature components; in this case Eq. (1.162) can be expressed as

$$x_{BP}(t) = x_I(t)\cos 2\pi f_0 t - x_Q(t)\sin 2\pi f_0 t$$

Eq. (1.165)

where $x_I(t)$ and $x_Q(t)$ are real LP signals referred to as the quadrature components (I-channel and Q-channel) and are given, respectively, by

$$x_I(t) = r(t)\cos\phi_x(t)$$
$$x_Q(t) = r(t)\sin\phi_x(t)$$

Eq. (1.166)

Figure 1.6 shows the quadrature components extraction process. First, the bandpass signal is split into two parts; one part is multiplied by $2\cos 2\pi f_0 t$ and the other is multiplied by $-2\sin 2\pi f_0 t$. From the figure, the two signals $z_1(t)$ and $z_2(t)$ are,

$$z_1(t) = 2x_I(t)(\cos 2\pi f_0 t)^2 - 2x_Q(t)\cos(2\pi f_0 t)\sin(2\pi f_0 t)$$

Eq. (1.167)

$$z_2(t) = -2x_I(t)\cos(2\pi f_0 t)\sin(2\pi f_0 t) + 2x_Q(t)(\sin 2\pi f_0 t)^2.$$

Eq. (1.168)

One can easily show using the appropriate trigonometric identities that the output of the low-pass filters are $x_I(t)$ and $x_Q(t)$.

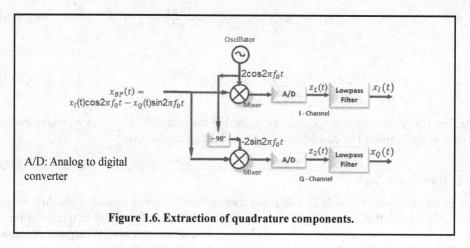

Figure 1.6. Extraction of quadrature components.

1.8.1. Analytic Signal (Pre-Envelope)

Given a real-valued signal $x(t)$, its Hilbert transform is

$$\mathcal{H}\{x(t)\} = \hat{x}(t) = \frac{1}{\pi}\int_{-\infty}^{\infty}\frac{x(u)}{t-u}\,du$$

Eq. (1.169)

Observation of Eq. (1.169) indicates that the Hilbert transform is computed as the convolution between the signals $x(t)$ and $h(t) = 1/(\pi t)$. More precisely,

$$\hat{x}(t) = x(t) \otimes \frac{1}{\pi t}.$$

Eq. (1.170)

The Fourier transform of $h(t)$ is

$$\mathcal{F}\{h(t)\} = \mathcal{F}\left\{\frac{1}{\pi t}\right\} = H(\omega) = e^{-j\frac{\pi}{2}}\,\text{sgn}(\omega)$$

Eq. (1.171)

where the function $\text{sgn}(\omega)$ is given by

$$\text{sgn}(\omega) = \frac{\omega}{|\omega|} = \begin{cases} 1 & ; \ \omega > 0 \\ 0; & \omega = 0 \\ -1 & ; \ \omega < 0 \end{cases}.$$

Eq. (1.172)

Thus, the effect of the Hilbert transform is to introduce a phase shift of $\pi/2$ on the signal $X(\omega)$. It follows that,

$$\mathcal{F}\{\hat{x}(t)\} = \hat{X}(\omega) = X(\omega) \times e^{-j\frac{\pi}{2}} \text{sgn}(\omega) = -X(\omega) \times \text{sgn}(\omega).$$

Eq. (1.173)

The analytic signal $\psi(t)$ corresponding to the real signal $x(t)$ is obtained by canceling the negative frequency contents of $X(\omega)$. Then, by definition

$$\Psi(\omega) = \begin{cases} 2X(\omega) & ; \omega > 0 \\ X(\omega) & ; \omega = 0 \\ 0 & ; \omega < 0 \end{cases}$$

Eq. (1.174)

or equivalently,

$$\Psi(\omega) = X(\omega)(1 + \text{sgn}(\omega)).$$

Eq. (1.175)

It follows that

$$\psi(t) = \mathcal{F}^{-1}\{\Psi(\omega)\} = x(t) + j\hat{x}(t).$$

Eq. (1.176)

The analytic signal is often referred to as the pre-envelope of $x(t)$ because the envelope of $x(t)$ can be obtained by simply taking the modulus of $\psi(t)$.

1.8.2. Pre-Envelope and Complex Envelope of Bandpass Signals

The Hilbert transform for the bandpass signal defined in Eq. (1.165) is

$$\hat{x}_{BP}(t) = \mathcal{H}\{x_{BP}(t)\} = x_I(t)\sin 2\pi f_0 t + x_Q(t)\cos 2\pi f_0 t.$$

Eq. (1.177)

The corresponding bandpass analytic signal (pre-envelope) is then given by

$$\psi_{BP}(t) = x_{BP}(t) + j\hat{x}_{BP}(t)$$

Eq. (1.178)

using Eq. (1.165) and Eq. (1.177) into Eq. (1.178) and collecting terms yields

$$\psi_{BP}(t) = [x_I(t) + jx_Q(t)]e^{j2\pi f_0 t} = \tilde{x}_{BP}(t)e^{j2\pi f_0 t}.$$

Eq. (1.179)

The signal $\tilde{x}_{BP}(t) = x_I(t) + jx_Q(t)$ is the complex envelope of $x_{BP}(t)$. Thus, the envelope signal and associated phase deviation are given by

$$a(t) = |\tilde{x}_{BP}(t)| = |x_I(t) + jx_Q(t)| = |\psi_{BP}(t)|$$

Eq. (1.180)

$$\phi(t) = \arg(\tilde{x}_{BP}(t)) = \angle\tilde{x}_{BP}(t).$$

Eq. (1.181)

In the remainder of this handbook, unless otherwise indicated, all signals will be considered to be bandpass signals and consequently the subscript BP will not be used. More specifically, a bandpass signal $x(t)$ and its corresponding pre-envelope (analytic signal) and complex envelope will be shown as

$$x(t) = x_I(t)\cos 2\pi f_0 t - x_Q(t)\sin 2\pi f_0 t$$

Eq. (1.182)

$$\psi(t) \doteq x(t) + j\hat{x}(t) \equiv \tilde{x}(t)e^{j2\pi f_0 t}$$

Eq. (1.183)

$$\tilde{x}(t) = x_I(t) + jx_Q(t).$$ **Eq. (1.184)**

Example:

Extract the quadrature components, frequency modulation, instantaneous frequency, analytic signal, and complex envelope for the signals:

(a) $x(t) = Rect\left(\dfrac{t}{\tau}\right)\cos(2\pi f_0 t)$; (b) $x(t) = Rect\left(\dfrac{t}{\tau}\right)\cos\left(2\pi f_0 t + \dfrac{\pi B}{\tau}t^2\right)$.

Solution:

(a) The quadrature components are extracted as described in Fig. 1.6. Define

$$z_1(t) = x(t) \times 2\cos(2\pi f_0 t), \quad z_2(t) = x(t) \times (-2)\sin(2\pi f_0 t),$$

then

$$z_1(t) = Rect\left(\frac{t}{\tau}\right)\cos(2\pi f_0 t) \times 2\cos(2\pi f_0 t) = Rect\left(\frac{t}{\tau}\right)\cos(0) + Rect\left(\frac{t}{\tau}\right)\cos(4\pi f_0 t)$$

$$z_2(t) = Rect\left(\frac{t}{\tau}\right)\cos(2\pi f_0 t) \times (-2)\sin(2\pi f_0 t) = Rect\left(\frac{t}{\tau}\right)\sin(0) - Rect\left(\frac{t}{\tau}\right)\sin(4\pi f_0 t).$$

Thus, the output of the LPFs are

$$x_I(t) = Rect\left(\frac{t}{\tau}\right) \quad ; \quad x_Q(t) = 0.$$

From Eq. (1.163) and Eq. (1.164) we get

$$f_m(t) = 0 \quad ; \quad f_i(t) = f_0.$$

Finally the complex envelope and the analytic signal are given by

$$\tilde{x}(t) = x_I(t) + jx_Q(t) = x_I(t) = Rect\left(\frac{t}{\tau}\right)$$

$$\psi(t) = \tilde{x}(t)e^{j2\pi f_0 t} = Rect\left(\frac{t}{\tau}\right)e^{j2\pi f_0 t}$$

(b)

$$z_1(t) = Rect\left(\frac{t}{\tau}\right)\cos\left(2\pi f_0 t + \frac{\pi B}{\tau}t^2\right) \times 2\cos(2\pi f_0 t)$$

which can be rewritten as

$$z_1(t) = Rect\left(\frac{t}{\tau}\right)\cos\left(\frac{\pi B}{\tau}t^2\right) + Rect\left(\frac{t}{\tau}\right)\cos\left(4\pi f_0 t + \frac{\pi B}{\tau}t^2\right)$$

and

$$z_2(t) = Rect\left(\frac{t}{\tau}\right)\cos\left(2\pi f_0 t + \frac{\pi B}{\tau}t^2\right) \times (-2)\sin(2\pi f_0 t),$$

which can be rewritten as

$$z_2(t) = Rect\left(\frac{t}{\tau}\right)\sin\left(\frac{\pi B}{\tau}t^2\right) - Rect\left(\frac{t}{\tau}\right)\sin\left(4\pi f_0 t + \frac{\pi B}{\tau}t^2\right).$$

Thus, the outputs of the low pass filters are

$$x_I(t) = Rect\left(\frac{t}{\tau}\right)\cos\left(\frac{\pi B}{\tau}t^2\right) \quad ; \quad x_Q(t) = Rect\left(\frac{t}{\tau}\right)\sin\left(\frac{\pi B}{\tau}t^2\right).$$

From Eq. (1.163) and Eq. (1.164) we get

$$f_m(t) = \frac{B}{\tau}t \qquad ; \ f_i(t) = f_0 + \frac{B}{\tau}t.$$

The complex envelope is

$$\tilde{x}(t) = x_I(t) + jx_Q(t) = Rect\left(\frac{t}{\tau}\right)\cos\left(\frac{\pi B}{\tau}t^2\right) + jRect\left(\frac{t}{\tau}\right)\sin\left(\frac{\pi B}{\tau}t^2\right),$$

which can be written as

$$\tilde{x}(t) = Rect\left(\frac{t}{\tau}\right)e^{j\left(\frac{\pi B}{\tau}t^2\right)}.$$

Finally, the analytic signal is

$$\psi(t) = \tilde{x}(t)e^{j2\pi f_0 t} = Rect\left(\frac{t}{\tau}\right)e^{j\left(\frac{\pi B}{\tau}t^2\right)}e^{j2\pi f_0 t} = Rect\left(\frac{t}{\tau}\right)e^{j\left(2\pi f_0 t + \frac{\pi B}{\tau}t^2\right)}.$$

1.8.3. Spectrum for a Linear Frequency Modulation Signal

Frequency or phase modulated signals can be used to achieve much wider instantaneous bandwidths. Linear frequency modulation (LFM) is very commonly used in many modern radar systems. In this case, the frequency is swept linearly across the pulse width, either upward (up-chirp) or downward (down-chirp). Figure 1.7 shows a typical example of an LFM waveform. The pulse width is τ_0, and the bandwidth is B.

The LFM up-chirp instantaneous phase can be expressed by

$$\phi(t) = 2\pi\left(f_0 t + \frac{\mu}{2}t^2\right) \qquad -\frac{\tau_0}{2} \leq t \leq \frac{\tau_0}{2}, \qquad\qquad \text{Eq. (1.185)}$$

where f_0 is the radar center frequency, and $\mu = (B/\tau_0)$ is the LFM coefficient. Thus, the instantaneous frequency is

$$f(t) = \frac{1}{2\pi}\frac{d}{dt}\phi(t) = f_0 + \mu t \qquad -\frac{\tau_0}{2} \leq t \leq \frac{\tau_0}{2}. \qquad\qquad \text{Eq. (1.186)}$$

Similarly, the down-chirp instantaneous phase and frequency are given, respectively, by

$$\phi(t) = 2\pi\left(f_0 t - \frac{\mu}{2}t^2\right) \qquad -\frac{\tau_0}{2} \leq t \leq \frac{\tau_0}{2} \qquad\qquad \text{Eq. (1.187)}$$

$$f(t) = \frac{1}{2\pi}\frac{d}{dt}\phi(t) = f_0 - \mu t \qquad -\frac{\tau_0}{2} \leq t \leq \frac{\tau_0}{2}. \qquad\qquad \text{Eq. (1.188)}$$

A typical up-chirp LFM waveform can be expressed by

$$x(t) = Rect\left(\frac{t}{\tau_0}\right)e^{j2\pi\left(f_0 t + \frac{\mu}{2}t^2\right)} \qquad\qquad \text{Eq. (1.189)}$$

where $Rect(t/\tau_0)$ denotes a rectangular pulse of width τ_0. Remember that the signal $x(t)$ in Eq. (1.189) is the analytic signal for the LFM waveform. It follows that,

$$x(t) = \tilde{x}(t) e^{j2\pi f_0 t}$$

Eq. (1.190)

$$\tilde{x}(t) = Rect\left(\frac{t}{\tau_0}\right) e^{j\pi\mu t^2}.$$

Eq. (1.191)

The spectrum of the signal $x(t)$ is determined from its complex envelope $\tilde{x}(t)$. The complex exponential term in Eq. (1.191) introduces a frequency shift about the center frequency f_o. Taking the Fourier transform of $\tilde{x}(t)$ yields

$$\tilde{X}(f) = \int_{-\infty}^{\infty} Rect\left(\frac{t}{\tau_0}\right) e^{j\pi\mu t^2} \ e^{-j2\pi ft} dt = \int_{-\frac{\tau_0}{2}}^{\frac{\tau_0}{2}} e^{j\pi\mu t^2} \ e^{-j2\pi ft} dt$$

Eq. (1.192)

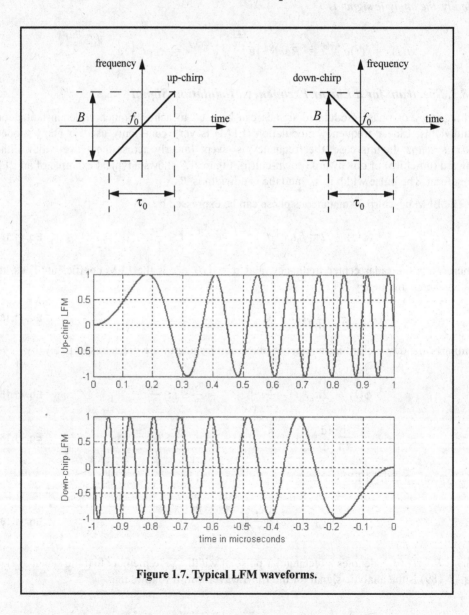

Figure 1.7. Typical LFM waveforms.

Let $\mu' = \pi\mu = \pi B/\tau_0$, and perform the change of variable

$$\left(z = \sqrt{\frac{2}{\pi}}\left(\sqrt{\mu'}t - \frac{\pi f}{\sqrt{\mu'}}\right)\right) \quad ; \quad \sqrt{\frac{\pi}{2\mu'}} \, dz = dt. \qquad \text{Eq. (1.193)}$$

Thus, Eq. (1.192) can be written as

$$\tilde{X}(f) = \sqrt{\frac{\pi}{2\mu'}} \; e^{-j(\pi f)^2/\mu'} \int_{-z_1}^{z_2} e^{j\pi z^2/2} \, dz \qquad \text{Eq. (1.194)}$$

$$\tilde{X}(f) = \sqrt{\frac{\pi}{2\mu'}} \; e^{-j(\pi f)^2/\mu'} \left\{ \int_0^{z_2} e^{j\pi z^2/2} \, dz - \int_0^{-z_1} e^{j\pi z^2/2} \, dz \right\} \qquad \text{Eq. (1.195)}$$

$$z_1 = -\sqrt{\frac{2\mu'}{\pi}}\left(\frac{\tau_0}{2} + \frac{\pi f}{\mu'}\right) = \sqrt{\frac{B\tau_0}{2}}\left(1 + \frac{f}{\frac{B}{2}}\right) \qquad \text{Eq. (1.196)}$$

$$z_2 = \sqrt{\frac{\mu'}{\pi}}\left(\frac{\tau_0}{2} - \frac{\omega}{\mu'}\right) = \sqrt{\frac{B\tau_0}{2}}\left(1 - \frac{f}{\frac{B}{2}}\right). \qquad \text{Eq. (1.197)}$$

The Fresnel integrals, denoted by $C(z)$ and $S(z)$, are defined by

$$C(z) = \int_0^z \cos\left(\frac{\pi \upsilon^2}{2}\right) d\upsilon \qquad \text{Eq. (1.198a)}$$

and

$$S(z) = \int_0^z \sin\left(\frac{\pi \upsilon^2}{2}\right) d\upsilon. \qquad \text{Eq. (1.198b)}$$

Fresnel integrals can be approximated by

$$C(z) \approx \frac{1}{2} + \frac{1}{\pi z}\sin\left(\frac{\pi}{2}z^2\right) \quad ; \quad z \gg 1 \qquad \text{Eq. (1.199)}$$

$$S(z) \approx \frac{1}{2} - \frac{1}{\pi z}\cos\left(\frac{\pi}{2}z^2\right) \quad ; \quad z \gg 1. \qquad \text{Eq. (1.200)}$$

Note that $C(-z) = -C(z)$ and $S(-z) = -S(z)$. Figure 1.8 shows a plot of both $C(z)$ and $S(z)$ for $0 \le z \le 4.0$.

Using Eqs. (1.198a) and (1.198b) into Eq. (1.195) and performing the integration yield

$$\tilde{X}(f) = \sqrt{\frac{\pi}{2\mu'}} \; e^{-j(\pi f)^2/(\mu')} \qquad \text{Eq. (1.201)}$$

$$\{[C(z_2) + C(z_1)] + j[S(z_2) + S(z_1)]\}$$

Figure 1.9 shows typical plots for the LFM real part, imaginary part, and amplitude spectrum. The square-like spectrum shown in Fig. 1.9c is widely known as the Fresnel spectrum.

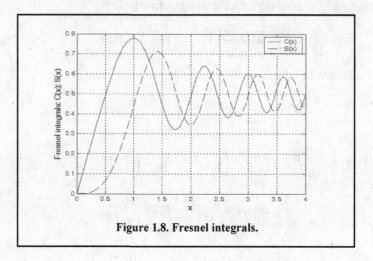

Figure 1.8. Fresnel integrals.

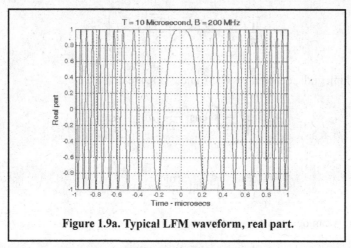

Figure 1.9a. Typical LFM waveform, real part.

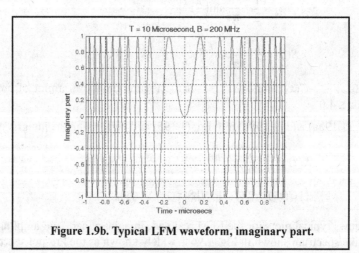

Figure 1.9b. Typical LFM waveform, imaginary part.

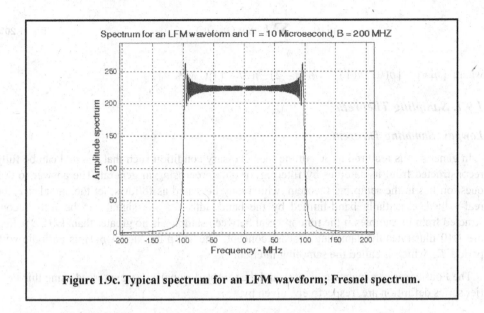

Figure 1.9c. Typical spectrum for an LFM waveform; Fresnel spectrum.

1.9. Discrete Time Systems and Signals

Advances in computer hardware and in digital technologies have completely revolutionized radar systems signals and data processing techniques. Virtually all modern radar systems use some form of a digital representation (signal samples) of their received signals for the purposes of signal and data processing. These samples of a time-limited signal are nothing more than a finite set of numbers (thought of as a vector) that represents discrete values of the continuous time domain signal. These samples are typically obtained by using Analog-to-Digital (A/D) conversion devices. Since in the digital world the radar receiver is now concerned with processing a set of finite numbers, its impulse response will also compose a set of finite numbers. Consequently, the radar receiver is now referred to as a discrete system. All input/output signal relationships are now carried out using discrete time samples. It must also be noted that just as in the case of continuous time-domain systems, the discrete systems of interest to radar applications must also be causal, stable, and linear time invariant.

Consider a continuous lowpass signal that is time-limited with duration τ and band-limited with bandwidth B. This signal (as will be shown in the next section) can be completely represented by a set of no more than $\{2\tau B\}$ samples. The value (τB) is widely known as the time-bandwidth product of a signal. Since a finite set of discrete values (samples) is used to represent the signal, it is common to represent this signal by a finite dimensional vector of the same size. This vector is denoted by $\mathbf{x}$, or simply by the sequence $x[n]$,

$$\mathbf{x} \equiv x[n] = [x(0) \; x(1) \; ...x(N-2) \; x(N-1)]'$$

Eq. (1.202)

where the superscript $'$ denotes transpose operation (not to be confused with the complex conjugate transpose symbol †). The value N is at least $2\tau B$ for a real lowpass limited signal $x(t)$ of duration τ and bandwidth B. If, however, the signal is complex, then N is at least τB and the components of the vector $\mathbf{x}$ are complex. The samples defined in Eq. (1.202) can be obtained from pulse-to-pulse samples at a fixed range (i.e., delay) of the radar echo signal. The PRF is denoted by f_r and the total observation interval is T_0; then N would be equal to $T_0 f_r$. Define the radar receiver transfer function as the discrete sequence $h[n]$ and the input signal sequence as $x[n]$; then the output sequence $y[n]$ is given by the convolution sum

$$y[n] = \sum_{m=0}^{M-1} h(m)x(n-m) \qquad\qquad \textbf{Eq. (1.203)}$$

where $\{h[n] = [h(0)\ \ h(1)\ \ ...h(M-2)\ \ h(M-1)];\ \ M \le N\}$.

1.9.1. Sampling Theorem

Lowpass Sampling Theorem

In general, it is required to determine the necessary condition such that a signal can be fully reconstructed from its samples by filtering, or data processing in general. The answer to this question lies in the sampling theorem, which may be stated as follows: let the signal $x(t)$ be real-valued, essentially band-limited by the bandwidth B; this signal can be fully reconstructed from its samples if the time interval between samples is no greater than $1/(2B)$. Figure 1.10 illustrates the sampling process concept. The sampling signal $p(t)$ is periodic with period T_s, which is called the sampling interval.

The Fourier series expansion of $p(t)$ and the sampled signal $x_s(t)$ expressed using this Fourier series definition are, respectively, given by

$$p(t) = \sum_{n=-\infty}^{\infty} P_n e^{j\frac{2\pi nt}{T_s}} \qquad\qquad \textbf{Eq. (1.204)}$$

$$x_s(t) = p(t) \cdot x(t) \qquad\qquad \textbf{Eq. (1.205)}$$

$$x_s(t) = \sum_{n=-\infty}^{\infty} x(t) P_n e^{j\frac{2\pi nt}{T_s}} \qquad\qquad \textbf{Eq. (1.206)}$$

where P_n are the Fourier series coefficients. Taking the Fourier transform of $x_s(t)$ yields

$$X_s(\omega) = \sum_{n=-\infty}^{\infty} P_n\, X\!\left(\omega - \frac{2\pi n}{T_s}\right) = P_0 X(\omega) + \sum_{\substack{n=-\infty \\ n \ne 0}}^{\infty} P_n\, X\!\left(\omega - \frac{2\pi n}{T_s}\right) \qquad \textbf{Eq. (1.207)}$$

where $X(\omega)$ is the Fourier transform of $x(t)$. Therefore, we conclude that the spectral density, $X_s(\omega)$, consists of replicas of $X(\omega)$ spaced $(2\pi/T_s)$ apart and scaled by the Fourier series coefficients P_n. A lowpass filter (LPF) of bandwidth B can then be used to recover the original signal $x(t)$.

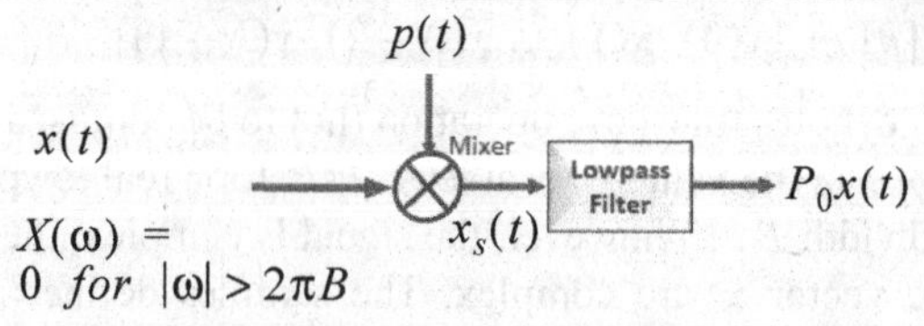

Figure 1.10. Concept of sampling.

When the sampling rate is increased (i.e., T_s decreases), the replicas of $X(\omega)$ move farther apart. Alternatively, when the sampling rate is decreased (i.e., T_s increases), the replicas get closer to one another. The value of T_s such that the replicas are tangent (touching) to one another defines the minimum required sampling rate so that $x(t)$ can be recovered from its samples by using an LPF. It follows that

$$\frac{2\pi}{T_s} = 2\pi(2B) \Leftrightarrow T_s = \frac{1}{2B}.$$ **Eq. (1.208)**

The sampling rate defined by Eq. (1.208) is known as the Nyquist sampling rate. When $T_s > (1/2B)$, the replicas of $X(\omega)$ overlap, and thus $x(t)$ cannot be recovered cleanly from its samples. This is known as aliasing. In practice, ideal LPF cannot be implemented; hence, practical systems tend to oversample in order to avoid aliasing.

It is desirable to develop a general expression from which any lowpass signal can be recovered from its samples, provided that Eq. (1.208) is satisfied. In order to do that, let $x(t)$ and $x_s(t)$ be the desired lowpass signal and its corresponding samples, respectively. Then an expression for $x(t)$ in terms of its samples can be derived as follows: First, obtain $X(\omega)$ by filtering the signal $X_s(\omega)$ using an ideal LPF whose transfer function is

$$H(\omega) = T_s Rect\left(\frac{\omega}{4\pi B}\right).$$ **Eq. (1.209)**

Thus,

$$X(\omega) = H(\omega)X_s(\omega) = T_s Rect\left(\frac{\omega}{4\pi B}\right)X_s(\omega).$$ **Eq. (1.210)**

The signal $x(t)$ is now obtained from the inverse Fourier transform of the right-hand side of Eq. (1.210) as

$$x(t) = \mathcal{F}^{-1}\left\{T_s Rect\left(\frac{\omega}{4\pi B}\right)X_s(\omega)\right\} = 2BT_s Sinc(2\pi Bt) \otimes x_s(t).$$ **Eq. (1.211)**

The sampled signal $x_s(t)$ can be represented using an ideal sampling signal

$$p(t) = \sum_n \delta(t - nT_s)$$ **Eq. (1.212)**

thus,

$$x_s(t) = \sum_n x(nT_s)\delta(t - nT_s).$$ **Eq. (1.213)**

Substituting Eq. (1.211) into Eq. (1.213) yields an expression for the signal $x(t)$ in terms of its samples

$$x_s(t) = 2BT_s \sum_n x(nT_s)\ Sinc(2\pi B(t - T_s))\ ; T_s \le \frac{1}{2B}$$ **Eq. (1.214)**

Bandpass Sampling Theorem

It was established earlier that any bandpass signal can be expressed using the quadrature components. It follows that it is sufficient to construct the bandpass signal $x(t)$ from samples of the quadrature components $\{x_I(t), x_Q(t)\}$. Let the signal $x(t)$ be essentially band-limited with bandwidth B, then each of the lowpass signals $x_I(t)$ and $x_Q(t)$ are also band-limited each with bandwidth $B/2$. Hence, if either or both of these lowpass signals are sampled at a rate $f_s \leq 1/B$, then the Nyquist criterion is not violated. Assume that both quadrature components are sampled synchronously, that is

$$x_I(t) = BT_s \sum_{n = -\infty}^{\infty} x_I(nT_s) \; Sinc(\pi B(t - nT_s)) \qquad \text{Eq. (1.215)}$$

$$x_Q(t) = BT_s \sum_{n = -\infty}^{\infty} x_Q(nT_s) \; Sinc(\pi B(t - nT_s)) \qquad \text{Eq. (1.216)}$$

where if the Nyquist rate is satisfied, then $BT_s = 1$ (unity time-bandwidth product). Substituting Eq. (1.215) and Eq. (1.216) into Eq. (1.165) yields

$$x(t) = BT_s \left\{ \sum_{n = -\infty}^{\infty} [x_I(nT_s)\cos 2\pi f_0 t - x_Q(nT_s)\sin 2\pi f_0 t] \; Sinc(\pi B(t - nT_s)) \right\} \qquad \text{Eq. (1.217)}$$

$$x(t) = Re\left\{ BT_s \sum_{n = -\infty}^{\infty} [x_I(nT_s) + jx_Q(nT_s)] e^{j2\pi f_0 t} Sinc(\pi B(t - nT_s)) \right\} \qquad \text{Eq. (1.218)}$$

where, of course, $T_s \leq 1/B$ is assumed. This leads to the conclusion that if the total period over which the signal $x(t)$ is sampled is T_0, then $2BT_0$ samples are required, BT_0 samples for $x_I(t)$ and BT_0 samples for $x_Q(t)$.

Example:

Assume that the sampling signal $p(t)$ is given by

$$p(t) = \sum_{n = -\infty}^{\infty} \delta(t - nT_s).$$

Compute an expression for $X_s(\omega)$.

Solution:

The signal $p(t)$ is called the Comb function, with exponential Fourier series

$$p(t) = \sum_{n = -\infty}^{\infty} \frac{1}{T_s} e^{2\frac{\pi n t}{T_s}}.$$

It follows that

$$x_s(t) = \sum_{n=-\infty}^{\infty} x(t)\frac{1}{T_s}e^{2\frac{\pi nt}{T_s}}.$$

Taking the Fourier transform of this equation yields

$$X_s(\omega) = \frac{2\pi}{T_s} \sum_{n=-\infty}^{\infty} X\left(\omega - \frac{2\pi n}{T_s}\right).$$

1.10. Z-Transform

The Z-transform is a transformation that maps samples of a discrete time-domain sequence into a new domain known as the z-domain. It is defined as

$$X(z) = Z\{x(n)\} = \sum_{n=-\infty}^{\infty} x(n)z^{-n} \qquad \text{Eq. (1.219)}$$

where $z = re^{j\omega}$, and for most cases, $r = 1$. It follows that Eq. (1.219) can be rewritten as

$$X(e^{j\omega}) = \sum_{n=-\infty}^{\infty} x(n)e^{-jn\omega}. \qquad \text{Eq. (1.220)}$$

In the z-domain, the region over which $X(z)$ is finite is called the region of convergence (ROC). A discrete LTI system has a transfer function $H(z)$ that describes how the system operates on its input sequence $x(n)$ in order to produce the output sequence $y(n)$. The output sequence $y(n)$ is computed from the discrete convolution between the sequences $x(n)$ and $h(n)$:

$$y(n) = \sum_{m=-\infty}^{\infty} x(m)h(n-m). \qquad \text{Eq. (1.221)}$$

However, since practical systems require the sequence $x(n)$ and $h(n)$ to be of finite length, we can rewrite Eq. (1.221) as

$$y(n) = \sum_{m=0}^{N} x(m)h(n-m). \qquad \text{Eq. (1.222)}$$

where N denotes the input sequence length. The Z-transform of Eq. (1.222) is

$$Y(z) = X(z)H(z) \qquad \text{Eq. (1.223)}$$

and the discrete system transfer function is

$$H(z) = Y(z)/X(z). \qquad \text{Eq. (1.224)}$$

Finally, the transfer function $H(z)$ can be written as

$$H(z)\big|_{z=e^{j\omega}} = |H(e^{j\omega})|e^{\angle H(e^{j\omega})} \qquad \text{Eq. (1.225)}$$

where $|H(e^{j\omega})|$ is the amplitude response, and $\angle H(e^{j\omega})$ is the phase response. Table 1.3 shows some common Z-transform pairs.

Table 1.3. Z-Transform Pairs.

$x(n)$; $n \geq 0$	$X(z)$	ROC; $|z| > R$
$\delta(n)$	1	0
1	$\dfrac{z}{(z-1)}$	1
n	$\dfrac{z}{(z-1)^2}$	1
n^2	$\dfrac{z(z+1)}{(z-1)^3}$	1
a^n	$\dfrac{z}{(z-a)}$	$|a|$
na^n	$\dfrac{az}{(z-a)^2}$	$|a|$
$\dfrac{a^n}{n!}$	$e^{a/z}$	0
$(n+1)a^n$	$\dfrac{z^2}{(z-a)^2}$	$|a|$
$\sin n\omega T$	$\dfrac{z\sin\omega T}{z^2 - 2z\cos\omega T + 1}$	1
$\cos n\omega T$	$\dfrac{z(z-\cos\omega T)}{z^2 - 2z\cos\omega T + 1}$	1
$a^n \sin n\omega T$	$\dfrac{az\sin\omega T}{z^2 - 2az\cos\omega T + a^2}$	$\dfrac{1}{|a|}$
$a^n \cos n\omega T$	$\dfrac{z(z - a^2\cos\omega T)}{z^2 - 2az\cos\omega T + a^2}$	$\dfrac{1}{|a|}$
$\dfrac{n(n-1)}{2!}$	$\dfrac{z}{(z-1)^3}$	1
$\dfrac{n(n-1)(n-2)}{3!}$	$\dfrac{z}{(z-1)^4}$	1
$\dfrac{(n+1)(n+2)a^n}{2!}$	$\dfrac{z^3}{(z-a)^3}$	$|a|$
$\dfrac{(n+1)(n+2)...(n+m)a^n}{m!}$	$\dfrac{z^{m+1}}{(z-a)^{m+1}}$	$|a|$

1.11. Discrete Fourier Transform

The discrete Fourier transform (DFT) is a mathematical operation that transforms a discrete sequence, usually from the time domain into the frequency domain, in order to explicitly determine the spectral information for the sequence. The time-domain sequence can be real or complex. The DFT has finite length N and is periodic with period equal to N. The discrete Fourier transform pairs for the finite sequence $x(n)$ are defined by

$$X(k) = \sum_{n=0}^{N-1} x(n) e^{-j\frac{2\pi nk}{N}} \qquad ; \ k = 0, ..., N-1 \qquad \text{Eq. (1.226)}$$

$$x(n) = \frac{1}{N} \sum_{k=0}^{N-1} X(k) e^{j\frac{2\pi nk}{N}} \qquad ; \ n = 0, ..., N-1. \qquad \text{Eq. (1.227)}$$

The fast Fourier transform (FFT) is not a new kind of transform different from the DFT. Instead, it is an algorithm used to compute the DFT more efficiently. There are numerous FFT algorithms that can be found in the literature. In this book we will interchangeably use the DFT and the FFT to mean the same thing. Furthermore, we will assume a radix-2 FFT algorithm, where the FFT size is equal to $N = 2^m$ for some integer m.

1.11.1. Discrete Power Spectrum

Practical discrete systems utilize DFTs of finite length as a means of numerical approximation for the Fourier transform. The input signals must be truncated to a finite duration (denoted by T) before they are sampled. This is necessary so that a finite length sequence is generated prior to signal processing. Unfortunately, this truncation process may cause some serious problems. To demonstrate this difficulty, consider the time-domain signal $x(t) = \sin 2\pi f_0 t$. The spectrum of $x(t)$ consists of two spectral lines at $\pm f_0$. Now, when $x(t)$ is truncated to length T seconds and sampled at a rate $T_s = T/N$, where N is the number of desired samples, we produce the sequence $\{x(n); \ n = 0, 1, ..., N-1\}$.

A truncated sequence $x(n)$ can be viewed as one period of some periodic sequence with period N. The discrete Fourier series expansion of $x(n)$ is

$$x(n) = \sum_{k=0}^{N-1} X_k e^{-j\frac{2\pi nk}{N}}. \qquad \text{Eq. (1.228)}$$

It can be shown that the coefficients X_k are given by

$$X_k = \frac{1}{N} \sum_{n=0}^{N-1} x(n) e^{-j\frac{2\pi nk}{N}} = \frac{1}{N} X(k) \qquad \text{Eq. (1.229)}$$

where $X(k)$ is the DFT of $x(n)$. Therefore, the discrete power spectrum (DPS), for the band-limited sequence $x(n)$ is the plot of $|X_k|^2$ versus k, where the lines are Δf apart,

$$P_0 = \frac{1}{N^2} |X(0)|^2 \qquad \text{Eq. (1.230)}$$

$$P_k = \frac{1}{N^2} \{|X(k)|^2 + |X(N-k)|^2\} \qquad ; \ k = 1, 2, ..., \frac{N}{2} - 1 \qquad \text{Eq. (1.231)}$$

$$P_{N/2} = \frac{1}{N^2}|X(N/2)|^2.$$ Eq. (1.232)

Note that the DPS is also called the discrete amplitude line spectrum, or simply, the line spectrum. In practice, radar systems employ time and / or frequency interpolation and will accordingly display the amplitude line spectrum in the form of a $|\sin(x)/x|$ instead of discrete amplitude lines. Recall that the DFT is a periodic function and the line power spectrum is computed as its modulus square.

Before proceeding to the next section, we will show how to select the FFT parameters. For this purpose, consider a band-limited signal $x(t)$ with bandwidth B. If the signal is not band-limited, an LPF can be first used to eliminate frequencies greater than B. In order to satisfy the sampling theorem, one must choose a sampling frequency $f_s = 1/t_s$, such that

$$f_s \geq 2B.$$ Eq. (1.233)

The truncated sequence duration T and the total number of samples N are related by

$$T = Nt_s$$ Eq. (1.234)

or equivalently,

$$f_s = \frac{N}{T}.$$ Eq. (1.235)

It follows that

$$f_s = \frac{N}{T} \geq 2B$$ Eq. (1.236)

and the frequency resolution is

$$\Delta f = \frac{1}{Nt_s} = \frac{f_s}{N} = \frac{1}{T} \geq \frac{2B}{N}.$$ Eq. (1.237)

1.11.2. Spectral Leakage and Fold-Over

Spectral Leakage

The DFT can be interpreted as a numerical approximation of the Fourier transform or the Fourier series. The periodicity of the DFT can present serious problems when estimating the discrete line power spectrum. To demonstrate this difficulty, consider the sine-wave signal $x(t) = \sin(2\pi t/T_0)$; ideally, the spectrum for this signal should consist of two symmetric lines located at $\pm f_0$, where $f_0 = 1/T_0$.

Define the truncated record (i.e., its samples) of $x(t)$ by $x_s(t)$ and let T be equal to the truncation period, it follows that the sampling interval for $x_s(t)$ is $t_s = T/N$, where N is the total number of samples. If by some chance the period T is a multiple-integer of T_0 and if f_0 is also a multiple-integer of ΔF, then indeed the discrete line power spectrum will be made of two discrete lines at $\pm f_0$. However, those two conditions are rarely met and as a result the line power spectrum will be made of many lines (i.e., spectral spread, spill-over, or leakage).

For example, let $T = 1.5T_0 = 32t_s$; in this case, the DFT algorithm assumes that the period is T instead of T_0. In other words, it assumes that $x(N-1) = 1$ while $x(N) = x(1) = 0$. This discontinuity created by the arbitrary selection of the record length is the main culprit behind the frequency spread and it cannot be avoided since T_0 is typically unknown. One can, however, effectively compress or reduce this spread by placing smaller weights onto samples near the edges of the record. This technique is known as windowing and will be discussed in the next section.

When the signal $x(t)$ is stationary and deterministic, then one record (i.e., one period) is sufficient to compute its discrete line power spectrum. The typical set of operations in a signal processing chain include: analog lowpass filtering, A/D conversion, windowing, DFT operation, and finally computation of the discrete line power spectrum. As described earlier, the inverse of the observation interval is the frequency resolution. Thus, for a given sampling frequency (bandwidth) the frequency resolution, ΔF, is improved as the record length is increased. Note that frequency interpolation of the DFT only improves the visual display of the DFT samples and does not improve its frequency resolution. This is a very common mistake made by many inexperienced engineers.

In general, signals in radar applications are not deterministic and one cannot guarantee the stationary condition; accordingly, one must compute the line power spectrum for several consecutive periods (records). Assume for example the signal $x(t)$ contains a decaying sine-wave with frequency f_0. Then the line spectrum for the *kth* record will contain a sine-wave of frequency f_0 and amplitude A_k, where A_k decreases as k is increased (i.e., over time). In this application the record duration should be a fraction of the transient time constant, even though this limits the frequency resolution.

More commonly in radar application, we analyze signals comprising a sum of a periodic and random components. The random component of the signal will vary unpredictably from one record to the next. The same holds true for its corresponding line power spectrum. Therefore, a first estimate of the power spectrum is obtained by performing an ensemble averaging on the set of line spectra. This estimate will still appear as random because the frequency resolution is greater than what the available information allows. Thus, the ensemble averaging is followed by frequency smoothing which acts like trade-off between resolution and smoothing.

To further demonstrate the concept of spectral leakage, consider a radar system with a dwell (coherent processing interval) equal to *20msec*, which corresponds to a frequency resolution $\Delta F = 50Hz$. Then, the amplitude line spectrum corresponding of two targets whose Doppler frequencies (or equivalently radial velocities) are separated by more than *50Hz* and are completely resolvable in the line spectrum. Furthermore, any two targets whose Doppler frequencies are separated by a multiple-integer of ΔF are completely resolvable even if they are located in two adjacent Doppler cells, as illustrated in Fig. 1.11. Alternatively, if the two targets are separated by less than *50Hz*, then their amplitude spectra will overlap (spill over to adjacent Doppler cells) and the two targets will not be resolved. The multiple-integer of ΔF condition is rarely the case in real world applications; and hence, target Doppler frequencies will almost always exhibit spectrum leakage (or spill over). The good news is that the spectral leakage will only impact three adjacent frequency cells, as shown in Fig. 1.12.

In order to better demonstrate spectral leakage, consider again Fig. 1.12 which shows four distinct cases demonstrating spectral leakage for a target whose Doppler frequency is $f_t = (\rho + n)\Delta F$ where $n \geq 0$ and $-0.5 \leq \rho \leq 0.5$. Figure 1.12-a shows the case for $\rho = -0.25$ in this case, although the target Doppler is within the *nth* Doppler bin, its line spectrum nonetheless will be split between the *(n-1)th* and the *nth* cell, with more of its power being in the *nth* cell. Figure 1.12-b shows the case where $\rho = 0$; clearly in this case the f_t is multiple integer of ΔF and little to no spectral leakage is spilled over to the adjacent cells. Figure 1.12-c shows the case where $\rho = 0.25$; here the line spectrum will cover the *nth* and the *(n+1)th* cells with most of the power being in the *nth* cell. Finally, Fig.1.12-d shows the case where $\rho = 0.5$, and the line spectrum will split evenly between the *nth* and the *(n+1)th* cells. It is worth noting that in all cases, the total sum of the power compromising the line spectrum is almost constant (or equal). Accordingly, the amplitudes of the individual lines in the spectrum will add up to a fixed value representing the total power associated with the target.

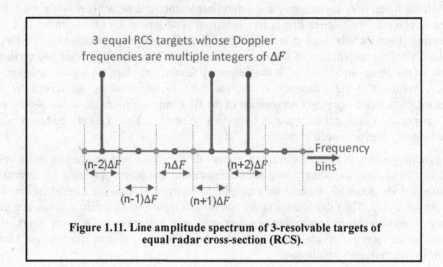

Figure 1.11. Line amplitude spectrum of 3-resolvable targets of equal radar cross-section (RCS).

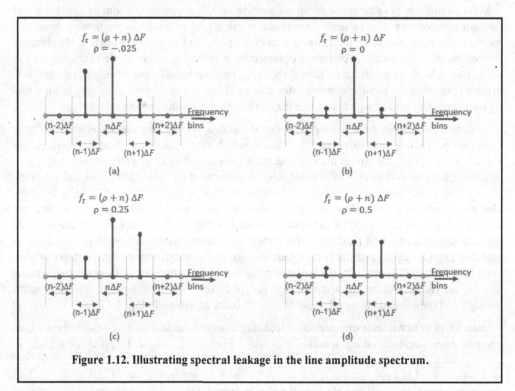

Figure 1.12. Illustrating spectral leakage in the line amplitude spectrum.

Spectral Fold-Over

Spectral fold-over occurs when using a DFT to detect the presence of signal whose frequency content is beyond the maximum resolvable frequency by that DFT. One must always satisfy Eq. (1.236) to avoid this condition. To demonstrate spectral fold-over, consider the same example from earlier, i.e., $T = 20msec$ and $\Delta f = 50Hz$. Let the number of DFT samples be $T = 64$. It follows that the corresponding DFT is capable of resolving targets whose Doppler frequencies range between $-1550Hz$ and $1600Hz$. Recall that the DFT is a periodic function; hence, the resulting amplitude spectrum will replicate itself every $3200Hz$ (i.e.,

$(\mp N/2)\Delta F$). Suppose this DFT is used to detect the presence of two targets whose Doppler frequencies are $f_1 = 300Hz$ and $f_2 = 1800Hz$. Clearly, the second target Doppler frequency falls on the *4th* Doppler bin of the next period, but fold-over occurs and a spectral line at the fourth DFT bin of the first period (i.e., $200Hz$) appears; the resulting amplitude line spectrum will show two targets at $300Hz$ and $200Hz$, as shown in Fig. 1.13.

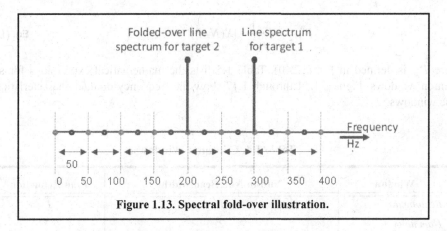

Figure 1.13. Spectral fold-over illustration.

1.11.3. Windowing Techniques

Truncation of the sequence $x(n)$ can be accomplished by computing the product

$$x_w(n) = x(n)w(n)$$

Eq. (1.238)

where

$$w(n) \le 1 \ for \ 0 \le n \le N-1 \ and \ 0 \ elsewhere.$$

Eq. (1.239)

The finite sequence $w(n)$ is called a windowing sequence, or simply a window. The windowing process should not impact the phase response of the truncated sequence. Consequently, the sequence $w(n)$ must retain linear phase. This can be accomplished by making the window symmetrical with respect to its central point. If $w(n) = 1$ for all n, we have what is known as the rectangular window. It leads to the Gibbs phenomenon, which manifests itself as an overshoot and a ripple before and after a discontinuity. Figure 1.14 shows the amplitude spectrum of a rectangular window. Note that the first sidelobe is at $-13.46dB$ below the main lobe. Windows that place smaller weights on the samples near the edges will have less overshoot at the discontinuity points (lower sidelobes); hence, they are more desirable than a rectangular window. However, reduction of the sidelobes is offset by a main lobe peak reduction and widening of the main lobe. Therefore, the proper choice of a windowing sequence is a trade-off between sidelobe reduction and mainlobe widening. Table 1.4 gives some commonly used windows and their impact on main beam widening and peak reduction. The multiplication process defined in Eq. (1.238) is equivalent to cyclic convolution in the frequency domain. It follows that $X_w(k)$ is a smeared (distorted) version of $X(k)$. To minimize this distortion, we would seek windows that have a narrow main lobe and small sidelobes. Additionally, using a window other than a rectangular window reduces the power by a factor P_w, where

$$P_w = \frac{1}{N}\sum_{n=0}^{N-1} w^2(n) = \sum_{k=0}^{N-1} |W(k)|^2 .$$

Eq. (1.240)

It follows that the DPS for the sequence $x_w(n)$ is now given by

$$P_0^w = \frac{1}{P_w N^2}|X(0)|^2$$

Eq. (1.241)

$$P_k^w = \frac{1}{P_w N^2}\{|X(k)|^2 + |X(N-k)|^2\} \quad ; \quad k = 1, 2, ..., \frac{N}{2} - 1$$

Eq. (1.242)

$$P_{N/2}^w = \frac{1}{P_w N^2}|X(N/2)|^2$$

Eq. (1.243)

where P_w is defined in Eq. (1.240). Table 1.5 lists the mathematical expressions for some common windows. Figures 1.14 through 1.17 show the frequency domain characteristics for these windows.

Table 1.4. Common Windows.

Window	Null-to-Null Beamwidth	Peak Reduction
Rectangular	1	1
Hamming	2	0.73
Hanning	2	0.664
Blackman	6	0.577
Kaiser ($\beta = 6$)	2.76	0.683
Kaiser ($\beta = 3$)	1.75	0.882

Table 1.5. Some Common Windows formulas, $n = 0, N-1$.

Window	Expression	First Side-lobe	Main Lobe Width
Rectangular	$w(n) = 1$	$-13.46\,dB$	1
Hamming	$w(n) = 0.54 - 0.46\cos\{(2\pi n)/(N-1)\}$	$-41\,dB$	2
Hanning	$w(n) = 0.5\left[1 - \cos\left(\dfrac{2\pi n}{N-1}\right)\right]$	$-27\,dB$	2
Kaiser	$w(n) = [I_0[\beta\sqrt{1-(2n/N)^2}]]/(I_0(\beta))$ I_0 : 0-order modified Bessel function of the 1st kind	$-46\,dB$ *for* $\beta = 2\pi$	$\sqrt{5}$ *for* $\beta = 2\pi$

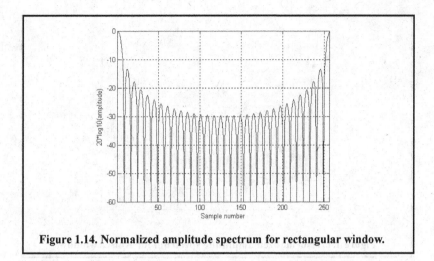

Figure 1.14. Normalized amplitude spectrum for rectangular window.

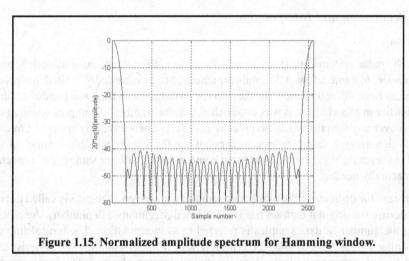

Figure 1.15. Normalized amplitude spectrum for Hamming window.

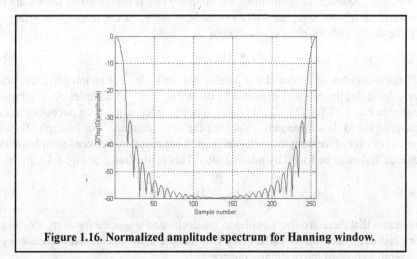

Figure 1.16. Normalized amplitude spectrum for Hanning window.

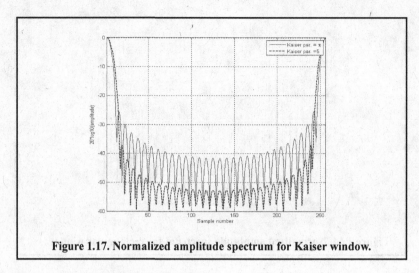

Figure 1.17. Normalized amplitude spectrum for Kaiser window.

1.11.4. Decimation and Interpolation

Decimation

Typically, radar systems use many signals for different functions, such as search, track, and discrimination, to name a few. All signals are assumed to be essentially limited; however, since these signals have different functions, they do not have the same time and bandwidth durations (τ, B). Earlier in this chapter, it was established that the number of samples required to sufficiently recover any signal from its samples is $N \geq 2\tau B$. Therefore, it is important to use an A/D with a high enough sampling rate to account for the largest possible number of samples required. As a result, it is often the case that some radar signals are sampled at a much higher rate than actually needed.

The process for decreasing the number of samples for a given sequence is called decimation. This is because the original data set has been reduced (decimated) in number. The process that increases the number of data samples is referred to as interpolation. The typical implementation for either operation is to alter the sampling rate, without violating the Nyquist sampling rate, of the input sequence. In decimation, the sampling rate is decreased by increasing the time steps between successive samples. More precisely, if the t_1 is the original sampling interval and t_2 is the decimated sampling interval, then

$$t_2 = Dt_1.$$ **Eq. (1.244)**

where D is the decimation ratio and it is greater than unity. If D is an integer, then decimation effectively decreases the original sequence by discarding $(D-1)$ samples of D samples. This is illustrated in Fig. 1.18 for $D = 3$. When D is not an integer, it is then necessary to first perform interpolation to determine new values for the new sequence. For example, if $D = 2.2$, then four out of every five samples in the decimated sequence are between samples in the original sequence and must be found by interpolation. This is illustrated in Fig. 1.19. In this case,

$$\left(t_2 = 2.2t_1 = \frac{11}{5}t_1\right) \Rightarrow 5t_2 = 11t_1,$$ **Eq. (1.245)**

which indicates that there are five samples in the decimated sequence for every eleven samples of the original sequence. Additionally, every fifth sample in the decimated sequence is equal to every eleventh sample of the original sequence.

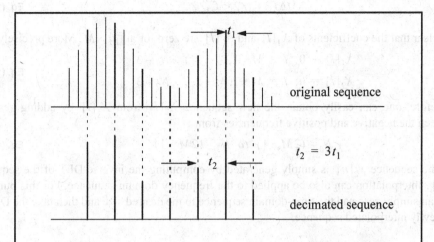

Figure 1.18. Decimation with $D = 3$. **Every sample of the decimated sequence coincides with every third sample of the original sequence.**

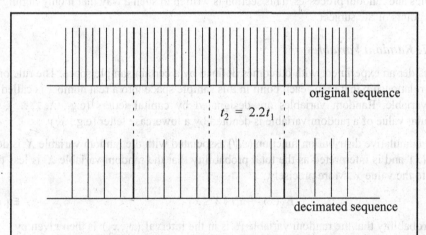

Figure 1.19. Decimation with $D = 2.2$. **Every fifth sample of the decimated sequence coincides with a sample in the original sequence.**

Interpolation

Suppose that a signal $x(t)$ whose duration is T seconds has been sampled at a sampling rate t_1 to obtain a sequence

$$\mathbf{x} = x[n] = \{x(nt_1), n = 0, 1, ..., N_1 - 1\} \qquad \text{Eq. (1.246)}$$

in this case, $N_1 = T/t_1$. Suppose you want to interpolate between the samples of $x[n]$ to generate a new sequence of size N_2 and sampling interval t_2, where $t_2 = t_1/k$. This effectively corresponds to a new sampling frequency $f_{s2} = kf_{s1}$ where $f_{s1} = 1/t_1$. A more efficient interpolation can be performed using the FFT, as will be described in the rest of this section. Denote the FFT of the sequences $x_1[n]$ and $x_2[n]$ by $X_1[l]$ and $X_2[l]$. Assume that the signal $x(t)$ is essentially band-limited with bandwidth $B = M\Delta f$ where M is an integer and $\Delta f = 1/T$. It follows that in order not to violate the sampling theorem

$$M\Delta f < f_{s1}/2 < f_{s2}/2 \,. \tag{Eq. (1.247)}$$

It is clear that the coefficients of $X_1[l]$ and $X_2[l]$ are zero for all $|l| > M$. More precisely,

$$X_1[l] = 0; \quad l = M+1, M+2, ..., N_1 - 3$$
$$X_2[l] = 0; \quad l = M+1, M+2, ..., N_2 - 3 \tag{Eq. (1.248)}$$

Therefore, one can easily obtain the new sequence $X_2[l]$ from $X_1[l]$ by adding zeros in between the negative and positive frequencies from

$$N_1 - (2M+1) \quad to \quad N_2 - (2M+1) \tag{Eq. (1.249)}$$

and the sequence $x_2[n]$ is simply generated by computing the inverse DFT of the sequence $X_2[l]$. Interpolation can also be applied to the frequency domain sequence. For this purpose, one can simply zero pad the time-domain sequence to the desired size and then take the DFT of the newly interpolated sequence.

1.12. Random Variables and Random Processes

The material in this section is presented as means for a quick top-level review of random variables and random processes. This section is written in such a way that it only highlights the major points of the subject.

1.12.1. Random Variables

Consider an experiment with outcomes defined by a certain sample space. The rule or functional relationship that maps each point in this sample space into a real number is called a random variable. Random variables are designated by capital letters (e.g., $X, Y, ...$), and a particular value of a random variable is denoted by a lowercase letter (e.g., $x, y, ...$).

The cumulative distribution function *(cdf)* associated with the random variable X is denoted as $F_X(x)$ and is interpreted as the total probability that the random variable X is less than or equal to the value x. More precisely,

$$F_X(x) = Pr\{X \le x\}\,. \tag{Eq. (1.250)}$$

The probability that the random variable X is in the interval (x_1, x_2) is then given by

$$F_X(x_2) - F_X(x_1) = Pr\{x_1 \le X \le x_2\}\,. \tag{Eq. (1.251)}$$

It is often practical to describe a random variable by the derivative of its *cdf*, which is called the probability density function *(pdf)*. The *pdf* of the random variable X is

$$f_X(x) = \frac{d}{dx}F_X(x) \tag{Eq. (1.252)}$$

or, equivalently,

$$F_X(x) = Pr\{X \le x\} = \int_{-\infty}^{x} f_X(\lambda)\,d\lambda \tag{Eq. (1.253)}$$

It follows that Eq. (1.251) can be written in the following equivalent form

$$F_X(x_2) - F_X(x_1) = Pr\{x_1 \le X \le x_2\} = \int_{x_1}^{x_2} f_X(\lambda)\,d\lambda \,. \tag{Eq. (1.254)}$$

The *cdf* has the following properties:

$$0 \le F_X(x) \le 1$$
$$F_X(-\infty) = 0$$
$$F_X(\infty) = 1$$
$$F_X(x_1) \le F_X(x_2) \Leftrightarrow x_1 \le x_2$$

Eq. (1.255)

Define the *nth* moment for the random variable X as

$$E[X^n] = \overline{X^n} = \int_{-\infty}^{\infty} x^n f_X(x) dx .$$

Eq. (1.256)

The first moment, $E[X]$, is called the mean value, while the second moment, $E[X^2]$, is called the mean squared value. When the random variable X represents an electrical signal across a 1Ω resistor, then $E[X]$ is the DC component, and $E[X^2]$ is the total average power.

The *nth* central moment is defined as

$$E[(X-\bar{X})^n] = \overline{(X-\bar{X})^n} = \int_{-\infty}^{\infty} (x-\bar{x})^n f_X(x) dx .$$

Eq. (1.257)

and thus the first central moment is zero. The second central moment is called the variance and is denoted by the symbol σ_X^2,

$$\sigma_X^2 = E[(X-\bar{X})^2] = \overline{(X-\bar{X})^2} .$$

Eq. (1.258)

In practice, the random nature of an electrical signal may need to be described by more than one random variable. In this case, the joint *cdf* and *pdf* functions need to be considered. The joint *cdf* and *pdf* for the two random variables X and Y are, respectively, defined by

$$F_{XY}(x, y) = Pr\{X \le x; Y \le y\}$$

Eq. (1.259)

$$f_{XY}(x, y) = \frac{\partial^2}{\partial x \partial y} F_{XY}(x, y) .$$

Eq. (1.260)

The marginal *cdf*s are obtained as follows:

$$F_X(x) = \int_{-\infty}^{\infty} \int_{-\infty}^{x} f_{UV}(u, v) du dv = F_{XY}(x, \infty)$$
$$F_Y(y) = \int_{-\infty}^{\infty} \int_{-\infty}^{y} f_{UV}(u, v) du dv = F_{XY}(\infty, y)$$

Eq. (1.261)

if the two random variables are statistically independent, then the joint *cdf*s and *pdf*s are, respectively, given by

$$F_{XY}(x, y) = F_X(x) F_Y(y)$$

Eq. (1.262)

$$f_{XY}(x, y) = f_X(x) f_Y(y) .$$

Eq. (1.263)

Consider a case when the two random variables X and Y are mapped into two new variables U and V through some transformations T_1 and T_2 defined by

$$U = T_1(X, Y) \qquad ; V = T_2(X, Y) .$$

Eq. (1.264)

The joint *pdf,* $f_{UV}(u, v)$, may be computed based on the invariance of probability under the transformation. For this purpose, one must first compute the matrix of derivatives; then the new joint *pdf* is computed as

$$f_{UV}(u, v) = f_{XY}(x, y)|\mathbf{J}|$$ Eq. (1.265)

$$|\mathbf{J}| = \begin{vmatrix} \dfrac{\partial x}{\partial u} & \dfrac{\partial x}{\partial v} \\ \dfrac{\partial y}{\partial u} & \dfrac{\partial y}{\partial v} \end{vmatrix}$$ Eq. (1.266)

where the determinant of the matrix of derivatives $|\mathbf{J}|$ is called the Jacobian determinant. In this notation, lower-case bold-faced letters indicate vectors, while upper-case bold-faced letter indicate matrices. The characteristic function for the random variable X is defined as

$$C_X(\omega) = E[e^{j\omega X}] = \int_{-\infty}^{\infty} f_X(x)e^{j\omega x}dx.$$ Eq. (1.267)

The characteristic function can be used to compute the *pdf* for a sum of independent random variables. More precisely, let the random variable Y be

$$Y = X_1 + X_2 + \ldots + X_M$$ Eq. (1.268)

where $\{X_m \; ; \; i = 1, \ldots, M\}$ is a set of independent random variables. It can be shown that

$$C_Y(\omega) = C_{X_1}(\omega)C_{X_2}(\omega)\ldots C_{X_M}(\omega)$$ Eq. (1.269)

and the *pdf* $f_Y(y)$ is computed as the inverse Fourier transform of $C_Y(\omega)$ as

$$f_Y(y) = \frac{1}{2\pi}\int_{-\infty}^{\infty} C_Y(\omega)e^{-j\omega y}d\omega.$$ Eq. (1.270)

The characteristic function can also be used to compute the *nth* moment as,

$$E[X^n] = (-j)^n \frac{d^n}{d\omega^n}C_X(\omega)\bigg|_{\omega = 0}.$$ Eq. (1.271)

1.12.2. Multivariate Gaussian Random Vector

Consider a joint probability for M random variables, $X_1, X_2, \ldots, X_M$. These variables can be represented as components of an $M \times 1$ random column vector, $\mathbf{x}$. More precisely,

$$\mathbf{x} = \begin{bmatrix} X_1 \\ X_2 \\ \vdots \\ X_M \end{bmatrix}.$$ Eq. (1.272)

The joint *pdf* for the vector $\mathbf{x}$ is

$$f_X(\mathbf{x}) = f_{X_1, X_2, \ldots, X_M}(x_1, x_2, \ldots, x_M).$$ Eq. (1.273)

The mean vector is defined as

$$\mu_{\mathbf{x}} = \begin{bmatrix} E[X_1] \\ E[X_2] \\ \vdots \\ E[X_M] \end{bmatrix}$$

Eq. (1.274)

and the covariance is an $M \times M$ matrix given by

$$\mathbf{C}_X = E[\mathbf{x} \ \mathbf{x}^\dagger] - \mu_{\mathbf{x}} \ \mu_{\mathbf{x}}^\dagger$$

Eq. (1.275)

where the superscript $\dagger$ indicates the complex conjugate transpose operation. Note that if the elements of the vector $\mathbf{x}$ are independent, then the covariance matrix is a diagonal matrix. A random vector $\mathbf{x}$ is multivariate Gaussian if its *pdf* is of the form

$$f_X(\mathbf{x}) = \frac{1}{\sqrt{(2\pi)^M |\mathbf{C}_X|}} \ \exp\left(-\frac{1}{2}(\mathbf{x} - \mu_{\mathbf{x}})^\dagger \mathbf{C}_X^{-1}(\mathbf{x} - \mu_{\mathbf{x}})\right)$$

Eq. (1.276)

where $\mu_{\mathbf{x}}$ is the mean vector, $\mathbf{C}_X$ is the covariance matrix, $\mathbf{C}_X^{-1}$ is the inverse of the covariance matrix, $|\mathbf{C}_X|$ is its determinant, and $\mathbf{x}$ is of dimension $M \times 1$. If $\mathbf{A}$ is a $K \times M$ matrix of rank K, then the random vector $\mathbf{y} = \mathbf{A}\mathbf{x}$ is a K-variate Gaussian vector with

$$\mu_{\mathbf{y}} = \mathbf{A}\mu_{\mathbf{x}}$$

Eq. (1.277)

$$\mathbf{C}_Y = \mathbf{A} \ \mathbf{C}_X \ \mathbf{A}^\dagger .$$

Eq. (1.278)

The characteristic function for a multivariate Gaussian *pdf* is defined by

$$C_X = E[\exp\{j(\omega_1 X_1 + \omega_2 X_2 + \dots + \omega_M X_M)\}] = \exp\left\{j\mu_{\mathbf{x}}^\dagger \omega - \frac{1}{2}\omega^\dagger \mathbf{C}_X \omega\right\}.$$

Eq. (1.279)

Then the moments for the joint distribution can be obtained by partial differentiation. For example,

$$E[X_1 X_2 X_3] = \frac{\partial^3}{\partial\omega_1 \partial\omega_2 \partial\omega_3} C_X(\omega_1, \omega_2, \omega_3) \qquad at \quad \omega = 0.$$

Eq. (1.280)

A special case of Eq. (1.278) is when the matrix $\mathbf{A}$ is given by

$$\mathbf{A} = \begin{bmatrix} a_1 a_2 \ \dots \ a_M \end{bmatrix}.$$

Eq. (1.281)

It follows that $\mathbf{y} = \mathbf{A}\mathbf{x}$ is a sum of random variables X_m, that is

$$Y = \sum_{m=1}^{M} a_m X_m.$$

Eq. (1.282)

The finding in Eq. (1.282) leads to the conclusion that the linear sum of Gaussian variables is also a Gaussian variable with mean and variance given by

$$\bar{Y} = a_1 \bar{X}_1 + a_2 \bar{X}_2 + \dots + a_M \bar{X}_M$$

Eq. (1.283)

$$\sigma_Y^2 = E[(Y - \bar{Y})^2] = E[a_1^2(X_1 - \bar{X}_1)^2] + \\ E[a_2^2(X_2 - \bar{X}_2)^2] + \dots + E[a_M^2(X_M - \bar{X}_M)^2]$$

Eq. (1.284)

and if the variables X_i are independent then Eq. (1.284) reduces to

$$\sigma_Y^2 = a_1^2\sigma_{X_1}^2 + a_2^2\sigma_{X_2}^2 + \ldots + a_M^2\sigma_{X_M}^2.$$

Eq. (1.285)

Finally, in this case, the probability density function $f_Y(y)$ is given by (which can also be derived from Eq. (1.269))

$$f_Y(y) = f_{X_1}(x_1) \otimes f_{X_2}(x_2) \otimes \ldots \otimes f_{X_M}(x_M)$$

Eq. (1.286)

where $\otimes$ indicates convolution.

1.12.3. Complex Multivariate Gaussian Random Vector

The complex envelope for the $M \times 1$ vector random variable $\tilde{X}$ is,

$$\tilde{\mathbf{x}} = \mathbf{x}_I + j\mathbf{x}_Q$$

Eq. (1.287)

where $\mathbf{x}_I$ and $\mathbf{x}_Q$ are real random multivariate Gaussian random vectors. The joint *pdf* for the complex random vector $\tilde{\mathbf{x}}$ is computed from the joint *pdf* of the two real vectors. The mean for the vector $\tilde{\mathbf{x}}$ is

$$E[\tilde{\mathbf{x}}] = E[\mathbf{x}_I] + jE[\mathbf{x}_Q].$$

Eq. (1.288)

The covariance matrix is also defined by

$$\mathbf{C}_{\tilde{X}} = E[(\tilde{\mathbf{x}} - E[\tilde{\mathbf{x}}])(\tilde{\mathbf{x}} - E[\tilde{\mathbf{x}}])^\dagger]$$

Eq. (1.289)

where the operator $\dagger$ indicates complex conjugate transpose.

The *pdf* for the vector $\tilde{\mathbf{x}}$ is

$$f_{\tilde{X}}(\tilde{\mathbf{x}}) = \frac{\exp[-(\tilde{\mathbf{x}} - E[\tilde{\mathbf{x}}])^\dagger \mathbf{C}_{\tilde{X}}^{-1}(\tilde{\mathbf{x}} - E[\tilde{\mathbf{x}}])]}{\pi^M |\mathbf{C}_{\tilde{X}}|}$$

Eq. (1.290)

with the following three conditions holding true

$$E[(\mathbf{x}_{I_i} - E[\mathbf{x}_{I_i}])(\mathbf{x}_{Q_i} - E[\mathbf{x}_{Q_i}])^\dagger] = \mathbf{0}$$

Eq. (1.291)

$$E[(\mathbf{x}_{I_i} - E[\mathbf{x}_{I_i}])(\mathbf{x}_{I_k} - E[\mathbf{x}_{I_k}])^\dagger] = E[(\mathbf{x}_{Q_i} - E[\mathbf{x}_{Q_i}])(\mathbf{x}_{Q_k} - E[\mathbf{x}_{Q_k}])^\dagger] \ ; \ all \ i, k$$

Eq. (1.292)

$$E[(\mathbf{x}_{I_i} - E[\mathbf{x}_{I_i}])(\mathbf{x}_{Q_k} - E[\mathbf{x}_{Q_k}])^\dagger] = -E[(\mathbf{x}_{Q_i} - E[\mathbf{x}_{Q_i}])(\mathbf{x}_{I_k} - E[\mathbf{x}_{I_k}])^\dagger] \ ; \ i \neq k.$$

Eq. (1.293)

1.12.4. Rayleigh Random Variables

Let X_I and X_Q be independent Gaussian random variables with zero mean and variance σ^2. Define two new random variables R and Φ as

$$\begin{aligned} X_I &= R\cos\Phi \\ X_Q &= R\sin\Phi \end{aligned}$$

Eq. (1.294)

The joint *pdf* of the two random variables X_I; X_Q is

$$f_{X_I X_Q}(x_I, x_Q) = \frac{1}{2\pi\sigma^2}\exp\left(-\frac{x_I^2 + x_Q^2}{2\sigma^2}\right) = \frac{1}{2\pi\sigma^2}\exp\left(-\frac{(r\cos\varphi)^2 + (r\sin\varphi)^2}{2\sigma^2}\right).$$

Eq. (1.295)

The joint *pdf* for the two random variables R; Φ is given by

$$f_{R\Phi}(r, \varphi) = f_{X_I X_Q}(x_I, x_Q)|\mathbf{J}|$$

Eq. (1.296)

where [**J**] is a matrix of derivatives defined by

$$[\mathbf{J}] = \begin{bmatrix} \dfrac{\partial x_I}{\partial r} & \dfrac{\partial x_I}{\partial \varphi} \\ \dfrac{\partial x_Q}{\partial r} & \dfrac{\partial x_Q}{\partial \varphi} \end{bmatrix} = \begin{bmatrix} \cos\varphi & -r\sin\varphi \\ \sin\varphi & r\cos\varphi \end{bmatrix}.$$

Eq. (1.297)

The determinant of the matrix of derivatives is called the Jacobian determinant, and in this case it is equal to,

$$|\mathbf{J}| = r$$

Eq. (1.298)

Substituting the right-hand side of Eq. (1.295) and Eq. (1.298) into Eq. (1.296) and collecting terms yields

$$f_{R\Phi}(r, \varphi) = \frac{r}{2\pi\sigma^2}\exp\left(-\frac{(r\cos\varphi)^2 + (r\sin\varphi)^2}{2\sigma^2}\right) = \frac{r}{2\pi\sigma^2}\exp\left(-\frac{r^2}{2\sigma^2}\right).$$

Eq. (1.299)

The *pdf* for R alone is obtained by integrating Eq. (1.299) over φ

$$f_R(r) = \int_0^{2\pi} f_{R\Phi}(r, \varphi)\, d\varphi = \frac{r}{\sigma^2}\exp\left(-\frac{r^2}{2\sigma^2}\right)\frac{1}{2\pi}\int_0^{2\pi} d\varphi$$

Eq. (1.300)

where the integral inside Eq. (1.300) is equal to 2π; thus,

$$f_R(r) = \frac{r}{\sigma^2}\exp\left(-\frac{r^2}{2\sigma^2}\right) \quad ; r \geq 0 .$$

Eq. (1.301)

The *pdf* described in Eq. (1.301) is referred to as a Rayleigh probability density function. The density function for the random variable Φ is obtained from

$$f_\Phi(\varphi) = \int_0^r f(r, \varphi)\ dr .$$

Eq. (1.302)

substituting Eq. (1.299) into Eq. (1.302) and performing integration by parts yields

$$f_\Phi(\varphi) = \frac{1}{2\pi} \quad ; \ 0 < \varphi < 2\pi ,$$

Eq. (1.303)

which is a uniform probability density function.

1.12.5. The Chi-Square Random Variables

Central Chi-Square Random Variable with N Degrees of Freedom

Let the random variables $\{X_1, X_2, \ldots, X_M\}$ be zero mean, statistically independent Gaussian random variables with unity variance. The variable

$$\chi_N^2 = \sum_{m=1}^M X_m^2$$

Eq. (1.304)

is the central chi-square random variable with M degrees of freedom. The chi-square *pdf* is

$$f_{\chi_M^2}(x) = \begin{cases} \dfrac{x^{(M-2)/2} \; e^{(-x/2)}}{2^{M/2} \; \Gamma(M/2)} & x \geq 0 \\ \\ 0 & x < 0 \end{cases}$$ **Eq. (1.305)**

where the Gamma function is defined as

$$\Gamma(m) = \int_0^\infty \lambda^{m-1} e^{-\lambda} \; d\lambda \; ; \; m > 0$$ **Eq. (1.306)**

with the following recursion

$$\Gamma(m+1) = m\Gamma(m)$$ **Eq. (1.307)**

and

$$\Gamma(m+1) = m! \qquad ; \; m = 0, 1, 2, ..., \text{ and } 0! = 1.$$ **Eq. (1.308)**

The mean and variance for the central chi-square are, respectively, given by

$$E[\chi_M^2] = M$$ **Eq. (1.309)**

$$\sigma_{\chi_M^2} = 2M.$$ **Eq. (1.310)**

Hence, the degrees of freedom M is the ratio of twice the squared mean to the variance

$$M = (2E^2[\chi_M^2])/\sigma_{\chi_M^2}.$$ **Eq. (1.311)**

Noncentral Chi-Square Random Variable with N Degrees of Freedom

In the general, the chi-square random variable requires that the Gaussian random variables $\{X_1, X_2, ..., X_M\}$ do not have zero means. Define a multivariate random variable **y** such that

$$Y_m = X_m + \mu_{X_m} \; ; m = 1, 2, ..., M$$ **Eq. (1.312)**

$$\mathbf{y} = \mathbf{x} + \mu_{\mathbf{x}}.$$ **Eq. (1.313)**

Consider the random variable

$$\chi_M'^2 = \sum_{m=1}^M Y_m^2 = \sum_{m=1}^M (X_m + \mu_{X_m})^2.$$ **Eq. (1.314)**

the variable $\chi_M'^2$ is called the noncentral chi-square random variable with M degrees of freedom and with a noncentral parameter λ, where

$$\lambda = \sum_{m=1}^M \mu_{X_m}^2 = \sum_{m=1}^M E^2[Y_m].$$ **Eq. (1.315)**

The noncentral chi-square *pdf* is

$$f_{\chi_M'^2}(x) = \begin{cases} \left(\dfrac{1}{2}\right)\left(\dfrac{x}{\lambda}\right)^{\frac{(M-2)}{4}} \exp\left\{(-(x+\lambda)/2)I_{\frac{(M-2)}{2}}(\sqrt{\lambda x})\right\} & x \geq 0 \\ \\ 0 & x < 0 \end{cases}$$ **Eq. (1.316)**

where I is the modified Bessel function (or occasionally called the hyperbolic Bessel function) of the first kind; and the subscripts are referred to as its order.

1.12.6. Random Processes

A random variable X is by definition a mapping of all possible outcomes of a random experiment to numbers. When the random variable becomes a function of both the outcome of the experiment and time, it is called a random process and is denoted by $X(t)$. Thus, one can view a random process as an ensemble of time-domain functions that are the outcome of a certain random experiment, as compared with single real numbers in the case of a random variable.

Since the *cdf* and *pdf* of a random process are time dependent, we will denote them as $F_X(x;t)$ and $f_X(x;t)$, respectively. The *nth* moment for the random process $X(t)$ is

$$E[X^n(t)] = \int_{-\infty}^{\infty} x^n f_X(x;t) dx.$$
Eq. (1.317)

A random process $X(t)$ is referred to as stationary to order one if all its statistical properties do not change with time. Consequently, $E[X(t)] = \bar{X}$, where $\bar{X}$ is a constant. A random process $X(t)$ is called stationary to order two (or wide-sense stationary) if

$$f_X(x_1, x_2; t_1, t_2) = f_X(x_1, x_2; t_1 + \Delta t, t_2 + \Delta t)$$
Eq. (1.318)

for all t_1, t_2 and Δt.

Define the statistical autocorrelation function for the random process $X(t)$ as

$$\Re_X(t_1, t_2) = E[X(t_1)X(t_2)].$$
Eq. (1.319)

The correlation $E[X(t_1)X(t_2)]$ is, in general, a function of (t_1, t_2). As a consequence of the wide-sense stationary definition, the autocorrelation function depends on the time difference $\tau = t_2 - t_1$, rather than on absolute time; and thus, for a wide-sense stationary process we have

$$E[X(t)] = \bar{X}$$
$$\Re_X(\tau) = E[X(t)X(t+\tau)]$$
Eq. (1.320)

If the time average and time correlation functions are equal to the statistical average and statistical correlation functions, respectively, then the random process is referred to as an ergodic random process. The following is true for an ergodic process:

$$\lim_{T \to \infty} \frac{1}{T} \int_{-T/2}^{T/2} x(t) dt = E[X(t)] = \bar{X}$$
Eq. (1.321)

$$\lim_{T \to \infty} \frac{1}{T} \int_{-T/2}^{T/2} x^*(t) x(t+\tau) dt = \Re_X(\tau).$$
Eq. (1.322)

The covariance of two random processes $X(t)$ and $Y(t)$ is defined by

$$C_{XY}(t, t+\tau) = E[\{X(t) - E[X(t)]\}\{Y(t+\tau) - E[Y(t+\tau)]\}],$$
Eq. (1.323)

which can also be written as

$$C_{XY}(t, t+\tau) = \Re_{XY}(\tau) - \bar{X}\bar{Y}.$$
Eq. (1.324)

1.12.7. Gaussian Random Process

Let $X(t)$ be a random process defined over the interval $\{0, T\}$, then $X(t)$ is said to be a Gaussian random process if every possible outcome of this process over this interval is a Gaussian process, provided that the mean square value of this process is finite. More precisely, $Y(t)$ will be a random process over the same interval $\{0, T\}$ defined by

$$Y(t) = \int_0^T x(t)z(t) \ dt$$

         Eq. (1.325)

where $z(t)$ is any function that yields $E[|Y|^2] < \infty$.

Gaussian random processes have a few unique properties that distinguish them from other types of random processes: (1) If the input to an LTI system is said to be a Gaussian random process, then its output is also a Gaussian random process. (2) If $X(t)$ is a Gaussian random process for any set of time occurrences $\{t_1, t_2, ..., t_M\}$, then the random variables $\{X(t_1), X(t_2), ..., X(t_M)\}$ are jointly Gaussian random variables. Finally, (3) any linear combination of a Gaussian process yields another jointly Gaussian random variable.

1.12.8. Lowpass Gaussian Random Processes

Let $X(t)$ be a real-valued Gaussian random process. If this process is an essentially band-limited process over the frequency interval $\{-B, B\}$, then the minimal number of samples required to represent this process is $M = 2TB$ real samples. Therefore, over the interval $\{0, T\}$, there are M random variables represented by the vector $\mathbf{x}$ made of M random variables, that is

$$\mathbf{x} = \begin{bmatrix} X(1/2B) \\ X(1/B) \\ \vdots \\ X(M/2B) \end{bmatrix} = \begin{bmatrix} X_1 \\ X_2 \\ \vdots \\ X_M \end{bmatrix}.$$

         Eq. (1.326)

If the random process $X(t)$ is a complex lowpass Gaussian process, represented by its complex envelope $\tilde{X}(t)$, then in this case, the minimal number of samples required to represent this process is $M = TB$ complex samples. The resulting jointly Gaussian complex random vector comprising $M = TB$ complex random variables is

$$\tilde{\mathbf{x}} = \begin{bmatrix} \tilde{X}(1/B) \\ \tilde{X}(2/B) \\ \vdots \\ \tilde{X}(M/B) \end{bmatrix} = \begin{bmatrix} \tilde{X}_1 \\ \tilde{X}_2 \\ \vdots \\ \tilde{X}_M \end{bmatrix}.$$

         Eq. (1.327)

If the power spectral destiny of a real Gaussian random process $X(t)$ is defined by

$$S_X(f) = \begin{cases} S_o & ; |f| < B \\ 0 & ; otherwise \end{cases},$$

         Eq. (1.328)

then the probability density function of the vector $\mathbf{x}$ is given by

$$f_X(x(t)) = \frac{1}{(4\pi S_o B)^{M/2}} \exp\left\{\left(-\frac{1}{4S_o B}\right) \sum_{m=1}^{M} X_m\right\} = \frac{1}{(4\pi S_o B)^{M/2}} \exp\left(-\frac{x^t x}{4S_o B}\right).$$ Eq. (1.329)

The mean of the random process defined in Eq. (1.327) is

$$\mu_{\mathbf{x}} = \begin{bmatrix} E[X_1] \\ E[X_2] \\ \vdots \\ E[X_M] \end{bmatrix} = \begin{bmatrix} \mu_1 \\ \mu_2 \\ \vdots \\ \mu_M \end{bmatrix}.$$ Eq. (1.330)

When the power spectral density of the process is non-white over the bandwidth, then in this case the random variables defined in Eq. (1.327) are no longer independent. Therefore, the *pdf* given in Eq. (1.329) is modified to

$$f_X(x(t)) = \frac{1}{\sqrt{(2\pi)^M \mathbf{C}_X}} \exp\left[\left(-\frac{1}{2}\right)(\mathbf{x} - \mu_{\mathbf{x}})^t \mathbf{C}_X^{-1}(\mathbf{x} - \mu_{\mathbf{x}})\right]$$ Eq. (1.331)

where the covariance matrix is

$$\mathbf{C}_X = E[(\mathbf{x} - \mu_{\mathbf{x}})(\mathbf{x} - \mu_{\mathbf{x}})^t].$$ Eq. (1.332)

1.12.9. Bandpass Gaussian Random Processes

It is customary to define the bandpass Gaussian random process through its complex envelope as

$$\tilde{X}(t) = X_I(t) + jX_Q(t)$$ Eq. (1.333)

where both $X_I(t)$ and $X_Q(t)$ are jointly lowpass statistically independent and stationary Gaussian random processes with zero mean and equal variance σ^2. The *pdf* for a sample $\tilde{X}(t_0)$ of the complex envelope is the joint *pdf* for $X_I(t)$ and $X_Q(t)$. That is,

$$f_X(\tilde{x}(t_0)) = \frac{1}{2\pi\sigma^2} \exp\left[-\frac{x_I^2(t_0) + x_Q^2(t_0)}{2\sigma^2}\right] = \frac{1}{2\pi\sigma^2} \exp\left[-\frac{|\tilde{x}(t_0)|^2}{2\sigma^2}\right].$$ Eq. (1.334)

Now, if both lowpass processes do not have zero mean and instead have a mean defined by

$$\mu(t) = \mu_I(t)\cos(2\pi f_0 t) + j\mu_Q(t)\sin(2\pi f_0 t),$$ Eq. (1.335)

the mean complex envelope is

$$\tilde{\mu}(t) = \mu_I(t) + j\mu_Q(t).$$ Eq. (1.336)

It follows that Eq. (1.334) can be rewritten as

$$f_X(\tilde{x}(t_0)) = \frac{1}{2\pi\sigma^2} e^{\left\{\frac{[x_I(t_0) - \mu_I(t_0)]^2 + [x_Q(t_0) - \mu_Q(t_0)]^2}{2\sigma^2}\right\}} = \frac{1}{2\pi\sigma^2} e^{\left\{\frac{|\tilde{x}(t_0) - \tilde{\mu}(t_0)|^2}{2\sigma^2}\right\}}.$$ Eq. (1.337)

Consider a duration of the process that spans the interval $\{0, T\}$. Then this segment of the complex envelope of the random process can be represented using a complex random variable vector of at least $M = BT$ elements where B is the bandwidth of the process. Define

$$\tilde{X}_i = \tilde{X}\left(\frac{m}{B}\right) \quad ;(i, m) = 1, 2, ..., BT = M \qquad \text{Eq. (1.338)}$$

$$\tilde{\mathbf{x}} = \begin{bmatrix} \tilde{X}_1 \\ \tilde{X}_2 \\ \vdots \\ \tilde{X}_M \end{bmatrix}. \qquad \text{Eq. (1.339)}$$

By definition, the covariance matrix $\tilde{\mathbf{c}}$ is

$$\tilde{\mathbf{c}}_X = E[(\tilde{\mathbf{x}} - \tilde{\mu}_{\mathbf{x}})(\tilde{\mathbf{x}} - \tilde{\mu}_{\mathbf{x}})^\dagger] = 2(\tilde{\mathbf{c}}_{X_I} + j\tilde{\mathbf{c}}_{X_{IQ}}) \qquad \text{Eq. (1.340)}$$

where

$$\tilde{\mathbf{c}}_{X_I} = E[(\tilde{\mathbf{x}}_I - \tilde{\mu}_{\mathbf{x}_I})(\tilde{\mathbf{x}}_I - \tilde{\mu}_{\mathbf{x}_I})^\dagger] \qquad \text{Eq. (1.341)}$$

$$\tilde{\mathbf{c}}_{X_{IQ}} = E[(\tilde{\mathbf{x}}_I - \tilde{\mu}_{\mathbf{x}_I})(\tilde{\mathbf{x}}_Q - \tilde{\mu}_{\mathbf{x}_Q})^\dagger]. \qquad \text{Eq. (1.342)}$$

Therefore, the *pdf* for the segment $\{\tilde{X}(t) \; ; 0 < t < T\}$ is

$$f_X(\tilde{\mathbf{x}}) = \frac{\exp[-(\tilde{\mathbf{x}} - \tilde{\mu}_{\mathbf{x}})^\dagger \tilde{\mathbf{c}}_X^{-1}(\tilde{\mathbf{x}} - \tilde{\mu}_{\mathbf{x}})]}{\pi^N |\tilde{\mathbf{c}}_X|}. \qquad \text{Eq. (1.343)}$$

1.12.10. Envelope of a Bandpass Gaussian Process

Consider the *pdf* of a segment of the envelope of a bandpass Gaussian random process. This process can be expressed as

$$X(t) = X_I(t)\cos(2\pi f_0 t) - X_Q(t)\sin(2\pi f_0 t) \qquad \text{Eq. (1.344)}$$

where $X_I(t)$ and $X_Q(t)$ are zero mean independent lowpass Gaussian processes. The envelope and phase are respectively denoted by $R(t)$ and $\Phi(t)$, where

$$R(t) = \sqrt{X_I(t)^2 + X_Q(t)^2} \qquad \text{Eq. (1.345)}$$

and

$$\Phi(t) = \left[\tan\left(\frac{X_Q(t)}{X_I(t)}\right)\right]^{-1} \qquad \text{Eq. (1.346)}$$

where

$$\begin{aligned} X_I(t) &= R(t)\cos(\Phi(t)) \\ X_Q(t) &= R(t)\sin(\Phi(t)) \end{aligned} \qquad \text{Eq. (1.347)}$$

The two processes $R(t)$ and $\Phi(t)$ are also independent, and their respective *pdfs* were derived earlier in this section.

Chapter 2

Radar Systems Basics

Bassem R. Mahafza

2.1. Radar Block Diagram

The emphasis of this book is on the radar signal types and associated signal processing and not on the radar system hardware subsystems and components. The word, radar, is an abbreviation for *ra*dio *d*etection *a*nd *r*anging. Radar systems use modulated bandpass radio frequency (RF) signals and directive antennas to search for targets within the radar field of view (FOV). When this RF signal is incident on a target, it interacts with the target in accordance with Maxwell's equations and RF energy is scattered out in all directions from the target. Some portion of the scattered energy (target return or echo) is in the direction of the radar. The radar, through its antenna, captures the echo signal and through signal processing (using specialized hardware along with signal/data processing algorithms), the radar extracts target information such as target range, target velocity, target angular position, etc. More specifically, the radar system emits a completely known waveform (signal) into free space with the expectation that a modified version of this transmitted signal scattered from the target will return to the radar. Accordingly, understanding the radar signal types and their associated radar signal processing techniques are key to understating how radars function. In this context, the radar system hardware becomes an enabler that generates the desired transmitted signals and facilitates the extraction of target information from the returned echoes.

Figure 2.1 shows a simplified radar system functional block diagram with its major subsystems identified along with their primary functions. The waveform generator produces a lowpass waveform (signal), and through modulation this signal is up-converted in frequency into a bandpass signal inside the transmitter. This bandpass signal goes through the radar directive antenna and is transformed into an electromagnetic (EM) wave that is propagated through free space. Accordingly, the signal is modified in both amplitude and phase as it travels through the propagation medium and it experiences significant changes as it interacts with the target. The target acts as an RF source and scatters the incident EM energy in many directions. Portions of this scattered energy usually return to the radar and enter its receiver through its antenna. The radar receiver's main purpose is to process received signals that resemble the original transmitted ones in order to extract the basic target attributes (range, size, range rate, angles, etc.). The signal processor reshapes the noisy received bandpass signal into a noisy copy of the originally transmitted lowpass signal. Finally, through sampling and quadrature components processing, the signal is transformed into data that is input into the radar data processor whereby using different algorithms the radar estimates the target kinematics such as its track information, classification and type. The time control box generates the synchronization timing signals required throughout the system, while the duplexer allows one single antenna to be used for both transmit and receive functions. The duplexer is not used in bistatic radar systems that use separate antennas for transmit and receive functions.

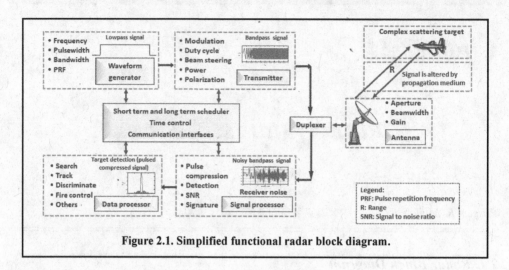

Figure 2.1. Simplified functional radar block diagram.

2.2. Radar Specific Terms

Figure 2.2 shows a simplified block diagram for the major radar subsystems. Basically, the waveform generator substitutes the transmitter subsystem, the antenna subsystem, and the receiver subsystem. As alluded to earlier, a radar system will extract target information by first transmitting a completely known signal (in the time and frequency and amplitude), and then through signal processing of a noisy version of the same signal. The target information extracted by the radar receiver subsystem may comprise, depending on the radar function and mission, a long list of target specific parameters. However, a short list of specific target parameters are always estimated by the radar. This section is concerned with presenting this short list along with associated physics models.

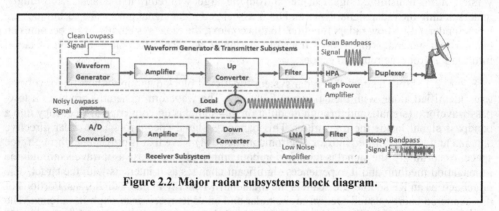

Figure 2.2. Major radar subsystems block diagram.

2.2.1. Range

Pulsed radars use a train of pulse waveforms (mainly with modulation). In this category, radar systems can be classified on the basis of the pulse repetition frequency (PRF), as low PRF, medium PRF, and high PRF radars. Low PRF radars are primarily used for ranging, at longer distances, where target velocity (Doppler shift) is not of interest. High PRF radars are mainly used to measure target velocity at shorter distances. Continuous wave as well as pulsed radars can measure both target range and radial velocity by utilizing different modulation schemes.

Consider the radar system in Fig. 2.3. The target's range, R, is computed by measuring the time delay, Δt, it takes a pulse to travel the two-way path between the radar and the target. Since electromagnetic waves travel at the speed of light, $c = 3 \times 10^8 m/s$, then range to the target is

$$R = \frac{c\Delta t}{2}$$

Eq. (2.1)

where R is in meters and Δt is in seconds. The factor of $1/2$ is used to account for the two-way time delay. In general, a pulsed radar transmits and receives a train of pulses, as illustrated by Fig. 2.4. The inter-pulse period (IPP) is T, and the pulse width is τ. The IPP is often referred to as the pulse repetition interval (PRI). The inverse of the PRI is the PRF, which is denoted by f_r,

$$f_r = \frac{1}{PRI} = \frac{1}{T}.$$

Eq. (2.2)

During each PRI the radar radiates energy only for τ seconds and listens for target returns for the rest of the PRI. The radar transmitting duty cycle (factor) d_t is then defined as the ratio $d_t = \tau/T$. Accordingly, the radar average transmitted power is

$$P_{av} = P_t \times d_t$$

Eq. (2.3)

where P_t denotes the radar peak transmitted power. The pulse energy is

$$E_p = P_t \tau = P_{av} T = \frac{P_{av}}{f_r}.$$

Eq. (2.4)

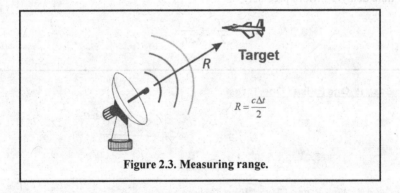

Figure 2.3. Measuring range.

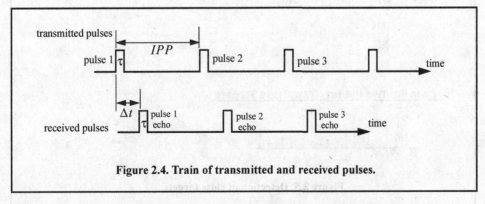

Figure 2.4. Train of transmitted and received pulses.

2.2.2. Unambiguous Range

Consider the target detection cases shown in Fig. 2.5. Clearly, in cases I and II where one radar pulse is used, the targets' ranges $R_1 = ct_1/2$ and $R_2 = ct_2/2$ are not ambiguous. Alternatively, in case III where two radar pulses are used, there will also be no ambiguity in determining range as long as the two targets are close and all echoes from pulse 1 are received by the radar before pulse 2 is transmitted. However, range ambiguity will exist in case III if the two targets are sufficiently far apart, such that the second target is beyond the second pulse, or stated alternatively, such that the return of the first pulse from the second target arrives after the second pulse has been transmitted. In this case, since each pulse is identical, the radar cannot (without further embellishment) immediately discern that this first pulse return from the second target is not just a closer range target, potentially closer than the first target (such the nature of range ambiguity).

To illustrate this range ambiguity, consider Fig. 2.6. In this case, range echo 1 represents the radar return from a target at range $R_1 = ct_1/2$ due to pulse 1. While, echo 2 could be interpreted as the return from the same target due to pulse 2, or it may be the return from a faraway target at range R_2 due to pulse 1 again. In this case,

$$R_2 = \frac{ct_1}{2} \qquad or \qquad R_2 = \frac{c(T + t_t)}{2}.$$ Eq. (2.5)

Clearly, range ambiguity is associated with echo 2. To prevent this ambiguity, once a pulse is transmitted the radar must wait a sufficient length of time so that returns from all targets out to the maximum range versus its expected targets are back before the next pulse is emitted. It follows that the maximum unambiguous range, R_u, must correspond to half of the PRI or the two-way time delay T. More precisely,

$$R_u = \frac{cT}{2} = \frac{c}{2f_r}.$$ Eq. (2.6)

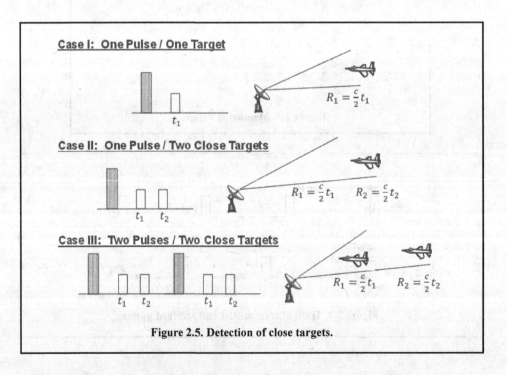

Figure 2.5. Detection of close targets.

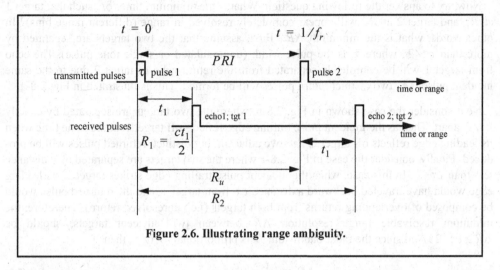

Figure 2.6. Illustrating range ambiguity.

2.2.3. Range Resolution

Range resolution, denoted by ΔR, is a radar metric that describes its ability to detect targets in close proximity with respect to each other as distinct objects. Radar systems are normally designed to operate between a minimum range R_{min} and maximum range R_{max}. The distance between R_{min} and R_{max} is then divided into M range bins (gates), each of width ΔR,

$$M = \frac{(R_{max} - R_{min})}{\Delta R}.$$

Eq. (2.7)

Targets separated by at least ΔR will be completely resolved in range, as illustrated in Fig. 2.7. Targets within the same range bin can be resolved in cross-range (azimuth) by isolating the targets in angle with narrow radar beams, and can sometimes (with suitable radar design) be resolved utilizing signal processing techniques.

Consider two targets located at ranges R_1 and R_2, corresponding to time delays t_1 and t_2, respectively. Denote the difference between those two ranges as ΔR:

$$\Delta R = R_2 - R_1 = c\frac{(t_2 - t_1)}{2} = c\frac{\delta t}{2}.$$

Eq. (2.8)

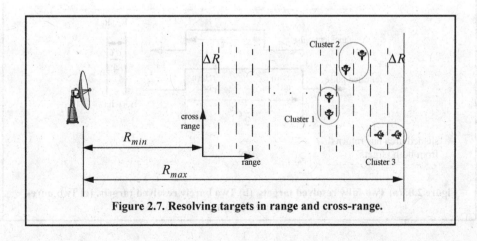

Figure 2.7. Resolving targets in range and cross-range.

Now, try to answer the following question: What is the minimum time, δt, such that target 1 at R_1 and target 2 at R_2 will appear completely resolved in range (different range bins)? In other words, what is the minimum ΔR? First, assume that the two targets are separated by more than $c\tau/2$, where τ is the pulse width (unmodulated or single tone pulse). The echo from target 1 will be completely separated from the return echo of target 2 due to the same incident pulse; i.e., two distinct return pulses will be formed. This is illustrated in Fig. 2.8-a.

Next consider the case shown in Fig. 2.8-b, where the two targets are separated by exactly $c\tau/2$ apart. Then as the incident pulse trailing edge reflects off target 1, at the same time when its leading edge reflects off target 2, and two adjacent, but distinct, returned pulses will be produced. Finally, consider the case in Fig. 2.8-c where the two targets are separated by a distance less than $c\tau/2$. In this case, when the incident pulse trailing edge strikes target 2, its leading edge would have traveled backward a distance $c\tau$ from target 1, and the returned pulse would be composed of overlapping returns from both targets (i.e., unresolved return). Therefore, the minimum resolvable range resolution ΔR between two adjacent targets, should be $\Delta R \geq c\tau/2$. And since the radar bandwidth B is proportional to $1/\tau$, then

$$\Delta R = \frac{c\tau}{2} = \frac{c}{2B}.$$

Eq. (2.9)

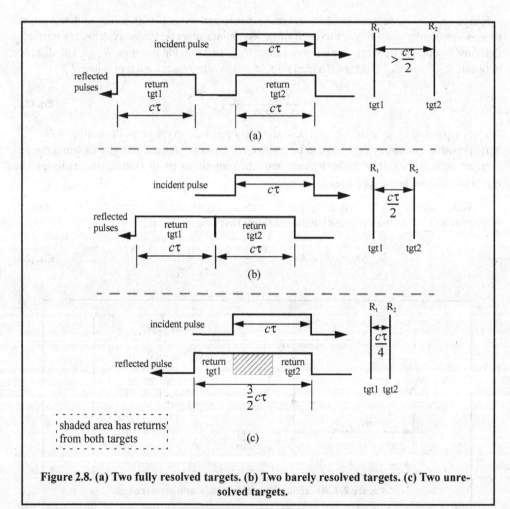

Figure 2.8. (a) Two fully resolved targets. (b) Two barely resolved targets. (c) Two unresolved targets.

In general, radar users and designers alike seek to minimize ΔR in order to enhance the radar target location performance. As suggested by Eq. (2.9), in order to achieve fine range resolution one must minimize the pulse width. However, this will reduce the average transmitted power and increase the instantaneous bandwidth. Achieving fine range resolution while maintaining adequate average transmitted power can be accomplished by using pulse compression techniques.

2.2.4. Doppler Frequency

Radars use Doppler frequency to extract target radial velocity (range rate), as well as to distinguish between moving and stationary targets or objects such as clutter. The Doppler phenomenon describes the shift in the center frequency of an incident waveform due to the target motion with respect to the source of radiation. Depending on the direction of the target's motion, this frequency shift may be positive or negative. A waveform incident on a target has equiphase wavefronts separated by λ, the wavelength. A closing target will cause the reflected equiphase wavefronts to compress and become closer to each other, resulting in a shorter wavelength of the reflected waveform, or equivalently a higher frequency. Alternatively, an opening or receding target (moving away from the radar) will cause the reflected equiphase wavefronts to expand, resulting in a longer wavelength of the reflected waveform or lower frequency. This is illustrated in Fig. 2.9.

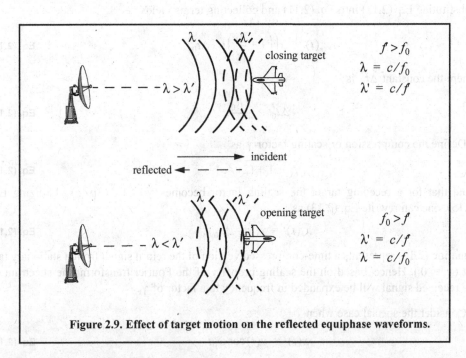

Figure 2.9. Effect of target motion on the reflected equiphase waveforms.

Doppler Frequency Extraction - Method I

Consider the closing (approaching) target shown in Fig. 2.10, and let the target radial velocity be v. Define R_0 as the target range at time t_0 (i.e., reference time); it follows that the range to the target at any other time t is

$$R(t) = R_0 - v(t - t_0).$$ **Eq. (2.10)**

For convenience $t_0 = 0$. The signal received by the radar is then given by

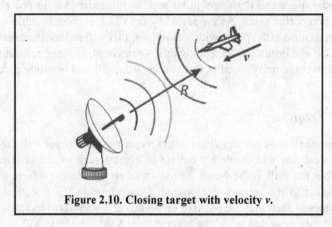

Figure 2.10. Closing target with velocity *v*.

$$x_r(t) = x(t - \Delta(t))$$

Eq. (2.11)

where $x(t)$ is the transmitted signal, and the delay $\Delta(t)$ is

$$\Delta(t) = \frac{2}{c}(R_0 - vt).$$

Eq. (2.12)

Substituting Eq. (2.12) into Eq. (2.11) and collecting terms yields

$$x_r(t) = x\left(\left(1 + \frac{2v}{c}\right)t - \Delta t_0\right)$$

Eq. (2.13)

where the constant Δt_0 is

$$\Delta t_0 = \frac{2R_0}{c}.$$

Eq. (2.14)

Define the compression or scaling factor γ as

$$\gamma = 1 + (2v/c)$$

Eq. (2.15)

Note that for a receding target the scaling factor becomes $\gamma = 1 - (2v/c)$. Utilizing Eq. (2.15), one can rewrite Eq. (2.13) as

$$x_r(t) = x(\gamma t - \Delta t_0).$$

Eq. (2.16)

Equation (2.16) represents a time-compressed version of the return signal from a stationary target ($v = 0$). Hence, based on the scaling property of the Fourier transform, the spectrum of the received signal will be expanded in frequency to a factor of γ.

Consider the special case when

$$x(t) = y(t)\cos\omega_0 t$$

Eq. (2.17)

where ω_0 is the radar center frequency in radians per second. The received signal $x_r(t)$ is then given by

$$x_r(t) = y(\gamma t - \psi_0)\cos(\gamma\omega_0 t - \psi_0).$$

Eq. (2.18)

The Fourier transform of Eq. (2.18) is

$$X_r(\omega) = \frac{1}{2\gamma}\left(Y\left(\frac{\omega}{\gamma} - \omega_0\right) + Y\left(\frac{\omega}{\gamma} + \omega_0\right)\right),$$

Eq. (2.19)

where for simplicity the effects of the constant delay Δt_0 have been ignored. The bandpass spectrum of the received signal is centered at $\pm \gamma \omega_0$ instead of $\pm \omega_0$. The difference between the two values corresponds to the amount of Doppler shift incurred due to the target motion,

$$\omega_d = \omega_0 \pm \gamma \omega_0 \Leftrightarrow f_d = f_0 \pm \gamma f_0. \qquad \text{Eq. (2.20)}$$

ω_d and f_d are the Doppler frequency in radians per second and in Hz, respectively. Substituting the value of γ in Eq. (2.20) yields

$$f_d = \pm \frac{2v}{c} f_0 = \pm \frac{2v}{\lambda} \qquad \text{Eq. (2.21)}$$

where $f_d > 0$ (i.e., positive) for a closing (incoming or inbound) target and $f_d < 0$ (i.e., negative) for an opening (receding or outbound) target.

Doppler Frequency Extraction - Method II

Consider the following transmitted radar signal

$$x_t(t) = a_t(t) \cos(2\pi f_0 t + \varphi_0) \qquad \text{Eq. (2.22)}$$

where $a_t(t)$ is the amplitude modulation, f_0 is the radar center operating frequency (i.e., carrier frequency), and φ_0 is a constant phase. The received radar signal is now of the form,

$$x_r(t) = a_r(t) \cos\left(2\pi f_0\left(t - \frac{2R(t)}{c}\right) + \varphi_0\right) \qquad \text{Eq. (2.23)}$$

Substituting Eq. (2.10) into Eq. (2.23), setting Δt_0 to zero, and collecting terms yield,

$$x_r(t) = a_r(t) \cos\left\{2\pi f_0\left(t - \frac{2R_0}{c}\right) + 2\pi f_0 \frac{2v}{c} t\right\}. \qquad \text{Eq. (2.24)}$$

It follows that the instantaneous frequency is

$$f_i = \frac{1}{2\pi} \frac{d}{dt}\left\{2\pi f_0\left(t - \frac{2R_0}{c}\right) + 2\pi f_0 \frac{2v}{c} t\right\} = f_0 + \frac{f_0}{c} 2v = f_0 + \frac{2}{\lambda} v. \qquad \text{Eq. (2.25)}$$

where λ is the wavelength and the relation $c = \lambda f_0$ was used in Eq. (2.25). Again, the difference between the transmitted center frequency and the received one is a measure of the Doppler frequency. More specifically,

$$f_d = f_0 + \frac{2}{\lambda} v - f_0 = \frac{2}{\lambda} v. \qquad \text{Eq. (2.26)}$$

Note the Doppler frequency given in Eq. (2.26) is positive (i.e., closing target). Alternatively for an opening target Eq. (2.10) is of the form

$$R(t) = R_0 + v(t - t_0) \qquad \text{Eq. (2.27)}$$

accordingly, the Doppler frequency is now given by

$$f_d = \frac{-2v}{\lambda}. \qquad \text{Eq. (2.28)}$$

Equations (2.26) and (2.28) are identical to Eq. (2.21).

The Doppler frequency shift for a closing and opening targets is illustrated in Fig. 2.11. It is important to note that the target velocity given in either one of Eqs. (2.21), (2.26), and (2.28) indicates the target radial velocity component on the radar line of sight and not the actual velocity of the target. Hence, a more accurate formula for the Doppler frequency is

$$f_d = \frac{\pm 2v_r}{\lambda}$$ Eq. (2.29)

where v_r is the target radial velocity along the radar line of sight. In the general case, the target radial velocity component is given by

$$v_r = v \cos\theta_e \; \cos\theta_a$$ Eq. (2.30)

where v is the target velocity, and the angles θ_e and θ_a are, respectively, the elevation and azimuth angles; see Fig. 2.12. As a further illustration, consider the three targets shown in Fig. 2.13. All three targets have the same velocity v. In this example, target 1 has zero Doppler shift; target 2 has maximum Doppler frequency as defined in Eq. (2.26). The amount of Doppler frequency of target 3 is $f_d = 2v\cos\theta/\lambda$, where $v\cos\theta$ is the radial velocity, and θ is the total angle between the radar line of sight and the target.

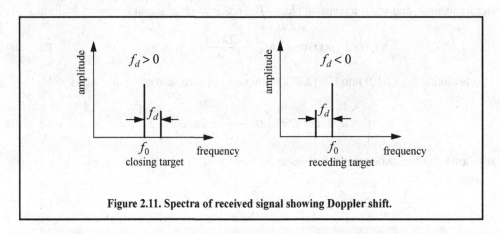

Figure 2.11. Spectra of received signal showing Doppler shift.

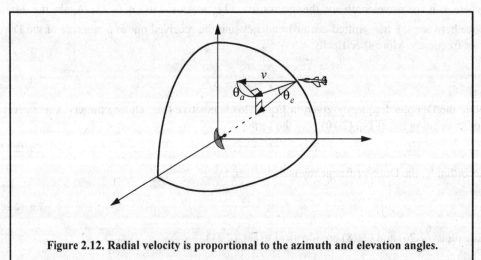

Figure 2.12. Radial velocity is proportional to the azimuth and elevation angles.

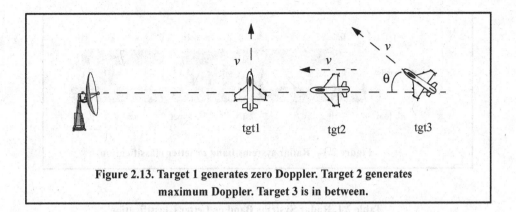

Figure 2.13. Target 1 generates zero Doppler. Target 2 generates maximum Doppler. Target 3 is in between.

2.3. Radar Systems Classifications and Bands

Radars can be classified as ground-based, airborne, spaceborne, or ship-based radar systems. They can also be classified into categories based on the specific radar characteristics, such as the frequency band, antenna type, and waveforms. Radar systems using continuous waveforms, modulated or otherwise, are classified as continuous wave (CW) radars. Alternatively, radar systems using time-limited pulsed waveforms are classified as pulsed radars. Another radar systems classification is concerned with the mission and/or the functionality of the specific radar. This includes: weather, acquisition and search, tracking, track-while-scan, fire control, early warning, over-the-horizon, terrain following, and terrain avoidance radars. Phased array radars utilize phased array antennas and are often called multifunction (multimode) radars. A phased array is a composite antenna formed from two or more basic radiators. Array antennas synthesize narrow directive beams that may be mechanically or electronically steered. Electronic steering is achieved by controlling the frequency, amplitude and /or phase of the electric current feeding the array elements, and thus the name phased arrays is adopted.

Historically, radars were first developed for military use. It is for this primary reason the most common radar systems classification is the letter or band designation originally used by the military during and after World War II. This letter or band designation has also been adopted as an IEEE (Institute of Electrical and Electronics Engineers) standard. In recent years, NATO (North Atlantic Treaty Organization) has adopted a new-band designation with easier abecedarian letters. Figure 2.14 shows the spectrum associated with these two letter or band radar classifications. Table 2.1 presents the same information in tabulated format.

2.3.1. High Frequency and Very HF Radars (A- and B-Bands)

Radar bands below *300 MHz* represented the frontier of radio technology at the time during World War II. However, in the modern radar era, these frequency bands are used mostly for early warning radars and radios. Special types of radars can utilize the electromagnetic waves' reflection off the ionosphere to detect targets beyond the horizon, and so they are called over-the-horizon radars (OTHR). At these frequencies, the electromagnetic wave atmospheric attenuation is small and can be overcome by using high-power transmitters. Radar angular measurement accuracies are limited in these bands because lower frequencies require antennas with significant physical size, thus limiting the radar's angle accuracy and angle resolution. Low-frequency systems can be used for foliage penetration (FoPen) applications, as well as in ground penetrating (G-Pen) applications. Other communication and broadcasting services typically use these frequency bands. Therefore, the available bandwidth for military radar systems is limited and highly contested throughout the world.

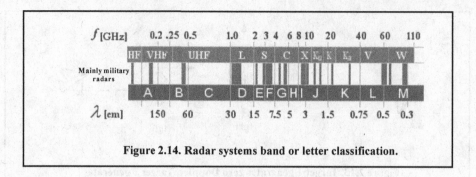

Figure 2.14. Radar systems band or letter classification.

Table 2.1. Radar Systems Band or Letter Classification.

Letter Designation	Frequency Range in GHz (IEEE Standard)	Frequency Range in GHz (NATO or New-Band Designation)
HF	0.003 - 0.03	A
VHF	0.03 - 0.3	A < 0.25; B > 0.25
UHF	0.3 - 1.0	B < 0.5; C > 0.5
L-band	1.0 - 2.0	D
S-band	2.0 - 4.0	E < 3.0; F > 3.0
C-band	4.0 - 8.0	G < 6.0; H > 6.0
X-band	8.0 - 12.5	I < 10.0; J > 10.0
Ku-band	12.5 - 18.0	J
K-band	18.0 - 26.5	J < 20.0; K > 20.0
Ka-band	26.5 - 40.0	K
V & W or Millimeter Wave (MMW)	Normally >34.0	L < 60.0; M > 60.0

2.3.2. Ultra High Frequency Radars (C-Band)

Ultra high frequency (UHF) bands are used for very long range early warning radars (EWR). This frequency band is also used for the detection and tracking of satellites and ballistic missiles at long ranges. In recent years, ultra wideband (UWB) radar applications use all frequencies in the A- to C-Bands. Some UWB radars can be used in ground penetration (G-Pen) applications as well as in see-through-the-wall (STTW) applications.

2.3.3. L-Band Radars (D-Band)

Radars in the L-band are primarily ground-based and ship-based systems that are used in long range military and air traffic control search operations for up to 250 *nautical miles* (~500 *km*). Due to earth curvature, their maximum achievable range is limited when detecting low-altitude targets which can disappear below the horizon line of sight (LOS). The air traffic management (ATM) long-range surveillance radars like the air route surveillance radar (ARSR), work in this frequency band. These radar systems are relatively large and demand sizable footprints. Historically, the designator L-band was adopted since the "L" represents the large antenna or long-range radars. But today, it refers explicitly to the frequency band irrespective of size or range of the radar.

2.3.4. S-Band Radars (E- and F-Bands)

Most ground- and ship-based medium range radars operate in the S-band. The atmospheric attenuation in this band is higher than in the NATO D-band, and they are also more susceptible to weather conditions than L-band. Radar in this band usually needs considerably high transmitting power as compared to the lower-frequency radars in order to achieve maximum detection range. Even with the considerable weather susceptibility, the National Weather Service next generation Doppler weather radar (NEXRAD) uses an S-band radar, because it can see beyond a severe storm. Special airport surveillance radars (ASR) used at some civilian airports are also in this band where they can detect aircrafts out to at least 60 *nautical miles*. The designator S-band (contrary to L-band) was adopted since the "S" represents the smaller antennas or shorter-range radars. Yet again, today it refers explicitly to the frequency band irrespective of size or range of the radar.

2.3.5. C-Band Radar (G-Band)

Many of the mobile military battlefield surveillance, missile-control and ground surveillance radar systems operate in this band. Most weather radar systems are also C-band radars. Medium range search, fire control military radars, and instrumentation radars are C-band systems. In this band, the size of the antenna allows for achieving adequate angular accuracies and resolution in trade of the aperture that is not excessively large, and hence more mobile. Performance of systems operating in this band can suffer from bad weather conditions and to counter that, they often employ antenna feeds with circular polarization.

2.3.6. X- and Ku-Band Radars (I- and J-Bands)

In the X-band frequency range (8 to 12 *GHz*), the relationship between the wave length and size of the antenna is considerably better than in lower-frequency bands yielding smaller size apertures with relatively high power density. Radar systems that require fine target detection capabilities and yet cannot tolerate the atmospheric attenuation of higher-frequency bands are typically X-band. The X- and Ku-bands are relatively popular radar frequency bands for military applications like airborne radars, since the small antenna size still provides good angular resolution performance as well as high gain. Missile guidance systems use the Ku-band (I- and J-bands) because of the small antenna size where weight and aperture size are limiting requirements. Space borne or airborne imaging radars used in synthetic aperture radar (SAR) for military electronic intelligence and civil geographic mapping typically use these frequency bands. These frequency bands are also widely used in maritime civil and military navigation radars.

2.3.7. K- and Ka- Band Radars (J- and K-Bands)

These high-frequency bands suffer severe weather and atmospheric attenuation. Therefore, radars utilizing these frequency bands are limited to short-range applications, such as vehicle collision avoidance (~24 *GHz*) police traffic radars (though many of these also operate in X-band), security motion detectors, short-range terrain avoidance, and terrain following radars. Alternatively, the achievable angular accuracies and range resolution are superior to other bands. In ATM applications these radars are often called surface movement radar (SMR) or airport surface detection equipment (ASDE) radars.

2.3.8. Millimeter Wave Radars (V- and W-Bands)

Radars operating in this frequency band also suffer from severe high atmospheric attenuation. Radar applications are limited to very short range of up to tens of meters. In the W-band maximum attenuation occurs at about 75 GHz and 96 GHz. Both of these frequencies are used in practice primarily in the automotive industry where very small radars (~75-76 GHz) are used for parking assistants, blind spots and brake assists. Some radar systems operating at 96 to 98 GHz are used as laboratory experimental or prototype systems. Radar systems above these frequencies are often called "Tera Hertz" radar systems and are an emerging new technology with new applications such as imaging through materials for security monitoring.

2.4. Decibel Arithmetic

The decibel (dB) is a logarithmic unit of measurement that represents a ratio of a physical quantity (such as voltage, power, or antenna gain) to a specific reference quantity of the same type. The unit dB is named after Alexander Graham Bell, who originated the unit as a measure of power attenuation in telephone lines. By Bell's definition, a unit of Bell gain is

$$\log\left(\frac{P_0}{P_i}\right)$$

Eq. (2.31)

where the logarithm operation is base 10, P_0 is the output power of a standard telephone line (almost one mile long), and P_i is the input power to the line. If voltage (or current) ratios are used instead of the power ratio, then a unit Bell gain is defined as

$$\log\left(\frac{V_0}{V_i}\right)^2 \qquad or \qquad \log(I_0/I_i)^2 .$$

Eq. (2.32)

Note that it is irrespective of any impedance or resistance, since it is a ratio of powers.

A decibel, dB, is $1/10$ of a Bell (recall that the prefix "*deci*" means 10^{-1}). It follows that a dB is defined as

$$10\log\left(\frac{P_0}{P_i}\right) = 10\log\left(\frac{V_0}{V_i}\right)^2 = 10\log(I_0/I_i)^2 .$$

Eq. (2.33)

The inverse dB is computed from the relations

$$P_0/P_i = 10^{dB/10}$$

$$V_0/V_i = 10^{dB/20}$$

Eq. (2.34)

$$I_0/I_i = 10^{dB/20}$$

The decibel nomenclature is widely used by radar designers and users for several reasons. Originally, it was used to facilitate calculations with slide rules, but today the most important one is that representing radar-related physical quantities using dBs drastically reduces the dynamic range that a designer or a user has to use. For example, an incoming radar signal may be as weak as $1 \times 10^{-9} V$, which can be expressed in dBs as $10\log(1 \times 10^{-9}) = -90dB$. Alternatively, a target may be located at range $R = 1000km$, which can be expressed in dBs as $60dB$. Another advantage of using dB in radar design and analysis is to facilitate the arithmetic associated with calculating the different radar parameters. This is true since multiplication in base-10 arithmetic translates into addition in dB-arithmetic, and division translates into subtraction. For example,

$$\frac{250 \times 0.0001}{455} \Leftrightarrow [10\log(250) + 10\log(0.0001) - 10\log(455)]dB = -42.6dB .$$

Eq. (2.35)

In general,

$$10\log\left(\frac{A \times B}{C}\right) = 10\log A + 10\log B - 10\log C \qquad \text{Eq. (2.36)}$$

$$10\log A^q = q \times 10\log A. \qquad \text{Eq. (2.37)}$$

Other *dB* ratios that are often used in radar analysis include the *dBsm* (*dB*, squared meters). In this case, the "power" is area in units m^2. This definition is very important when referring to target radar cross-section (RCS), whose units are in squared meters. More precisely, a target whose RCS is σ (in units m^2) can be expressed in *dBsm* as $10\log(\sigma)$. For example, a $10 m^2$ target is often referred to as a $10 dBsm$ target, and a target with RCS $0.01 m^2$ is equivalent to a $-20 dBsm$. Finally, the units *dBm* (*dB*, milliwatt) and *dBw* (*dB*, Watt) are power ratios of *dB*s with reference to one milliwatt and one Watt, respectively.

$$dBm = 10\log\left(\frac{P}{1mW}\right) \qquad \text{Eq. (2.38)}$$

$$dBw = 10\log\left(\frac{P}{1W}\right) \qquad \text{Eq. (2.39)}$$

To find *dBm* from *dBw*, add 30*dB*, and to find *dBw* from *dBm*, subtract 30*dB*. Other common *dB* units include *dBz* and *dBi*. The *dBz* is used to measure weather radar reflectivity representing the amount of returned power received by the radar referenced to (mm^6/m^{-3}). The unit *dBi* (*dB*, isotropic) represents the forward gain of an antenna compared to an ideal isotropic antenna that emits energy equally in all directions.

2.5. Electromagnetic Waves (RF Waves)

As stated earlier, the radar waveform generator outputs a fully known (both in time and frequency and potentially amplitude) baseband waveform which is then up-converted into an RF waveform through the transmitter subsystem. Hence, the output of the transmitter comprises a high energy complex bandpass waveform with specific amplitude, phase, and or frequency modulation. The complex bandpass waveform is then transfered through a set of RF circuitry to the antenna. The antenna's primary job is to convert its high energy input complex bandpass waveform into an electromagnetic RF signal propagating away from the radar at the speed of light. To increase the antenna's efficiency in converting oscillating electrical signal into an RF signal, the antenna has to be appropriately designed to match the frequency (or wavelength) of the radiated RF waves. The relationship between waveform frequency and wavelength is

$$f = \frac{c}{\lambda}, \qquad \text{Eq. (2.40)}$$

where c is the speed of light.

The RF signal has two components, the electric field **E** and the magnetic field **H**. The fields are orthogonal with respect to one another and with respect to the propagation path, as illustrated in Fig. 2.15. Most radar systems extract target information from the electric field component. The normalized electric field incident on a target is,

$$E_i = e^{jk(\mathbf{r}_i \bullet \mathbf{r})} \qquad \text{Eq. (2.41)}$$

where $\mathbf{r}_i$ is the direction vector of incidence and $\mathbf{r}$ is the range vector to the target, each with respect to the transmission phase center. The • symbol indicates the dot product operation.

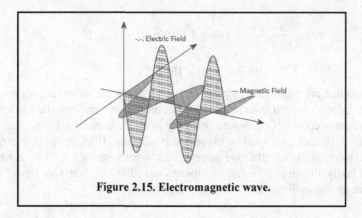

Figure 2.15. Electromagnetic wave.

2.5.1. Polarization

The term, polarization, defines the direction of the tip of the electric field vector (phaser) along the propagation path. More specifically, if the tip of the electric field vector traces a line over each full wavelength along the propagation path, the wave is said to be linearly polarized. If this plane is horizontal, the waveform polarization is refereed to as being horizontal, and alternatively if this plane is vertical, the polarization is said to be vertical. If the tip of the electric field vector traces a circle along the propagation path and over each full wavelength, wherein the aforementioned plane now twists about the propagation path axis into the shape of an Archimedes' screw, then the waveform is said to be circularly polarized. If this motion of the electric field trace is clock-wise, the waveform is right circularly polarized, and conversely if it is counter-clock-wise, then the waveform is left circularly polarized. This is illustrated in Fig. 2.16.

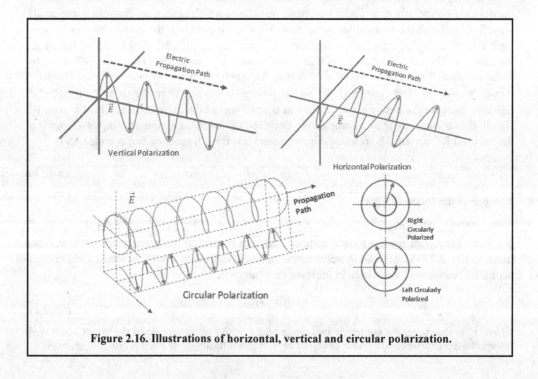

Figure 2.16. Illustrations of horizontal, vertical and circular polarization.

In the general case, the x and y electric field components for a wave traveling along the positive z direction are given by

$$E_x = E_1 \sin(\omega t - kz) \qquad \text{Eq. (2.42)}$$

$$E_y = E_2 \sin(\omega t - kz + \delta) \qquad \text{Eq. (2.43)}$$

where $k = 2\pi/\lambda$, ω is the wave frequency, the angle δ is the time phase angle at which E_y leads E_x, and finally, E_1 and E_2 are, respectively, the wave amplitudes along the x and y directions. The combined vector traces an ellipse (i.e., elliptical polarization) reducing to a circle for circular polarization when observed in the x-y plane. This is illustrated in Fig. 2.17.

The ratio of the major to the minor axes of the polarization ellipse is called the axial ratio (AR). When AR is unity, the polarization ellipse becomes a circle (i.e., circular polarization). Alternatively, when $E_1 = 0$ (hence, the minor axis in this case) and $AR = \infty$, the wave becomes linearly polarized. Equations (2.42) and (2.43) can be combined to give the instantaneous total electric field,

$$\mathbf{E} = \hat{\mathbf{a}}_x E_1 \sin(\omega t - kz) + \hat{\mathbf{a}}_y E_2 \sin(\omega t - kz + \delta) \qquad \text{Eq. (2.44)}$$

where $\hat{\mathbf{a}}_x$ and $\hat{\mathbf{a}}_y$ are unit vectors along the x and y directions, respectively. For vertical polarization $E_2 = 0$, horizontal polarization $E_1 = 0$, and circular polarization $\delta = \pm\pi/2$ (left- or right-hand circular polarization, respectively). When $z = 0$, $E_x = E_1 \sin(\omega t)$ and $E_y = E_2 \sin(\omega t + \delta)$, then by replacing $\sin(\omega t)$ by the ratio E_x/E_1 and by using trigonometry properties Eq. (2.44) can be rewritten as

$$\frac{E_x^2}{E_1^2} - \frac{2 E_x E_y \cos\delta}{E_1 E_2} + \frac{E_y^2}{E_2^2} = (\sin\delta)^2. \qquad \text{Eq. (2.45)}$$

Note that Eq. (2.45) has no dependency on ωt and it has the general form for the equation of an ellipse. In the general case, the polarization ellipse may have any orientation, as illustrated in Fig. 2.18. The angle ξ is called the tilt angle of the ellipse. In this case, AR is given by

$$AR = \frac{OA}{OB} \qquad (1 \le AR \le \infty). \qquad \text{Eq. (2.46)}$$

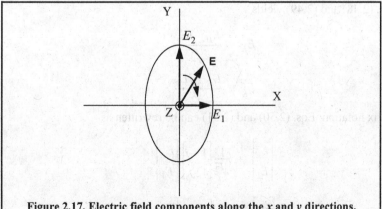

Figure 2.17. Electric field components along the x and y directions. The positive z direction is off the page.

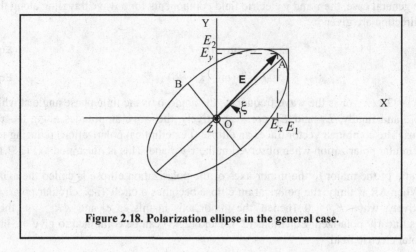

Figure 2.18. Polarization ellipse in the general case.

When $E_1 = 0$, the wave is said to be linearly polarized in the y direction, while if $E_2 = 0$, the wave is said to be linearly polarized in the x direction. Polarization can also be linear at an angle of $45°$ when $E_1 = E_2$ and $\xi = 45°$. When $E_1 = E_2$ and $\delta = 90°$, the wave is said to be left circularly polarized (LCP), while if $\delta = -90°$ the wave is said to right circularly polarized (RCP). It is a common notation to call the linear polarizations along the x and y directions by the names horizontal and vertical polarizations, respectively.

In general, an arbitrarily polarized electric field may be written as the sum of two circularly polarized fields. More precisely,

$$\mathbf{E} = \mathbf{E}_R + \mathbf{E}_L \qquad\qquad \text{Eq. (2.47)}$$

where $\mathbf{E}_R$ and $\mathbf{E}_L$ are the RCP and LCP fields, respectively. Similarly, the RCP and LCP waves can be written as

$$\mathbf{E}_R = \mathbf{E}_V + j\mathbf{E}_H \qquad\qquad \text{Eq. (2.48)}$$

$$\mathbf{E}_L = \mathbf{E}_V - j\mathbf{E}_H \qquad\qquad \text{Eq. (2.49)}$$

where $\mathbf{E}_V$ and $\mathbf{E}_H$ are the fields with vertical and horizontal polarizations, respectively. Combining Eqs. (2.48) and (2.49) yields

$$E_R = \frac{E_H - jE_V}{\sqrt{2}} \qquad\qquad \text{Eq. (2.50)}$$

$$E_L = \frac{E_H + jE_V}{\sqrt{2}}. \qquad\qquad \text{Eq. (2.51)}$$

Using matrix notation, Eqs. (2.50) and (2.51) can be rewritten as

$$\begin{bmatrix} E_R \\ E_L \end{bmatrix} = \frac{1}{\sqrt{2}} \begin{bmatrix} 1 & -j \\ 1 & j \end{bmatrix} \begin{bmatrix} E_H \\ E_V \end{bmatrix} \qquad\qquad \text{Eq. (2.52)}$$

$$\begin{bmatrix} E_H \\ E_V \end{bmatrix} = \frac{1}{\sqrt{2}} \begin{bmatrix} 1 & 1 \\ j & -j \end{bmatrix} \begin{bmatrix} E_R \\ E_L \end{bmatrix}. \qquad\qquad \text{Eq. (2.53)}$$

More extensive descriptions of polarization phenomena can be described by other matrices called Jones and Mueller as well as Stokes parameters (Stokes vectors), which can be useful for characterizing targets tracked by radars.

2.6. Coherence

A radar is said to be coherent if the phase of any two transmitted pulses is consistent, i.e., there is a continuity in the signal phase from one pulse to the next, as illustrated in Fig. 2.19-a. One can view coherence as the radar's ability to maintain an integer multiple of wavelengths between the equiphase wavefront from the end of one pulse to the equiphase wavefront at the beginning of the next pulse. Alternatively, when the phase continuity condition is not maintained between consecutive pulses, then the pulse train is said to be non-coherent, as illustrated in Fig. 2.19-b.

Coherence can be achieved by using a STAble Local Oscillator (STALO). A radar is said to be coherent-on-receive or quasi-coherent if it stores in its memory a record of the phases of all transmitted pulses, albeit, these records must all be very accurately calibrated to a stable reference of the transmitted pulse. In this case, the receiver phase reference is normally the phase of the most recent transmitted pulse. Coherence also refers to the radar's ability to accurately measure the received signal phase. Since Doppler represents a frequency shift in the received signal, then only coherent or coherent-on-receive radars can extract Doppler information. This is because the instantaneous frequency of a signal is proportional to the time derivative of the signal phase. More precisely,

$$f_i = \frac{1}{2\pi} \frac{\mathrm{d}}{\mathrm{d}t} \phi(t)$$

Eq. (2.54)

where f_i is the instantaneous frequency, and $\phi(t)$ is the signal phase.

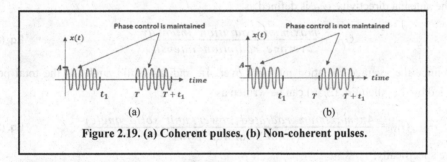

Figure 2.19. (a) Coherent pulses. (b) Non-coherent pulses.

2.7. Radar Antenna

The radar antenna is a transducer device that transfers electrical signal energy into electromagnetic (EM) radiation energy on transmit and converts collected EM radiation energy into electrical signal energy on receive. Most transmit antennas are designed to efficiently (with high radiation efficiency) focus or concentrate the radiated energy toward a particular angular region or point in space. Likewise, most receive antennas are designed to efficiently emphasize the radiation approaching from a particular angular region or point in space. This angular region is referred to as the radar antenna mainbeam which is typically described by an antenna mainbeam gain and an antenna beamwidth. A monostatic radar antenna (i.e., using the same antenna for both transmit and receive) typically can take advantage of the concept of EM reciprocity (transmit and receive EM phenomenology is the same except for the opposite direction of propagation), and therefore the transmit and receive beams have very similar antenna beam patterns. In addition to forming beams, the antenna is typically responsible for steering (mechanically or electronically) the mainbeam to a desired location within an angular region for which there is also a region in range of interest. A mechanically steerable antenna can be, for example, a rotating dish antenna. An electronically steerable antenna can be a phase weighted array of elemental antennas.

The angular and range volume in space, where targets are to be detected, is referred to as the radar field of regard. The field of regard has range, azimuthal and elevation extents with respect to the radar antenna coordinates (typically measured from the center of the antenna of the radar system). The antenna, when properly designed, during transmit will efficiently (with low loss) transition the complex bandpass voltage or current signal coming from the transmitter, and radiate electromagnetic RF energy characterized by its electrical and magnetic fields into the propagation path. Of interest to the radar system is the electric field emitted by an ideal antenna (infinitesimal and isotropic but not realizable) which is a spherical wave. The equiphase wavefronts (separated by a full wavelength) of a spherical wave define a sphere whose surface area is

$$A_{sphere} = 4\pi R^2$$ Eq. (2.55)

where R is the radius of the sphere.

2.7.1. Antenna Directivity and Gain

The most basic characteristic of an antenna is its radiation intensity pattern (or simply, radiation intensity) which mathematically describes how the radiated power is distributed in space once emitted from the antenna. In this context, the radiation intensity is the power-per-unit solid angle in the direction (θ, ϕ) and denoted by $P(\theta, \phi)$, where $0 \leq \theta \leq \pi$ is the elevation angle and $0 \leq \phi \leq 2\pi$ is the azimuth angle.

The antenna directivity G_D is defined as

$$G_D = \frac{maximum\ radiation\ intensity}{average\ radiation\ intensity},$$ Eq. (2.56)

and since the average radiation intensity over 4π radians (solid angle) is the total power divided by 4π, then Eq. (2.56) can be written as

$$G_D = \frac{4\pi(maximum\ radiated\ power/unit\ solid\ angle)}{total\ radiated\ power}.$$ Eq. (2.57)

More specifically,

$$G_D = 4\pi\ \frac{P(\theta, \phi)_{max}}{\int_0^\pi \int_0^{2\pi} P(\theta, \phi)\, d\theta\, d\phi}.$$ Eq. (2.58)

A widely accepted approximation for the directivity is

$$G_D \approx \frac{4\pi}{\theta_3 \phi_3},$$ Eq. (2.59)

where θ_3 and ϕ_3 are the antenna half-power ($3dB$) beamwidths in either direction. The antenna power gain and its directivity are related by

$$G = \rho_r G_D,$$ Eq. (2.60)

where ρ_r is the radiation efficiency factor.

The radiation efficiency factor is ratio between the incident power (i.e., delivered to the antenna by the transmitter) to the actual power radiated by the antenna into space. Amongst other factors, the radiation efficiency factor accounts for the ohmic losses associated with the antenna. Therefore, the antenna gain and antenna directivity have similar mathematical representations, denoted in Eq. (2.58). In the case of directivity the denominator represents the total radiated power, while in the case of gain the denominator is replaced with the total incident power. In radar applications, antenna gain is more meaningful, and accordingly emphasis is on it rather the antenna directivity.

The antenna gain G and its effective aperture A_e are related by

$$G = \frac{4\pi A_e}{\lambda^2}$$
Eq. (2.61)

where λ is the radar operating wavelength. The relationship between the antenna's effective aperture A_e and the physical aperture A is

$$A_e = \rho_a A; \quad 0 \le \rho \le 1$$
Eq. (2.62)

where ρ_a is referred to as the aperture efficiency, and good antennas require $\rho_a \to 1$. In practice, $\rho_a \approx 0.7$ is widely accepted. In this book, unless otherwise noted, A and A_e are used interchangeably to refer to the antenna's aperture, and will assume that antennas have the same gain in the transmitting and receiving modes. Using simple algebraic manipulations of Eqs. (2.59) through (2.61) (assuming that $\rho_r = 1$) yields

$$G = \frac{4\pi A_e}{\lambda^2} \approx \frac{4\pi}{\theta_3 \phi_3} .$$
Eq. (2.63)

The right-hand side of Eq. (2.63) becomes an equality using an approximation constant, k_a, more precisely,

$$G = k_a \frac{4\pi}{\theta_e \theta_a}$$
Eq. (2.64)

where $k_a \le 1$ and depends on the physical aperture shape, and the angles θ_e and θ_a are, respectively, the antenna's elevation and azimuth beamwidths in radians. An excellent commonly used approximation of Eq. (2.64) is

$$G \approx \frac{26000}{\theta_e \theta_a}$$
Eq. (2.65)

where in this case the azimuth and elevation beamwidths are given in degrees.

2.7.2. Antenna Power Radiation Pattern

The graphical representation (either 2-dimensional (2-D) or 3-dimensional (3-D)) of the radiation intensity is referred to as the antenna power radiation pattern (radiation pattern or power pattern). In radar application using the radiation power pattern is often sufficient to completely describe the radar antenna radiation properties. The type of antenna that radiates power equally in all directions is called an isotropic antenna. A normalized 3-D antenna power pattern for an isotropic antenna is shown in Fig. 2.20. Since isotropic antennas have spherical radiation power patterns, one can define the peak power density (power per unit area) at any point in space away from the radar as

$$P_D = \frac{Peak\ transmitted\ power}{area\ of\ a\ sphere} \quad \frac{Watts}{m^2} .$$
Eq. (2.66)

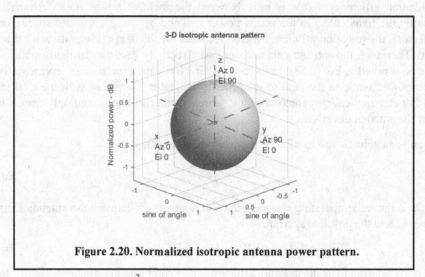

Figure 2.20. Normalized isotropic antenna power pattern.

The power density, in $Watts/m^2$, at range R away from the radar (assuming a lossless propagation medium) is

$$P_D = \frac{P_t}{4\pi R^2} \qquad\qquad \text{Eq. (2.67)}$$

where P_t is the peak transmitted power and $4\pi R^2$ is the surface area of a sphere of radius R.

In radar applications, using isotropic antennas or omni-directional antennas (i.e., antennas that radiate power in all directions), does not lend itself to effective utilization of the radar transmitted power. Accordingly, radar systems will almost always use directional antennas of finite aperture that can direct the emitted power in a certain angular volume (sector). Figure 2.21 shows a typical far-field antenna power pattern for a directive antenna. Compared to an isotropic antenna, the radiated energy is now primarily focused within the antenna mainbeam, whose beamwidth is θ_{3dB}.

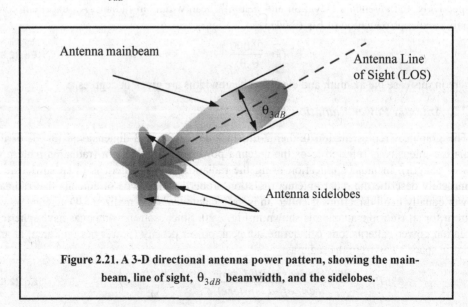

Figure 2.21. A 3-D directional antenna power pattern, showing the mainbeam, line of sight, θ_{3dB} beamwidth, and the sidelobes.

The ratio of the peak power of the mainbeam to that of an isotropic antenna is referred to as the antenna gain, and is denoted by G, as illustrated in Fig. 2.22. Some of the radiated energy is now located in the pattern's sidelobes. Antenna sidelobes are not desirable since they take away some of the radiated energy away from the mainbeam. To reduce the sidelobe levels, one must avoid using uniform illumination of the aperture. This can be accomplished by applying physical tapering (i.e, windowing) of the aperture or by controlling the amplitude and phase distribution of the signal feeding the antenna. Figure 2.23 shows an example of the mainbeam to the sidelobe levels of a typical circular aperture antenna before and after applying a Hamming window taper. Observation of Fig. 2.23 indicates that the maximum sidelobe level went down to -42 *dB* below the mainbeam after tapering as compared to just -13.46 *dB* before tapering. This reduction of sidelobe levels comes at the price of widening the 3 *dB* beamwidth and lowering the maximum gain. Even with this price, tapering remains a desirable feature and is almost always utilized in radar systems.

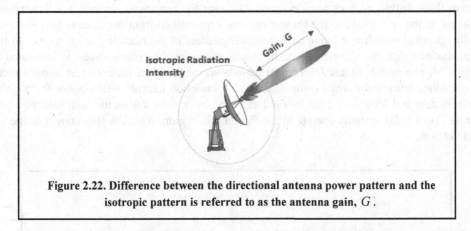

Figure 2.22. Difference between the directional antenna power pattern and the isotropic pattern is referred to as the antenna gain, G.

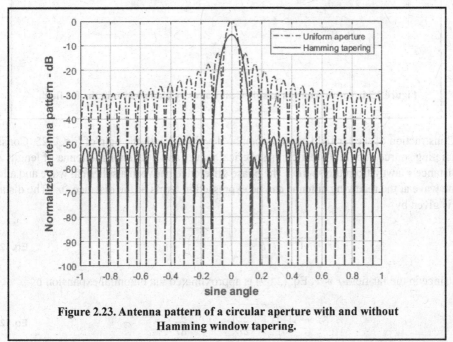

Figure 2.23. Antenna pattern of a circular aperture with and without Hamming window tapering.

The antenna beamwidth (typically measured by its 3 *dB* point) is inversely proportional to the aperture physical dimensions in relation to the wavelength. It follows that small antenna apertures will produce wider beams and vice versa. As a rule of thumb, the 3 *dB* antenna beam width is

$$\theta_{3dB} = k_0 \frac{\lambda}{L} \qquad (radians) \qquad \text{Eq. (2.68)}$$

where k_0 is a constant, λ is the wavelength of the radiated energy, and L is the length of the aperture. For example, $k_0 = 1.02$ for a uniformly illuminated circular antenna rapture, and $k_0 = 1.25$ for a tapered aperture; in both cases L is the diameter of the circular antenna.

2.7.3. Near and Far Fields

Based on the distance from the face of the antenna, where the radiated electric field is measured, three distinct regions are identified. They are the near field, Fresnel, and Fraunhofer regions. In the near field and the Fresnel regions, rays emitted from the antenna have substantially spherical wavefronts (equiphase fronts) regardless of the radiating antenna type. In the Fraunhofer region, the wavefronts can be locally represented by plane waves, as illustrated in Fig. 2.24. The near field and the Fresnel regions are normally of little interest to most radar applications, except for when computing the RF radiation hazards safety zones for a given radar system and for deriving the far field antenna power pattern from the near field measurements. Most radar systems operate in the Fraunhofer region, which is also known as the far field region.

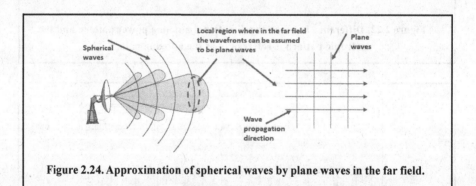

Figure 2.24. Approximation of spherical waves by plane waves in the far field.

Construction of the far field criterion can be developed with the help of Fig. 2.25. Consider a radiating source at point O that emits spherical waves and a receiving antenna of length d is at distance r away from the source. The phase difference between a spherical wave and a local plane wave at the receiving antenna can be expressed in terms of the distance δr. The distance δr is given by

$$\delta r = \overline{AO} - \overline{OB} = \sqrt{r^2 + \left(\frac{d}{2}\right)^2} - r, \qquad \text{Eq. (2.69)}$$

and since in the far field $r \gg d$, Eq. (2.69) is approximated via binomial expansion by

$$\delta r = r\left(\sqrt{1 + \left(\frac{d}{2r}\right)^2} - 1\right) \approx \frac{d^2}{8r}. \qquad \text{Eq. (2.70)}$$

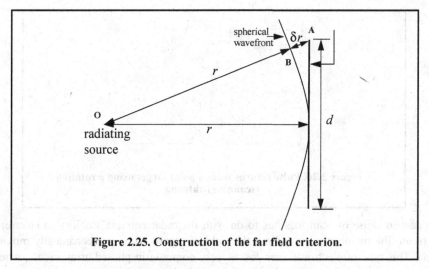

Figure 2.25. Construction of the far field criterion.

It is customary to assume far field when the distance δr corresponds to less than $1/16$ of a wavelength (i.e., $22.5°$). More precisely, if

$$\delta r = \frac{d^2}{8r} \leq \frac{\lambda}{16}, \qquad \qquad \text{Eq. (2.71)}$$

then a useful expression for far field is

$$r \geq \frac{2d^2}{\lambda}. \qquad \qquad \text{Eq. (2.72)}$$

Note that far field is a function of both the antenna size and the operating wavelength.

2.7.4. Beam Shape Loss and Scan Loss

Beam Shape Loss

Typically, the maximum antenna gain is defined as the ratio of the power produced by the antenna on its line of sight (boresight) to the power produced by a hypothetical lossless isotropic antenna. When the target is not on the antenna mainbeam center, the incident power on the target is less than maximum, and accordingly the gain is also less than maximum. The loss in the signal power due to not having maximum antenna gain on the target at all times is called the antenna pattern (shape) loss. Once an antenna has been selected for a given radar, the amount of antenna power pattern loss can be measured or mathematically predicted.

Antenna Scan Loss

Antenna scan loss is caused by the radar antenna's mechanical motion (rotation) and / or the electronic beam steering (particularly when using a phased array antennas). Scan loss in mechanically steerable antennas is always a function of the antenna scan rate. In this case, if the scan rate is fast enough so that the antenna gain on a given target is not always maximum (i.e., center of the mainbeam), then scan loss occurs. This loss can manifest itself even further when the radar employs multiple pulses per beam as the antenna rotates. More specifically, during a single scan a given target may enter the antenna beam at the *3dB* point, reach maximum gain at the center of the beam, and finally leave the beam at the other side *3dB* point, as illustrated in Fig. 2.26. Clearly, returns from pulses hitting the target do not have equal returns.

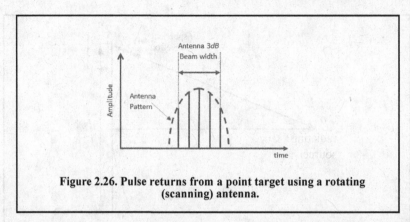

Figure 2.26. Pulse returns from a point target using a rotating (scanning) antenna.

The second cause of scan loss has to do with the radar antenna's ability to electronically point (scan) the mainbeam throughout the field of regard without mechanically moving the antenna. This type of electronic scan loss is very common in phased array radars, where the radar aperture comprises many radiating elements (antennas) that are grouped together using some form of a grid. This grid may be linear or planar, and may take on many different forms.

Additionally, the antenna mainbeam is broadened when electronically steered away from the physical normal of the array's face (antenna boresight). This broadening is a function of the *sine* of the steering angle. In this case, in the far field, the area of a perpendicular plane intersecting the steered-beam is larger than that perpendicular plane intersecting the same beam when it is on the antenna boresight. Therefore, when the radar peak radiated power is fixed, then the radar power density ($Watts/m^2$) incident on a target from a steered-beam is lower than that of the non-steered-beam. Beam broadening is illustrated in Fig 2.27. The 2-way antenna scan loss is given by

$$L_{scan} \approx (\cos\alpha)^{2.5}$$

Eq. (2.73)

where α refers to either azimuth or elevation scan angle measured from the antenna boresight. For example, when $\alpha = 0°, 45°, 60°$, then the 2-way antenna scan loss (reducing the antenna gain value used in the radar equation) is $0, -3.76, -7.53$ *dB,* respectively. In order to limit the scan loss to some acceptable practical values, most arrays do not scan electronically beyond about $\alpha = 60°$. Such arrays are called full field of view (FFOV) arrays.

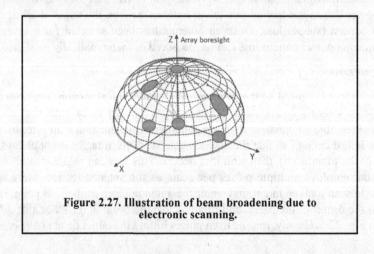

Figure 2.27. Illustration of beam broadening due to electronic scanning.

The FFOV arrays typically employ element spacing of $d \leq 0.6\lambda$ (where λ is the wavelength) to avoid grating lobes within the FOV. Arrays that limit electronic scanning to under $\alpha = 60°$ are referred to as limited field of view (LFOV) arrays. In this case the scan loss is

$$L_{scan} = \left[\frac{\sin\left(\frac{\pi d}{\lambda}\sin\alpha\right)}{\left(\frac{\pi d}{\lambda}\sin\alpha\right)} \right]^{-4}.$$

Eq. (2.74)

Figure 2.28 shows a plot for scan loss versus scan angle.

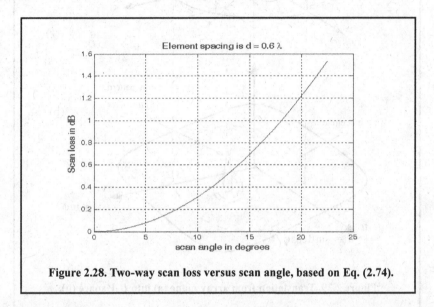

Figure 2.28. Two-way scan loss versus scan angle, based on Eq. (2.74).

Phased array antennas can electronically steer the mainbeam in both azimuth, φ and/or elevation angles θ. This steering however is not a linear function of the azimuth and elevation angles; it is instead linear in the "sine-space" of these angles (i.e., $\sin\varphi$ and $\sin\theta$). Therefore, it is more convenient to convert the array's radiation pattern which is originally a function of φ and θ into a linear function of the sines of these angles. For this purpose, one can define the following change of variables,

$$u = \sin\theta\cos\varphi$$
$$v = \sin\theta\sin\varphi$$

Eq. (2.75)

$$\varphi = \tan^{-1}\left(\frac{v}{u}\right)$$

Eq. (2.76)

$$\theta = \sin^{-1}(\sqrt{v^2 + u^2})$$

These two new variables define a linear space known as the *U-V* space, as illustrated in Fig. 2.29. In the *U-V* space, the antenna pattern will be confined graphically to within a unit circle, more precisely the visible region of the *U-V* space (i.e., the region of angular space that a real beam can be scanned over) is then defined by

$$\sqrt{u^2 + v^2} \leq 1.$$

Eq. (2.77)

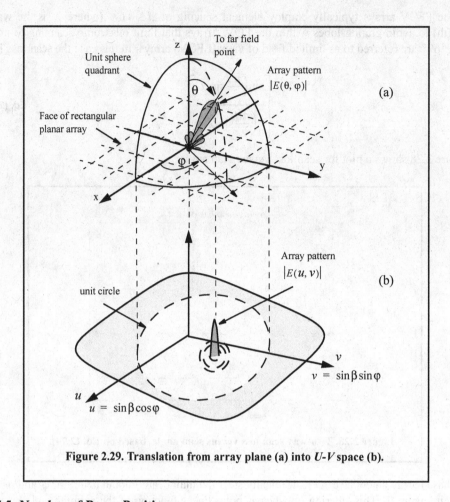

Figure 2.29. Translation from array plane (a) into *U-V* space (b).

2.7.5. Number of Beam Positions

One of the primary radar system functions is to search a predetermined search volume of space (constrained by detection sensitivity and the minimum and maximum azimuth and elevation angles of the radar). For this purpose, the radar system will, in accordance with a known search pattern, move the antenna beam to cover the entire search volume. Clearly and as one would expect, the antenna *3dB* beamwidth is much smaller than the field of regard and it will take the radar many beam positions, $n_B > 1$, to cover the entire field of regard.

The search volumes are normally specified by a search solid angle Ω in steradians. Define the radar search volume extent for both azimuth and elevation as Θ_A and Θ_E. Consequently, the search volume is computed as

$$\Omega = \frac{(\Theta_A \Theta_E)}{(57.296)^2} \; steradians$$

Eq. (2.78)

where both Θ_A and Θ_E are given in degrees. The radar antenna *3dB* beamwidth is typically expressed in terms of its azimuth and elevation beamwidths θ_a and θ_e, respectively. It follows that the antenna solid angle coverage is $\theta_a \theta_e$ and, thus, the number of antenna beam positions n_B required to cover a solid angle Ω is

$$n_B = \frac{\Omega}{(\theta_a \theta_e)/(57.296)^2}. \qquad \text{Eq. (2.79)}$$

It can be shown that when Ω represents the entire hemisphere, then Eq. (2.79) can be approximated (i.e., rule-of-thumb approximation) by

$$n_B > \frac{2\pi}{\theta_a \theta_e} \approx \frac{2\pi A_e}{\lambda^2} \approx \frac{G}{2}. \qquad \text{Eq. (2.80)}$$

Recall however, that the antenna steering is a linear function in the *U-V* space and not in the angle space. Additionally for phased array antenna, beam widening is expected when the steering angle is moved away from the antenna boresight. Therefore, the formulas in Eq. (2.79) and (2.80) are not exact, and instead, for phased array antenna, one should use the sine-space calculations to compute the required number of beam positions needed to search the entire radar search volume with the minimum number of beams. The following example will illustrate this computation method.

Consider a radar whose search volume is $\pm 45°$ in azimuth and $8°$ in elevation. Assume a pencil beam with a *3dB* beamwidth equal to $1°$. Using Eq. (2.79) yields,

$$\Omega = \frac{(\Theta_A \Theta_E)}{(57.296)^2} = \frac{(45+45)\times 8}{(57.296)^2} = 0.21932 \ \textit{steradians} \ \Rightarrow$$

$$\qquad \text{Eq. (2.81)}$$

$$n_B = \frac{0.21932}{\{1\times 1/(57.296)^2\}} = \frac{0.21932}{3.0461\times 10^{-4}} = 720 \ \textit{beam positions}$$

however, using the sine-space computation approach yields

$$n_{az} = 2\times \frac{\sin(45)}{\sin(1)} = 2\times \frac{0.707}{0.01745} = 81 \ \textit{azimuth beam positions} \qquad \text{Eq. (2.82)}$$

$$n_{el} = \frac{\sin(8)}{\sin(1)} = \frac{0.1392}{0.01745} = 8 \ \textit{elevation beam positions} \qquad \text{Eq. (2.83)}$$

it follows that

$$n_B = n_{az}\times n_{el} = 81\times 8 = 648 \ \textit{beam positions}. \qquad \text{Eq. (2.84)}$$

In conclusion, one can easily see that *648* beam positions, using sine-space (i.e., *U-V* space), are needed to cover the entire field of regard and not *720* beam positions as indicated earlier.

2.8. Radar Cross-Section

Electromagnetic waves, with any specified polarization, are normally diffracted or scattered in all directions when incident on a target. These scattered waves are broken down into two parts. The first part is made of waves that have the same polarization as the receiving antenna. The other portion of the scattered waves will have a different polarization to which the receiving antenna may not respond. The two polarizations are orthogonal and are referred to as the principal polarization (PP) and orthogonal polarization (OP), respectively. The intensity of the backscattered energy that has the same polarization as the radar's receiving antenna principal polarization is used to define the target radar cross-section (RCS). When a target is illuminated by RF energy, it acts like an antenna, and will have near and far fields. Waves reflected and measured in the near field are, in general, spherical. Alternatively, in the far field, the wavefronts are decomposed into a linear combination of plane waves.

Assume the power density of a wave incident on a target located at range R away from the radar is P_{Di}, as illustrated in Fig. 2.30. The amount of reflected power from the target is

$$P_r = \sigma P_{Di} \qquad \text{Eq. (2.85)}$$

σ denotes the target cross-section. Define P_{Dr} as the power density of the scattered waves at the receiving antenna. It follows that

$$P_{Dr} = \frac{P_r}{4\pi R^2} \qquad \text{Eq. (2.86)}$$

Equating Eqs. (2.85) and (2.86) yields

$$\sigma = 4\pi R^2 \left(\frac{P_{Dr}}{P_{Di}}\right). \qquad \text{Eq. (2.87)}$$

In order to ensure that the radar receiving antenna is in the far field (i.e., scattered waves received by the antenna are planar), Eq. (2.87) is modified

$$\sigma = 4\pi \lim_{R \to \infty} R^2 \left(\frac{P_{Dr}}{P_{Di}}\right) \qquad \text{Eq. (2.88)}$$

The RCS defined by Eq. (2.88) is often referred to as either the monostatic RCS, the backscattered RCS, or simply target RCS.

As indicated by Eq. (2.88) the units for σ is m^2, which is often expressed in *dBsm*. The RCS does not represent nor should it be interpreted as a measure of the physical area of the target in m^2. As a matter of fact, this is never the case except for a target made of conductive sphere whose radius is much larger than the incident wavelength; in this case, the RCS for the sphere is $\sigma_{sphere} = \pi r^2$; where r is the radius of the sphere. Accordingly, one can interpret the target RCS as the electronic area of the target as projected on the radar line of sight and is frequency dependent. The target RCS is dependent on many factors, including its physical shape, orientation (i.e., aspect angle with respect to the radar), material, coating, number and spacing of its scattering centers (major reflection points), and polarization. Table 2.1 shows a list of objects and their corresponding RCS.

The backscattered RCS is measured from all waves scattered in the direction of the radar and that has the same polarization as the receiving antenna. It represents a portion of the total scattered target RCS σ_t, where $\sigma_t > \sigma$. Assuming a spherical coordinate system defined by (ρ, θ, φ), then at range ρ the target scattered cross-section is a function of (θ, φ). Let the angles (θ_i, φ_i) define the direction of propagation of the incident waves. Also, let the angles (θ_s, φ_s) define the direction of propagation of the scattered waves. The special case, when $\theta_s = \theta_i$ and $\varphi_s = \varphi_i$, defines the monostatic RCS. The RCS measured by the radar at angles $\theta_s \neq \theta_i$ and $\varphi_s \neq \varphi_i$ is called the bistatic RCS. The total target scattered RCS is given by

$$\sigma_t = \frac{1}{4\pi} \int_{\varphi_s = 0}^{2\pi} \int_{\theta_s = 0}^{\pi} \sigma(\theta_s, \varphi_s) \sin\theta_s \ d\theta \ d\varphi_s. \qquad \text{Eq. (2.89)}$$

The amount of backscattered waves from a target is proportional to the ratio of the target extent (size) to the wavelength, λ, of the incident waves. In fact, a radar will not be able to detect targets much smaller than its operating wavelength. For example, if weather radars use L-band frequency, rain drops become nearly invisible to the radar since they are much smaller than the wavelength. RCS measurements in the frequency region, where the target extent and the wavelength are comparable, are referred to as the Rayleigh region. Alternatively, the frequency region where the target extent is much larger than the radar operating wavelength is referred to as the optical region. In practice, the majority of radar systems are designed to operate in the optical region of their intended targets.

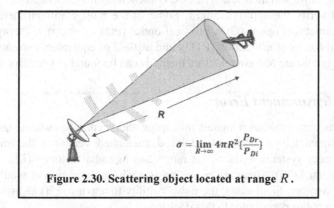

$$\sigma = \lim_{R \to \infty} 4\pi R^2 \{\frac{P_{Dr}}{P_{Di}}\}$$

Figure 2.30. Scattering object located at range R.

Table 2.1. Common Objects and Their Corresponding RCS.

Object	RCS in m^2	RCS in *dBsm*
Truck	*200+*	*23+*
Car	*100+*	*20+*
Large civilian aircraft	*100+*	*20+*
Bomber or large aircraft	*40*	*16*
Boat	*10*	*10*
Fighter aircraft	*2*	*3*
Adult human	*1*	*0*
Bird	*0.01*	*-20*
Insect	*0.00001*	*-50*

2.8.1. RCS Prediction Methods

Most radar systems use RCS as a means of classification. Therefore, accurate prediction of target RCS is critical in order to design and develop robust classification algorithms. Additionally, measuring and identifying the scattering centers (sources) for a given target aid in developing RCS reduction techniques. Radar cross-section calculations require broad and extensive technical knowledge; thus, many scientists and scholars find the subject challenging and intellectually motivating. Two categories of RCS prediction methods are available: exact and approximate.

Exact methods of RCS prediction are very complex even for simple-shaped objects. This is because they require solving either differential or integral equations that describe the scattered waves from an object under the proper set of boundary conditions. Such boundary conditions are governed by Maxwell's equations. Even when exact solutions are achievable, they are often difficult to interpret and to program using digital computers. Due to the difficulties associated with the exact RCS prediction, approximate methods become the viable alternative. The majority of the approximate methods are valid in the optical region (i.e., the radar wavelength is smaller than the object under consideration), and each has its own strengths and limitations. Most approximate methods can predict RCS within few *dBsm* of the truth.

In general, such a variation is quite acceptable by radar engineers and designers. Approximate methods are usually the main source for predicting RCS of complex and extended targets such as aircrafts, ships, and missiles. When experimental results are available, they can be used to validate and verify the approximations. Some of the most commonly used approximate methods are geometrical optics (GO), physical optics (PO), geometrical theory of diffraction (GTD), physical theory of diffraction (PTD), and method of equivalent currents (MEC). More details on RCS prediction and computation methods can be found in Chapters 11 and 12.

2.9. Radar Measurement Errors

Radar systems transmit known signals into space and attempt to estimate target parameters from the echo signal, which comprises a delayed, attenuated, version of the emitted signal. Of importance to radar systems is the target range and its radial velocity (i.e., range rate with respect to the radar LOS). There are many reasons why a radar system would use a certain waveform over another. In all cases, the radar's ability to maximize its measurement in range or range rate is a major contributor to this decision.

Radar systems extract target information (attributes) such as target RCS, range, range rate, and angular position relative to the radar location by processing the radar echoes. To this end, a radar echo (or simply a radar measurement) passes through three distinct phases. They are, measurement availability, measurement quality, and measurement accuracy. Each phase is typically characterized by the signal-to-noise ratio (SNR) value at the output of the radar receiver (matched filter). Initially, a measurement availability occurs at low SNR values (~6 to 8 dB), where the received signal is large enough to surpass a pre-determined threshold value (i.e., detection). Next, when the measurement quality is good enough (SNR ~ 13dB), the radar data processor establishes distinct track files (i.e, tracking occurs) for each detected target. Finally, when the measured SNR value becomes large, the radar is said to have enough SNR (15dB or more) to achieve certain measurement accuracy. Typically, range, range rate, and angle measurement accuracy limits are pre-determined in the radar design process.

Before discussing the radar range measurement, range rate measurement, and angular measurement accuracies, we will first introduce the definition for the term *accuracy*. At the heart of this discussion are the range and velocity (i.e., Doppler) resolutions. The term, resolution, describes the radar's ability to distinguish close proximity targets (in range or Doppler) as distinct separable targets. In others words, any two adjacent targets separated by this resolution value in any one coordinate are completely resolved along that coordinate. The radar's ability to discern a very small change in range or Doppler measurements is referred to as a measurement *precision*, while measurement accuracy refers to the correctness of the measurement. Accuracy is an indication of how close is a measured (i.e., measured by the radar) target attribute (range, range rate, etc.) to its true value.

Precision is an indication of how close the radar measurements are with respect to each other when the same measurement is repeated multiple times. The objective is to make the radar measurement both accurate and precise. However, due to measurement biases (a condition often true in radar systems) radar systems measurements may not be readily usable by the radar signal processor even when those measurements are both accurate and precise. This is illustrated using the experiment shown in Fig. 2.31.

Radar systems use measurement accuracy as a means to measure the total measurement error. On the other hand, radar systems use precision to measure the noise error only, since a random noise signal will always interfere with the radar signal.

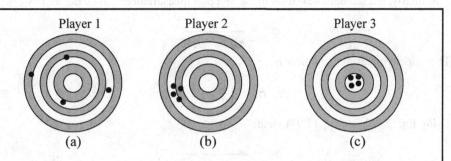

Figure 2.31. (a) Inaccurate and imprecise measurements. (b) Accurate and precise but biased measurements. (c) Precise and accurate measurements.

In this experiment, consider three dart players, each with 4 darts, attempting to hit the bull's eye on the dart board. Figure 2.31-a shows the results for player 1, while Figures 2.31-b and 2.31-c show the results for players 2 and 3. Using the definitions introduced above for precision and accuracy, one can conclude the following: player 1 is inaccurate and imprecise; player 2 is accurate and precise but suffers severe bias; finally, player 3 is both accurate and precise.

The mathematical formulations for both range and Doppler resolutions were introduced earlier. The range resolution, ΔR is

$$\Delta R = \frac{c\tau}{2} \Rightarrow \Delta R = \frac{c}{2B} \qquad \text{Eq. (2.90)}$$

where τ is the pulse width, c the speed of light, and B is the signal bandwidth. The Doppler frequency f_d is

$$f_d = \frac{2v}{\lambda} \qquad \text{Eq. (2.91)}$$

where v is the target radial velocity on the radar line of sight, and λ is the wavelength. It follows that the velocity resolution Δv is given by

$$\Delta v = \frac{\lambda \Delta f_d}{2} \Rightarrow \Delta v = \frac{\lambda}{T_i}, \qquad \text{Eq. (2.92)}$$

where T_i is the integration time. Note that $T_i = \tau$ when a single pulse is used for the measurement. The standard deviation describing the integration time error is

$$\sigma_\tau = \frac{1}{B\sqrt{2 \times SNR}}, \qquad \text{Eq. (2.93)}$$

where B is the signal bandwidth and SNR is the measured signal-to-noise ratio. From Eq. (2.90), the range measurement error is

$$\sigma_R = \frac{c\sigma_\tau}{2}. \qquad \text{Eq. (2.94)}$$

Substituting Eq. (2.93) into Eq. (2.94) yields,

$$\sigma_R = \frac{c}{2B\sqrt{2 \times SNR}}. \qquad \text{Eq. (2.95)}$$

Similarly, the standard deviation in the Doppler measurement can be derived as

$$\sigma_{f_d} = \frac{1}{\tau\sqrt{2 \times SNR}} \ .$$

Eq. (2.96)

The velocity measurement error is

$$\sigma_v = \left(\frac{\lambda}{2}\right)\sigma_{fd} \ .$$

Eq. (2.97)

Using Eq. (2.96) into Eq. (2.97) yields

$$\sigma_v = \frac{\lambda}{2\tau\sqrt{2 \times SNR}} \ .$$

Eq. (2.98)

The standard deviation of the error in the angle measurement is

$$\sigma_\theta = \frac{\Theta}{k\sqrt{2 \times SNR}}$$

Eq. (2.99)

where Θ is the antenna beamwidth of the angular coordinate of the measurement (azimuth or elevation), k is the monopulse slope between *1.5* and *1.7* and the value $k = 1.56$ is widely accepted.

Chapter 3

Radar Equation

Bassem R. Mahafza

3.1. Radar Range Equation

Consider a radar that employs an isotropic antenna; since isotropic antennas have spherical radiation patterns, then the effective power out of the radar (at the antenna physical aperture) is

$$P_{eff} = \frac{P_t}{L_t},$$

Eq. (3.1)

where P_t is the peak transmitted in *Watts* and L_t is the total transmit losses. The power density, in *Watts/m²*, at range R away from the radar is

$$P_D = \frac{P_t}{4\pi R^2 L_t}$$

Eq. (3.2)

where $4\pi R^2$ is the surface area of a sphere of radius R. Using an isotropic antenna in radar applications where the transmitted energy is spread equally in all directions wastes its resources, since radar systems are typically interested in only searching a limited volume in space referred to as the "field of regard". Accordingly, radar systems utilize directional antennas in order to focus their radiated energy in a certain direction. Figure 3.1 shows a representative 3-dimensional (3-D) isotropic and directional antennas radiation patterns. Simply put, going from an isotropic antenna to a directional antenna, the radar system will mainly emit energy into a small volume of space controlled by the antenna radiation pattern. This is characterized by its *3dB* azimuth and elevation beamwidths, θ_a and θ_e, respectively. The mainbeam is a function of the antenna physical aperture shape, dimensions, and is impacted by many factors. As shown in Fig. 3.1, using directional antennas places some of the radar radiated energy in the antenna pattern sidelobes, an undesirable feature that radar antenna designers try to minimize. Note that the difference between the maximum of the mainbeam and the isotropic radiation level is referred to as the antenna gain, G. In this case the effective radiated power (ERP_r) of the radar is given by,

$$ERP_r = \frac{P_t G_t}{L_t}$$

Eq. (3.3)

where G_t is the transmits antenna gain for the radar. In almost all cases of monostatic radars (i.e., a radar using the same antenna for transmit and receive), the receive antenna gain G_r is set equal to G_t. Therefore, and for ease of notation, the subscripts are dropped and we will simply use the symbol G to represent both the transmit and receive antenna gains.

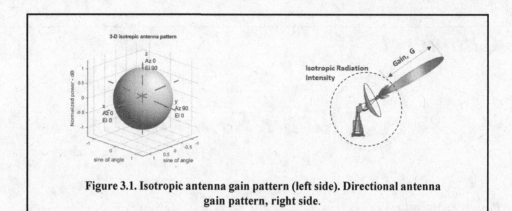

Figure 3.1. Isotropic antenna gain pattern (left side). Directional antenna gain pattern, right side.

The antenna gain is related to its effective aperture A_e as follows

$$G = \frac{4\pi A_e}{\lambda^2}$$ Eq. (3.4)

where λ is the radar operating wavelength; clearly and as indicated by Eq. (3.4) the antenna gain is unitless. The relationship between the antenna's effective aperture A_e and its physical aperture A is

$$A_e = \rho A \qquad 0 \le \rho \le 1$$ Eq. (3.5)

where ρ is referred to as the aperture efficiency. Good antenna designs require $\rho \to 1$. In this book, unless otherwise noted, A and A_e are used interchangeably to refer to the antenna's aperture. In practice, $\rho \approx 0.7$ is widely accepted.

Some of the antenna rules of thumb were introduced in Chapter 2, and are repeated here for convenience. First, the antenna gain, G, is related to the antenna's $3dB$ azimuth and elevation beamwidths by

$$G = K\frac{4\pi}{\theta_a \theta_e} \qquad ,(\theta_a, \theta_e) \ in \ radians$$ Eq. (3.6)

where $K \le 1$ depends on the physical aperture shape and (θ_a, θ_e) are the antenna's azimuth and elevation beamwidths, respectively. An excellent commonly used approximation of Eq. (3.6) is

$$G \approx \frac{26000}{\theta_a \theta_e} \qquad ,(\theta_a, \theta_e) \ in \ degrees$$ Eq. (3.7)

Accordingly, when using a directional antenna, the emitted radar power density incident upon a target located at range R on the radar line of sight (antenna boresight) is given by

$$P_D = \frac{P_t G}{4\pi R^2} \frac{1}{L_t} \frac{1}{L_{atm_1}} \qquad \left(\frac{W}{m^2}\right).$$ Eq. (3.8)

where L_{atm_1} is the one-way (from the radar to the target) radio frequency (RF) propagation medium loss, or atmospheric loss. When the radar radiated energy impinges upon a target, the induced surface currents on that target radiate electromagnetic energy in all directions.

The amount of the radiated energy is proportional to the target size, orientation, physical shape, and material, which are all lumped together in one target-specific parameter called the radar cross-section (RCS) denoted by the Greek letter σ. The RCS is defined as the ratio of the power reflected back to the radar to the power density incident on the target,

$$\sigma = \frac{P_r}{P_D} \quad (m^2)$$

Eq. (3.9)

where P_r is the power reflected from the target in the direction of the radar. Thus, the total power density at the antenna aperture is

$$P_{Dr} = \frac{P_t G \sigma}{4\pi R^2} \frac{1}{L_t L_{atm_1} L_{atm_1} 4\pi R^2} \quad \left(\frac{W}{m^2}\right)$$

Eq. (3.10)

where the second $1/4\pi R^2$ term signifies the power density incident on the radar, and the second L_{atm_1} is used to account for the atmospheric loss from the target to the radar. It is more practical to simply use the two-way atmospheric loss, L_{atm}. It follows that Eq. (3.10) can now be written as

$$P_{Dr} = \frac{P_t G \sigma}{(4\pi)^2 R^4} \frac{1}{L_t \ L_{atm}} \quad \left(\frac{W}{m^2}\right).$$

Eq. (3.11)

The amount of signal power delivered to the radar through its antenna is

$$P_r = \frac{P_t G \sigma}{(4\pi)^2 R^4} \frac{1}{L_t \ L_{atm}} A_e \frac{1}{L_r} \quad (W),$$

Eq. (3.12)

where L_r is the total receive losses through the antenna. Substituting the value of A_e from Eq. (3.4) into Eq. (3.12) yields

$$P_r = \frac{P_t G \sigma}{(4\pi)^2 R^4} \frac{1}{L_t L_{atm} L_r} \frac{G \lambda^2}{4\pi} \Rightarrow P_r = \frac{P_t G^2 \lambda^2 \sigma}{(4\pi)^3 R^4 L_t L_{atm} L_r} \quad (W).$$

Eq. (3.13)

In practical situations the returned signal received by the radar will be corrupted with additive noise (deliberate and or natural), which introduces unwanted voltages at all radar frequencies. The natural input noise signal comprises many random sources and in accordance with the central limit theorem, the noise signal is assumed to be Gaussian. Furthermore, the input noise power spectrum density is assumed to be white (i.e., has constant power at all frequencies). However, in most practical systems the noise is considered to be band-limited white Gaussian noise (i.e., limited to at least the radar instantaneous bandwidth). The input noise power going through the antenna into the radar receiver is N_i. More specifically,

$$N_i = k T_s B \quad \left(\frac{Joule}{Kelvin} \cdot Kelvin \cdot Hz\right)$$

Eq. (3.14)

where $k = 1.38 \times 10^{-23}$ *Joule/degree Kelvin* is Boltzmann's constant, and T_s is the total effective system noise temperature in degrees *Kelvin*. The combined signal (noise plus target echo signal) goes through the radar receiver hardware before it is presented to the radar signal processor whose primary function is to extract the relevant target attributes (range, range rate, target RCS etc.). The fidelity of the radar receiver is normally described by a figure of merit referred to as the noise figure, F. The noise figure is defined as

$$F = \frac{(SNR)_i}{(SNR)_o} = \frac{S_i / N_i}{S_o / N_o} \quad (unitless)$$

Eq. (3.15)

where $(SNR)_i$ and $(SNR)_o$ are, respectively, the signal-to-noise ratios at the input and output of the receiver. The input signal power is S_i, while the input noise power is N_i. The values S_o and N_o are, respectively, the output signal and noise powers. From Eq. (3.15), the input signal power is

$$S_i = N_i F(SNR)_o \qquad (unitless).$$

Eq. (3.16)

Using Eq. (3.14) in Eq. (3.16) yields,

$$S_i = F \cdot kT_s B \cdot (SNR)_o.$$

Eq. (3.17)

The receiver effective noise temperature excluding the antenna is

$$T_e = T_o(F-1)$$

Eq. (3.18)

where $T_0 = 290K$ and F is the receiver noise figure from Eq. (3.15). It follows that the total effective system noise temperature T_s is given by

$$T_s = T_e + T_a = T_0(F-1) + T_a \Rightarrow T_s = T_o F - T_o + T_a$$

Eq. (3.19)

where T_a is the antenna temperature. In many radar applications it is desirable to set the antenna temperature T_a to T_0 and thus, Eq. (3.19) is reduced to

$$T_s = T_o F.$$

Eq. (3.20)

Using Eq. (3.20) in Eq. (3.17) yields

$$S_i = kT_o BF(SNR)_o.$$

Eq. (3.21)

Recall that the signal power was derived earlier and is given in Eq. (3.13). Using the result from Eq. (3.20) into Eq. (3.13) yields,

$$\frac{P_t G^2 \lambda^2 \sigma}{(4\pi)^3 R^4} \frac{1}{L_t L_{atm} L_r} = kT_o BF(SNR)_o.$$

Eq. (3.22)

Rearranging the terms of Eq. (3.22) yields the $(SNR)_o$ at the output of the radar receiver as

$$(SNR)_o = \frac{P_t G^2 \lambda^2 \sigma}{(4\pi)^3 R^4} \frac{1}{kT_o BF} \frac{1}{L_t L_{atm} L_r}.$$

Eq. (3.23)

By combining the different losses (L_t, L_{atm}, L_r) into one combined total radar loss denoted by L_T, the SNR at the output of the radar receiver can be expressed as

$$SNR = \frac{P_t G^2 \lambda^2 \sigma}{(4\pi)^3 R^4 kT_o BF L_T} \qquad (unitless),$$

Eq. (3.24)

where the subscript from the term SNR is dropped for ease of notation. Equation (3.24) is commonly known as the *radar range equation*, or simply the *radar equation*. Other forms of the radar equation exist and will be discussed later in this chapter. But for now, if one uses Eq. (3.20) in Eq. (3.24) the radar equation can be written as,

$$SNR = \frac{P_t G^2 \lambda^2 \sigma}{(4\pi)^3 R^4 kT_s BL_T}.$$

Eq. (3.25)

Finally, by using the relationship $\tau = 1/B$ where τ is the radar pulse width and B is the radar instantaneous bandwidth of the radar range equation can be expressed as,

$$SNR = \frac{P_t G^2 \lambda^2 \sigma \tau}{(4\pi)^3 R^4 k T_s L_T} \qquad OR \qquad SNR = \frac{P_t G^2 \lambda^2 \sigma \tau}{(4\pi)^3 R^4 k T_0 F L_T}. \qquad \text{Eq. (3.26)}$$

The *SNR* defined in Eq. (3.26) is often referred to as the *radar sensitivity*. It is very common to use the two terms (i.e., *SNR* and sensitivity) interchangeably. The phrase *radar sensitivity* is widely used to indicate the radar's ability to detect (i.e., measurement availability), track (i.e., measurement quality), and classify (i.e., measurement accuracy) targets within its field of regard (search volume). As a rule of thumb, the measurement availability sensitivity is $SNR \geq 6 \sim 8dB$, the measurement quality sensitivity is $SNR \geq 10 \sim 13dB$, and finally the measurement accuracy sensitivity is $SNR \geq 15dB$.

3.1.1. Maximum Detection Range

From the radar equation, one can easily observe that the maximum radar range R_{max} corresponds to the minimum detectable signal power in the radar, $(SNR)_{min}$. It follows that,

$$R_{max} = \left(\frac{P_t G^2 \lambda^2 \sigma \tau}{(4\pi)^3 k T_s L_T} \frac{1}{(SNR)_{min}} \right)^{1/4}. \qquad \text{Eq. (3.27)}$$

Consider a new detection range R_{new} that is twice the maximum range R_{max}. More precisely, let the new range R_{new} be

$$R_{new} = 2R_{max}, \qquad \text{Eq. (3.28)}$$

it follows that

$$R_{new}^4 = (2R_{max})^4 = 16R_{max}^4. \qquad \text{Eq. (3.29)}$$

Clearly, increasing the left-hand side Eq. (3.27) *16-folds* can be achieved through increasing the peak transmitted power, P_t by a factor of *16*. Alternatively, substituting Eq. (3.4) into Eq. (3.27) yields,

$$R_{max} = \left(\frac{P_t \lambda^2 \sigma \tau}{(4\pi)^3 k T_s L_T} \left(\frac{4\pi}{\lambda^2} A_e \right)^2 \frac{1}{(SNR)_{min}} \right)^{1/4}. \qquad \text{Eq. (3.30)}$$

Accordingly, to gain a factor of *16* on the left-hand side of Eq. (3.30) the aperture area can be increased by a factor of *4*. Therefore, in order to double the radar range, one must increase the peak transmitted power P_t *16* times; or equivalently, increase the effective aperture area four times.

A graphical step-by-step derivation of the radar equation is shown in Fig. 3.2. In this case, the transmit and receive antenna gains are respectively denoted by G_t and G_r, and the same is held true for the transmit and receive losses, L_t and L_r. Finally L_{atm_1} denotes the one-way atmospheric loss, L_{atm} is the two-way atmospheric loss, and L_T denotes the combined total radar losses.

Plots of the SNR versus range are widely known as sensitivity plots. Figures 3.3-a and 3.3-b show sensitivity plots (using semi-log and linear scales) generated using following inputs into the radar equation: Peak power $P_t = 1.5MW$, operating frequency $f_0 = 5.6GHz$, antenna gain $G = 45dB$, radar losses $L = 6dB$, noise figure $F = 3dB$. The bandwidth is $B = 5MHz$. The radar minimum and maximum detection ranges are $R_{min} = 25Km$ and $R_{max} = 165Km$.

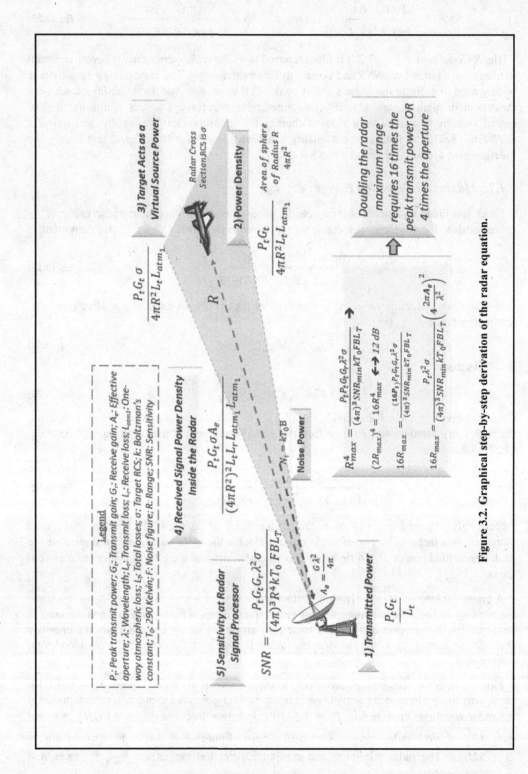

Figure 3.2. Graphical step-by-step derivation of the radar equation.

Legend

P_t: Peak transmit power; G_t: Transmit gain; G_r: Receive gain; A_e: Effective aperture; λ: Wavelength; L_t: Transmit loss; L_r: Receive loss; L_{atm_1}: One-way atmospheric loss; L_T: Total losses; σ: Target RCS; k: Boltzman's constant; T_0: 290 Kelvin; F: Noise figure; R: Range; SNR: Sensitivity

3) Target Acts as a Virtual Source Power

Radar Cross Section,RCS is σ

$$\frac{P_t G_t \; \sigma}{4\pi R^2 L_t L_{atm_1}}$$

2) Power Density

Area of sphere of Radius R

$4\pi R^2$

$$\frac{P_t G_t}{4\pi R^2 L_t L_{atm_1}}$$

Doubling the radar maximum range requires 16 times the peak transmit power OR 4 times the aperture

R

4) Received Signal Power Density Inside the Radar

$$\frac{P_t G_t \; \sigma A_e}{(4\pi R^2)^2 L_t L_r L_{atm_1} L_{atm_1}}$$

Noise Power

$$N_t = kT_0B$$

$$R_{max}^4 = \frac{P_t P_t G_t G_r \lambda^2 \sigma}{(4\pi)^3 SNR_{min} kT_0 FBL_T}$$

$$(2R_{max})^4 = 16R_{max}^4 \; \longleftarrow 12 \; dB$$

$$16R_{max} = \frac{(16P_t)P_t G_t G_r \lambda^2 \sigma}{(4\pi)^3 SNR_{min} kT_0 FBL_T}$$

$$16R_{max} = \frac{P_t \lambda^2 \sigma}{(4\pi)^3 SNR_{min} kT_0 FBL_T} \left(4\frac{2\pi A_e}{\lambda^2}\right)^2$$

5) Sensitivity at Radar Signal Processor

$$SNR = \frac{P_t G_t G_r \lambda^2 \sigma}{(4\pi)^3 R^4 kT_0 \; FBL_T}$$

$$A_e = \frac{G \lambda^2}{4\pi}$$

1) Transmitted Power

$$\frac{P_t G_t}{L_t}$$

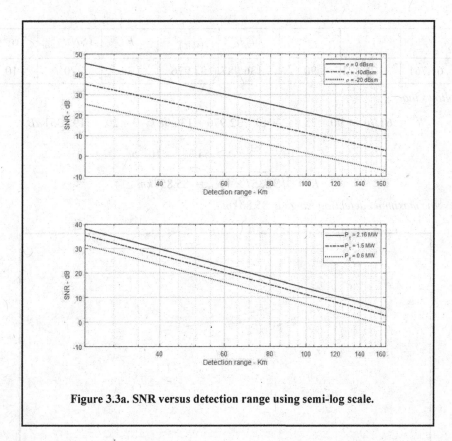

Figure 3.3a. SNR versus detection range using semi-log scale.

Example:

Assume a certain C-band radar with the following parameters: Peak power $P_t = 1.5MW$, operating frequency $f_0 = 5.6GHz$, antenna gain $G = 45dB$, total loss $L_T = 0$, temperature $T_o = 290K$, pulse width $\tau = 0.2\mu sec$. The radar threshold is $(SNR)_{min} = 20dB$. Assume target cross-section $\sigma = 0.1m^2$. Compute the maximum range.

Solution:

The radar bandwidth is

$$B = \frac{1}{\tau} = \frac{1}{0.2 \times 10^{-6}} = 5MHz.$$

The wavelength is

$$\lambda = \frac{c}{f_0} = \frac{3 \times 10^8}{5.6 \times 10^9} = 0.054m.$$

From the radar equation one gets

$$(R^4)_{dB} = (P_t + G^2 + \lambda^2 + \sigma - (4\pi)^3 - kT_oB - F - (SNR)_{min})_{dB}$$

where, before summing, the dB calculations are carried out for each of the individual parameters on the right-hand side. One can now construct the following table with all parameters computed in dB:

P_t	λ^2	G^2	kT_oB	$(4\pi)^3$	F	$(SNR)_{min}$	σ
61.761	−25.421	90	−136.987	32.976	3	20	−10

It follows that

$$R^4 = 61.761 + 90 - 25.352 - 10 - 32.976 + 136.987 - 3 - 20 = 197.351\,dB$$

$$R^4 = 10^{(197.351/10)} = 54.337 \times 10^{18}\,m^4$$

$$R = \sqrt[4]{54.357 \times 10^{18}} = 85.857\,km \,.$$

Thus, the maximum detection range is $85.86\,km$.

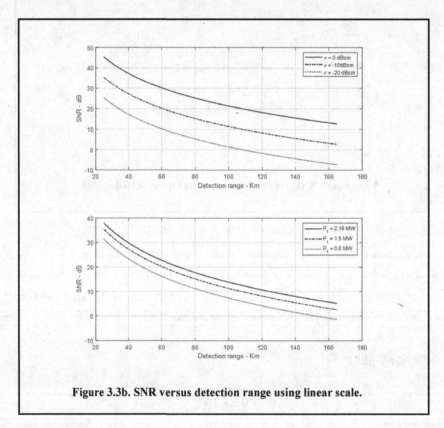

Figure 3.3b. SNR versus detection range using linear scale.

3.1.2. Blake Chart

A graphical presentation of the radar equation in the form of sensitivity plots as a function of range-angle-height is often referred to as a Blake chart plot. In practice, it is very common to also represent the radar equation in a tabulated format referred to as the Blake chart. In this context, a tabulated Blake chart represents a single data point (i.e., a specific elevation angle) on the Blake chart plot where the antenna gain is considered to be maximum (i.e., the radar line of sight). Figure 3.4 shows a sample tabulated Blake chart for a hypothetical S-band air defense radar. The output of the table is either the sensitivity (i.e., SNR) for a given range and target RCS, or the maximum range for a given SNR and target RCS.

$$SNR = \frac{P_t G^2 \lambda^2 \sigma \tau}{(4\pi)^3 R^4 k T_o FL}$$

Item	Sub-Item	Symbol	Value	Units	Value
Example Blake Chart Worksheet					
Peak power		P_t	1.0	MW	60.00 dB
Transmit antenna gain		G_t		none	44.76 dB
Receive antenna gain		G_r		none	45.76 dB
Wavelength		λ^2	100.0	cm²	-20.00 dB
Target RCS		σ	1.0	m²	0.00 dBsm
Pulse width		τ	110	μsec	-39.58 dB
$(4\pi)^3$		N/A		none	-32.98 dB
KT_0		N/A		Joules	203.98 dB
Noise figure		F		none	-7.61 dB
Range (370 km)		R	370,400.0	m⁴	-222.75 dB
	Atmospheric	L_{atm}		none	3.30 dB (round trip)
	Radome	L_{rdm}		none	0.50 dB
	RF front end	L_{RF}		none	4.2 dB
Losses	Receive channel	L_r		none	3.0 dB
	Beam shape	L_{bs}		none	3.20 dB
	Scanning	L_{scn}		none	5.50 dB
	Other losses	L_{othr}		none	0.85 dB
Total losses					-21.55 dB
Sensitivity	**SNR**				**10.031 dB**

Figure 3.4. Tabulated Blake chart for a hypothetical S-band air defense radar.

3.1.3. Low Pulse Repetition Frequency Radar Equation

Consider a pulsed radar with pulse width τ, pulse repetition interval (PRI) T, and peak transmitted power P_t. The pulse repetition frequency (PRF), f_r, is equal to $1/T$. The average transmitted power is $P_{av} = P_t d_t$, where $d_t = \tau/T$ is the transmission duty factor. One can define the receiving duty factor d_r as

$$d_r = \frac{T-\tau}{T} = 1 - \tau f_r.$$ **Eq. (3.31)**

For low PRF radars where $T \gg \tau$, the receiving duty factor is $d_r \approx 1$. Define the "time on target" T_i (the time that a target is illuminated by the beam) as

$$T_i = \frac{n_p}{f_r} \Rightarrow n_p = T_i f_r$$ **Eq. (3.32)**

where n_p is the total number of pulses that strike the target. Assuming low PRF, the single pulse radar equation is given by

$$(SNR)_1 = \frac{P_t G^2 \lambda^2 \sigma}{(4\pi)^3 R^4 k T_o B F L_T},$$ **Eq. (3.33)**

and for n_p coherently integrated pulses we get

$$(SNR)_{n_p} = \frac{P_t G^2 \lambda^2 \sigma \, n_p}{(4\pi)^3 R^4 k T_o B F L_T}.$$ **Eq. (3.34)**

Now by using Eq. (3.32) and using $B = 1/\tau$, the low PRF radar equation can be written as

$$(SNR)_{n_p} = \frac{P_t G^2 \lambda^2 \sigma T_i f_r \tau}{(4\pi)^3 R^4 k T_o F L_T}.$$ **Eq. (3.35)**

Figures 3.5 and 3.6 show typical sensitivity plots for a low PRF radar with the following parameters: Peak power $P_t = 1.5MW$, operating frequency $f_0 = 5.6GHz$, antenna gain $G = 45dB$, radar losses $L = 6dB$, noise figure $F = 3dB$. The bandwidth is $B = 5MHz$. The target RCS is $\sigma = 0.1m^2$.

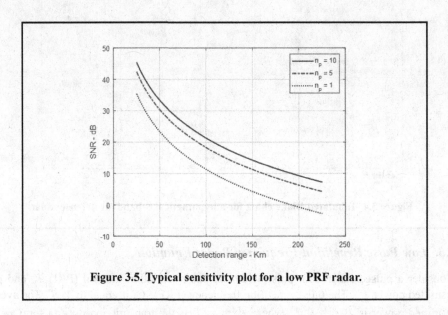

Figure 3.5. Typical sensitivity plot for a low PRF radar.

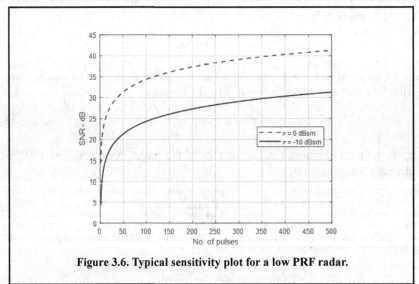

Figure 3.6. Typical sensitivity plot for a low PRF radar.

3.1.4. High PRF Radar Equation

In high PRF radars, the transmitted signal is assumed to be a periodic train of pulses, with pulse width τ and period T. This pulse train can be represented using an exponential Fourier series, where the central power spectrum line (dc-component) for this series contains most of the signal's power. Its value is $(\tau/T)^2$, and it is equal to the square of the transmit duty factor. Thus, the single pulse radar equation for a high PRF radar is

$$SNR = \frac{P_t G^2 \lambda^2 \sigma d_t^2}{(4\pi)^3 R^4 k T_o B F L_T d_r} \qquad \text{Eq. (3.36)}$$

where, in this case, one needs to account for the receive duty factor (which was ignored), since its value is comparable to the transmit duty factor. In fact, $d_r \approx d_t = \tau f_r$. Additionally, the operating radar bandwidth is now matched to the radar integration time (i.e., time-on-target), $B = 1/T_i$. It follows that

$$SNR = \frac{P_t \tau f_r T_i G^2 \lambda^2 \sigma}{(4\pi)^3 R^4 k T_o F L_T} \qquad \text{Eq. (3.37)}$$

and finally,

$$SNR = \frac{P_{av} T_i G^2 \lambda^2 \sigma}{(4\pi)^3 R^4 k T_o F L_T} \qquad \text{Eq. (3.38)}$$

where P_{av} was substituted for $P_t \tau f_r$. Note that the product $P_{av} T_i$ is a "kind of energy" product which indicates that high PRF radars can enhance detection performance by using relatively low power and longer integration time.

Example:

Compute the single pulse SNR for a high PRF radar with the following parameters: peak power $P_t = 100 KW$, antenna gain $G = 20 dB$, operating frequency $f_0 = 5.6 GHz$, losses $L_T = 8 dB$, noise figure $F = 5 dB$, dwell interval $T_i = 2 s$, duty factor $d_t = 0.3$. The range of interest is $R = 50 Km$. Assume target RCS $\sigma = 0.01 m^2$.

Solution:

From Eq. (3.38) we have

$$(SNR)_{dB} = (P_{av} + G^2 + \lambda^2 + \sigma + T_i - (4\pi)^3 - R^4 - kT_o - F - L_T)_{dB}$$

The following table gives all parameters in dB:

P_{av}	G^2	λ^2	T_i	$(4\pi)^3 kT_0$	L_T	R^4	σ
44.771	40	−25.421	3.01	−171.00	8	187.959	−20

$SNR = 44.771 + 40 - 25.421 - 20 + 3.01 - 32.976 + 203.977 - 187.959 - 5 - 8 = 12.4 dB$.

3.1.5. Surveillance Radar Equation

The primary job for surveillance radars is to continuously scan a specified volume of space searching for targets of interest. Once detection is established, target information such as range, angular position, and possibly target velocity are extracted by the radar signal and data processors. Depending on the radar design and antenna, different search patterns can be adopted. Search volumes are normally specified by a search solid angle Ω in steradians, as illustrated in Fig. 3.7. Define the radar search volume extent for both azimuth and elevation as Θ_A and Θ_E. Consequently, the search volume is computed as

$$\Omega = \Theta_A \Theta_E / (57.296)^2 \ steradians \qquad \text{Eq. (3.39)}$$

where both Θ_A and Θ_E are given in degrees. The radar antenna *3dB* beamwidth can be expressed in terms of its azimuth and elevation *3dB* beamwidths θ_a and θ_e, respectively. It follows that the antenna solid angle coverage is $\theta_a \theta_e$ and, thus, the number of antenna beam positions n_B required to cover a solid angle Ω is

$$n_B = \frac{\Omega}{(\theta_a \theta_e)/(57.296)^2}. \qquad \text{Eq. (3.40)}$$

In order to develop the search radar equation, start with

$$SNR = \frac{P_t G^2 \lambda^2 \sigma}{(4\pi)^3 kT_o BFL_T R^4}. \qquad \text{Eq. (3.41)}$$

Using the relations $\tau = 1/B$ and $P_t = P_{av} T/\tau$, where T is the PRI and τ is the pulse width, yields

$$SNR = \frac{T}{\tau} \frac{P_{av} G^2 \lambda^2 \sigma \tau}{(4\pi)^3 kT_o FL_T R^4}. \qquad \text{Eq. (3.42)}$$

Define the time it takes the radar to scan a volume defined by the solid angle Ω as the scan time T_{sc}. The time on target can then be expressed in terms of T_{sc} as

$$T_i = \frac{T_{sc}}{n_B} = \frac{T_{sc}}{\Omega} \theta_a \theta_e. \qquad \text{Eq. (3.43)}$$

Assume that during a single scan only one pulse per beam per PRI illuminates the target. It follows that $T_i = T$ and, thus, Eq. (3.42) can be written as

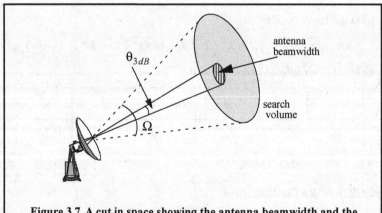

Figure 3.7. A cut in space showing the antenna beamwidth and the search volume.

$$SNR = \frac{P_{av}G^2\lambda^2\sigma}{(4\pi)^3 kT_oFL_TR^4}\frac{T_{sc}}{\Omega}\theta_a\theta_e.$$ Eq. (3.44)

Substituting Eqs. (3.4) and (3.6) into Eq. (3.44) and collecting terms yields the search radar equation (based on a single pulse per beam per PRI) as

$$SNR = \frac{P_{av}A_e\sigma}{4\pi kT_oFLR^4}\frac{T_{sc}}{\Omega}.$$ Eq. (3.45)

The quantity $P_{av}A$ in Eq. (3.45) is known as the power aperture product. In practice, the power aperture product is widely used to categorize the radar's ability to fulfill its search mission. Normally, a power aperture product is computed to meet a predetermined SNR and radar cross-section for a given search volume defined by Ω.

As a special case, assume a radar using a circular aperture (antenna) with diameter D. The $3dB$ antenna beamwidth θ_{3dB} is

$$\theta_{3dB} \approx \frac{\lambda}{D},$$ Eq. (3.46)

and when aperture tapering is used, $\theta_{3dB} \approx 1.25\lambda/D$. Substituting Eq. (3.46) into Eq. (3.40) and collecting terms yields

$$n_B = \frac{D^2}{\lambda^2}\,\Omega.$$ Eq. (3.47)

In this case, the scan time T_{sc} is related to the time-on-target by

$$T_i = \frac{T_{sc}}{n_B} = \frac{T_{sc}\lambda^2}{D^2\Omega}.$$ Eq. (3.48)

Substitute Eq. (3.48) into Eq. (3.42) to get

$$SNR = \frac{P_{av}G^2\lambda^2\sigma}{(4\pi)^3 R^4 kT_oFL}\frac{T_{sc}\lambda^2}{D^2\Omega},$$ Eq. (3.49)

and by using Eq. (3.4) in Eq. (3.49) one can define the search radar equation for a circular aperture as

$$SNR = \frac{P_{av}A\sigma}{16R^4 kT_oLF}\frac{T_{sc}}{\Omega}$$ Eq. (3.50)

where the relation $A = \pi D^2/4$ (aperture area) was used.

Plots of the power aperture product versus range and plots of the average power versus aperture area for three RCS choices are shown in Fig. 3.8. In this case, the following radar parameters were used:

σ	T_{sc}	$\theta_e = \theta_a$	R	$F+L$	SNR
$0.1\ m^2$	$2.5\,\mathrm{sec}$	$2°$	$250Km$	$13dB$	$15dB$

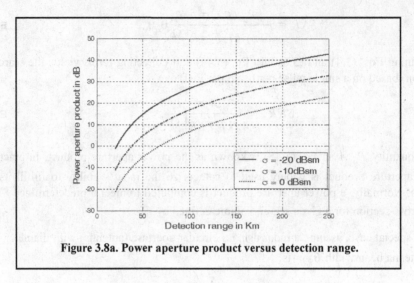

Figure 3.8a. Power aperture product versus detection range.

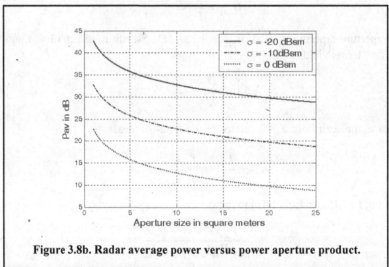

Figure 3.8b. Radar average power versus power aperture product.

3.2. Bistatic Radar Equation

Radar systems that use the same antenna for both transmitting and receiving are called "monostatic radars". Bistatic radars use transmit and receive antennas that are placed at different locations. Under this definition continuous wave (CW) radars, although they use separate transmit and receive antennas, are not considered bistatic radars unless the distance between the two antennas is considerable. Figure 3.9 shows the geometry associated with bistatic radars. The angle, β, is called the bistatic angle. A synchronization link between the transmitter and receiver is necessary in order to maximize the receiver's knowledge of the transmitted signal so that it can extract maximum target information.

The synchronization link may provide the receiver with the following information: (1) the transmitted frequency in order to compute the Doppler shift, and (2) the transmit time or phase reference in order to measure the total scattered path ($R_t + R_r$). Frequency and phase reference synchronization can be maintained through line-of-sight communications between the transmitter and receiver. However, if this is not possible, the receiver may use a stable reference oscillator for synchronization. One major distinction between monostatic and bistatic radar operations has to do with the measured bistatic target RCS, denoted by σ_B. In the case of a small bistatic angle, the bistatic RCS is similar to the monostatic RCS; but, as the bistatic angle approaches $180°$, the bistatic RCS becomes very large and can be approximated by

$$\sigma_{B_{max}} \approx \frac{4\pi A_t^2}{\lambda^2} \qquad \text{Eq. (3.51)}$$

where λ is the wavelength, and A_t is the target projected area.

The bistatic radar equation can be derived in a similar fashion to the monostatic radar equation. Referring to Fig. 3.9, the power density at the target is

$$P_D = \frac{P_t G_t}{4\pi R_t^2} \qquad \text{Eq. (3.52)}$$

where P_t is the peak transmitted power, G_t is the gain of the transmitting antenna, and R_t is the range from the radar transmitter to the target.

The effective power scattered off a target with bistatic RCS σ_B is

$$P' = P_D \sigma_B \qquad \text{Eq. (3.53)}$$

and the power density at the receiver antenna is

$$P_{refl} = \frac{P'}{4\pi R_r^2} = \frac{P_D \sigma_B}{4\pi R_r^2}. \qquad \text{Eq. (3.54)}$$

R_r is the range from the target to the receiver. Substituting Eq. (3.52) into Eq. (3.54) yields

$$P_{refl} = \frac{P_t G_t \sigma_B}{(4\pi)^2 R_t^2 R_r^2}. \qquad \text{Eq. (3.55)}$$

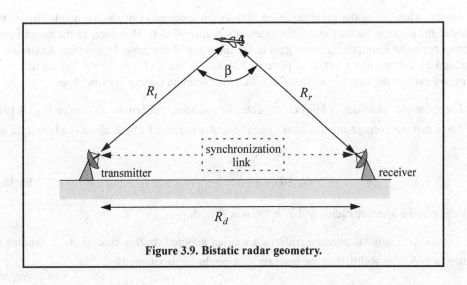

Figure 3.9. Bistatic radar geometry.

The total power delivered to the signal processor by a receiver antenna with aperture A_e is

$$P_{Dr} = \frac{P_t G_t \sigma_B A_e}{(4\pi)^2 R_t^2 R_r^2}.$$

Eq. (3.56)

Substituting $(G_r \lambda^2 / 4\pi)$ for A_e yields

$$P_{Dr} = \frac{P_t G_t G_r \lambda^2 \sigma_B}{(4\pi)^3 R_t^2 R_r^2}$$

Eq. (3.57)

where G_r is the gain of the receive antenna. Finally, when transmitter and receiver losses, L_t and L_r, are taken into consideration, the bistatic radar equation can be written as

$$P_{Dr} = \frac{P_t G_t G_r \lambda^2 \sigma_B}{(4\pi)^3 R_t^2 R_r^2 L_t L_r}.$$

Eq. (3.58)

3.3. Radar Losses

As indicated by the radar equation, the receiver SNR is inversely proportional to the radar losses. Hence, any increase in radar losses causes a drop in the SNR. This decreases the radar sensitivity and accordingly its probability of detection since it is a function of the SNR. Often, the principal difference between a good radar design and a poor radar design is the radar losses. Radar losses include ohmic (resistance) losses and statistical losses. In this section, a brief summary of radar losses is presented.

3.3.1. Transmit and Receive Losses

Transmit and receive losses occur between the radar transmitter and antenna input port, and between the antenna output port and the receiver front end, respectively. Such losses are often called "plumbing losses". Typically, plumbing losses are on the order of *1* to *2 dB*.

3.3.2. Antenna Pattern Loss and Scan Loss

So far, when using the radar equation, maximum antenna gain was assumed. This is true only if the target is located along the antenna's boresight axis. However, as the target moves across the radar beam, the antenna gain in the direction of the target is less than maximum, as defined by the antenna's radiation pattern. The loss in the SNR due to not having maximum antenna gain on the target at all times is called the "antenna pattern" (shape) loss.

For example, consider a $|\sin(x)/x|$ antenna radiation pattern as shown in Fig. 3.10. It follows that the average antenna gain over an angular region of $\pm\theta/2$ about the boresight axis is

$$G_{av}(\theta) \approx 1 - \left(\frac{\pi r}{\lambda}\right)^2 \frac{\theta^2}{36}$$

Eq. (3.59)

where r is the aperture radius and λ is the wavelength.

In practice, Gaussian antenna patterns are often adopted. In this case, if θ_{3dB} denotes the antenna *3dB* beamwidth, then the antenna gain can be approximated by

$$G(\theta) = \exp\left(-\frac{2.776\theta^2}{\theta_{3dB}^2}\right).$$ **Eq. (3.60)**

If the antenna mechanical scanning rate is so fast that the gain on receive is not the same as on transmit, additional scan loss has to be calculated and added to the beam shape loss. Scan loss can be computed in a similar fashion to beam shape loss. Phased array radars are often prime candidates for both beam shape and scan losses.

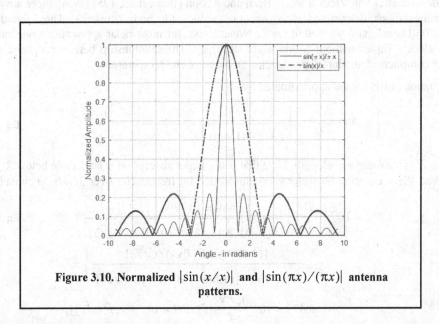

Figure 3.10. Normalized $|\sin(x/x)|$ and $|\sin(\pi x)/(\pi x)|$ antenna patterns.

3.3.3. Atmospheric Loss

Radar electromagnetic waves travel in free space without suffering any energy loss. However, due to gases (mainly oxygen) and water vapor present along the radar wave propagation path, a loss in radar energy occurs. This loss is known as atmospheric attenuation. Most of this lost radar energy is normally absorbed by gases and water vapor and transformed into heat, while a small portion of this lost energy is used in molecular transformation of the atmosphere particles. This section will analyze atmospheric attenuation in the context of most radar application within the atmosphere.

Atmospheric Absorption

The atmospheric absorption due to oxygen was derived by Van Vleck (Van Vleck, 1947a) as

$$\gamma_O = 28.809\frac{P\nu^2}{T^2}\left\{\frac{[(1.704P\nu_1)/(\sqrt{T})]}{\nu^2 + [(1.704\times10^{-12}P\nu_1)/(\sqrt{T})]^2}\right.$$ **Eq. (3.61)**

$$+\frac{[(1.704P\nu_2)/(\sqrt{T})]}{(\nu_0-\nu)^2 + [(1.704\times10^{-12}P\nu_2)/(\sqrt{T})]^2}$$

$$\left.+\frac{[(1.704P\nu_2)/(\sqrt{T})]}{(\nu_0+\nu)^2 + [(1.704\times10^{-12}P\nu_2)/(\sqrt{T})]^2}\right\}$$

where γ_O is the total oxygen absorption in dB/km; ν is the reciprocal of the wavelength in cm^{-1}, ν_0 is the resonance wave number for oxygen and is equal to $2\,cm^{-1}$, ν_1 is a constant related to the non-resonance part of absorption in cm^{-1}, ν_2 is a constant related to the resonance part of absorption in cm^{-1}, P is the atmospheric pressure in *millibars,* and T is the atmospheric temperature in degrees *Kelvin.*

Using data derived from his experiments, Van Vleck suggested using equal values for both ν_1 and ν_2; more specifically, he recommended using $\nu_1 = \nu_2 = 0.02\,cm^{-1}$. However, a decade later after Van Vleck's work, Bean and Abbott (Bean et al., 1957) using more advanced experimentations determined more accurate values for both constants. They found that $\nu_1 = 0.018\,cm^{-1}$ and $\nu_2 = 0.05\,cm^{-1}$. Nonetheless, for most radar applications one can use Van Vleck's values without losing much accuracy. The relationship between ν_1 and ν_2 is rather complicated and has dependencies on pressure and temperature.

Equation (3.61) can be approximated by

$$\gamma_O = \left\{0.4909\frac{P^2}{T^{5/2}}\nu_1\right\}\left\{\frac{1}{1 + 2.904 \times 10^{-4}\lambda^2 P^2 T^{-1}\nu_1^2}\right\}\left\{1 + \frac{0.5\nu_2}{\lambda^2\nu_1}\right\} \qquad \text{Eq. (3.62)}$$

where λ is the radar wavelength. Note that water vapor absorption is negligible below $3\,GHz$. The Van Vleck equation for water vapor absorption for frequencies over $3\,GHz$ is given by

$$\gamma_w = 1.012 \times 10^{-3}\frac{\rho_w P\nu^2}{T}\left\{\frac{[1.689 \times 10^{-2}P\nu_3/(\sqrt{T})]}{(\nu_w - \nu)^2 + [1.689 \times 10^{-2}P\nu_3/(\sqrt{T})]^2} + \right. \qquad \text{Eq. (3.63)}$$

$$\left. \frac{[(1.689 \times 10^{-2}P\nu_3)/(\sqrt{T})]}{(\nu_w + \nu)^2 + [(1.689 \times 10^{-2}P\nu_3)/(\sqrt{T})]^2}\right\} +$$

$$3.471 \times 10^{-3}\frac{\rho_w P\nu^2}{T}[(1.689 \times 10^{-2}P\nu_4)/(\sqrt{T})]$$

where all variables are as defined before in Eq. (3.61) except for: γ_w is the water vapor absorption in dB/km, ρ_w is the water vapor density in m^{-3}, ν_w is a constant equal to $0.742\,cm^{-1}$, ν_3 is a constant related to water vapor resonance at $22.2\,GHz$, and ν_4 is a constant related to water vapor resonance above $22.2\,GHz$. Van Vleck suggested using $\nu_3 = \nu_4 = 0.1\,cm^{-1}$, which was later updated by Bean and Abbott to the more accurate values of at $\nu_3 = 0.1\,cm^{-1}$ and $\nu_4 = 0.3\,cm^{-1}$. Equation (3.63) can be approximated by

$$\gamma_w = 1.852 \times 3.165 \times 10^{-6}\frac{\rho_w P^2}{T^{3/2}}\left\{\frac{1}{(1 - 0.742\lambda)^2 + 2.853 \times 10^{-6}\lambda^2 P^2 T^{-1}} \right. \qquad \text{Eq. (3.64)}$$

$$\left. + \frac{1}{(1 + 0.742\lambda)^2 + 2.853 \times 10^{-6}\lambda^2 P^2 T^{-1}} + \frac{3.43}{\lambda^2}\right\}$$

The atmospheric temperature for altitudes less than 12 *km* is given by

$$T = 288 - 6.5h \qquad \text{Eq. (3.65)}$$

where T is the temperature in degrees *Kelvin*, and h is the altitude in *km*. Assuming that air pressure at sea level is *1015 millibars,* then the air pressure in *millibars* at any altitude for up to 12 *km* is given by

$$P = 1015(1 - 0.02257h)^{5.2561} \qquad \text{Eq. (3.66)}$$

Using Eqs. (3.65) and (3.66), one can construct Table 3.1, which shows some representative data for air pressure, atmospheric pressure, and their corresponding water vapor density. Figure 3.11 shows the total atmospheric absorption in *dB* and the attenuation due to oxygen alone versus range using the data in Table 3.1.

Table 3.1. Sample Atmospheric Data.

$h - km$	P - millibars	T - degrees Kelvin	Water vapor density - g/m^3
0.0	1015.0	288.0	6.18
0.7620	925.86	282.89	4.93
1.5240	843.18	277.79	3.74
3.0480	695.73	267.58	2.01
6.0960	463.10	247.16	0.34
9.1440	297.91	226.74	0.05
12.1920	184.04	206.31	<0.01

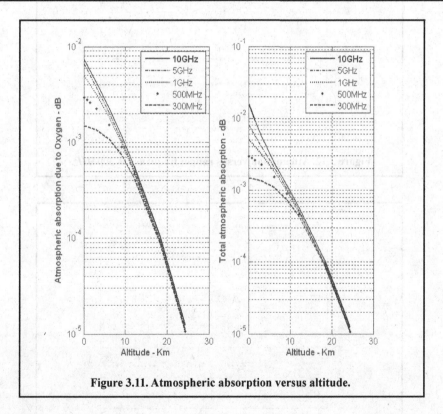

Figure 3.11. Atmospheric absorption versus altitude.

Atmospheric Attenuation Plots

To compute the total atmospheric attenuation experienced by a radar, one must first compute the two-way total absorption along the radar wave path, from the radar to the target and back. Then, the total atmospheric attenuation is computed from the integral of $\gamma_{atm} = \gamma_O + \gamma_w$ along the ray path. Clearly, γ_{atm} is not only a function of pressure, temperature, water vapor, and frequency, but it is also a function of the radar waves path and its initial elevation angle. More specifically, one would expect the radar wave ray to go through more atmosphere at lower elevation angles, and thus experience more atmospheric attenuation. The total two-way atmospheric attenuation at range R_i using the elevation angle β and the wavelength λ as parameters is then given by

$$\kappa_{atm}(R_i; \beta, \lambda) = 2 \int_0^{R_i} \gamma_{atm}(R_i; \beta, \lambda) \ dR \qquad \text{Eq. (3.67)}$$

where the factor *2* is used to account for the two-way loss or attenuation. Figure 3.12 shows a typical two-way atmospheric attenuation plot versus range at $300MHz$, with the elevation angle as a parameter. Figure. 3.13 is similar to Fig. 3.12, except it is for $3GHz$.

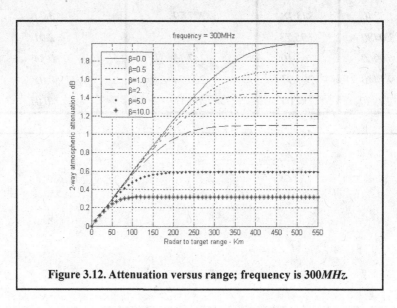

Figure 3.12. Attenuation versus range; frequency is 300*MHz*.

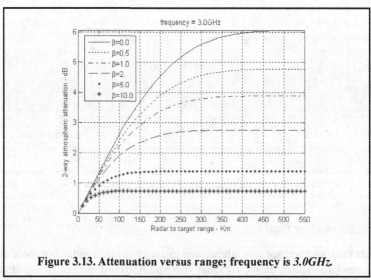

Figure 3.13. Attenuation versus range; frequency is *3.0GHz*.

Attenuation Due to Precipitation

Radar waves propagating through rain precipitation suffer loss in signal power. This power loss is due to absorption by and scattering from the rain droplets. Clearly, heavier rain rate will result in more absorption and scattering, thus leading to more power loss. Attenuation due to rain is also a function radar wavelength. For example, the one-way attenuation, measured in dB/km, due to rain precipitation is given by

$$A_r = \begin{cases} 3.43 \times 10^{-4} r^{0.97} & \lambda = 10cm \\ 1.8 \times 10^{-3} r^{1.05} & \lambda = 5cm \\ 1.0 \times 10^{-2} r^{1.21} & \lambda = 3.2cm \end{cases} \qquad \text{Eq. (3.68)}$$

where r is the rainfall rate in *mm/hr*. A more general formula for this attenuation is given by

$$A_r = K_A f^\alpha r \qquad \text{Eq. (3.69)}$$

where f is the frequency in *GHz*, K_A and α are constants yet to be defined. Almost all open literature sources do not agree on specific values for these two constants, where α varies from about *2.25* to *3.84* while K_A varies from 1.21×10^{-5} to 8.33×10^{-6}. This author recommends using $K_A = 0.0002$ and $\alpha = 2.25$. It follows that

$$A_r = 0.0002 \; f^{2.25} r \; \frac{dB}{km}. \qquad \text{Eq. (3.70)}$$

Figure 3.14 illustrates the behavior of rain attenuation as a function of frequency. Clearly, and as one would expect, as the wavelength becomes smaller, the rain attenuation becomes more dominant.

The one-way attenuation in dB/km due to snow precipitation has been reported in the literature as one of the following two formulas

$$A_s = \frac{0.035 r^2}{\lambda^4} + \frac{0.0022 r}{\lambda} \qquad \text{Eq. (3.71)}$$

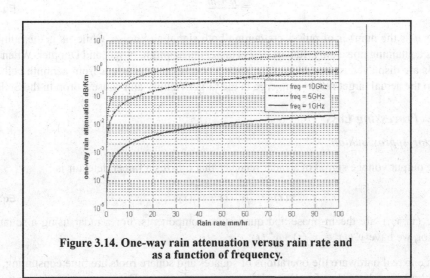

Figure 3.14. One-way rain attenuation versus rain rate and as a function of frequency.

$$A_s = \frac{0.00349r^{1.6}}{\lambda^4} + \frac{0.00224r}{\lambda}$$ **Eq. (3.72)**

where r is the snow fall rate in *millimeters* of water content per hour and λ is the radar wavelength in *centimeters*. Equations (3.69) and (3.72) both give fairly accurate results with Eq. (3.71) having the edge. Figure 3.15 illustrates the behavior of snow attenuation as a function of frequency. Clearly, and as one would expect, as the wavelength becomes smaller, the snow attenuation becomes more dominant.

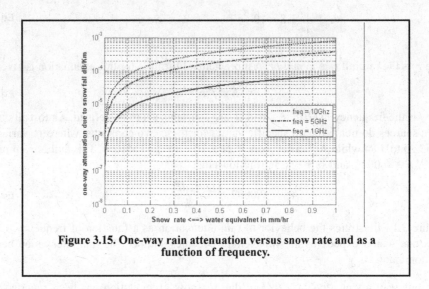

Figure 3.15. One-way rain attenuation versus snow rate and as a function of frequency.

3.3.4. Collapsing Loss

When the number of integrated returned noise pulses is larger than the target returned pulses, a drop in the *SNR* occurs. This is called "collapsing loss". The collapsing loss factor is

$$\rho_c = \frac{n+m}{n}$$ **Eq. (3.73)**

where n is the number of pulses containing both signal and noise, while m is the number of pulses containing noise only. Radars detect targets in azimuth, range, and Doppler. When target returns are displayed in one coordinate, such as range, noise sources from azimuth cells adjacent to the actual target return converge in the target vicinity and cause a drop in the SNR.

3.3.5. Processing Loss

Detector Approximation

The output voltage signal of a radar receiver that utilizes a linear detector is

$$v(t) = \sqrt{v_I^2(t) + v_Q^2(t)}$$ **Eq. (3.74)**

where (v_I, v_Q) are the in-phase and quadrature components. For a radar using a square law detector, we have $v^2(t) = v_I^2(t) + v_Q^2(t)$.

Since in real hardware the operations of squares and square roots are time consuming, many algorithms have been developed for detector approximation. These approximations result in a loss of signal power, typically *0.5* to *1dB*.

Constant False Alarm Rate Loss

In many cases the radar detection threshold is constantly adjusted as a function of the receiver noise level in order to maintain a constant false alarm rate. For this purpose, constant false alarm rate (CFAR) processors are utilized. This keeps the number of false alarms under control in a changing and unknown background of interference. CFAR processing can cause a loss in the SNR level on the order of *1* to *3dB*.

Three different types of CFAR processors are primarily used. They are adaptive threshold CFAR, nonparametric CFAR, and nonlinear receiver techniques. Adaptive CFAR assumes that the interference distribution is known and approximates the unknown parameters associated with these distributions. Nonparametric CFAR processors tend to accommodate unknown interference distributions. Nonlinear receiver techniques attempt to normalize the root-mean-square amplitude of the interference.

Quantization Loss

Finite word length (number of bits) and quantization noise cause an increase in the noise power density at the output of the analog-to-digital (A/D) converter. The A/D noise level is $q^2/12$, where q is the quantization level.

Range Gate Straddle Loss

The radar receiver is normally implemented as a series of contiguous range gates (bins). Each range bin is implemented as an integrator matched to the transmitted pulse width. Since the radar receiver acts as a filter that smears (smooths), the received target echoes. Typically, the smoothed target return envelope straddles more than one range gate.

Typically, three gates are affected; they are called the early, on, and late gates. If a point target is located exactly at the center of a range gate, then the early and late samples are equal. However, as the target starts to move into the next gate, the late sample becomes larger while the early sample gets smaller. The amplitudes of all three samples should always roughly add up to the same value. Since the target is likely to fall anywhere between two adjacent range bins, a loss in the SNR occurs (per range gate). More specifically, a target's returned energy is spread over three range bins. Typically, straddle loss of about *2* to *3dB* is not unusual.

Doppler Filter Straddle Loss

Doppler filter straddle is similar to range gate straddle. However, in this case the Doppler filter spectrum is spread (widened) due to weighting functions. Weighting functions are normally used to reduce the sidelobe levels. Since the target Doppler frequency can fall anywhere between two Doppler filters, signal loss occurs.

Other Losses

Other losses may include equipment losses due to aging radar hardware, matched filter loss, and antenna efficiency loss. Tracking radars suffer from cross-over (squint) loss.

3.4. Noise Figure

Any signal other than the target returns in the radar receiver is considered to be noise. This includes interfering signals from outside the radar and thermal noise generated within the receiver itself. Thermal noise (thermal agitation of electrons) and shot noise (variation in carrier density of a semiconductor) are the two main internal noise sources within a radar receiver. The analysis in this section follows Berkowitz (1965).

The power spectral density of thermal noise is given by

$$S_n(\omega) = \frac{|\omega| h}{\pi \left[\exp\left(\frac{|\omega| h}{2\pi k T}\right) - 1 \right]}$$ Eq. (3.75)

where $|\omega|$ is the absolute value of the frequency in radians per second, T is the temperature of the conducting medium in degrees *Kelvin*, k is Boltzman's constant, and h is Planck's constant ($h = 6.625 \times 10^{-34}$ *Joule s*). When the condition $|\omega| \ll 2\pi k T / h$ is true, it can be shown that Eq. (3.75) is approximated by

$$S_n(\omega) \approx 2kT$$ Eq. (3.76)

This approximation is widely accepted, since, in practice, radar systems operate at frequencies less than $100 GHz$; and, for example, if $T = 290 K$, then $2\pi k T / h \approx 6000 GHz$.

The mean-square noise voltage (noise power) generated across a $1 ohm$ resistance is then

$$\langle n^2 \rangle = \frac{1}{2\pi} \int_{-2\pi B}^{2\pi B} 2kT \ d\omega = 4kTB$$ Eq. (3.77)

where B is the system bandwidth in Hertz.

Any electrical system containing thermal noise and having input resistance R_{in} can be replaced by an equivalent noiseless system with a series combination of a noise equivalent voltage source and a noiseless input resistor R_{in} added at its input, as illustrated in Fig. 3.16.

The amount of noise power that can physically be extracted from $\langle n^2 \rangle$ is one fourth the value computed in Eq. (3.77). Consider a noisy system with power gain A_P, as shown in Fig. 3.17. The noise figure is defined by

$$F_{dB} = 10 \ \log \frac{total \ noise \ power \ out}{noise \ power \ out \ due \ to \ R_{in} \ alone}.$$ Eq. (3.78)

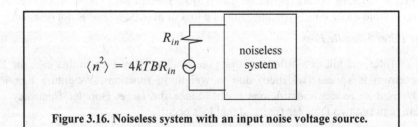

Figure 3.16. Noiseless system with an input noise voltage source.

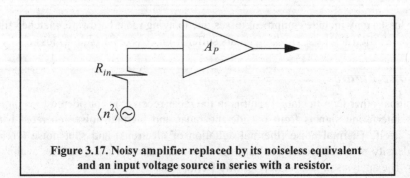

**Figure 3.17. Noisy amplifier replaced by its noiseless equivalent
and an input voltage source in series with a resistor.**

More precisely,

$$F_{dB} = 10 \log \frac{N_o}{N_i \, A_p}$$

Eq. (3.79)

where N_o and N_i are, respectively, the noise power at the output and input of the system. If we define the input and output signal power by S_i and S_o, respectively, then the power gain is

$$A_P = \frac{S_o}{S_i}.$$

Eq. (3.80)

It follows that

$$F_{dB} = 10\log\left(\frac{S_i/N_i}{S_o/N_o}\right) = \left(\frac{S_i}{N_i}\right)_{dB} - \left(\frac{S_o}{N_o}\right)_{dB}$$

Eq. (3.81)

where

$$\left(\frac{S_i}{N_i}\right)_{dB} > \left(\frac{S_o}{N_o}\right)_{dB}.$$

Eq. (3.82)

Thus, the noise figure is the loss in the signal-to-noise ratio due to the added thermal noise of the amplifier $((SNR)_o = (SNR)_i - F \ in \ dB)$.

One can also express the noise figure in terms of the system's effective temperature T_e. Consider the amplifier shown in Fig. 3.17, and let its effective temperature be T_e. Assume the input noise temperature is T_o. Thus, the input noise power is

$$N_i = kT_oB$$

Eq. (3.83)

and the output noise power is

$$N_o = kT_oB \, A_p + kT_eB \, A_p$$

Eq. (3.84)

where the first term on the right-hand side of Eq. (3.84) corresponds to the input noise, and the latter term is due to thermal noise generated inside the system. It follows that the noise figure can be expressed as

$$F = \frac{(SNR)_i}{(SNR)_o} = \frac{S_i}{kT_oB} \, kBA_p \, \frac{T_o + T_e}{S_o} = 1 + \frac{T_e}{T_o}.$$

Eq. (3.85)

Equivalently, we can write

$$T_e = (F-1)T_o.$$

Eq. (3.86)

Consider a cascaded system as in Fig. 3.18. Network 1 is defined by noise figure F_1, power gain G_1, bandwidth B, and temperature T_{e1}. Similarly, network 2 is defined by F_2, G_2, B, and T_{e2}. Assume the input noise has temperature T_0. The output signal power is

$$S_o = S_iG_1G_2.$$

Eq. (3.87)

The input and output noise powers are, respectively, given by

$$N_i = kT_oB$$

Eq. (3.88)

$$N_o = kT_0BG_1G_2 + kT_{e1}BG_1G_2 + kT_{e2}BG_2$$

Eq. (3.89)

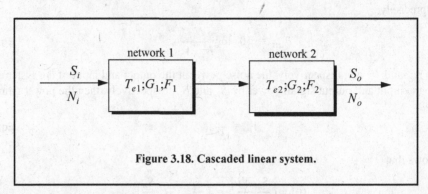

Figure 3.18. Cascaded linear system.

where the three terms on the right-hand side of Eq. (3.89), respectively, correspond to the input noise power, thermal noise generated inside network 1, and thermal noise generated inside network 2.

Now, use the relation $T_e = (F-1)T_0$ along with Eq. (3.88) and Eq. (3.89) to express the overall output noise power as

$$N_o = F_1 N_i G_1 G_2 + (F_2 - 1)N_i G_2 .$$ **Eq. (3.90)**

It follows that the overall noise figure for the cascaded system is

$$F = \frac{(S_i/N_i)}{(S_o/N_o)} = F_1 + \frac{F_2 - 1}{G_1}$$ **Eq. (3.91)**

In general, for an n-stage system we get

$$F = F_1 + \frac{F_2 - 1}{G_1} + \frac{F_3 - 1}{G_1 G_2} + ... + \frac{F_n - 1}{G_1 G_2 G_3 \, \cdot \, \cdot \, \cdot \, G_{n-1}} .$$ **Eq. (3.92)**

Also, the n-stage system effective temperatures can be computed as

$$T_e = T_{e1} + \frac{T_{e2}}{G_1} + \frac{T_{e3}}{G_1 G_2} + ... + \frac{T_{en}}{G_1 G_2 G_3 \, \cdot \, \cdot \, \cdot \, G_{n-1}} .$$ **Eq. (3.93)**

As suggested by Eqs. (3.92) and (3.93), the overall noise figure is mainly dominated by the first stage. Thus, radar receivers employ low-noise power amplifiers in the first stage in order to minimize the overall receiver noise figure. However, for radar systems that are built for low RCS operations, every stage should be included in the analysis.

3.5. Continuous Wave Radars

As mentioned earlier, in order to avoid interruption of the continuous radar energy emission, two antennas are used in continuous wave (CW) radars, one for transmission and one for reception. Figure 3.19 shows a simplified CW radar block diagram. The appropriate values of the signal frequency at different locations are noted on the diagram. The individual narrow band filters (NBF) must be as narrow as possible in bandwidth in order to allow accurate Doppler measurements and minimize the amount of noise power. In theory, the operating bandwidth of a CW radar is infinitesimal (since it corresponds to an infinite duration continuous sine-wave). However, systems with infinitesimal bandwidths cannot physically exist, and thus, the bandwidth of CW radars is assumed to correspond to that of a gated CW waveform.

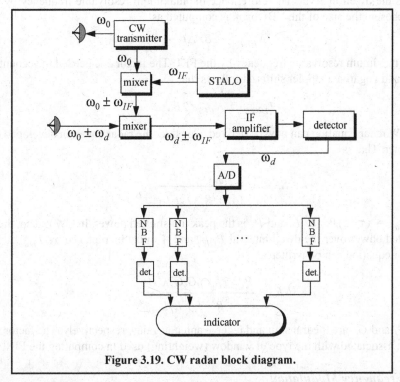

Figure 3.19. CW radar block diagram.

The NBF bank (Doppler filter bank) can be implemented using a fast Fourier transform (FFT). The Doppler filter bank is implemented using an FFT of size N_{FFT}. If the individual NBF bandwidth (FFT bin) is Δf, then the effective radar Doppler bandwidth is $N_{FFT}\Delta f/2$. The one-half factor is used to account for both negative and positive Doppler shifts. The frequency resolution, Δf, is proportional to the inverse of the integration time.

Since range is computed from the radar echoes by measuring a two-way time delay, single frequency CW radars cannot measure target range. In order for CW radars to be able to measure target range, the transmit and receive waveforms must have some sort of timing marks. By comparing the timing marks at transmit and receive, CW radars can extract target range. The timing mark can be implemented by modulating the transmit waveform. One commonly used technique is linear frequency modulation (LFM). Before we discuss LFM signals, we will first introduce the CW radar equation and briefly address general frequency modulated (FM) waveforms using sinusoidal modulating signals.

3.5.1. CW Radar Equation

As indicated by Fig. 3.19, the CW radar receiver declares detection at the output of a particular Doppler bin if that output value passes the detection threshold within the detector box. Since the NBF bank is implemented by an FFT, only finite length data sets can be processed at a time. The length of such blocks is normally referred to as the dwell interval, integration time, or coherent processing interval. The dwell interval determines the frequency resolution or the bandwidth of the individual NBFs. More precisely,

$$\Delta f = \frac{1}{T_{Dwell}}.$$

Eq. (3.94)

T_{Dwell} is the dwell interval. Therefore, once the maximum resolvable frequency by the NBF bank is chosen, the size of the NBF bank is computed as

$$N_{FFT} = 2B/\Delta f.$$

Eq. (3.95)

B is the maximum resolvable frequency by the FFT. The factor 2 is needed to account for both positive and negative Doppler shifts. It follows that

$$T_{Dwell} = N_{FFT}/2B.$$

Eq. (3.96)

The CW radar equation can now be derived. Consider the radar equation developed earlier in this chapter. That is

$$SNR = \frac{P_{av}TG^2\lambda^2\sigma}{(4\pi)^3R^4kT_oFL_T}$$

Eq. (3.97)

where $P_{av} = (\tau/T)P_t$, τ/T, and P_t is the peak transmitted power. In CW radars, the average transmitted power over the dwell interval P_{CW}, and T must be replaced by T_{Dwell}. Thus, the CW radar equation can be written as

$$SNR = \frac{P_{CW}T_{Dwell}G_tG_r\lambda^2\sigma}{(4\pi)^3R^4kT_oFL_TL_{win}}$$

Eq. (3.98)

where G_t and G_r are the transmit and receive antenna gains, respectively. The factor L_{win} is a loss term associated with the type of window (weighting) used in computing the FFT.

3.5.2. Frequency Modulation

The discussion presented in this section will be restricted to sinusoidal modulating signals. In this case, the general formula for an FM waveform can be expressed by

$$x(t) = A\cos\left(2\pi f_0 t + k_f\int_0^t \cos(2\pi f_m u)\,du\right).$$

Eq. (3.99)

The radar operating frequency (carrier frequency) is f_0, $\cos 2\pi f_m t$ is the modulating signal, A is a constant, and $k_f = 2\pi\Delta f_{peak}$, where Δf_{peak} is the peak frequency deviation. The phase is given by

$$\psi(t) = 2\pi f_0 t + 2\pi\Delta f_{peak}\int_0^t \cos(2\pi f_m u)\,du = 2\pi f_0 t + \beta\sin 2\pi f_m t$$

Eq. (3.100)

where β is the FM modulation index given by

$$\beta = \frac{\Delta f_{peak}}{f_m}.$$

Eq. (3.101)

Let $x_r(t)$ be the received radar signal from a target at range R. It follows that

$$x_r(t) = A_r\cos(2\pi f_0(t - \Delta t) + \beta\sin 2\pi f_m(t - \Delta t))$$

Eq. (3.102)

where the delay Δt is

$$\Delta t = \frac{2R}{c}.$$

Eq. (3.103)

c is the speed of light. CW radar receivers utilize phase detectors in order to extract target range from the instantaneous frequency, as illustrated in Fig. 3.20. A good measurement of the phase detector output $y(t)$ implies a good measurement of Δt, and hence range.

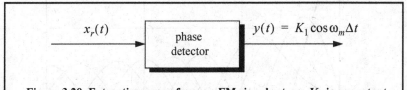

Figure 3.20. Extracting range from an FM signal return. K_1 is a constant.

Consider the FM waveform $x(t)$ given by

$$x(t) = A\cos(2\pi f_0 t + \beta\sin 2\pi f_m t)$$

Eq. (3.104)

which can be written as

$$x(t) = A Re\{e^{j2\pi f_0 t}\ e^{j\beta\sin 2\pi f_m t}\}$$

Eq. (3.105)

where $Re\{\ \}$ denotes the real part. Since the signal $\exp(j\beta\sin 2\pi f_m t)$ is periodic with period $T = 1/f_m$, it can be expressed using the complex exponential Fourier series as

$$e^{j\beta\sin 2\pi f_m t} = \left(\sum_{n=-\infty}^{\infty} C_n e^{jn2\pi f_m t}\right)$$

Eq. (3.106)

where the Fourier series coefficients C_n are given by

$$C_n = \frac{1}{2\pi}\int_{-\pi}^{\pi} e^{j\beta\sin 2\pi f_m t}\ e^{-jn2\pi f_m t}\ dt .$$

Eq. (3.107)

Make the change of variable $u = 2\pi f_m t$, and recognize that the Bessel function of the first kind of order n is

$$J_n(\beta) = \frac{1}{2\pi}\int_{-\pi}^{\pi} e^{j(\beta\sin u - nu)}\ du .$$

Eq. (3.108)

Thus, the Fourier series coefficients are $C_n = J_n(\beta)$, and consequently Eq. (3.106) can now be written as

$$e^{j\beta\sin 2\pi f_m t} = \left(\sum_{n=-\infty}^{\infty} J_n(\beta)e^{jn2\pi f_m t}\right) .$$

Eq. (3.109)

which is known as the Bessel-Jacobi equation. Figure 3.21 shows a plot of Bessel functions of the first kind for $n = 0, 1, 2, 3$. The total power in the signal $x(t)$ is

$$P = \frac{1}{2}A^2 \sum_{n=-\infty}^{\infty} |J_n(\beta)|^2 = \frac{1}{2}A^2 .$$

Eq. (3.110)

Substituting Eq. (3.109) into Eq. (3.105) yields

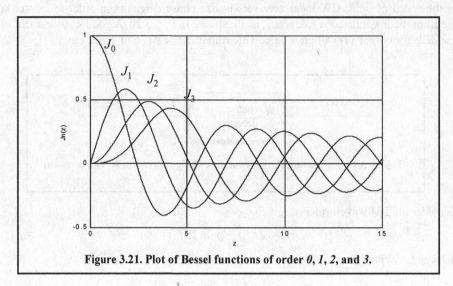

Figure 3.21. Plot of Bessel functions of order *0*, *1*, *2*, and *3*.

$$x(t) = A Re\left\{ e^{j2\pi f_0 t} \sum_{n=-\infty}^{\infty} J_n(\beta) e^{jn2\pi f_m t} \right\}.$$ **Eq. (3.111)**

Expanding Eq. (3.111) yields

$$x(t) = A \sum_{n=-\infty}^{\infty} J_n(\beta) \cos(2\pi f_0 + n2\pi f_m)t .$$ **Eq. (3.112)**

Finally, since $J_n(\beta) = J_{-n}(\beta)$ for n odd and $J_n(\beta) = -J_{-n}(\beta)$ for n even one can rewrite Eq. (3.112) as

$$x(t) = A\{J_0(\beta)\cos 2\pi f_0 t + J_1(\beta)[\cos(2\pi f_0 + 2\pi f_m)t - \cos(2\pi f_0 - 2\pi f_m)t]$$ **Eq. (3.113)**
$$+ J_2(\beta)[\cos(2\pi f_0 + 4\pi f_m)t + \cos(2\pi f_0 - 4\pi f_m)t]$$
$$+ J_3(\beta)[\cos(2\pi f_0 + 6\pi f_m)t - \cos(2\pi f_0 - 6\pi f_m)t]$$
$$+ J_4(\beta)[\cos((2\pi f_0 + 8\pi f_m)t + \cos(2\pi f_0 - 8\pi f_m)t)] + \ldots\}$$

which can be rewritten as

$$x(t) = A\left\{ J_0(\beta)\cos 2\pi f_0 t + \sum_{n=even}^{\infty} J_n(\beta)[\cos(2\pi f_0 + 2n\pi f_m)t + \right.$$ **Eq. (3.114)**

$$\left. \cos(2\pi f_0 - 2n\pi f_m)t] + \sum_{q=odd}^{\infty} J_q(\beta)[\cos(2\pi f_0 + 2q\pi f_m)t - \cos(2\pi f_0 - 2q\pi f_m)t] \right\}$$

The spectrum of $x(t)$ is composed of pairs of spectral lines centered at f_0, as sketched in Fig. 3.22. The spacing between adjacent spectral lines is f_m. The central spectral line has an amplitude equal to $AJ_o(\beta)$, while the amplitude of the *nth* spectral line is $AJ_n(\beta)$.

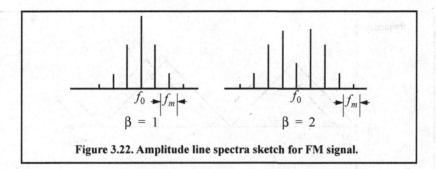

Figure 3.22. Amplitude line spectra sketch for FM signal.

As indicated by Eq. (3.114) the bandwidth of FM signals is infinite. However, the magnitudes of spectral lines of the higher orders are small, and thus the bandwidth can be approximated using Carson's rule,

$$B \approx 2(\beta + 1)f_m$$ **Eq. (3.115)**

When β is small, only $J_0(\beta)$ and $J_1(\beta)$ have significant values. Thus, Eq. (3.114) becomes,

$$x(t) \approx A\{J_0(\beta)\cos 2\pi f_0 t + J_1(\beta)[\cos(2\pi f_0 + 2\pi f_m)t - \cos(2\pi f_0 - 2\pi f_m)t]\}.$$ **Eq. (3.116)**

Finally, for small β, the Bessel functions can be approximated by

$$J_0(\beta) \approx 1$$ **Eq. (3.117)**

$$J_1(\beta) \approx \beta/2.$$ **Eq. (3.118)**

Thus, Eq. (3.116) may be approximated by

$$x(t) \approx A\left\{\cos 2\pi f_0 t + \frac{1}{2}\beta[\cos(2\pi f_0 + 2\pi f_m)t - \cos(2\pi f_0 - 2\pi f_m)t]\right\}.$$ **Eq. (3.119)**

3.5.3. Linear Frequency Modulated CW Radar

Continuous wave radars may use LFM waveforms so that both range and Doppler information can be measured. In practical CW radars, the LFM waveform cannot be continually changed in one direction, and thus, periodicity in the modulation is normally utilized. Figure 3.23 shows a sketch of a triangular LFM waveform.

The modulation does not need to be triangular; it may be sinusoidal, sawtoothed, or some other form. The dashed line in Fig. 3.23 represents the return waveform from a stationary target at range R. The beat frequency f_b is also sketched in Fig. 3.23. It is defined as the difference (due to heterodyning) between the transmitted and received signals. The time delay Δt is a measure of target range; that is,

$$\Delta t = (2R)/c.$$ **Eq. (3.120)**

In practice, the modulating frequency f_m is selected such that

$$f_m = 1/(2t_0).$$ **Eq. (3.121)**

The rate of frequency change, $\dot{f}$, is

$$\dot{f} = \frac{\Delta f}{t_0} = \frac{\Delta f}{(1/2f_m)} = 2f_m \Delta f$$ **Eq. (3.122)**

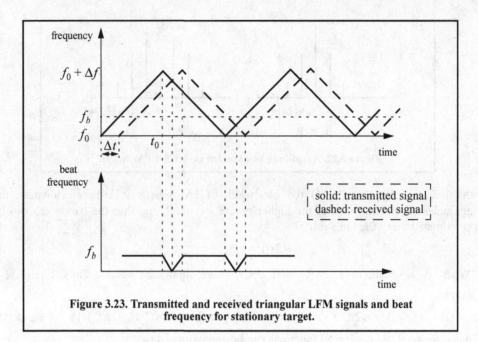

Figure 3.23. Transmitted and received triangular LFM signals and beat frequency for stationary target.

where Δf is the peak frequency deviation. The beat frequency f_b is given by

$$f_b = \Delta t \dot{f} = \frac{2R}{c} \dot{f}.$$ **Eq. (3.123)**

Equation (3.123) can be rearranged as

$$\dot{f} = \frac{c}{2R} f_b.$$ **Eq. (3.124)**

Equating Eqs. (3.122) and (3.124) and solving for f_b yields

$$f_b = (4Rf_m\Delta f)/c.$$ **Eq. (3.125)**

Now consider the case when Doppler is present (i.e., non-stationary target). The corresponding triangular LFM transmitted and received waveforms are sketched in Fig. 3.24, along with the corresponding beat frequency. As previously noted the beat frequency is defined as

$$f_b = f_{received} - f_{transmitted}.$$ **Eq. (3.126)**

When the target is not stationary, the received signal will contain a Doppler shift term in addition to the frequency shift due to the time delay Δt. In this case, the Doppler shift term subtracts from the beat frequency during the positive portion of the slope. Alternatively, the two terms add up during the negative portion of the slope. Denote the beat frequency during the positive (up) and negative (down) portions of the slope, respectively, as f_{bu} and f_{bd}. It follows that

$$f_{bu} = \frac{2R}{c}\dot{f} - \frac{2\dot{R}}{\lambda}$$ **Eq. (3.127)**

where $\dot{R}$ is the range rate or the target radial velocity as seen by the radar. The first term of the right-hand side of Eq. (3.127) is due to the range delay defined by Eq. (3.120), while the second term is due to the target Doppler. Similarly,

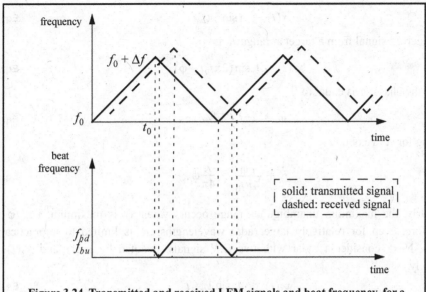

Figure 3.24. Transmitted and received LFM signals and beat frequency, for a moving target.

$$f_{bd} = \frac{2R}{c}\dot{f} + \frac{2\dot{R}}{\lambda}.$$

Eq. (3.128)

Range is computed by adding Eq. (3.127) and Eq. (3.128). More precisely,

$$R = \frac{c}{4\dot{f}}(f_{bu} + f_{bd}).$$

Eq. (3.129)

The range rate is computed by subtracting Eq. (3.127) from Eq. (3.128),

$$\dot{R} = \frac{\lambda}{4}(f_{bd} - f_{bu}).$$

Eq. (3.130)

As indicated by Eqs. (3.129) and (3.130), CW radars utilizing triangular LFM can extract both range and range rate information. In practice, the maximum time delay Δt_{max} is normally selected as

$$\Delta t_{max} = 0.1 t_0.$$

Eq. (3.131)

Thus, the maximum range is given by

$$R_{max} = \frac{0.1 c t_0}{2} = \frac{0.1 c}{4 f_m}$$

Eq. (3.132)

and the maximum unambiguous range will correspond to a shift equal to $2t_0$.

3.5.4. Multiple Frequency CW Radar

Continuous wave radars do not have to use LFM waveforms in order to obtain good range measurements. Multiple frequency schemes allow CW radars to compute very adequate range measurements without using frequency modulation. In order to illustrate this concept, first consider a CW radar with the following waveform

$$x(t) = A \sin 2\pi f_0 t.$$ Eq. (3.133)

The received signal from a target at range R is

$$x_r(t) = A_r \sin(2\pi f_0 t - \varphi)$$ Eq. (3.134)

where the phase φ is equal to

$$\varphi = 2\pi f_0 (2R/c).$$ Eq. (3.135)

Solving for R we obtain

$$R = \frac{c\varphi}{4\pi f_0} = \frac{\lambda}{4\pi}\varphi.$$ Eq. (3.136)

Clearly, the maximum unambiguous range occurs when φ is maximum, i.e., $\varphi = 2\pi$. Therefore, even for relatively large radar wavelengths, R is limited to impractical small values. Next, consider a radar with two CW signals, denoted by $x_1(t)$ and $x_2(t)$. More precisely,

$$x_1(t) = A_1 \sin 2\pi f_1 t$$ Eq. (3.137)

$$x_2(t) = A_2 \sin 2\pi f_2 t.$$ Eq. (3.138)

The received signals from a moving target are

$$x_{1r}(t) = A_{r_1} \sin(2\pi f_1 t - \varphi_1)$$ Eq. (3.139)

$$x_{2r}(t) = A_{r_2} \sin(2\pi f_2 t - \varphi_2)$$ Eq. (3.140)

where $\varphi_1 = (4\pi f_1 R)/c$ and $\varphi_2 = (4\pi f_2 R)/c$. After heterodyning (mixing) with the carrier frequency, the phase difference between the two received signals is

$$\varphi_2 - \varphi_1 = \Delta\varphi = \frac{4\pi R}{c}(f_2 - f_1) = \frac{4\pi R}{c}\Delta f.$$ Eq. (3.141)

Again R is maximum when $\Delta\varphi = 2\pi$; it follows that the maximum unambiguous range is now

$$R = c/2\Delta f$$ Eq. (3.142)

and since $\Delta f \ll c$, the range computed by Eq. (3.142) is much greater than that computed using Eq. (3.136), thus, indicating an increase in the unambiguous range when using more than one frequency.

Chapter 4

Radar Propagation Medium

Bassem R. Mahafza

4.1. Earth's Impact on the Radar Equation

So far in this book, all analysis presented implicitly assumed that the radar electromagnetic waves travel as if they were in free space. Simply put, all analysis presented did not account for the effects of the earth's atmosphere nor the effects of the earth's surface. Despite the fact that *free space analysis* may be adequate to provide a general understanding of radar systems, it is only an approximation. In order to accurately predict radar performance, one must modify free space analysis to include the effects of the earth and its atmosphere. These modifications should account for ground reflections from the surface of the earth, diffraction of electromagnetic waves, bending or refraction of radar waves due to the earth's atmosphere, Doppler errors, rotation of the polarization plane, time delays, dispersion effects, and attenuation or absorption of radar energy by the gases constituting the atmosphere.

The earth's impact on the radar equation manifests itself by introducing an additional power term in the radar equation. This term is referred to as the *pattern propagation factor* and is symbolically denoted by F_p. The propagation factor can actually introduce constructive as well as destructive interference onto the SNR depending on the radar frequency and the geometry under consideration. In general, the pattern propagation factor is defined as

$$F_p = \left| \frac{E}{E_0} \right| \qquad \text{Eq. (4.1)}$$

where E is the electric field in the medium and E_0 is the free space electric field. In this case, the radar equation is now given by

$$SNR = \frac{P_t G^2 \lambda^2 \sigma}{(4\pi)^3 k T_0 BFLR^4} F_p^4. \qquad \text{Eq. (4.2)}$$

4.2. Earth's Atmosphere

The earth's atmosphere is comprised of several layers, as illustrated in Fig. 4.1. The first layer, which extends in altitude to about $30km$, is known as the troposphere. Electromagnetic waves refract (generally bend downward) as they travel in the troposphere. The troposphere refractive effect is related to its dielectric constant profile in altitude, which is a function of the altitude profile in pressure, temperature, water vapor, and gaseous content. Additionally, due to gases and water vapor in the atmosphere, radar energy suffers a loss. This loss is known as the atmospheric attenuation. Atmospheric attenuation increases in the presence of rain, fog, dust, and clouds. The region above the troposphere (altitude from 30 to 85km) behaves like free space, and little refraction occurs in this region, this region is called the interference zone.

The ionosphere extends from about 85km to about 1000km. It has very low gas density compared to the troposphere. It contains a significant amount of ionized free electrons. The ionization is primarily caused by the sun's ultraviolet and X-rays. This presence of free electrons in the ionosphere affects electromagnetic wave propagation in different ways. These effects include refraction, absorption, noise emission, and polarization rotation. The degree of degradation depends heavily on the frequency of the incident waves. For example, frequencies lower than about 4 to 6MHz are completely reflected from the lower region of the ionosphere. Frequencies higher than 30MHz may penetrate the ionosphere with some level of attenuation. In general, as the frequency is increased, most of the ionosphere's effects become less prominent. The region below the horizon, close to the earth's surface, is called the diffraction region. Diffraction is a term used to describe the bending of radar waves around physical objects. In this region, two types of diffraction are common.

In free space, electromagnetic waves travel in straight lines. However, in the presence of the earth's atmosphere, they bend (refract), as illustrated in Fig. 4.2. Refraction is a term used to describe the deviation of radar wave propagation from straight lines. The deviation from straight line propagation is caused by the variation of the index of refraction. The index of refraction is defined as

$$n = c/v \qquad \text{Eq. (4.3)}$$

where c is the velocity of electromagnetic waves in free space and v is the wave phase velocity in the medium. In the troposphere, the index of refraction decreases uniformly with altitude, while in the ionosphere the index of refraction is minimum at the level of maximum electron density. Alternatively, the interference zone acts like free space and in it the index of refraction is unity.

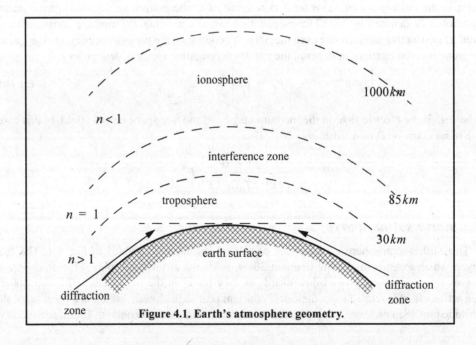

Figure 4.1. Earth's atmosphere geometry.

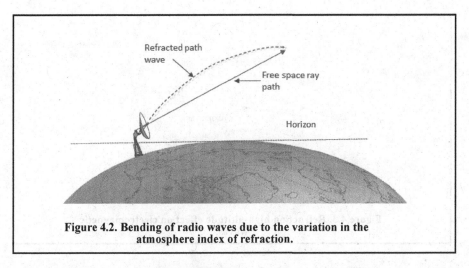

Figure 4.2. Bending of radio waves due to the variation in the atmosphere index of refraction.

In order to effectively study the effects of the atmosphere on the propagation of radar waves, it is necessary to have accurate knowledge of the height variation of the index of refraction in the troposphere and the ionosphere. The index of refraction is a function of the height above mean sea level, geographic location on the earth, weather, time of day or night, and the season of the year. Therefore, analyzing the atmospheric propagation effects under all parametric conditions becomes an overwhelming task. Typically, this problem is simplified by analyzing atmospheric models that are representative of an average of atmospheric conditions.

In most applications, including radars, one can assume a *well-mixed atmosphere* condition, where the index of refraction decreases in a smooth monotonic fashion with height. The rate of change of the earth's index of refraction n with altitude h is normally referred to as the refractivity gradient, dn/dh. As a result of the negative rate of change in dn/dh, electromagnetic waves travel at slightly higher velocities in the upper troposphere than in the lower part. As a result of this, waves traveling horizontally in the troposphere gradually bend downward. In general, since the rate of change in the refractivity index is very slight, waves do not curve downward appreciably unless they travel very long distances through the atmosphere.

Refraction affects radar waves in two different ways depending on height. For targets that have altitudes typically above $100m$, the effect of refraction is illustrated in Fig. 4.3. In this case, refraction imposes limitations on the radar's capability to measure target position, and introduces an error in measuring the elevation angle. In a well-mixed atmosphere and very low altitudes (less than $100m$), the refractivity gradient close to the earth's surface is almost constant. However, temperature changes and humidity lapses close to the earth's surface may cause serious changes in the refractivity profile. When the refractivity index gradient becomes large (negatively) enough, electromagnetic waves bend around the curve of the earth. Consequently, the radar's range to the horizon is extended.

Electromagnetic energy can become confined to a channel or duct (low loss within the duct, high loss outside the duct) within the atmosphere, refracting or reflecting between two layers, one at higher altitudes and the other at lower altitudes (when there are index of refraction inversion conditions) or at the earth's surface. This phenomenon is called ducting, and is illustrated in Fig. 4.4. Ducting can be serious over the sea surface, particularly during a hot summer.

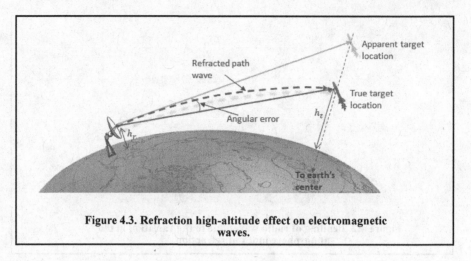

Figure 4.3. Refraction high-altitude effect on electromagnetic waves.

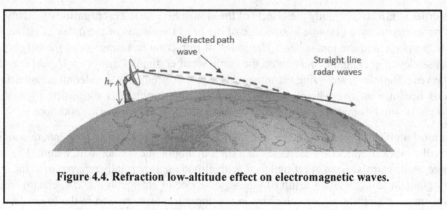

Figure 4.4. Refraction low-altitude effect on electromagnetic waves.

4.3. Atmospheric Models

The amount of bending electromagnetic waves experience due to refraction has a lot to do with the medium propagation index of refraction n, defined in Eq. (4.3). Because the index of refraction is not constant as one rises in altitude, it is necessary to analyze the formulas for the index of refraction as a function of height or altitude. Over the last several decades, this topic has been a subject of study by many scientists and physicists; thus, open source references on the subject are abundant in the literature. However, due to differences in notation used as well as the application being studied, it is rather difficult to sift through all available information in a timely and productive manner, particularly for the non-experts in the field. In this chapter, the subject is analyzed in the context of radar wave propagation in the atmosphere. In order to simplify the presentation of the theory, the index of refraction is first analyzed in the troposphere, then the ionosphere.

4.3.1. Index of Refraction in the Troposphere

As mentioned earlier, the index of refraction is a function of water vapor, air temperature, and air pressure in the medium, which all vary as a function of height. Because the rate of change of the index of refraction as a function of height is so small, it is very common to introduce a new quantity referred to as *refractivity N*, where

$$N = (n-1) \cdot 1 \times 10^6.$$ **Eq. (4.4)**

Using this notation, refractivity in the troposphere is given by

$$N = \frac{K_1}{T}\left(P + \frac{K_2 P_w}{T}\right)$$ **Eq. (4.5)**

where T is the air temperature of the medium in degrees *Kelvin*, P is the total air pressure in *millibars*, P_w is the partial pressure of water vapor in *millibars*, and K_1, K_2 are constants. The first term of Eq. (4.5) (i.e., $(K_1 P)/T$) applies to all frequencies, while the second term (i.e., $(K_1 K_2 P_w)/T$) is applicable to radio frequencies only. Experts in the field differ on the exact values for K_1, K_2 based on their relevant applications. However, for most radar applications K_1 can be assumed to be $77.6°$ *Kelvin/millibar* and K_2 is $4810°$ *Kelvin*. Therefore, Eq. (4.5) can now be written as,

$$N = \frac{77.6}{T}\left(P + \frac{4810 P_w}{T}\right).$$ **Eq. (4.6)**

The lowest values of N occur in dry areas where both P and P_w are low. In the United States, the surface value of N, denoted by N_0, varies between 285 and 345 in the winter, and from 275 to 385 in the summer. Note that Eq. (4.6) is valid for heights up to $h \le 50 km$.

If the values for T, P, and P_w are known everywhere and at all times, then N can be computed everywhere. However, knowing these variables everywhere and at all times is a very daunting task. Therefore, approximations are made for N, where the assumption that pressure and water vapor tend to decrease with height in a well-mixed atmosphere is taken into consideration. On average, the refractivity will decrease exponentially from N_0 in accordance with the following relation,

$$N = N_0 e^{-c_e \cdot h}$$ **Eq. (4.7)**

where h is the altitude in *km* and c_e is a constant (in km^{-1}) related to refractivity by

$$c_e = -\frac{\left(\frac{d}{dh}N\right)\Big|_{h=0}}{N_0}.$$ **Eq. (4.8)**

In general, c_e can be computed from Eq. (4.7) using two different altitudes. For example,

$$c_e = -\ln\left(\frac{N|_{1Km}}{N_0}\right).$$ **Eq. (4.9)**

The International Telecommunication Union (ITU) has established that for an average atmosphere, $N_0 = 315$ and $c_e = 0.1360 km^{-1}$. In the United States, the average values are given by $N_0 = 313$ and $c_e = 0.1439 km^{-1}$. Table 4.1 lists a few values for these variables.

4.3.2. Index of Refraction in the Ionosphere

Unlike the troposphere, refraction in the ionosphere occurs because of the high electron density (ionization) inside the ionosphere and not due to water vapor or other variables. The average electron density as a function of height is given by the Chapman function as

$$\rho_e = \rho_{max} \cdot e^{\frac{1-z-e^{-z}}{2}}$$ **Eq. (4.10)**

Table 4.1. Published Values for the Parameters in Eq. (4.7).

N_0	c_e (h in km)	c_e (h in $feet$)
200	0.1184	3.609×10^{-5}
250	0.1256	3.829×10^{-5}
301	0.1396	4.256×10^{-5}
313	0.1439	4.385×10^{-5}
350	0.1593	4.857×10^{-5}
400	0.1867	5.691×10^{-5}
450	0.2233	6.805×10^{-5}

where ρ_e is the electron density in electrons per cubic meters, ρ_{max} is the maximum electron density along the propagation path, and z is the normalized altitude or normalized height. The normalized height is given by

$$z = \frac{h - h_m}{H}$$

Eq. (4.11)

where h_m is the height of maximum electron density and the height scale H is given by

$$H = \frac{kT}{mg}$$

Eq. (4.12)

where k is Boltzmann's constant, T is the temperature in degrees *Kelvin*, m is the mean molecular mass of an air particle, and g is the gravitational constant ($9.81 m/s^2$). Table 4.2 shows some representative values for H, h_m and the corresponding values for ρ_{max}.

Electrons in the ionosphere travel in spiral paths along the earth's magnetic field lines at an angular rate ϖ_p given by

$$\varpi_p^2 = \frac{\rho_e Q^2}{m \varepsilon_0}$$

Eq. (4.13)

where ϖ_p is called the angular plasma frequency, critical frequency, or plasma frequency of oscillation, Q is the charge of an electron ($1.6022 \times 10^{-19} Columbs$), m is the mass of an electron, and ε_0 is the permittivity of free space ($8.8542 \times 10^{-12} Columbs/m$). The index of refraction is given by

$$n = \sqrt{1 - \left(\frac{\varpi_p}{\omega}\right)^2}$$

Eq. (4.14)

where $\omega = 2\pi f$ is the radar wave frequency in radians and f is the frequency in Hertz. Substituting Eq. (4.13) into Eq. (4.14) and collecting terms yields

$$n = \sqrt{1 - \frac{80.6 \rho_e}{f^2}} \approx 1 - \frac{40.3 \rho_e}{f^2}.$$

Eq. (4.15)

Note that Eq. (4.15) is valid for $h > 50km$ and the refractivity is given by

$$N \approx -\frac{40.3\rho_e \times 10^6}{f^2} .$$

Eq. (4.16)

Table 4.2. Representative Values for H, h_m and ρ_{max}.

$h_m - km$	$H - km$	$\rho_{max} - electron/cm^3$
100	10	1.5×10^5
200	35	3.0×10^5
300	70	12.5×10^5

4.3.3. Mathematical Model for Computing Refraction

Consider the geometry shown in Fig 4.5. The different variables shown in this figure are defined as follows: R is the range to the target in free space, R_a is the actual refracted range to the target, r_0 is the earth's radius and is equal to $6375km$, r is the distance from the center of earth to the target, h is the target height above the earth's surface, β_f is the elevation angle of the free space range ray, β_0 is the elevation angle of the actual refracted range ray, β is the target elevation angle, the rest of the variables are as defined in the figure. From the geometry, ds and dr are related by the relationships

$$(ds)^2 = (dr)^2 + r^2(d\theta)^2 ,$$

Eq. (4.17)

and

$$\sin\beta = \frac{dr}{ds} .$$

Eq. (4.18)

Hence,

$$\cos\beta = \sqrt{1 - \left(\frac{dr}{ds}\right)^2} .$$

Eq. (4.19)

From Eq. (4.3), the time it takes a radar wave to travel from point r_1 to r_2 is given by

$$t = \frac{1}{c}\int_{r_1}^{r_2} n \ dr .$$

Eq. (4.20)

In radar applications, this time represents the time difference between the time it takes the wave to travel from its source to the target using the refracted and the free space rays. From the law of sines,

$$\sin\left(\frac{\pi}{2} + \beta_f\right) = \frac{r_0 + h}{R}\sin\theta \Rightarrow \beta_f = \cos^{-1}\left(\frac{r_0 + h}{R}\sin\theta\right)$$

Eq. (4.21)

and the free space range using the law of cosines is given by

$$R = \sqrt{r_0^2 + (r_0 + h)^2 - 2r_0(r_0 + h)\cos\theta} .$$

Eq. (4.22)

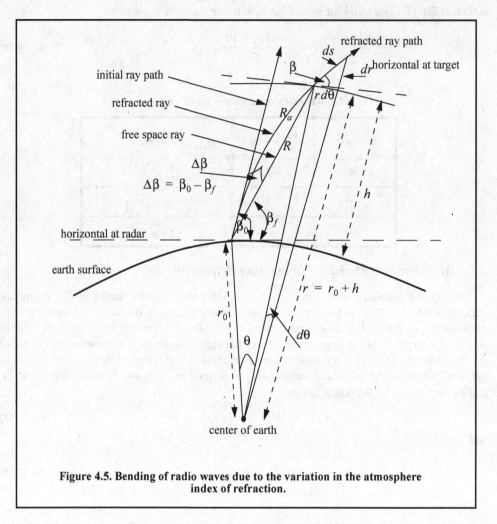

Figure 4.5. Bending of radio waves due to the variation in the atmosphere index of refraction.

Clearly the range error due to refraction is the difference between the apparent range R_a and the free space range R, which is defined in Eq. (4.22). More precisely,

$$\delta R = R_a - R.$$

Eq. (4.23)

Calculating the error in Eq. (4.23) can be a cumbersome task; it requires minimizing the integral defined in Eq. (4.20) using Fermat's principle. This process is well documented in the literature and only the results are shown here. One can easily show that

$$\sin\beta = \sqrt{1 - \left(\frac{n_0 r_0 \cos\beta_0}{nr}\right)^2}$$

Eq. (4.24)

where n_0 and n are, respectively, the medium indices of refraction at the radar and at the target. From Eq. (4.20) the apparent range is

$$R_a = \int_{r_0}^{r} n dr.$$

Eq. (4.25)

It can be shown that Eq. (4.25) can be expressed in the troposphere as

$$R_a\big|_{troposphere} = \frac{1}{n_0 r_0 \cos\beta_0} \int_{r_0}^{r} \frac{n^2 r\, dr}{\sqrt{\left(\dfrac{nr}{n_0 r_0 \cos\beta_0}\right)^2 - 1}} \qquad \textbf{Eq. (4.26)}$$

and in the ionosphere it can be expressed as

$$R_a\big|_{ionosphere} = \frac{1}{n_0 r_0 \cos\beta_0} \int_{r_0}^{r} \frac{r\, dr}{\sqrt{\left(\dfrac{nr}{n_0 r_0 \cos\beta_0}\right)^2 - 1}}. \qquad \textbf{Eq. (4.27)}$$

4.3.4. Stratified Atmospheric Refraction Model

In this section, an excellent approximation method is presented for calculating the range measurement errors and the time-delay errors experienced by radar waves due to refraction. This method is referred to as the *stratified atmospheric model* and is capable of producing very accurate theoretical estimates of the propagation errors. The basic assumption for this approach is that the atmosphere is stratified into M spherical layers, each is of thickness $\{h_m; \ m = 1, ..., M\}$ and a constant refractive index $\{n_m; \ m = 1, ..., M\}$, as illustrated in Fig. 4.6. In this figure, β_o is the apparent elevation angle and β_{oM} is the true elevation angle. The free space path is denoted by R_{oM}, while the refracted path comprises the sum of $\{R_1, R_2, ..., R_M\}$. From the figure,

$$r_m = r_o + \sum_{j=1}^{m} h_j \qquad ;m = 1, 2, ..., M \qquad \textbf{Eq. (4.28)}$$

where r_o is the actual radius of the earth.

Using the law of sines, the angle of incidence α_o is given by

$$\frac{\sin\alpha_1}{r_0} = \frac{\sin(\pi/2 + \beta_o)}{r_1}. \qquad \textbf{Eq. (4.29)}$$

Using Snell's law for spherically symmetrical surfaces, the angle β_{m+1} that the ray makes with the horizon in layer *(m+1)* is given by

$$n_m r_m \cos\beta_m = n_{(m+1)} r_{(m+1)} \cos\beta_{(m+1)} \qquad ,m = 0, 1, ..., M-1. \qquad \textbf{Eq. (4.30)}$$

Consequently,

$$\beta_{(m+1)} = \cos^{-1}\left(\frac{n_m r_m}{n_{(m+1)} r_{(m+1)}} \cos\beta_m\right) \qquad ,m = 0, 1, ..., M-1. \qquad \textbf{Eq. (4.31)}$$

Recall that β_0 and β_1 are defined to be one and the same, and so are n_0 and n_1. From Eq. (4.29), one can write the general expression for the angle of incidence. More precisely,

$$\alpha_m = \sin^{-1}\left(\frac{r_{(m-1)}}{r_m} \cos\beta_m\right) \qquad ;m = 1, 2, ..., M. \qquad \textbf{Eq. (4.32)}$$

Applying the law of sines of the direct path R_{0m} yields

$$\beta_{om} = \cos^{-1}\left(\frac{r_m}{R_{om}} \sin\left(\sum_{j=1}^{m} \theta_j\right)\right) \qquad ;m = 1, 2, ..., M \qquad \textbf{Eq. (4.33)}$$

where

$$R_{om}^2 = r_o^2 + r_m^2 - 2r_o r_m \cos\left(\sum_{j=1}^{m} \theta_j\right) \qquad ;m = 1, 2, ..., M \qquad \textbf{Eq. (4.34)}$$

$$\theta_m = \frac{\pi}{2} - \beta_m - \alpha_m \qquad ;m = 1, 2, ..., M. \qquad \textbf{Eq. (4.35)}$$

The refraction angle error is measured as the difference between the apparent and true elevation angles. Thus, it is given by

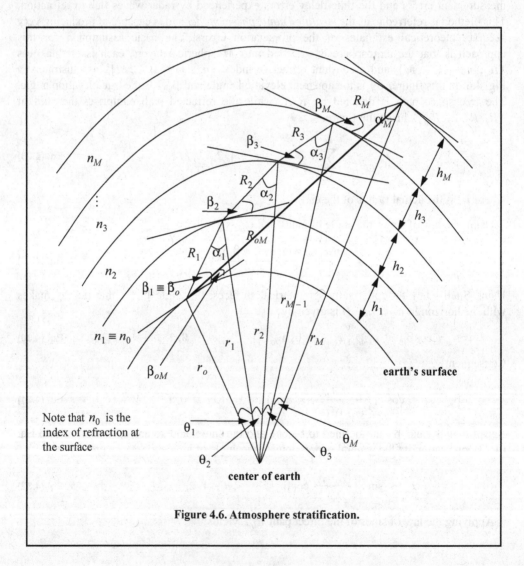

Figure 4.6. Atmosphere stratification.

$$\Delta\beta_m = \beta_o - \beta_{om}.$$ Eq. (4.36)

In this notation, $\beta_{01} = \beta_0$; thus, when $m = 1$, then

$$R_{o1} = R_1; \quad and \quad \Delta\beta_1 = 0.$$ Eq. (4.37)

Furthermore, when $\beta_o = 90°$,

$$R_{oM} = \sum_{m=1}^{M} h_m.$$ Eq. (4.38)

Now, in order to determine the time-delay error due to refraction, refer again to Fig. 4.6. The time it takes an electromagnetic wave to travel through a given layer, $\{R_m; \ m = 1, 2, ..., M\}$, is defined as $\{t_m; \ m = 1, 2, ..., M\}$ where

$$t_m = R_m / v_{\varphi_m}$$ Eq. (4.39)

and where v_{φ_m} is the phase velocity in the mth layer and is defined by

$$v_{\varphi_m} = \frac{c}{n_m}.$$ Eq. (4.40)

It follows that the total time of travel of the refracted wave in a stratified atmosphere is

$$t_T = \frac{1}{c} \sum_{j=1}^{M} n_j R_j.$$ Eq. (4.41)

The free space travel time of an unrefracted wave is denoted by t_{oM},

$$t_{oM} = \frac{R_{oM}}{c}.$$ Eq. (4.42)

Therefore, the range error resulting from refraction at the mth is δR_m and is given by

$$\delta R_m = \sum_{j=1}^{m} n_j R_j - R_{om} \qquad ; m = 1, 2, ..., M.$$ Eq. (4.43)

By using the law of cosines, one computes R_m as

$$R_m^2 = r_{(m-1)}^2 + r_m^2 - 2r_m r_{(m-1)} \cos\theta_m \qquad ; m = 1, 2, ..., M.$$ Eq. (4.44)

The results stated in Eqs. (4.41) and (4.43) are valid only in the troposphere. In the ionosphere, which is a dispersive medium, the index of refraction is also a function of frequency. In this case, the group velocity must be used when estimating the range errors of radar measurements. The group velocity is

$$v = nc.$$ Eq. (4.45)

Thus, the total time of travel in the medium is now given by

$$t_T = \frac{1}{c} \sum_{j=1}^{M} \frac{R_j}{n_j}.$$ Eq. (4.46)

Finally, the range error at the mth in the ionosphere is

$$\delta R_m = \sum_{j=1}^{m} \frac{R_j}{n_j} - R_{om} \qquad ; m = 1, 2, ..., M.$$ Eq. (4.47)

Figure 4.7 shows a plot for the total range error incurred versus range due to refraction at $f = 9.5 GHz$ for a few elevation angles.

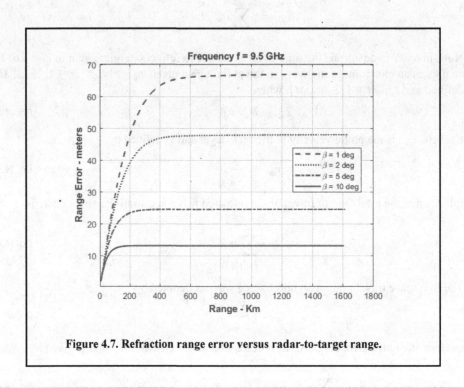

Figure 4.7. Refraction range error versus radar-to-target range.

4.4. Four-Third Earth Model

A very common way of dealing with refraction is to replace the actual earth with an imaginary earth whose effective radius is $r_e = kr_0$, where r_0 is the actual earth radius, and k is

$$k = \frac{1}{1 + \dot{r}_0 \left(\frac{dn}{dh} \right)}.$$ Eq. (4.48)

When the refractivity gradient is assumed to be constant with altitude and is equal to 39×10^{-9} per meter, then $k = 4/3$. Using an effective earth radius $r_e = (4/3)r_0$ produces what is known as the *four-third earth model*. In general, choosing

$$r_e = r_0(1 + 6.37 \times 10^{-3}(dn/dh))$$ Eq. (4.49)

produces a propagation model where waves travel in straight lines. Selecting the correct value for k depends heavily on the region's meteorological conditions. At low altitudes (typically less than $10km$) when using the four-third earth model, one can assume that radar waves (beams) travel in straight lines and do not refract. This is illustrated in Fig. 4.8.

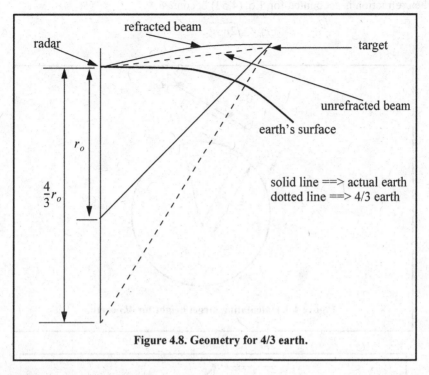

Figure 4.8. Geometry for 4/3 earth.

4.4.1. Target Height Equation

Using ray tracing (geometric optics), an integral relating range to target height with the elevation angle as a parameter can be derived and calculated. However, such computations are complex and numerically intensive. Thus, in practice, radar systems deal with refraction in two different ways, depending on height. For altitudes higher than $3km$, actual target heights are estimated from look-up tables or from charts of target height versus range for different elevation angles. Blake (1986) derives the *height-finding equation* for the four-third earth (see Fig. 4.9); it is

$$h = h_r + 6076R\sin\theta + 0.6625R^2\cos^2(\theta) \qquad \text{Eq. (4.50)}$$

where h and h_r are in feet and R is nautical miles.

The distance to the horizon for a radar located at height h_r can be calculated with the help of Fig. 4.10. For the right-angle triangle OBA (see Fig. 4.10 for position of the points A, B, and O) we get

$$r_h = \sqrt{(r_0 + h_r)^2 - r_0^2} \qquad \text{Eq. (4.51)}$$

where r_h is the distance to the horizon. By expanding Eq. (4.51) and collecting terms, one can derive the expression for the distance to the horizon as

$$r_h^2 = 2r_0 h_r + h_r^2. \qquad \text{Eq. (4.52)}$$

Finally, since $r_0 \gg h_r$ Eq. (4.52) is approximated by

$$r_h \approx \sqrt{2r_0 h_r}, \qquad \text{Eq. (4.53)}$$

and when refraction is accounted for, Eq. (4.53) becomes

$$r_h \approx \sqrt{2r_e h_r}.$$

Eq. (4.54)

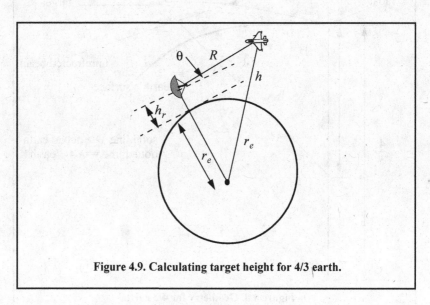

Figure 4.9. Calculating target height for 4/3 earth.

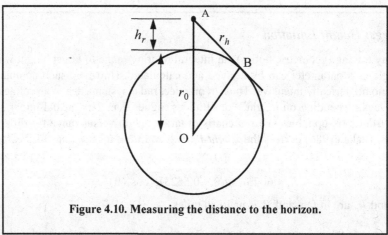

Figure 4.10. Measuring the distance to the horizon.

4.5. Ground Reflection

When radar waves are reflected from the earth's surface, they suffer a loss in amplitude and a change in phase. Three factors that contribute the overall ground reflection coefficient are the reflection coefficient for a flat surface, the divergence factor due to earth's curvature, and the surface roughness.

4.5.1. Smooth Surface Reflection Coefficient

The smooth surface reflection coefficient depends on the frequency, the surface dielectric coefficient, and the radar grazing angle. The vertical polarization and the horizontal polarization reflection coefficients are

$$\Gamma_v = \frac{\varepsilon \sin\psi_g - \sqrt{\varepsilon - (\cos\psi_g)^2}}{\varepsilon \sin\psi_g + \sqrt{\varepsilon - (\cos\psi_g)^2}} \qquad \text{Eq. (4.55)}$$

$$\Gamma_h = \frac{\sin\psi_g - \sqrt{\varepsilon - (\cos\psi_g)^2}}{\sin\psi_g + \sqrt{\varepsilon - (\cos\psi_g)^2}} \qquad \text{Eq. (4.56)}$$

where ψ_g is the grazing angle (incident angle) and ε is the complex dielectric constant of the surface, and are given by

$$\varepsilon = \varepsilon' - j\varepsilon'' = \varepsilon' - j60\lambda\sigma \qquad \text{Eq. (4.57)}$$

where λ is the wavelength and σ the medium conductivity in mhos/meter. Typical values of ε' and ε'' can be found tabulated in the literature. Tables 4.3 through 4.5 show some typical values for the electromagnetic properties of soil, lake water, and seawater, respectively. Note that when $\psi_g = 90°$ one gets

$$\Gamma_h = \frac{1 - \sqrt{\varepsilon}}{1 + \sqrt{\varepsilon}} = \frac{\varepsilon - \sqrt{\varepsilon}}{\varepsilon + \sqrt{\varepsilon}} = -\Gamma_v \qquad \text{Eq. (4.58)}$$

while when the grazing angle is very small ($\psi_g \approx 0$), one has

$$\Gamma_h = -1 = \Gamma_v. \qquad \text{Eq. (4.59)}$$

Table 4.3. Electromagnetic Properties of Soil.

Frequency GHz	Moisture content by volume							
	0.3%		10%		20%		30%	
	ε'	ε''	ε'	ε''	ε'	ε''	ε'	ε''
0.3	2.9	0.071	6.0	0.45	10.5	0.75	16.7	1.2
3.0	2.9	0.027	6.0	0.40	10.5	1.1	16.7	2.0
8.0	2.8	0.032	5.8	0.87	10.3	2.5	15.3	4.1
14.0	2.8	0.350	5.6	1.14	9.4	3.7	12.6	6.3
24.0	2.6	0.030	4.9	1.15	7.7	4.8	9.6	8.5

Table 4.4. Electromagnetic Properties of Lake Water.

Frequency GHz	Temperature					
	$T = 0°C$		$T = 10°C$		$T = 20°C$	
	ε'	ε''	ε'	ε''	ε'	ε''
0.1	85.9	68.4	83.0	91.8	79.1	115.2
1.0	84.9	15.66	82.5	15.12	78.8	15.84
2.0	82.1	20.7	81.1	16.2	78.1	14.4
3.0	77.9	26.7	78.9	20.6	76.9	16.2
4.0	72.6	31.5	75.9	24.8	75.3	19.4
6.0	61.1	39.0	68.7	33.0	71.0	24.9
8.0	50.3	40.5	60.7	36.0	65.9	29.3

Table 4.5. Electromagnetic Properties of Sea Water.

Frequency GHz	Temperature					
	$T = 0°C$		$T = 10°C$		$T = 20°C$	
	ε'	ε''	ε'	ε''	ε'	ε''
0.1	77.8	522	75.6	684	72.5	864
1.0	77.0	59.4	75.2	73.8	72.3	90.0
2.0	74.0	41.4	74.0	45.0	71.6	50.4
3.0	71.0	38.4	72.1	38.4	70.5	40.2
4.0	66.5	39.6	69.5	36.9	69.1	36.0
6.0	56.6	42.0	63.2	39.0	65.4	36.0
8.0	47.0	42.8	56.2	40.5	60.8	36.0

Fig. 4.11 shows the corresponding magnitude plots for Γ_h and Γ_v, while Fig. 4.12 shows the phase plots for seawater at $28°C$ where $\varepsilon' = 65$ and $\varepsilon'' = 30.7$ at the X-band. The plots shown in these figures show the general typical behavior of the reflection coefficient. Figures 4.13 and 4.14 show the magnitudes of the horizontal and vertical reflection coefficients as a function of grazing angle for four soils at $8GHz$.

Observation of Figs. 4.11 and 4.12 yields the following conclusions: (1) The magnitude of the reflection coefficient with horizontal polarization is equal to unity at very small grazing angles and it decreases monotonically as the angle is increased. (2) The magnitude of the vertical polarization has a well-defined minimum. The angle that corresponds to this condition is called "Brewster's polarization angle". For this reason, airborne radars in the look-down mode utilize mainly vertical polarization to significantly reduce the terrain bounce reflections. (3) For horizontal polarization, the phase is almost π; however, for vertical polarization, the phase changes to zero around Brewster's angle. (4) For very small angles (less than $2°$), both $|\Gamma_h|$ and $|\Gamma_v|$ are nearly one; $\angle\Gamma_h$ and $\angle\Gamma_v$ are nearly π. Thus, little difference in the propagation of horizontally or vertically polarized waves exists at low (i.e., very small) grazing angles.

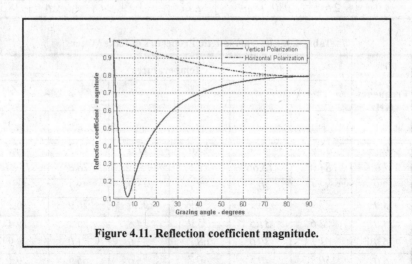

Figure 4.11. Reflection coefficient magnitude.

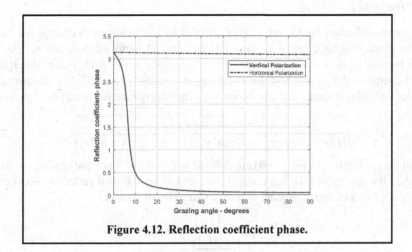

Figure 4.12. Reflection coefficient phase.

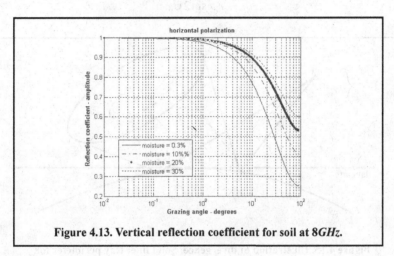

Figure 4.13. Vertical reflection coefficient for soil at 8*GHz*.

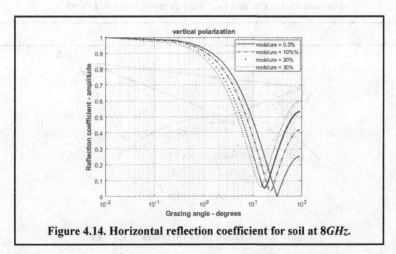

Figure 4.14. Horizontal reflection coefficient for soil at 8*GHz*.

4.5.2. Divergence

The overall reflection coefficient is also affected by the round earth divergence factor, D. When an electromagnetic wave is incident on a round earth surface, the reflected wave diverges because of the earth's curvature. This is illustrated in Fig. 4.15. Due to divergence, the reflected energy is defocused, and the radar power density is reduced. The divergence factor can be derived using geometrical considerations. The divergence factor can be expressed as

$$D = \sqrt{\frac{r_e \, r \, \sin\psi_g}{[(2r_1r_2/\cos\psi_g) + r_e r \sin\psi_g](1 + h_r/r_e)(1 + h_t/r_e)}} \qquad \text{Eq. (4.60)}$$

where all the parameters in Eq. (4.60) are defined in Fig. 4.16. Since the grazing ψ_g is always small when the divergence D has a significant impact on the total reflection coefficient, the following approximation is adequate in most radar cases of interest,

$$D \approx \frac{1}{\sqrt{1 + \dfrac{4r_1r_2}{r_e r \sin 2\psi_g}}} . \qquad \text{Eq. (4.61)}$$

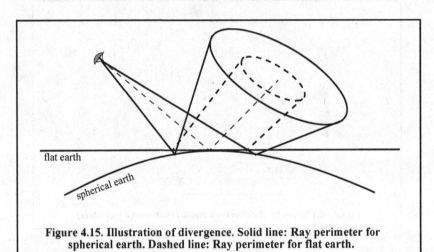

Figure 4.15. Illustration of divergence. Solid line: Ray perimeter for spherical earth. Dashed line: Ray perimeter for flat earth.

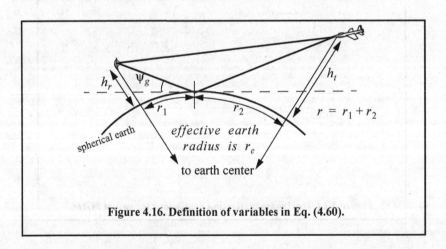

Figure 4.16. Definition of variables in Eq. (4.60).

4.5.3. Rough Surface Reflection

In addition to divergence, surface roughness also affects the reflection coefficient. Surface roughness is given by

$$S_r = e^{-2\left(\frac{2\pi h_{rms}\sin\psi_g}{\lambda}\right)^2}$$

Eq. (4.62)

where h_{rms} is the rms surface height irregularity. Another form for the rough surface reflection coefficient that is more consistent with experimental results is given by

$$S_r = e^{-z}I_0(z)$$

Eq. (4.63)

$$z = 2\left(\frac{2\pi h_{rms}\sin\psi_g}{\lambda}\right)^2$$

Eq. (4.64)

where I_0 is the modified Bessel function of order zero. Figure 4.17 shows a plot of the rough surface reflection coefficient versus $f_{MHz}h_{rms}\sin\psi_g$. The solid line uses Eq. (4.62), while the dashed line uses Eq. (4.63).

4.5.4. Total Reflection Coefficient

In general, rays reflected from rough surfaces undergo changes in phase and amplitude, which results in the diffused (non-coherent) portion of the reflected signal. Combining the effects of smooth surface reflection coefficient, divergence, and the rough surface reflection coefficient, one can express the total reflection coefficient Γ_t as

$$\Gamma_t = \Gamma_{(h,\,v)}DS_r,$$

Eq. (4.65)

where $\Gamma_{(h,\,v)}$ is the horizontal or vertical smooth surface reflection coefficient, D is divergence, and S_r is the rough surface reflection coefficient.

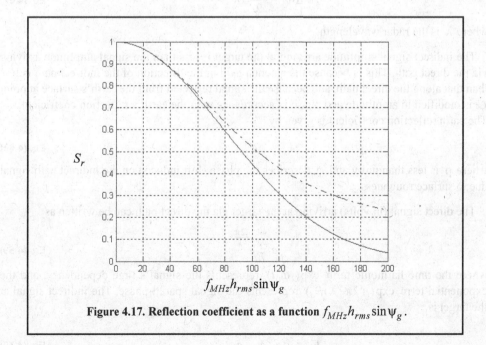

Figure 4.17. Reflection coefficient as a function $f_{MHz}h_{rms}\sin\psi_g$.

4.6. Pattern Propagation Factor

In general, the pattern propagation factor is a term used to describe the wave propagation when free space conditions are not met. This factor is defined separately for the transmitting and receiving paths. The propagation factor also accounts for the radar antenna pattern effects. The basic definition of the propagation factor is

$$F_p = \left| \frac{E}{E_0} \right|,$$

Eq. (4.66)

where E is the electric field in the medium and E_0 is the free space electric field.

Near the surface of the earth, multipath propagation effects dominate the formation of the propagation factor. In this section, a general expression for the propagation factor due to multipath will be developed. In this sense, the propagation factor describes the constructive/destructive interference of the electromagnetic waves diffracted from the earth's surface (which can be assumed to be either flat or curved). The subsequent sections derive the specific forms of the propagation factor due to flat and curved earth. The analysis in this section is after Blake (1986).

Consider the geometry shown in Fig. 4.18. The radar is located at height h_r. The target is at range R and is located at a height h_t. The grazing angle is ψ_g. The radar energy emanating from its antenna will reach the target via two paths: the "direct path" AB and the "indirect path" ACB. The lengths of the paths AB and ACB are normally very close to one another, and thus the difference between the two paths is very small. Denote the direct path as R_d, the indirect path as R_i, and the difference as $\Delta R = R_i - R_d$. It follows that the phase difference between the two paths is given by

$$\Delta \Phi = \frac{2\pi}{\lambda} \Delta R$$

Eq. (4.67)

where λ is the radar wavelength.

The indirect signal amplitude arriving at the target is less than the signal amplitude arriving via the direct path. This is because the antenna gain in the direction of the indirect path is less than that along the direct path, and because the signal reflected from the earth's surface at point C is modified in amplitude and phase in accordance with the earth's reflection coefficient, Γ. The earth reflection coefficient is given by

$$\Gamma = \rho e^{j\varphi}$$

Eq. (4.68)

where ρ is less than unity and φ describes the phase shift induced on the indirect path signal due to surface roughness.

The direct signal (in volts) arriving at the target via the direct path can be written as

$$E_d = e^{j\omega_0 t} e^{j\frac{2\pi}{\lambda} R_d}$$

Eq. (4.69)

where the time harmonic term $\exp(j\omega_0 t)$ represents the signal's time dependency, and the exponential term $\exp(j(2\pi/\lambda)R_d)$ represents the signal spatial phase. The indirect signal at the target is

$$E_i = \rho e^{j\varphi} e^{j\omega_0 t} e^{j\frac{2\pi}{\lambda} R_i}$$

Eq. (4.70)

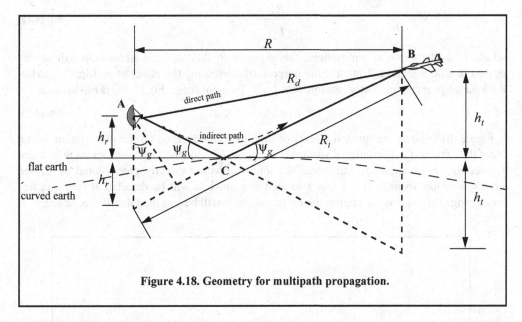

Figure 4.18. Geometry for multipath propagation.

where $\rho \exp(j\varphi)$ is the surface reflection coefficient. Therefore, the overall signal arriving at the target is

$$E = E_d + E_i = e^{j\omega_0 t} e^{j\frac{2\pi}{\lambda}R_d} \left(1 + \rho e^{j\left(\varphi + \frac{2\pi}{\lambda}(R_i - R_d)\right)} \right). \qquad \text{Eq. (4.71)}$$

Due to reflections from the earth's surface, the overall signal strength is then modified at the target by the ratio of the signal strength in the presence of earth to the signal strength at the target in free space. By using Eqs. (4.69) and (4.71) into Eq. (4.66) the propagation factor is computed as

$$F_p = \left| \frac{E_d + E_i}{E_d} \right| = \left| 1 + \rho e^{j\varphi} e^{j\Delta\Phi} \right|, \qquad \text{Eq. (4.72)}$$

which can be rewritten as

$$F_p = \left| 1 + \rho e^{j\alpha} \right| \qquad \text{Eq. (4.73)}$$

where $\alpha = \Delta\Phi + \varphi$, using Euler's identity ($e^{j\alpha} = \cos\alpha + j\sin\alpha$), Eq. (4.73) is written as

$$F_p = \sqrt{1 + \rho^2 + 2\rho\cos\alpha}. \qquad \text{Eq. (4.74)}$$

It follows that the signal power at the target is modified by the factor F_p^2. By using reciprocity, the received signal power at the radar is computed by multiplying the radar equation by the factor F_p^4. In the following two sections, we will develop exact expressions for the propagation factor for flat and curved earth.

The propagation factor for free space and no multipath is $F_p = 1$. Denote the radar detection range in free space (i.e., $F_p = 1$) as R_0. It follows that the detection range in the presence of the atmosphere and multipath interference is

$$R = \frac{R_0 F_p}{(L_a)^{1/4}}$$

Eq. (4.75)

where L_a is the two-way atmospheric loss at range R. Atmospheric attenuation will be discussed in a later section. Thus, for the purpose of illustrating the effect of multipath interference on the propagation factor, assume that $L_a = 1$. In this case, Eq. (4.75) is modified to

$$R = R_0 F_p.$$

Eq. (4.76)

Figure 4.19 shows the general effects of multipath interference on the propagation factor. Note that, due to the presence of surface reflections, the antenna elevation coverage is transformed into a lobed pattern structure. The lobe widths are directly proportional to λ, and inversely proportional to h_r. A target located at a maxima will be detected at twice its free space range. At many other angles, the detection range will be less than that in free space.

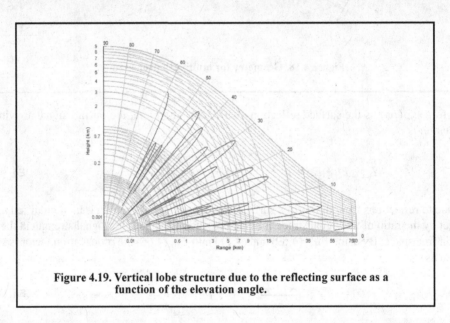

Figure 4.19. Vertical lobe structure due to the reflecting surface as a function of the elevation angle.

4.6.1. Flat Earth

Using the geometry of Fig. 4.18, the direct and indirect paths are computed as

$$R_d = \sqrt{R^2 + (h_t - h_r)^2}$$

Eq. (4.77)

$$R_i = \sqrt{R^2 + (h_t + h_r)^2}.$$

Eq. (4.78)

Equations (4.77) and (4.78) can be approximated using the truncated binomial series expansion as

$$R_d \approx R + \frac{(h_t - h_r)^2}{2R}$$

Eq. (4.79)

$$R_i \approx R + \frac{(h_t + h_r)^2}{2R}.$$

Eq. (4.80)

This approximation is valid for low grazing angles, where $R \gg h_t, h_r$. It follows that

$$\Delta R = R_i - R_d \approx \frac{2h_t h_r}{R}.$$ Eq. (4.81)

Substituting Eq. (4.81) into Eq. (4.67) yields the phase difference due to multipath propagation between the two signals (direct and indirect) arriving at the target. More precisely,

$$\Delta \Phi = \frac{2\pi}{\lambda} \Delta R \approx \frac{4\pi h_t h_r}{\lambda R}.$$ Eq. (4.82)

At this point, assume a smooth surface with reflection coefficient $\Gamma = -1$. This assumption means that waves reflected from the surface suffer no amplitude loss, and that the induced surface phase shift is equal to $180°$. Using Eq. (4.67) and Eq. (4.74) along with these assumptions yields

$$F_p^2 = 2 - 2\cos\Delta\Phi = 4\sin^2\left(\frac{\Delta\Phi}{2}\right).$$ Eq. (4.83)

Substituting Eq. (4.82) into Eq. (4.83) yields

$$F_p^2 = 4\sin^2\left(\frac{2\pi h_t h_r}{\lambda R}\right).$$ Eq. (4.84)

By using reciprocity, the expression for the propagation factor at the radar is then given by

$$F_p^4 = 16\sin^4\left(\frac{2\pi h_t h_r}{\lambda R}\right).$$ Eq. (4.85)

Finally, the signal power at the radar is computed by multiplying the radar equation by the factor F_p^4,

$$P_r = \frac{P_t G^2 \lambda^2 \sigma}{(4\pi)^3 R^4} 16\sin^4\left(\frac{2\pi h_t h_r}{\lambda R}\right).$$ Eq. (4.86)

Since the sine function varies between 0 and 1, the signal power will then vary between 0 and 16. Therefore, the fourth power relation between signal power and the target range results in varying the target range from 0 to twice the actual range in free space. In addition to that, the field strength at the radar will now have holes that correspond to the nulls of the propagation factor.

The nulls of the propagation factor occur when the sine is equal to zero. More precisely,

$$\frac{2h_r h_t}{\lambda R} = n$$ Eq. (4.87)

where $n = \{0, 1, 2, \dots\}$. The maxima occur at

$$\frac{4h_r h_t}{\lambda R} = n + 1.$$ Eq. (4.88)

The target heights that produce nulls in the propagation factor are $\{h_t = n(\lambda R / 2h_r); n = 0, 1, 2, \dots\}$, and the peaks are produced from target heights $\{h_t = n(\lambda R / 4h_r); n = 1, 2, \dots\}$. Therefore, due to the presence of surface reflections, the antenna elevation coverage is transformed into a lobed pattern structure as illustrated by Fig. 4.19. A target located at a maxima will be detected at no more than twice its free space range. Alternatively, at many other angles, the detection range will be less than that in free space. At angles defined by Eq. (4.86), there would be no measurable target returns. For small angles, Eq. (4.86) can be approximated by

$$P_r \approx \frac{4\pi P_t G^2 \sigma}{\lambda^2 R^8} (h_t h_r)^4, \qquad \text{Eq. (4.89)}$$

thus, the received signal power varies as the eighth power of the range instead of the fourth power. Also, the factor $G\lambda$ is now replaced by G/λ.

4.6.2. Spherical Earth

In order to model the effects of multipath propagation on radar performance more accurately, we need to remove the flat earth condition and account for the earth's curvature. When considering round earth, electromagnetic waves travel in curved paths because of the atmospheric refraction. And as mentioned earlier, the most commonly used approach to reducing the effects of atmospheric refraction is to replace the actual earth by an imaginary earth such that electromagnetic waves travel in straight lines. The effective radius of the imaginary earth is

$$r_e = kr_0 \qquad \text{Eq. (4.90)}$$

where k is a constant and r_0 is the actual earth radius. Using the geometry in Fig. 4.20, the direct and indirect path difference is

$$\Delta R = R_1 + R_2 - R_d. \qquad \text{Eq. (4.91)}$$

The propagation factor is computed by using ΔR from Eq. (4.91) in Eq. (4.67) and substituting the result in Eq. (4.74). To compute (R_1, R_2, and R_d), the following cubic equation must first be solved for r_1:

$$2r_1^3 - 3rr_1^2 + (r^2 - 2r_e(h_r + h_t))r_1 + 2r_e h_r r = 0. \qquad \text{Eq. (4.92)}$$

The solution is

$$r_1 = \frac{r}{2} - p\sin\frac{\xi}{3} \qquad \text{Eq. (4.93)}$$

where

$$p = \frac{2}{\sqrt{3}}\sqrt{r_e(h_t + h_r) + \frac{r^2}{4}} \qquad \text{Eq. (4.94)}$$

$$\xi = \sin^{-1}\left(\frac{2r_e r(h_t - h_r)}{p^3}\right). \qquad \text{Eq. (4.95)}$$

Next, we solve for R_1, R_2, and R_d. From Fig. 4.20,

$$\phi_1 = \frac{r_1}{r_e}; \quad \phi_2 = \frac{r_2}{r_e} \qquad \text{Eq. (4.96)}$$

and

$$\phi = \frac{r}{r_e}. \qquad \text{Eq. (4.97)}$$

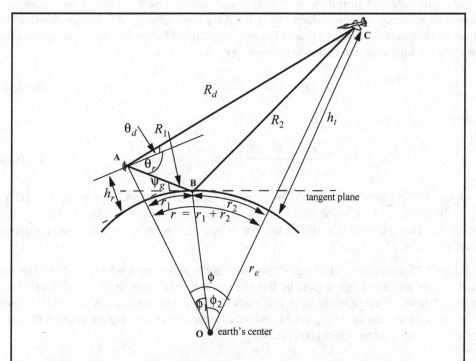

Figure 4.20. Geometry associated with multipath propagation over round earth.

Using the law of cosines to the triangles ABO and BOC yields

$$R_1 = \sqrt{r_e^2 + (r_e + h_r)^2 - 2r_e(r_e + h_r)\cos\phi_1} \qquad\qquad \text{Eq. (4.98)}$$

$$R_2 = \sqrt{r_e^2 + (r_e + h_t)^2 - 2r_e(r_e + h_t)\cos\phi_2}. \qquad\qquad \text{Eq. (4.99)}$$

Equations (4.98) and (4.99) can be written in the following simpler forms:

$$R_1 = \sqrt{h_r^2 + 4r_e(r_e + h_r)\sin^2\!\left(\frac{\phi_1}{2}\right)} \qquad\qquad \text{Eq. (4.100)}$$

$$R_2 = \sqrt{h_t^2 + 4r_e(r_e + h_t)\sin^2\!\left(\frac{\phi_2}{2}\right)} \qquad\qquad \text{Eq. (4.101)}$$

Using the law of cosines on the triangle AOC yields

$$R_d = \sqrt{(h_r - h_t)^2 + 4(r_e + h_t)(r_e + h_r)\sin^2\!\left(\frac{\phi_1 + \phi_2}{2}\right)}. \qquad\qquad \text{Eq. (4.102)}$$

Additionally,

$$r = r_e \cos^{-1}\!\left(\sqrt{\frac{(r_e + h_r)^2 + (r_e + h_t)^2 - R_d^2}{2(r_e + h_r)(r_e + h_t)}}\right). \qquad\qquad \text{Eq. (4.103)}$$

Substituting Eqs. (4.100) through (4.102) directly into Eq. (4.91) may not be conducive to numerical accuracy. A more suitable form for the computation of ΔR is then derived. The detailed derivation is in Blake (1986). The results are listed below. For better numerical accuracy, use the following expression to compute ΔR:

$$\Delta R = \frac{4 R_1 R_2 \sin^2 \psi_g}{R_1 + R_2 + R_d}$$

Eq. (4.104)

where

$$\psi_g = \sin^{-1}\left(\frac{2 r_e h_r + h_r^2 - R_1^2}{2 r_e R_1}\right) \approx \sin^{-1}\left(\frac{h_r}{R_1} - \frac{R_1}{2 r_e}\right).$$

Eq. (4.105)

Figure 4.21 presents a plot for the propagation factor loss versus range using $f = 3 GHz$; $h_r = 30.48 m$; and $h_t = 60.96 m$. In this case, the target reference range is at $R_o = 185.2 km$. Divergence effects are not included; neither is the reflection coefficient. More precisely, $D = \Gamma_t = 1$.

Figure 4.22 shows the relative signal level with and without multipath losses. Note that multipath losses affect the signal level by introducing numerous nulls in the signal level. These nulls will typically cause the radar to lose track of targets passing through such nulls. Figures 4.23 and 4.24 are similar to Figs. 4.21 and 4.22, except these new figures account for divergence. All plots assume vertical polarization.

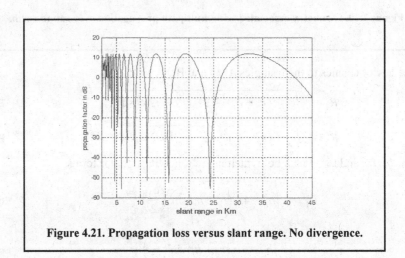

Figure 4.21. Propagation loss versus slant range. No divergence.

4.7. Diffraction

Diffraction is a term used to describe the phenomenon of electromagnetic waves bending around obstacles. It is of major importance to radar systems operating at very low altitudes. Hills and ridges diffract radio energy and make it possible to perform detection in regions that are physically shadowed. In practice, experimental data measurements provide the dominant source of information available on this phenomenon. Some theoretical analyses of diffraction are also available. However, in these cases many assumptions are made, and perhaps the most important assumption is that obstacles are chosen to be perfect conductors.

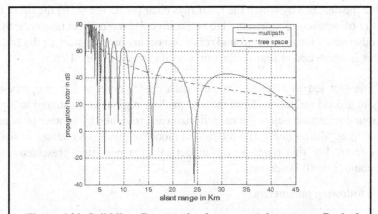

Figure 4.22. Solid line: Propagation loss versus slant range. Dashed line: Free space loss. No divergence.

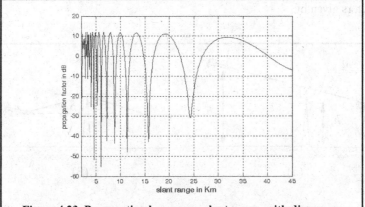

Figure 4.23. Propagation loss versus slant range, with divergence.

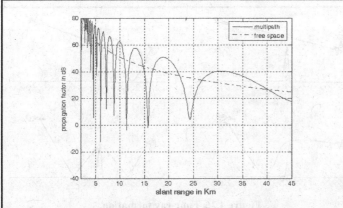

Figure 4.24. Solid line: Propagation loss versus slant range. Dashed line: Free space loss, with divergence.

The problem of propagation over a knife edge on a plane can be described with the help of Fig. 4.25. The target and radar heights are denoted, respectively, by h_t and h_r. The edge height is h_e. Denote the distance by which the radar rays clear (or do not clear) the tip of the edge by δ. As a matter of notation, δ is assumed to be positive when the direct rays clear the edge, and is negative otherwise. Because the ground reflection occurs on both sides of the edge, the propagation factor is composed of four distinct rays, as illustrated in Fig. 4.26.

The analysis that led to creating the multipath model described in the previous section applies only to ground reflections from the intermediate region, as illustrated in Fig. 4.27. The effects of ground reflection below the radar horizon are governed by another physical phenomenon referred to as "diffraction". The diffraction model requires calculations of the Airy function and its roots. For this purpose, the numerical approximation presented in Shatz and Polychronopoulos (1990) is adopted.

Define the following parameters,

$$x = \frac{R}{r_0} \;,\quad y = \frac{h_r}{h_0} \;,\quad t = \frac{h_t}{h_0} \qquad\qquad \textbf{Eq. (4.106)}$$

where h_r is the radar altitude, h_t is target altitude, R is range to the target, h_0 and r_0 are normalizing factors given by

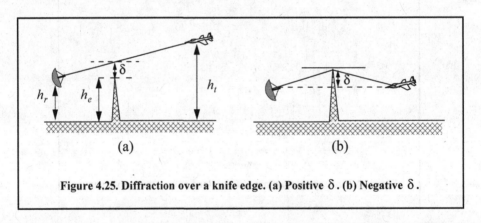

Figure 4.25. Diffraction over a knife edge. (a) Positive δ. (b) Negative δ.

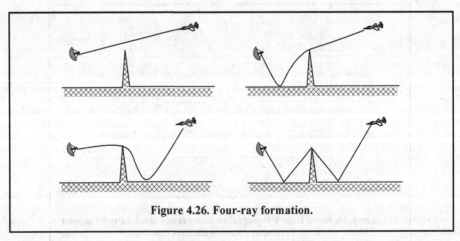

Figure 4.26. Four-ray formation.

$$h_0 = \frac{1}{2}(r_e\lambda^2/\pi^2)^{1/3}$$

Eq. (4.107)

$$r_0 = (r_e^2\lambda/\pi)^{1/3}.$$

Eq. (4.108)

λ is the wavelength and r_e is the effective earth radius. Let $A_i(u)$ denote the Airy function defined by

$$A_i(u) = \frac{1}{\pi}\int_0^\infty \cos\left(\frac{q^3}{3} + uq\right) dq.$$

Eq. (4.109)

The general expression for the propagation factor in the diffraction region is equal to

$$F = 2\sqrt{\pi x}\sum_{n=1}^\infty f_n(y)f_n(t)\exp[(e^{j\pi/6})a_n x]$$

Eq. (4.110)

where (x, y, t) are defined in Eq. (4.106) and

$$f_n(u) = \frac{A_i(a_n + ue^{j\pi/3})}{e^{j\pi/3}A_i'(a_n)}$$

Eq. (4.111)

where a_n is the *n*th root of the Airy function and A_i' is the first derivative of the Airy function. Shatz and Polychronopoulos (1990) showed that Eq. (4.110) can be approximated by

$$F = 2\sqrt{\pi x}\sum_{n=1}^\infty \frac{\widehat{A_i}(a_n + ye^{j\pi/3})}{e^{j\pi/3}A_i'(a_n)}\frac{\widehat{A_i}(a_n + te^{j\pi/3})}{e^{j\pi/3}A_i'(a_n)}$$

Eq. (4.112)

$$\exp\left[\frac{1}{2}(\sqrt{3} + j)a_n x - \frac{2}{3}(a_n + ye^{j\pi/3})^{3/2} - \frac{2}{3}(a_n + te^{j\pi/3})^{3/2}\right]$$

where

$$\widehat{A_i}(u) = A_i(u)e^{j\frac{2}{3}u^{3/2}}.$$

Eq. (4.113)

Shatz and Polychronopoulos showed that the sum in Eq. (4.112) represents accurate computation of the propagation factor within the diffraction region. Note that the variables x, y, and t were defined in Eq. (4.106).

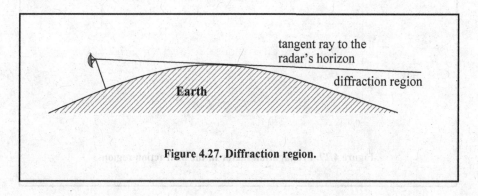

Figure 4.27. Diffraction region.

Figure 4.28 (after Shatz) shows a typical output generated by this program for $h_t = 1000m$, $h_r = 8000m$, and *frequency* $= 167MHz$. Figure 4.29 is similar to Fig. 4.28 except in this case the following parameters are used: $h_t = 3000m$, $h_r = 200m$, and *frequency* $= 428MHz$. Figure 4.30 shows a plot for the propagation factor using the same parameters in Fig. 4.29; however, in this figure, both intermediate and diffraction regions are shown.

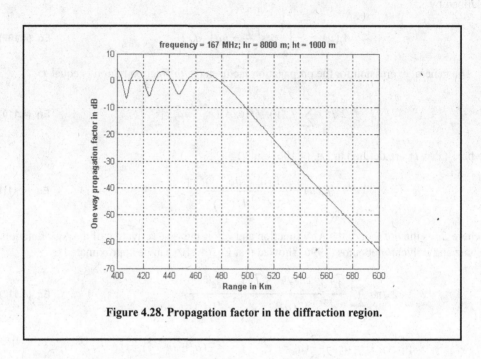

Figure 4.28. Propagation factor in the diffraction region.

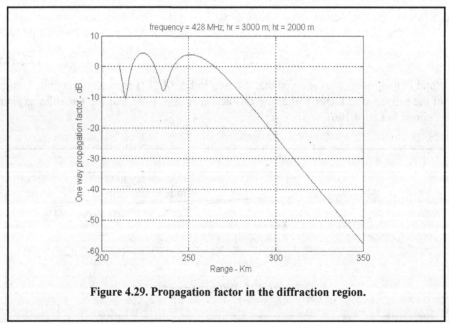

Figure 4.29. Propagation factor in the diffraction region.

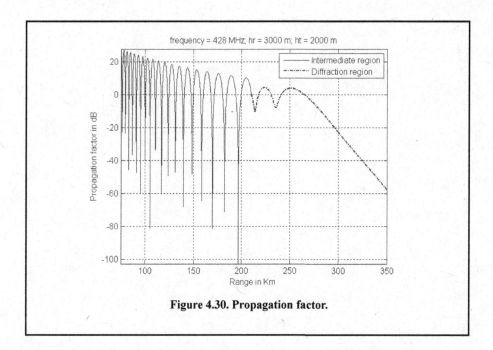

Figure 4.30. Propagation factor.

Chapter 5

Radar Electronic Warfare Techniques

Bassem R. Mahafza and Robert J. Balla

5.1. Electronic Warfare Classes

The term electronic warfare (EW) describes any electronic deliberate attempt (technique or tactic) to use electromagnetic (EM) energy (actively or passively) to collect data on and / or disrupt normal operations of radar, communications device, or any other device that operates in the EM spectrum. Although the physics of EW and its counter-measures are well understood and known, specific tactical embodiments quickly acquire a cloak of secrecy due to their potential tactical advantage to an adversary if revealed. Consequently, the presentation given here will be highly abridged with only the rudimentary framework of the field of EW given for orientation. The interested reader is directed to the more comprehensive EW literature for further enlightenment on this interesting field. There are three major classes of EW: electronic support measures (ESM), electronic counter-measures (ECM) (also called electronic attack (EA)), and electronic counter-counter measures (ECCM) (also called electronic protection (EP)). Figure 5.1 shows a breakdown of the most common classes of EW techniques. In this chapter the emphasis is on jamming of radar systems.

Electronic support measures (ESM) describe the actions taken to detect and identify the electromagnetic characteristics of an adversary radar system or other electronic emitters such as radios and altimeters, and is commonly referred to as signal intelligence (SIGINT). Signal intelligence comprises four categories:

1. Detection and analysis of enemy radar systems waveforms, which is often called electronic intelligence (ELINT)

2. Detection and analysis of enemy communication signals, which is often called communications intelligence (COMINT)

3. Identification and analysis of an adversary instrumentation signals, and is often referred to as foreign intelligence (FISINT), and finally

4. Measurements of signature intelligence (MASINT) which focuses on unintentionally transmitted signals and associated information characteristics.

Parameters collected by SIGINT may include frequency, bandwidth, modulation, waveform type, and polarization to name a few. Sound intelligence and engineering assessments of ESM data are used to identify specific system weaknesses that can be exploited with the optimum noise, deception, or combination of jamming techniques. To this end, ESM information is programmed into jamming systems to counter specific victim-radars' capabilities.

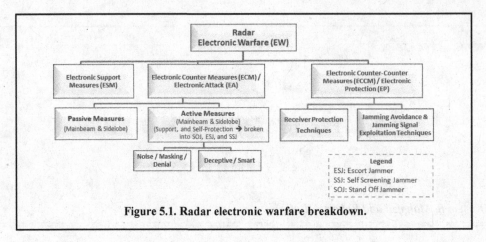

Figure 5.1. Radar electronic warfare breakdown.

Electronic counter-measures (ECM) involve the use of the electromagnetic energy to impede the adversaries' defensive capabilities. It is broken down into two major categories, active and passive ECM techniques. The effectiveness of ECM relies heavily on having adequate and sufficient information on the victim-radar; accordingly, the ESM collected data provides the foundation for developing the appropriate passive and / or active ECM technique. Passive ECM techniques include chaff, radar decoys, and radar cross-section (RCS) alterations such as radio frequency absorbing materials (RAM). Passive ECM is often placed on the threat itself or deployed to remain physically close to it.

Active ECM techniques involve utilizing active jamming devices to disrupt defense radar systems normal operations. Active ECM techniques may be categorized either based on their deployment method or based on the jamming technique they employ. Jammers deployed into the victim-radar mainbeam are referred to as *self-protection jammers* which include escort jamming (ESJ) that accompany the attacking aircraft and self-screening jamming (SSJ) that are typically deployed on-board the attacking platform. Jamming directed into the victim-radar sidelobes is referred to as *support jammers* and include stand-off jamming (SOJ) which are typically deployed at ranges greater than the attacking aircraft, and precursor jamming (PrJ) which are deployed at ranges closer than the attacking aircraft. Alternatively, classifications of active ECM based on their jamming technique are either *noise jamming* (also called masking or denial) or *deception jamming* (also called smart jamming). Most deceptive jammers utilize digital radio frequency memory (DRFM) devices with field programmable gate arrays (FPGA). These devices can synthesize a multiplicity of false targets that are substantially identical to the true target to confuse the defense.

Electronic counter-counter measures (ECCM) techniques are broken down into receiver protection techniques and jamming exploitation techniques. The first category is concerned with ensuring the integrity of the radar receiver chain. The second category is concerned with developing anti-jamming techniques that can exploit jamming device weaknesses.

5.2. Passive Jamming Techniques

Passive jamming techniques include RAM, chaff, decoys, and other techniques that do not require an active power source. Chaff is the only passive ECM technique discussed here. Chaff consists of a large number of ribbon-like pieces of metallic materials or metalized plastic with large RCS values that are dispensed by the offense to mask or screen the attacking objects. The radar reflections off the chaff pieces may cause the tracking radar to lose target track and / or lock on false target tracks. The chaff material is generally cut into small pieces where the size is dependent upon the victim-radar operating frequency effectively masking returns from the attacking objects. At *1/2* wavelength, chaff acts as a resonant dipole and reflects much of the incident energy.

The maximum chaff RCS occurs when the chaff dipole length L is *1/2* the radar wavelength. The average RCS for a single *1/2* wavelength dipole when viewed broadside is

$$\sigma_{ch1} \approx 0.88\lambda^2 \qquad \text{Eq. (5.1)}$$

where λ is the wavelength. For an average aspect angle, the chaff RCS drops to

$$\sigma_{ch1} \approx 0.15\lambda^2. \qquad \text{Eq. (5.2)}$$

The subscript $ch1$ is used to indicate a single dipole, and λ is the radar wavelength. The total chaff RCS within a radar resolution volume (cell) is

$$\sigma_{ch} \approx 0.15\lambda^2 N_D \qquad \text{Eq. (5.3)}$$

where N_D is the total number of chaff dipoles. Equation (5.3) is valid when the chaff volume is larger than the radar resolution cell. Alternatively, when the radar resolution cell is larger than the chaff volume, then the total chaff RCS within a radar resolution volume is

$$\sigma_{ch} \approx \frac{0.15\lambda^2 N_D V_{CS}}{L_{beam} V_R} \qquad \text{Eq. (5.4)}$$

where V_R is the radar resolution cell volume, V_{CS} is the chaff scattering volume, and L_{beam} is the radar antenna beam shape loss for the chaff cloud.

Echoes from a chaff cloud are typically random and have thermal noise-like characteristics because the individual clutter components (scatterers) have random phases and amplitudes. Due to these characteristics, chaff is often statistically described by a probability distribution function. The type of distribution depends on the nature of the chaff cloud itself, radar operating parameters, and the viewing angle of the radar. Thus, the signal-to-chaff ratio is given by

$$\frac{S}{C_{ch}} = \frac{\sigma}{\sigma_{ch}} CCR \qquad \text{Eq. (5.5)}$$

where σ is the target RCS and CCR is the chaff-cancellation-ratio. The value of CCR depends on the type of chaff mitigation techniques adopted by the radar signal and data processors. Since chaff is a form of volumetric clutter, signal processing and moving target indicator (MTI) techniques developed for rain and other forms of volumetric clutter can be applied to mitigate many of the effects of chaff. Chaff can be categorized into two types: (1) denial chaff, and (2) deceptive chaff. In the first case, the chaff is deployed in order to screen targets that reside within or near the deployed chaff cloud. In the second case, the chaff cloud is dispersed to complicate and / or overwhelm the tracking and processing functions of the radar by luring the tracker away from the target and / or creating multiple false targets.

5.3. Radar Equation with Jamming

The radar equation for a target located at range R and with RCS σ is given by,

$$SNR = \frac{P_t G_t G_r \lambda^2 \sigma G_{pc}}{(4\pi)^3 k T_o B_r F L_t L_r R^4}. \qquad \text{Eq. (5.6)}$$

where SNR is the signal-to-noise power ratio, P_t is the peak transmitted power, G_t is the antenna gain at transmit, G_r is the antenna gain at receive, λ is the wavelength, G_{pc} is the pulse compression gain (i.e., the time-bandwidth product), k is Boltzmann's constant, T_0 is $290°K$, B_r is the instantaneous receiver bandwidth, F is the receiver noise figure, L_t total transmit radar losses, and L_r is the total receive radar losses. The SNR is a very important metric. It quantifies the radar sensitivity and establishes its ability to effectively detect the presence of a target, track it and even classify it. When jamming is present, the radar detection capability is determined by receiver signal-to-noise-plus-interference ratio rather than SNR alone. From Eq. (5.6), the signal power at the radar receiver input is

$$S = \frac{P_t G_t G_r \lambda^2 \sigma G_{pc}}{(4\pi)^3 L_t L_r R^4}.$$ Eq. (5.7)

In general, a jammer is characterized by its operating bandwidth B_J and effective radiated power, J_{ERP}, which is proportional to the jammer transmitter power P_J. More precisely,

$$J_{ERP} = \frac{P_J G_J}{L_J}$$ Eq. (5.8)

where G_J is the jammer antenna gain, and L_J is the total jammer transmit losses. Let R_j be the radar-to-jammer range, it follows that the jamming power at the radar receiver input is

$$J = \frac{P_J G_J A_r B_r}{4\pi R_J^2 L_J L_r B_J}$$ Eq. (5.9)

where A_r is the effective aperture of the radar receiving antenna. The term $4\pi R_J^2$ is the surface area of a sphere whose radius is R_J. Note that the ratio of the radar bandwidth to jammer bandwidth is included in Eq. (5.9). This accounts for that portion of jamming power that coincides with the radar instantaneous bandwidth. Typically, and for the jammer to be effective, the jammer bandwidth must be greater than the radar instantaneous bandwidth, i.e., $B_J > B_r$. Recall the relationship $A_r = (G'\lambda^2)/(4\pi)$, where G' is the effective receive antenna gain in the direction of the jammer. Using this relation in Eq. (5.9) yields,

$$J = \frac{P_J G_J}{4\pi R_J^2} \frac{G'\lambda^2}{4\pi} \frac{B_r}{L_J B_J} \frac{1}{L_r} = \frac{P_J G_J}{L_J} \frac{G'\lambda^2}{(4\pi)^2 R_J^2} \frac{B_r}{B_J} \frac{1}{L_r}.$$ Eq. (5.10)

It follows that the jammer-to-noise ratio at the radar receiver input is

$$JNR = \frac{P_J G_J}{L_J} \frac{G'\lambda^2}{(4\pi)^2 R_J^2} \frac{B_r}{B_J} \frac{1}{k T_o B_r F L_r},$$ Eq. (5.11)

where $k T_o B_r F$ is the noise power, and L_r is the radar receive losses. Dividing Eq. (5.6) by Eq. (5.11) leads to an expression for the signal-to-jammer-ratio (S/J). More precisely,

$$\frac{S}{J} = \frac{P_t}{J_{ERP}} \frac{G_t G_r \sigma}{4\pi G'} \frac{R_J^2}{R^4} \frac{B_J}{B_r} \frac{G_{pc}}{L_t}.$$ Eq. (5.12)

Finally, assuming a monostatic radar (i.e., $G_t = G_r = G$) then the general expression for the S/J is expressed as

$$\frac{S}{J} = \frac{P_t}{J_{ERP}} \frac{\sigma}{4\pi} \frac{G^2}{G'} \frac{R_J^2}{R^4} \frac{B_J}{B_r} \frac{G_{pc}}{L_t}.$$ Eq. (5.13)

A graphical step-by-step derivation of the signal-to-jammer ratio is in Fig. 5.2.

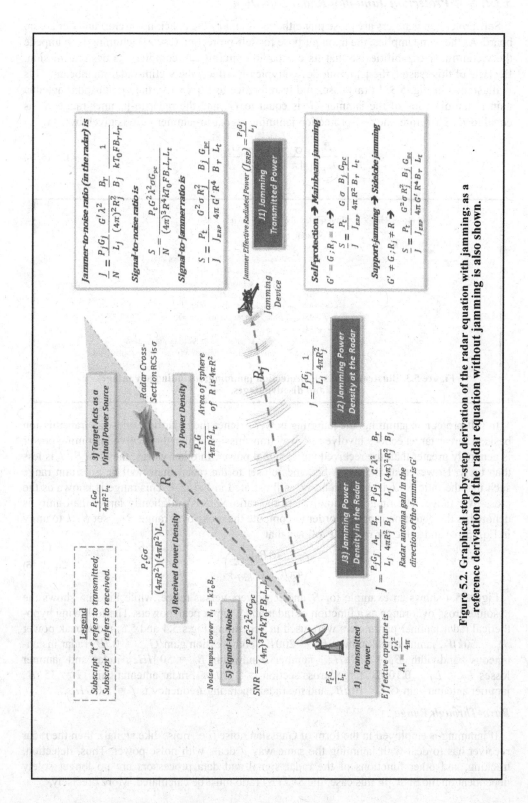

Figure 5.2. Graphical step-by-step derivation of the radar equation with jamming; as a reference derivation of the radar equation without jamming is also shown.

5.3.1. Self-Protection Jamming Radar Equation

Self-protection jammers are those that either accompany the attacking aircraft and / or are on board. As the name implies, the main purpose for self-protection (escort) jamming is to impede the victim-radar capabilities so that its companion aircraft can complete its desired mission. Because of this reason, the jamming device typically affects the victim-radar mainbeam. This is illustrated in Fig. 5.3. In this case, and in reference to Eq. (5.13), the victim-radar antenna gain in the direction of the jammer G' is equal to G, and the radar-to-jammer range R_J is equal to R. Therefore, the self-protection jamming signal-to-jammer ratio is given by

$$\frac{S}{J} = \frac{P_t}{J_{ERP}} \frac{\sigma}{4\pi} \frac{G}{R^2} \frac{B_J}{B_r} \frac{G_{pc}}{L_t}.$$

Eq. (5.14)

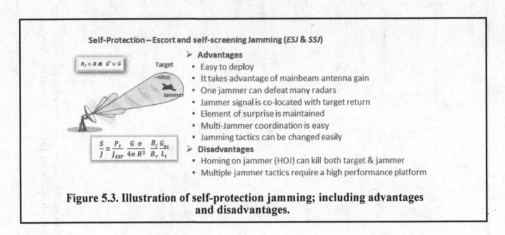

Figure 5.3. Illustration of self-protection jamming; including advantages and disadvantages.

In self-protection jamming, the jamming power reaches the radar on a one-way transmission basis, whereas target echoes involve two-way transmission. Thus, the received jamming power is generally greater than the received target signal power. In other words, the ratio S/J is less than unity. However, as the target becomes closer to the radar, there will be a certain range such that the ratio S/J is equal to unity, as illustrated in Fig. 5.4. This range is known as the cross-over range. The range window where the ratio S/J is sufficiently larger than unity is denoted as the detection range. In order to compute the cross-over range R_{co}, set S/J to unity in Eq. (5.14) and solve for range. It follows that

$$(R_{CO})_{SSJ} = \left(\frac{P_t G \sigma B_J G_{pc}}{4\pi B_r L_t (J_{ERP})} \right)^{1/2}.$$

Eq. (5.15)

Figure 5.4 shows an example for S and J powers versus range, while Fig. 5.5 shows the absolute cross-over range as a function of radar and jammer peak powers. The following hypothetical radar/jammer parameters were used in generating Fig.s 5.4 and 5.5: radar peak power $P_t = 50kW$, jammer peak power $P_J = 200W$, compression gain $G_{pc} = 0dB$, radar instantaneous bandwidth $B_r = 667kHz$, jammer bandwidth $B_J = 50MHz$, radar and jammer losses $L_T = L_J = 0.10dB$, target cross section $\sigma = 10.m^2$, radar antenna gain $G = 35dB$, jammer antenna gain $G_J = 10dB$, and the radar operating frequency is $f = 5.6GHz$.

Burn-Through Range

If jamming is employed in the form of Gaussian noise (i.e., noise-like signal), then the radar receiver has to deal with jamming the same way it deals with noise power. Thus, detection, tracking, and other functions of the radar signal and data processors are no longer solely dependent on the SNR. In this case, the $S/(J+N)$ ratio must be calculated. More precisely,

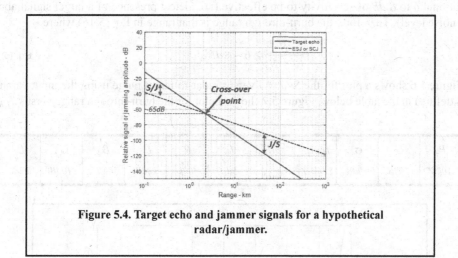

Figure 5.4. Target echo and jammer signals for a hypothetical radar/jammer.

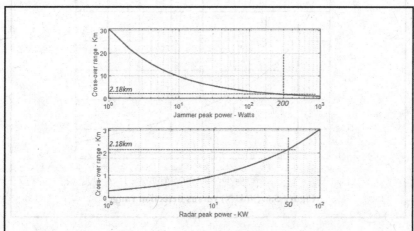

Figure 5.5. Cross-over range versus jammer and radar peak powers for a hypothetical radar/jammer.

$$\frac{S}{(J+N)} = \frac{[P_t G_t G_r \lambda^2 \sigma G_{pc} n_p]/[(4\pi)^3 R^4 L_t L_r]}{\left(J_{ERP}\left[\dfrac{G_r \lambda^2 B_r}{(4\pi)^2 R_j^2 B_J L_r}\right] + kT_0 B_r F\right)},$$

Eq. (5.16)

where n_p is the number of integrated radar pulses and all other parameters have been previously defined.

The $S/(J+N)$ ratio should be used in place of the SNR. The range at which the radar can detect and perform proper measurements for a given $S/(J+N)$ value is defined as the burn-through range. It is fairly common in the literature to assume the burn-through range and the cross-over range to be the same. Although from a mathematical view point this assumption is valid, it is not a practical assumption. Because, at the cross-over range the signal power, S and the jammer power J are equal (i.e., $J/S = 0 dB$); however, the radar system needs at least an additional *6* to *8 dB* of sensitivity to be effective (i.e., detect presence of a target signal above the noise level). Therefore, the burn-through range is that range in Eq. (5.16) where

$$\frac{S}{(J+N)} \geq 6 \sim 8\,dB\,.$$

Eq. (5.17)

Figure 5.6 shows a plot for the *S/(J+N)* versus radar-to-target range using the input parameters defined in the table below. Figure 5.7 shows a plot for the burn-through range versus J_{ERP}.

P_t	G	σ	$freq$	$\tau = B_r^{-1}$	L_t	R	P_J	B_J	G_J	L_j
50kW	*35dB*	*10dB*	*5.6GHZ*	*50μs*	*5dB*	*400km*	*200W*	*50MHz*	*10dB*	*0.3dB*

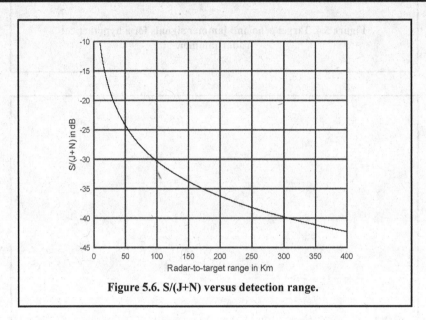

Figure 5.6. S/(J+N) versus detection range.

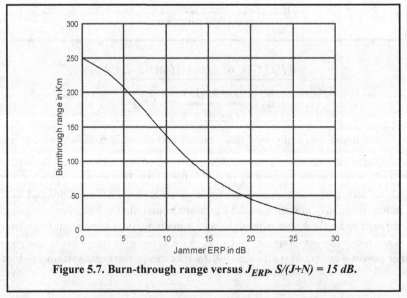

Figure 5.7. Burn-through range versus J_{ERP}. S/(J+N) = 15 dB.

5.3.2. Support Jamming Radar Equation

If noise jamming is directed into the victim-radar sidelobes it will require, in order for it to be effective, significantly more J_{ERP} and / or must operate at a much shorter range than main-beam jammers. Sidelobe jammers are often deployed to interfere with a specific victim-radar. Since they do not have to be deployed close to the attacking aircraft, they have a wide variety of standoff deployment options. There are two main types of support jamming techniques: stand-off jammers (SOJ) and precursor jammers (PrJ). Typically, support jammers emit ECM signals from long ranges that are beyond the defense's lethal capability. Figure 5.8 shows how support jammers are deployed along with the advantages and disadvantages of their deployment methods.

In the case of support jamming, the victim-radar antenna gain in the direction of the jammer G' is not equal to G, and the radar-to-jammer range R_J is not equal to R. Therefore, higher J_{ERP} is required for support jamming than for self protection jamming. Also, due to the R^2 factor stand off jamming requires higher J_{ERP} than stand-in jamming. The support jamming signal to jammer ratio is given by

$$\frac{S}{J} = \frac{P_t}{J_{ERP}} \frac{\sigma}{4\pi} \frac{G^2}{G'} \frac{R_J^2}{R^4} \frac{B_J}{B_r} \frac{G_{PC}}{L_t}.$$

Eq. (5.18)

The *S/(J+N)* is given by

$$\frac{S}{(J+N)} = \frac{[P_t G_t G_r \lambda^2 \sigma G_{pc} n_p]/[(4\pi)^3 R^4 L_t L_r]}{\left(J_{ERP}\left[\dfrac{G'\lambda^2 B_r}{(4\pi)^2 R_j^2 B_J L_r}\right] + kT_0 B_r F\right)}.$$

Eq. (5.19)

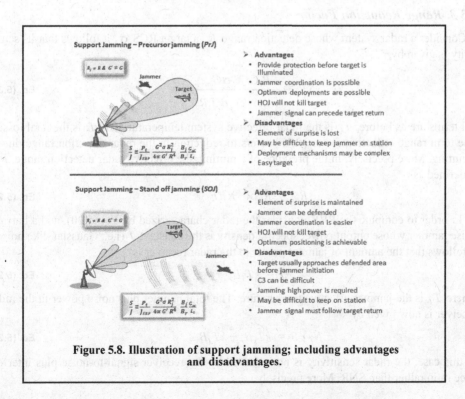

Figure 5.8. Illustration of support jamming; including advantages and disadvantages.

Figure 5.9 shows a plot for a hypothetical radar/SOJ case. This plot shows the powers for the target signal, S, the SOJ signal, J, versus radar-to-target range using semi-log scale. The cross-over range is identified as the range at which $S = J$. As discussed before, if support jamming is employed in the form of Gaussian noise, then the radar receiver deals with the jamming signal the same way it deals with noise power in the radar. This will be discussed further in the next section.

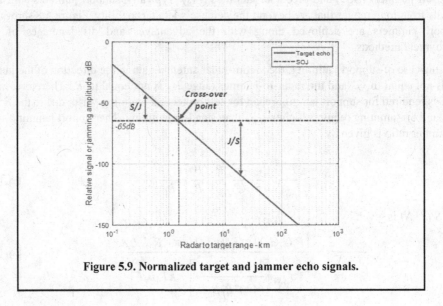

Figure 5.9. Normalized target and jammer echo signals.

5.3.3. Range Reduction Factor

Consider a radar system whose detection range R, a target RCS σ, it follows that its sensitivity is given by,

$$SNR = \frac{P_t G^2 \lambda^2 \sigma G_{pc}}{(4\pi)^3 k T_s B_r L R^4}.$$

Eq. (5.20)

All terms are as before, T_s is the radar effective system temperature and L is the total losses. The term range reduction factor (RRF) refers to reduction in the radar detection range due to jamming. More precisely, in the presence of jamming, the effective radar detection range, R_{dj}, is defined as

$$R_{dj} = R \times RRF.$$

Eq. (5.21)

In order to compute the RRF, consider the radar characterized by Eq. (5.20), and a barrage noise jammer whose output power spectral density is the constant J (i.e., Gaussian-like noise). It follows that the amount of jammer power in the radar receiver is

$$J = k T_J B_r$$

Eq. (5.22)

where T_J is the jammer effective temperature. The total jammer plus noise power in the radar receiver is now given by

$$N_i + J = k T_s B_r + k T_J B_r.$$

Eq. (5.23)

In this case, the radar sensitivity is now limited by the receiver signal-to-noise plus interference ratio rather than SNR. More precisely,

$$\left(\frac{S}{J+N}\right) = \frac{P_t G^2 \lambda^2 \sigma G_{pc}}{(4\pi)^3 k(T_s + T_J)B_r L R^4} \; . \qquad \text{Eq. (5.24)}$$

The amount of reduction in the signal-to-noise plus interference ratio because of the jammer is computed from the difference between Eqs. (5.24) and (5.20). It is expressed (in *dB*) by

$$\Upsilon = 10.0 \times \log\left(1 + \frac{T_J}{T_s}\right). \qquad \text{Eq. (5.25)}$$

Consequently, the RRF is

$$RRF = 10^{\frac{-\Upsilon}{40}}. \qquad \text{Eq. (5.26)}$$

5.4. Noise (Denial) Jamming Techniques

Noise jamming (also called masking or denial jamming) generates "noise-like" signals spread in frequency over the entire victim-radar operating bandwidth. It works by raising the receiver noise floor level, thus, lowering the victim-radar sensitivity (SNR). Noise jamming increases the victim-radar noise floor across its entire operating bandwidth. This effectively makes it very difficult to detect the desired targets. This is the reason why noise jammers are often called maskers (since they mask the target returns) or denial jammers (since they practically deny victim-radars the ability to detect the presence of targets). Noise jamming can be deployed in the main beam or in the sidelobes of the victim-radar antenna.

Noise jamming is typically produced by modulating an RF carrier signal matched to the victim-radar carrier frequency with noise and / or random amplitude changes and then transmitting this signal in the direction of the victim-radar. It requires higher J_{ERP} to saturate the victim-radar receiver when employed against the radar's antenna sidelobes.

5.4.1. Barrage Noise Jamming

The most critical aspect of barrage jamming is its noise power spectral density. It works by injecting noise-like signals into the victim-radar operating bandwidth. If the jammer covers a narrow frequency range of the victim-radar operating bandwidth, it is referred to as narrow-band barrage noise jammer. It covers a wide frequency range, called wide-band barrage noise jammer. This is illustrated in Fig. 5.10.

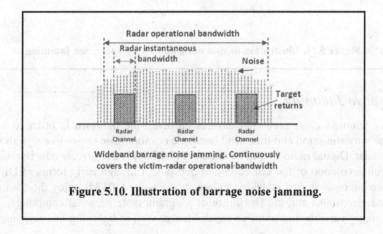

Wideband barrage noise jamming. Continuously covers the victim-radar operational bandwidth

Figure 5.10. Illustration of barrage noise jamming.

Barrage noise jammers can be responsive (i.e., transmit some and listen some) to counter the victim-radar frequency agility. Barrage jamming requires high power to ensure continuous coverage of the victim-radar entire operating bandwidth. This is because the jamming signal is spread over a wide frequency range, which lowers the J_{ERP} at any single frequency. Wideband barrage jamming is useful against frequency-agile radars and against multiple radar systems operating in a specific frequency band. Barrage jamming is simple and can cover a wide portion of the electromagnetic spectrum. The main disadvantage of barrage jamming is its low power density, especially when a high jamming-to-signal (J/S) ratio is needed.

5.4.2. Spot Noise and Sweep Spot Noise Jamming

Spot noise jamming is typically used to alleviate the need for high power sources when applying barrage noise. In this case, only a portion of the victim-radar operational bandwidth needs to be jammed and thus requires less jamming power. This is illustrated in Fig. 5.11-a for a single victim-radar and Fig. 5.11-b for multiple victim-radars. This narrow band spot jamming is tuned to the anticipated frequency of the victim-radar. When it is necessary to simultaneously jam a number of radars at different frequencies, more than one spot noise jamming device is used. The narrow band jamming bandwidth can be up to *10-20 MHz*. Victim-radars can use frequency agility to mitigate the effects of spot noise jamming.

In the case of swept noise, the jamming noise signal is swept across a broad frequency window at varying rates over the entire victim-radar operational bandwidth, as illustrated in Fig. 5.11-c. With this technique, a number of radar systems can be simultaneously jammed, and because of the potentially high jamming power, swept-spot jammers are able to cover a number of radars operating in a broad frequency range.

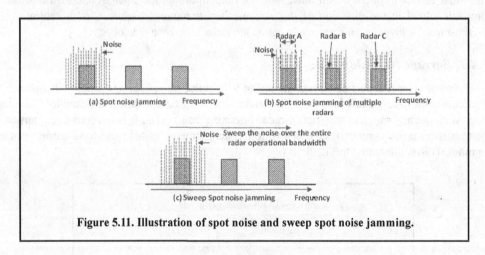

Figure 5.11. Illustration of spot noise and sweep spot noise jamming.

5.5. Deceptive Jamming

Deceptive jammers carry receiving devices on-board the platform in order to analyze the victim-radar's transmission and then send back one or more false target-like signals to confuse the victim-radar. Digital radio frequency memory (DRFM) is a relatively new byproduct of the digital circuit revolution of the last couple of decades. Although early forms of DRFMs have existed since jammers started attacking radars, modern-day DRFMs enjoy the compactness of miniaturized electronics and the flexibility of programmable personal computers. This gives them both highly variable and adaptive capabilities as well as lightning fast responsiveness.

The primary function of a DRFM is to receive a victim radar's transmitted signal, store it, characterize it, and then retransmit one or more copies of it at a selected later time(s), either as a pure copy of what was received, or with specific added modifications (modulations) which impart some false information onto the retransmitted signal. The victim-radar receives this retransmitted signal and, due to its added delay in arriving, is mistaken for an additional target at longer range. If the signal has been modified by the DRFM, the modifications are designed to fool the radar into thinking the false target has alternative attributes like a different range or different velocity than the DRFM.

As suggested above, DRFMs can replicate and retransmit signals received from the victim radar and / or modify those signals before retransmission. If they just repeat the received signal, they are sometimes referred to as repeaters or coherent repeaters. For each delayed retransmission of the stored pulse received from the victim-radar, a separate additional false target is created and then received by the victim radar. The victim-radar then is subjected to multiple false targets (MFT) which it cannot tell apart. In other employments, a DRFM may repeat only one or few pulses with an intent other than the production of MFTs. In these cases the repeated (and usually modified) pulses are usually referred to as "cover pulses".

Cover pulse jamming is a modification to the spot noise jamming technique. In this case, the noise signal is made *responsive* for short periods of time; and accordingly, the jammer acts as a transponder. It receives several victim-radar pulses and determines its pulse repetition frequency. It uses this data to predict when the next radar pulse should arrive. By using an oscillator that is gated for a period of time based on predicted pulse arrival time, a noise-modulated signal is amplified and transmitted to the victim-radar. Effectively, cover pulses mask the target return in range by being much stronger than the target echoes, thus, burying the true target return within them. Although this strong signal is readily detected, it can last long enough to raise the noise floor level. This forces the victim-radar to raise its constant false alarm (CFAR) threshold in a manner that causes the real target returns to fall below this higher threshold level.

Range gate stealer / range gate pull off (RGPO) is another technique of deceptive jamming. It uses DRFMs to create or inject false targets in the victim-radar. This technique works effectively against a radar with a steady pulse repetition frequency. It first employs a cover pulse on top of the target return to take over the range gate. Then the RGPO jammer will slowly over time delay the jamming echoes. It forces the victim-radar to follow the jamming signal to the right or left, as illustrated in Fig. 5.12-a.

Velocity gate pull off (VGPO) is similar to RGPO except in this case the jamming devices work on the Doppler bins of the victim-radar receiver, as illustrated in Fig. 5.12.b. Angle deception jamming is another common technique and its main objective is to introduce angle tracking errors in the victim-radar receiver. Several techniques have been devised to introduce tracking errors in monopulse radars, but they all require high quality information on the victim-radar's parameters, which may not be always available. More robust jamming techniques capable of defeating monopulse include cross-eye and cross-polarization.

Cross-polarization jamming exploits the difference in the victim-radar monopulse antenna patterns to generate a jamming pulse that is orthogonally polarized with respect to the victim-radar principal polarization. The antenna pattern for a monopulse radar using sum and two delta channels shows the tracking point to be between the two beams. However, when the radar also has a receiving pattern for the orthogonally polarized signal, then the cross-polarization jammer shifts its signal one beamwidth (right and left) to confuse the victim-radar using the orthogonally polarized signal. This shift in the tracking axes results in a target tracking signal that is *180°* out of phase with the real signal.

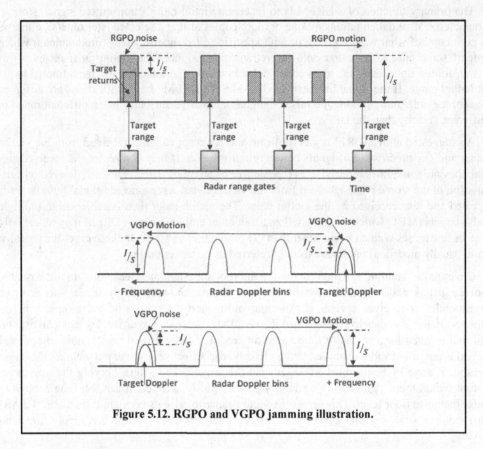

Figure 5.12. RGPO and VGPO jamming illustration.

Once a cross-polarized jammer receives and measures the polarization of the victim monopulse radar, it transmits a very high power (~*25-30 dB* stronger) jamming signal at the same frequency using an orthogonal polarization to the victim-radar to exploit the tracking errors in the cross-polarized antenna pattern. To be effective, a cross-polarized jammer must be able to generate a powerful jamming pulse that is orthogonally polarized with respect to the victim-radar main polarization and the radar's antenna pattern contains as a set of cross-polarized lobes called "Condon lobes". This is illustrated in Fig. 5.13. It should be noted that cross-polarized jamming may not affect flat antennas, such as active electronically scanned array (AESA) and passive electronically scanned array (PESA) since there is no radial geometry that is the typical origin of the Condon lobes.

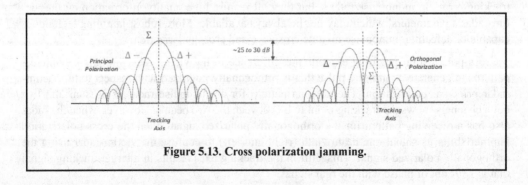

Figure 5.13. Cross polarization jamming.

5.6. Electronic Counter-Counter Measure Techniques

Electronic counter-counter measures (ECCM) describe the techniques used by the defense to mitigate or eliminate the effectiveness of ECM. The ECCM techniques are divided into two major categories. In the first category the intent is to preserve or protect the radar receiver from an ECM attack. While, in the second, the radar uses a combination of hardware and software (mainly algorithms) and advanced waveforms to exploit the attacking ECM device.

5.6.1. Receiver Protection Techniques

In the first category, sensitivity time control (STC) is perhaps the simplest technique utilized by air-defense radar systems. Typically, STC is used to counter receiver front-end saturation caused by close-in chaff, close-in clutter and / or biological clutter like insects and birds. The radar receiver simply reduces its automatic gain control (AGC), i.e., reducing its sensitivity. This ensures that returns from close-in small RCS objects do not saturate the receiver. Accordingly, the receiver gain is set at normal for long ranges and reduced for close-in ranges. One major problem with using STC is that close-in small RCS targets, like unmanned aerial vehicles (UAVs), may be missed if STC is improperly adjusted. Additionally, and perhaps more importantly, at least for ambiguous pulse Doppler radars, the $1/R^3$ STC attenuation curve folds over at the beginning of each ambiguous range interval, greatly enlarging the range blinds at each ambiguous range interval, and undoubtedly at longer range where the radar is already challenged by $1/R^4$ sensitivity roll off.

Automatic gain control is another technique used inside the radar receiver to counter chaff, clutter, and most types of barrage jamming. In this case, the AGC senses the signal level of a receiver's output and develops a back-bias, producing a constant output level. The main drawback of AGC is its slow response time.

Another technique intended to ensure the proper working of the receiver chain is using a logarithmic receiver with a fast time constant. This technique, typically counters narrowband noise jamming, chaff, and clutter. In this technique, the receiver amplifies and demodulates large dynamic-range signals in logarithmic amplifiers, thus, producing "amplitude compression" of the strong signals. The main limitation of this technique includes that the receiver output is nearly constant, so the radar operator cannot always tell when jamming is present. Additionally, this technique is not as effective against wideband barrage noise jamming, or fast-swept jamming, since it causes a broadening of displayed jam sector as well as degrading bearing accuracy on the jamming source.

5.6.2. Jamming Avoidance and Exploitation Techniques

One very common jamming exploitation technique is using frequency agility to counter narrowband jamming and some types of repeater and deception jamming. Frequency agility enables the radar to make rapid changes of transmitter and receiver operating frequency, sometimes on a pulse-to-pulse basis. This prevents the jamming device from locking on the radar center frequency. Caution should be exercised, however, since manual frequency changes may cause mutual interference with other closeby radars. Frequency diversity is similar to frequency agility and works well against narrowband jamming and some types of repeaters and transponders. In this case, the multiple radars are a priori assigned different operating frequencies that are separated to reduce mutual interference and their susceptibility to jamming.

Polarization diversity is another technique used to counter chaff. Also, polarization diversity attenuates jamming input to a radar receiver by using antenna polarization different from the jammer polarization, and usually involves separate radars of different polarization. There are two precautions when using polarization diversity. First, ground clutter worsens when using vertical polarization in the case of air-defense applications. Second, close coordination is necessary if separate radars are used. To this end, one radar can be horizontally polarized radar and another can be vertically polarized radar.

Jamming strobe indicator is another ECCM technique used by radar systems. In this case, the radar counters any transmitted jamming signal with a high-duty-cycle modulation signal. The jamming strobe indicator is a variable marker on the radar display that moves in range proportionally to the jamming signal strength. The indicator traces an antenna lobe pattern on the display, showing the azimuth coordinates of the jamming source. Concerns with jamming strobe indicator is that it interrupts normal radar operations, and sometimes inverse or sidelobe jamming can cause erroneous strobes. Finally, jam strobes do not react to unmodulated continuous wave or low-duty-cycle jamming signals.

Passive angle tracking counters most types of jamming signals by allowing the radar to acquire and to angle-track the jamming signal's source. The primary concerns with this technique include blinking jamming devices which can cause severe instability in the radar receiver. Additionally, the range to the jammer is unavailable until the target reaches burn-through range. Finally, homing on jamming techniques allows the defensive weapon system to lock on the jammer which are typically co-located with the attacking object.

Sidelobe suppression (SLS) is used to counter sidelobe response to chaff, clutter, barrage jamming, sidelobe jamming, as well as deception jamming. In this case, an auxiliary antenna approximates the pattern and gain of sidelobes of the main antenna and produces a signal for comparison with the signal received in the main antenna. If the signal in the auxiliary antenna is greater, the signal in the main antenna channel is blanked and / or canceled. This permits bearings to be obtained on a jamming source to reject it.

5.7. Case Studies

As stated earlier in this chapter, burn-through is one technique that can be used by a victim-radar to mitigate barrage noise jamming. Burn-through techniques include: (1) using longer pulses to increase the victim-radar average transmitted power while utilizing pulse compression techniques (see Chapter 7) to achieve fine range resolution; (2) using pulse integration to effectively increase time (i.e., power) on target; and (3) utilizing wider operational bandwidths to force the jammer to dilute its effective radiated power when it covers the entire victim-radar operational bandwidth.

Using higher transmit antenna gain and / or lowering the receive antenna sidelobe levels can be used to help performance against sidelobe jammers. Lower sidelobe levels reduces the energy introduced by support jammers into the victim-radar. Higher antenna gain forces the escort jammer to remain very close to the target, to remain within the victim-radar main beam. In the following section, two hypothetical case studies are analyzed. The intent of the two case studies is to demonstrate the mitigation techniques discussed in this chapter and they do not trace to any practical scenarios. Simply put, the case studies introduced are a purely mathematical exercise.

5.7.1. Hypothetical Victim-Radar Parameters

Consider a hypothetical C-band radar with the following parameters: operating frequency $f_0 = 5.6 GHz$, peak transmit power $P_t = 50 kW$, operating bandwidth $B_r = 66.7 MHz$, equal transmit and receive antenna gains $G_t = G_r = 35 dB$, transmit losses $L_t = 4 dB$, receive losses $L_r = 3 dB$, and noise figure $F = 5 dB$. Assume that $G_{pc} = 0 dB$. Table 5.1 shows a tabulated Blake chart of this hypothetical radar.

Let the required radar sensitivity to detect and track a target whose RCS is $\sigma = 10 m^2$ using a single pulse with pulse width $\tau = 1.5 \mu s$ be $SNR = 13 dB$. It follows that target range is

$$R = \left(\frac{P_t G_t G_r \lambda^2 \sigma G_{pc} n_p}{(4\pi)^3 k T_0 F B_r L_t L_r (SNR)} \right)^{1/4}$$

Eq. (5.27)

where n_p is the number of coherently integrated pulses. Substituting the values from Table 5.1 into Eq. (5.27) yields

$$R = \left(\frac{((50000) \cdot (10^{3.5})^2 \cdot (0.05375)^2 \cdot (10) \cdot (1) \cdot (1))}{(1984.4) \cdot (4 \times 10^{-21}) \cdot (666.7 \times 10^3) \cdot (10^{(0.5 + 0.4 + 0.3)}) \cdot (10^{1.3})} \right)^{1/4}$$

Eq. (5.28)

$$= (85.7255 \times 10^9)^{1/4} = 54.1 km$$

Alternatively, using the Blake chart (i.e., decibel arithmetic) yields,

$$R^4 \big|_{dB} = 189.333 dB \Leftrightarrow R = 10^{(189.333/40)} = 54.1 km .$$

Eq. (5.29)

The signal power at the radar receiver input is

$$S = P_t + G_r + G_t + \lambda^2 + \sigma + G_{pc} + n_p - (4\pi)^3 - L_t - L_r - R^4$$

Eq. (5.30)

$$= 46.99 + 35.00 + 35.00 - 25.42 - 10.00 - 32.98 - 4.00 - 3.00 - 189.33$$

$$= -127.74 dB \Leftrightarrow 1.68 \times 10^{-13} W .$$

The noise power at the radar receiver input is

$$N = KT_0 + B_r + F = -203.98 + 58.24 + 5 = -140.72 dB \Leftrightarrow 8.47 \times 10^{-15} W .$$

Eq. (5.31)

It follows that the SNR is

$$SNR = \frac{S}{N} = -127.74 + 140.72 = 12.99 dB .$$

Eq. (5.32)

Figure 5.14 shows the SNR ratio versus range. One can clearly see that when the $SNR = 13 dB$, the corresponding target range is $R = 54.1 km$.

5.7.2. Self-Screening Jamming Case

Assume a hypothetical SSJ with the following parameters: jammer power $P_J = 100 W$, jammer antenna gain $G_J = 10 dB$, jammer transmit loss $L_J = 5 dB$, and jammer bandwidth $B_J = 60 MHz$. The jammer effective radiated power is

$$J_{ERP} = \frac{P_J G_j}{L_j} \Rightarrow J_{ERP} \big|_{dB} = 20.00 + 10.00 - 5.00 = 25.00 dB .$$

Eq. (5.33)

Table 5.2 is the jammer Blake chart. The jammer power at the receiver input is

$$J = \frac{P_J G_J}{L_J} \frac{G' \lambda^2}{(4\pi)^2 R_J^2} \frac{B_r}{B_J} \frac{1}{L_r} .$$

Eq. (5.34)

Table 5.1. Hypothetical C-Band Radar Parameters.

Parameter	Symbol	Value	Units	dB Value	Designator
Peak Power	P_t	50,000.00	W	46.99	Numerator
Transmit Gain	G_t	3,162.278	none	35.00	Numerator
Receive Gain	G_r	3,162.278	none	35.00	Numerator
Wavelength	λ^2	$(0.05357)^2$	m^2	-25.42	Numerator
Target RCS	σ	10	m^2	10.00	Numerator
Constant-1	$(4\pi)^3$	1,984.402	none	32.98	Denominator
Constant-2	kT_0	4.002×10^{-21}	W/Hz	-203.98	Denominator
Radar Instanta-neous Bandwidth	B_r	666.67×10^3	Hz	58.24	Denominator
Noise Figure	F	3.162	none	5.00	Denominator
Transmit Loss	L_t	2.512	none	4.00	Denominator
Receive Loss	L_r	1.995	none	3.00	Denominator
Signal-to-Noise Ratio	SNR	19.953	none	13.00	Denominator
Pulse Comp. Gain	G_{pc}	1.00	none	0.00	Numerator
Number of Pulses	n_p	1.00	none	0.00	Numerator
Subtotal				*189.333*	

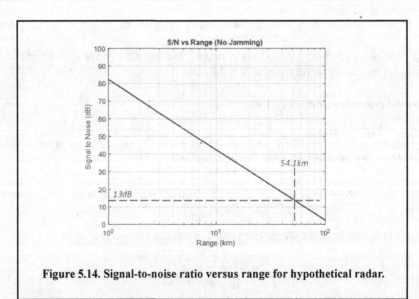

Figure 5.14. Signal-to-noise ratio versus range for hypothetical radar.

Table 5.2. Hypothetical SSJ Blake Chart.

Parameter	Symbol	Value	Units	dB Value	Designator
Peak Power	P_J	100.00	W	20.00	Numerator
Antenna Gain	G_J	10.00	none	10	Numerator
Radar Gain at the Jammer	G'	3,162.278	none	35.00	Numerator
Wavelength	λ^2	$(0.05357)^2$	m^2	-25.42	Numerator
Radar Instantaneous Bandwidth	B_r	666.67×10^3	Hz	58.24	Numerator
Constant-1	$(4\pi)^2$	157.91	none	21.98	Denominator
Jammer Range	R_J^2	$(54.1 \times 10^3)^2$	m^2	94.60	Denominator
Jammer Losses	L_J	3.162	none	5.00	Denominator
Jammer Bandwidth	B_J	60.0×10^6	Hz	77.8	Denominator
Receive Loss	L_r	2.51	none	3.00	Denominator
Subtotal	J			**-104.56**	

Recall that in the case of an SSJ, we have $G' = G_r$ and $R_J = R$. From Table 5.2 and Eq. (5.31), the J/N at *54.1km* is

$$JNR|_{dB} = -104.56 - (-140.72) = 36.16 dB .$$ **Eq. (5.35)**

The jammer power is *36.16 dB* or *4,130* times > noise power. The *S/J* ratio is

$$\left.\frac{S}{J}\right|_{dB} = -127.74 - (-104.56) = -23.2 dB .$$ **Eq. (5.36)**

More specifically, the jammer power at the radar receiver input is *23.2dB* or ~*209* times > signal power. The cross-over range is computed using Eq. (5.15). The cross-over range is

$$(R_{CO})_{SSJ} = \left(\frac{P_t G \sigma B_J G_{pc}}{4\pi B_r L_t (J_{ERP})}\right)^{1/2} .$$ **Eq. (5.37)**

It follows that

$$(R_{co})_{SSJ}|_{dB} = \sqrt{46.99 + 35.00 + 10.00 + 77.78 + 0.00 - 10.99 - 58.28 - 4.00 - 25.00}$$ **Eq. (5.38)**

$$= \sqrt{71.5} = 35.75 dB \Leftrightarrow (R_{co})_{SSJ} = 10^{3.575} = 3.76 km \cdot$$

One can easily verify this result by calculating the signal power and jammer power at *3.76 km*. More specifically,

$$S = 46.99 + 3.500 + 35.0 - 25.42 + 10.0 - 32.98 - 143.0 - 4.0 - 3.0 = -81.4 dB.$$ **Eq. (5.39)**

$$J = 20.0 + 10.0 + 35.0 - 25.42 + 58.24 - 21.98$$
$$- 71.5 - 77.78 - 3.0 - 5.0 = -81.4 dB$$

Eq. (5.40)

Figure 5.15 shows a plot of the signal and jammer powers versus range. Observation of Fig. 5.15 shows that at long range the jammer power at the radar receiver input far exceeds both the signal power and noise power. The target signal power is an R^4 ($40dB$/decade) relationship and the jammer power is an R^2 ($20dB$/decade) relationship. Therefore, as the target gets closer to the radar, you reach a cross-over range where $S/J = 0dB$. Then, as the target gets even closer to radar, you reach a burn-through range when $S/(J+N)$ become large enough (~ *6 to 8 dB*) for the radar to detect the target in the presence of the SSJ. A $S/(J+N)$ of ~ *13 dB* is typically required for stable tracking.

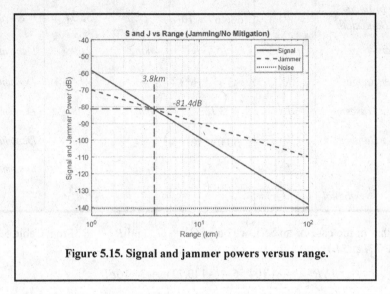

Figure 5.15. Signal and jammer powers versus range.

In this case study, the SSJ has effectively masked the target. By reviewing the analysis and curves, we observe there are several radar design modifications shown below that can be used to help mitigation of the SSJ.

Increase the radar operating bandwidth and use frequency agility

This method forces the jammer designer to increase the jammer operating bandwidth to ensure it covers the entire radar operating bandwidth. This essentially reduces (dilutes) the jammer power relative to the radar's instantaneous bandwidth.

Increase P_t

Although, mathematically, this is the simplest method to burn-through the jamming, it is nonetheless very expensive and accordingly is not recommended.

Increase the radar pulse width (τ)

This method increases the radar energy on the target and pulse compression ensures adequate radar range resolution. Recall, the pulse compression gain, G_{pc} is equal to the time-bandwidth product $B\tau$. However, the maximum pulse width is constrained by the transmitter design and target eclipsing.

Employ coherent or non-coherent pulse integration

Pulse integration (i.e., using $n_p \geq 2$), coherently or non-coherently, increases target signal input power to the receiver and improves sensitivity (i.e., SNR) by a factor of n_p when using coherent integration and a factor of $\sim \sqrt{n_p}$ when employing non-coherent integration (more information on pulse integration can be found in Chapter 8).

By evaluating the above calculations and curves, we observe that the jammer power >> than the noise power at the target ranges of interest. Therefore, J/S is the figure of merit for this scenario. The *J/S* is *23.2dB* at *53 Km* away from the radar in this jamming environment. Therefore, to achieve a *S/J* ratio of *13dB* one must "buy-back" $\sim 39\ dB$ of sensitivity. We will use the following mitigation steps:

1. Keep the radar transmit power at $P_t = 50kW$.

2. Increase the radar operating bandwidth from *56* to *560MHz*. This forces the jammer to increase its operating bandwidth from *60* to *600MHz* to effectively jam the entire radar operating bandwidth. This reduces the effective jammer signal power and *J/S* by a factor of *10* or *10dB*.

3. Increase the radar pulse width from $\tau = 1.5\mu s$ to $\tau = 150\mu s$. This increases the energy on the target by a factor of *100* or 20dB. We recall the radar eclipsing range (i.e., minimum detection range) decreases as τ is increased. Since, the un-eclipsed range is given by $R_m = c\tau/2$, then a $150\mu s$ pulse will eclipse targets at ranges less than *22.5km*. For our design, we will use $150\mu s$ pulses for ranges > *25 Km*, $75\mu s$ pulses at ranges between *12.5* and *25 km* (*12.5km < R < 25km*), $37.5\mu s$ pulses for ranges between *6* and *12.5*, and $18.5\mu s$ pulses for ranges between *3* and *6km*. The pulse compression gain is a factor of *20dB* for the $150\mu s$ pulse, a factor of 17dB for the $75\mu s$ pulse, a factor of *14dB* for the $37.5\mu s$ pulse, and a factor of *11dB* for the $18.5\mu s$ pulse.

4. Use coherent pulse integration. If one coherently integrates *10* pulses to increase the receiver signal input power increases by *10dB* (i.e., a factor of *10*).

These mitigation steps provide S/J of greater than *11dB* for target ranges up to *40km*. The corresponding performance curves are shown in Figs. 5.16 and 5.17. The step-like changes in these plots indicate a *3dB* change corresponding to the different pulses used to avoid eclipsing in the mitigation process. The S/J improvements are clearly indicated in Fig. 5.17.

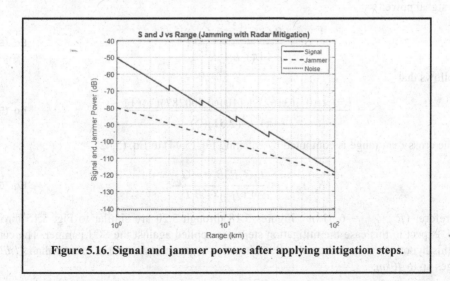

Figure 5.16. Signal and jammer powers after applying mitigation steps.

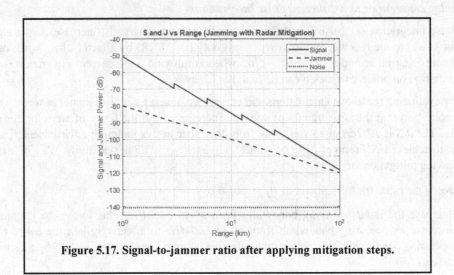

Figure 5.17. Signal-to-jammer ratio after applying mitigation steps.

5.7.3. Support Jamming Case

In this case, assume a hypothetical side lobe jammer is employed with the following parameters: $P_J = 5000\,W$, jammer antenna gain $G_J = 30\,dB$, radar-to-jammer range $R = 20\,km$, and jammer transmit losses $L_J = 5\,dB$. The radar antenna gain in the direction of the jammer is $G' = 3\,dB$ (typically this value is taken as the rms value of the radar antenna's sidelobe gain). The jamming power at the radar receiver is

$$J = \frac{P_J G_J}{L_J} \cdot \frac{G'\lambda^2}{(4\pi)^2 R_J^2} \frac{B_r}{B_J} \frac{1}{L_r}.$$
Eq. (5.41)

It follows that

$$J = \frac{(5000)(1000)(2)(0.000287)(667 \times 10^3)}{(2.16)(157.9)(20 \times 10^3)(60 \times 10^6)(2)} = 87.99 \times 10^{-10}\,W \Leftrightarrow J = -90.97\,dB .$$
Eq. (5.42)

The signal power is

$$S = \frac{P_t G_t G_r \lambda^2 \sigma n_p G_{pc}}{(4\pi)^3 L_t L_r R^4},$$
Eq. (5.43)

It follows that

$$S = \frac{(50 \times 10^3)(3162.3)^2(10)(0.000287)(1)(1)}{(4\pi)^3 R^4 (2.51)(2)}.$$
Eq. (5.44)

The cross-over range is computed by equating Eq. (5.44) to Eq. (5.42),

$$(R_{co})_{SOJ} = \frac{P_t G^2 R_J^2 B_J \sigma n_p G_{pc}}{4\pi J_{ERP} G' B_r L_t}.$$
Eq. (5.45)

Therefore, $(R_{co})_{SOJ} = 6.51\,km$. Figures 5.18 through 5.20 are similar to Fig. 5.15 through 5.17, expect in this case the mitigation steps are applied against the SOJ jammer. The curves for this hypothetical case show that the mitigation steps achieve a S/J of greater than *11dB* for ranges up to *40km*.

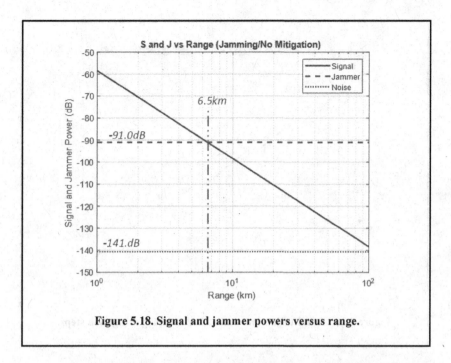

Figure 5.18. Signal and jammer powers versus range.

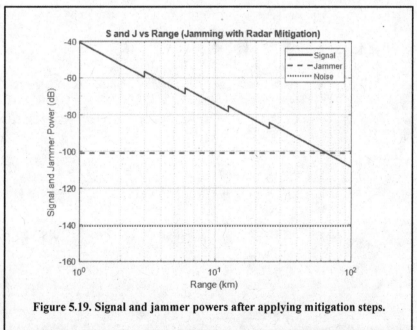

Figure 5.19. Signal and jammer powers after applying mitigation steps.

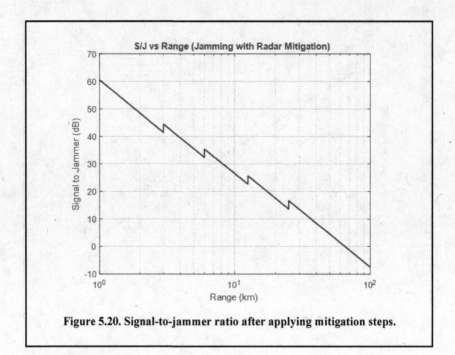

Figure 5.20. Signal-to-jammer ratio after applying mitigation steps.

Chapter 6

Matched Filter
Receiver

Bassem R. Mahafza

6.1. Matched Filtering

The topics of matched filtering and pulse compression are central to almost all radar systems. Pulse compression is a signal processing application made possible through the use of a linear time invariant (LTI) filter known as the matched filter. The most unique characteristic of the matched filter is that it produces the maximum achievable instantaneous signal-to-noise ratio (SNR) at its output when a signal plus additive white noise is present at the input. Maximizing the SNR means increasing the radar sensitivity, which significantly improves the extraction of target specific attributes from the radar echoes or returned signal. Accordingly, it is important to use a radar receiver which can be modeled as an LTI system that maximizes the signal's SNR at its output. For this purpose, the basic radar receiver of interest is often referred to as the "matched filter receiver". The matched filter is an optimum filter in the sense of SNR because the SNR at its output is maximized at some delay t_0 that corresponds to the true target range R_0 (i.e., $t_0 = (2R_0)/c$).

Figure 6.1 shows a simplified block diagram for the radar receiver of interest. In order to derive the general expression for the transfer function and the impulse response of this optimum filter, adopt the following notation:

$h(t)$ is the optimum filter impulse response

$H(f)$ is the optimum filter transfer function

$x_i(t) = a_i x(t - t_0)$ is a scaled and delayed copy of the radar transmitted signal $x(t)$

$X_i(f)$ is the Fourier transform of the signal $x_i(t)$

$x_o(t)$ is the output signal due to the input signal $x_i(t)$

$X_o(f)$ is the Fourier transform of the signal $x_o(t)$

$n_i(t)$ is the input noise signal

$N_i(f)$ is the input noise power spectrum density

$n_o(t)$ is the output noise signal

$N_o(f)$ is the output noise power spectrum density

The filter input signal is

$$s_i(t) = x_i(t) + n_i(t) \Rightarrow s_i(t) = a_i x(t - t_0) + n_i(t)$$

Eq. (6.1)

183

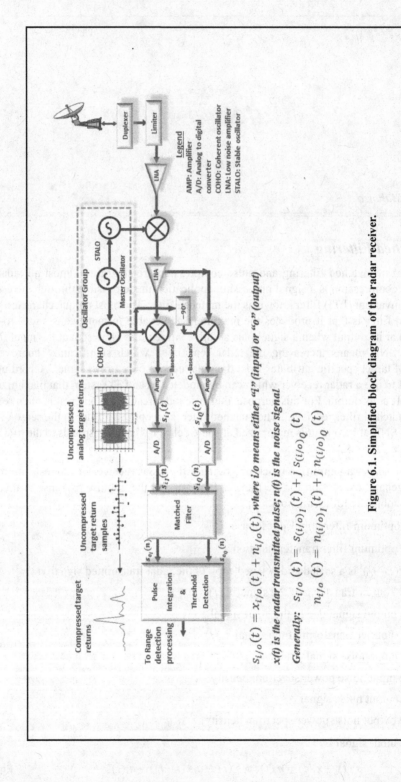

Figure 6.1. Simplified block diagram of the radar receiver.

$$s_o(t) = x_o(t) + n_o(t) \qquad\qquad \text{Eq. (6.2)}$$

$$n_o(t) = n_i(t) \otimes h(t) = \int_{-\infty}^{\infty} n_i(u) h(t-u) du \qquad\qquad \text{Eq. (6.3)}$$

$$x_o(t) = x_i(t) \otimes h(t) = a_i x(t - t_0) \otimes h(t) = \int_{-\infty}^{\infty} a_i x(u - t_0) h(t-u) du. \qquad \text{Eq. (6.4)}$$

The constant a_i can be set to unity without any loss of generality. The desired objective is to determine the impulse response $h(t)$ for the optimum filter so that the SNR at its output is maximum at some time $t = t_0$, more specifically

$$max\{SNR(t)\} = SNR(t)\big|_{t_0} = \frac{P_{x_o}\big|_{t_0}}{\sigma_{n_o}^2}, \qquad\qquad \text{Eq. (6.5)}$$

where P_{xo} is the normalized output signal power and $\sigma_{n_o}^2$ is the total output noise power.

Output Signal Power

The normalized signal power at the output of the optimum filter is

$$P_{xo} = |x_o(t)|^2. \qquad\qquad \text{Eq. (6.6)}$$

Using Eq. (6.4) and the Fourier transform properties, the signal $x_o(t)$ may be expressed in the form

$$x_o(t) = x_i(t) \otimes h(t) = \mathcal{F}^{-1}\{X_i(f) H(f)\} = \int_{-\infty}^{\infty} X_i(f) H(f) e^{j2\pi ft} \, df, \qquad \text{Eq. (6.7)}$$

where $X_i(f)$ and $H(f)$ are, respectively, the Fourier transform for $x_i(t)$ and $h(t)$. The signal power at the output can then be written as,

$$P_{x_o} = \left| \int_{-\infty}^{\infty} X_i(f) H(f) e^{j2\pi ft} \, df \right|^2. \qquad\qquad \text{Eq. (6.8)}$$

Since we are interested in maximizing the SNR at $t = t_0$, we can rewrite Eq. (6.8) at t_0 as

$$P_{x_o}\big|_{t_0} = \left| \int_{-\infty}^{\infty} X_i(f) H(f) e^{j2\pi ft_0} \, df \right|^2. \qquad\qquad \text{Eq. (6.9)}$$

Output Noise Power

A special case of great interest to radar applications is when the input noise is bandlimited stationary white noise with zero mean. Therefore, the input noise auto-correlation function is

$$\overline{\mathcal{R}}_{n_i}(t) = \frac{\eta_0}{2} \delta(t) \qquad\qquad \text{Eq. (6.10)}$$

where η_0 is constant. The corresponding input noise power spectrum density is then given by

$$S_{n_i}(f) = \mathcal{F}\left\{ \frac{\eta_0}{2} \delta(t) \right\} = \frac{\eta_0}{2} \qquad \left(\frac{Watts}{Hz} \right) \qquad \text{Eq. (6.11)}$$

The auto-correlation for the output noise signal $n_o(t)$ is

$$\overline{\mathcal{R}}_{n_o}(t) = \frac{\eta_0}{2}|H(f)|^2$$

Eq. (6.12)

It follows that the total output noise power is

$$\sigma_{n_o}^2 = \int_{-\infty}^{\infty} \frac{\eta_0}{2}|H(f)|^2 df = \frac{\eta_0}{2}\int_{-\infty}^{\infty} |H(f)|^2 df.$$

Eq. (6.13)

Signal-to-Noise Ratio

The SNR at the output of the optimum filter is determined from Eqs. (6.9) and (6.13) as

$$SNR(t_0) = \frac{\left|\int_{-\infty}^{\infty} X_i(f)H(f)e^{j2\pi ft_0} \, df\right|^2}{\frac{\eta_0}{2}\int_{-\infty}^{\infty} |H(f)|^2 df}.$$

Eq. (6.14)

The $SNR(t_0)$ is maximum when the numerator of Eq. (6.14) is maximum. Remember the Cauchy-Schwarz's inequality of the form

$$\left|\int_{-\infty}^{\infty} X_1(u)X_2^*(u) \, du\right|^2 \le \int_{-\infty}^{\infty} |X_1(u)|^2 \, du \int_{-\infty}^{\infty} |X_2(u)|^2 \, du,$$

Eq. (6.15)

The left-hand side of the Cauchy-Schwarz's inequality is similar to the numerator of Eq. (6.14). Clearly the maximum value for the left-hand side of Eq. (6.15) occurs when the left-hand side is equal to the right-hand side. It is well documented in the literature that equality in Eq. (6.15) occurs when $X_1(u) = KX_2(u)$ for some arbitrary constant K, which can be set to unity. Applying the Cauchy-Schwarz's inequality to Eq. (6.14) yields

$$SNR(t_0) = \frac{\left|\int_{-\infty}^{\infty} X_i(f)H(f)e^{j2\pi ft_0} \, df\right|^2}{\frac{\eta_0}{2}\int_{-\infty}^{\infty} |H(f)|^2 df} \le \frac{\int_{-\infty}^{\infty} |X_i(f)|^2 \, df \int_{-\infty}^{\infty} |H(f)|^2 \, df}{\frac{\eta_0}{2}\int_{-\infty}^{\infty} |H(f)|^2 df},$$

Eq. (6.16)

or

$$SNR(t_0) \le \frac{\int_{-\infty}^{\infty} |X_i(f)|^2 \, df}{\frac{\eta_0}{2}}.$$

Eq. (6.17)

Equality in Eq. (6.17) holds if and only if

$$H(f) = X_i^*(f)e^{-j2\pi ft_0}.$$

Eq. (6.18)

The impulse response $h(t)$ is determined from

$$h(t) = \mathcal{F}^{-1}\{X_i^*(f)e^{-j2\pi ft_0}\} = \int_{-\infty}^{\infty} X_i^*(f)e^{-j2\pi ft_0}e^{j2\pi ft} df =$$

Eq. (6.19)

$$\int_{-\infty}^{\infty} X_i^*(f)e^{-j2f(t_0-t)} df = \left[\int_{-\infty}^{\infty} X_i(f)e^{j2f(t_0-t)} df\right]^* = x_i^*(t_0-t)$$

This means that the transfer function of the optimum filter is matched to the conjugate of a time reversed and delayed copy of the signal $x_i(t)$.

When the condition in Eq. (6.19) is satisfied, the maximum SNR at the output of the filter is determined from Eq. (6.17) as

$$max\{SNR(t)\} = SNR(t_0) = \frac{\int_{-\infty}^{\infty} |X_i(f)|^2 \, df}{\dfrac{\eta_0}{2}}. \qquad \text{Eq. (6.20)}$$

However, the energy, E_{x_i}, for the signal $x_i(t)$ is

$$E_{x_i} = \int_{-\infty}^{\infty} |X_i(f)|^2 \, df. \qquad \text{Eq. (6.21)}$$

Consequently, the maximum output (i.e., peak) instantaneous SNR for the optimum filter is

$$SNR(t_0) = \frac{2E_{x_i}}{\eta_0}. \qquad \text{Eq. (6.22)}$$

Note that Eq. (6.22) is unitless since the units for η_0 are in *Watts/Hertz* (or Joules). Observation of Eq. (6.22) indicates that the maximum SNR depends on the input signal energy and the input noise power density and is independent of the waveform.

6.1.1. Matched Filter Impulse Response

Equation (6.19) indicates that the impulse response for the desired optimum filter that maximizes the instantaneous SNR at its output is

$$h(t) = x_i^*(t_0 - t). \qquad \text{Eq. (6.23)}$$

But from Eq. (6.1) the input signal $x_i(t)$ is an amplitude scaled delayed copy of the radar transmitted pulse $x(t)$, more specifically

$$x_i(t) = a_i x(t - t_0). \qquad \text{Eq. (6.24)}$$

Set a_i to unity and substitute Eq. (6.24) into Eq. (6.23) yield

$$h(t) = x_i^*(t_0 - t) = x^*(t_0 - t + t_0) = x^*(-t). \qquad \text{Eq. (6.25)}$$

This means that the non-casual (i.e., not physically realizable) impulse response of the optimum filter is matched to the conjugate of a time reversed copy of the radar transmitted signal. Accordingly the term *matched filter* is adopted.

To ensure causality, an additional time delay term $\tau_0 \geq T$ is added, where T is the transmitted signal duration. Thus, the realizable matched filter response is given by

$$h(t) = x^*(\tau_0 - t). \qquad \text{Eq. (6.26)}$$

6.1.2. The Replica

Again, consider a radar system that uses a finite duration energy signal $x(t)$ and assume that a matched filter receiver is utilized. From Eq. (6.1) the input signal can be written as,

$$s_i(t) = x(t - t_0) + n_i(t). \qquad \text{Eq. (6.27)}$$

The causal matched filter output $s_o(t)$ is determined from the convolution integral between the filter's impulse response and $s_i(t)$:

$$s_0(t) = \int_{-\infty}^{\infty} s_i(u)h(t-u)du.$$

Eq. (6.28)

Substituting Eq. (6.26) into Eq. (6.28) yields

$$s_o(t) = \int_{-\infty}^{\infty} s_i(u)x^*(u-t+\tau_0)du = \overline{\mathscr{R}}_{sx}(t-\tau_0)$$

Eq. (6.29)

where $\overline{\mathscr{R}}_{sx}(t-\tau_0)$ is the cross-correlation between $s(t)$ and $x(t-\tau_0)$. Thus, the causal matched filter output can be computed from the cross-correlation between the radar received signal and a delayed replica of the transmitted waveform. If the input signal is the same as the transmitted signal, the output of the matched filter would be the autocorrelation function of the received (or transmitted) signal. In practice, replicas of the transmitted waveforms are normally computed and stored in memory for use by the radar signal processor when needed.

6.1.3. Mean and Variance of the Matched Filter Output

Since the matched filter is an LTI filter, when its input statistics are Gaussian, its output statistics are also Gaussian. For this purpose, consider the following two hypotheses. Hypothesis H_0 is when the input to the matched filter consists of noise only. That is,

$$H_0 \Leftrightarrow s(t) = n_i(t)$$

Eq. (6.30)

where $n_i(t)$ is stationary zero mean Gaussian bandlimited white noise with power spectrum density $\eta_0/2$. Hypothesis H_1 is when the input consists of signal plus noise. That is,

$$H_1 \Leftrightarrow s(t) = x(t) + n_i(t).$$

Eq. (6.31)

Denote the conditional means and variances for both hypotheses by: $E[s_o/H_0]$ is the mean value of $s_0(\tau_0)$, when the signal is absent; $E[s_o/H_1]$ is the mean value of $s_0(\tau_0)$ when the signal is present; $Var[s_o/H_0]$ is the variance of $s_0(\tau_0)$ when the signal is absent; and $Var[s_o/H_1]$ is the variance of $s_0(\tau_0)$ when the signal is present. It follows that

$$E[s_o/H_0] = 0$$

Eq. (6.32)

$$E[s_o/H_1] = \int_{-\infty}^{\infty} |x_i(t)|^2 \, dt = E_x$$

Eq. (6.33)

where E_x is the signal energy. Finally,

$$Var[s_o/H_0] = Var[s_o/H_1] = \int_{-\infty}^{\infty} \left(\frac{\eta_0}{2}\right)|H(f)|^2 df.$$

Eq. (6.34)

6.2. General Formula for the Output of the Matched Filter

Two cases are analyzed: the first is when a stationary target is present, and the second case is concerned with a moving target whose velocity is constant. Assume the range to the target is

$$R(t) = R_0 - v(t-t_0)$$

Eq. (6.35)

where v is the target radial velocity (i.e., the target velocity component on the radar line of sight.) The initial detection range R_0 is given by

$$R_0 = \frac{ct_0}{2} \Rightarrow t_0 = \frac{2R_0}{c}$$

Eq. (6.36)

where c is the speed of light and t_0 is the round trip delay it takes a certain radar pulse to travel from the radar to the target at range R_0 and back.

The general expression for the transmitted radar bandpass signal is

$$x(t) = x_I(t)\cos(2\pi f_0 t) - x_Q(t)\sin(2\pi f_0 t)$$

Eq. (6.37)

which can be written using its pre-envelope (analytic signal, see Chapter 1) as

$$x(t) = Re\{\psi(t)\} = Re\{\tilde{x}(t)e^{j2\pi f_0 t}\}$$

Eq. (6.38)

where $Re\{\ \}$ indicates "the real part of," and $\tilde{x}(t)$ is the complex envelope.

6.2.1. Stationary Target Case

In this case, the received radar return, assuming a normalized amplitude, is given by

$$s_r(t) = x\left(t - \frac{2R_0}{c}\right) = x(t - t_0) = Re\{\tilde{x}(t - t_0)e^{j2\pi f_0(t - t_0)}\}.$$

Eq. (6.39)

It follows that the received analytic and complex envelope signals are, respectively, given by

$$\psi_r(t) = \tilde{x}(t - t_0)e^{-j2\pi f_0 t_0}e^{j2\pi f_0 t} = \tilde{s}_r(t)e^{j2\pi f_0 t}$$

Eq. (6.40)

$$\tilde{s}_r(t) = \tilde{x}(t - t_0)e^{-j2\pi f_0 t_0}.$$

Eq. (6.41)

Observation of Eq. (6.41) clearly indicates that the received complex envelope is more than just a delayed version of the transmitted complex envelope. It actually contains an additional phase shift φ_0 which represents the phase corresponding to the two-way optical length for the target range. That is,

$$\varphi_0 = -2\pi f_0 t_0 = -2\pi f_0 2\frac{R_0}{c} = -\frac{2\pi}{\lambda}2R_0$$

Eq. (6.42)

where λ is the radar wavelength and is equal to c/f_0. Since a very small change in range can produce significant change in this phase term, this phase is often treated as a random variable with uniform probability density function over the interval $\{0, 2\pi\}$. Furthermore, the radar signal processor will first attempt to remove (correct for) this phase term through a process known as phase unwrapping.

The output of the causal matched filter is determined through the convolution between the input signal and the transfer function, it is

$$s_o(t) = \int_{-\infty}^{\infty} \tilde{s}_r(u)h(t - u)du$$

Eq. (6.43)

where the impulse response $h(t)$ is in Eq. (6.26). It follows that

$$s_o(t) = \int_{-\infty}^{\infty} \tilde{x}(u - t_0)e^{-j2\pi f_0 t_0}\ \tilde{x}^*(u - t + \tau_0)du.$$

Eq. (6.44)

Make the following change of variables:

$$z = u - t_0 \Rightarrow dz = du.$$

Eq. (6.45)

Therefore, the output of the matched filter when a stationary target is present is

$$s_o(t) = e^{-j2\pi f_0 t_0} \int_{-\infty}^{\infty} \tilde{x}(z)\tilde{x}^*(z - t + \tau_0 + t_0)dz = e^{-j2\pi f_0 t_0} \mathcal{R}_x(t - \tau_0 - t_0) \qquad \text{Eq. (6.46)}$$

where $\mathcal{R}_x(t)$ is the autocorrelation function for the signal $\tilde{x}(t)$ and has a peak equal to $\mathcal{R}_x(0)$ which occurs at $t = \tau_0 + t_0$.

6.2.2. Moving Target Case

In this case, the received signal is not only delayed in time by t_0, but it also has a Doppler frequency shift f_d corresponding to the target velocity, where

$$f_d = \frac{2vf_0}{c} = \frac{2v}{\lambda}. \qquad \text{Eq. (6.47)}$$

The pre-envelope of the received signal, assuming a normalized amplitude, can be written as

$$\psi_r(t) = \psi\left(t - \frac{2R(t)}{c}\right) = \tilde{x}\left(t - \frac{2R(t)}{c}\right)e^{j2\pi f_0\left(t - \frac{2R(t)}{c}\right)} \qquad \text{Eq. (6.48)}$$

substituting Eq. (6.35) into Eq. (6.48) yields

$$\psi_r(t) = \tilde{x}\left(t - \frac{2R_0}{c} + \frac{2vt}{c} - \frac{2vt_0}{c}\right)e^{j2\pi f_0\left(t - \frac{2R_0}{c} + \frac{2vt}{c} - \frac{2vt_0}{c}\right)}, \qquad \text{Eq. (6.49)}$$

collecting terms yields

$$\psi_r(t) = \tilde{x}\left(t\left(1 + \frac{2v}{c}\right) - t_0\left(1 + \frac{2v}{c}\right)\right)e^{j2\pi f_0\left(t - \frac{2R_0}{c} + \frac{2vt}{c} - \frac{2vt_0}{c}\right)}. \qquad \text{Eq. (6.50)}$$

Define the scaling factor γ as

$$\gamma = 1 + \frac{2v}{c} \qquad \text{Eq. (6.51)}$$

then Eq. (6.50) can be written as

$$\psi_r(t) = \tilde{x}(\gamma(t - t_0))e^{j2\pi f_0\left(t - \frac{2R_0}{c} + \frac{2vt}{c} - \frac{2vt_0}{c}\right)}. \qquad \text{Eq. (6.52)}$$

Since $c \gg v$, the following approximation can be used

$$\tilde{x}(\gamma(t - t_0)) \approx \tilde{x}(t - t_0). \qquad \text{Eq. (6.53)}$$

It follows that Eq. (6.52) can now be rewritten as

$$\psi_r(t) = \tilde{x}(t - t_0)e^{j2\pi f_0 t}e^{-j2\pi f_0 \frac{2R_0}{c}}e^{j2\pi f_0 \frac{2vt}{c}}e^{-j2\pi f_0 \frac{2vt_0}{c}}. \qquad \text{Eq. (6.54)}$$

Recognizing that $f_d = (2vf_0)/c$ and $t_0 = (2R_0)/c$, the received pre-envelope signal is

$$\psi_r(t) = \tilde{x}(t - t_0)e^{j2\pi f_0 t}e^{-j2\pi f_0 t_0}e^{j2\pi f_d t}e^{-j2\pi f_d t_0} = \tilde{s}(t - t_0)e^{j2\pi(f_0 + f_d)(t - t_0)} \qquad \text{Eq. (6.55)}$$

or

$$\psi_r(t) = \{\tilde{x}(t - t_0)e^{j2\pi f_d t}e^{-j2\pi(f_0 + f_d)t_0}\}e^{j2\pi f_0 t}. \qquad \text{Eq. (6.56)}$$

Then by inspection, the complex envelope of the received signal is

$$\tilde{x}_r(t) = \tilde{x}(t - t_0) e^{j2\pi f_d t} e^{-j2\pi(f_0 + f_d)t_0}.$$

Eq. (6.57)

Finally, it is concluded that the complex envelope of the received signal when the target is moving at a constant velocity v is a delayed (by t_0) version of the complex envelope signal of the stationary target case except that:

1. An additional phase shift term corresponding to the target's Doppler frequency is present,

2. The phase shift term $(-2\pi f_d t_0)$ is present.

The output of the matched filter was given in Eq. (6.28). Substituting Eq. (6.57) into Eq. (6.28) yields

$$s_o(t) = \int_{-\infty}^{\infty} \tilde{x}(u - t_0) e^{j2\pi f_d u} e^{-j2\pi(f_0 + f_d)t_0} \tilde{x}^*(u - t + \tau_0) \; du.$$

Eq. (6.58)

Applying the change of variables given in Eq. (6.45) and collecting terms provide

$$s_o(t) = e^{-j2\pi f_0 t_0} \int_{-\infty}^{\infty} \tilde{x}(z)\tilde{x}^*(z - t + \tau_0 + t_0) e^{j2\pi f_d z} e^{j2\pi f_d t_0} e^{-j2\pi f_d t_0} \; dz.$$

Eq. (6.59)

Observation of Eq. (6.59) indicates that the output is a function of both t and f_d. Thus, it is more appropriate to rewrite the output of the matched filter as a two-dimensional function of both variables. That is,

$$s_o(t;f_d) = e^{-j2\pi f_0 t_0} \int_{-\infty}^{\infty} \tilde{x}(z)\tilde{x}^*(z - t + \tau_0 + t_0) e^{j2\pi f_d z} \; dz.$$

Eq. (6.60)

6.3. Waveform Resolution

As indicated by Eq. (6.22), the radar sensitivity (in the case of white additive noise) depends only on the total energy of the received signal and is independent of the shape of the specific waveform. This leads to the following question: If the radar sensitivity is independent of the waveform, then what is the best choice for the transmitted waveform? The answer depends on many factors; however, perhaps the most important consideration next to sensitivity lies in the waveform's range and Doppler resolution characteristics, which can be determined from the output of the matched filter.

6.3.1. Range Resolution

Consider radar returns from two equal-sized stationary targets (i.e., zero Doppler) separated in range by distance ΔR. Ask the question: What is the smallest value of ΔR so that the returned signal is interpreted by the radar as two distinct targets? In order to answer this question, assume that the radar transmitted bandpass pulse is denoted by $x(t)$,

$$x(t) = r(t)\cos(2\pi f_0 t + \phi(t))$$

Eq. (6.61)

where f_0 is the carrier frequency, $r(t)$ is the amplitude modulation, and $\phi(t)$ is the phase modulation. The signal $x(t)$ can then be expressed as the real part of the pre-envelope signal $\psi(t)$, where

$$\psi(t) = r(t)e^{j(2\pi f_0 t - \phi(t))} = \tilde{x}(t)e^{2\pi f_0 t}$$

Eq. (6.62)

and the complex envelope is

$$\tilde{x}(t) = r(t)e^{-j\phi(t)}, \qquad\qquad\qquad \text{Eq. (6.63)}$$

it follows that

$$x(t) = Re\{\psi(t)\}. \qquad\qquad\qquad \text{Eq. (6.64)}$$

The returns from two close targets are, respectively, given by

$$x_1(t) = \psi(t - \tau_0) \qquad\qquad\qquad \text{Eq. (6.65)}$$

$$x_2(t) = \psi(t - \tau_0 - \tau) \qquad\qquad\qquad \text{Eq. (6.66)}$$

where τ is the difference in delay between the two target returns. One can assume that the reference time is τ_0, and thus without any loss of generality, one may set $\tau_0 = 0$. It follows that the two targets are distinguishable by how large or small the delay τ can be.

In order to measure the difference in range between the two targets, consider the integral square error between $\psi(t)$ and $\psi(t - \tau)$. Denoting this error as ε_R^2, it follows that

$$\varepsilon_R^2 = \int_{-\infty}^{\infty} |\psi(t) - \psi(t - \tau)|^2 \ dt \qquad\qquad\qquad \text{Eq. (6.67)}$$

which can be written as

$$\varepsilon_R^2 = \int_{-\infty}^{\infty} |\psi(t)|^2 dt + \int_{-\infty}^{\infty} |\psi(t - \tau)|^2 dt - \int_{-\infty}^{\infty} \{(\psi(t)\psi^*(t - \tau) + \psi^*(t)\psi(t - \tau))dt\} \quad \text{Eq. (6.68)}$$

Using Eq. (6.62) into Eq. (6.68) yields

$$\varepsilon_R^2 = 2\int_{-\infty}^{\infty} |\tilde{x}(t)|^2 \ dt - 2Re\left\{\int_{-\infty}^{\infty} \psi^*(t)\psi(t - \tau) \ dt\right\} = \qquad \text{Eq. (6.69)}$$

$$2\int_{-\infty}^{\infty} |\tilde{x}(t)|^2 \ dt - 2Re\left\{e^{-j\omega_0\tau}\int_{-\infty}^{\infty} \tilde{x}^*(t)\tilde{x}(t - \tau) \ dt\right\}.$$

This squared error is minimum when the second portion of the right-hand side of Eq. (6.69) is positive and maximum. Note that the first term in the right-hand side of Eq. (6.69) represents the total signal energy and is assumed to be constant. The second term is a varying function of τ with its fluctuation tied to the carrier frequency. The modulus square of the integral inside the right-most side of this equation is defined as the range ambiguity function,

$$\chi_R(\tau) = \left|\int_{-\infty}^{\infty} \tilde{x}^*(t)\tilde{x}(t - \tau) \ dt\right|^2. \qquad\qquad\qquad \text{Eq. (6.70)}$$

This range ambiguity function is modulus square of the right-hand side of Eq. (6.46). A comparison between Eqs. (6.70) and (6.46) indicates that the output of the matched filter and the range ambiguity function have similar envelopes (in this case, the Doppler shift f_d is set to zero). This indicates that the matched filter, in addition to providing the maximum instantaneous SNR at its output, also preserves the signal range resolution properties. The value of $\chi_R(\tau)$ that minimizes the squared error in Eq. (6.69) occurs when $\tau = 0$. Target resolvability in range is measured by the function $\chi_R(\tau)$. As a consequence, the most desirable shape for $\chi_R(\tau)$ is a very sharp peak (thumbtack shape) centered at $\tau = 0$ and falls very quickly away from the peak. However, this ideal thumbtack shape is not physically realizable since physically realizable waveforms have finite effective duration and finite effective bandwidth.

The minimum range resolution corresponding to a time duration τ_e or effective bandwidth B_e is

$$\Delta R = \frac{c\tau_e}{2} = \frac{c}{2B_e}.$$ **Eq. (6.71)**

Define the effective time duration and bandwidth for any waveform $\tilde{x}(t)$ as

$$\tau_e = \frac{\left[\int_{-\infty}^{\infty} |\tilde{x}(t)|^2 dt\right]^2}{\int_{-\infty}^{\infty} |\tilde{x}(t)|^4 dt}$$ **Eq. (6.72)**

$$B_e = \frac{\left[\int_{-\infty}^{\infty} |\tilde{X}(f)|^2 df\right]^2}{\int_{-\infty}^{\infty} |\tilde{X}(f)|^4 df}$$ **Eq. (6.73)**

where $\tilde{X}(f)$ is the Fourier transform for $\tilde{x}(t)$.

6.3.2. Doppler Resolution

The Doppler shift corresponding to the target radial velocity is

$$f_d = \frac{2v}{\lambda} = \frac{2vf_0}{c}$$ **Eq. (6.74)**

where v is the target radial velocity, λ is the wavelength, f_0 is the frequency, and c is the speed of light.

The Fourier transform of the pre-envelope is

$$\Psi(f) = \int_{-\infty}^{\infty} \psi(t)e^{-j2\pi ft} dt.$$ **Eq. (6.75)**

The Doppler shift associated with the target causes the received signal spectrum to shift by f_d. In other words, the received spectrum can be represented by $\Psi(f-f_d)$. In order to distinguish between the two targets located at the same range but having different velocities, one may use the integral square error. More precisely,

$$\varepsilon_f^2 = \int_{-\infty}^{\infty} |\Psi(f) - \Psi(f-f_d)|^2 df.$$ **Eq. (6.76)**

Using similar analysis as that which led to Eq. (6.69), one should maximize

$$Re\left\{\int_{-\infty}^{\infty} \Psi^*(f)\Psi(f-f_d) df\right\}.$$ **Eq. (6.77)**

Taking the Fourier transform of the pre-envelope (analytic signal) defined in Eq. (6.62) yields

$$\Psi(f) = \mathcal{F}\{\psi(t)\} = \tilde{X}(2\pi f - 2\pi f_0)$$ **Eq. (6.78)**

thus,

$$\int_{-\infty}^{\infty} \tilde{X}^*(2\pi f)\tilde{X}(2\pi f - 2\pi f_d) \ df = \int_{-\infty}^{\infty} \tilde{X}^*(2\pi f - 2\pi f_0)\tilde{X}(2\pi f - 2\pi f_0 - 2\pi f_d) \ df. \qquad \textbf{Eq. (6.79)}$$

The complex frequency correlation function is then defined as

$$\chi_f(f_d) = \left| \int_{-\infty}^{\infty} \tilde{X}^*(2\pi f)\tilde{X}(2\pi f - 2\pi f_d) \ df \right|^2. \qquad \textbf{Eq. (6.80)}$$

The velocity resolution (Doppler resolution) is by definition

$$\Delta v = \frac{c\Delta f_d}{2f_0} \qquad \textbf{Eq. (6.81)}$$

where Δf_d is the minimum resolvable Doppler difference between the Doppler frequencies corresponding to two moving targets, i.e., $\Delta f_d = f_{d1} - f_{d2}$, where f_{d1} and f_{d2} are the two individual Doppler frequencies for targets 1 and 2, respectively. The Doppler resolution Δf_d is equal to the inverse of the total effective duration of the waveform. Thus,

$$\Delta f_d = \frac{\displaystyle\int_{-\infty}^{\infty} |\chi_f(f_d)|^2 df_d}{\chi_f^2(0)} = \frac{\displaystyle\int_{-\infty}^{\infty} |\tilde{x}(t)|^4 dt}{\left(\displaystyle\int_{-\infty}^{\infty} |\tilde{x}(t)|^2 dt\right)^2} = \frac{1}{\tau_e}. \qquad \textbf{Eq. (6.82)}$$

6.3.3. Combined Range and Doppler Resolution

In this general case, one needs to use a two-dimensional function in the pair of variables (τ, f_d). For this purpose, assume that the pre-envelope of the transmitted waveform is

$$\psi(t) = \tilde{x}(t)e^{j2\pi f_0 t}. \qquad \textbf{Eq. (6.83)}$$

Then the delayed and Doppler-shifted signal is

$$\psi(t - \tau) = \tilde{x}(t - \tau)e^{j2\pi(f_0 - f_d)(t - \tau)}. \qquad \textbf{Eq. (6.84)}$$

Computing the integral square error between Eq. (6.83) and Eq. (6.84) yields

$$\varepsilon^2 = \int_{-\infty}^{\infty} |\psi(t) - \psi(t - \tau)|^2 dt \qquad \textbf{Eq. (6.85)}$$

$$\varepsilon^2 = 2\int_{-\infty}^{\infty} |\psi(t)|^2 dt - 2Re\left\{\int_{-\infty}^{\infty} \psi^*(t) - \psi(t - \tau) dt\right\} \qquad \textbf{Eq. (6.86)}$$

which can be written as

$$\varepsilon^2 = 2\int_{-\infty}^{\infty} |\tilde{x}(t)|^2 \ dt - 2Re\left\{ e^{j2\pi(f_0 - f_d)\tau}\int_{-\infty}^{\infty} \tilde{x}(t)\tilde{x}^*(t - \tau)e^{j2\pi f_d t} dt\right\}. \qquad \textbf{Eq. (6.87)}$$

Again, in order to maximize this squared error for $\tau \neq 0$, one must minimize the last term of Eq. (6.87). The combined range and Doppler correlation function is referred to as the ambiguity function

$$\chi(\tau, f_d) = \left| \int_{-\infty}^{\infty} \tilde{x}(t)\tilde{x}^*(t - \tau)e^{j2\pi f_d t} dt \right|^2, \qquad \textbf{Eq. (6.88)}$$

where

$$\chi_R(\tau) = \chi(\tau, 0); \quad and \quad \chi_f(\tau) = \chi(0, f_d).$$

Eq. (6.89)

In order to achieve the best range and Doppler resolution, the modulus square of this function must be minimized at $\tau \neq 0$ and $f_d \neq 0$. Note that the modulus square of the matched filter output, except for a phase term, is identical to that given in Eq. (6.88). This means that the output of the filter exhibits maximum instantaneous SNR as well as the most achievable range and Doppler resolutions. The ambiguity function is often used by radar designers and analysts to determine the *goodness* of a given radar waveform, where this *goodness* is measured by its range and Doppler resolutions. Remember that since the matched filter is used, maximum SNR is guaranteed. This will be discussed further in Chapter 7.

6.4. Range and Doppler Uncertainty

The formula derived in Eq. (6.88) represents the output of the matched filter when the signal at its input comprises target returns only and has no noise components. This assumption cannot be true in practical situations. In general, the input at the matched filter contains both target and noise returns. The noise signal is assumed to be an additive random process that is uncorrelated with the target and has bandlimited white spectrum. Referring to Eq. (6.88), a peak at the output of the matched filter at (τ_1, f_{d1}) represents a target whose delay (range) corresponds to τ_1 and Doppler frequency equal to f_{d1}. Therefore, measuring the targets' exact range and Doppler frequency is determined from measuring peak locations occurring in the two-dimensional space (τ, f_d). This last statement, however, is correct only if noise is not present at the input of the matched filter. When noise is present and because noise is random, it will generate ambiguity (uncertainty) about the exact location of the ambiguity function peaks in the (τ, f_d) space. The analysis presented closely follows Burdic (1968) and Cook and Bernfeld (1993).

6.4.1. Range Uncertainty

Consider the case when the return signal complex envelope is (assuming stationary target)

$$\tilde{s}_r(t) = \tilde{x}_r(t) + \tilde{n}(t)$$

Eq. (6.90)

where $\tilde{x}_r(t)$ is the target return signal complex envelope and $\tilde{n}(t)$ is the noise signal complex envelope. The integral squared error between the total received signal (target plus noise) and the shift (delayed) transmitted waveform is

$$\varepsilon^2 = \int_0^{T_{max}} |\tilde{x}(t-\tau) - \tilde{s}_r(t)|^2 \, dt$$

Eq. (6.91)

T_{max} corresponds to maximum range under consideration. Expanding this squared error yields

$$\varepsilon^2 = 2\int_0^{T_{max}} |\tilde{x}(t)|^2 \, dt + 2\int_0^{T_{max}} |\tilde{n}(t)|^2 \, dt - 2Re\left\{\int_0^{T_{max}} \tilde{x}^*(t-\tau)\tilde{s}_r(t)dt\right\}$$

Eq. (6.92)

which can be written as

$$\varepsilon^2 = E_x + E_n - 2Re\left\{\int_0^{T_{max}} \tilde{x}^*(t-\tau)\tilde{x}_r(t)dt + \int_0^{T_{max}} \tilde{x}^*(t-\tau)\tilde{n}(t)dt\right\}.$$

Eq. (6.93)

This expression is minimum at some value τ that makes the integral term inside Eq. (6.93) maximum and positive. More precisely, the following functions must be maximized

$$\mathcal{R}_{x_r x}(\tau) = \int_0^{T_{max}} \tilde{x}^*(t-\tau)\tilde{x}_r(t)\,dt \qquad \text{Eq. (6.94)}$$

$$\mathcal{R}_{nx}(\tau) = \int_0^{T_{max}} \tilde{x}^*(t-\tau)\tilde{n}(t)\,dt. \qquad \text{Eq. (6.95)}$$

However, since the noise signal is unknown, then only Eq. (6.94) must be maximized in order to reduce the squared error which can be written as

$$\varepsilon^2 = E - 2Re\{\mathcal{R}_{x_r x}(\tau) + \mathcal{R}_{nx}(\tau)\}. \qquad \text{Eq. (6.96)}$$

Expanding the quantity $\{\mathcal{R}_{x_r x}(\tau)\}$ using Taylor series expansion about the point $\tau = t_0$, where $t_0 = 2R_0/c$, and R_0 is the exact target range leads to

$$\mathcal{R}_{x_r x}(\tau) = \mathcal{R}_{x_r x}(t_0) + \mathcal{R}'_{x_r x}(t_0)(\tau - t_0) + \frac{\mathcal{R}''_{x_r x}(t_0)(\tau - t_0)^2}{2!} + \dots \qquad \text{Eq. (6.97)}$$

where $\mathcal{R}'$ and $\mathcal{R}''$, respectively, indicate the first and second derivatives with respect to delay. Remember that since the real part of the correlation function is an even function, all its odd number derivatives are equal to zero. Truncate the right-hand side of Eq. (6.97) by using the first three terms (note that term 2 is zero) to get

$$Re\{\mathcal{R}_{x_r x}(\tau)\} \approx \mathcal{R}_{x_r x}(t_0) + \frac{\mathcal{R}''_{x_r x}(t_0)(\tau - t_0)^2}{2}. \qquad \text{Eq. (6.98)}$$

There is some value τ_1 close to the exact target range, t_0, that will maximize the expression in Eq. (6.98). In order to find this value, differentiate the quantity $Re\{\mathcal{R}_{x_r x}(\tau) + \mathcal{R}_{nx}(\tau)\}$ with respect to τ and set the result equal to zero to find τ_1. More specifically,

$$Re\left\{\frac{d}{d\tau}\mathcal{R}_{x_r x}(\tau) + \frac{d}{d\tau}\mathcal{R}_{nx}(\tau)\right\}\Bigg|_{\tau = \tau_1} = Re\{\mathcal{R}_{x_r x}(\tau) + \mathcal{R}_{nx}(\tau)(\tau)\}\Big|_{\tau = \tau_1} = 0, \qquad \text{Eq. (6.99)}$$

the derivative of the $Re\{\mathcal{R}_{x_r x}(\tau)\}$ can be found from Eq. (6.98) as

$$Re\left\{\frac{d}{d\tau}\mathcal{R}_{x_r x}(\tau)\right\} = \frac{d}{d\tau}\left(\mathcal{R}_{x_r x}(t_0) + \frac{\mathcal{R}''_{x_r x}(t_0)(\tau - t_0)^2}{2!}\right) = \mathcal{R}''_{x_r x}(t_0)(\tau - t_0). \qquad \text{Eq. (6.100)}$$

Evaluating Eq. (6.100) at $\tau = \tau_1$ and substituting the result into Eq. (6.99) yield

$$(\tau_1 - t_0) = -\frac{Re\{\mathcal{R}_{nx}(\tau_1)\}}{\mathcal{R}''_{x_r x}(t_0)}. \qquad \text{Eq. (6.101)}$$

The value $(\tau_1 - t_0)$ represents the amount of target range measurement error. It is more meaningful, since noise is random, to compute this error in terms of the standard deviation of its rms value. Hence, the standard deviation for range measurement error is

$$\sigma_\tau = (\tau_1 - t_0)_{rms} = -\frac{Re\{\mathcal{R}_{nx}(\tau_1)\}_{rms}}{\mathcal{R}''_{x_r x}(t_0)}. \qquad \text{Eq. (6.102)}$$

By using the differentiation property of the Fourier transform and Parseval's theorem, the denominator of Eq. (6.102) can be determined by

$$\mathcal{R}''_{x_r x}(t_0) = (2\pi)^2 \int_{-\infty}^{\infty} f^2 \; |X(f)|^2 df.$$

Eq. (6.103)

The Fourier transform of $\mathcal{R}_{nx}(\tau)$ as

$$\mathcal{F}\{\mathcal{R}_{nx}(\tau)\} = X^*(f)\frac{\eta_0}{2}$$

Eq. (6.104)

where $\eta_0/2$ is the noise power spectrum density value (i.e., white noise). Again, from the Fourier transform properties, the Fourier transform of the derivative of $\mathcal{R}_{nx}(\tau)$ is

$$\mathcal{F}\{\mathcal{R}'_{nx}(\tau)\} = (j2\pi f)\left(X^*(f)\frac{\eta_0}{2}\right) = (j2\pi f)S_{nx}(f).$$

Eq. (6.105)

The rms value for $\mathcal{R}_{nx}(\tau)$ is by definition

$$\{\mathcal{R}_{nx}(\tau)\}_{rms} = \sqrt{\lim_{T_{max}} \frac{1}{T_{max}} \int_0^{T_{max}} \mathcal{R}_{nx}(\tau) \; d\tau}$$

Eq. (6.106)

which can be rewritten using Parseval's theorem as

$$\{\mathcal{R}_{nx}(\tau)\}_{rms} = \sqrt{\int_0^{T_{max}} |\mathcal{F}\{\mathcal{R}_{nx}(\tau)\}|^2 \; df},$$

Eq. (6.107)

substituting Eq. (6.105) into Eq. (6.107) yields

$$\{\mathcal{R}_{nx}(\tau)\}_{rms} = \sqrt{\frac{\eta_0}{2}(2\pi)^2 \int_0^{T_{max}} f^2 \; |X(f)|^2 \; df}.$$

Eq. (6.108)

Finally, the standard deviation for range measurement error can be written as

$$\sigma_\tau = \frac{\sqrt{\eta_0/2}}{\sqrt{(2\pi)^2 \int_{-\infty}^{\infty} f^2 \; |X(f)|^2 df}}.$$

Eq. (6.109)

Define the bandwidth rms value (in units *radians/sec* not *Hz*), B_{rms}^2, as

$$B_{rms}^2 = \frac{(2\pi)^2 \int_{-\infty}^{\infty} f^2 \; |X(f)|^2 df}{\int_{-\infty}^{\infty} |X(f)|^2 df}.$$

Eq. (6.110)

It follows that Eq. (6.109) can now be written as

$$\sigma_\tau = \frac{\sqrt{\eta_0/2}}{B_{rms}\sqrt{\int_{-\infty}^{\infty} |X(f)|^2 df}} = \frac{\sqrt{\eta_0/2}}{B_{rms}\sqrt{E_x}} = \frac{1}{B_{rms}\sqrt{2E_x/\eta_0}}$$

Eq. (6.111)

which leads to the conclusion that the uncertainty in range measurement is inversely proportional to the rms bandwidth and the square root of the ratio of signal energy to the noise power density (square root of the SNR). Note that B_{rms} is a characteristic of the waveform and it is not the actual bandwidth. The actual bandwidth is B_e.

6.4.2. Doppler (Velocity) Uncertainty

For this purpose, assume that the target range is completely known. Denote the signal transmitted by the radar as $x(t)$ and the received signal (target plus noise) as $s_r(t)$. The integral square difference between the two returns can be written as

$$\varepsilon^2 = \int_0^{f_{max}} |X(f-f_c) - S_r(f)|^2 \, df \qquad \text{Eq. (6.112)}$$

where $X(f)$ is the Fourier transform of $x(t)$, $S_r(f)$ is the Fourier transform of $s_r(t)$, and f_{max} is the maximum anticipated target Doppler. Again expand Eq. (6.112) to get

$$\varepsilon^2 = \int_0^{f_{max}} |X(f)|^2 \, df + \int_0^{f_{max}} |S_r(f)|^2 \, df - 2Re\left\{ \int_0^{f_{max}} |X^*(f-f_c) S_r(f)|^2 \, df \right\}. \qquad \text{Eq. (6.113)}$$

Minimizing the error squared in Eq. (6.113) requires maximizing the value

$$Re\left\{ \int_0^{f_{max}} |X^*(f-f_c) S_r(f)|^2 \, df \right\}. \qquad \text{Eq. (6.114)}$$

Conducting similar analysis as that performed in the previous section, the signal duration rms, τ_{rms}^2, value can be defined as

$$\tau_{rms}^2 = (2\pi)^2 \frac{\displaystyle\int_{-\infty}^{\infty} t^2 \, |x(t)|^2 dt}{\displaystyle\int_{-\infty}^{\infty} |x(t)|^2 dt}. \qquad \text{Eq. (6.115)}$$

The standard deviation in the Doppler measurement can be derived as

$$\sigma_{f_d} = \frac{1}{\tau_{rms}\sqrt{2E_x/\eta_0}}. \qquad \text{Eq. (6.116)}$$

Comparison of Eq. (6.116) and Eq. (6.111) indicates that the error in estimating Doppler is inversely proportional to the signal duration, while the error in estimating range is inversely proportional to the signal bandwidth. Therefore, and as expected, larger bandwidths minimize the range measurement errors and longer integration periods minimize the Doppler measurement errors.

6.5. Combined Range-Doppler Uncertainty

In the previous section, range estimate error and Doppler estimate error were derived by assuming that they are uncoupled estimates. In other words, range error was derived assuming stationary target, while Doppler error was derived assuming completely known target range. In this section a general formula for the combined range and Doppler errors is derived, where we analyze both target range and target Doppler that are not known.

The analytic signal for this case was given in Eq. (6.55). By setting $t_0 = 0$ in Eq. (6.55), then the analytic signal can be expressed as

$$\psi_r(t) = \tilde{s}(t) e^{j2\pi(f_0 + f_d)t} = r(t) e^{j\varphi(t)} e^{j2\pi(f_0 + f_d)t} \qquad \text{Eq. (6.117)}$$

where the complex envelope signal, $\tilde{s}(t)$, can be expressed as

$$\tilde{s}(t) = r(t)e^{j\varphi(t)}. \qquad \text{Eq. (6.118)}$$

The estimate for the range error, as established earlier, is determined by maximizing the function

$$Re\{\mathcal{R}_s(\tau, f_d) + \mathcal{R}_{ns}(\tau)\}. \qquad \text{Eq. (6.119)}$$

It follows that for some fixed value f_{d1} there is a value τ_1 close to $t_0 = 0$ that will maximize Eq. (6.119); that is,

$$Re\{\mathcal{R}'_s(\tau_1, f_{d1}) + \mathcal{R}'_{ns}(\tau_1)\} = 0. \qquad \text{Eq. (6.120)}$$

Again, the Taylor series expansion of $\mathcal{R}_s$ about $\tau = 0$ is

$$\mathcal{R}_s(\tau, f_d) = Re\left\{ \mathcal{R}_s(0, f_{d1}) + \mathcal{R}'_s(0, f_{d1})(\tau) + \frac{\mathcal{R}''_s(0, f_{d1})\tau^2}{2!} + \ldots \right\}. \qquad \text{Eq. (6.121)}$$

Thus,

$$Re\left\{ \frac{d}{d\tau}\mathcal{R}_s(\tau, f_d) \right\} \approx Re\{\mathcal{R}'_s(0, f_{d1}) + \mathcal{R}''_s(0, f_{d1})\tau\}. \qquad \text{Eq. (6.122)}$$

Substituting Eq. (6.122) into Eq. (6.120) and solving for τ_1 yields

$$\tau_1 = -\frac{Re\{\mathcal{R}'_{ns}(\tau_1) + \mathcal{R}'_s(0, f_{d1})\}}{Re\{\mathcal{R}''_s(0, f_{d1})\}}. \qquad \text{Eq. (6.123)}$$

Since $f_{d1} \to 0$ (i.e., very small), then the value of $\mathcal{R}''_s(0, f_{d1})$ is not much different from $\mathcal{R}''_s(0, 0)$; thus,

$$\tau_1 \approx -\frac{Re\{\mathcal{R}'_{ns}(\tau_1) + \mathcal{R}'_s(0, f_{d1})\}}{\mathcal{R}''_s(0, 0)}. \qquad \text{Eq. (6.124)}$$

To evaluate the term $\mathcal{R}'_s(0, f_{d1})$, start with the definition of $\mathcal{R}_s(\tau, f_d)$,

$$\mathcal{R}_s(\tau, f_d) = \int_{-\infty}^{\infty} r(t-\tau)e^{-j\varphi(t-\tau)}r(t)e^{j(\varphi(t) + 2\pi f_d t)}dt, \qquad \text{Eq. (6.125)}$$

compute the derivative of Eq. (6.125) with respect to τ

$$\mathcal{R}'_s(\tau, f_d) = -\int_{-\infty}^{\infty} \{r'(t-\tau)r(t) - j\varphi'(t-\tau)r(t-\tau)r(t)\}e^{j(\varphi(t) - \varphi(t-\tau) + 2\pi f_d t)}dt. \qquad \text{Eq. (6.126)}$$

Evaluating Eq. (6.126) at $\tau = 0$ and $f_d = f_{d1}$ gives

$$\mathcal{R}'_s(0, f_{d1}) = -\int_{-\infty}^{\infty} \{r'(t)r(t) - j\varphi'(t)r^2(t)\} \times e^{j2\pi f_{d1}t}dt. \qquad \text{Eq. (6.127)}$$

The complex exponential term can be approximated using small angle approximation as

$$e^{j2\pi f_{d1}t} = \cos(2\pi f_{d1}t) + j\sin(2\pi f_{d1}t) \approx 1 + j2\pi f_{d1}t. \qquad \text{Eq. (6.128)}$$

Next substitute Eq. (6.128) into Eq. (6.127), collect terms, and compute its real part to get

$$Re\{\mathcal{R}'_s(0, f_{d1})\} = -\int_{-\infty}^{\infty} r'(t)r(t)dt - \int_{-\infty}^{\infty} t\varphi'(t)r^2(t)dt.$$

Eq. (6.129)

The first integral is evaluated (using Fourier transform properties and Parseval's theorem) as

$$\int_{-\infty}^{\infty} r'(t)r(t)dt = (j2\pi)\int_{-\infty}^{\infty} f_d|\mathcal{R}(f)|^2 df.$$

Eq. (6.130)

Remember that since the envelope function $r(t)$ is a real lowpass signal, its Fourier transform is an even function. Using this result, Eq. (6.129) becomes

$$Re\{\mathcal{R}'_s(0, f_{d1})\} = (j2\pi)\int_{-\infty}^{\infty} f_d|\mathcal{R}(f)|^2 df.$$

Eq. (6.131)

Substitute Eq. (6.131) into Eq. (6.124) to get

$$\tau_1 = -\frac{Re\{\mathcal{R}'_{ns}(\tau_1)\} - 2\pi f_{d1}\int_{-\infty}^{\infty} t\varphi'(t)r^2(t)dt}{\mathcal{R}''_s(0, 0)}.$$

Eq. (6.132)

The integral on the left-hand side of Eq. (6.132) provides a measure of how much the output of the matched filter will shift away from its true location, along the delay axis, due to target motion. Define the normalized time-phase constant α as

$$\alpha = \frac{2\pi\int_{-\infty}^{\infty} t\varphi'(t)|\tilde{s}(t)|^2 dt}{\int_{-\infty}^{\infty} |\tilde{s}(t)|^2 dt}.$$

Eq. (6.133)

Using similar analysis we can determine the spectral cross correlation constant, γ, which provides an indication of how much the output of the matched filter will shift away from its true location, along the Doppler axis. This spectral cross correlation constant is given by

$$\gamma = 2\pi\frac{\int_{-\infty}^{\infty} f^2 \Phi'(f)|\tilde{S}(f)|^2 df}{\int_{-\infty}^{\infty} |\tilde{S}(f)|^2 df}$$

Eq. (6.134)

where $\Phi(f)$ is the Fourier transform of $\varphi(t)$.

To gain better understating of the implications of the two constants α and γ, consider a linear frequency modulated (LFM) waveform $\tilde{s}(t)$, whose phase is

$$\varphi(t) = \mu t^2$$

Eq. (6.135)

where $\mu = (\pi B)/\tau_0$, B is the LFM bandwidth, and τ_0 is the pulse width. Substituting the derivative of Eq. (6.135) into Eq. (6.133) yields

$$\alpha = \frac{4\pi\mu\int_{-\infty}^{\infty} t^2|\tilde{s}(t)|^2 dt}{\int_{-\infty}^{\infty} |\tilde{s}(t)|^2 dt}$$

Eq. (6.136)

which can be, using Eq. (6.115), rewritten as

$$\alpha = \left(\frac{\mu}{\pi}\right)\left\{(2\pi)^2\frac{\int_{-\infty}^{\infty}t^2|\tilde{s}(t)|^2 dt}{\int_{-\infty}^{\infty}|\tilde{s}(t)|^2 dt}\right\} = \frac{\mu}{\pi}\tau_{rms}^2 . \qquad \text{Eq. (6.137)}$$

It follows that Eq. (6.111) is now modified to

$$\sigma_\tau^2 = \frac{\eta_0}{B_{rms}^2 2E_x} + \frac{f_{d1}^2\alpha^2}{B_{rms}^4} . \qquad \text{Eq. (6.138)}$$

Similarly for Doppler uncertainty, Eq. (6.116) is now modified to

$$\sigma_{f_d}^2 = \frac{\eta_0}{\tau_{rms}^2 2E_x} + \frac{t_1^2\gamma^2}{\tau_{rms}^4} . \qquad \text{Eq. (6.139)}$$

where f_{d1} and t_1 are constants. Since estimates of range or Doppler when noise is present cannot be 100% exact, it is better to replace these constants with their equivalent mean-squared errors. That is, let

$$f_{d1}^2 = \sigma_{fd}^2$$
$$t_1^2 = \sigma_\tau^2 \qquad \text{Eq. (6.140)}$$

where σ_τ^2 is as in Eq. (6.138) and σ_{fd}^2 is in Eq. (6.139). Thus, Eq. (6.138) can be written as

$$\sigma_\tau^2 = \frac{\eta_0}{B_{rms}^2 2E_x} + \frac{\alpha^2}{B_{rms}^4}\sigma_{fd}^2 . \qquad \text{Eq. (6.141)}$$

Substituting Eq. (6.139) for σ_{fd}^2 yields,

$$\sigma_\tau^2 = \frac{\eta_0}{B_{rms}^2 2E_x} + \frac{\alpha^2}{B_{rms}^4}\left(\frac{\eta_0}{\tau_{rms}^2 2E_x} + \frac{\gamma^2\sigma_\tau^2}{\tau_{rms}^4}\right) . \qquad \text{Eq. (6.142)}$$

Similarly, Eq. (6.139) can now be written as,

$$\sigma_{f_d}^2 = \frac{\eta_0}{\tau_{rms}^2 2E_x} + \frac{\gamma^2}{\tau_{rms}^4}\sigma_\tau^2 . \qquad \text{Eq. (6.143)}$$

Substituting Eq. (6.138) for σ_τ^2 yields,

$$\sigma_{f_d}^2 = \frac{\eta_0}{\tau_{rms}^2 2E_x} + \frac{\gamma^2}{\tau_{rms}^4}\left(\frac{\eta_0}{B_{rms}^2 2E_x} + \frac{\alpha^2\sigma_{fd}^2}{B_{rms}^4}\right) . \qquad \text{Eq. (6.144)}$$

In summary, Eqs. (6.111) and (6.116) may lead to the conclusion that one can estimate the peak position of the matched filter output in the delay-Doppler space with the desired precision provided that the rms time-bandwidth product (i.e., $B_{rms} \cdot \tau_{rms}$) is very large. However, as indicated by Eqs. (6.141) and (6.144), this conclusion is true only if the factors α and γ are fairly small.

6.6. *Target Parameter Estimation*

Target parameters of interest to radar applications include, but are not limited to, target range (delay), amplitude, phase, Doppler, and angular location (azimuth and elevation). Target information (parameters) is typically embedded in the return signal amplitude and phase. Different classes of waveforms are used by the radar signal and data processors to extract various target parameters more efficiently than others. Since radar echoes typically comprise signal plus additive noise, most if not all of the ability to extract target information is governed by the statistics of the input noise, whose statistical parameters most likely are not known but can be estimated. Thus, statistical estimates of the target parameters (amplitude, phase, delay, Doppler, etc.) are utilized. The general form of the radar signal can be expressed in the following form

$$x(t) = Ar(t - t_0)\cos[2\pi(f_0 + f_d)(t - t_0) + \phi(t - t_0) + \phi_0] \qquad \text{Eq. (6.145)}$$

where A is the signal amplitude, $r(t)$ is the envelope lowpass signal, ϕ_0 is some constant phase, f_0 is the carrier frequency, t_0 and f_d are the target delay and Doppler, respectively. The analysis in this section closely follows Melsa and Cohn (1978).

6.6.1. *What Is an Estimator?*

It is usually safe to assume, due to the central limit theorem, that the input noise is Gaussian and white with mainly unknown parameters. Furthermore, following receiver processing, one can assume that this noise is bandlimited white Gaussian noise. Consequently, the primary question that needs to be answered is as follows: Given that the probability density function of the observation is known (Gaussian in this case) and given a finite number of independent measurements, can one determine an estimate of a given parameter (such as range, Doppler, amplitude, or phase)? Let $f_X(x;\theta)$ be the *pdf* of a random variable X with an unknown parameter θ. Define the values $\{x_1, x_2, ..., x_N\}$ as N observed independent values of the variable X. Define the function or estimator $\theta(x_1, x_2, ..., x_N)$ as an estimate of the unknown parameter θ. The estimation bias is

$$E[\hat{\theta} - \theta] = b \qquad \text{Eq. (6.146)}$$

where $E[\ ]$ represents the "expected value of." The estimator $\hat{\theta}$ is referred to as an unbiased estimator if and only if

$$E[\hat{\theta}] = \theta. \qquad \text{Eq. (6.147)}$$

One of the most popular and common measures of the quality or effectiveness of an estimator is the mean square deviation (MSD) referred to symbolically as $\Delta^2(\theta)$. For an unbiased estimator,

$$\Delta^2(\hat{\theta}) = \sigma_{\hat{\theta}}^2 \qquad \text{Eq. (6.148)}$$

where $\sigma_{\hat{\theta}}^2$ is the estimator variance. It can be shown that the Cramer-Rao bound for this MSD is given by

$$\sigma^2(\hat{\theta}) \geq \sigma_{min}^2(\theta) = \cfrac{1}{N\int_{-\infty}^{\infty} \left(\frac{\partial}{\partial\theta}\log\{f_X(x;\theta)\}\right)^2 f_X(x;\theta)\ dx}. \qquad \text{Eq. (6.149)}$$

The efficiency of this unbiased estimator is defined by

$$\varepsilon(\hat{\theta}) = \frac{\sigma_{min}^2(\theta)}{\sigma^2(\hat{\theta})} .$$

Eq. (6.150)

When $\varepsilon(\hat{\theta}) = 1$ the unbiased estimator is called an efficient estimate.

Consider an essentially time limited signal $x(t)$ with effective duration τ_e and assume a bandlimited white noise with PSD $\eta_0/2$. In this case, Eq. (6.149) is equivalent to

$$\sigma^2(\hat{\theta}_i) \geq \frac{1}{\frac{2N}{\eta_0} \int_0^{T_r} \left(\frac{\partial}{\partial \theta_i} x(t)\right)^2 dt}$$

Eq. (6.151)

where $\hat{\theta}_i$ is the estimate for the *ith* parameter of interest and T_r is the pulse repetition interval for the pulsed sequence. In the next two sections, estimates of the target amplitude and phase are derived. It must be noted that since these estimates represent independent random variables, they are referred to as uncoupled estimates. That is, the computation of one estimate does not depend on a priori knowledge of the other estimates.

6.6.2. Amplitude Estimation

The signal amplitude A in Eq. (6.145) is the parameter of interest, in this case. Taking the partial derivative of Eq. (6.145) with respect to A and squaring the result yields

$$\left(\frac{\partial}{\partial A} x(t)\right)^2 = [r(t-t_0)\cos(2\pi(f_0+f_d)(t-t_0) + \phi(t-t_0) + \phi_0)]^2 .$$

Eq. (6.152)

Thus,

$$\int_0^{NT_r} \left(\frac{\partial}{\partial A} x(t)\right)^2 dt = \int_0^{NT_r} x^2(t) \ dt = NE_x$$

Eq. (6.153)

where E_x is the signal energy (from Parseval's theorem). Substituting the right-hand side of Eq. (6.153) into Eq. (6.151) and collecting terms yield the variance for the amplitude estimate,

$$\sigma_A^2 \geq \frac{\eta_0}{2NE_x} = \frac{1}{N \ SNR} .$$

Eq. (6.154)

In this case Eq. (6.22) is used in Eq. (6.154). The *SNR* represents the nominal signal-to-noise ratio of the signal at the output of the matched filter due to N pulses. This clearly indicates that the signal amplitude estimate is improved as the SNR is increased.

6.6.3. Phase Estimation

In this case, it is desired to compute the best estimate for the signal phase ϕ_0. Taking the partial derivative of the signal in Eq. (6.145) with respect to ϕ_0 and squaring the result yield

$$\left(\frac{\partial}{\partial \phi_0} x(t)\right)^2 = (-r(t-t_0)\sin[2\pi(f_0+f_d)(t-t_0) + \phi(t-t_0) + \phi_0])^2 ,$$

Eq. (6.155)

it follows that

$$\int_0^{NT_r} \left(\frac{\partial}{\partial \phi_0} x(t)\right)^2 dt = \int_0^{NT_r} (x(t))^2 \ dt = NE_x .$$

Eq. (6.156)

Thus, the variance of the phase estimate is

$$\sigma^2_{\phi_0} \geq \frac{1}{\dfrac{2}{\eta_0} N E_x} = \frac{1}{N \; SNR}.$$

Eq. (6.157)

6.7. Pulse Compression

Range resolution for a given radar can be significantly improved by using very short pulses. Unfortunately, utilizing short pulses decreases the average transmitted power, hence reducing the SNR. Since the average transmitted power is directly linked to the receiver SNR, it is often desirable to increase the pulse width (i.e., the average transmitted power) while simultaneously maintaining adequate range resolution. This can be made possible by using pulse compression techniques with a matched filter receiver. Pulse compression allows us to achieve the average transmitted power of a relatively long pulse while obtaining the range resolution corresponding to a short pulse. Two pulse compression techniques are discussed. The first technique is known as "correlation processing" which is predominantly used for narrow band and some medium band radar operations. The second technique is called "stretch processing" and is normally used for extremely wide band radar operations.

6.7.1. Time-Bandwidth Product

Consider a radar system that employs a matched filter receiver. Let the matched filter receiver bandwidth be denoted as B. Then, the noise power available within the matched filter bandwidth is given by

$$N_i = 2 \; \frac{\eta_0}{2} \; B,$$

Eq. (6.158)

where the factor of two is used to account for both negative and positive frequency bands, and η_0 is termed the two-sided noise spectral density, as illustrated in Fig. 6.2. The average input signal power over a pulse duration τ_0 is

$$S_i = \frac{E_x}{\tau_0}$$

Eq. (6.159)

where E_x is the signal energy. Consequently, the matched filter input SNR is given by

$$(SNR)_i = \frac{S_i}{N_i} = \frac{E_x}{\eta_0 B \tau_0}.$$

Eq. (6.160)

Using Eq. (6.22) and Eq. (6.160), the output peak instantaneous SNR to the input SNR ratio is

$$\frac{SNR(t_0)}{(SNR)_i} = 2B\tau_0.$$

Eq. (6.161)

The quantity $B\tau_0$ is referred to as the time-bandwidth product for a given waveform or its corresponding matched filter. The factor $B\tau_0$ by which the output SNR is increased over that at the input is called the matched filter gain, or simply the compression gain. The time-bandwidth product of a pulse can be made much greater than unity by using frequency or phase modulation. If the radar receiver transfer function is perfectly matched to that of the input waveform, then the compression gain is equal to $B\tau_0$. Clearly, the compression gain becomes smaller than $B\tau_0$ as the spectrum of the matched filter deviates from that of the input signal.

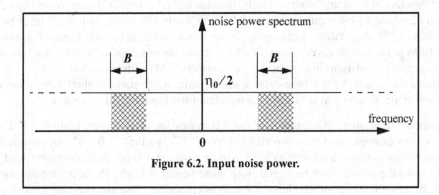

Figure 6.2. Input noise power.

6.7.2. Radar Equation with Pulse Compression

The radar equation for a pulsed radar can be written as,

$$SNR = \frac{P_t \tau_0 G^2 \lambda^2 \sigma}{(4\pi)^3 R^4 k T_0 F L_T}$$

Eq. (6.162)

where P_t is peak power, τ_0 is pulse width, G is antenna gain, σ is target RCS, R is range, k is Boltzmann's constant, T_0 is 290 degrees Kelvin, F is noise figure, and L_T is total radar losses.

Pulse compression radars transmit relatively long pulses (with modulation) and process the radar echo into very short pulses (compressed). One can view the transmitted pulse as being composed of a series of very short subpulses (duty is 100%), where the width of each subpulse is equal to the desired compressed pulse width. Denote the compressed pulse width as τ_c. Thus, for an individual subpulse, Eq. (6.162) can be written as

$$(SNR)_{\tau_c} = \frac{P_t \tau_c G^2 \lambda^2 \sigma}{(4\pi)^3 R^4 k T_0 F L_T}$$

Eq. (6.163)

The SNR for the uncompressed pulse is then derived from Eq. (6.163) as

$$SNR = \frac{P_t (\tau_0 = n_P \tau_c) G^2 \lambda^2 \sigma}{(4\pi)^3 R^4 k T_0 F L_T}$$

Eq. (6.164)

where n_P is the number of subpulses. Equation (6.164) is denoted as the radar equation with pulse compression. Observation of Eq. (6.162) and Eq. (6.164) indicates the following (note that both equations have the same form): For a given set of radar parameters, and as long as the transmitted pulse remains unchanged, the SNR is also unchanged regardless of the signal bandwidth. More precisely, when pulse compression is used, the detection range is maintained while the range resolution is drastically improved by keeping the pulse width unchanged and by increasing the bandwidth. Recall that range resolution is proportional to the inverse of the signal bandwidth:

$$\Delta R = c/2B.$$

Eq. (6.165)

6.7.3. Basic Principle of Pulse Compression

For this purpose, consider a long pulse with LFM modulation and a matched filter receiver. The output of the matched filter (along the delay axis, i.e., range) is an order of magnitude narrower than that at its input. More precisely, the matched filter output is compressed by a factor $\xi = B\tau_0$, where τ_0 is the pulse width and B is the bandwidth. Thus, by using long pulses and wide band LFM modulation, large compression ratios can be achieved. Figure 6.3 shows an ideal LFM pulse compression process. Part (a) shows the envelope of a pulse; part (b) shows the frequency modulation (in this case it is an upchirp LFM) with bandwidth $B = f_2 - f_1$. Part (c) shows the matched filter time-delay characteristic, while part (d) shows the compressed pulse envelope. Finally part (e) shows the matched filter input/output waveforms.

Figure 6.4 illustrates the advantage of pulse compression using a more realistic LFM waveform. In this example, two targets with RCS, $\sigma_1 = 1m^2$ and $\sigma_2 = 0.5m^2$, are detected. The two targets are not separated enough in time to be resolved without pulse compression. Figure 6.4-a shows the composite echo signal from those targets. Clearly, the target returns overlap, and thus, they are not resolved. Figure 6.4-b shows that after pulse compression the two pulses are completely separated and are resolved as two distinct targets. In fact, when using LFM, returns from neighboring targets are resolved as long as they are separated in time by τ_c, the compressed pulse width.

When using pulse compression, it is desirable to use modulation schemes that can accomplish a maximum pulse compression ratio and can significantly reduce the sidelobe levels of the compressed waveform. This is illustrated in Fig. 6.5; in this case, the output of a matched filter is shown for three distinct cases: LFM pulse with $B = 10MHz$, an LFM pulse with bandwidth $B = 25MHz$, and an LFM pulse with bandwidth $B = 50MHz$. Clearly, the resolution (null-to-null) of the compressed pulse becomes narrower (i.e., better resolution) as the time-bandwidth product is increased.

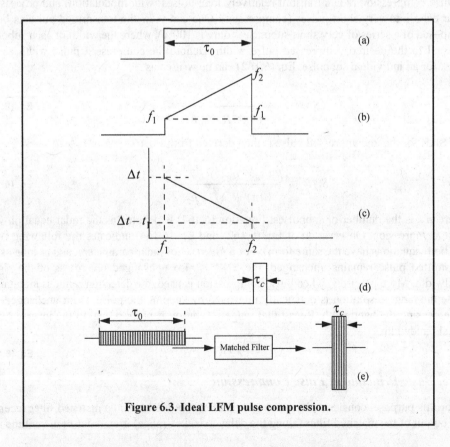

Figure 6.3. Ideal LFM pulse compression.

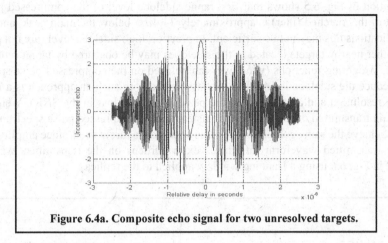

Figure 6.4a. Composite echo signal for two unresolved targets.

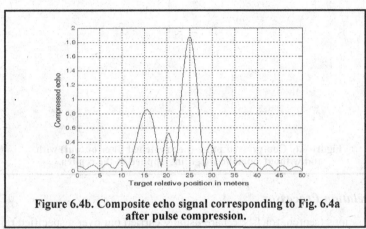

Figure 6.4b. Composite echo signal corresponding to Fig. 6.4a after pulse compression.

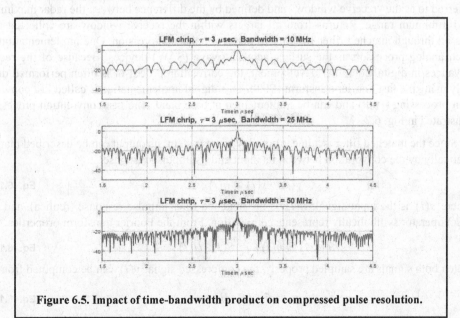

Figure 6.5. Impact of time-bandwidth product on compressed pulse resolution.

Observation of Fig. 6.5 shows that first range sidelobe level of the compressed pulse (i.e., the output of the matched filter) is approximately $13.4 dB$ below the main peak, and for most radar applications this may not be sufficient. In practice, high sidelobe levels are not preferable because other nearby targets located in the sidelobes may be obscured by target returns in the main lobe. Weighting functions (windows) can be used on the compressed pulse spectrum in order to reduce the sidelobe levels. The cost associated with such an approach is a loss in the main lobe resolution and a reduction in the peak value (i.e., loss in the SNR). Weighting the time domain transmitted or received signal instead of the compressed pulse spectrum will theoretically achieve the same goal. However, this approach is rarely used, since amplitude modulating the transmitted waveform introduces extra burdens on the transmitter. Weighting is illustrated in Fig. 6.6 using a Hanning window applied to the replica.

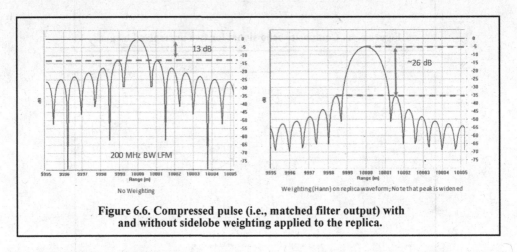

Figure 6.6. Compressed pulse (i.e., matched filter output) with and without sidelobe weighting applied to the replica.

6.7.4. Correlation Processor

Radar operations (search, track, etc.) are usually carried out over a specified range window, referred to as the "receive window" and defined by the difference between the radar maximum and minimum range. Returns from all targets within the receive window are collected and passed through matched filter circuitry to perform pulse compression. One implementation of such analog processors is the surface acoustic wave (SAW) devices. Because of the recent advances in digital computer development, the correlation processor is often performed digitally using the fast Fourier transform (FFT). This digital implementation is called fast convolution processing (FCP) and can be implemented at base band. The fast convolution process is illustrated in Fig. 6.7.

Since the matched filter is a linear time invariant system, its output can be described mathematically by the convolution between its input and its impulse response,

$$y(t) = s(t) \otimes h(t) \qquad \qquad \text{Eq. (6.166)}$$

where $s(t)$ is the input signal, $h(t)$ is the matched filter impulse response (replica), and the ($\otimes$) operator symbolically represents convolution. From the Fourier transform properties,

$$\mathcal{F}\{s(t) \otimes h(t)\} = S(f) \cdot H(f) . \qquad \qquad \text{Eq. (6.167)}$$

When both signals are sampled properly, the compressed signal $y(t)$ can be computed from

$$y = \mathcal{F}^{-1}\{S \cdot H\} \qquad \qquad \text{Eq. (6.168)}$$

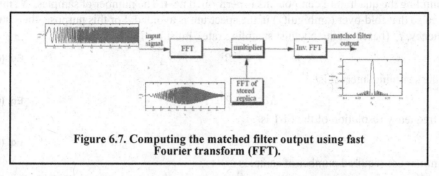

Figure 6.7. Computing the matched filter output using fast Fourier transform (FFT).

where $\mathcal{F}^{-1}$ is the inverse Fourier transform. Consider a radar system that utilizes a correlation processor receiver (i.e., matched filter). The receive window in meters is defined by

$$R_{rec} = R_{max} - R_{min}$$ **Eq. (6.169)**

where R_{max} and R_{min}, respectively, define the maximum and minimum range over which the radar performs detection. Typically R_{rec} is limited to the extent of the target complex. The normalized LFM complex transmitted signal has the form

$$s(t) = \exp\left(j2\pi\left(f_0 t + \frac{\mu}{2}t^2\right)\right) \qquad 0 \le t \le \tau_0$$ **Eq. (6.170)**

τ_0 is the transmitted pulse width, $\mu = B/\tau_0$, and B is the instantaneous bandwidth.

The radar echo signal is similar to the transmitted one with the exception of a time delay and an amplitude change that correspond to the target RCS and other factors. Consider a target at range R_1. The echo received by the radar from this target is

$$s_r(t) = a_1 \exp\left(j2\pi\left(f_0(t - t_1) + \frac{\mu}{2}(t - t_1)^2\right)\right)$$ **Eq. (6.171)**

where a_1 is proportional to target RCS, antenna gain, and range attenuation. The time delay t_1 is given by

$$t_1 = 2R_1/c.$$ **Eq. (6.172)**

The first step of the processing consists of removing the frequency f_0. This is accomplished by mixing $s_r(t)$ with a reference signal whose phase is $2\pi f_0 t$. The phase of the resultant signal, after lowpass filtering, is then given by

$$\phi(t) = 2\pi\left(-f_0 t_1 + \frac{\mu}{2}(t - t_1)^2\right)$$ **Eq. (6.173)**

and the instantaneous frequency is

$$f_i(t) = \frac{1}{2\pi}\frac{d}{dt}\phi(t) = \mu(t - t_1) = \frac{B}{\tau_0}\left(t - \frac{2R_1}{c}\right).$$ **Eq. (6.174)**

The term (Bt/τ_0) is a frequency corruption term which can, in almost all radar applications, be ignored. The quadrature components are

$$\begin{pmatrix} x_I(t) \\ x_Q(t) \end{pmatrix} = \begin{pmatrix} \cos\phi(t) \\ \sin\phi(t) \end{pmatrix}.$$ **Eq. (6.175)**

Sampling the quadrature components is performed next. The number of samples, N, must be chosen so that fold-over (ambiguity) in the spectrum is avoided. For this purpose, the sampling frequency, f_s (based on the Nyquist sampling rate), must be

$$f_s \geq 2B \qquad\qquad \text{Eq. (6.176)}$$

and the sampling interval is

$$\Delta t \leq 1/(2B). \qquad\qquad \text{Eq. (6.177)}$$

The frequency resolution of the FFT is

$$\Delta f = 1/\tau_0 \qquad\qquad \text{Eq. (6.178)}$$

The minimum required number of samples is

$$N = \frac{1}{\Delta f \Delta t} = \frac{\tau_0}{\Delta t}. \qquad\qquad \text{Eq. (6.179)}$$

Equating Eqs. (6.177) and (6.179) yields

$$N \geq 2B\tau_0. \qquad\qquad \text{Eq. (6.180)}$$

Consequently, a total of $2B\tau_0$ real samples, or $B\tau_0$ complex samples, is sufficient to completely describe an LFM waveform of duration τ_0 and bandwidth B. For example, an LFM signal of duration $\tau_0 = 20 \ \mu s$ and bandwidth $B = 5 \ MHz$ requires 200 real samples to determine the input signal (100 samples for the I-channel and 100 samples for the Q-channel).

For better implementation of the FFT, N is extended to the next power of two, by zero padding. Thus, the total number of samples, for some positive integer m, is

$$N_{FFT} = 2^m \geq N. \qquad\qquad \text{Eq. (6.181)}$$

The final steps of the FCP processing include (1) taking the FFT of the sampled sequence, (2) multiplying the frequency domain sequence of the signal with the FFT of the matched filter impulse response, and (3) performing the inverse FFT of the composite frequency domain sequence in order to generate the time domain compressed pulse. Of course, weighting, antenna gain, and range attenuation compensation must also be performed.

Assume that I targets at ranges R_1, R_2, and so forth are within the receive window. From superposition, the phase of the down-converted signal is

$$\phi(t) = \sum_{i=1}^{I} 2\pi\left(-f_0 t_i + \frac{\mu}{2}(t - t_i)^2\right) \qquad\qquad \text{Eq. (6.182)}$$

where $\{t_i = (2R_i/c); \ i = 1, 2, ..., I\}$ represent the two-way time delays, where t_1 coincides with the start of the receive window. As an example, the following case:

# targets	R_{rec}	pulse width	Bandwidth	targets range	Target RCS	Window type
3	200m	5 μs	20MHz	[20 80 120] m	[1 1 1]m^2	none

Note that the compressed pulsed range resolution is $\Delta R = 7.5m$. Figure 6.8 shows the real and imaginary parts of the replica used for this example. Figure 6.9 shows the uncompressed echo, while Fig. 6.10 shows the compressed matched filter output. Figure 6.11 is similar to Fig. 6.10, except in this case the first and second targets are less than 7.5 meters apart (they are at 78 and 80 meters). Clearly, in this case those two targets are not resolved. However, if the bandwidth is changed to 50 MHz (i.e., $\Delta R = 3.0m$) then the two targets begin to be resolved, as shown in Fig. 6.12.

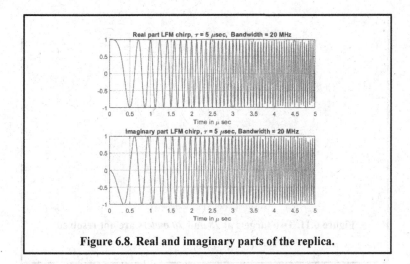

Figure 6.8. Real and imaginary parts of the replica.

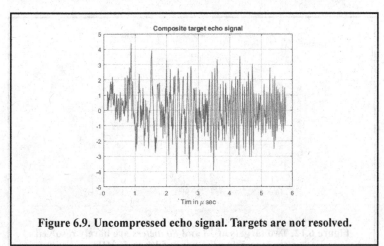

Figure 6.9. Uncompressed echo signal. Targets are not resolved.

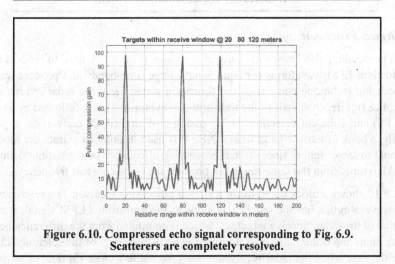

Figure 6.10. Compressed echo signal corresponding to Fig. 6.9.
Scatterers are completely resolved.

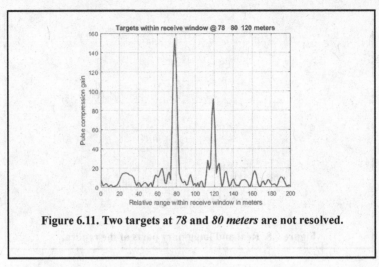

Figure 6.11. Two targets at *78* and *80 meters* are not resolved.

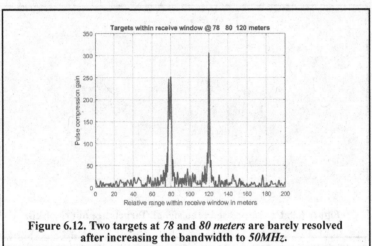

**Figure 6.12. Two targets at *78* and *80 meters* are barely resolved
after increasing the bandwidth to *50MHz*.**

6.7.5. Stretch Processor

Stretch processing, also known as *active correlation,* is normally used to process extremely high-bandwidth LFM waveforms (or equivalently large time-bandwidth product waveforms). This processing technique consists of the following steps: First, the radar returns are mixed with a replica (reference signal) of the transmitted waveform. This is followed by low pass filtering (LPF) and coherent detection. Next, analog-to-digital (A/D) conversion is performed; and finally, a bank of narrow band filters (NBFs) is used in order to extract the tones that are proportional to target range, since stretch processing effectively converts time delay into frequency. All returns from the same range bin produce the same constant frequency.

Figure 6.13 shows a block diagram for a stretch processing receiver. The reference signal is an LFM waveform that has the same LFM slope as the transmitted LFM signal. It exists over the duration of the radar "receive window," which is computed from the difference between the radar maximum and minimum range. Denote the start frequency of the reference chirp as f_r. Consider the case when the radar receives returns from a few close (in time or range) targets, as illustrated in Fig. 6.13.

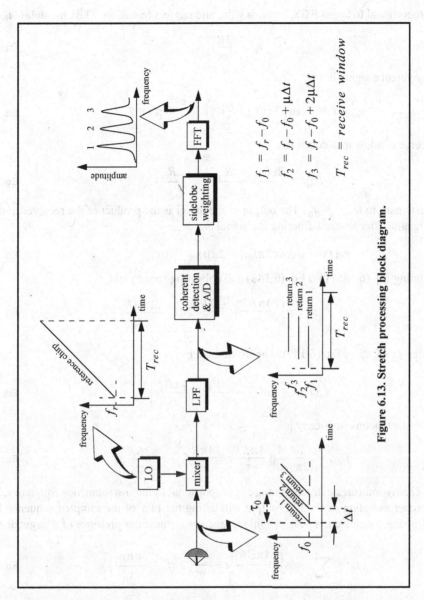

Figure 6.13. Stretch processing block diagram.

$$f_1 = f_r - f_0$$
$$f_2 = f_r - f_0 + \mu\Delta t$$
$$f_3 = f_r - f_0 + 2\mu\Delta t$$

$$T_{rec} = receive \ window$$

Mixing with the reference signal and performing lowpass filtering are effectively equivalent to subtracting the return frequency chirp from the reference signal. Thus, the LPF output consists of constant tones corresponding to the targets' positions. The normalized transmitted signal can be expressed by

$$s_1(t) = \cos\left(2\pi\left(f_0 t + \frac{\mu}{2}t^2\right)\right) \qquad 0 \le t \le \tau_0 \qquad \textbf{Eq. (6.183)}$$

where $\mu = B/\tau_0$ is the LFM coefficient and f_0 is the chirp start frequency. Assume a point scatterer at range R. The signal received by the radar is

$$s_r(t) = a\cos\left[2\pi\left(f_0(t - t_0) + \frac{\mu}{2}(t - t_0)^2\right)\right] \qquad \textbf{Eq. (6.184)}$$

a is proportional to target RCS, antenna gain, and range attenuation. The time delay t_0 is

$$t_0 = \frac{2R}{c}.$$

Eq. (6.185)

The reference signal is

$$s_{ref}(t) = 2\cos\left(2\pi\left(f_r t + \frac{\mu}{2}t^2\right)\right) \qquad 0 \le t \le T_{rec},$$

Eq. (6.186)

the receive window in seconds is

$$T_{rec} = \frac{2(R_{max} - R_{min})}{c} = \frac{2R_{rec}}{c}.$$

Eq. (6.187)

It is customary to let $f_r = f_0$. The output of the mixer is the product of the received and reference signals. After lowpass filtering the signal is

$$s_0(t) = a\cos(2\pi f_0 t_0 + 2\pi\mu t_0 t - \pi\mu(t_0)^2).$$

Eq. (6.188)

Substituting Eq. (6.185) into Eq. (6.188) and collecting terms yield

$$s_0(t) = a \ \cos\left[\left(\frac{4\pi BR}{c\tau_0}\right)t + \frac{2R}{c}\left(2\pi f_0 - \frac{2\pi BR}{c\tau_0}\right)\right]$$

Eq. (6.189)

and since $\tau_0 \gg 2R/c$, Eq. (6.189) is approximated by

$$s_0(t) \approx a \ \cos\left[\left(\frac{4\pi BR}{c\tau_0}\right)t + \frac{4\pi R}{c}f_0\right].$$

Eq. (6.190)

The instantaneous frequency is

$$f_{inst} = \frac{1}{2\pi} \frac{d}{dt}\left(\left(\frac{4\pi BR}{c\tau_0}t + \frac{4\pi R}{c}f_0\right)\right) = \frac{2BR}{c\tau_0}$$

Eq. (6.191)

which clearly indicates that target range is proportional to the instantaneous frequency. Therefore, proper sampling of the LPF output and taking the FFT of the sampled sequence lead to the following conclusion: a peak at some frequency f_1 indicates presence of a target at range

$$s_o(t) = \sum_{i=1}^{I} a_i\cos\left[\left(\frac{4\pi BR_i}{c\tau_0}\right)t + \frac{2R_i}{c}\left(2\pi f_0 - \frac{2\pi BR_i}{c\tau_0}\right)\right].$$

Eq. (6.192)

Hence, target returns appear as constant frequency tones that can be resolved using the FFT. Consequently, determining the proper sampling rate and FFT size is very critical. The rest of this section presents a methodology for computing the proper FFT parameters required for stretch processing.

Assume a radar system using a stretch processor receiver. The pulse width is τ_0 and the chirp bandwidth is B. Since stretch processing is normally used in extreme bandwidth cases (i.e., very large B), the receive window over which radar returns will be processed is typically limited to from a few meters to possibly less than *100 meters*. The compressed pulse range resolution is computed from Eq. (6.165). Declare the FFT size to be N and its frequency resolution to be Δf. The frequency resolution is computed using the following procedure: Consider two adjacent point scatterers at ranges R_1 and R_2. The minimum frequency separation, Δf, between those scatterers so that they are resolved can be computed from Eq. (6.191) as

$$\Delta f = f_2 - f_1 = \frac{2B}{c\tau_0}(R_2 - R_1) = \frac{2B}{c\tau_0}\Delta R.$$

Eq. (6.193)

Substituting Eq. (6.165) into Eq. (6.193) yields

$$\Delta f = \frac{2B}{c\tau_0}\frac{c}{2B} = \frac{1}{\tau_0}.$$

Eq. (6.194)

The maximum frequency resolvable by the FFT is limited to the region $\pm N\Delta f/2$. Thus, the maximum resolvable frequency is

$$\frac{N\Delta f}{2} > \frac{2B(R_{max} - R_{min})}{c\tau_0} = \frac{2BR_{rec}}{c\tau_0}.$$

Eq. (6.195)

Using Eqs. (6.187) and (6.195) into Eq. (6.193) and collecting terms yield

$$N > 2BT_{rec}.$$

Eq. (6.196)

For better implementation of the FFT, choose an FFT of size

$$N_{FFT} \geq N = 2^m$$

Eq. (6.197)

where m is a nonzero positive integer. The sampling interval is then given by

$$\Delta f = \frac{1}{T_s N_{FFT}} \Rightarrow T_s = \frac{1}{\Delta f N_{FFT}}.$$

Eq. (6.198)

As an example, consider the radar whose parameters are shown in the following table:

# targets	R_{rec}	pulse width	Bandwidth	Target range	Target RCS	Window type
3	30m	10ms	1GHz	[2 5 10] m	[1 1 2]m²	Kaiser

Note that the compressed pulse range resolution, without using a window, is $\Delta R = 0.15m$. Figures 6.14 and 6.15, respectively, show the uncompressed and compressed echo signals corresponding to this example. Figures 6.16-a and 6.16-b are similar to Fig. 6.14 and Fig. 6.15 except in this case two of the targets are less than *15cm* apart (i.e., unresolved targets at $R_{relative} = [3, 3.1]m$).

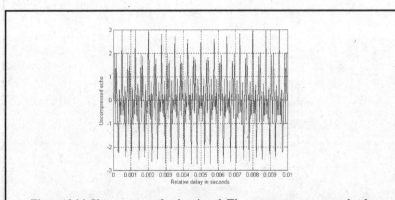

Figure 6.14. Uncompressed echo signal. Three targets are unresolved.

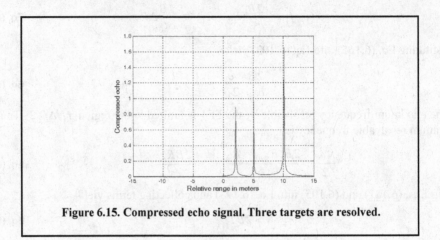

Figure 6.15. Compressed echo signal. Three targets are resolved.

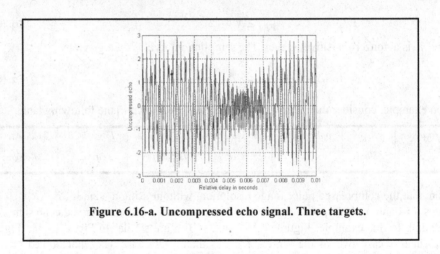

Figure 6.16-a. Uncompressed echo signal. Three targets.

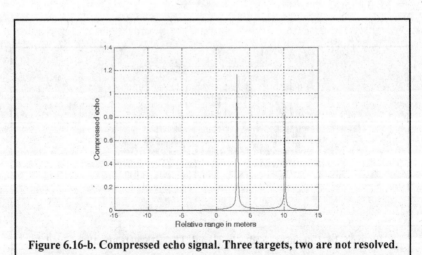

Figure 6.16-b. Compressed echo signal. Three targets, two are not resolved.

6.7.6. Stepped Frequency Waveforms

Stepped frequency waveforms (SFW) is a class of radar waveforms that are used in extremely wide bandwidth applications where very large time-bandwidth product is required. One may think of SFW as a special case of an extremely wide bandwidth LFM waveform. For this purpose, consider an LFM signal whose bandwidth is B_i and whose pulse width is T_i and refer to it as the primary LFM. Divide this long pulse into N subpulses each of width τ_0 to generate a sequence of pulses whose PRI is denoted by T. It follows that $T_i = (n-1)T$. One reason SFW may be chosen over an extremely wideband LFM pulse is that it may be very difficult for the transmit hardware to maintain a phase error-free large time-bandwidth product LFM slope within a single pulse. By using SFW, the same equivalent bandwidth can be achieved; however, the requirements on the hardware are relaxed as phase errors are minimized since the LFM is chirped over a much shorter duration. Define the beginning frequency for each subpulse as that value measured from the primary LFM at the leading edge of each subpulse, as illustrated in Fig. 6.17. That is

$$f_i = f_0 + i\Delta f; \quad i = 0, N-1 \qquad \text{Eq. (6.199)}$$

where Δf is the frequency step from one subpulse to another. The set of n subpulses is often referred to as a burst. Each subpulse can have its own LFM modulation. To this end, assume that each subpulse is of width τ_0 and bandwidth B, then the LFM slope of each pulse is

$$\mu = B/\tau_0. \qquad \text{Eq. (6.200)}$$

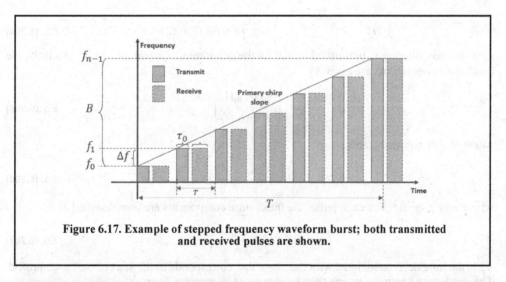

Figure 6.17. Example of stepped frequency waveform burst; both transmitted and received pulses are shown.

The SFW operation and processing involve the following steps:

1. A series of N narrow-band LFM pulses is transmitted. The chirp beginning frequency from pulse to pulse is stepped by a fixed frequency step Δf. Each group of N pulses is referred to as a burst.
2. The LFM slope (quadratic phase term) is first removed from the received signal, as described in Fig. 6.17. The reference slope must be equal to the combined primary LFM and single subpulse slopes. Thus, the received signal is reduced to a series of subpulses.
3. These subpulses are then sampled at a rate that coincides with the center of each pulse, sampling rate equivalent to $(1/T)$.
4. The quadrature components for each burst are collected and stored.

5. Spectral weighting (to reduce the range sidelobe levels) is applied to the quadrature components. Corrections for target velocity, phase, and amplitude variations are applied.
6. The inverse discrete Fourier transform of the weighted quadrature components of each burst is calculated to synthesize a range profile for that burst. The process is repeated for M bursts to obtain consecutive high resolution range profiles.

Within a burst, the transmitted waveform for the ith step can be described as

$$x_i(t) = \left(C_i \frac{1}{\sqrt{\tau_0}} Rect\left(\frac{t}{\tau_0}\right) e^{j2\pi\left(f_i t + \frac{\mu}{2}t^2\right)} \qquad \begin{array}{c} iT \leq t \leq iT + \tau_0 \\ elsewhere \end{array} \right) \qquad \text{Eq. (6.201)}$$

where C_i are constants. The received signal from a target located at range R_0 is then given by

$$x_{ri}(t) = C_i' e^{j2\pi\left[f_i(t - \Delta(t)) - \frac{\mu}{2}(t - \Delta(t))^2\right]} \qquad , \quad iT + \Delta(t) \leq t \leq iT + \tau_0 + \Delta(t) \qquad \text{Eq. (6.202)}$$

where C_i' are constant and the round trip delay $\Delta(t)$ is given by

$$\Delta(t) = \frac{R_0 - vt}{c/2} \qquad \text{Eq. (6.203)}$$

where c is the speed of light and v is the target radial velocity. In order to remove the quadratic phase term, mixing is first performed with the reference signal given by

$$y_i(t) = e^{j2\pi\left(f_i t + \frac{\mu}{2}t^2\right)} \qquad ; \quad iT \leq t \leq iT + \tau_0, \qquad \text{Eq. (6.204)}$$

next lowpass filtering is performed to extract the quadrature components. More precisely, the quadrature components are given by

$$\begin{pmatrix} x_I(t) \\ x_Q(t) \end{pmatrix} = \begin{pmatrix} A_i \cos\phi_i(t) \\ A_i \sin\phi_i(t) \end{pmatrix} \qquad \text{Eq. (6.205)}$$

where A_i are constants, and

$$\phi_i(t) = -2\pi f_i\left(\frac{2R_0}{c} - \frac{2vt}{c}\right) \qquad \text{Eq. (6.206)}$$

where now $f_i = \Delta f$. For each pulse, the quadrature components are then sampled at

$$t_i = iT + \frac{\tau_r}{2} + \frac{2R_0}{c} \qquad \text{Eq. (6.207)}$$

τ_r is the time delay associated with the range that corresponds to the start of the range profile. The quadrature components can then be expressed in complex form as

$$X_i = A_i e^{j\phi_i}. \qquad \text{Eq. (6.208)}$$

Equation (6.208) represents samples of the target reflectivity, due to a single burst, in the frequency domain. This information can then be transformed into a series of range delay reflectivity (i.e., range profile) values by using the inverse discrete Fourier transform. It follows that

$$H_l = \frac{1}{N} \sum_{i=0}^{N-1} X_i \exp\left(j\frac{2\pi li}{N}\right) \qquad ; \quad 0 \leq l \leq N-1. \qquad \text{Eq. (6.209)}$$

Substituting Eq. (6.205) and Eq. (6.208) into (6.209) and collecting terms yield

$$H_l = \frac{1}{N} \sum_{i=0}^{N-1} A_i \ \exp\left\{j\left(\frac{2\pi li}{N} - 2\pi f_i\left(\frac{2R_0}{c} - \frac{2vt_i}{c}\right)\right)\right\}$$

Eq. (6.210)

By normalizing with respect to N, assuming that $A_i = 1$, and that the target is stationary (i.e., $v = 0$), then the range profile can be written as

$$H_l = \sum_{i=0}^{N-1} \exp\left\{j\left(\frac{2\pi li}{N} - 2\pi f_i\frac{2R_0}{c}\right)\right\}$$

Eq. (6.211)

and by using $f_i = i\Delta f$ yields

$$H_l = \sum_{i=0}^{N-1} \exp\left\{j\frac{2\pi i}{N}\left(-\frac{2NR_0\Delta f}{c} + l\right)\right\}$$

Eq. (6.212)

which can be simplified to

$$H_l = \frac{\sin \pi\zeta}{\sin\frac{\pi\zeta}{N}} \ \exp\left(j\frac{N-1}{2} \ \frac{2\pi\zeta}{N}\right)$$

Eq. (6.213)

where

$$\zeta = \frac{-2NR_0\Delta f}{c} + l.$$

Eq. (6.214)

Finally, the synthesized range profile is

$$|H_l| = \left|\frac{(\sin \pi\zeta)}{\left(\sin\frac{\pi\zeta}{N}\right)}\right|.$$

Eq. (6.215)

Range Resolution and Range Ambiguity in SFW

As usual, range resolution is determined from the overall system instantaneous bandwidth. Assuming an SFW with N steps and step size Δf, then the corresponding range resolution is equal to

$$\Delta R = \frac{c}{2N\Delta f}.$$

Eq. (6.216)

Range ambiguity associated with an SFW can be determined by examining the phase term that corresponds to a stationary point scatterer located at range R_0. More precisely,

$$\phi_i(t) = 2\pi f_i\frac{2R_0}{c},$$

Eq. (6.217)

it follows that

$$\frac{\Delta\phi}{\Delta f} = \frac{4\pi(f_{i+1} - f_i)R_0}{(f_{i+1} - f_i)c} = \frac{4\pi R_0}{c},$$

Eq. (6.218)

or equivalently,

$$R_0 = \frac{\Delta\phi}{\Delta f}\frac{c}{4\pi}.$$

Eq. (6.219)

It is clear from Eq. (6.219) that range ambiguity exists for $\Delta\phi = \Delta\phi + 2N\pi$. Therefore,

$$R_0 = \frac{\Delta\phi + 2N\pi}{\Delta f}\frac{c}{4\pi} = R_0 + N\left(\frac{c}{2\Delta f}\right)$$ Eq. (6.220)

and the unambiguous range window is

$$R_u = \frac{c}{2\Delta f}.$$ Eq. (6.221)

A range profile synthesized using a particular SFW represents the relative range reflectivity for all scatterers within the unambiguous range window, with respect to the absolute range that corresponds to the burst time delay. Additionally, if a specific target extent is larger than R_u, then all scatterers falling outside the unambiguous range window will fold over and appear in the synthesized profile. This fold-over problem is identical to the spectral fold-over that occurs when using a fast Fourier transform (FFT) to resolve certain signal frequency contents. For example, consider an FFT with frequency resolution $\Delta f = 50Hz$ and size $NFFT = 64$. In this case, this FFT can resolve frequency tones between $-1600Hz$ and $1600Hz$. When this FFT is used to resolve the frequency content of a sine-wave tone equal to $1800Hz$, fold-over occurs and a spectral line at the fourth FFT bin (i.e., $200Hz$) appears. Therefore, in order to avoid fold-over in the synthesized range profile, the frequency step, Δf, must be

$$\Delta f \le c/2E$$ Eq. (6.222)

where E is the target extent in meters. Additionally, the pulse width must also be large enough to contain the whole target extent. Thus,

$$\Delta f \le 1/\tau_0$$ Eq. (6.223)

and in practice,

$$\Delta f \le 1/2\tau_0.$$ Eq. (6.224)

This is necessary in order to reduce the amount of contamination of the synthesized range profile caused by the clutter surrounding the target under consideration. For example, assume that the range profile starts at $R_0 = 900m$ with the following parameters:

# targets	Pulse width	N	Δf	1/T	v
3	$100\mu s$	64	$10MHz$	$100KHz$	0.0

In this case, $\Delta R = 0.235m$, and $R_u = 15m$. Thus, targets that are more than 0.235 meters apart will appear as distinct peaks in the synthesized range profile. Assume two cases; in the first case, the targets located at *[908, 910, 912]* meters within the receive window, and in the second case, they are at *[908, 910, 910.2]* meters. In both cases, the target RCS are, respectively, *[100, 10, 1]* meters squared. Figure 6.18 shows the synthesized range profiles.

Figure 6.19 is similar to Fig. 6.18, except in this case the Hamming window is used. Figure 6.20 shows the synthesized range profile that corresponds to the second case (Hamming window is used). Note that all three targets were resolved in Fig. 6.18 and Fig. 6.19; however, the last two scatterers are not resolved in Fig. 6.20, because they are separated by less than ΔR. Next, consider another case where the targets are located at = *[908, 912, 916]* meters. Figure 6.21 shows the corresponding range profile. In this case, fold-over occurs, and the last target appears at the lower portion of the synthesized range profile. Also, consider the case where the targets are at *[908, 910, 923]* meters. Figure 6.22 shows the corresponding range profile. In this case, ambiguity is associated with the first and third scatterers since they are separated by $15m$. Both appear at the same range bin.

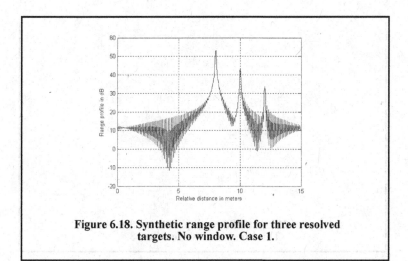

Figure 6.18. Synthetic range profile for three resolved targets. No window. Case 1.

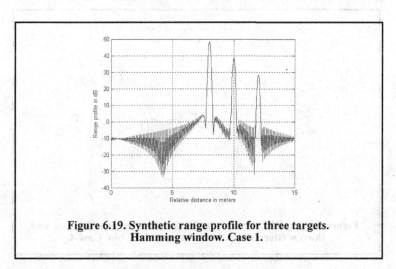

Figure 6.19. Synthetic range profile for three targets. Hamming window. Case 1.

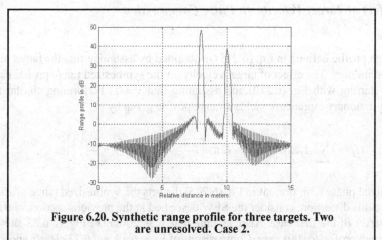

Figure 6.20. Synthetic range profile for three targets. Two are unresolved. Case 2.

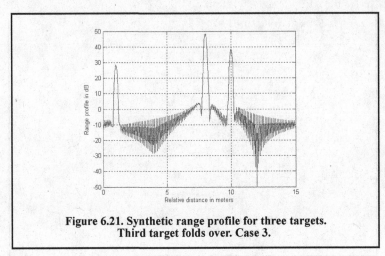

Figure 6.21. Synthetic range profile for three targets. Third target folds over. Case 3.

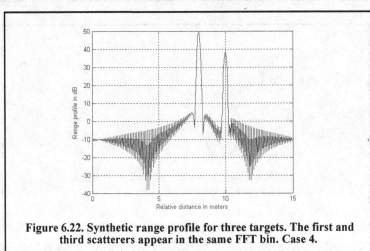

Figure 6.22. Synthetic range profile for three targets. The first and third scatterers appear in the same FFT bin. Case 4.

6.7.7. Effect of Target Velocity on Pulse Compression

SFW Case

The range profile defined in Eq. (6.215) is obtained by assuming that the target under examination is stationary. The effect of target velocity on the synthesized range profile can be determined by starting with Eq. (6.210) and assuming that $v \neq 0$. Performing similar analysis as that of the stationary target case yields a range profile given by

$$H_l = \sum_{i=0}^{N-1} A_i \exp\left\{ j\frac{2\pi l i}{N} - j2\pi f_i \left[\frac{2R}{c} - \frac{2v}{c}\left(iT + \frac{\tau_r}{2} + \frac{2R}{c} \right) \right] \right\}$$

Eq. (6.225)

The additional phase term present in Eq. (6.225) distorts the synthesized range profile. In order to illustrate this distortion, consider the SFW described in the previous section, and assume the three scatterers of the first case. Also, assume that $v = 200 m/s$. Figure 6.23 shows the synthesized range profile for this case. Comparisons of Figs. 6.19 and 6.23 clearly show the distortion effects caused by the uncompensated target velocity. Figure 6.24 is similar to Fig. 6.23

except in this case, $v = -200 m/s$. Note in either case, the targets have moved from their expected positions (to the left or right) by $Disp = 2 \times n \times v / PRF$ *(1.28 m)*, where the term *Disp* indicates displacement. This distortion can be eliminated by multiplying the complex received data at each pulse by the phase term

$$\Phi = \exp\left(-j2\pi f_i\left[\frac{2\hat{v}}{c}\left(iT + \frac{\tau_r}{2} + \frac{2\hat{R}}{c}\right)\right]\right)$$

Eq. (6.226)

$\hat{v}$ and $\hat{R}$ are, respectively, estimates of the target velocity and range. This process of modifying the phase of the quadrature components is often referred to as "phase rotation." In practice, when good estimates of $\hat{v}$ and $\hat{R}$ are not available, then the effects of target velocity are reduced by using frequency hopping between the consecutive pulses within the SFW. In this case, the frequency of each individual pulse is chosen according to a predetermined code. Waveforms of this type are often called frequency coded waveforms (FCW). Costas waveforms or signals are a good example of this type of waveform. Figure 6.25 shows a synthesized range profile for a moving target whose RCS is $\sigma = 10 m^2$ and $v = 10 m/s$. The initial target range is at $R = 912 m$. All other parameters are as before.

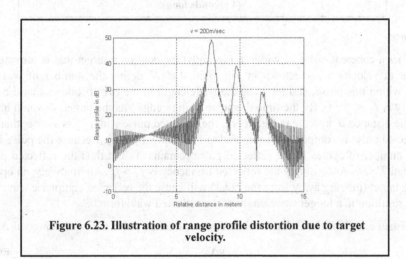

Figure 6.23. Illustration of range profile distortion due to target velocity.

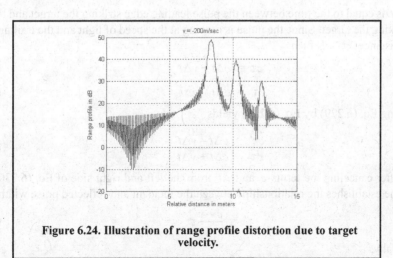

Figure 6.24. Illustration of range profile distortion due to target velocity.

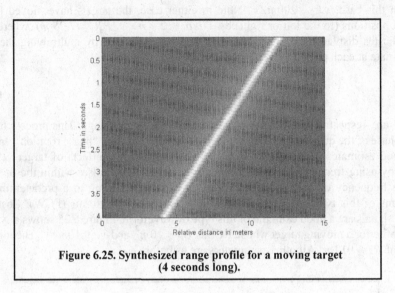

**Figure 6.25. Synthesized range profile for a moving target
(4 seconds long).**

LFM Case

Consider a coherent pulse of width τ (seconds) incident on a target that is moving toward the radar at velocity v, as shown in Fig. 6.26. Let N define the number of wavelengths (cycles) within this pulse, and let λ be the wavelength in meters. It follows that the incident frequency is $f_0 = N/\tau$. By the time the pulse trailing edge hits the target, it would have traveled some distance d into the pulse; hence, the reflected pulse width τ' is shorter than τ (i.e., the reflected pulse is compressed compared to the incident pulse). Because the pulse is coherent, the number of cycles in the reflected pulse remains N and thus the reflected pulse has wavelength $\lambda' < \lambda$. Accordingly the reflected frequency is $f_0' > f_0$. Alternatively, an opening or receding target (moving away from the radar) will cause the reflected equiphase wavefronts to expand, resulting in a longer wavelength of the reflected waveform.

The distance d (in meters) that the target moves into the pulse during the interval Δt,

$$d = v\Delta t \qquad\qquad \text{Eq. (6.227)}$$

where Δt is equal to the time between the pulse leading edge striking the target and the trailing edge striking the target. Since the pulse is moving at the speed of light and the trailing edge has moved distance $c\tau - d$, then

$$c\tau = c\Delta t + v\Delta t \qquad\qquad \text{Eq. (6.228)}$$

$$c\tau' = c\Delta t - v\Delta t. \qquad\qquad \text{Eq. (6.229)}$$

Dividing Eq. (6.229) by Eq. (6.228) yields

$$\frac{c\tau'}{c\tau} = \frac{c\Delta t - v\Delta t}{c\Delta t + v\Delta t} \qquad\qquad \text{Eq. (6.230)}$$

which, after canceling the terms c and Δt from the left and right side of Eq. (6.230), respectively, one establishes the relationship between the incident and reflected pulse widths as

$$\tau' = \frac{c-v}{c+v}\tau. \qquad\qquad \text{Eq. (6.231)}$$

Additionally,

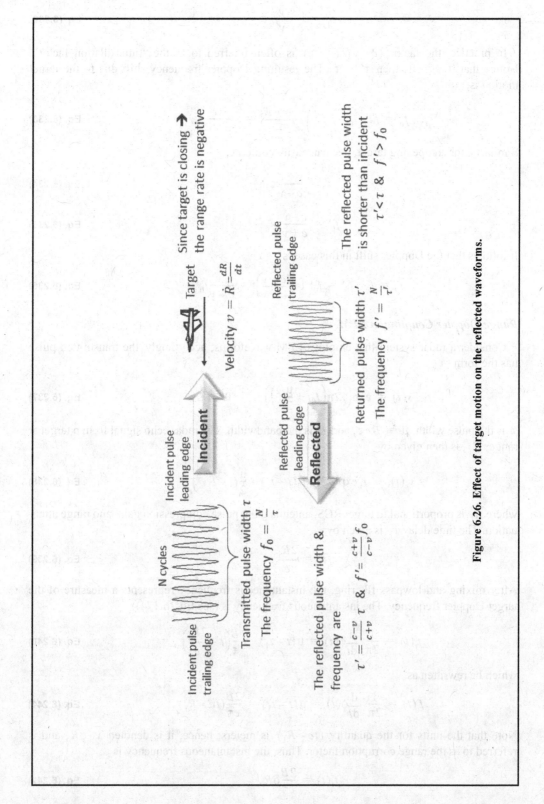

Figure 6.26. Effect of target motion on the reflected waveforms.

$$f_0' = \frac{c+v}{c-v}f_0.$$

Eq. (6.232)

In practice, the factor $(c-v)/(c+v)$ is often referred to as the "time dilation factor". Notice that if $v = 0$, then $\tau' = \tau$. The resulting Doppler frequency shift due to the target motion is,

$$f_d = f_0 - f_0' = f_0\left(1 - \frac{c+v}{c-v}\right) = -\frac{2v}{c-v}f_0.$$

Eq. (6.233)

Similarly, for an opening target, one can easily compute,

$$\tau' = \frac{v+c}{c-v}\tau,$$

Eq. (6.234)

$$f_0' = \frac{c-v}{c+v}f_0.$$

Eq. (6.235)

It follows that the Doppler shift in this case is

$$f_d = f_0 - f_0' = f_0\left(1 - \frac{c-v}{c+v}\right) = \frac{2v}{c-v}f_0.$$

Eq. (6.236)

Range-Doppler Coupling in LFM

Consider a radar system that employs LFM waveforms; accordingly, the transmitted pulse has the form

$$s(t) = \exp\left(j2\pi\left(f_0 t + \frac{\mu}{2}t^2\right)\right) \qquad 0 \le t \le \tau$$

Eq. (6.237)

τ is the pulse width, $\mu = B/\tau$, and B is the bandwidth. The radar echo signal from a target at range, R_1, is then given by

$$s_r(t) = a_1 \exp\left(j2\pi\left(f_0(t-t_1) + \frac{\mu}{2}(t-t_1)^2\right)\right)$$

Eq. (6.238)

where a_1 is proportional to target RCS, antenna gain, pulse compression gain, and range attenuation. The time delay t_1 is given by

$$t_1 = \frac{2R_1}{c}.$$

Eq. (6.239)

After mixing and lowpass filtering, the instantaneous frequency represents a measure of the target Doppler frequency. The instantaneous frequency is (see Eq. (6.174))

$$f_i(t) = \frac{1}{2\pi}\frac{d}{dt}\phi(t) = \mu(t-t_1) = \frac{B}{\tau}\left(t - \frac{2R_1}{c}\right),$$

Eq. (6.240)

which be rewritten as

$$f_i(t) = \frac{1}{2\pi}\frac{d}{dt}\phi(t) = \mu(t-t_1) = \frac{2B}{c\tau}(tc - R_1).$$

Eq. (6.241)

Note that the units for the quantity $(tc - R_1)$ is meters; hence, it is denoted as δR, and is referred to as the range corruption factor. Thus, the instantaneous frequency is

$$f_i(t) = \frac{2B}{c\tau}\delta R.$$

Eq. (6.242)

Equating the right-hand side òf Eq. (6.235) and Eq. (6.242) yields,

$$\frac{2v}{c-v}f_0 = \frac{2B}{c\tau}\delta R,$$

Eq. (6.243)

rearranging terms; yields the range corruption factor as

$$\delta R = \left(\frac{c\tau}{B}\right)\left(\frac{v}{c-v}\right)f_0 \cong \frac{\tau}{B}vf_0,$$

Eq. (6.244)

where the approximation $(c-v) \cong c$ was utilized. As clearly indicated from Eq. (6.244) target motion will corrupt the measurement. Therefore, for a moving target, the pulsed compressed output will be shifted left or right by the amount of the range error given in Eq. (6.244). This error is often referred to as the range Doppler coupling error.

For example, assume a hypothetical case with the following parameters:

Bandwidth	Pulse width	f_0	v
100MHz	$2.5\,\mu s$	16 GHz	-5000 m/s

It follows that $\delta R = 2m$. Figure 6.27 shows the impact of this range error on the estimated target location. As shown in this example, the peak of the compressed pulse is at *198m* instead the true target location at $R = 200m$ within the receive window.

Intuitively, if one can a priori, estimate the target range rate $\dot{R}$, then the radar might transmit a pulse that is either longer or shorter (depending on the sign of $\dot{R}$) by the amount it estimates the time dilation factor. However, doing that can be a very challenging task, and it is more practical to modify the transmit center frequency and bandwidth in anticipation of range measurement corruption. More specifically, if the desired nominal radar frequency and bandwidth are respectively, f_0 and B, then the radar will transmit a pulse whose frequency and bandwidth are $f_r = \gamma f_0$ and $B_r = \gamma B$ where γ is the time dilation factor, $\gamma = (c+v)/(c-v)$ for a closing target and is equal to the reciprocal of it in the case of an opening target.

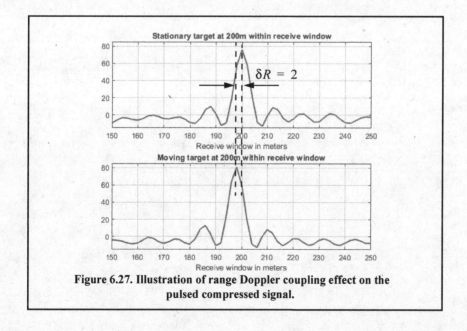

Figure 6.27. Illustration of range Doppler coupling effect on the pulsed compressed signal.

Chapter 7

Radar Ambiguity
Function

Bassem R. Mahafza

7.1. Ambiguity Function Definition

Consider a radar system that employs the matched filter receiver. The general form for the radar transmitted bandpass signal is

$$x(t) = x_I(t)\cos 2\pi f_0 t - x_Q(t)\sin 2\pi f_0 t.$$

Eq. (7.1)

The output of the matched filter due to a moving target with Doppler frequency f_d is

$$x_o(\tau; f_d) = e^{-j2\pi f_0 t_0}\int_{-\infty}^{\infty} \tilde{x}(t)\tilde{x}^*(\tau-t)e^{j2\pi f_d t}\, dt.$$

Eq. (7.2)

where $\tilde{x}(t)$ is the complex envelope, and t_0 is the round trip delay it takes a certain radar pulse to travel from the radar to the target at range R_0 and back; it is given by

$$t_0 = \frac{2R_0}{c}$$

Eq. (7.3)

as always, c is the speed of light.

The modulus square of Eq. (7.2) is referred to as the ambiguity function $\chi(\tau, f_d)$. That is,

$$\chi(\tau, f_d) = |x_o(\tau; f_d)|^2 = \left|\int_{-\infty}^{\infty} \tilde{x}(t)\tilde{x}^*(t-\tau)e^{j2\pi f_d t}\, dt\right|^2.$$

Eq. (7.4)

Let E_x as the energy of the signal $\tilde{x}(t)$,

$$E_x = \int_{-\infty}^{\infty} |\tilde{x}(t)|^2\, dt.$$

Eq. (7.5)

The properties for the radar ambiguity function are listed below:

1) The maximum value for the ambiguity function occurs at $(\tau, f_d) = (0, 0)$ and is equal to $4E_x^2$,

$$max\{\chi(\tau; f_d)\} = \chi(0; 0) = (2E_x)^2$$

Eq. (7.6)

$$\chi(\tau; f_d) \leq \chi(0; 0),$$

Eq. (7.7)

2) The ambiguity function is symmetric,

$$\chi(\tau;f_d) = \chi(-\tau;-f_d),$$

Eq. (7.8)

3) The total volume under the ambiguity function is constant,

$$\iint (\chi(\tau;f_d)) \; d\tau \; df_d = (2E_x)^2,$$

Eq. (7.9)

4) If the function $X(f)$ is the Fourier transform of the signal $x(t)$, then by using Parseval's theorem we get

$$\chi(\tau;f_d) = \left| \int X^*(f)X(f-f_d)e^{-j2\pi f\tau} df \right|^2.$$

Eq. (7.10)

5) Suppose that $\chi(\tau;f_d)$ is the ambiguity function for the signal $\tilde{x}(t)$. Adding a quadratic phase modulation term to $\tilde{x}(t)$ yields

$$\tilde{x}_1(t) = \tilde{x}(t)e^{j\pi\mu t^2}$$

Eq. (7.11)

where μ is a constant. It follows that the ambiguity function for the signal $\tilde{x}_1(t)$ is given by

$$\chi_1(\tau;f_d) = \chi(\tau;(f_d+\mu\tau)).$$

Eq. (7.12)

The radar ambiguity function describes the interference caused by the range and/or Doppler shift of a target when compared to a reference target of equal radar cross-section (RCS). The ambiguity function evaluated at $(\tau,f_d) = (0,0)$ is equal to the matched filter output that is perfectly matched to the signal reflected from the target of interest. In other words, returns from the nominal target are located at the origin of the ambiguity function. Thus, the ambiguity function at nonzero τ and f_d represents returns from some range and Doppler different from those for the nominal target. The ambiguity function is normally used by radar designers as a means of studying different waveforms. It can provide insight about how different radar waveforms may be suitable for the various radar applications. It is also used to determine the range and Doppler resolutions for the waveform. The three-dimensional (3-D) plot of the ambiguity function versus frequency and time delay is called the "radar ambiguity diagram".

The ideal radar ambiguity function is represented by a spike of infinitesimal width that peaks at the origin and is zero everywhere else, as illustrated in Fig. 7.1. An ideal ambiguity function provides perfect resolution between neighboring targets regardless of how close they may be to each other. Unfortunately, an ideal ambiguity function cannot physically exist because the ambiguity function must have a finite peak value equal to $(2E_x)^2$ and a finite volume also equal to $(2E_x)^2$. Clearly, the ideal ambiguity function cannot meet those conditions.

The instantaneous signal-to-noise ratio (SNR) at the output of the matched filter, assuming a signal plus additive white noise at its input, is optimum at some delay t_0 (that corresponds to the true target range R_0), and is given by

$$SNR(t_0) = \frac{E_x}{(\eta_0/2)},$$

Eq. (7.13)

where $(\eta_0/2)$ is the input noise power spectrum density. Equation (7.13) shows that the output instantaneous SNR depends on the ratio of the signal energy, E_x, to the input noise power density and is independent of the waveform used by the radar. This result, may intuitively lead to conclusion, in order to improve the radar sensitivity (i.e., SNR), one would employ a matched filter receiver and a signal $x(t)$ whose energy is maximum. However, recall that the pulse compression gain, G_{pc}, (a measure of SNR) at the output of the matched filter is equal to the time-bandwidth product of the signal $x(t)$.

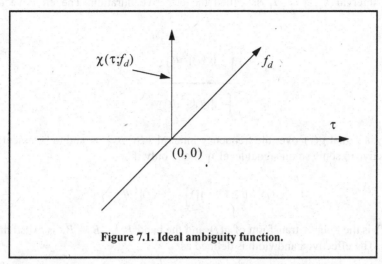

Figure 7.1. Ideal ambiguity function.

Recall that radar range resolution is improved as the signal bandwidth is increased. The bandwidth is computed as the reciprocal of the waveform (pulse) time resolution constant. This approximation that is widely used and accepted, even though it is not quite 100% accurate. This is true since using one value or the other for the bandwidth does not make much difference in the overall calculation of the SNR when using the radar equation. So, the answer to what signal characteristics are best for radar applications revolves around the output of the matched filter (i.e., the ambiguity function $\chi(\tau;f_d)$). The best pulse is the one that can provide simultaneous precision in range and Doppler, and maximize the matched filter pulse compression gain computed as the time-bandwidth product. The rest of this chapter is dedicated to studying these waveform metrics.

7.2. Effective Signal Bandwidth and Duration

The signal bandwidth is the range of frequency over which its spectrum is a nonzero. In general, any signal can be defined using its duration (pulse width) and bandwidth. A signal is said to be band-limited if it has finite bandwidth. Signals that have finite durations (time-limited) will have infinite bandwidths. Band-limited signals have infinite durations. The extreme case is a continuous sine-wave, whose bandwidth is infinitesimal.

Radar signal processing can be performed in either the time domain or frequency domain. In either case, the radar signal processor assumes signals to be of finite duration (time-limited) and finite bandwidth (band-limited). The trouble with this assumption is that time-limited and band-limited signals cannot simultaneously exist. That is, a signal cannot have finite duration and have finite bandwidth. Because of this, it is customary to assume that radar signals are essentially limited in time and frequency. Essentially time-limited signals are considered to be very small outside a certain finite time duration. If the Fourier transform of a signal is very small outside a certain finite frequency bandwidth, the signal is called an essentially band-limited signal. A signal $g(t)$ over the time interval $\{t_1, t_2\}$ is said to be essentially time-limited relative to some very small signal level ε if and only if

$$\int_{t_1}^{t_2} |g(t)|^2 dt \geq (1-\varepsilon)\int_{-\infty}^{\infty} |g(t)|^2 dt$$

Eq. (7.14)

where the interval $\tau_e = t_2 - t_1$ is called the effective duration. The effective duration is defined as

$$\tau_e = \frac{\left(\int_{-\infty}^{\infty} |g(t)|^2 dt\right)^2}{\int_{-\infty}^{\infty} |g(t)|^4 dt}.$$

Eq. (7.15)

Similarly, a signal $g(t)$ over the frequency interval $\{B_1, B_2\}$ is said to be essentially band-limited relative to some small signal level η if and only if

$$\int_{B_1}^{B_2} |G(f)|^2 df \geq (1-\eta) \int_{-\infty}^{\infty} |G(f)|^2 df$$

Eq. (7.16)

where $G(f)$ is the Fourier transform of $g(t)$ and the band $B_e = B_2 - B_1$ is called the effective bandwidth. The effective bandwidth is defined as

$$B_e = \frac{\left(\int_{-\infty}^{\infty} |G(f)|^2 df\right)^2}{\int_{-\infty}^{\infty} |G(f)|^4 df}.$$

Eq. (7.17)

Different, but equivalent, definitions for the effective bandwidth and effective duration can be found in the literature. In this book, the definitions cited in Burdic (1968) are adopted. The quantity $B_e \tau_e$ is referred to as the time-bandwidth product.

7.3. Single Pulse Ambiguity Function

The complex envelope of a single pulse is $\tilde{x}(t)$ defined by

$$\tilde{x}(t) = \frac{1}{\sqrt{\tau_0}} x(t) = \frac{1}{\sqrt{\tau_0}} Rect\left(\frac{t}{\tau_0}\right)$$

Eq. (7.18)

where

$$x(t) = Rect\left(\frac{t}{\tau_0}\right) = \begin{cases} 1 & \frac{-\tau_0}{2} < 0 < \frac{\tau_0}{2} \\ 0 & elsewhere \end{cases}.$$

Eq. (7.19)

The corresponding autocorrelation function for the envelop $\tilde{x}(t)$ is,

$$\mathcal{R}_x(\tau) = \begin{cases} \frac{1}{\tau_0}(\tau_0 + t) & -\tau_0 \leq t \leq 0 \\ \frac{1}{\tau_0}(\tau_0 - t) & 0 \leq t \leq \tau_0 \\ 0 & elsewhere \end{cases} \Leftrightarrow \left(1 - \frac{|\tau|}{\tau_0}\right) \quad |\tau| \leq \tau_0.$$

Eq. (7.20)

7.3.1. Time-Bandwidth Product

The effective bandwidth for the complex envelope of a rectangular pulse, $\tilde{x}(t)$, is computed using Eq. (7.17). For this purpose, the denominator is

$$\int_{-\infty}^{\infty} |\tilde{X}(f)|^4 \, df = \int_{-\infty}^{\infty} |\mathcal{R}_x(\tau)|^2 \, d\tau = \frac{2}{3} \qquad \text{Eq. (7.21)}$$

and its numerator is computed as

$$\left(\int_{-\infty}^{\infty} |\tilde{X}(f)|^2 \, df \right)^2 = |\mathcal{R}_x(0)|^2 = 1. \qquad \text{Eq. (7.22)}$$

Note that Eq. (7.22) represents the square of the signal total energy. Therefore, the effective bandwidth is

$$B_e = \frac{\left(\int_{-\infty}^{\infty} |\tilde{X}(f)|^2 \, df \right)^2}{\int_{-\infty}^{\infty} |\tilde{X}(f)|^4 \, df} = \frac{(\tau_0^2)}{\left(\frac{2\tau_0^3}{3} \right)} = \frac{3}{2}. \qquad \text{Eq. (7.23)}$$

The effective duration for the signal $\tilde{x}(t)$ is computed from Eq. (7.15) as

$$\tau_e = \frac{\left(\int_{-\infty}^{\infty} |\tilde{x}(t)|^2 \, dt \right)^2}{\int_{-\infty}^{\infty} |\tilde{x}(t)|^4 \, dt} \qquad \text{Eq. (7.24)}$$

$$\tau_e = \frac{\left(\int_{-\tau_0/2}^{\tau_0/2} (1)^2 \, dt \right)^2}{\int_{-\tau_0/2}^{\tau_0/2} (1)^4 \, dt} = \frac{\tau_0^2}{\tau_0^2} = 1. \qquad \text{Eq. (7.25)}$$

Finally, the time-bandwidth product for this signal is

$$B_e \tau_e = \frac{3}{2} \times 1 = \frac{3}{2}. \qquad \text{Eq. (7.26)}$$

7.3.2. Ambiguity Function

In accordance with Eq. (7.2), the output of the matched filter is

$$x_o(\tau; f_d) = e^{-j2\pi f_0 t_0} \int_{-\infty}^{\infty} \tilde{x}(t) \tilde{x}^*(\tau - t) e^{j2\pi f_d t} \, dt \qquad \text{Eq. (7.27)}$$

the complex envelope $\tilde{x}(t)$ is as defined in Eq. (7.18). It follows that the ambiguity function is

$$\chi(\tau;f_d) = \left| \int_{-\infty}^{\infty} \tilde{x}(t)\tilde{x}^*(t-\tau)e^{j2\pi f_d t}dt \right|^2 .$$ **Eq. (7.28)**

Substituting Eq. (7.18) into Eq. (7.28) and performing the integration yields

$$\chi(\tau;f_d) = \left| \left(1 - \frac{|\tau|}{\tau_0}\right) \frac{\sin(\pi f_d(\tau_0 - |\tau|))}{\pi f_d(\tau_0 - |\tau|)} \right|^2 \qquad |\tau| \le \tau_0 .$$ **Eq. (7.29)**

Figures 7.2-a and 7.2-b show 3-D and contour plots of single pulse ambiguity function. The ambiguity function cut along the time-delay axis τ is obtained by setting $f_d = 0$,

$$\chi(\tau;0) = \left(1 - \frac{|\tau|}{\tau_0}\right)^2 \qquad |\tau| \le \tau_0 .$$ **Eq. (7.30)**

Note that the time autocorrelation function of the signal $\tilde{x}(t)$ is equal to $\chi(\tau;0)$ (which as one would expect, it is equal to the square of Eq. (7.20)). Similarly, the cut along the Doppler axis is

$$\chi(0;f_d) = \left| \frac{\sin \pi \tau_0 f_d}{\pi \tau_0 f_d} \right|^2 .$$ **Eq. (7.31)**

Figures 7.3 and 7.4, respectively, show the plots of the ambiguity function cuts defined by Eqs. (7.30) and (7.31). Since the zero Doppler cut along the time-delay axis extends between $-\tau_0$ and τ_0, close targets will be unambiguous if they are at least τ_0 seconds apart. The zero time cut along the Doppler frequency axis has a $(\sin(x)/x)^2$ shape. It extends from $-\infty$ to ∞. The first null occurs at $f_d = \pm 1/\tau_0$. Hence, it is possible to detect two targets that are shifted by $1/\tau_0$, without any ambiguity. Thus, the single pulse range and Doppler resolutions are limited by the pulse width τ_0. Fine range resolution requires that a very short pulse be used. Unfortunately, using very short pulses requires very large operating bandwidths and may limit the radar average transmitted power to impractical values.

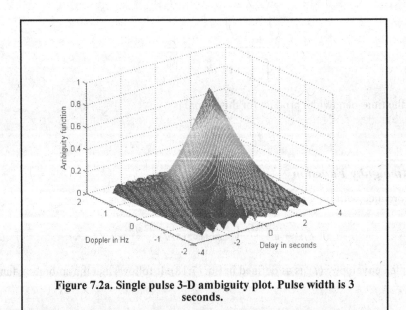

Figure 7.2a. Single pulse 3-D ambiguity plot. Pulse width is 3 seconds.

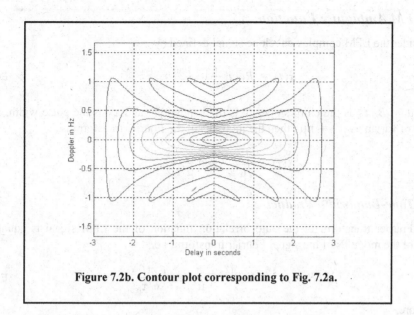

Figure 7.2b. Contour plot corresponding to Fig. 7.2a.

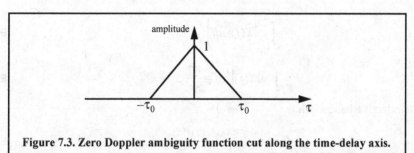

Figure 7.3. Zero Doppler ambiguity function cut along the time-delay axis.

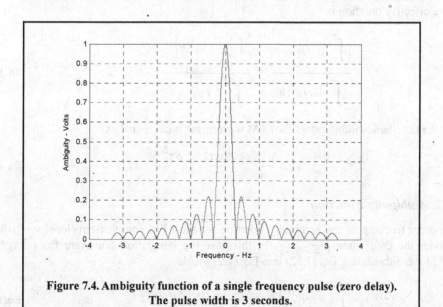

Figure 7.4. Ambiguity function of a single frequency pulse (zero delay).
The pulse width is 3 seconds.

7.4. LFM Ambiguity Function

Consider the LFM complex envelope signal defined by

$$\tilde{x}(t) = Rect\left(\frac{t}{\tau_0}\right) e^{j\pi\mu t^2} \quad , \qquad\qquad \textbf{Eq. (7.32)}$$

where $\mu = B/\tau_0$ is the chirp slope, B is the bandwidth, and τ_0 is the pulse width. Make a change of variables $\mu' = \pi\mu$, then the modulus of the Fourier transform is

$$|\tilde{X}(f)| \approx \sqrt{\frac{\pi}{\mu'}} \; Rect\left(\frac{\pi f}{\mu'\tau_0}\right). \qquad\qquad \textbf{Eq. (7.33)}$$

7.4.1. Time-Bandwidth Product

The Fourier transform of the autocorrelation function of the LFM signal is equal to the square of the modulus of the signal Fourier transform, i.e.,

$$\mathcal{F}\{R_x(\tau)\} = |\tilde{X}(f)|^2 = \frac{\pi}{\mu'}Rect\left(\frac{\pi f}{\mu'\tau_0}\right) \quad . \qquad\qquad \textbf{Eq. (7.34)}$$

Therefore,

$$\left(\int_{-\infty}^{\infty} |\tilde{X}(f)|^2 df\right)^2 \approx \tau_0^2 \qquad\qquad \textbf{Eq. (7.35)}$$

$$\int_{-\infty}^{\infty} |\tilde{X}(f)|^4 df \cong \frac{\pi\tau_0}{\mu'} \; . \qquad\qquad \textbf{Eq. (7.36)}$$

Then the effective bandwidth is

$$B_e \approx \tau_0^2 / \left(\frac{\pi\tau_0}{\mu'}\right) = \frac{\mu'\tau_0}{\pi} \; . \qquad\qquad \textbf{Eq. (7.37)}$$

The effective duration is

$$\tau_e = \frac{\left(\int_{-\infty}^{\infty} |\tilde{x}(t)|^2 dt\right)^2}{\int_{-\infty}^{\infty} |\tilde{x}(t)|^4 dt} = \frac{\left(\int_{-\tau_0/2}^{\tau_0/2} (1)^2 dt\right)^2}{\int_{-\tau_0/2}^{\tau_0/2} (1)^4 dt} = \frac{\tau_0^2}{\tau_0} = \tau_0 \; . \qquad\qquad \textbf{Eq. (7.38)}$$

And the time-bandwidth product for LFM waveforms is computed as

$$B_e\tau_e \approx \frac{\mu'\tau_0}{\pi}\tau_0 = \frac{\mu'\tau_0^2}{\pi} = \frac{\pi\mu\tau_0^2}{\pi} = \frac{B\tau_0^2}{\tau_0} = B\tau_0 \; . \qquad\qquad \textbf{Eq. (7.39)}$$

7.4.2. Ambiguity Function

In order to compute the ambiguity function for the LFM complex envelope, we will first consider the case when $0 \le \tau \le \tau_0$. In this case the integration limits are from $-\tau_0/2$ to $(\tau_0/2) - \tau$. Substituting Eq. (7.32) into Eq. (7.2) yields

$$x_o(\tau;f_d) = \int_{-\infty}^{\infty} Rect\left(\frac{t}{\tau_0}\right) Rect\left(\frac{t-\tau}{\tau_0}\right) e^{j\pi\mu t^2} e^{-j\pi\mu(t-\tau)^2} e^{j2\pi f_d t} \; dt \; . \qquad \textbf{Eq. (7.40)}$$

It follows that

$$x_o(\tau;f_d) = e^{-j\pi\mu\tau^2} \int_{\frac{-\tau_0}{2}}^{\frac{\tau_0}{2}-\tau} e^{j2\pi(\mu\tau+f_d)t} \, dt.$$ **Eq. (7.41)**

Finishing the integration process in Eq. (7.41) yields

$$x_o(\tau;f_d) = e^{j\pi\tau f_d}\left(1-\frac{\tau}{\tau_0}\right)\frac{\sin(\pi\tau_0(\mu\tau+f_d)(1-\tau/\tau_0))}{\pi\tau_0(\mu\tau+f_d)(1-\tau/\tau_0)} \qquad 0 \le \tau \le \tau_0.$$ **Eq. (7.42)**

Similar analysis for the case when $-\tau_0 \le \tau \le 0$ can be carried out, where, in this case, the integration limits are from $(-\tau_0/2)-\tau$ to $\tau_0/2$. Then by using the symmetry property of the ambiguity function, one can compute an expression for $x_o(\tau;f_d)$ that is valid for any τ,

$$x_o(\tau;f_d) = e^{j\pi\tau f_d}\left(1-\frac{|\tau|}{\tau_0}\right)\frac{\sin(\pi\tau_0(\mu\tau+f_d)(1-|\tau|/\tau_0))}{\pi\tau_0(\mu\tau+f_d)(1-|\tau|/\tau_0)} \qquad |\tau| \le \tau_0$$ **Eq. (7.43)**

and finally, the up-chirp LFM ambiguity function is

$$\chi(\tau;f_d) = \left|\left(1-\frac{|\tau|}{\tau_0}\right)\frac{\sin(\pi\tau_0(\mu\tau+f_d)(1-|\tau|/\tau_0))}{\pi\tau_0(\mu\tau+f_d)(1-|\tau|/\tau_0)}\right|^2 \qquad |\tau| \le \tau_0.$$ **Eq. (7.44)**

Similarly, the ambiguity function for a down-chirp LFM waveform is given by

$$\chi(\tau;f_d) = \left|\left(1-\frac{|\tau|}{\tau_0}\right)\frac{\sin(\pi\tau_0(\mu\tau-f_d)(1-|\tau|/\tau_0))}{\pi\tau_0(\mu\tau-f_d)(1-|\tau|/\tau_0)}\right|^2 \qquad |\tau| \le \tau_0.$$ **Eq. (7.45)**

Figures 7.5-a and 7.5-b show 3-D and contour plots for the LFM ambiguity functions for $\tau_0 = 1$ second and $B = 5Hz$ for a down-chirp pulse. The up-chirp ambiguity function cut along the time-delay axis τ is

$$\chi(\tau;0) = \left|\left(1-\frac{|\tau|}{\tau_0}\right)\frac{\sin(\pi\mu\tau_0\tau(1-|\tau|/\tau_0))}{\pi\mu\tau_0\tau(1-|\tau|/\tau_0)}\right|^2 \qquad |\tau| \le \tau_0.$$ **Eq. (7.46)**

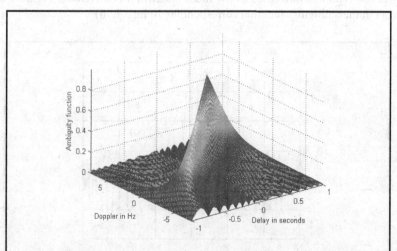

Figure 7.5a. Down-chirp LFM 3-D ambiguity plot. Pulse width is 1 second, and bandwidth is 5*Hz*.

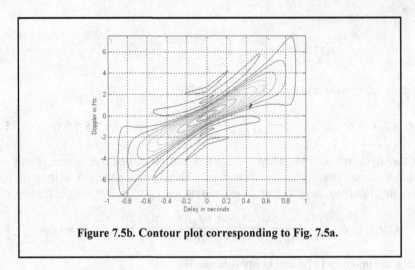

Figure 7.5b. Contour plot corresponding to Fig. 7.5a.

Note that the LFM ambiguity function cut along the Doppler frequency axis (i.e., $\chi(0, f_d)$) is similar to that of the single pulse given in Eq. (7.31). This should not be surprising since the pulse shape has not changed (only frequency modulation was added). However, the cut along the time-delay axis changes significantly; it is now much narrower compared to the unmodulated pulse cut. In this case, the first null occurs at

$$\tau_{n1} \approx 1/B \,.$$ **Eq. (7.47)**

Equation (7.47) shows that the effective pulse width (compressed pulse width) of the matched filter output is determined by the radar bandwidth. It follows that the LFM ambiguity function cut along the time-delay axis is narrower than that of the unmodulated pulse by a factor

$$\xi = \tau_0/(1/B) = \tau_0 B$$ **Eq. (7.48)**

where ξ is referred to as the compression ratio (also called the time-bandwidth product and compression gain). All three names can be used interchangeably. As indicated by Eq. (7.48), the compression ratio also increases as the radar bandwidth is increased. Figure 7.6 shows a plot for a cut in the ambiguity function corresponding to Eq. (7.46).

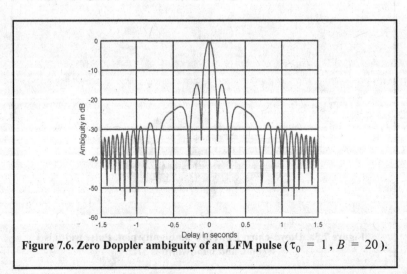

Figure 7.6. Zero Doppler ambiguity of an LFM pulse ($\tau_0 = 1$, $B = 20$).

Example:

Compute the range resolution before and after pulse compression corresponding to an LFM waveform whose bandwidth is $B = 1GHz$ and pulse width is $\tau_0 = 10ms$.

Solution:

The range resolution before pulse compression is

$$\Delta R_{uncomp} = \frac{c\tau_0}{2} = \frac{3 \times 10^8 \times 10 \times 10^{-3}}{2} = 1.5 \times 10^6 \ meters.$$

Using Eq. (7.47) yields

$$\tau_{n1} = \frac{1}{1 \times 10^9} = 1 \ ns \ and \ \Delta R_{comp} = \frac{c\tau_{n1}}{2} = \frac{3 \times 10^8 \times 1 \times 10^{-9}}{2} = 15 \ cm.$$

7.5. Coherent Pulse Train Ambiguity Function

Figure 7.7 shows a plot of a coherent pulse train. The pulse width is denoted as τ_0 and the pulse repetition interval is T. The number of pulses in the train is N; hence, the train's length is $T_t = NT$ seconds. A normalized individual pulse $\tilde{x}(t)$ is defined by

$$\tilde{x}_1(t) = \frac{1}{\sqrt{\tau_0}} Rect\left(\frac{t}{\tau_0}\right). \qquad \text{Eq. (7.49)}$$

When coherency is maintained between the consecutive pulses, then an expression for the normalized train is

$$\tilde{x}(t) = \frac{1}{\sqrt{N}} \sum_{i=0}^{N-1} \tilde{x}_1(t - iT). \qquad \text{Eq. (7.50)}$$

7.5.1. Time-Bandwidth Product

The finite duration train complex envelope is given by

$$\tilde{x}(t) = Rect\left(\frac{t}{NT}\right) \sum_{n=0}^{N-1} Rect\left(\frac{t - nT}{\tau_0}\right). \qquad \text{Eq. (7.51)}$$

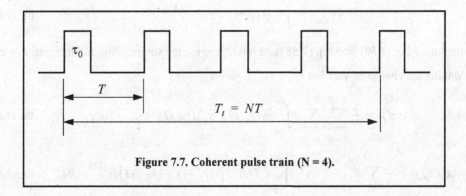

Figure 7.7. Coherent pulse train (N = 4).

The corresponding Fourier transform is

$$\tilde{X}(f) = \frac{T_t \tau_0}{T} Sinc(fT_t) \otimes \sum_{n=-\infty}^{\infty} Sinc(nf_r \tau_0) \delta(f - nf_r).$$ **Eq. (7.52)**

The total energy for this signal is

$$\int_{-\infty}^{\infty} |\tilde{X}(f)|^2 df = \frac{T_t \tau_0}{T}$$ **Eq. (7.53)**

It can also be shown that

$$\int_{-\infty}^{\infty} |\mathcal{R}_x(\tau)|^2 d\tau = \int_{-\infty}^{\infty} |\tilde{X}(f)|^4 df \cong \left(\frac{4}{3}\right)\left(\frac{T_t}{T}\right)^3 \left(\frac{2}{3}\right)(\tau_0)^3.$$ **Eq. (7.54)**

It follows that the effective bandwidth is

$$B_e \approx \frac{(T_t \tau_0 / T)^2}{(4/3)(T_t/T)^3 (2/3)(\tau_0)^3} = \left(\frac{3T}{4T_t}\right)\left(\frac{3}{2\tau_0}\right).$$ **Eq. (7.55)**

The result of Eq. (7.55) clearly indicates that the effective bandwidth of the pulse train decreases as the length of the train is increased. This should intuitively make a lot of sense, since the bandwidth is inversely proportional to signal duration.

The effective duration of this signal can be computed using Eq. (7.15). Again, the numerator represents the square of the total signal energy. In this case, the denominator is equal to unity. Thus, the effective duration is

$$\tau_e = \frac{T_t \tau_0}{T}$$ **Eq. (7.56)**

and the time-bandwidth product of this waveform is

$$B_e \tau_e \approx \left(\frac{3T}{4T_t}\right)\left(\frac{3}{2\tau_0}\right)\left(\frac{T_t \tau_0}{T}\right) = \frac{9}{8}.$$ **Eq. (7.57)**

7.5.2. Ambiguity Function

The output of the matched filter is

$$x_o(\tau; f_d) = \int_{-\infty}^{\infty} \tilde{x}(t)\tilde{x}^*(t-\tau)e^{j2\pi f_d t} dt.$$ **Eq. (7.58)**

Substituting Eq. (7.50) into Eq. (7.58) and interchanging the summations and integration yield

Making the change of variable $t_1 = t - iT$ yields

$$x_o(\tau; f_d) = \frac{1}{N} \sum_{i=0}^{N-1} \sum_{j=0}^{N-1} \int_{-\infty}^{\infty} \tilde{x}_1(t-iT) \ \tilde{x}_1^*(t-jT-\tau)e^{j2\pi f_d t} dt.$$ **Eq. (7.59)**

$$x_0(\tau; f_d) = \frac{1}{N} \sum_{i=0}^{N-1} e^{j2\pi f_d iT} \sum_{j=0}^{N-1} \int_{-\infty}^{\infty} \tilde{x}_1(t_1) \ \tilde{x}_1^*(t_1 - [\tau - (i-j)T])e^{j2\pi f_d t_1} dt_1.$$ **Eq. (7.60)**

The integral inside Eq. (7.60) represents the output of the matched filter for a single pulse and is denoted by $x_o^{(1)}$. It follows that

$$x_0(\tau;f_d) = \frac{1}{N} \sum_{i=0}^{N-1} e^{j2\pi f_d iT} \sum_{j=0}^{N-1} x_o^{(1)}[\tau - (i-j)T;f_d].$$ **Eq. (7.61)**

When the relation $q = i - j$ is used, then the following relation is true:

$$\sum_{i=0}^{N} \sum_{m=0}^{N} = \left. \sum_{q=-(N-1)}^{0} \sum_{i=0}^{N-1-|q|} \right|_{for\ j=i-q} + \left. \sum_{q=1}^{N-1} \sum_{j=0}^{N-1-|q|} \right|_{for\ i=j+q}.$$ **Eq. (7.62)**

Applying the result of Eq. (7.62) into Eq. (7.61) gives

$$x_o(\tau;f_d) = \frac{1}{N} \sum_{q=-(N-1)}^{0} \left\{ x_o^{(1)}(\tau - qT;f_d) \sum_{i=0}^{N-1-|q|} e^{j2\pi f_d iT} \right\}$$

$$+ \frac{1}{N} \sum_{q=1}^{N-1} \left\{ e^{j2\pi f_d qT} x_o^{(1)}(\tau - qT;f_d) \sum_{j=0}^{N-1-|q|} e^{j2\pi f_d jT} \right\}$$ **Eq. (7.63)**

Setting $z = \exp(j2\pi f_d T)$, and using the relation

$$\sum_{j=0}^{N-1-|q|} z^j = \frac{1-z^{N-|q|}}{1-z}$$ **Eq. (7.64)**

yields

$$\sum_{i=0}^{N-1-|q|} e^{j2\pi f_d iT} = e^{[j\pi f_d(N-1-|q|T)]} \frac{\sin[\pi f_d(N-1-|q|)T]}{\sin(\pi f_d T)}.$$ **Eq. (7.65)**

Using Eq. (7.65) in Eq. (7.61) yields two complementary sums for positive and negative q. Both sums can be combined as

$$x_0(\tau;f_d) = \frac{1}{N} \sum_{q=-(N-1)}^{N-1} x_o^{(1)}(\tau - qT;f_d) e^{[j\pi f_d(N-1+q)T]} \frac{\sin[\pi f_d(N-|q|)T]}{\sin(\pi f_d T)}.$$ **Eq. (7.66)**

The second part of the right-hand side of Eq. (7.66) is the impact of the train on the ambiguity function. The first part is primarily responsible for its shape details (according to the pulse type being used).

Finally, the ambiguity function associated with the coherent pulse train is computed as the modulus square of Eq. (7.66). For $\tau_0 < T/2$, the ambiguity function reduces to

$$\chi(\tau;f_d) = \left| \frac{1}{N} \sum_{q=-(N-1)}^{N-1} x_o^{(1)}(\tau - qT;f_d) \left| \frac{\sin[\pi f_d(N-|q|)T]}{\sin(\pi f_d T)} \right| \right|^2 ; |\tau| \le NT.$$ **Eq. (7.67)**

Within the region $|\tau| \le \tau_0 \Rightarrow q = 0$, Eq. (7.67) can be written as

$$\chi(\tau;f_d) = \chi_1(\tau;f_d) \left| \frac{\sin[\pi f_d NT]}{N\sin(\pi f_d T)} \right|^2 \; ; |\tau| \le \tau_0 . \qquad \text{Eq. (7.68)}$$

Where $\chi_1(\tau;f_d)$ is the ambiguity function for the signal $x_o^{(1)}$ (i.e., single rectangular pulse). Thus, the ambiguity function for a coherent pulse train is the superposition of the individual pulse's ambiguity function. The ambiguity function cuts along the time-delay and the Doppler axes are, respectively, given by

$$\chi(\tau;0) = \left| \sum_{q=-(N-1)}^{N-1} \left(1 - \frac{|q|}{N}\right)\left(1 - \frac{|\tau - qT|}{\tau_0}\right) \right|^2 ; \; |\tau - qT| < \tau_0 \qquad \text{Eq. (7.69)}$$

$$\chi(0;f_d) = \left| \frac{1}{N} \frac{\sin(\pi f_d \tau_0)}{\pi f_d \tau_0} \frac{\sin(\pi f_d NT)}{\sin(\pi f_d T)} \right|^2 . \qquad \text{Eq. (7.70)}$$

Figures 7.8-a and 7.8-b show the 3-D ambiguity plot and the corresponding contour plot for $N = 5$, $\tau_0 = 0.4$, and $T = 1$. Figures 7.8-c and 7.8-d, respectively, show sketches of the zero Doppler and zero delay cuts of the ambiguity function. The ambiguity function peaks along the frequency axis are located at multiple integers of the frequency $f = 1/T$. Alternatively, the peaks are at multiple integers of T along the delay axis. The width of the ambiguity function peaks along the delay axis $2\tau_0$. The peak width along the Doppler axis is $1/(N-1)T$.

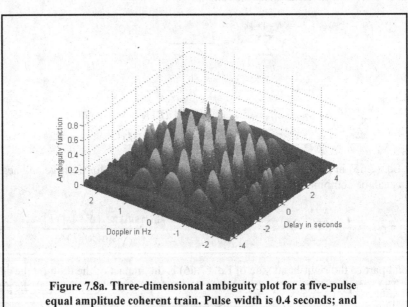

Figure 7.8a. Three-dimensional ambiguity plot for a five-pulse equal amplitude coherent train. Pulse width is 0.4 seconds; and PRI is 1 second, N=5.

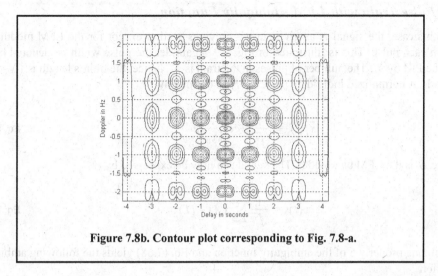

Figure 7.8b. Contour plot corresponding to Fig. 7.8-a.

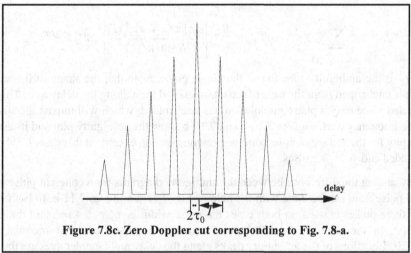

Figure 7.8c. Zero Doppler cut corresponding to Fig. 7.8-a.

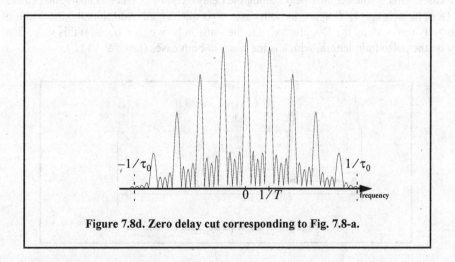

Figure 7.8d. Zero delay cut corresponding to Fig. 7.8-a.

7.6. Pulse Train with LFM Ambiguity Function

In this case, the signal is as given in the previous section except for the LFM modulation within each pulse. This is illustrated in Fig. 7.9. Again, let the pulse width be denoted by τ_0 and the PRI by T. The number of pulses in the train is N; hence, the train's length is $(N-1)T$ seconds. A normalized individual pulse $\tilde{x}_1(t)$ is defined by

$$\tilde{x}_1(t) = \frac{1}{\sqrt{\tau_0}} Rect\left(\frac{t}{\tau_0}\right) e^{j\pi\frac{B}{\tau_0}t^2} \qquad \text{Eq. (7.71)}$$

where B is the LFM bandwidth. The signal can now be expressed by

$$\tilde{x}(t) = \frac{1}{\sqrt{N}} \sum_{i=0}^{N-1} \tilde{x}_1(t-iT). \qquad \text{Eq. (7.72)}$$

Utilizing property 5 of the ambiguity function and Eq. (7.68) yields the following ambiguity function

$$\chi(\tau;f_d) = \sum_{q=-(N-1)}^{N-1} \chi_1\left(\tau-qT;f_d+\frac{B}{\tau_0}\tau\right) \left|\frac{\sin\left[\pi f_d(N-|q|)T\right]}{N\sin(\pi f_d T)}\right|^2 \quad ;|\tau|\leq NT \qquad \text{Eq. (7.73)}$$

where χ_1 is the ambiguity function of the single pulse. Note that the shape of the ambiguity function is unchanged from the case of the unmodulated train along the delay axis. This should be expected since only a phase modulation has been added, which will impact the shape only along the frequency axis. Figures 7.10-a and 7.10-b show the ambiguity plot and its associated contour plot for the same example from the previous section except, in this case, LFM modulation is added and $N = 3$ pulses.

Understanding the difference between the ambiguity diagrams for a coherent pulse train and an LFM pulse train can be done with the help of Fig. 7.11-a and Fig. 7.11-b. In both figures a train of three pulses is used; in both cases the pulse width is $\tau_0 = 0.4 \, sec$, and the period is $T = 1 \, sec$. In the case of the LFM pulse train, each pulse has LFM modulation with $B\tau_0 = 20$. Locations of the ambiguity peaks along the delay and Doppler axes are the same in both cases. This is true because peaks along the delay axis are T seconds apart and peaks along the Doppler axis are $1/T$ apart; in both cases T is unchanged. Additionally, the width of the ambiguity peaks along the Doppler axis are the same in both cases, because this value depends only on the pulse train length, which is the same in both cases (i.e., $(N-1)T$).

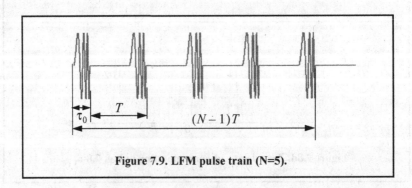

Figure 7.9. LFM pulse train (N=5).

The width of the ambiguity peaks along the delay axis are significantly different, however. In the case of the coherent pulse train, this width is approximately equal to twice the pulse width. Alternatively, this value is much smaller in the case of the LFM pulse train. This clearly leads to the expected conclusion that the addition of LFM modulation significantly enhances the range resolution. Finally, the presence of the LFM modulation introduces a slope change in the ambiguity diagram; again, a result that is also expected.

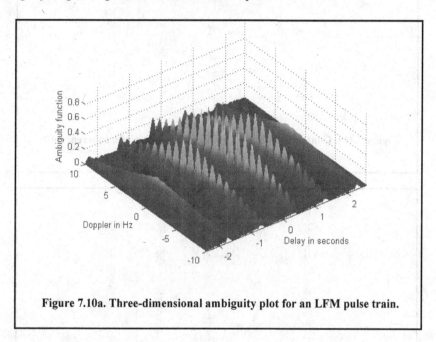

Figure 7.10a. Three-dimensional ambiguity plot for an LFM pulse train.

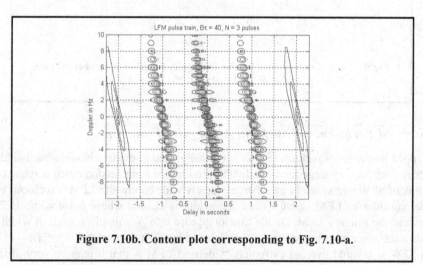

Figure 7.10b. Contour plot corresponding to Fig. 7.10-a.

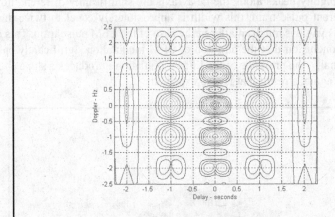

Figure 7.11a. Contour plot for the ambiguity function of a coherent pulse train. $N = 3; \tau_0 = 0.4;\ T = 1$.

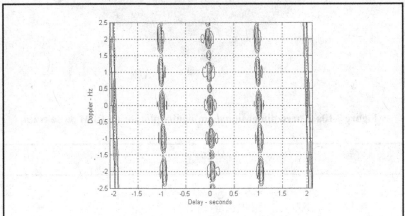

Figure 7.11b. Contour plot for the ambiguity function of a coherent pulse train. $N = 3;\ B\tau_0 = 20;\ T = 1$.

7.7. Stepped Frequency Waveform Ambiguity Function

A stepped frequency waveform (SFW) is typically used in extremely wide bandwidth radar applications where very large time-bandwidth product (or compression ratio) is required. One may think of SFW as a special case of an extremely wide bandwidth LFM waveform. For this purpose, consider an LFM signal whose bandwidth is B_i and whose pulse width is T_i, and refer to it as the primary LFM. Divide this long pulse into N subpulses, each of width τ_0, to generate a sequence of pulses whose PRI is denoted by T. It follows that $T_i = (n-1)T$. One reason SFW is favored over an extremely wideband LFM is that it may be very difficult to maintain the LFM slope when the time-bandwidth product is large. By using SFW, the same equivalent bandwidth can be achieved; however, phase errors are minimized since the LFM is chirped over a much shorter duration.

Define the beginning frequency for each subpulse as that value measured from the primary LFM at the leading edge of each subpulse, as illustrated in Fig. 7.12. That is

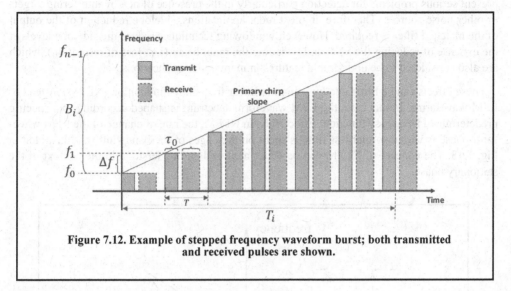

Figure 7.12. Example of stepped frequency waveform burst; both transmitted and received pulses are shown.

$$f_i = f_0 + i\Delta f; \quad i = 0, N-1 \qquad\qquad \textbf{Eq. (7.74)}$$

where Δf is the frequency step from one subpulse to another. The set of n subpulses is often referred to as a burst. Each subpulse can have its own LFM modulation. To this end, assume that the subpulse LFM modulation corresponds to an LFM slope of $\mu = B/\tau_0$.

The complex envelope of a single subpulse with LFM modulation is

$$\tilde{x}_1 = \frac{1}{\sqrt{\tau_0}} Rect\left(\frac{t}{\tau_0}\right) e^{j\pi\mu t^2}. \qquad\qquad \textbf{Eq. (7.75)}$$

Of course if the subpulses do not have any LFM modulation, then the same equation holds true by setting $\mu = 0$. The overall complex envelope of the whole burst is

$$\tilde{x}(t) = \frac{1}{\sqrt{N}} \sum_{i=0}^{N-1} \tilde{x}_1(t - iT). \qquad\qquad \textbf{Eq. (7.76)}$$

The ambiguity function of the matched filter corresponding to Eq. (7.76) can be obtained from that of the coherent pulse train developed in an earlier section along with property 5 of the ambiguity function, resulting in

$$\chi(\tau;f_d) = \sum_{q=-(N-1)}^{N-1} \chi_1\left(\tau - qT; \left(f_d + \frac{B}{\tau_0}\tau\right)\right) \left| \frac{\sin\left[\pi\left(f_d + \frac{\Delta f}{T}\tau\right)(N - |q|)T\right]}{N\sin\left(\pi\left(f_d + \frac{\Delta f}{T}\tau\right)T\right)} \right|^2 \quad ; |\tau| \leq NT \quad \textbf{Eq. (7.77)}$$

where χ_1 is the ambiguity function of the single pulse.

7.8. Nonlinear Frequency Modulation

As clearly shown by Fig. 7.6, the output of the matched filter corresponding to an LFM pulse has sidelobe levels similar to those of the $|\sin(x)/x|^2$ signal, that is, $13.4dB$ below the main beam peak. In many radar applications, these sidelobe levels are considered too high and may present serious problems for detection particularly in the presence of nearby interfering targets or other noise sources. Therefore, in most radar applications, sidelobe reduction of the output of the matched filter is required. However, windowing techniques reduce the sidelobe levels at the expense of reducing the SNR and widening the main beam (i.e., loss of resolution), which are also considered to be undesirable features in many radar applications.

These effects can be mitigated by using nonlinear frequency modulation (NLFM) instead of LFM waveforms. In this case, the LFM waveform spectrum is shaped according to a specific predetermined frequency function. Effectively, in NLFM, the rate of change of the LFM wave-form phase is varied so that less time is spent on the edges of the bandwidth, as illustrated in Fig. 7.13. The concept of NLFM can be better analyzed and understood in the context of the stationary phase.

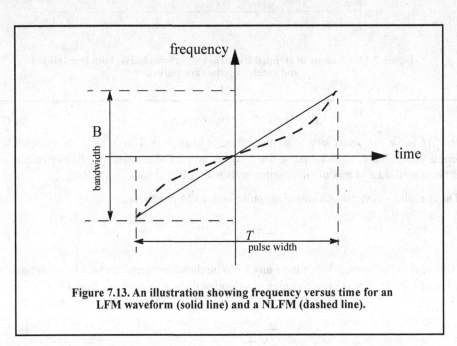

Figure 7.13. An illustration showing frequency versus time for an LFM waveform (solid line) and a NLFM (dashed line).

7.8.1. Concept of Stationary Phase

Consider the following bandpass signal

$$x(t) = x_I(t)\cos(2\pi f_0 t + \phi(t)) - x_Q(t)\sin(2\pi f_0 t + \phi(t)),\qquad \text{Eq. (7.78)}$$

where $\phi(t)$ is the frequency modulation. The corresponding analytic signal (pre-envelope) is

$$\psi(t) = \tilde{x}(t)e^{j2\pi f_0 t} = r(t)e^{j\phi(t)}e^{j2\pi f_0 t}\qquad \text{Eq. (7.79)}$$

where $\tilde{x}(t)$ is the complex envelope and is given by

$$\tilde{x}(t) = r(t)e^{j\phi(t)},\qquad \text{Eq. (7.80)}$$

The lowpass signal $r(t)$ represents the envelope of the transmitted signal; it is given by

$$r(t) = \sqrt{x_I^2(t) + x_Q^2(t)}.\qquad \text{Eq. (7.81)}$$

It follows that the Fourier transform of the signal $\tilde{x}(t)$ can then be written as

$$X(\omega) = \int_{-\infty}^{\infty} r(t)e^{j(-\omega t + \phi(t))} \, dt,$$

Eq. (7.82)

$$X(\omega) = |X(\omega)|e^{j\Phi(\omega)}$$

Eq. (7.83)

where $|X(\omega)|$ is the modulus of the Fourier transform and $\Phi(\omega)$ is the corresponding phase frequency response. It is clear that the integrand is an oscillating function of time varying at a rate of

$$\frac{d}{dt}[\omega t - \phi(t)].$$

Eq. (7.84)

Most contribution to the Fourier transform spectrum occurs when this rate of change is minimal. More specifically, it occurs when

$$\frac{d}{dt}[\omega t - \phi(t)] = 0 \Rightarrow \omega - \phi'(t) = 0 .$$

Eq. (7.85)

The expression in Eq. (7.85) is parametric since it relates two independent variables. Thus, for each value ω_n there is only one specific $\phi'(t_n)$ that satisfies Eq. (7.85). Thus, the time when this phase term is stationary will be different for different values of ω_n. Expanding the phase term in Eq. (7.85) about an incremental value t_n using Taylor series expansion yields

$$\omega_n t - \phi(t) = \omega_n t_n - \phi(t_n) + (\omega_n - \phi'(t_n))(t - t_n) - \frac{\phi''(t_n)}{2!}(t - t_n)^2 + \dots$$

Eq. (7.86)

An acceptable approximation of Eq. (7.86) is obtained by using the first three terms, provided that the difference $(t - t_n)$ is very small. Now, using the right-hand side of Eq. (7.85) into Eq. (7.86) and terminating the expansion at the first three terms yields

$$\omega_n t - \phi(t) = \omega_n t_n - \phi(t_n) - \frac{\phi''(t_n)}{2!}(t - t_n)^2 .$$

Eq. (7.87)

By substituting Eq. (7.87) into Eq. (7.82) and using the fact that $r(t)$ is relatively constant (slow varying) when compared to the rate at which the carrier signal is varying, gives

$$X(\omega_n) = r(t_n)\int_{t_n^-}^{t_n^+} e^{-j\left(\omega_n t_n - \phi(t_n) - \frac{\phi''(t_n)}{2}(t - t_n)^2\right)} \, dt$$

Eq. (7.88)

t_n^+ and t_n^- represent infinitesimal changes about t_n. Equation (7.88) can be written as

$$X(\omega_n) = r(t_n)e^{j(-\omega_n t_n - \phi(t_n))}\int_{t_n^-}^{t_n^+} e^{j\left(\frac{\phi''(t_n)}{2}(t - t_n)^2\right)} \, dt .$$

Eq. (7.89)

Consider the changes of variables

$$t - t_n = \lambda \Rightarrow dt = d\lambda$$

Eq. (7.90)

$$\sqrt{\phi''(t_n)}\lambda = \sqrt{\pi} \; y \Rightarrow d\lambda = \frac{\sqrt{\pi}}{\sqrt{\phi''(t_n)}}dy .$$

Eq. (7.91)

Using these changes of variables leads to

$$X(\omega_n) = \frac{2\sqrt{\pi}\ r(t_n)}{\sqrt{\phi''(t_n)}} e^{j(-\omega_n t_n - \phi(t_n))} \int_0^{y_0} e^{j\left(\frac{\pi y^2}{2}\right)}\ dy \qquad \text{Eq. (7.92)}$$

where

$$y_0 = \sqrt{\frac{|\phi''(t_n)|}{\pi}}. \qquad \text{Eq. (7.93)}$$

The integral in Eq. (7.92) is of the form of a Fresnel integral, which has an upper limit approximated by

$$\exp\left(j\frac{\pi}{4}\right) / \sqrt{2}. \qquad \text{Eq. (7.94)}$$

Substituting Eq. (7.94) into Eq. (7.92) yields

$$X(\omega_n) = \frac{\sqrt{2\pi}\ r(t_n)}{\sqrt{\phi''(t_n)}} e^{j\left(-\omega_n t_n - \phi(t_n) + \frac{\pi}{4}\right)}. \qquad \text{Eq. (7.95)}$$

Thus, for all possible values of ω

$$|X(\omega_t)|^2 \approx 2\pi \frac{r^2(t)}{|\phi''(t)|} \Rightarrow |X(\omega)| = \frac{\sqrt{2\pi}}{\sqrt{|\phi''(t)|}}\ r(t). \qquad \text{Eq. (7.96)}$$

The subscript t was used to indicate the dependency of ω on time.

Using a similar approach that led to Eq. (7.96), an expression for $\tilde{x}(t_n)$ can be obtained. From Eq. (7.83), the signal $\tilde{x}(t)$

$$\tilde{x}(t) = \frac{1}{2\pi} \int_{-\infty}^{\infty} |X(\omega)|\ e^{j(\Phi(\omega) + \omega t)}\ d\omega. \qquad \text{Eq. (7.97)}$$

The phase term $\Phi(\omega)$ is (using Eq. (7.87))

$$\Phi(\omega) = -\omega t - \phi(t) + \frac{\pi}{4}. \qquad \text{Eq. (7.98)}$$

Differentiating with respect to ω yields

$$\frac{d}{d\omega}\Phi(\omega) = -t - \frac{dt}{d\omega}\left[\omega - \frac{d}{dt}\phi(t)\right] = \Phi'(\omega)\ . \qquad \text{Eq. (7.99)}$$

Using the stationary phase relation in Eq. (7.85) (i.e., $\omega - \phi'(t) = 0$) yields

$$\Phi'(\omega) = -t \qquad \text{Eq. (7.100)}$$

and

$$\Phi''(\omega) = -\frac{dt}{d\omega}. \qquad \text{Eq. (7.101)}$$

Define the signal group time-delay function as

$$T_g(\omega) = -\Phi'(\omega), \qquad \text{Eq. (7.102)}$$

then the signal instantaneous frequency is the inverse of $T_g(\omega)$. Figure 7.14 shows a drawing illustrating this inverse relationship between the NLFM and the corresponding group time-delay function.

Comparison of Eq. (7.97) and Eq. (7.82) indicates that both equations have similar form. Thus, if one substitutes $X(\omega)/2\pi$ for $r(t)$, $\Phi(\omega)$ for $\phi(t)$, ω for t, and $-t$ for ω in Eq. (7.82), a similar expression to Eq. (7.95) can be derived. That is,

$$\left|\tilde{x}(t_\omega)\right|^2 \approx \frac{1}{2\pi}\frac{\left|X(\omega)\right|^2}{\left|\Phi''(\omega)\right|}.$$

Eq. (7.103)

The subscript ω was used to indicate the dependency of t on frequency. However, from Eq. (7.80)

$$\left|\tilde{x}(t)\right|^2 = \left|r(t)e^{j\phi(t)}\right|^2 = r^2(t).$$

Eq. (7.104)

It follows that Eq. (7.103) can be rewritten as

$$r^2(t_\omega) \approx \frac{1}{2\pi}\frac{\left|X(\omega)\right|^2}{\left|\Phi''(\omega)\right|} \Rightarrow r(t) = \frac{\left|X(\omega)\right|}{\sqrt{2\pi\left|\Phi''(\omega)\right|}}.$$

Eq. (7.105)

Substituting Eq. (7.104) into Eq. (7.105) yields a general relationship for any t

$$r^2(t)\ dt = \frac{1}{2\pi}\left|X(\omega)\right|^2 d\omega,$$

Eq. (7.106)

Clearly, the functions $r(t)$, $\phi(t)$, $X(\omega)$, and $\Phi(\omega)$ are related to each other as Fourier transform pairs, as given by

$$r(t)e^{j\phi(t)} = \frac{1}{2\pi}\int_{-\infty}^{\infty}\left|X(\omega)\right|\ e^{j(\Phi(\omega)+\omega t)}\ d\omega$$

Eq. (7.107)

$$\left|X(\omega)\right|\ e^{j\Phi(\omega)} = \int_{-\infty}^{\infty}r(t)\ e^{-j(\omega t-\phi(t))}\ d\omega.$$

Eq. (7.108)

They are also related using Parseval's theorem by

$$\int_{-\infty}^{t}r^2(\zeta)\ d\zeta = \frac{1}{2\pi}\int_{-\infty}^{\infty}\left|X(\lambda)\right|^2\ d\lambda.$$

Eq. (7.109)

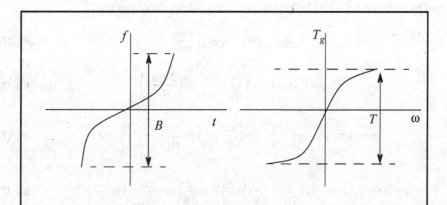

Figure 7.14. Matched filter time delay and frequency modulation for a NLFM waveform.

The formula for the output of the matched filter was derived earlier and is repeated here as Eq. (7.110)

$$x_o(\tau, f_d) = \int_{-\infty}^{\infty} \tilde{x}(t)\tilde{x}^*(t-\tau)e^{j2\pi f_d t} dt. \qquad \text{Eq. (7.110)}$$

Substituting the right-hand side of Eq. (7.80) into Eq. (7.110) yields

$$x_o(\tau, f_d) = \int_{-\infty}^{\infty} r(t)r^*(t-\tau)e^{j2\pi f_d t} dt. \qquad \text{Eq. (7.111)}$$

It follows that the zero Doppler and zero delay cuts of the ambiguity function can be written as

$$\chi(\tau, 0) = \frac{1}{2\pi}\int_{-\infty}^{\infty} |X(\omega)|^2 e^{j\omega\tau} d\omega \qquad \text{Eq. (7.112)}$$

$$\chi(0, f_d) = \int_{-\infty}^{\infty} |r(t)|^2 e^{j2\pi f_d t} dt. \qquad \text{Eq. (7.113)}$$

These two equations imply that the shapes of the ambiguity function cuts are controlled by selecting different functions X and r. In other words, the ambiguity function main beam and its delay axis sidelobes can be controlled (shaped) by the specific choices of these two functions; hence, the term *spectrum shaping* is used. Using this concept of spectrum shaping, one can control the frequency modulation of an LFM (see Fig. 7.13) to produce an ambiguity function with the desired sidelobe levels.

7.8.2. Frequency Modulated Waveform Spectrum Shaping

One class of frequency modulation (FM) waveforms which takes advantage of the stationary phase principles to control (shape) the spectrum is

$$|X(\omega; n)|^2 = \left(\cos\pi\left(\frac{\pi\omega}{B_n}\right)\right)^n \qquad ; \ |\omega| \le \frac{B_n}{2} \qquad \text{Eq. (7.114)}$$

where the value n is an integer greater than zero. It can be easily shown using direct integration and by utilizing Eq. (7.114) that the group time-delay functions are

$$n = 1 \Rightarrow T_{g1}(\omega) = \frac{T}{2}\sin\left(\frac{\pi\omega}{B_1}\right) \qquad \text{Eq. (7.115)}$$

$$n = 2 \Rightarrow T_{g2}(\omega) = T\left[\frac{\omega}{B_2} + \frac{1}{2\pi}\sin\left(\frac{2\pi\omega}{B_2}\right)\right] \qquad \text{Eq. (7.116)}$$

$$n = 3 \Rightarrow T_{g3}(\omega) = \frac{T}{4}\left\{\sin\left(\frac{\pi\omega}{B_3}\right)\left[\left(\cos\frac{\pi\omega}{B_3}\right)^2 + 2\right]\right\} \qquad \text{Eq. (7.117)}$$

$$n = 4 \Rightarrow T_{g4}(\omega) = T\left\{\frac{\omega}{B_4} + \frac{1}{2\pi}\sin\frac{2\pi\omega}{B_4} + \frac{2}{3\pi}\left(\cos\frac{\pi\omega}{B_4}\right)^3\sin\frac{\pi\omega}{B_4}\right\} \qquad \text{Eq. (7.118)}$$

Figure 7.15 shows a plot for Eq. (7.115) through Eq. (7.118). These plots assume $T = 1$ and the x-axis is normalized, with respect to B. The Doppler mismatch (i.e., a peak of the ambiguity function at a delay value other than zero) is proportional to the amount of Doppler frequency f_d. Hence, an error in measuring target range is always expected when LFM waveforms are used. To achieve sidelobe levels for the output of the matched filter that do not exceed a predetermined level, use this class of NLFM waveform

$$|X(\omega;n;k)|^2 = k + (1-k)\left(\cos\pi\left(\frac{\pi\omega}{B_n}\right)\right)^n \qquad ;|\omega| \le \frac{B_n}{2}. \qquad \text{Eq. (7.119)}$$

For example, using the combination $n = 2$, $k = 0.08$ yields sidelobe levels less than $-40dB$.

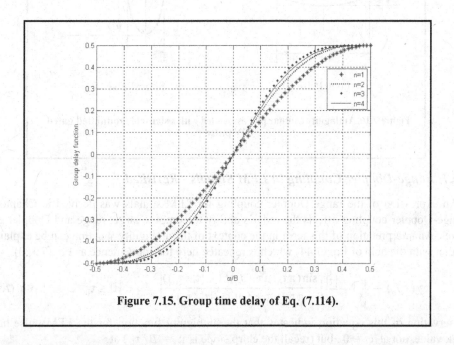

Figure 7.15. Group time delay of Eq. (7.114).

7.9. Ambiguity Diagram Contours

Plots of the ambiguity function are called "ambiguity diagrams". For a given waveform, the corresponding ambiguity diagram is normally used to determine the waveform properties such as the target resolution capability, measurements (time and frequency) accuracy, and its response to clutter. The ambiguity diagram contours are cuts in the 3-D ambiguity plot at some value, Q, such that $Q < \chi(0, 0)$. The resulting plots are ellipses. The width of a given ellipse along the delay axis is proportional to the signal effective duration, τ_e. Alternatively, the width of an ellipse along the Doppler axis is proportional to the signal effective bandwidth, B_e.

Figure 7.16 shows a sketch of typical ambiguity contour plots associated with a single unmodulated pulse. As illustrated in Fig. 7.16, narrow pulses provide better range accuracy than long pulses. Alternatively, the Doppler accuracy is better for a wider pulse than it is for a short one. This trade-off between range and Doppler measurements comes from the uncertainty associated with the time-bandwidth product of a single sinusoidal pulse, where the product of uncertainty in time (range) and uncertainty in frequency (Doppler) cannot be much smaller than unity. Figure 7.17 shows the ambiguity contour plot associated with an LFM waveform. The slope is an indication of the LFM modulation.

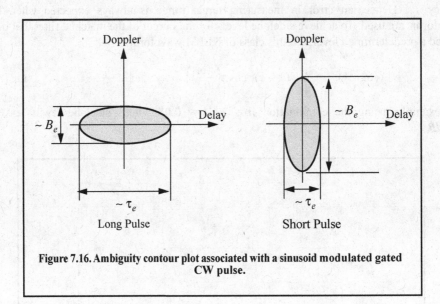

Figure 7.16. Ambiguity contour plot associated with a sinusoid modulated gated CW pulse.

7.9.1. Range-Doppler Coupling in LFM Signals - Revisited

An expression of the range-Doppler coupling for LFM signals was derived in Chapter 6. Range-Doppler coupling affects the radar's ability to compute target range and Doppler estimates. An interpretation of this term in the context of the ambiguity function can be explained further with the help of Eq. (7.44) which is repeated here for convenience as Eq. (7.120),

$$\chi(\tau; f_d) = \left| \left(1 - \frac{|\tau|}{\tau_0}\right) \frac{\sin(\pi\tau_0(\mu\tau + f_d)(1 - |\tau|/\tau_0))}{\pi\tau_0(\mu\tau + f_d)(1 - |\tau|/\tau_0)} \right|^2 \qquad |\tau| \le \tau_0. \qquad \textbf{Eq. (7.120)}$$

Observation of this equation indicates that the ambiguity function for the LFM pulse has a peak value, not at $\tau = 0$, but (recall the chirp slope is $\mu = B/\tau_0$) at

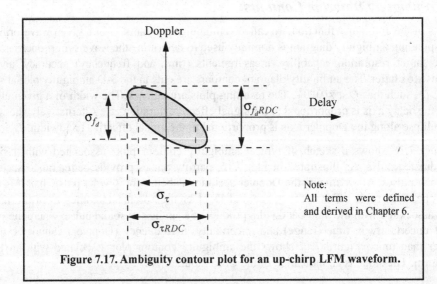

Figure 7.17. Ambiguity contour plot for an up-chirp LFM waveform.

$$\left(\frac{B}{\tau_0}\right)\tau + f_d = 0 \Rightarrow \tau = -f_d\left(\frac{\tau_0}{B}\right).$$

Eq. (7.121)

This Doppler mismatch (i.e., a peak of the ambiguity function at a delay value other than zero) is proportional to the amount of Doppler frequency f_d. This coupling introduces a range measurement corruption, δR, given by

$$\delta R = \frac{c\delta\tau}{2}$$

Eq. (7.122)

where c is the speed of light and the factor of 2 is needed to account for the two-way delay from the radar to the target. Substituting Eq. (7.121) into Eq. (7.122) and using the relationship $f_d = -2v/\lambda$ yield,

$$\delta R = \left(\frac{c}{2}\right)\left(\frac{\tau_0}{B}\right)\left(\frac{2v}{\lambda}\right) = \frac{\tau_0}{B}vf_0$$

Eq. (7.123)

where v is the target redial velocity, λ is the wavelength, and f_0 is the radar operating frequency (recall that $c = \lambda f_0$). Equation (7.123) is the same as Eq. (6.244) from Chapter 6, where the range Doppler coupling corruption factor, δR, was derived earlier.

Modern radar systems using LFM waveforms can correct for the effect of range-Doppler coupling by repeating the measurement with an LFM waveform of the opposite slope and averaging the two measurements. This way, the range measurement error is negated and the true target range is extracted from the averaged value.

Some radar systems, particularly those used for long-range surveillance applications, may actually take advantage of range-Doppler coupling effect; and here is how it works: Typically, radars during the search mode utilize very wide range bins which may contain many targets with different distinct Doppler frequencies. It follows that the output of the matched filter has several targets that have equal delay but different Doppler mismatches. All targets with Doppler mismatches greater than $1/\tau_0$ are significantly attenuated by the ambiguity function (because of the sharp decaying slope of the ambiguity function along the Doppler axis), and thus will most likely go undetected along the Doppler axis. The combined target complex within that range bin is then detected using an LFM waveform as if all targets had a Doppler mismatch corresponding to the target whose Doppler mismatch is less than or equal to $1/\tau_0$. Thus, all targets within that wide range bin are detected as one narrow band target. Because of this range-Doppler coupling, LFM waveforms are often referred to as "Doppler intolerant (insensitive) waveforms".

7.10. Discrete Code Signal Representation

The general form for a discrete code signal was presented in Cook (1993) as

$$x(t) = e^{j\omega_0 t}\sum_{n=1}^{N}u_n(t) = e^{j\omega_0 t}\sum_{n=1}^{N}P_n(t)e^{j(\omega_n t + \theta_n)}$$

Eq. (7.124)

where ω_0 is the carrier frequency in radians, (ω_n, θ_n) are constants, N is the code length (number of bits in the code), and the signal $P_n(t)$ is given by

$$P_n(t) = a_n Rect\left(\frac{t}{\tau_0}\right).$$

Eq. (7.125)

The constant a_n is either (1) or (0), and

$$Rect\left(\frac{t}{\tau_0}\right) = \begin{cases} 1 & ; \quad 0 < t < \tau_0 \\ 0 & ; \quad elsewhere \end{cases}.$$ Eq. (7.126)

Using this notation, the discrete code can be described through the sequence

$$U[n] = \{u_n, n = 1, 2, ..., N\}$$ Eq. (7.127)

which, in general, is a complex sequence depending on the values of ω_n and θ_n. The sequence $U[n]$ is called the code, and for convenience it will be denoted by U.

In general, the output of the matched filter is

$$x_o(\tau, f_d) = \int_{-\infty}^{\infty} x^*(t)x(t+\tau)e^{-j2\pi f_d t} dt,$$ Eq. (7.128)

substituting Eq. (7.124) into Eq. (7.128) yields

$$x_o(\tau, f_d) = \sum_{n=1}^{N} \sum_{k=1}^{N} \int_{-\infty}^{\infty} u_n^*(t)u_k(t+\tau)e^{-j2\pi f_d t} dt.$$ Eq. (7.129)

Depending on the choice of combination for a_n, ω_n, and θ_n, different class of codes can be generated. To this end, pulse-train codes are generated when

$$\theta_n = \omega_n = 0 \quad ; \ and \ a_n = 1, or \ 0.$$ Eq. (7.130)

Binary phase codes and polyphase codes are generated when

$$\omega_n = 0 \quad ; \ and \ a_n = 1,$$ Eq. (7.131)

finally, frequency codes are generated when

$$\theta_n = 0 \quad ; \ and \ a_n = 1, or \ 0.$$ Eq. (7.132)

7.10.1. Pulse-Train Codes

The idea behind this class of code is to divide a relatively long pulse of length T_P into N subpulses, each being a rectangular pulse with pulse width τ_0 and amplitude of 1 or 0. It follows that the code U is the sequence of 1s and 0s. More precisely, the signal representing this class of code can be written as (after Cook 1993)

$$x(t) = e^{j\omega_0 t} \sum_{n=1}^{N} P_n(t) = e^{j\omega_0 t} \sum_{n=1}^{N} a_n Rect\left(\frac{t}{\tau_0}\right).$$ Eq. (7.133)

One way to generate a pulse-train class code can be by setting

$$a_n = \begin{cases} 1 & n-1 = 0 \ modulu \ q \\ 0 & n-1 \neq 0 \ modulu \ q \end{cases}$$ Eq. (7.134)

where q is a positive integer that divides evenly into $N-1$. That is,

$$M-1 = \frac{(N-1)}{q}$$ Eq. (7.135)

where M is the number of 1s in the code. For example, when $N = 21$ and $q = 5$, then $M = 5$, and the resulting code is

$$\{U\} = \{10000 \quad 10000 \quad 10000 \quad 10000 \quad 1\}.$$ Eq. (7.136)

This is illustrated in Fig. 7.18. For an analog (continuous time) signal, this code would have been represented by the following continuous time domain signal

$$x_1(t) = e^{j\omega_0 t} \sum_{m=0}^{4} Rect\left(\frac{t - mT}{\tau_0}\right),$$ Eq. (7.137)

where the period is $T = 5\tau_0$. Using this analogy yields

$$\frac{T_p}{M-1} \equiv T$$ Eq. (7.138)

and Eq. (7.133) can now be written as

$$x(t) = e^{j\omega_0 t} \sum_{m=1}^{M-1} Rect\left(\frac{t - m\left(\frac{T_p}{M-1}\right)}{\tau_0}\right).$$ Eq. (7.139)

Earlier in this chapter, an expression for the ambiguity function for a coherent train of pulses was derived. Comparison of Eq. (7.139) and Eq. (7.50) shows that the two equations are equivalent when the condition in Eq. (7.138) is true except for some constants. It follows that the ambiguity function for the signal defined in Eq. (7.139) is

$$\chi(\tau; f_d) = \sum_{k=-M}^{M} \left| \frac{\sin\left[\pi f_d\left([M - |k|]\frac{T_p}{M-1}\right)\right]}{\sin\left(\pi f_d \frac{T_p}{M-1}\right)} \right| \left| \frac{\sin\left[\pi f_d\left(\tau_0 - \left|\tau - \frac{kT_p}{M-1}\right|\right)\right]}{\pi f_d} \right|.$$ Eq. (7.140)

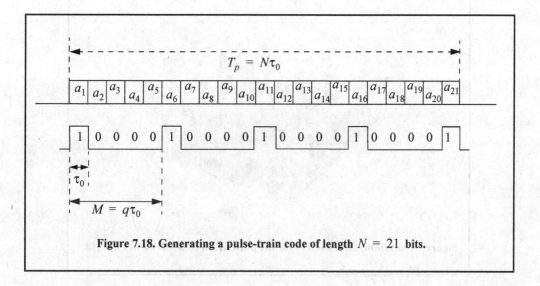

Figure 7.18. Generating a pulse-train code of length $N = 21$ bits.

As indicated by Eq. (7.140), the ambiguity function is periodic in both time, τ, and frequency, fd. The delay period is determined from the second part of the right-hand side of Eq. (7.140) and is equal to $kT_p/(M-1)$, while the period in frequency is obtained from the first part and is equal to $(M-1)/T_p$. The zero Doppler and zero delay cuts of the ambiguity function are derived from Eq. (7.140). They are given by

$$\chi(\tau;0) = M\tau_0 \sum_{k=-M}^{M} \left[1 - \frac{|k|}{M}\right]\left(1 - \frac{\left|\tau - \dfrac{kT_p}{M-1}\right|}{\tau_0}\right)$$

Eq. (7.141)

$$\chi(0;f_d) = \sum_{k=-M}^{M} \left|\frac{\sin\left[\pi M f_d\left(\dfrac{T_p}{M-1}\right)\right]}{\sin\left(\pi f_d \dfrac{T_p}{M-1}\right)}\right| \left|\frac{\sin(\pi f_d \tau_0)}{\pi f_d \tau_0}\right|.$$

Eq. (7.142)

Figure 7.19-a shows the three-dimensional ambiguity plot for the code shown in Fig. 7.18, while Fig. 7.19-b shows the corresponding contour plot.

A cartoon showing contour cuts of the ambiguity function for a pulse-train code is shown in Fig. 7.19-c. Clearly, the width of the ambiguity function main lobe (i.e., resolution) is directly tied to the code length. As one would expect, longer codes will produce a narrower main lobe and thus have better resolution than shorter ones. Further observation of Fig. 7.19 shows that this ambiguity function has a strong grating lobe structure along with high sidelobe levels. The presence of such strong lobing structure limits the effectiveness of the code and will cause detection ambiguities. These lobes are a direct result from the uniform equal spacing between the 1s within a code (i.e., periodicity of the code). These lobes can be significantly reduced by getting rid of the periodic structure of the code, i.e., placing the pulses at nonuniform spacing. This is called code "staggering" (PRF staggering).

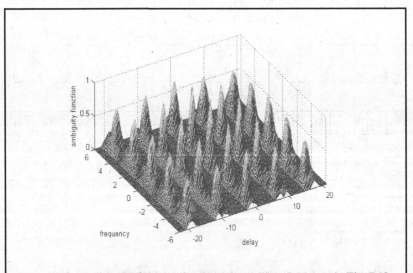

Figure 7.19a. Ambiguity function for the pulse-train code shown in Fig. 7.18.

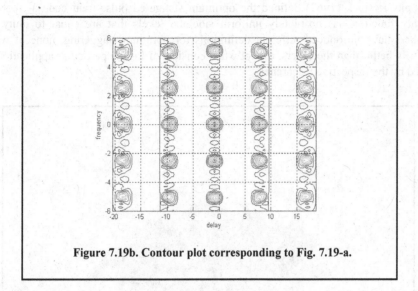

Figure 7.19b. Contour plot corresponding to Fig. 7.19-a.

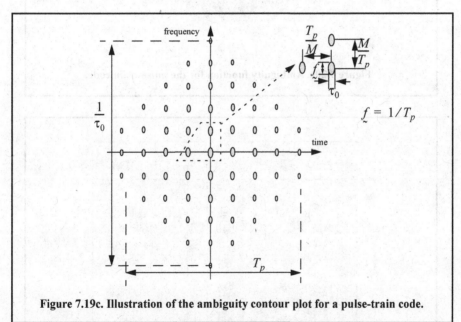

Figure 7.19c. Illustration of the ambiguity contour plot for a pulse-train code.

For example, consider a pulse-train code of length $N = 21$. A staggered pulse-train code can then be obtained by using the following sequence a_n

$$\{a_n\} = 1 \qquad n = 1, 4, 6, 12, 15, 21 .$$ Eq. (7.143)

Thus, the resulting code is

$$\{U\} = \{100101000001001000001\} .$$ Eq. (7.144)

Figure 7.20 shows the ambiguity plot corresponding to this code. As indicated by Fig. 7.20, the ambiguity function corresponding to a staggered pulse-train code approaches a thumbtack shape. The choice of the optimum staggered code has been researched extensively by numerous people. Resnick (1962) defined the optimum staggered pulse-train code as that whose ambiguity function has absolutely uniform sidelobe levels that are equal to unity. Other researchers have introduced different definitions for optimum staggering, none of which is necessarily better than the others, except when considered for the particular application being analyzed by the respective researcher.

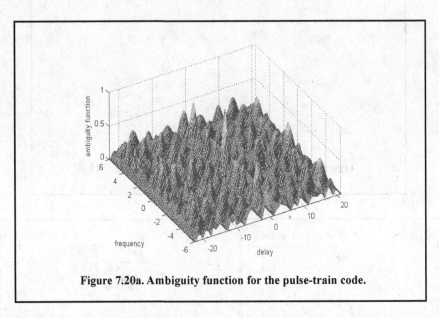

Figure 7.20a. Ambiguity function for the pulse-train code.

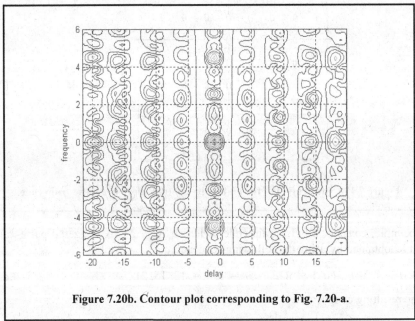

Figure 7.20b. Contour plot corresponding to Fig. 7.20-a.

7.11. Phase Coding

The signal corresponding to this class of code is obtained from Eq. (7.124) by letting $\omega_n = 0$. It follows that

$$x(t) = e^{j\omega_0 t} \sum_{n=1}^{N} u_n(t) = e^{j\omega_0 t} \sum_{n=1}^{N} P_n(t) e^{j\theta_n}.$$

Eq. (7.145)

Two subclasses of phase codes are analyzed: the binary phase codes and polyphase codes.

7.11.1. Binary Phase Codes

In this case, the phase θ_n is set equal to either (0) or (π), and hence, the term *binary* is used. For this purpose, define the coefficient D_n as

$$D_n = e^{j\theta_n} = \pm 1.$$

Eq. (7.146)

The ambiguity function for this class of code is derived by substituting Eq. (7.146) into Eq. (7.128). The resulting ambiguity function was given in Cook (1993) as

$$\chi(\tau;f_d) = \begin{cases} \chi_0(\tau',f_d) \displaystyle\sum_{n=1}^{N-k} D_n D_{n+k} e^{-j2\pi f_d(n-1)\tau_0} + \\[2em] \chi_0(\tau_0-\tau',f_d) \displaystyle\sum_{n=1}^{N-(k+1)} D_n D_{n+k+1} e^{-j2\pi f_d n\tau_0} \end{cases} \quad 0 < \tau < N\tau_0$$

Eq. (7.147)

where

$$\tau = k\tau_0 + \tau' \quad \begin{cases} 0 < \tau' < \tau_0 \\ k = 0, 1, 2, \ldots, N \end{cases}$$

Eq. (7.148)

$$\chi_0(\tau',f_d) = \int_0^{\tau_0-\tau'} \exp(-j2\pi f_d t)\, dt \quad 0 < \tau' < \tau_0.$$

Eq. (7.149)

The corresponding zero Doppler cut is then given by

$$\chi(\tau;0) = \tau_0\left(1 - \frac{|\tau'|}{\tau_0}\right) \sum_{n=1}^{N-|k|} D_n D_{n+k} + |\tau'| \sum_{n=1}^{N-|k+1|} D_n D_{n+k+1},$$

Eq. (7.150)

and when $\tau' = 0$ then

$$\chi(k;0) = \tau_0 \sum_{n=1}^{N-|k|} D_n D_{n+k}.$$

Eq. (7.151)

Barker Code

Barker code is one of the most commonly known codes from the binary phase code class. In this case, a long pulse of width T_p is divided into N smaller pulses; each is of width $\tau_0 = T_p/N$. Then, the phase of each subpulse is chosen as either 0 or π radians relative to some code. It is customary to characterize a subpulse that has 0 phase (amplitude of +1 volt) as either "1" or "+." Alternatively, a subpulse with phase equal to π (amplitude of -1 volt) is characterized by either "0" or "-." The Barker code is optimum in accordance with the definition set by Resnick. Figure 7.21 illustrates this concept for a Barker code of length seven. A Barker code of length N is denoted as B_N. There are only seven known Barker codes that share this unique property; they are listed in Table 7.1. Note that B_2 and B_4 have complementary forms that have the same characteristics.

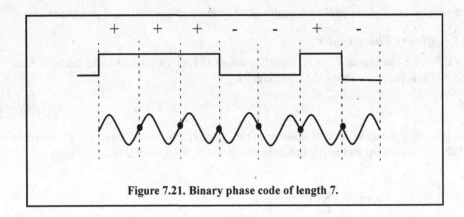

Figure 7.21. Binary phase code of length 7.

Table 7.1. Barker Code.

Code Symbol	Code Length	Code Elements	Side Lobe Reduction (dB)
B_2	2	+- OR ++	6.0
B_3	3	++-	9.5
B_4	4	++-+ OR +++-	12.0
B_5	5	+++-+	14.0
B_7	7	+++--+-	16.9
B_{11}	11	+++---+--+-	20.8
B_{13}	13	+++++--++-+-+	22.3

In general, the autocorrelation function (which is an approximation for the matched filter output) for a B_N Barker code will be $2N\tau_0$ wide. The main lobe is $2\tau_0$ wide; the peak value is equal to N. There are $(N-1)/2$ sidelobes on either side of the main lobe; this is illustrated in Fig. 7.22 for a B_{13}. Notice that the main lobe is equal to *13*, while all sidelobes are unity. The most sidelobe reduction offered by a Barker code is $-22.3\,dB$, which may not be sufficient for the desired radar application. However, Barker codes can be combined to generate much longer codes. In this case, a B_M code can be used within a B_N code (M within N) to generate a code of length MN. The compression ratio for the combined B_{MN} code is equal to MN. As an example (see Fig. 7.23) a combined B_{54} is given by

$$B_{54} = \{11101, 11101, 00010, 11101\}.$$ **Eq. (7.152)**

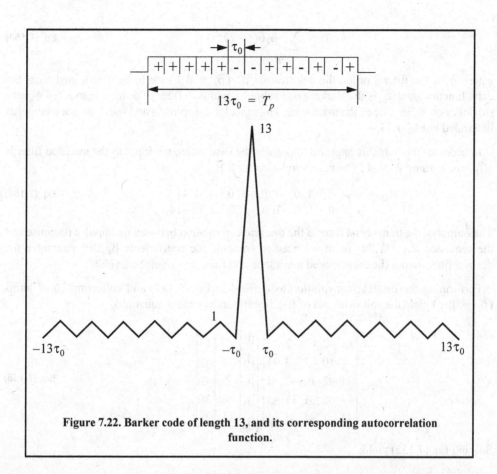

Figure 7.22. Barker code of length 13, and its corresponding autocorrelation function.

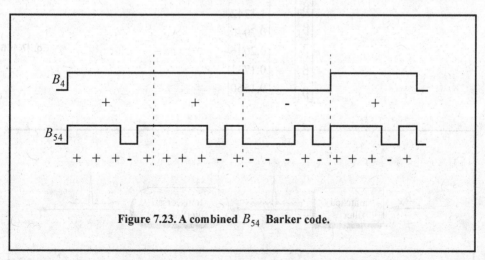

Figure 7.23. A combined B_{54} Barker code.

Unfortunately, the sidelobes of a combined Barker code autocorrelation function are no longer equal to unity. Some sidelobes of a combined Barker code autocorrelation function can be reduced to zero if the matched filter is followed by a linear transversal filter with impulse response given by

$$h(t) = \sum_{k=-N}^{N} \beta_k \delta(t - 2k\tau_0)$$

Eq. (7.153)

where N is the filter's order, the coefficients β_k ($\beta_k = \beta_{-k}$) are to be determined, δ is the delta function, and τ_0 is the Barker code subpulse width. A filter of order N produces N zero sidelobes on either side of the main lobe. The main lobe amplitude and width do not change, as illustrated in Fig. 7.24.

In order to illustrate this approach, consider the case where the input to the matched filter is B_{11}, and assume $N = 4$. The autocorrelation for a B_{11} is

$$R_{11} = \{-1, 0, -1, 0, -1, 0, -1, 0, -1, 0, 11, \\ 0, -1, 0, -1, 0, -1, 0, -1, 0, -1\}$$

Eq. (7.154)

The output of the transversal filter is the discrete convolution between its impulse response and the sequence R_{11}. At this point we need to compute the coefficients β_k that guarantee the desired filter output (i.e., unchanged main lobe and four zero sidelobe levels).

Performing the discrete convolution as defined in Eq. (7.153) and collecting equal terms ($\beta_k = \beta_{-k}$) yield the following set of five linearly independent equations,

$$\begin{bmatrix} 11 & -2 & -2 & -2 & -2 \\ -1 & 10 & -2 & -2 & -1 \\ -1 & -2 & 10 & -2 & -1 \\ -1 & -2 & -1 & 11 & -1 \\ -1 & -1 & -1 & -1 & 11 \end{bmatrix} \begin{bmatrix} \beta_0 \\ \beta_1 \\ \beta_2 \\ \beta_3 \\ \beta_4 \end{bmatrix} = \begin{bmatrix} 11 \\ 0 \\ 0 \\ 0 \\ 0 \end{bmatrix}.$$

Eq. (7.155)

Solving Eq. (7.155) yields

$$\begin{bmatrix} \beta_0 \\ \beta_1 \\ \beta_2 \\ \beta_3 \\ \beta_4 \end{bmatrix} = \begin{bmatrix} 1.1342 \\ 0.2046 \\ 0.2046 \\ 0.1731 \\ 0.1560 \end{bmatrix}.$$

Eq. (7.156)

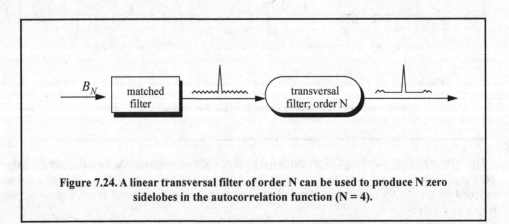

Figure 7.24. A linear transversal filter of order N can be used to produce N zero sidelobes in the autocorrelation function (N = 4).

Note that setting the first equation equal to 11 and all other equations to 0 and then solving for β_k guarantees that the main peak remains unchanged, and that the next four sidelobes are zeros. So far we have assumed that coded pulses have rectangular shapes. Using other pulses of other shapes, such as Gaussian, may produce better sidelobe reduction and a larger compression ratio.

Figure 7.25 shows the output of this function when B_{13} is used as an input. Figure 7.26 is similar to Fig. 7.25, except in this case B_7 is used as an input. Figure 7.27 a-c show the ambiguity function, the zero Doppler cut, and the contour plot for the combined Barker code defined in Fig. 7.26.

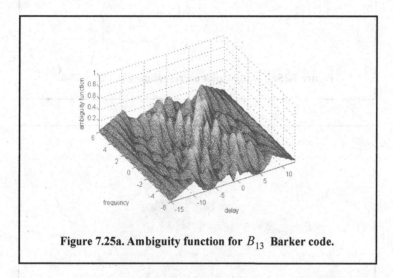

Figure 7.25a. Ambiguity function for B_{13} Barker code.

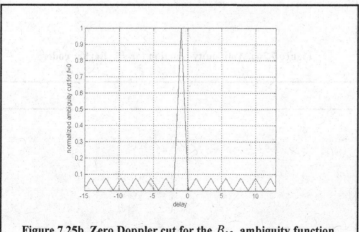

Figure 7.25b. Zero Doppler cut for the B_{13} ambiguity function.

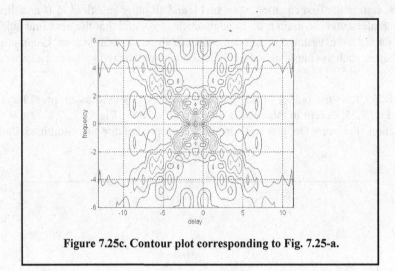

Figure 7.25c. Contour plot corresponding to Fig. 7.25-a.

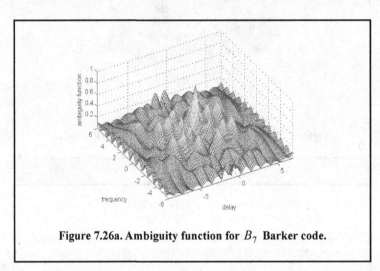

Figure 7.26a. Ambiguity function for B_7 Barker code.

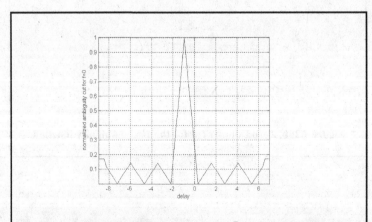

Figure 7.26b. Zero Doppler cut for the B_7 ambiguity function.

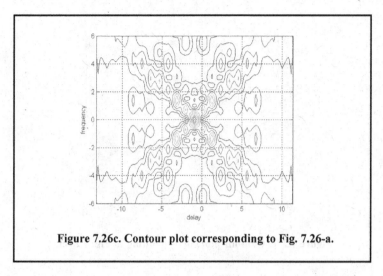

Figure 7.26c. Contour plot corresponding to Fig. 7.26-a.

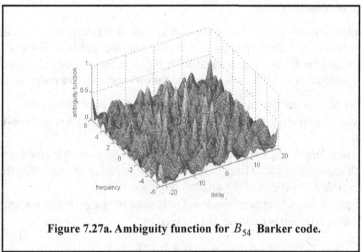

Figure 7.27a. Ambiguity function for B_{54} Barker code.

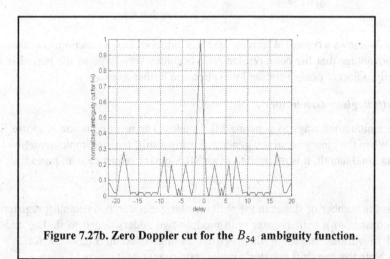

Figure 7.27b. Zero Doppler cut for the B_{54} ambiguity function.

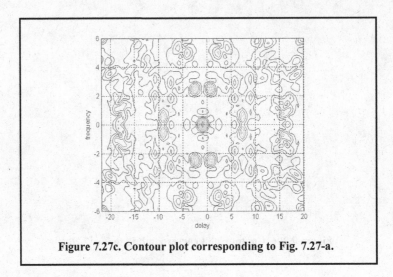

Figure 7.27c. Contour plot corresponding to Fig. 7.27-a.

Pseudo-Random Number Codes

Pseudo-random number (PRN) codes are also known as maximal length sequences (MLS) codes. These codes are called pseudo-random because the statistics associated with their occurrence are similar to those associated with the coin-toss sequences. Maximum length sequences are periodic. The MLS codes have the following distinctive properties:

1. The number of ones per period is one more than the number of minus ones.
2. Half the runs (consecutive states of the same kind) are of length one and one-fourth are of length two.
3. Every maximal length sequence has the "shift and add" property. This means that, if a maximal length sequence is added (modulo 2) to a shifted version of itself, then the resulting sequence is a shifted version of the original sequence.
4. Every n-tuple of the code appears once and only once in one period of the sequence.
5. The correlation function is periodic and is given by

$$\phi(n) = \begin{Bmatrix} L & n = 0, \pm L, \pm 2L, ... \\ -1 & elsewhere \end{Bmatrix}.$$ **Eq. (7.157)**

Figure 7.28 shows a typical sketch for an MLS autocorrelation function. Clearly these codes have the advantage that the compression ratio becomes very large as the period is increased. Additionally, adjacent peaks (grating lobes) become farther apart.

Linear Shift Register Generators

There are numerous ways to generate MLS codes. The most common is to use linear shift registers. When the binary sequence generated using a shift register implementation is periodic and has maximal length, it is referred to as an MLS binary sequence with period L,

$$L = 2^n - 1$$ **Eq. (7.158)**

where n is the number of stages in the shift register generator. A linear shift register generator basically consists of a shift register with modulo-two adders added to it. The adders can be connected to various stages of the register, as illustrated in Fig. 7.29 for $n = 4$ (i.e., $L = 15$). Note that the shift register's initial state cannot be 0.

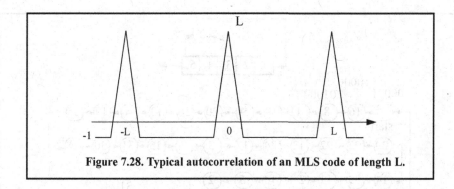

Figure 7.28. Typical autocorrelation of an MLS code of length L.

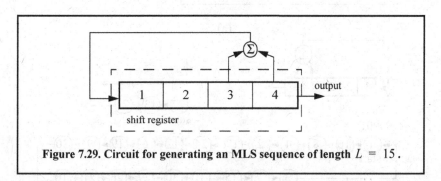

Figure 7.29. Circuit for generating an MLS sequence of length $L = 15$.

The feedback connections associated with a shift register generator determine whether the output sequence will be maximal. For a given size shift register, only a few feedback connections lead to maximal sequence outputs. In order to illustrate this concept, consider the two 5-stage shift register generators shown in Fig. 7.30. The shift register generator shown in Fig. 7.30-a generates a maximal length sequence, as clearly depicted by its state diagram. However, the shift register generator shown in Fig. 7.30-b produces three non-maximal length sequences (depending on the initial state). Given an n-stage shift register generator, one would be interested in knowing how many feedback connections will yield maximal length sequences. Zierler (1955) showed that the number of maximal length sequences possible for a given n-stage linear shift register generator is

$$N_L = (\varphi(2^n - 1))/n. \qquad \text{Eq. (7.159)}$$

φ is the Euler's totient (Euler's phi) function and is defined by

$$\varphi(k) = k \prod_i (p_i - 1)/p_i \qquad \text{Eq. (7.160)}$$

where p_i are the prime factors of k. Note that when p_i has multiples, only one of them is used. Also note that when k is a prime number, the Euler's phi function is

$$\varphi(k) = k - 1. \qquad \text{Eq. (7.161)}$$

For example, a 3-stage shift register generator will produce

$$N_L = \frac{\varphi(2^3 - 1)}{3} = \frac{\varphi(7)}{3} = \frac{7-1}{3} = 2, \qquad \text{Eq. (7.162)}$$

and a 6-stage shift register,

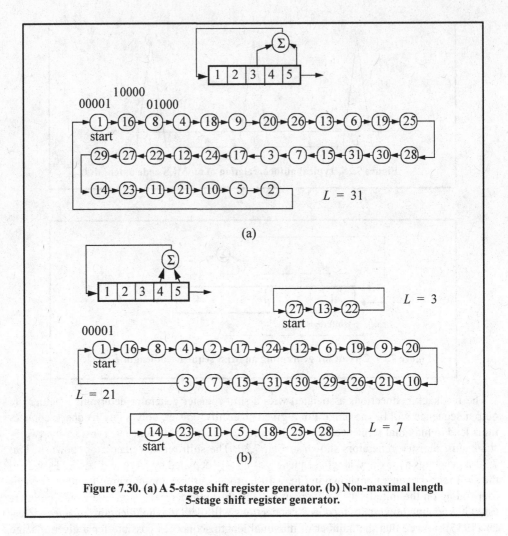

Figure 7.30. (a) A 5-stage shift register generator. (b) Non-maximal length
5-stage shift register generator.

$$N_L = \frac{\varphi(2^6 - 1)}{6} = \frac{\varphi(63)}{6} = \frac{63}{6} \times \frac{(3-1)}{3} \times \frac{(7-1)}{7} = 6.$$ **Eq. (7.163)**

Maximal Length Sequence Characteristic Polynomial

Consider an n-stage maximal length linear shift register whose feedback connections correspond to n, k, m, etc. This maximal length shift register can be described using its characteristic polynomial defined by

$$x^n + x^k + x^m + \ldots + 1$$ **Eq. (7.164)**

where the additions are modulo 2. Therefore, if the characteristic polynomial for an n-stage shift register is known, one can easily determine the register feedback connections and consequently deduce the corresponding maximal length sequence. For example, consider a 6-stage shift register whose characteristic polynomial is

$$x^6 + x^5 + 1,$$ **Eq. (7.165)**

and the shift register which generates a maximal length sequence is shown in Fig. 7.31.

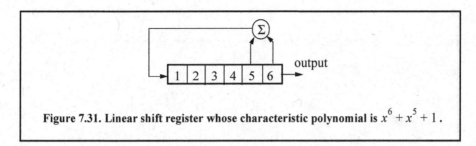

Figure 7.31. Linear shift register whose characteristic polynomial is $x^6 + x^5 + 1$.

One of the most important issues associated with generating a maximal length sequence using a linear shift register is determining the characteristic polynomial. This has been and continues to be a subject of research for many radar engineers and designers. It has been shown that polynomials which are both irreducible (not factorable) and primitive will produce maximal length shift register generators. A polynomial of degree n is irreducible if it is not divisible by any polynomial of degree less than n. It follows that all irreducible polynomials must have an odd number of terms. Consequently, only linear shift register generators with an even number of feedback connections can produce maximal length sequences. An irreducible polynomial is primitive if and only if it divides $x^n - 1$ for no value of n less than $2^n - 1$. Figure 7.32 shows the contour and 3-D ambiguity plots corresponding to a 31-bit PRN code.

$$u31 = [1\ -1\ -1\ -1\ -1\ 1\ -1\ 1\ -1\ 1\ 1\ 1\ -1\ 1\ 1\ -1\ -1\ -1\ 1\ 1\ 1\ 1\ 1\ -1\ -1\ 1\ 1\ 1\ -1\ 1\ -1\ -1].$$

Figure 7.33 is similar to Fig. 7.32, except in this case the input maximal length sequence is

$$u15=[1\ -1\ -1\ -1\ 1\ 1\ 1\ 1\ 1\ -1\ 1\ -1\ 1\ 1\ -1\ -1].$$

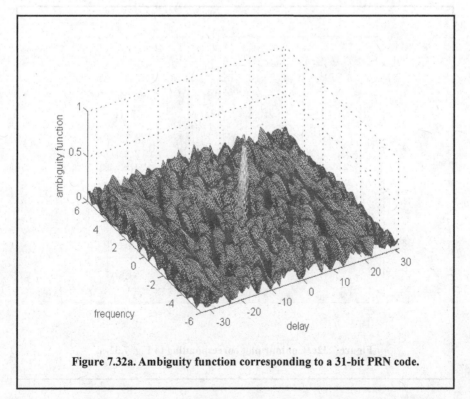

Figure 7.32a. Ambiguity function corresponding to a 31-bit PRN code.

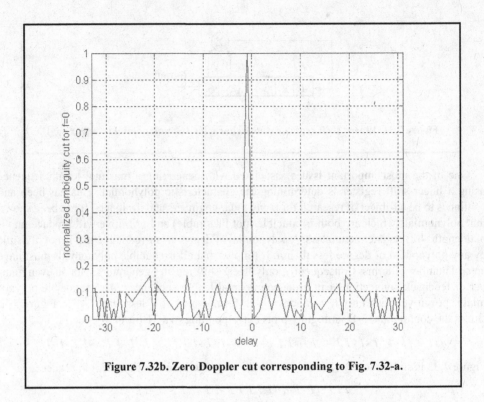

Figure 7.32b. Zero Doppler cut corresponding to Fig. 7.32-a.

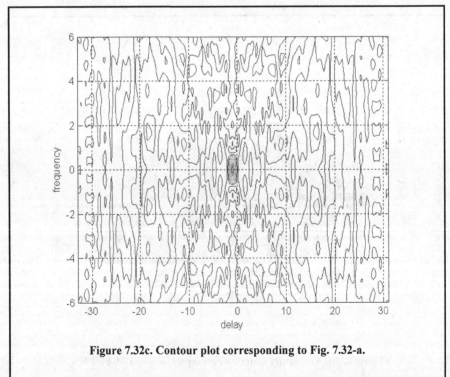

Figure 7.32c. Contour plot corresponding to Fig. 7.32-a.

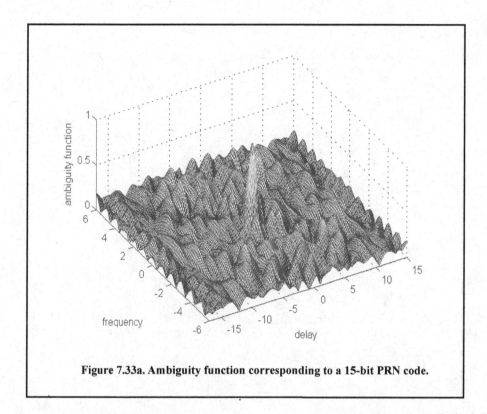

Figure 7.33a. Ambiguity function corresponding to a 15-bit PRN code.

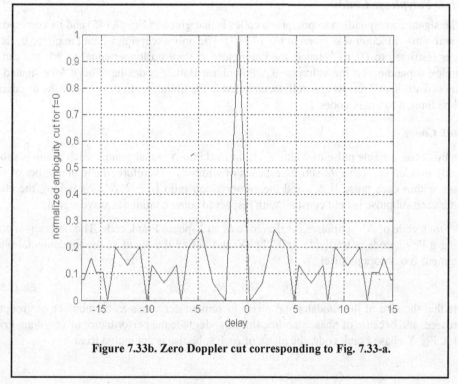

Figure 7.33b. Zero Doppler cut corresponding to Fig. 7.33-a.

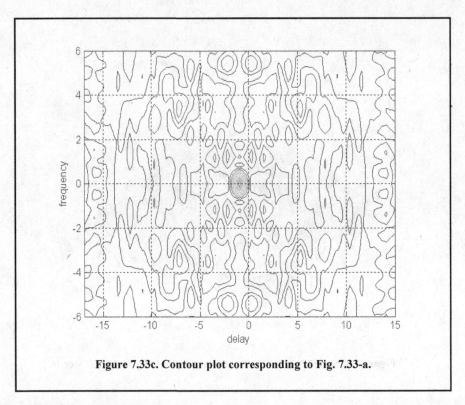

Figure 7.33c. Contour plot corresponding to Fig. 7.33-a.

7.11.2. Polyphase Codes

The signal corresponding to polyphase codes is that given in Eq. (7.145) and its corresponding ambiguity function was given in Eq. (7.147). The only exception is that the phase θ_n is no longer restricted to $(0, \pi)$. Hence, the coefficient D_n are no longer equal to ± 1 but can be complex depending on the value of θ_n. Polyphase Barker codes have been investigated by many scientists, and results are well documented in the literature. In this chapter the discussion will be limited to Frank codes.

Frank Codes

In this case, a single pulse of width T_p is divided into N equal groups; each group is subsequently divided into other N subpulses, each of width τ_0. Therefore, the total number of subpulses within each pulse is N^2, and the compression ratio is $\xi \doteq N^2$. As before, the phase within each subpulse is held constant with respect to some continuous wave signal.

A Frank code of N^2 subpulses is referred to as an N-phase Frank code. The first step in computing a Frank code is to divide $360°$ by N and define the result as the fundamental phase increment $\Delta\varphi$. More precisely,

$$\Delta\varphi = 360°/N. \qquad\qquad \text{Eq. (7.166)}$$

Note that the size of the fundamental phase increment decreases as the number of groups is increased, and because of phase stability, this may degrade the performance of very long Frank codes. For N-phase Frank code, the phase of each subpulse is computed from

$$
\left(
\begin{array}{cccccc}
0 & 0 & 0 & 0 & \cdots & 0 \\
0 & 1 & 2 & 3 & \cdots & N-1 \\
0 & 2 & 4 & 6 & \cdots & 2(N-1) \\
\cdots & \cdots & \cdots & \cdots & \cdots & \cdots \\
\cdots & \cdots & \cdots & \cdots & \cdots & \cdots \\
0 & (N-1) & 2(N-1) & 3(N-1) & \cdots & (N-1)^2
\end{array}
\right) \Delta\varphi
$$

Eq. (7.167)

where each row represents a group, and a column represents the subpulses for that group. For example, a 4-phase Frank code has $N = 4$, and the fundamental phase increment is $\Delta\varphi = (360°/4) = 90°$. It follows that

$$
\left(
\begin{array}{cccc}
0 & 0 & 0 & 0 \\
0 & 90° & 180° & 270° \\
0 & 180° & 0 & 180° \\
0 & 270° & 180° & 90°
\end{array}
\right)
\Rightarrow
\left(
\begin{array}{cccc}
1 & 1 & 1 & 1 \\
1 & j & -1 & -j \\
1 & -1 & 1 & -1 \\
1 & -j & -1 & j
\end{array}
\right).
$$

Eq. (7.168)

Therefore, a Frank code of 16 elements is given by

$$
F_{16} = \{1 \ 1 \ 1 \ 1 \ 1 \ j \ -1 \ -j \ 1 \ -1 \ 1 \ -1 \ 1 \ -j \ -1 \ j\}.
$$

Eq. (7.169)

A plot of the ambiguity function for F_{16} is shown in Fig. 7.34. Note the thumbtack shape of the ambiguity function. The phase increments within each row represent a step-wise approximation of an up-chirp LFM waveform. The phase increments for subsequent rows increase linearly versus time. Thus, the corresponding LFM chirp slopes also increase linearly for subsequent rows. This is illustrated in Fig. 7.35, for F_{16}.

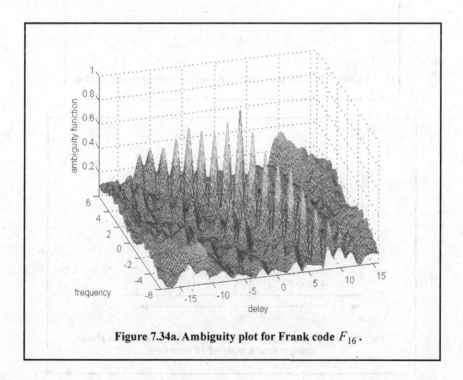

Figure 7.34a. Ambiguity plot for Frank code F_{16}.

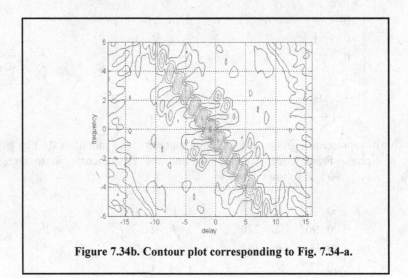

Figure 7.34b. Contour plot corresponding to Fig. 7.34-a.

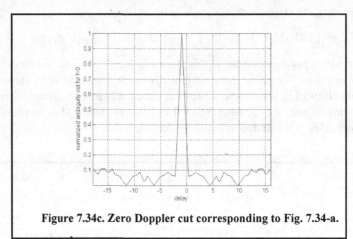

Figure 7.34c. Zero Doppler cut corresponding to Fig. 7.34-a.

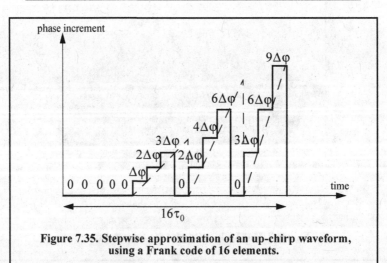

**Figure 7.35. Stepwise approximation of an up-chirp waveform,
using a Frank code of 16 elements.**

7.12. Frequency Codes

Frequency codes are derived from Eq. (7.124) under the condition stated in Eq. (7.132) (i.e., $\theta_n = 0$; *and* $a_n = 1, or\ 0$). The stepped frequency waveform (SFW) discussed in the previous chapter is considered to be a code under this class of discrete coded waveforms. The discussion in this section is limited to Costas codes. Construction of Costas codes can be understood in the context of SFW. In SFW, a relatively long pulse of length T_p is divided into N subpulses, each of width τ_0 $(T_p = N\tau_0)$. Each group of N subpulses is called a burst. Within each burst, the frequency is increased by Δf from one subpulse to the next. The overall burst bandwidth is $N\Delta f$. More precisely,

$$\tau_0 = T_p/N \qquad \text{Eq. (7.170)}$$

and the frequency for the *ith* subpulse is

$$f_i = f_0 + i\Delta f; \quad i = 1, N \qquad \text{Eq. (7.171)}$$

where f_0 is a constant frequency and $f_0 \gg \Delta f$. It follows that the time-bandwidth product of this waveform is

$$\Delta f T_p = N^2. \qquad \text{Eq. (7.172)}$$

Costas (1984) signals (or codes) are similar to SFW, except that the frequencies for the subpulses are selected in a random fashion, according to some predetermined rule or logic. For this purpose, consider the $N \times N$ matrix shown in Fig. 7.36-b. In this case, the rows are indexed from $i = 1, 2, ..., N$ and the columns are indexed from $j = 0, 1, 2, ..., (N-1)$. The rows are used to denote the subpulses, and the columns are used to denote the frequency. A *dot* indicates the frequency value assigned to the associated subpulse. In this fashion, Fig. 7.36-a shows the frequency assignment associated with an SFW. Alternatively, the frequency assignments in Fig. 7.36-b are chosen randomly. For a matrix of size $N \times N$, there are a total of $N!$ possible ways of assigning the dots (i.e., $N!$ possible codes).

The sequences of dot assignments for which the corresponding ambiguity function approaches an ideal or a *thumbtack* response are called "Costas codes". A near thumbtack response was obtained by Costas using the following logic: There is only one frequency per time slot (row) and per frequency slot (column). Therefore, for an $N \times N$ matrix, the number of possible Costas codes is drastically less than $N!$. For example, there are $N_c = 4$ possible Costas codes for $N = 3$, and $N_c = 40$ possible codes for $N = 5$. It can be shown that the code density, defined as the ratio $N_c/N!$, gets significantly smaller as N becomes larger. There are numerous analytical ways to generate Costas codes. In this section we will describe two of these methods. First, let q be an odd prime number, and choose the number of subpulses as

$$N = q - 1. \qquad \text{Eq. (7.173)}$$

Define γ as the primitive root of q. A primitive root of q (an odd prime number) is defined as γ such that the powers $\gamma, \gamma^2, \gamma^3, ..., \gamma^{q-1}$ modulo q generate every integer from 1 to $q - 1$. In the first method, for an $N \times N$ matrix, label the rows and columns, respectively, as

$$\begin{aligned} i &= 0, 1, 2, ..., (q-2) \\ j &= 1, 2, 3, ..., (q-1) \end{aligned} \qquad \text{Eq. (7.174)}$$

Place a dot in the location (i, j) corresponding to f_i if and only if

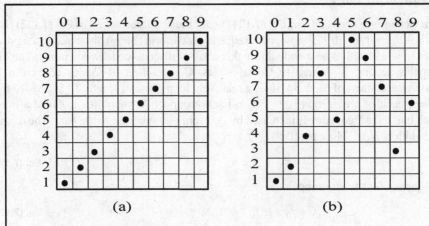

Figure 7.36. Frequency assignment for a burst of N subpulses. (a) SFW (stepped LFM); (b) Costas code of length *Nc = 10*.

$$i = (\gamma)^j \ (modulo \ q).$$ Eq. (7.175)

In the next method, Costas code is first obtained from the logic described above; then by deleting the first row and first column from the matrix, a new code is generated. This method produces a Costas code of length $N = q - 2$.

Define the normalized complex envelope of the Costas signal as

$$x(t) = \frac{1}{\sqrt{N\tau_0}} \sum_{l=0}^{N-1} x_l(t - l\tau_0)$$ Eq. (7.176)

$$x_l(t) = \begin{pmatrix} \exp(j2\pi f_l t) & 0 \le t \le \tau_0 \\ 0 & elsewhere \end{pmatrix}.$$ Eq. (7.177)

Costas showed that the output of the matched filter is

$$\chi(\tau, f_d) = \frac{1}{N} \sum_{l=0}^{N-1} \exp(j2\pi l f_d \tau) \left(\Phi_{ll}(\tau, f_d) + \sum_{\substack{q=0 \\ q \ne l}}^{N-1} \Phi_{lq}(\tau - (l-q)\tau_0, f_d) \right)$$ Eq. (7.178)

$$\Phi_{lq}(\tau, f_d) = \left(\tau_0 - \frac{|\tau|}{\tau_0}\right) \frac{\sin\alpha}{\alpha} \ \exp(-j\beta - j2\pi f_q \tau) \qquad , \ |\tau| \le \tau_1$$ Eq. (7.179)

$$\alpha = \pi(f_l - f_q - f_d)(\tau_0 - |\tau|)$$ Eq. (7.180)

$$\beta = \pi(f_l - f_q - f_d)(\tau_0 + |\tau|).$$ Eq. (7.181)

An ambiguity function of Costas signal has a near thumb-tack response. All sidelobes, except for a few around the origin, have amplitude $1/N$. A few sidelobes close to the origin have amplitude $2/N$, which is typical of Costas codes. The compression ratio of a Costas code is approximately N.

Chapter 8

Target Detection

Bassem R. Mahafza

Part I
Single Pulse Detection

In Part I of this chapter, target detection is introduced in the context of single pulse detection with completely known (i.e., deterministic) amplitude and phase in one case, and known amplitude with random phase in another. The underlying assumption is that radar targets are made of non-varying (non-fluctuating) scatterers. However, in practice that it is rarely the case. First, one would expect the radar to receive multiple returns (pulses) from any given target in its field of view. Furthermore, real-world targets will fluctuate over the duration of a single pulse or from pulse to pulse. Accordingly, Part II of this chapter extends the analysis to account for target fluctuation as well as for target detection where multiple returned pulses are taken into consideration. Multiple returned pulses can be integrated (combined) coherently or noncoherently. The process of combining radar returns from many pulses is called "radar pulse integration". Pulse integration can be performed on the quadrature components prior to the envelope detector. This is called "coherent integration" or pre-detection integration. Coherent integration preserves the phase relationship between the received pulses. Thus, a buildup in the signal amplitude is expected. Alternatively, pulse integration performed after the envelope detector (where the phase relation is lost) is called noncoherent or post-detection integration, and a buildup in the signal amplitude is guaranteed.

8.1. Single Pulse with Known Parameters

In its simplest form, a radar signal can be represented by a single pulse comprising a sinusoid of known amplitude and phase. Consequently, a returned signal will also comprise a sinusoid. Under the assumption of completely known signal parameters, a returned pulse from a target has known amplitude and known phase with no random components. The radar signal processor will attempt to maximize the probability of detection for a given probability of false alarm. In this case, detection is referred to as "coherent detection" or coherent demodulation. A radar system will declare detection with a certain probability of detection if the received voltage signal envelope exceeds a pre-set threshold value. For this purpose, the radar receiver is said to employ an envelope detector.

Figure 8.1 shows a simplified block diagram of a radar matched filter receiver followed by a threshold decision logic. The signal at the input of the matched filter $s(t)$ is composed of the target echo signal $x(t)$ and additive zero mean Gaussian noise (white noise is assumed in the analysis presented in this chapter) random process $n(t)$, with variance σ^2. The input noise is assumed to be spatially incoherent and uncorrelated with the signal. The matched filter impulse response is $h(t)$, and its output is denoted by the signal $v(t)$, and is given by

$$v(t) = \int_{-\infty}^{\infty} s(t)h(t-u) \ du.$$

Eq. (8.1)

Recall that if $n(t)$ is a Gaussian random process, then so is $s(t)$. Since $x(t)$ is a deterministic signal, its only effect is a shift of the mean of the random process. Following the definition of the Gaussian process (see Chapter 1 for a refresher), one concludes that the signal $v(t)$ is also a Gaussian random process, and over a coherent processing interval $\{0, T\}$, two hypotheses are considered:

H_0 when the signal $s(t)$ is made of noise only, and

H_1 when the signal $s(t)$ is made of signal plus noise.

More specifically,

$$H_0 \Leftrightarrow \mathbf{s} = \mathbf{n} \qquad ; 0 < t < T$$

Eq. (8.2)

$$H_1 \Leftrightarrow \mathbf{s} = \mathbf{n} + \mathbf{x} \qquad ; 0 < t < T$$

Eq. (8.3)

where all vectors are of size $M \times 1$ ($M = 2TB$), and B is the operating bandwidth of the receiver. It follows that,

$$E[\mathbf{n}] = \mathbf{0}$$
$$E[\mathbf{n}\mathbf{n}^\dagger] = \mathbf{C}_n$$
$$E[\mathbf{s}/H_1] = \mathbf{x}$$

Eq. (8.4)

where $\mathbf{C}_n$ is the noise covariance matrix.

When the noise $n(t)$ is white, or it is band-limited white over the frequency band $\{-B, B\}$, then its power spectrum density is given by

$$\bar{S}_n(f) = \frac{\eta_o}{2} \qquad ; -B < f < B$$

Eq. (8.5)

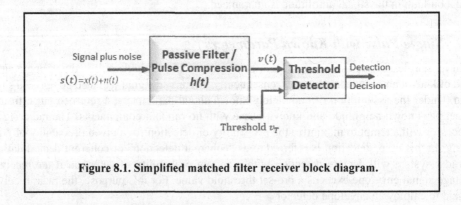

Figure 8.1. Simplified matched filter receiver block diagram.

where η_o is a constant. The conditional probability for the H_0 is

$$f(\mathbf{s}/H_0) = \frac{1}{(2\pi\eta_o B)^{M/2}} \exp\left(-\frac{\mathbf{s}^\dagger \mathbf{s}}{2\eta_o B}\right).$$ Eq. (8.6)

where the symbol $\dagger$ indicates the complex conjugate operation. Notionally, bold-faced letters denote vectors, and bold-faced capital letters indicate matrices. Alternatively, the conditional probability for H_1 is identical to Eq. (8.6) except in this case, one must replace $\mathbf{s}$ by $\mathbf{s} - \mathbf{x}$. It follows that

$$f(\mathbf{s}/H_1) = \frac{1}{(2\pi\eta_o B)^{M/2}} \exp\left(-\frac{(\mathbf{s}-\mathbf{x})^\dagger(\mathbf{s}-\mathbf{x})}{2\eta_o B}\right).$$ Eq. (8.7)

Recall that the statistics associated with the random process $v(t)$ over the interval $\{0, T\}$ is Gaussian. In general, a Gaussian *pdf* function is given by

$$f_V(v) = \frac{1}{\sigma\sqrt{2\pi}} \exp\left(-\frac{(v-\overline{V})^2}{2\sigma^2}\right)$$ Eq. (8.8)

where σ^2 is the variance and $\overline{V}$ is the mean value. It follows that

$$E[V/H_0] = 0$$ Eq. (8.9)

$$Var[V/H_0] = \frac{E_x \eta_o}{2} = \sigma^2$$ Eq. (8.10)

$$E[V/H_1] = \int_0^T x^*(t)x(t) \ dt = E_x$$ Eq. (8.11)

$$Var[V/H_1] = \frac{E_x \eta_o}{2} = \sigma^2$$ Eq. (8.12)

where E_x is the signal's energy.

Assuming the H_0 hypothesis, then the probability of a false P_{fa} alarm is computed from Eq. (8.8) when the signal $v(t)$ exceeds a set threshold value v_T. More specifically,

$$P_{fa} = Pr\{v(t) > v_T/H_0\} = \int_{v_T}^\infty \frac{1}{\sigma\sqrt{2\pi}} \exp\left(-\frac{v^2}{2\sigma^2}\right) dv.$$ Eq. (8.13)

Note that the value $v^2/(2\sigma^2)$ is a measure of the signal-to-noise ratio at the output of the matched filter. Substituting the variance as computed in Eq. (8.10) into Eq. (8.13) yields,

$$P_{fa} = \int_{v_T}^\infty \frac{1}{\sqrt{\pi E_x \eta_o}} \exp\left(-\frac{v^2}{E_x \eta_o}\right) dv.$$ Eq. (8.14)

Making the change of variable $\zeta = v/(\sqrt{E_x \eta_o})$ yields

$$P_{fa} = \int_{\frac{v_T}{\sqrt{E_x \eta_o}}}^\infty \frac{1}{\sqrt{\pi}} e^{-\zeta^2} d\zeta.$$ Eq. (8.15)

Multiplying and dividing Eq. (8.15) by 2 yields

$$P_{fa} = \frac{2}{2}\frac{1}{\sqrt{\pi}}\int_{\frac{v_T}{\sqrt{E_x\eta_o}}}^{\infty} e^{-\zeta^2}\, d\zeta = \frac{1}{2}erfc\left(\frac{v_T}{\sqrt{E_x\eta_o}}\right) \qquad \text{Eq. (8.16)}$$

where *erfc* is the complementary error function defined by

$$erfc(z) = \frac{2}{\sqrt{\pi}}\int_{z}^{\infty} e^{-\zeta^2}\, d\zeta . \qquad \text{Eq. (8.17)}$$

The error function *erf* is related to the complementary error function using the relation

$$erfc(z) = 1 - erf(z) = 1 - \frac{2}{\sqrt{\pi}}\int_{0}^{z} e^{-\zeta^2}\, d\zeta . \qquad \text{Eq. (8.18)}$$

Using similar analysis, one can derive the probability of detection as

$$P_d = Pr\{v(t) > v_T / H_1\} = \frac{1}{2}erfc\left(\frac{v_T - Ex}{\sqrt{E_x\eta_o}}\right) . \qquad \text{Eq. (8.19)}$$

Table 8.1 gives samples of the single pulse SNR corresponding to few values of P_d and P_{fa}, using Eq. (8.19). For example, if $P_d = 0.99$ and $P_{fa} = 10^{-10}$, then the minimum single pulse SNR is $SNR = 16.12dB$.

Table 8.1. Single Pulse SNR (in dB).

P_d	10^{-3}	10^{-4}	10^{-5}	10^{-6}	10^{-7}	10^{-8}	10^{-9}	10^{-10}	10^{-11}	10^{-12}
.1	4.00	6.19	7.85	8.95	9.94	10.44	11.12	11.62	12.16	12.65
.2	5.57	7.35	8.75	9.81	10.50	11.19	11.87	12.31	12.85	13.25
.3	6.75	8.25	9.50	10.44	11.10	11.75	12.37	12.81	13.25	13.65
.4	7.87	8.85	10.18	10.87	11.56	12.18	12.75	13.25	13.65	14.00
.5	8.44	9.45	10.62	11.25	11.95	12.60	13.11	13.52	14.00	14.35
.6	8.75	9.95	11.00	11.75	12.37	12.88	13.50	13.87	14.25	14.62
.7	9.56	10.50	11.50	12.31	12.75	13.31	13.87	14.20	14.59	14.95
.8	10.18	11.12	12.05	12.62	13.25	13.75	14.25	14.55	14.87	15.25
.9	10.95	11.85	12.65	13.31	13.85	14.25	14.62	15.00	15.45	15.75
.95	11.50	12.40	13.12	13.65	14.25	14.64	15.10	15.45	15.75	16.12
.98	12.18	13.00	13.62	14.25	14.62	15.12	15.47	15.85	16.25	16.50
.99	12.62	13.37	14.05	14.50	15.00	15.38	15.75	16.12	16.47	16.75
.995	12.85	13.65	14.31	14.75	15.25	15.71	16.06	16.37	16.65	17.00
.998	13.31	14.05	14.62	15.06	15.53	16.05	16.37	16.7	16.89	17.25
.999	13.62	14.25	14.88	15.25	15.85	16.13	16.50	16.85	17.12	17.44
.9995	13.84	14.50	15.06	15.55	15.99	16.35	16.70	16.98	17.35	17.55
.9999	14.38	14.94	15.44	16.12	16.50	16.87	17.12	17.35	17.62	17.87

8.2. *Single Pulse with Known Amplitude and Unknown Phase*

In this case of a single pulse with known amplitude and unknown phase, the returned signal comprises a sinusoid of a deterministic amplitude and random phase whose *pdf* is uniform over the interval $\{0, 2\pi\}$. The output of the matched filter receiver that employs an envelope detector is denoted by $v(t)$ (see Fig. 8.2), and it can be written as a bandpass random process as

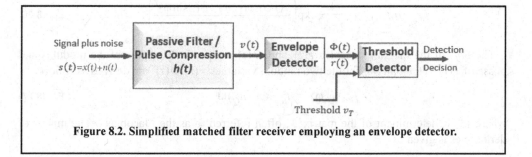

Figure 8.2. Simplified matched filter receiver employing an envelope detector.

$$v(t) = v_I(t)\cos\omega_0 t + v_Q(t)\sin\omega_0 t = r(t)\cos(\omega_0 t - \Phi(t))$$

$$v_I(t) = r(t)\cos\Phi(t) \qquad \text{Eq. (8.20)}$$

$$v_Q(t) = r(t)\sin\Phi(t)$$

$$r(t) = \sqrt{[v_I(t)]^2 + [v_Q(t)]^2} \qquad and \qquad \Phi(t) = \left[\tan\left(\frac{v_Q(t)}{v_I(t)}\right)\right]^{-1} \qquad \text{Eq. (8.21)}$$

where $\omega_0 = 2\pi f_0$ is the radar operating frequency, $r(t)$ is the envelope of $v(t)$, the phase is $\Phi(t) = \text{atan}(v_Q/v_I)$, and the subscripts I and Q, respectively, refer to the in-phase and quadrature components. A target is detected when $r(t)$ exceeds the threshold value v_T, where the decision hypotheses are

$$H_1 \Leftrightarrow s(t) = x(t) + n(t) \qquad and \qquad r(t) > v_T \Rightarrow Detection$$

$$H_0 \Leftrightarrow s(t) = n(t) \qquad and \qquad r(t) > v_T \Rightarrow False \;\; alarm \qquad \text{Eq. (8.22)}$$

The case when the noise subtracts from the signal (while a target is present) to make $r(t)$ smaller than the threshold is called a "miss". The matched filter output is a complex random variable that comprises either noise alone or noise plus target returns (i.e., sine wave of amplitude A and random phase).

The quadrature components corresponding to the noise only case are

$$v_I(t) = n_I(t) \qquad \text{Eq. (8.23)}$$

$$v_Q(t) = n_Q(t)$$

where the noise quadrature components $n_I(t)$ and $n_Q(t)$ are uncorrelated zero mean lowpass Gaussian noise with equal variances, σ^2. In the second case (signal plus noise), the quadrature components are

$$v_I(t) = A + n_I(t) = r(t)\cos\Phi(t) \Rightarrow n_I(t) = r(t)\cos\Phi(t) - A$$

$$v_Q(t) = n_Q(t) = r(t)\sin\Phi(t) \qquad \text{Eq. (8.24)}$$

The joint probability density function (*pdf*) of the two random variables $n_I; n_Q$ is

$$f_{n_I n_Q}(n_I, n_Q) = \frac{1}{2\pi\sigma^2}\exp\left(-\frac{n_I^2 + n_Q^2}{2\sigma^2}\right) = \frac{1}{2\pi\sigma^2}\exp\left(-\frac{(r\cos\varphi - A)^2 + (r\sin\varphi)^2}{2\sigma^2}\right), \qquad \text{Eq. (8.25)}$$

which can be written as

$$f_{n_I n_Q}(n_I, n_Q) = \frac{1}{2\pi\sigma^2} \exp\left(-\frac{(r\cos\varphi - A)^2 + (r\sin\varphi)^2}{2\sigma^2}\right).$$

Eq. (8.26)

The *pdfs* of the random variables $r(t)$ and $\Phi(t)$, respectively, represent the modulus and phase of $v(t)$. The joint *pdf* for the two random variables $r(t); \Phi(t)$ are derived as follows,

$$f_{R\Phi}(r, \varphi) = f_{n_I n_Q}(n_I, n_Q)|J|$$

Eq. (8.27)

where $|J|$ is determinant of the matrix J, often referred to as the "Jacobian". The matrix of derivatives is given by

$$J = \begin{bmatrix} \dfrac{\partial n_I}{\partial r} & \dfrac{\partial n_I}{\partial \varphi} \\[2mm] \dfrac{\partial n_Q}{\partial r} & \dfrac{\partial n_Q}{\partial \varphi} \end{bmatrix} = \begin{bmatrix} \cos\varphi & -r\sin\varphi \\ \sin\varphi & r\cos\varphi \end{bmatrix}.$$

Eq. (8.28)

It follows that the Jacobian is

$$|J| = r(t).$$

Eq. (8.29)

Substituting Eq. (8.26) and Eq. (8.29) into Eq. (8.27) and collecting terms yields

$$f_{R\Phi}(r, \varphi) = \frac{r}{2\pi\sigma^2} \exp\left(-\frac{r^2 + A^2}{2\sigma^2}\right) \exp\left(\frac{rA\cos\varphi}{\sigma^2}\right).$$

Eq. (8.30)

The *pdf* for $r(t)$ alone is obtained by integrating Eq. (8.30) over φ. That is,

$$f_R(r) = \int_0^{2\pi} f_{R\Phi}(r, \varphi)\, d\varphi = \frac{r}{\sigma^2} \exp\left(-\frac{r^2 + A^2}{2\sigma^2}\right) \frac{1}{2\pi}\int_0^{2\pi} \exp\left(\frac{rA\cos\varphi}{\sigma^2}\right) d\varphi$$

Eq. (8.31)

where the integral inside Eq. (8.31) is known as the modified Bessel function of zero order,

$$I_0(\beta) = \frac{1}{2\pi}\int_0^{2\pi} e^{\beta\cos\theta}\, d\theta.$$

Eq. (8.32)

Thus,

$$f_R(r) = \frac{r}{\sigma^2} I_0\left(\frac{rA}{\sigma^2}\right) \exp\left(-\frac{r^2 + A^2}{2\sigma^2}\right),$$

Eq. (8.33)

which is the Rician probability density function. The case when $A/\sigma^2 = 0$ (noise alone) the resulting *pdf* is a Rayleigh probability density function

$$f_R(r) = \frac{r}{\sigma^2} \exp\left(-\frac{r^2}{2\sigma^2}\right).$$

Eq. (8.34)

When (A/σ^2) is very large, Eq. (8.33) becomes a Gaussian probability density function of mean A and variance σ^2:

$$f_R(r) \approx \frac{1}{\sqrt{2\pi\sigma^2}} \exp\left(-\frac{(r - A)^2}{2\sigma^2}\right).$$

Eq. (8.35)

Figure 8.3 shows plots for the Rayleigh and Gaussian densities. The density function for the random variable Φ is obtained from

$$f_\Phi(\varphi) = \int_0^r f_{R\Phi}(r, \varphi) \ dr .$$

Eq. (8.36)

While the detailed derivation is lengthy and is beyond the scope of this chapter, the result is

$$f_\Phi(\varphi) = \frac{1}{2\pi} \ \exp\left(\frac{-A^2}{2\sigma^2}\right) + \frac{A\cos\varphi}{\sqrt{2\pi\sigma^2}} \ \exp\left(\frac{-(A\sin\varphi)^2}{2\sigma^2}\right) \ F\left(\frac{A\cos\varphi}{\sigma}\right)$$

Eq. (8.37)

where

$$F(x) = \int_{-\infty}^x \frac{1}{\sqrt{2\pi}} \ e^{-\zeta^2/2} \ d\zeta .$$

Eq. (8.38)

The function $F(x)$ can be found tabulated in most mathematical formula reference books. Note that for the case of noise alone ($A = 0$), Eq. (8.38) collapses to a uniform *pdf* over the interval $\{0, 2\pi\}$. One excellent approximation for the function $F(x)$ is

$$F(x) = 1 - \left(\frac{1}{0.661x + 0.339\sqrt{x^2 + 5.51}}\right)\frac{1}{\sqrt{2\pi}}e^{-x^2/2} \qquad x \geq 0 .$$

Eq. (8.39)

and for negative values of x

$$F(-x) = 1 - F(x) .$$

Eq. (8.40)

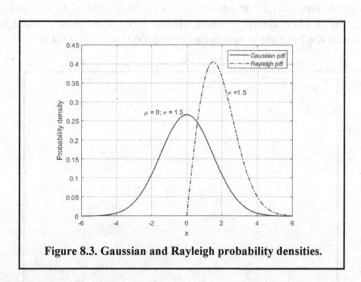

Figure 8.3. Gaussian and Rayleigh probability densities.

8.2.1. Probability of False Alarm

The probability of false alarm P_{fa} is defined as the probability that a sample r of the signal $r(t)$ will exceed the threshold voltage v_T when noise alone is present in the radar:

$$P_{fa} = \int_{v_T}^\infty \frac{r}{\sigma^2}\exp\left(-\frac{r^2}{2\sigma^2}\right) \ dr = \exp\left(\frac{-v_T^2}{2\sigma^2}\right)$$

Eq. (8.41)

$$v_T = \sqrt{2\sigma^2 \ln\left(\frac{1}{P_{fa}}\right)} \, .$$

Eq. (8.42)

Figure 8.4 shows a plot of the normalized threshold versus the probability of false alarm. It is evident from this figure that P_{fa} is very sensitive to small changes in the threshold value. The false alarm time T_{fa} is related to the probability of false alarm by

$$T_{fa} = t_{int}/P_{fa}$$

Eq. (8.43)

where t_{int} represents the radar integration time, or the average time that the output of the envelope detector will pass the threshold voltage. Since the radar operating bandwidth B is the inverse of t_{int}, by using the right-hand side of Eq. (8.41) and Eq. (8.42), one can rewrite T_{fa} as

$$T_{fa} = \frac{1}{B}\exp\left(\frac{v_T^2}{2\sigma^2}\right).$$

Eq. (8.44)

Minimizing T_{fa} means increasing the threshold value, and as a result, the radar maximum detection range is decreased. The choice of an acceptable value for T_{fa} becomes a compromise depending on the radar mode of operation. The false alarm number is defined as

$$n_{fa} = \frac{-\ln(2)}{\ln(1 - P_{fa})} \approx \frac{\ln(2)}{P_{fa}} \, .$$

Eq. (8.45)

Other slightly different definitions for the false alarm number exist in the literature, causing a source of confusion for many non-expert readers. Other than the definition in Eq. (8.45), the most commonly used definition for the false alarm number is the one introduced by Marcum (1960). Marcum defines the false alarm number as the reciprocal of P_{fa}. In this text, the definition given in Eq. (8.45) is always assumed. Hence, a clear distinction is made between Marcum's definition of the false alarm number and the definition in Eq. (8.45).

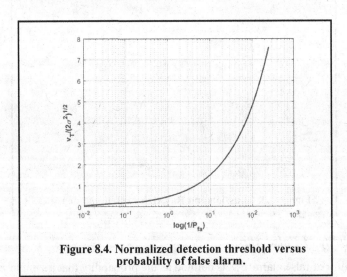

Figure 8.4. Normalized detection threshold versus probability of false alarm.

8.2.2. Probability of Detection

The probability of detection P_d is the probability that a sample r of $r(t)$ will exceed the threshold voltage in the case of noise plus signal,

$$P_d = \int_{v_T}^{\infty} \frac{r}{\sigma^2} I_0\left(\frac{rA}{\sigma^2}\right) \exp\left(-\frac{r^2 + A^2}{2\sigma^2}\right) dr .$$

Eq. (8.46)

Assuming that the radar signal is a sinusoid of amplitude A (completely known), then its power is $A^2/2$. Now, by using $SNR = A^2/2\sigma^2$ (single-pulse SNR) and $(v_T^2/2\sigma^2) = \ln(1/P_{fa})$, then Eq. (8.46) can be rewritten as

$$P_d = \int_{\sqrt{2\sigma^2 \ln(1/P_{fa})}}^{\infty} \frac{r}{\sigma^2} I_0\left(\frac{rA}{\sigma^2}\right) \exp\left(-\frac{r^2 + A^2}{2\sigma^2}\right) dr = Q\left[\sqrt{\frac{A^2}{\sigma^2}}, \sqrt{2\ln\left(\frac{1}{P_{fa}}\right)}\right]$$

Eq. (8.47)

where

$$Q[a, b] = \int_{b}^{\infty} \zeta I_0(a\zeta) e^{-(\zeta^2 + a^2)/2} \, d\zeta .$$

Eq. (8.48)

Q is called Marcum's Q-function. When P_{fa} is small and P_d is relatively large so that the threshold is also large, the probability of detection can be approximated by

$$P_d \approx F\left(\frac{A}{\sigma} - \sqrt{2\ln\left(\frac{1}{P_{fa}}\right)}\right) .$$

Eq. (8.49)

$F(x)$ is given by Eq. (8.38). Many other approximations for the probability of detection can be found throughout the literature. One very accurate approximation presented by North (1963) is given by

$$P_d \approx 0.5 \times erfc(\sqrt{-\ln P_{fa}} - \sqrt{SNR + 0.5})$$

Eq. (8.50)

where the complementary error function was defined in Eq. (817). The integral given in Eq. (8.47) is complicated and can be computed using numerical integration techniques. Parl (1980) developed an excellent algorithm to numerically compute this integral. It is summarized as follows:

$$Q[a, b] = \begin{cases} \dfrac{\alpha_n}{2\beta_n} \exp\left(\dfrac{(a-b)^2}{2}\right) & a < b \\ 1 - \left(\dfrac{\alpha_n}{2\beta_n} \exp\left(\dfrac{(a-b)^2}{2}\right)\right) & a \geq b \end{cases}$$

Eq. (8.51)

$$\alpha_n = d_n + \frac{2n}{ab}\alpha_{n-1} + \alpha_{n-2}$$

Eq. (8.52)

$$\beta_n = 1 + \frac{2n}{ab}\beta_{n-1} + \beta_{n-2}$$

Eq. (8.53)

$$d_{n+1} = d_n d_1$$

Eq. (8.54)

$$\alpha_0 = \begin{cases} 1 & a < b \\ 0 & a \geq b \end{cases}$$

Eq. (8.55)

$$d_1 = \begin{cases} a/b & a < b \\ b/a & a \geq b \end{cases} .$$

Eq. (8.56)

$\alpha_{-1} = 0.0$, $\beta_0 = 0.5$, and $\beta_{-1} = 0$. The recursive of Eq. (8.52) through Eq. (8.56) are computed continuously until $\beta_\eta > 10^p$ for values of $p \geq 3$. The accuracy of the algorithm is enhanced as the value of p is increased. Figure 8.5 shows plots of the probability of detection, P_d, versus the single pulse SNR, with the P_{fa} as a parameter.

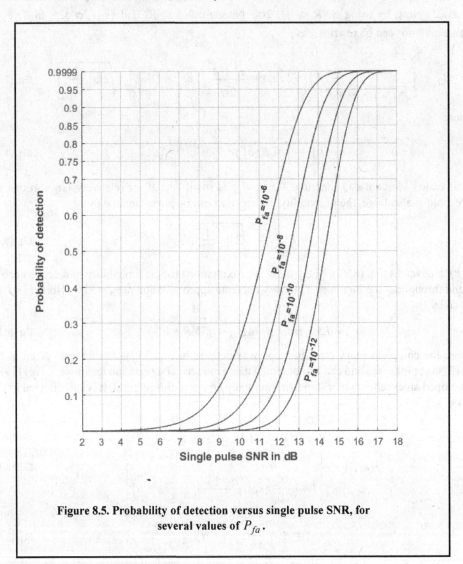

Figure 8.5. Probability of detection versus single pulse SNR, for several values of P_{fa}.

Part II
Detection of Fluctuating Targets

8.3. Pulse Integration

Combining the returns from all pulses returned by a given target during a single scan is very likely to increase the radar sensitivity (i.e., SNR). The number of returned pulses from a given target depends on the antenna scan rate, the antenna beam width, and the radar pulse repetition frequency (PRF). More precisely, the number of pulses returned from a given target is given by

$$n_P = \frac{\theta_a T_{sc} f_r}{2\pi} \qquad \text{Eq. (8.57)}$$

where θ_a is the azimuth antenna beam width, T_{sc} is the scan time, and f_r is the radar pulse repetition frequency. The number of reflected pulses may also be expressed as

$$n_P = \frac{\theta_a f_r}{\dot{\theta}_{scan}} \qquad \text{Eq. (8.58)}$$

where $\dot{\theta}_{scan}$ is the antenna scan rate in degrees per second. Note that when using Eq. (8.57), θ_a is expressed in radians, while when using Eq. (8.58), it is expressed in degrees. As an example, consider a radar with an azimuth antenna beam width $\theta_a = 3°$, antenna scan rate $\dot{\theta}_{scan} = 45°/\sec$ (antenna scan time, $T_{sc} = 8\sec$), and a PRF $f_r = 300 Hz$. Using either Eq. (8.57) or Eq. (8.58) yields $n_P = 20$ pulses.

Pulse integration will very likely improve the receiver SNR. Nonetheless, caution should be exercised when attempting to account for how much SNR is attained through pulse integration. This is true for the following reasons: First, during an antenna scan, a given target will not always be located at the center of the radar beam (i.e., have maximum gain). In fact, during a scan, a target will first enter the antenna beam at the *3-dB* point, reach maximum gain, and finally leave the beam at the *3-dB* point again. Thus, the returns do not have the same amplitude even though the target RCS may be constant and all other factors that may introduce signal loss remain the same. Other factors that may introduce further variation to the amplitude of the returned pulses include target radar cross-section (RCS) and propagation path fluctuations. Additionally, when the radar employs a very fast scan rate, an additional loss term is introduced due to the motion of the beam between transmission and reception. This is referred to as "scan loss". A distinction should be made between scan loss due to a rotating antenna (which is described here) and the term scan loss that is normally associated with phased array antennas (which takes on a different meaning in that context).

Finally, since coherent integration utilizes the phase information from all integrated pulses, it is critical that any phase variation between all integrated pulses be known with a great level of confidence. Consequently, target dynamics (such as target range, range rate, tumble rate, RCS fluctuation) must be estimated or computed accurately so that coherent integration can be meaningful. In fact, if a radar coherently integrates pulses from targets without proper knowledge of the target dynamics, it may suffer a loss in SNR rather than the expected SNR buildup. Knowledge of target dynamics is not as critical when employing noncoherent integration; nonetheless, target range rate must be estimated so that only the returns from a given target within a specific range bin are integrated. In other words, one must avoid range walk (i.e., having a target cross between adjacent range bins during a single scan).

A comprehensive analysis of pulse integration should also take into account issues such as the probability of detection P_d, probability of false alarm P_{fa}, the target statistical fluctuation model, and the noise or interference of statistical models. This is the subject of the rest of this chapter.

8.3.1. Coherent Integration

In coherent integration, and when a perfect integrator is used (100% efficiency) to integrate n_P pulses, the SNR is improved by the same factor. Otherwise, integration loss occurs, which is always the case for noncoherent integration. Coherent integration loss occurs when the integration process is not optimum. This could be due to target fluctuation, instability in the radar local oscillator, or propagation path changes.

Denote the single pulse SNR required to produce a given probability of detection as $(SNR)_1$. The SNR resulting from coherently integrating n_P pulses is then given by

$$(SNR)_{CI} = n_P(SNR)_1.$$ 	Eq. (8.59)

Coherent integration cannot be applied over a long interval of time, particularly if the target RCS is varying rapidly. If the target radial velocity is known and constant acceleration is assumed, the maximum coherent integration time is limited to

$$t_{CI} = \sqrt{\frac{\lambda}{2a_r}}$$ 	Eq. (8.60)

where λ is the radar wavelength and a_r is the target radial acceleration. Coherent integration time can be extended if the target radial acceleration can be compensated for by the radar.

In order to demonstrate the improvement in the SNR using coherent integration, consider the case where the radar return signal contains both signal plus additive noise. The *mth* pulse is

$$x_m(t) = s(t) + n_m(t)$$ 	Eq. (8.61)

where $s(t)$ is the radar signal return of interest and $n_m(t)$ is white uncorrelated additive noise signal with variance σ^2. Coherent integration of n_P pulses yields

$$z(t) = \frac{1}{n_P}\sum_{m=1}^{n_P} x_m(t) = \sum_{m=1}^{n_P} \frac{1}{n_P}[s(t) + n_m(t)] = s(t) + \sum_{m=1}^{n_P} \frac{1}{n_P} n_m(t).$$ 	Eq. (8.62)

The total noise power in $z(t)$ is equal to the variance. More precisely,

$$\sigma_{n_P}^2 = E\left[\left(\sum_{m=1}^{n_P} \frac{1}{n_P} n_m(t)\right)\left(\sum_{l=1}^{n_P} \frac{1}{n_P} n_l(t)\right)^*\right]$$ 	Eq. (8.63)

where E is the expected value operator. It follows that

$$\sigma_{n_P}^2 = \frac{1}{n_P^2}\sum_{m,l=1}^{n_P} E[n_m(t)n_l^*(t)] = \frac{1}{n_P^2}\sum_{m,l=1}^{n_P} \sigma_{ny}^2 \delta_{ml} = \frac{1}{n_P}\sigma_{ny}^2$$ 	Eq. (8.64)

where σ_{ny}^2 is the single pulse noise power and δ_{ml} is equal to zero for $m \neq l$ and unity for $m = l$. Observation of Eq. (8.64) indicates that the desired signal power after coherent integration is unchanged, while the noise power is reduced by the factor $1/n_P$. Thus, the SNR after coherent integration is improved by n_P.

8.3.2. Noncoherent Integration

When the phase of the integrated pulses is not known, so that coherent integration is no longer possible, another form of pulse integration is done. In this case, pulse integration is performed by adding (integrating) the individual pulses' envelopes or the square of their envelopes. Thus, the term noncoherent integration is adopted. A block diagram of a radar receiver utilizing noncoherent integration is illustrated in Fig. 8.6. The performance difference (measured in SNR) between the linear envelope detector and the quadratic (square law) detector is practically negligible. Robertson (1967) showed that this difference is typically less than $0.2\,dB$; he showed that the performance difference is higher than $0.2\,dB$ only for cases where $n_P > 100$ and $P_d < 0.01$. Both of these conditions are of no practical significance in radar applications. It is much easier to analyze and implement the square law detector in real hardware than is the case for the envelope detector. Therefore, most authors make no distinction between the type of detector used when referring to noncoherent integration and the square law detector is almost always assumed. The analysis presented in this book will always assume, unless indicated otherwise, noncoherent integration using the square law detector.

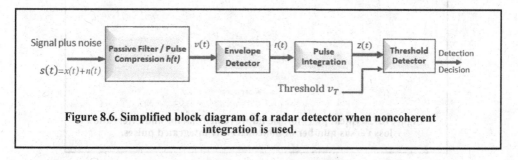

Figure 8.6. Simplified block diagram of a radar detector when noncoherent integration is used.

8.3.3. Improvement Factor and Integration Loss

Noncoherent integration is less efficient than coherent integration. Actually, the noncoherent integration gain is always smaller than the number of noncoherently integrated pulses. This loss in integration is referred to as "post-detection" or square-law detector loss. Define $(SNR)_{NCI}$ as the SNR required to achieve a specific P_d given a particular P_{fa} when n_P pulses are integrated noncoherently. Also denote the single pulse SNR as $(SNR)_1$. Thus,

$$(SNR)_{NCI} = (SNR)_1 \times I(n_P) \qquad \text{Eq. (8.65)}$$

where $I(n_P)$ is called the integration improvement factor. An empirically derived expression for the improvement factor that is accurate within $0.8\,dB$ is reported in Peebles (1998) as

$$[I(n_P)]_{dB} = 6.79(1 + 0.253 P_D)\left(1 + \frac{\log(1/P_{fa})}{46.6}\right)\log(n_P) \qquad \text{Eq. (8.66)}$$

$$(1 - 0.140\log(n_P) + 0.018310(\log n_P)^2)$$

The integration loss in dB is defined as

$$[L_{NCI}]_{dB} = 10\log n_P - [I(n_P)]_{dB}. \qquad \textbf{Eq. (8.67)}$$

Figure 8.7 shows plots of the improvement factor versus the number of integrated pulses using different combinations of P_d and P_{fa}. The top part of Fig. 8.7 shows plots of the integration improvement factor as a function of the number of integrated pulses with P_d and P_{fa} as parameters using Eq. (8.66). While, the lower part of Fig. 8.7 shows plots of the corresponding integration loss versus n_P with P_d and P_{fa} as parameters.

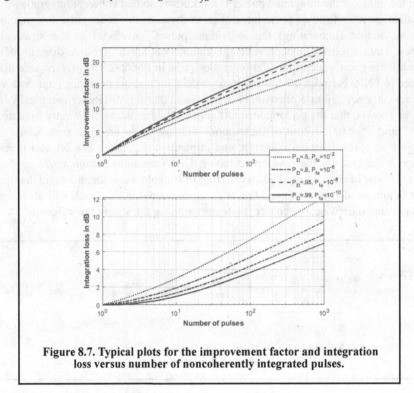

Figure 8.7. Typical plots for the improvement factor and integration loss versus number of noncoherently integrated pulses.

Swerling V, or Swerling 0, targets have constant amplitude over one antenna scan or observation interval; however, a Swerling I target amplitude varies independently from scan to scan according to a chi-square probability density function with two degrees of freedom. The amplitude of Swerling II targets fluctuates independently from pulse to pulse according to a chi-square probability density function with two degrees of freedom.

Target fluctuation associated with a Swerling III model is from scan to scan according to a chi-square probability density function with four degrees of freedom. Finally, the fluctuation of Swerling IV targets is from pulse to pulse according to a chi-square probability density function with four degrees of freedom.

Swerling showed that the statistics associated with Swerling I and II models apply to targets consisting of many small scatterers of comparable RCS values, while the statistics associated with Swerling III and IV models apply to targets consisting of one large RCS scatterer and many small equal RCS scatterers. Noncoherent integration can be applied to all four Swerling models; however, coherent integration cannot be used when the target fluctuation is either Swerling II or Swerling IV. This is because the target amplitude decorrelates from pulse to pulse (fast fluctuation) for Swerling II and IV models, and thus phase coherency cannot be maintained.

The chi-square *pdf* with $2N$ degrees of freedom can be written as

$$f_X(x) = \frac{N}{(N-1)! \sqrt{\sigma_x^2}} \left(\frac{Nx}{\sigma_x}\right)^{N-1} \exp\left(-\frac{Nx}{\sigma_x}\right) \qquad \text{Eq. (8.68)}$$

where σ_x is the standard deviation for the RCS value. Using this equation, the *pdf* associated with Swerling I and II targets can be obtained by letting $N = 1$, which yields a Rayleigh *pdf*. More precisely,

$$f_X(x) = \frac{1}{\sigma_x} \exp\left(-\frac{x}{\sigma_x}\right) \qquad x \geq 0 . \qquad \text{Eq. (8.69)}$$

Letting $N = 2$ yields the *pdf* for Swerling III and IV type targets,

$$f_X(x) = \frac{4x}{\sigma_x^2} \exp\left(-\frac{2x}{\sigma_x}\right) \qquad x \geq 0 . \qquad \text{Eq. (8.70)}$$

8.3.4. Probability of False Alarm Formulation for a Square Law Detector

Computation of the general formula for the probability of false alarm P_{fa} and subsequently the rest of square law detection theory requires knowledge and a good understating of the incomplete Gamma function. Hence, those readers who are not familiar with this function are advised to read Section 8.9 before proceeding with the rest of this chapter. DiFranco and Rubin (1980) derived a general form relating the threshold and P_{fa} for any number of pulses when noncoherent integration is used. The square law detector under consideration is shown in Fig. 8.8. There are $n_P \geq 2$ pulses integrated noncoherently and the noise power (variance) is σ^2.

The complex envelope in terms of the quadrature components is given by

$$\tilde{r}(t) = r_I(t) + j r_Q(t) , \qquad \text{Eq. (8.71)}$$

thus the square of the complex envelope is

$$|\tilde{r}(t)|^2 = r_I^2(t) + r_Q^2(t) . \qquad \text{Eq. (8.72)}$$

The samples $|\tilde{r}_k|^2$ are computed from the samples of $\tilde{r}(t)$ evaluated at $t = t_k;\ k = 1, 2, ..., n_P$. It follows that

$$Z = \frac{1}{2\sigma^2} \sum_{k=1}^{n_P} [r_I^2(t_k) + r_Q^2(t_k)] . \qquad \text{Eq. (8.73)}$$

The random variable Z is the sum of $2n_P$ squares of random variables, each of which is a Gaussian random variable with variance σ^2. Thus, the *pdf* for the random variable Z is given by

$$f_Z(z) = \begin{cases} \dfrac{z^{n_P - 1} e^{-z}}{\Gamma(n_P)} & z \geq 0 \\ 0 & z < 0 \end{cases} . \qquad \text{Eq. (8.74)}$$

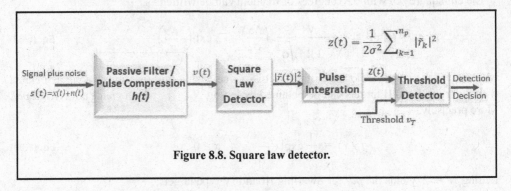

Figure 8.8. Square law detector.

Consequently, the probability of false alarm given a threshold value v_T is

$$P_{fa} = Prob\{Z \ge v_T\} = \int_{v_T}^{\infty} \frac{z^{n_p-1} e^{-z}}{\Gamma(n_P)} \, dz.$$

Eq. (8.75)

and using analysis provided in Section 8.9 yields

$$P_{fa} = 1 - \Gamma_I\left(\frac{v_T}{\sqrt{n_P}}, n_P - 1\right).$$

Eq. (8.76)

Using the algebraic expression for the incomplete Gamma function, the probability of false alarm can be expressed as

$$P_{fa} = e^{-v_T} \sum_{k=0}^{n_P-1} \frac{v_T^k}{k!} = 1 - e^{-v_T} \sum_{k=n_P}^{\infty} \frac{v_T^k}{k!}.$$

Eq. (8.77)

Next, the threshold value v_T can then be approximated by the recursive formula used in the Newton-Raphson method. More precisely,

$$v_{T,m} = v_{T,m-1} - \frac{G(v_{T,m-1})}{G'(v_{T,m-1})} \qquad ; \ m = 1, 2, 3, \dots$$

Eq. (8.78)

The iteration is terminated when $|v_{T,m} - v_{T,m-1}| < v_{T,m-1}/10000.0$. The functions G and G' are

$$G(v_{T,m}) = (0.5)^{n_P/n_{fa}} - \Gamma_I(v_T, n_P)$$

Eq. (8.79)

$$G'(v_{T,m}) = -\frac{e^{-v_T} v_T^{n_P-1}}{(n_P-1)!}.$$

Eq. (8.80)

The initial value for the recursion is

$$v_{T,0} = n_P - \sqrt{n_P} + 2.3 \sqrt{-\log P_{fa}} \left(\sqrt{-\log P_{fa}} + \sqrt{n_P} - 1\right).$$

Eq. (8.81)

Figure 8.9 shows plots of the threshold value versus the number of integrated pulses for several values of n_{fa}; remember that $P_{fa} \approx \ln(2)/n_{fa}$.

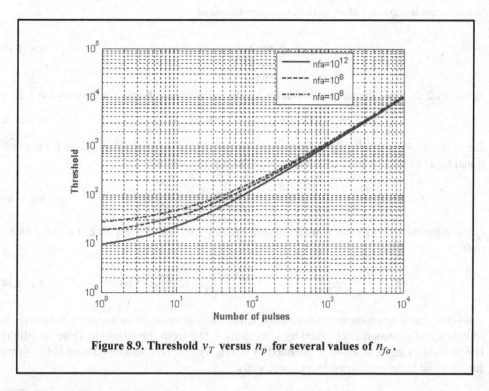

Figure 8.9. Threshold v_T versus n_p for several values of n_{fa}.

8.3.5. Square Law Detection

The *pdf* for the linear envelope $r(t)$ was derived earlier in Part I of this chapter. Define a new dimensionless variable y as

$$y_n = \frac{r_n}{\sigma}$$

Eq. (8.82)

where the subscript n denotes the *nth* pulse. Also define

$$\Re_p = \frac{A^2}{\sigma^2} = 2SNR.$$

Eq. (8.83)

σ^2 is the noise variance. It follows that the *pdf* for the new variable is

$$f_{Y_n}(y_n) = f_{R_n}(r_n)\left|\frac{dr_n}{dy_n}\right| = y_n \, I_0(y_n\sqrt{\Re_p}) \, \exp\left(\frac{-(y_n^2 + \Re_p)}{2}\right).$$

Eq. (8.84)

The output of a square law detector for the *nth* pulse is proportional to the square of its input. Thus, it is convenient to define a change variable,

$$z_n = \frac{1}{2}y_n^2.$$

Eq. (8.85)

The *pdf* for the variable at the output of the square law detector is given by

$$f_{Z_n}(x_n) = f(y_n)\left|\frac{dy_n}{dz_n}\right| = \exp\left(-\left(z_n + \frac{\Re_p}{2}\right)\right)I_0(\sqrt{2z_n\Re_p}).$$

Eq. (8.86)

Noncoherent integration of n_p pulses is implemented as

$$z = \sum_{n=1}^{n_P} \frac{1}{2} y_n^2 .$$ **Eq. (8.87)**

Again, $n_P \geq 2$. Since the random variables y_n are independent, the *pdf* for the variable z is

$$f_Z(z) = f((y_1) \otimes f(y_2) \otimes \ldots \otimes f(y_{n_p})) .$$ **Eq. (8.88)**

The operator $\otimes$ symbolically indicates convolution. The characteristic functions for the individual *pdf*s can then be used to compute the joint *pdf*, the result is

$$f_Z(z) = \left(\frac{2z}{n_P \Re_p}\right)^{(n_P - 1)/2} \exp\left(-z - \frac{1}{2} n_P \Re_p\right) I_{n_P - 1}(\sqrt{2 n_P z \Re_p}) .$$ **Eq. (8.89)**

$I_{n_P - 1}$ is the modified Bessel function of order $n_P - 1$. Substituting Eq. (8.83) into Eq. (8.89) yields

$$f_Z(z) = \left(\frac{z}{n_P SNR}\right)^{(n_P - 1)/2} e^{(-z - n_P SNR)} I_{n_P - 1}(2\sqrt{n_P z SNR}) .$$ **Eq. (8.90)**

When target fluctuation is not present (referred to as Swerling 0 or Swerling V target), the probability of detection is obtained by integrating $f_Z(z)$ from the threshold value to infinity. The probability of false alarm is obtained by letting $\Re_p$ be zero and integrating the *pdf* from the threshold value to infinity. More specifically,

$$P_d\big|_{SNR} = \int_{v_T}^{\infty} \left(\frac{z}{n_P SNR}\right)^{(n_P - 1)/2} e^{(-z - n_P SNR)} I_{n_P - 1}(2\sqrt{n_P z SNR}) dz ,$$ **Eq. (8.91)**

which can be rewritten as

$$P_d\big|_{SNR} = e^{-n_P SNR} \left(\sum_{k=0}^{\infty} \frac{(n_P SNR)^k}{k!}\right) \left(\sum_{j=0}^{n_P - 1 + k} \frac{e^{-v_T} v_T^j}{j!}\right) .$$ **Eq. (8.92)**

Alternatively, when target fluctuation is present, the *pdf* is calculated using the conditional probability density function of Eq. (8.90) with respect to the SNR value of the target fluctuation type. In general, given a fluctuating target with SNR^F, where the superscript indicates fluctuation, the expression for the probability of detection is

$$P_d\big|_{SNR^F} = \int_0^{\infty} P\big|_{SNR} f_Z(z^F / SNR^F)(dz) d =$$ **Eq. (8.93)**

$$\int_0^{\infty} P_d\big|_{SNR} \left(\frac{z^F}{n_P SNR^F}\right)^{(n_P - 1)/2} e^{(-z^F - n_P SNR^F)} I_{n_P - 1}(2\sqrt{n_P z^F SNR^F}) dz$$

Remember that target fluctuation introduces an additional loss term in the SNR. It follows that for the same P_d given the same P_{fa} and the same n_P, $SNR^F > SNR$. One way to calculate this additional SNR is to first compute the required SNR given no fluctuation, then add to it the amount of target fluctuation loss to get the required value for SNR^F. How to calculate this fluctuation loss will be addressed later on in this chapter. Meanwhile, hereinafter, the superscript $\{^F\}$ will be dropped and it will always be assumed.

8.4. Probability of Detection Calculation

Marcum defined the probability of false alarm for the case when $n_P > 1$ as

$$P_{fa} \approx \ln(2)\left(\frac{n_P}{n_{fd}}\right).$$

Eq. (8.94)

The single pulse probability of detection for nonfluctuating targets was derived in Part I of this chapter. When $n_P > 1$, the probability of detection is computed using the Gram-Charlier series. In this case, the probability of detection is

$$P_d \cong \frac{erfc(V/\sqrt{2})}{2} - \frac{e^{-V^2/2}}{\sqrt{2\pi}}[C_3(V^2 - 1) + C_4 V(3 - V^2) - C_6 V(V^4 - 10V^2 + 15)]$$

Eq. (8.95)

the constants C_3, C_4, and C_6 are the Gram-Charlier series coefficients, and the variable V is

$$V = \frac{v_T - n_P(1 + SNR)}{\varpi}.$$

Eq. (8.96)

In general, values for C_3, C_4, C_6, and ϖ vary depending on the target fluctuation type.

8.4.1. Detection of Swerling 0 (Swerling V) Targets

For Swerling 0 (Swerling V) target fluctuations, the general form for the probability of detection is calculated using Eq. (8.94). In this case, the Gram-Charlier series coefficients are

$$C_3 = -\frac{SNR + 1/3}{\sqrt{n_p}(2SNR + 1)^{1.5}}$$

Eq. (8.97)

$$C_4 = \frac{SNR + 1/4}{n_p(2SNR + 1)^2}$$

Eq. (8.98)

$$C_6 = C_3^2/2$$

Eq. (8.99)

$$\varpi = \sqrt{n_p(2SNR + 1)}.$$

Eq. (8.100)

Figure 8.10 shows a plot for the probability of detection of Swerling V target versus SNR for cases $n_p = 1, 5, 10$. Note that it requires less SNR, with ten pulses integrated noncoherently, to achieve the same probability of detection as in the case of a single pulse. Hence, for any given P_D, the SNR improvement can be read from the plot.

8.4.2. Detection of Swerling I Targets

The exact formula for the probability of detection for Swerling I type targets is

$$P_d = e^{-(v_T)/(1 + SNR)} \qquad ; n_P = 1$$

Eq. (8.101)

and for $n_P > 1$, it is given by

$$P_d = 1 - \Gamma_I(v_T, n_P - 1) + \left(1 + \frac{1}{n_P SNR}\right)^{n_p - 1} \Gamma_I\left(\frac{v_T}{1 + \frac{1}{n_P SNR}}, n_P - 1\right) e^{-v_T/(1 + n_P SNR)}.$$

Eq. (8.102)

Figure 8.11 shows a plot of the probability of detection as a function of SNR for $n_p = 1$ and $P_{fa} = 10^{-6}$ for both Swerling I and V (Swerling 0) type fluctuations. Note that it requires more SNR, with fluctuation, to achieve the same P_d as in the case with no fluctuation. Figure 8.12 is similar to Fig. 8.11, except in this case $P_{fa} = 10^{-6}$ and $n_P = 5$.

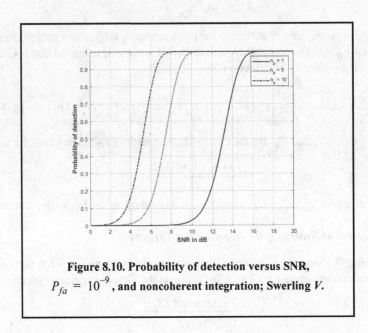

Figure 8.10. Probability of detection versus SNR,
$P_{fa} = 10^{-9}$**, and noncoherent integration; Swerling V.**

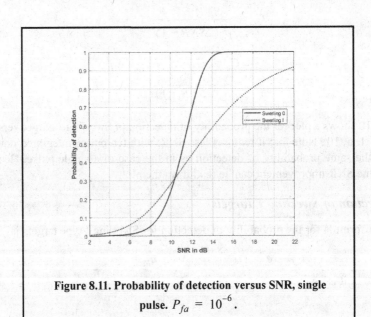

Figure 8.11. Probability of detection versus SNR, single
pulse. $P_{fa} = 10^{-6}$.

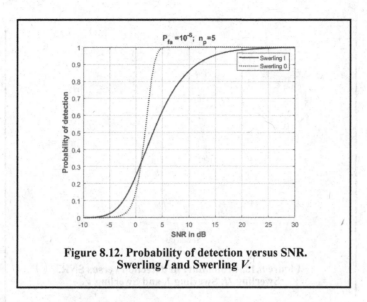

Figure 8.12. Probability of detection versus SNR.
Swerling *I* and Swerling *V*.

8.4.3. Detection of Swerling II Targets

In the case of Swerling II targets, the probability of detection is given by

$$P_d = 1 - \Gamma_I\!\left(\frac{v_T}{(1 + SNR)}, n_p\right) \qquad ; \; n_P \le 50 \;.$$

Eq. (8.103)

For the case when $n_P > 50$ the probability of detection is computed using the Gram-Charlier series. In this case,

$$C_3 = -\frac{1}{3\sqrt{n_p}} \qquad , \; C_6 = \frac{C_3^2}{2}$$

Eq. (8.104)

$$C_4 = \frac{1}{4n_p}$$

Eq. (8.105)

$$\varpi = \sqrt{n_p}\,(1 + SNR)\;.$$

Eq. (8.106)

Figure 8.13 shows a plot of the probability of detection for Swerling *V*, Swerling *I*, and Swerling *II* with $n_P = 5$, where $P_{fa} = 10^{-7}$. Figure 8.14 is similar to Fig. 8.13 except in this case $n_P = 2$.

8.4.4. Detection of Swerling III Targets

The exact formulas, developed by Marcum, for the probability of detection for Swerling *III* type targets when $n_P = 1, 2$

$$P_d = \exp\!\left(\frac{-v_T}{1 + \frac{n_P SNR}{2}}\right)\!\left(1 + \frac{2}{n_P SNR}\right)^{n_P - 2}\!\left(1 + \frac{v_T}{1 + \frac{n_P SNR}{2}} - \frac{2}{n_P SNR}(n_P - 2)\right)\;.$$

Eq. (8.107)

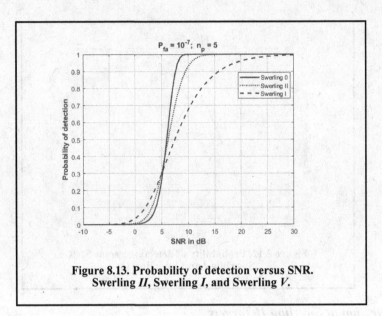

**Figure 8.13. Probability of detection versus SNR.
Swerling *II*, Swerling *I*, and Swerling *V*.**

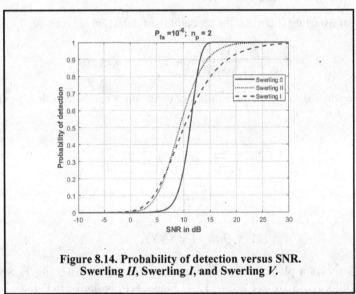

**Figure 8.14. Probability of detection versus SNR.
Swerling *II*, Swerling *I*, and Swerling *V*.**

For $n_P > 2$ the expression is

$$P_d = \frac{v_T^{n_P-1} e^{-V_T}}{(1 + n_P SNR/2)(n_P - 2)!} + 1 - \Gamma_I(v_T, n_P - 1) + K_0 \quad .$$ Eq. (8.108a)

$$\times \ \Gamma_I\left(\frac{v_T}{1 + 2/n_p SNR}, n_p - 1\right)$$

where K_0 is given by

$$K_0 = 1 + \frac{v_T}{1 + n_P SNR/2} - \frac{2}{n_p SNR}(n_P - 2) .$$ Eq. (8.108b)

Figure 8.15 shows a plot of the probability of detection as a function of SNR for $n_p = 1, 10, 50, 100$, where $P_{fa} = 10^{-9}$. Figure 8.16 shows a plot of the probability of detection for Swerling V, Swerling I, Swerling II, and Swerling III with $n_p = 5$ and $P_{fa} = 10^{-7}$. Notice that as the target fluctuation becomes more rapid, as in the case of Swerling I type targets, it requires more SNR to achieve the same probability of detection when considering lesser fluctuating targets as in the case of Swerling V, for example.

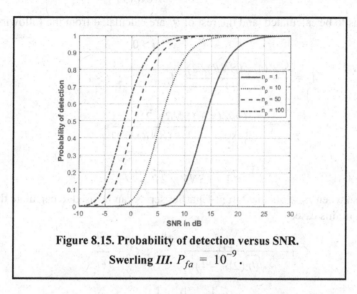

Figure 8.15. Probability of detection versus SNR.
Swerling *III*. $P_{fa} = 10^{-9}$.

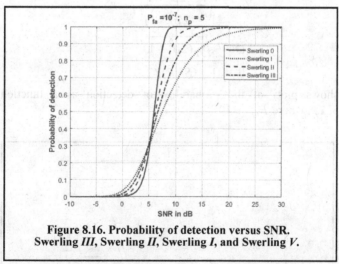

Figure 8.16. Probability of detection versus SNR.
Swerling *III*, Swerling *II*, Swerling *I*, and Swerling *V*.

8.4.5. Detection of Swerling IV Targets

The expression for the probability of detection for Swerling IV targets for $n_p < 50$ is

$$P_d = 1 - \left[\gamma_0 + \left(\frac{SNR}{2}\right) n_P \gamma_1 + \left(\frac{SNR}{2}\right)^2 \frac{n_P(n_P - 1)}{2!} \gamma_2 + \dots + \right.$$
$$\left. \left(\frac{SNR}{2}\right)^{n_P} \gamma_{n_P} \right] \bigg/ \left(1 + \frac{SNR}{2}\right)^{-n_P} \qquad \text{Eq. (8.109)}$$

$$\gamma_i = \Gamma_I\left(\frac{v_T}{1 + (SNR)/2} , n_P + i\right). \qquad\qquad \textbf{Eq. (8.110)}$$

By using the recursive formula

$$\Gamma_I(x, i+1) = \Gamma_I(x, i) - \frac{x^i}{i! \exp(x)}, \qquad\qquad \textbf{Eq. (8.111)}$$

only γ_0 needs to be calculated, and the rest of γ_i are calculated from the following recursion:

$$\gamma_i = \gamma_{i-1} - A_i \qquad ; \; i > 0 \qquad\qquad \textbf{Eq. (8.112)}$$

$$A_i = \frac{v_T/(1 + (SNR)/2)}{n_P + i - 1} A_{i-1} \qquad ; \; i > 1 \qquad\qquad \textbf{Eq. (8.113)}$$

$$A_1 = \frac{(v_T/(1 + (SNR)/2))^{n_P}}{n_P! \exp(v_T/(1 + (SNR)/2))} \qquad\qquad \textbf{Eq. (8.114)}$$

$$\gamma_0 = \Gamma_I\left(\frac{v_T}{(1 + (SNR)/2)} , n_P\right). \qquad\qquad \textbf{Eq. (8.115)}$$

For the case when $n_P \geq 50$, the Gram-Charlier series can be used to calculate the probability of detection. In this case,

$$C_3 = \frac{1}{3\sqrt{n_P}} \frac{2\beta^3 - 1}{(2\beta^2 - 1)^{1.5}} \qquad ; \; C_6 = \frac{C_3^2}{2} \qquad\qquad \textbf{Eq. (8.116)}$$

$$C_4 = \frac{1}{4n_P} \frac{2\beta^4 - 1}{(2\beta^2 - 1)^2} \qquad\qquad \textbf{Eq. (8.117)}$$

$$\varpi = \sqrt{n_P(2\beta^2 - 1)} \qquad\qquad \textbf{Eq. (8.118)}$$

$$\beta = 1 + (SNR)/2. \qquad\qquad \textbf{Eq. (8.119)}$$

Figure 8.17 shows plots of the probability of detection as a function of SNR for $n_P = 1, 10, 25, 75$, where $P_{fa} = 10^{-6}$.

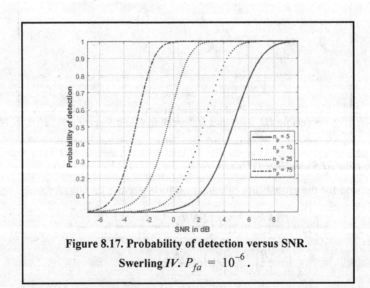

Figure 8.17. Probability of detection versus SNR.

Swerling *IV*. $P_{fa} = 10^{-6}$.

8.5. *Cumulative Probability of Detection*

Denote the range at which the single pulse SNR is unity (*0 dB*) as R_0, and refer to it as the reference range. Then, for a specific radar, the single pulse SNR at R_0 is defined by the radar equation and is given by

$$(SNR)_{R_0} = \frac{P_t G^2 \lambda^2 \sigma}{(4\pi)^3 kT_0 BFLR_0^4} = 1.$$ Eq. (8.120)

The single pulse SNR at any range R is

$$SNR = \frac{P_t G^2 \lambda^2 \sigma}{(4\pi)^3 kT_0 BFLR^4}.$$ Eq. (8.121)

Dividing Eq. (8.121) by Eq. (8.120) yields

$$\frac{SNR}{(SNR)_{R_0}} = \left(\frac{R_0}{R}\right)^4.$$ Eq. (8.122)

Therefore, if the range R_0 is known, then the SNR at any other range R is

$$(SNR)_{dB} = 40\log\left(\frac{R_0}{R}\right).$$ Eq. (8.123)

Also, define the range R_{50} as the range at which $P_d = 0.5 = P_{50}$. Normally, the radar unambiguous range R_u is set equal to $2R_{50}$. The cumulative probability of detection refers to detecting the target at least once by the time it is at range R. More precisely, consider a target closing on a scanning radar, where the target is illuminated only during a scan (frame). As the target gets closer to the radar, its probability of detection increases since the SNR is increased. Suppose that the probability of detection during the *nth* frame is P_{d_n}; then, the cumulative probability of detecting the target at least once during the *nth* frame (see Fig. 8.18) is given by

$$P_{C_n} = 1 - \prod_{i=1}^{n}(1 - P_{d_i}).$$ Eq. (8.124)

P_{d_1} is usually selected to be very small. Clearly, the probability of not detecting the target during the *nth* frame is $1 - P_{C_n}$. The probability of detection for the *ith* frame, P_{d_i}, is computed as discussed in the previous section.

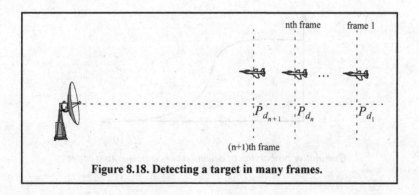

Figure 8.18. Detecting a target in many frames.

Example:

A radar detects a closing target at $R = 10km$, with probability of detection P_d equal to 0.5. Assume $P_{fa} = 10^{-7}$. Compute and sketch the single look probability of detection as a function of normalized range (with respect to $R = 10km$), over the interval $(2-20)km$. If the range between two successive frames is $1km$, what is the cumulative probability of detection at $R = 8km$?

Solution:

From Table 8.1 the SNR corresponding to $P_d = 0.5$ and $P_{fa} = 10^{-7}$ is approximately $12dB$. By using a similar analysis to that which led to Eq. (8.123), we can express the SNR at any range R as

$$(SNR)_R = (SNR)_{10} + 40 \ \log\frac{10}{R} = 52 - 40 \ \log R.$$

By using the function Marcumsq's algorithm, we can construct the following table:

R km	(SNR) dB	P_d
2	39.09	0.999
4	27.9	0.999
6	20.9	0.999
8	15.9	0.999
9	13.8	0.9
10	12.0	0.5
11	10.3	0.25
12	8.8	0.07
14	6.1	0.01
16	3.8	ε
20	0.01	ε

where ε is very small. A sketch of P_d versus normalized range is shown in the figure below.

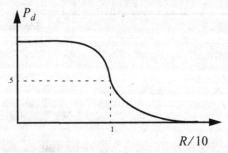

Cumulative probability of detection versus normalized range.

The cumulative probability of detection is given in Eq. (8.124), where the probability of detection of the first frame is selected to be very small. Thus, we can arbitrarily choose frame 1 to be at $R = 16km$. Note that selecting a different starting point for frame 1 would have a negligible effect on the cumulative probability (we only need P_{d_1} to be very small). Below is a range listing for frames 1 through 9, where frame 9 corresponds to $R = 8km$.

frame	1	2	3	4	5	6	7	8	9
range in *km*	16	15	14	13	12	11	10	9	8

The cumulative probability of detection at 8Km is then

$$P_{C_9} = 1 - (1 - 0.999)(1 - 0.9)(1 - 0.5)(1 - 0.25)(1 - 0.07)$$
$$(1 - 0.01)(1 - \varepsilon)^2 \approx 0.9998$$

8.6. Constant False Alarm Rate

The detection threshold is computed so that the radar receiver maintains a constant predetermined probability of false alarm. The relationship between the threshold value v_T and the probability of false alarm P_{fa} was derived earlier in this chapter, and for convenience is repeated here as Eq. (8.125):

$$v_T = \sqrt{2\sigma^2 \ln(1/P_{fa})}.$$ **Eq. (8.125)**

If the noise power σ^2 is constant, then a fixed threshold can satisfy Eq. (8.125). However, due to many reasons, this condition is rarely true. Thus, in order to maintain a constant probability of false alarm, the threshold value must be continuously updated based on the estimates of the noise variance. The process of continuously changing the threshold value to maintain a constant probability of false alarm is known as the constant false alarm rate (CFAR).

Three different types of CFAR processors are primarily used: adaptive threshold CFAR, nonparametric CFAR, and nonlinear receiver techniques. Adaptive CFAR assumes that the interference distribution is known and approximates the unknown parameters associated with these distributions. Nonparametric CFAR processors tend to accommodate unknown interference distributions. Nonlinear receiver techniques attempt to normalize the root-mean-square amplitude of the interference. In this book, only the analog cell-averaging CFAR (CA-CFAR) technique is examined. The analysis presented in this section closely follows Urkowitz[1].

8.6.1. Cell-Averaging CFAR (Single Pulse)

The CA-CFAR processor is shown in Fig. 8.19. Cell averaging is performed on a series of range and/or Doppler bins (cells). The echo return for each pulse is detected by a square-law detector. In analog implementation, these cells are obtained from a tapped delay line. The cell under test (CUT) is the central cell. The immediate neighbors of the CUT are excluded from the averaging process due to a possible spillover from the CUT. The output of M reference cells ($M/2$ on each side of the CUT) is averaged. The threshold value is obtained by multiplying the averaged estimate from all reference cells by a constant K_0 (used for scaling). A detection is declared in the CUT if

---

1. Urkowitz, H., Decision and Detection Theory, unpublished lecture notes. Lockheed Martin Co., Moorestown, NJ (undated).

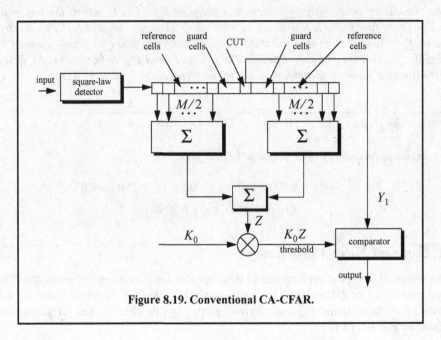

Figure 8.19. Conventional CA-CFAR.

$$Y_1 \geq K_0 Z. \qquad \text{Eq. (8.126)}$$

CA-CFAR assumes that the target of interest is in the CUT and all reference cells contain zero-mean independent Gaussian noise of variance σ^2. Therefore, the output of the reference cells, Z, represents a random variable with gamma probability density function (special case of the chi-square) with $2M$ degrees of freedom. In this case, the gamma *pdf* is

$$f(z) = \frac{z^{(M/2)-1} e^{(-z/2\sigma^2)}}{2^{M/2} \sigma^M \Gamma(M/2)} \qquad ; \ z > 0. \qquad \text{Eq. (8.127)}$$

The probability of false alarm corresponding to a fixed threshold was derived earlier. When CA-CFAR is implemented, then the probability of false alarm can be derived from the conditional false alarm probability, which is averaged over all possible values of the threshold in order to achieve an unconditional false alarm probability. The conditional probability of false alarm when $y = v_T$ can be written as

$$P_{fa}(v_T = y) = e^{-y/2\sigma^2}. \qquad \text{Eq. (8.128)}$$

It follows that the unconditional probability of false alarm is

$$P_{fa} = \int_0^\infty P_{fa}(v_T = y)f(y)\,dy \qquad \text{Eq. (8.129)}$$

where $f(y)$ is the *pdf* of the threshold, which except for the constant K_0, is the same as that defined in Eq. (8.127). Therefore,

$$f(y) = \frac{y^{M-1} e^{(-y/2K_0\sigma^2)}}{(2K_0\sigma^2)^M \Gamma(M)} \qquad ; \ y \geq 0. \qquad \text{Eq. (8.130)}$$

Substituting $f(y)$ in Eq. (8.129) and performing the integration yields

$$P_{fa} = 1/(1 + K_0)^M.$$
Eq. (8.131)

Observation of Eq. (8.131) shows that the probability of false alarm is now independent of the noise power, which is the objective of CFAR processing. Figures 8.20-a and 8.20-b, respectively show the probability of detection, P_d, versus SNR with and without CFAR. For a given P_d, note the amount of additional SNR is required to achieve this probability. This difference, is referred to as CFAR loss and it should be part of the loss budget inside the Blake chart table, when determining the radar sensitivity.

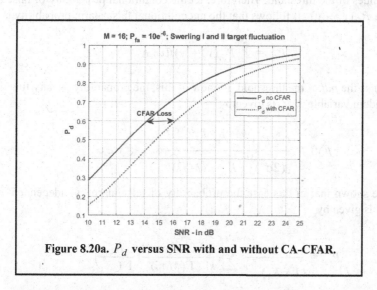

Figure 8.20a. P_d versus SNR with and without CA-CFAR.

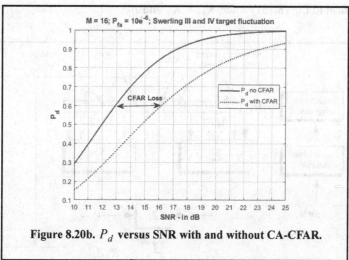

Figure 8.20b. P_d versus SNR with and without CA-CFAR.

8.6.2. Cell-Averaging CFAR with Noncoherent Integration

In practice, CFAR averaging is often implemented after noncoherent integration, as illustrated in Fig. 8.21. Now, the output of each reference cell is the sum of n_P squared envelopes. It follows that the total number of summed reference samples is Mn_P. The output Y_1 is also the sum of n_P squared envelopes. When noise alone is present in the CUT, Y_1 is a random variable whose *pdf* is a gamma distribution with $2n_p$ degrees of freedom. Additionally, the summed output of the reference cells is the sum of Mn_P squared envelopes. Thus, Z is also a random variable which has a gamma *pdf* with $2Mn_P$ degrees of freedom. The probability of false alarm is then equal to the probability that the ratio Y_1/Z exceeds the threshold is,

$$P_{fa} = Prob\{Y_1/Z > K_1\}. \qquad \text{Eq. (8.132)}$$

Equation (8.132) implies that one must first find the joint *pdf* for the ratio Y_1/Z. However, this can be avoided if P_{fa} is first computed for a fixed threshold value V_T, then averaged over all possible values of the threshold. Therefore, let the conditional probability of false alarm when $y = v_T$ be $P_{fa}(v_T = y)$. It follows that the unconditional false alarm probability is

$$P_{fa} = \int_0^\infty P_{fa}(v_T = y)f(y)\,dy \qquad \text{Eq. (8.133)}$$

where $f(y)$ is the *pdf* of the threshold. In view of this, the probability density function describing the random variable $K_1 Z$ is given by

$$f(y) = \frac{(y/K_1)^{Mn_P - 1}\, e^{(-y/2K_1\sigma^2)}}{(2\sigma^2)^{Mn_P} K_1\, \Gamma(Mn_P)} \qquad ; \; y \geq 0. \qquad \text{Eq. (8.134)}$$

It can be shown that in this case the probability of false alarm is independent of the noise power and is given by

$$P_{fa} = \frac{1}{(1+K_1)^{Mn_P}} \sum_{k=0}^{n_P - 1} \frac{1}{k!} \frac{\Gamma(Mn_P + k)}{\Gamma(Mn_P)} \left(\frac{K_1}{1+K_1}\right)^k, \qquad \text{Eq. (8.135)}$$

which is identical to Eq. (8.131) when $K_1 = K_0$ and $n_P = 1$.

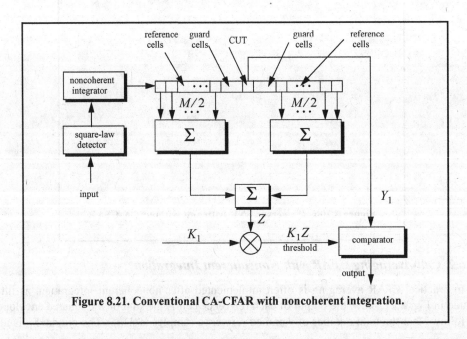

Figure 8.21. Conventional CA-CFAR with noncoherent integration.

8.7. M-out-of-N Detection

A few sources in the literature refer to the *M-out-of-N* detection as *binary integration* and / or as *double threshold* detection; nonetheless, *M-out-of-N* is the most commonly used name. The basic idea behind the *M-out-of-N* detection technique is as follows: In any given resolution cell (range, Doppler, or angle) the detection process is repeated *N* times, where the outcome of each decision cycle is either a "detection" or "no detection," hence the term *binary* is used in the literature. For each decision cycle, the probability of detection and the probability of false alarm are computed. The final decision criterion declares a target detection if *M-out-of-N* decision cycles have resulted in a detection. Clearly, the decision criterion associated with this technique follows a binomial distribution.

To elaborate further on this concept of detection, assume a non-fluctuating target whose single trial probability of detection is P_d and its probability of false alarm is P_{fa}. Denote the total probability of detection resulting from the *M-out-of-N* detection technique as P_{dmn}. It follows that after *N* independent trials of detection, one gets

$$P_{dmn} = 1 - (1 - P_D)^N .$$

Eq. (8.136)

Similarly, the probability of false alarm after the same number of trials is

$$P_{FA} = 1 - (1 - P_{fa})^N .$$

Eq. (8.137)

For example, if the desired P_{dmn} is *0.99*, then by using Eq. (8.136), one finds that a $P_D = 0.9$ will accomplish the desired P_{dmn} after 2 trials (i.e., *N=2*); alternatively, when using a $P_d = 0.2$, it will take 20 trials to reach the desired P_{dmn}. Furthermore, Eq. (8.136) implicitly indicates that as the number of trials increases so does P_{dmn}, but this buildup in detection probability is somewhat costly. That is true because as the number of trials is increased, the overall probability of false alarm P_{FA} is also increased; obviously, a very undesirable result.

A slight modification to the *M-out-of-N* detection process that guarantees an increase or buildup in P_{Dmn} while simultaneously keeping P_{FA} in check is as follows:

1. A specific P_{fa} value is chosen; typically it is a design constraint
2. For each value M, compute the corresponding P_{FA} from Eq. (8.137)
3. Using any of the techniques developed in this book to calculate the threshold value v_T so that P_{fa} is maintained, compute its corresponding SNR
4. Calculate P_d that corresponds to the SNR computed in step 3
5. Use Eq. (8.136) to compute the probability of detection P_{dmn}, and compute the corresponding SNR so that the threshold value computed in step 3 is maintained; therefore, P_{dmn} is also maintained
6. Repeat for each M to establish the specific combination of M (i.e., yielding P_{FA}) so that the SNR is minimized for a given P_{dmn}

Following this modified approach, P_{dmn} and P_{FA} are given by

$$P_{dmn} = \sum_{k=M}^{N} C_k^N \, P_d^k \, (1 - P_d)^{N-k}$$

Eq. (8.138)

$$P_{FA} = \sum_{k=M}^{N} C_k^N \, P_{fa}^k \, (1 - P_{fa})^{N-k} \qquad \text{Eq. (8.139)}$$

where

$$C_k^N = \frac{N!}{k!(N-k)!} . \qquad \text{Eq. (8.140)}$$

For small values of P_d, Eq. (8.138) keeps the overall detection probability P_{dmn} to less than or equal to P_d. Alternatively, for larger values of P_d, a quick buildup in the value of P_{dmn} occurs.

Selecting the specific combination of N and M that yields a desired P_{dmn} is typically a design constraint. In any case, once the choice is made, one must take target fluctuating into account. In this case, the optimal value for M is

$$M_{opt} = 10^{\alpha} N^{\beta} \qquad \text{Eq. (8.141)}$$

where α and β are constants that vary depending on the target fluctuation type, Table 8.2 shows their values corresponding to different Swerling targets.

Table 8.2. Parameters of Eq. (8.141).

Fluctuation Type	α	β	Range of N
Swerling 0	0.8	-0.02	5-700
Swerling I	0.8	-0.02	6-700
Swerling II	0.91	-0.38	9-700
Swerling III	0.8	-0.02	6-700
Swerling IV	0.873	-0.27	10-700

8.8. Radar Equation-Revisited

The radar equation developed in Chapter 3 assumed a constant target RCS and did not account for integration loss. In this section, a more comprehensive form of the radar equation is introduced. In this case, the radar equation is given by

$$R^4 = \frac{P_{av} G_t G_r \lambda^2 \sigma I(n_P)}{(4\pi)^3 k T_o F B \tau f_r L_t L_f \, (SNR)_1} \qquad \text{Eq. (8.142)}$$

where $P_{av} = P_t \tau f_r$ is the average transmitted power, P_t is the peak transmitted power, τ is the pulse width, f_r is PRF, G_t is the transmitting antenna gain, G_r is the receiving antenna gain, λ is the wavelength, σ is the target cross-section, $I(n_P)$ is the improvement factor, n_P is the number of integrated pulses, k is Boltzmann constant, T_o is 290 Kelvin, F is the system noise figure, B is the receiver bandwidth, L_t is the total system losses including integration loss, L_f is the loss due to target fluctuation, and $(SNR)_1$ is the minimum single pulse SNR required for detection.

Assuming that the radar parameters such as power, antenna gain, wavelength, losses, bandwidth, effective temperature, and noise figure are known, the steps one should follow to solve for range are shown in Fig. 8.22. Note that both sides of the bottom half of Fig. 8.22 are identical. Nevertheless, two paths are purposely shown so that a distinction between scintillating and nonfluctuating targets is made.

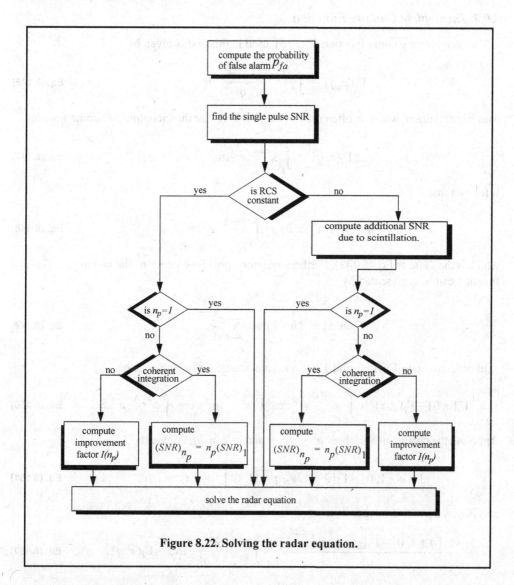

Figure 8.22. Solving the radar equation.

8.9. Gamma Function

Define the Gamma function (not the incomplete Gamma function) of the variable z (generally complex) as

$$\Gamma(z) = \int_0^\infty x^{z-1} e^{-x} \, dx$$

Eq. (8.143)

and when z is a positive integer, then

$$\Gamma(z) = (z-1)! \, .$$

Eq. (8.144)

One very useful and frequently used property is

$$\Gamma(z+1) = z\Gamma(z).$$

Eq. (8.145)

8.9.1. Incomplete Gamma Function

The incomplete gamma function $\Gamma_I(u, q)$ used in this text is given by

$$\Gamma_I(u, q) = \int_0^{u\sqrt{q+1}} \frac{e^{-x} x^q}{q!} \, dx.$$

Eq. (8.146)

Another definition, which is often used in the literature, for the incomplete Gamma function

$$\Gamma_I[z, q] = \int_0^\infty x^{z-1} e^{-x} dx.$$

Eq. (8.147)

It follows that

$$\Gamma_I[z, q] = \Gamma_I[z, 0] = \int_0^\infty x^{z-1} e^{-x} dx.$$

Eq. (8.148)

which is the same as Eq. (8.143). Furthermore, for a positive integer n, the incomplete Gamma function can be represented by

$$\Gamma_I[n, z] = (n-1)! e^{-z} \sum_{k=0}^{n-1} \frac{z^k}{k!}.$$

Eq. (8.149)

In order to relate $\Gamma_I[n, z]$ and $\Gamma_I(u, q)$, compute the following relation

$$\Gamma_I[a, 0] - \Gamma_I[a, z] = \int_0^\infty x^{a-1} e^{-x} dx - \int_z^\infty x^{a-1} e^{-x} dx = \int_0^z x^{a-1} e^{-x} dx.$$

Eq. (8.150)

Applying the change of variables $a = q+1$ and $z = u\sqrt{q+1}$ yields

$$\Gamma_I[q+1, 0] - \Gamma_I[q+1, u\sqrt{q+1}] = \int_0^{u\sqrt{q+1}} x^q e^{-x} dx,$$

Eq. (8.151)

and if q is a positive integer then

$$\frac{\Gamma_I[q+1, 0] - \Gamma_I[q+1, u\sqrt{q+1}]}{q!} = \int_0^{u\sqrt{q+1}} \frac{x^q e^{-x}}{q!} dx = \Gamma_I(u, q).$$

Eq. (8.152)

Which can be rewritten as

$$\Gamma_I(u, q) = 1 - \frac{(q+1-1)! e^{-u\sqrt{q+1}}}{q!} \sum_{k=0}^q \frac{(u\sqrt{q+1})^k}{k!}.$$

Eq. (8.153)

Finally, the incomplete Gamma function can be written as

$$\Gamma_I(u, q)' = 1 - e^{-u\sqrt{q+1}} \sum_{k=0}^{q} \frac{(u\sqrt{q+1})^k}{k!}.$$

Eq. (8.154)

The two limiting values for Eq. (8.154) are

$$\Gamma_I(0, q) = 0 \qquad \Gamma_I(\infty, q) = 1.$$

Eq. (8.155)

Figure 8.23 shows the incomplete gamma function for $q = 1, 3, 5, 8$.

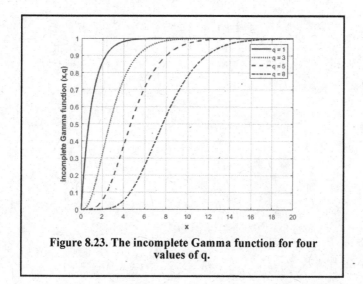

Figure 8.23. The incomplete Gamma function for four values of q.

Chapter 9

Radar Signal Processing in Clutter

Scott C. Winton

9.1. Introduction

This chapter discusses radar clutter and the various techniques used to improve radar performance in the presence of clutter. It begins with an overview of clutter and how it is quantified. Clutter is usually described stochastically, so it is worth looking at what distributions are utilized. Doppler processing techniques are utilized in order to improve detection of moving targets embedded in clutter and determine their radial velocities.

Moving target indicator (MTI) filters will be introduced and described. Use of Doppler processing requires that range samples be collected at the pulse repetition interval (PRI), which can lead to range or Doppler ambiguities, or both. This chapter includes an overview of these ambiguities and how to resolve them. Finally, pulse Doppler processing, which tends to use shorter PRIs, uses frequency analysis to determine the radial velocity and other attributes of a target. Both pulse Doppler and the use of the discrete Fourier transform (DFT) are introduced and discussed.

9.2. Clutter Definition

Taken at its most general level, clutter is radar returns that have not originated off the targets of interest. Backscatter off land or sea, often termed area clutter, is a particular problem for ground-looking airborne and space-based radars, but also for ground-based systems seeking target returns near the horizon. Volume clutter can create problems for almost any radar and may include weather, airborne objects such as birds or even insects and manmade objects, such as chaff.

The amount of clutter entering the radar will be dependent on the system parameters, such as the frequency band, polarization and beam width. The situation is further complicated by the type of clutter. For example, land clutter will be dependent on the amount and types of vegetation, rock, or buildings. Sea clutter is dependent on the sea state. The sea state is a numeric delineation of wave parameters, such as height and length, used in oceanography.

Not surprisingly, clutter is almost always modeled stochastically. Probability moments are developed for both amplitude and spectra, the latter being extremely useful when trying to detect moving targets within clutter. Most of this data is developed empirically. The literature is replete with empirical studies of clutter, some are included in the Bibliography.

Returns from clutter are based on the characteristics of the clutter itself, same as a target. Therefore, clutter does not, in general, spread over all resolution cells like noise. So, like targets, clutter can best be described as having a radar cross-section (RCS). A simplified way of looking at area or volume clutter is to attempt to determine an area RCS clutter density, σ^0 or volume RCS, η^0, the first has units (m^2/m^2), while the latter has units of $1/m$ and acts as a mean or median RCS value per unit area or volume.

9.3. Volume Clutter

Volume clutter may have very large spatial extents, especially weather, such as rain. Thunderstorms can produce rain that has vertical extents up to about *10 km*. Rain, in general, may have horizontal extents that may reach hundreds of kilometers in all directions. Biological clutter, such as insects and birds, may be more localized. The vertical extent of chaff is limited to the altitude of the dispensing aircraft, but winds can disperse chaff horizontally over larger horizontal regions and last for at least several hours.

Volume Cell

If η^0 can be determined for volume clutter, the RCS for clutter in a given resolution cell σ_c may be found by

$$\sigma_c = \eta^0 V_r \qquad\qquad \text{Eq. (9.1)}$$

where V_r is the volume of the resolution cell. The volume of the resolution cell is given by

$$V_r = \frac{R^2 \theta_a \theta_e \tau c}{2L^2} \qquad\qquad \text{Eq. (9.2)}$$

where R is range, θ_a and θ_e are the azimuth and elevation beam widths in radians, respectively, τ is the pulse width, c is the speed of light, and L is the beam shape loss. The resolution cell is shown in Fig. 9.1.

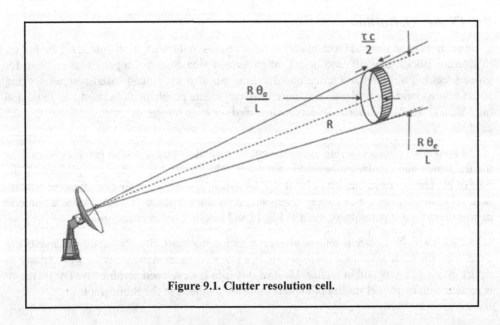

Figure 9.1. Clutter resolution cell.

Rain

For small, spherical raindrops, it is appropriate to assume Rayleigh scattering, where the scatterers are significantly smaller than the wavelength. In this case, the volume RCS density is

$$\eta^0 = \sum_{i=1}^{N} \frac{\pi^5}{\lambda^4} D_i^6 |K|^2 \qquad \text{Eq. (9.3)}$$

where λ is the wavelength of the radar energy, D is the diameter of the raindrops, and K is approximated by

$$|K|^2 = \frac{\varepsilon' - 1}{\varepsilon' + 2} \qquad \text{Eq. (9.4)}$$

where ε' is the dielectric constant of the raindrops. In practice, K is also dependent on both λ and the temperature of the raindrops.

If the precipitation radar reflectivity factor Z is defined as

$$Z = \sum_{i=1}^{N} D_i^6, \qquad \text{Eq. (9.5)}$$

then Eq. (9.3) becomes

$$\eta^0 = \frac{\pi^5}{\lambda^4} K^2 Z. \qquad \text{Eq. (9.6)}$$

Because number of drops within the volume is dependent on the rain rate, another form of the precipitation radar reflectivity factor is

$$Z = ar^b, \qquad \text{Eq. (9.7)}$$

where r is the rain rate, and the constants a and b are determined empirically. When using Eq. (9.7) in Eq. (9.6), η^0 is now a function of the rain rate.

Chaff

Chaff is a radar countermeasure designed to confuse or deceive the radar. Chaff is commonly made of thin aluminum or silver strips or wires that are cut to size for a given frequency as to present a resonant dipole to the radar. Chaff is usually dispensed by placing it in a cartridge and ejecting it from an airborne platform. Before it is well dispersed, large amounts of chaff can present clouds of adjacent volume cells that can hide real targets. Smaller deployments of chaff can be used to create false targets.

If the chaff closely resembles a resonant dipole, it will present a maximum RCS of

$$\sigma_i = 0.86\lambda^2 \qquad \text{Eq. (9.8)}$$

where σ_i has units of m^2. As with any target, this value will change with aspect angle. Averaged over aspect angles, the RCS will become

$$\sigma_{ia} = C\lambda^2. \qquad \text{Eq. (9.9)}$$

where C will be approximately in the range of $0.14 \Rightarrow 0.18$. Because the resonance region is relatively small, chaff may be cut to different lengths to encompass the entire radar band.

As with rain, the RCS of the chaff within a resolution cell will depend on the number of chaff particles, N, within that cell. Therefore,

$$\sigma_c = \sum_{i=1}^{N} \sigma_{ia}.$$

Eq. (9.10)

where V_r was found by Eq. (9.2). The density of the chaff will depend on a variety of factors including the volume and mass of the chaff dispersed, the altitude of release and the prevailing winds.

9.3.1. Radar Range Equation in Volume Clutter

The power density presented to the receive antenna of the radar due to a target is

$$P_{Dr} = \frac{P_t G^2 \lambda^2 \sigma_t}{(4\pi)^3 R^4},$$

Eq. (9.11)

where P_{Dr} is the power density at the radar receive antenna due to reflections from the target, P_t is the peak transmitted power, G is the gain of the radar antenna, λ is the wavelength of the radar, σ_t is the RCS of the target, and R is the range from the antenna to the target. The power density presented to the receive antenna due to volume clutter is

$$P_c = \frac{P_t G^2 \lambda^2 \sigma_c}{(4\pi)^3 R^4},$$

Eq. (9.12)

where σ_c is the clutter RCS within a resolution cell, and is given by

$$\sigma_c = V_r \eta^0,$$

Eq. (9.13)

σ_i is the RCS of a single clutter component such as a rain drop or a piece of chaff. Finally, the signal-to-clutter ratio for volume clutter $(SCR)_V$ can be obtained by taking the ratio of P_{Dr} to P_c. More specifically,

$$(SCR)_V = \frac{P_{Dr}}{P_c} = \frac{\sigma_t}{V_r \eta^0}$$

Eq. (9.14)

9.3.2. Volume Clutter Spectra

Volume clutter, regardless of the type, will invariably have components of motion that are radial to the radar. Therefore, radars that measure Doppler will also measure the radial component of the velocity of the clutter. The radial velocity of the clutter will vary based on the type of clutter and atmospheric effects, predominantly wind.

Nathanson (1991) provides the equation for the variance of the radial velocity of rain and chaff clutter that includes four dominant factors

$$\sigma_v = \sqrt{\sigma_{fl}^2 + \sigma_{sh}^2 + \sigma_{tb}^2 + \sigma_{bb}^2},$$

Eq. (9.15)

where σ_v is the standard deviation of the radial component of the clutter velocity, σ_{fl} is the standard deviation due to distribution of the clutter fall velocity, σ_{sh} is the standard deviation due to wind shear, σ_{tb} is the standard deviation due to turbulence, and σ_{bb} is the standard deviation due to beam broadening.

Because not all rain is the same size, it also does not have the same fall velocity. The spread of falling velocities creates a spread velocity seen by the radar. Without the influence of wind, rain has a maximum fall velocity of approximately *10 m/sec*. Fortunately, the average fall rate is not far removed from that. Therefore, the standard deviation of the fall velocity is somewhere around an order of magnitude less than the maximum fall velocity. Including the impact of the elevation angle of the radar, the standard deviation is

$$\sigma_{fl} = (\sin\theta_e), \qquad \text{Eq. (9.16)}$$

where θ_e is the elevation angle of the radar. At lower angles, σ_{fl} is small compared to other components of Eq. (9.15), since in this case, the small angle approximation applies.

Wind shear is the term used to describe the difference in wind speed with altitude. Wind shear can cause a widening of the variance of precipitation radial velocity. If it is assumed that the wind shear is constant, that is, a constant gradient, and the antenna pattern is Gaussian, then Nathanson reports the standard deviation of wind shear as

$$\sigma_{sh} = 0.42kR\psi^2, \qquad \text{Eq. (9.17)}$$

where k is the constant gradient, R is the slant range from the radar to the resolution cell in kilometers and ψ^2 2 is the two-way elevation beam width in radians. The suggested value of k for narrow beam antennas is *4.0 m/sec/km* for an arbitrary azimuth. Figure 9.2 shows the variance due to wind shear for various values of the elevation beam width. The value of σ_{sh} does not increase without bound and is limited to a value of about *6 m/sec* for small beamwidths.

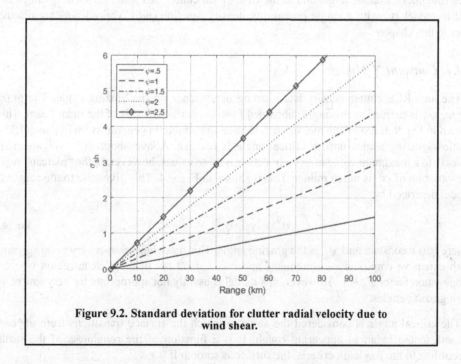

Figure 9.2. Standard deviation for clutter radial velocity due to wind shear.

Turbulence is the unpredictable flow of air resulting from various atmospheric phenomena. It can also be viewed as the fluctuation of wind speed about some mean. That said, empirically derived values for the variance of radial velocity due to turbulence are relatively independent of altitude, with the standard deviation for altitudes over a few kilometers being

$$\sigma_{tb} \approx 0.6, \qquad \text{Eq. (9.18)}$$

where the units of σ_{tb} are in *m/sec*.

Finally, there is an additional spread due to the radial components of tangential winds blowing across the radar beam. The standard deviation is similar to that of wind sheer and is

$$\sigma_{bb} = 0.42 v_0 \theta_2 \sin\varphi, \qquad \text{Eq. (9.19)}$$

where v_0 is the wind velocity at the center of the beam, θ_2 is the two-way azimuth beamwidth and φ is the azimuth angle relative to the wind direction at beam center. In general, it is expected that σ_{bb} will be much smaller than the spread due to wind shear or turbulence.

If the platform is moving or the beam is being scanned during the dwell, these will also broaden the spectrum of the clutter radial velocity. These situations are discussed in Section 9.7. The use of Eq. (9.15) requires that the components are interdependent. While it is not strictly true, it makes for a useful approximation.

9.4. Area Clutter

Area clutter is quite often the limiting environment for down looking radars. As mentioned previously, it can also create problems for ground based systems pointing near the horizon. Unlike volume clutter, area clutter has a limited range extent. The area RCS clutter density, σ^0, is dependent numerous parameters including terrain type, wavelength, polarization, surface roughness, grazing angle and in the case of sea clutter, sea state. As such, it can be difficult to model σ^0 with a single probability density function (*pdf*). Various *pdf*s are discussed later in this chapter.

9.4.1. Constant γ Model

The area RCS clutter density has a strong dependence on the grazing angle. The grazing angle, ψ_g is defined as the angle subtended from the surface to axis of the radar beam. This is shown in Fig. 9.3. Extensive measurements have shown that in general, σ^0 will rise quickly at shallow grazing angles until a critical angle is reached. Above about $60°$, σ^0 again rises quickly to a maximum value at $90°$. In between these values, however, in the "plateau" region, the variation of σ^0 is much milder. This is shown in Fig. 9.4. This gives rise to the constant-γ model described by

$$\sigma^0 = \gamma \sin\psi_g, \qquad \text{Eq. (9.20)}$$

where γ is a constant and ψ_g is the grazing angle. This model has shown very good agreement with extensive empirical measurements and may extend out of the plateau region where the propagation factor $F_p \approx 1$. However, this model is usually not appropriate for very low or very high grazing angles.

The critical angle is considered the angle in which the surface transitions from appearing smooth to the radar, to appearing rough. It is a function of the roughness of the surface. According to the Rayleigh criteria, the surface is smooth if

$$\frac{(4\pi h_{rms})\sin\psi_g}{\lambda} < \frac{\pi}{2}$$ **Eq. (9.21)**

where h_{rms} is the root mean square of the surface height and λ is the wavelength. Consider Figure 9.5. Because of the differences in height, the "rough path" is longer than the "smooth path." This equates to a phase difference of

$$\Delta\psi = \frac{2\pi}{\lambda}\ 2h_{rms}\sin\psi_g.$$ **Eq. (9.22)**

The critical angle ψ_{gc} is then computed when $\Delta\psi = \pi$ (first null), it is given by,

$$\psi_{gc} = arc\sin(\lambda/4h_{rms})$$ **Eq. (9.23)**

In a similar manner, for sea clutter, h_{rms} will be related to the sea state.

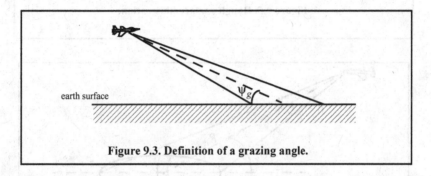

Figure 9.3. Definition of a grazing angle.

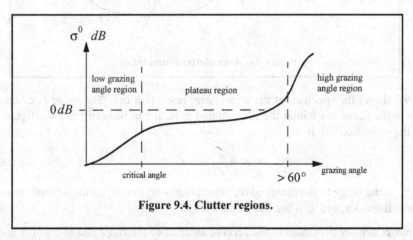

Figure 9.4. Clutter regions.

9.4.2. Signal to Clutter, Airborne Radar

If the area RCS clutter density σ^0 is known, then the clutter RCS is simply

$$\sigma_c = \sigma^0 A_c$$ **Eq. (9.24)**

where σ_c is the clutter RCS and A_c is the area of the resolution cell. The area of the resolution cell is dependent on the antenna beam, the grazing angle and the radar pulse width. Figure 9.6 shows the general situation for area clutter, where the radar beam illuminates a portion of the ground proportional to the antenna beamwidth. However, the illumination region represents multiple range cells.

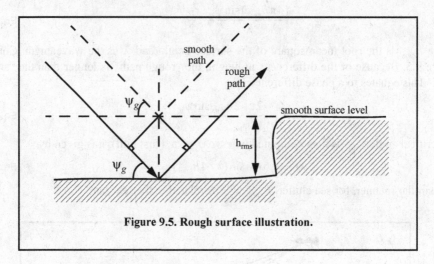

Figure 9.5. Rough surface illustration.

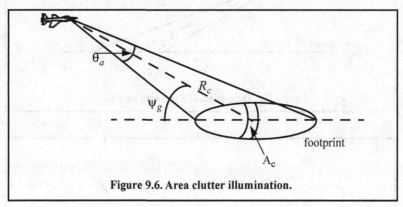

Figure 9.6. Area clutter illumination.

Figure 9.7 shows the specifics of the area clutter resolution cell. The value $(c\tau/2)sec\psi_g$ is the size of the range bin within the illumination area. It can be seen from the figure that the area of the resolution cell is

$$A_c = R_c\theta_a\frac{c\tau}{2L}\sec\psi_g.$$

Eq. (9.25)

where R_c is the range to the center of the illumination region, θ_a is the azimuth beam width, τ is the pulse width, and L is the beam shape loss.

The power density presented to the receive antenna of the radar due to a target and due to clutter were provided as Eqs. (9.11) and (9.12) and repeated here

$$P_{Dr} = \frac{P_tG^2\lambda^2\sigma_t}{(4\pi)^3R^4},$$

Eq. (9.26)

$$P_c = \frac{P_tG^2\lambda^2\sigma_c}{(4\pi)^3R^4}.$$

Eq. (9.27)

Using Eqs. (9.24) and (9.25) in the ratio of Eq. (9.26) to Eq.(9.27) provides the signal to clutter ratio for area clutter $(SCR)_A$

$$(SCR)_C = \frac{2\sigma_t L \cos\psi_g}{\sigma^0 \theta_a R_c \tau}.$$ **Eq. (9.28)**

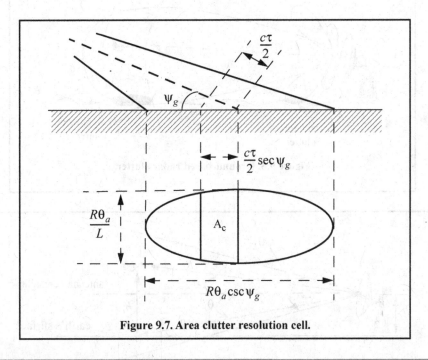

Figure 9.7. Area clutter resolution cell.

9.5. Clutter RCS, Ground-Based

The calculation of $(SCR)_A$ for ground-based radar systems follows from the previous section; however, due to their proximity to the ground, these systems may have to contend with sidelobe clutter. The situation is even further complicated for high pulse repetition frequency (PRF) systems.

9.5.1. Low PRF Case

For low PRF systems (range unambiguous), the general situation is shown in Fig. 9.8. Depending on the radar antenna pattern and the pointing angle, a portion of the main beam and sidelobes will illuminate the ground. Sidelobes may illuminate the ground even when the main beam does not. Clutter power will compete with the power from the target when it is received at the same time, that is, within the same range bin. If clutter is received from both the main beam and side lobe, the clutter RCS will have two components

$$\sigma_c = \sigma_{MBc} + \sigma_{SLc}.$$ **Eq. (9.29)**

As with the airborne radars, the clutter RCS for ground-based systems is a function of the illumination area. Figure 9.9 shows an example with a ground-based radar. From Figure 9.9, the ground-based radar has a *3dB* azimuth beam width θ_A and first null-to-null elevation beam width θ_E. The main beam is pointed at an elevation angle θ_e to illuminate the target. The value R is the slant range to the target. The values h_r and h_t are the heights of the radar and the target, respectively. The angle θ_r is the angle from the $0°$ elevation angle to the ground at range R. Finally, ΔR is the range resolution of the radar.

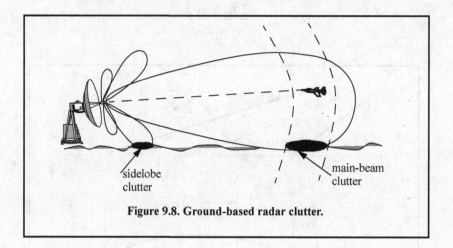

Figure 9.8. Ground-based radar clutter.

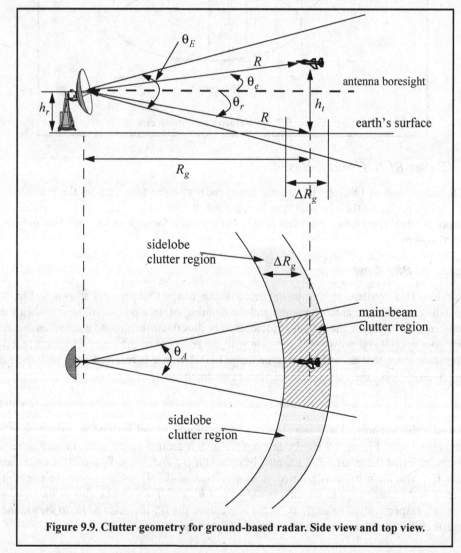

Figure 9.9. Clutter geometry for ground-based radar. Side view and top view.

From the figure, it can be shown

$$\theta_r = \operatorname{asin}\left(\frac{h_r}{R}\right) \qquad \text{Eq. (9.30)}$$

$$\Delta R_g = \Delta R \cos\theta_r \qquad \text{Eq. (9.31)}$$

$$R_g = R\cos\theta_r . \qquad \text{Eq. (9.32)}$$

From these, the areas of illumination for the mainbeam and sidelobe are

$$A_{mb} = \frac{\Delta R_g\ R_g\ \theta_A}{L} \qquad \text{Eq. (9.33)}$$

$$A_{sl} \approx \Delta R_g\ \pi R_g\ , \qquad \text{Eq. (9.34)}$$

where it is assumed that the sidelobe areas exist between $-90°$ and $90°$ azimuth. The value L is the beam shape loss.

From Eq. (9.24), the respective RCS values are

$$\sigma_{mb} = \sigma^0 A_{mb} \qquad \text{Eq. (9.35)}$$

and the sidelobe clutter RCS is

$$\sigma_{sl} = \sigma^0 A_{sl} . \qquad \text{Eq. (9.36)}$$

Because the radar antenna is pointed at the target, the illumination areas shown in Fig. 9.9 will not be illuminated by the maximum gain of the antenna. If the antenna has a normalized gain pattern $G(\theta)$ where θ is subtended from the pointing angle and the maximum gain exists at $G(0)$, then, from Fig. 9.9, the main beam of the antenna will illuminate the ground with gain $G(\theta_e + \theta_r)$. If sum $(\theta_e + \theta_r)$ exceeds the first null of the gain pattern, it is assumed that the ground is illuminated only with antenna sidelobes. The assumed gain for the sidelobe area is the root-mean-square (*rms*) sidelobe level taken over the hemisphere, $G(SSL)$. This reduction in gain is accounted for in the clutter RCS and as such

$$\sigma_{mb} = \sigma^0 A_{mb} G^2(\theta_e + \theta_r) = \frac{1}{L}\sigma^0 \Delta R_g\ R_g\ \theta_A G^2(\theta_e + \theta_r) \qquad \text{Eq. (9.37)}$$

and

$$\sigma_{sl} = \sigma^0 A_{sl} G^2(SSL) = \sigma^0 \Delta R_g\ \pi R_g G^2(SSL) . \qquad \text{Eq. (9.38)}$$

Finally, for long range, it is important to take into account refraction and the curvature of the earth. A range dependence can be included with the total clutter calculations as

$$\sigma_c(R) = \frac{\sigma_{mb} + \sigma_{sl}}{(1 + (R/R_h)^4)} \qquad \text{Eq. (9.39)}$$

where R_h is the radar range to the horizon calculated as

$$R_h = \sqrt{8 h_r r_o / 3} \qquad \text{Eq. (9.40)}$$

where r_o is the Earth's radius equal to $6375 Km$.

9.5.2. High PRF Case

For the high PRF case (Doppler unambiguous), it is likely that the time between pulses is smaller than what is needed for the desired range. Because, in the high PRF case, the receiver is integrating multiple pulses, the receiver will receive clutter power from multiple pulses. The total clutter power at the receiver over the coherent integration time NT (number of pulses times PRI) is given by

$$P_{ct} = \sum_{n=0}^{N} P_{cs} Rect\left(\frac{t-nT}{\tau}\right) \qquad \text{Eq. (9.41)}$$

where P_{cs} is the clutter from a single pulse, such as in the low PRF Case, τ is the pulse width and t is anytime delay (range) in which the receiver is on. The receiver will be shut off for at least every τ but will likely also include a guard band. The symbol "*Rect*" denotes the rectangular pulse function.

9.6. Amplitude Distribution

Finding the value of σ^0 is of limited utility for the radar system unless a probability density function can be found. Because σ^0 is usually determined empirically and because σ^0 has great variability due to the reasons mentioned previously, more than one *pdf* may be utilized for σ^0 depending on the grazing angle or type of clutter.

For very large grazing angles, the log normal distribution or exponential (Rayleigh amplitude) distributions may accurately represent the distribution of σ^0. Like the normal distribution, the log normal distribution has a mean $\bar{\sigma}^0$ and standard deviation σ_d, but the *pdf* of log normal distribution has the natural log function included as shown in Eq. (9.42),

$$f(\sigma^\circ) = \frac{1}{\sigma^0 \sigma_d \sqrt{2\pi}} \exp\left(\frac{-(\log\sigma^0 - \bar{\sigma}^0)^2}{2\sigma_d^2}\right); \quad \sigma^\circ \geq 0. \qquad \text{Eq. (9.42)}$$

For grazing angles that begin to approach ψ_c, it is common to use a Rayleigh distribution. The *pdf* for a Rayleigh distribution is

$$f(\sigma^\circ) = \frac{\sigma^0}{b^2} \exp\left\{\frac{-(\sigma^0)^2}{2b^2}\right\}; \quad \sigma^\circ \geq 0 \qquad \text{Eq. (9.43)}$$

where b is a parameter that controls the height and width of the *pdf*. Figure 9.10 shows the Rayleigh *pdf* for several values of b.

For cases where the grazing angle approaches ψ_c and below, the more general Weibull distribution may be more appropriate. The *pdf* for the Weibull distribution is

$$f(\sigma^\circ) = \frac{a}{b}\left(\frac{\sigma^\circ}{b}\right)^{a-1} \exp\left\{-\left(\frac{\sigma^\circ}{b}\right)^a\right\}; \quad \sigma^\circ \geq 0 \qquad \text{Eq. (9.44)}$$

If $b = 1/\lambda$ and $a = 1$, the *pdf* is now

$$f(\sigma^\circ) = \lambda e^{-\lambda\sigma^\circ} = \frac{1}{\bar{\sigma}^0} e^{(-\sigma^\circ/\bar{\sigma}^0)}; \quad \sigma^\circ \geq 0 \qquad \text{Eq. (9.45)}$$

which is the *pdf* for an exponential (Rayleigh amplitude) distribution.

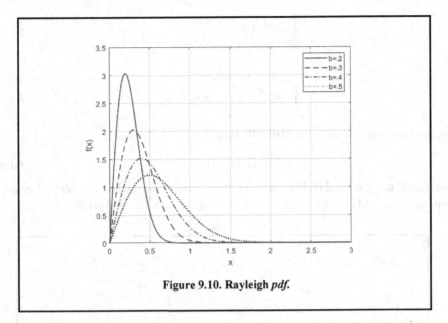

Figure 9.10. Rayleigh *pdf*.

Another common parameterization of the *pdf* of the Weibull distribution is to let $\alpha = b^a$. Then Eq. (9.44)

$$f(\sigma^\circ) = \frac{a(\sigma^\circ)^{a-1}}{\alpha} \exp\left\{\frac{-(\sigma^\circ)^a}{\alpha}\right\};\ \ \sigma^\circ \geq 0. \qquad \textbf{Eq. (9.46)}$$

Finally, if $\rho = 1/a$, Eq. (9.46) becomes

$$f(\sigma^\circ) = \frac{(\sigma^\circ)^{1/\rho}}{\rho\alpha\sigma^\circ} \exp\left\{\frac{-(\sigma^\circ)^{1/\rho}}{\alpha}\right\};\ \ \sigma^\circ \geq 0. \qquad \textbf{Eq. (9.47)}$$

The parameters ρ and α determine the mean and spread of the distribution, the latter being characterized by the median. Weibull *pdf* can be characterized by the ratio of the mean to the median. The mean can be found by the standard first moment of the distribution, that is

$$\bar{\sigma}^0 = \int_0^\infty \sigma^0 f(\sigma^0)\, d\sigma^0 \qquad \textbf{Eq. (9.48)}$$

Using Eq. (9.46) with the change of variable $q = (\sigma^0)^a/\alpha$ and letting $\rho = 1/a$ yields

$$\bar{\sigma}^0 = \alpha^\rho \int_0^\infty q^\rho e^{-q}\, dq . \qquad \textbf{Eq. (9.49)}$$

The integral in Eq. (9.49) should be recognized as the incomplete Gamma integral, which means that

$$\bar{\sigma}^0 = \alpha^\rho \Gamma(1+\rho). \qquad \textbf{Eq. (9.50)}$$

By definition, the median of a probability distribution is the value σ_m^0 such that

$$\int_{0}^{\sigma_{m}^{0}} f(\sigma^{0}) d\sigma^{0} = 0.5,$$

Eq. (9.51)

or

$$\int_{\sigma_{m}^{0}}^{\infty} f(\sigma^{0}) d\sigma^{0} = 0.5.$$

Eq. (9.52)

It can be shown that for the Weibull distribution

$$\sigma_{m}^{0} = [\alpha \ln(2)]^{\rho}$$

Eq. (9.53)

Comparing Eqs. (9.50) and (9.53), the ratio of the mean to the median is described by a single parameter. Figure 9.11 shows the mean to median ratio (in *dB)* for values of ρ .

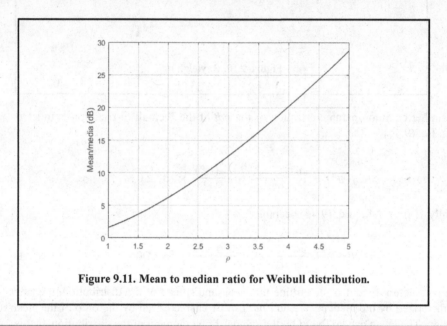

Figure 9.11. Mean to median ratio for Weibull distribution.

9.7. Area Clutter Spectrum

There are several models for clutter power spectrum. However, it is mathematically convenient, and therefore common, to represent the spectrum as Gaussian with frequency. Some types of area clutter, such as sea clutter, may not have zero mean. Furthermore, it is generally accepted that wind blown land clutter has wider tails than a Gaussian. However, the Gaussian power spectrum density (PSD) is sufficient to motivate the discussions of moving target indicator (MTI) and pulse Doppler processing in subsequent sections. The Gaussian PSD is

$$S_c(f) = \frac{P_c}{T\sigma_f \sqrt{2\pi}} \sum_{k=-\infty}^{\infty} \exp\left(-\frac{(f-kf_r)^2}{2\sigma_f^2}\right)$$

Eq. (9.54)

where P_c is the clutter power or clutter mean square power, f_r is the PRF, T is the PRI (i.e., $1/f_r$), and σ_f is the clutter spectral spreading parameter as defined in Eq. (9.61), described shortly. As clearly indicated by Eq. (9.54), the clutter PSD is periodic with period equal to f_r. Assuming zero mean, the maximum of the PSD is centered on multiples of the PRF.

Because the PSD is periodic, the mean square clutter power is

$$P_c = T\int_{-f_r/2}^{f_r/2} S_c(f)\,df.$$

Eq. (9.55)

A typical clutter PSD is shown in Fig. 9.12. The spreading parameter σ_f is the sum of three components that are the principal sources of spreading of the clutter spectrum. These are:

1. σ_s, due to the scanning of the antenna.

2. σ_w, due to clutter motion caused by wind.

3. σ_p, due to the motion of the radar platform.

When the antenna is scanned mechanically, or electronically during a dwell, clutter returns will vary from pulse to pulse. This will amplitude modulate the clutter returns and spread the clutter spectrum. The standard deviation of this spread is given by

$$\sigma_s = \frac{\sqrt{\ln 2}}{2\pi\theta_a}\omega_s\lambda,$$

Eq. (9.56)

where θ_a is the azimuth beam width of the radar antenna and ω_s is the scan rate, in units of radians and radians/sec, respectively, and λ is the wavelength of the waveform.

Most land clutter will have a large return at zero frequency due to the fact that the land, in general, is not moving. However, the motion of trees and other vegetation due to the wind creates a small spread. This spread is related to the *rms* value of the vegetation movement v_{rms} by

$$\sigma_w = (2v_{rms})/\lambda.$$

Eq. (9.57)

If the radar platform is moving, the overall spectrum of clutter will be shifted by

$$f_c = \frac{2v_p\cos\theta}{\lambda},$$

Eq. (9.58)

where $v_p\cos\theta$ is the radial velocity component of the radar platform in the direction of the clutter. The clutter components will vary within the azimuth beam width of the radar antenna, creating a broadening of the main lobe clutter. This broadening is,

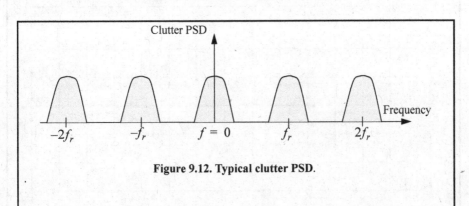

Figure 9.12. Typical clutter PSD.

$$B_p = \frac{2v_p\theta_a\cos\theta}{\lambda}.$$ **Eq. (9.59)**

The standard deviation of this broadening is

$$\sigma_p = \frac{v_p\sin\theta}{\lambda}.$$ **Eq. (9.60)**

Finally, the spreading parameter σ_f is

$$\sigma_f = \sqrt{\sigma_s + \sigma_w + \sigma_p}.$$ **Eq. (9.61)**

9.8. Doppler Processing

Doppler processing usually refers to the processing that analyzes or takes advantage of the Doppler shift of a target or interference. The best known forms of Doppler processing are MTI and pulsed Doppler. The MTI attempts to enhance the detectability of targets in areas of high clutter power. Doppler processing also performs that function but also analyzes the Doppler of a target to estimate its speed and other attributes.

9.8.1. Range and Doppler Processing

Figure 9.13 shows the two-dimensional signal processing grid. Each cube represents one complex sample of a coherently demodulated base band return. Each row represents the samples from the time delays of a single pulse. These discrete time delays each represent a specific discrete range. Each column represents the samples for different pulses at the same discrete range. In general, the sampling for the range processing will be at least $1/B$, where B is the bandwidth of the transmitted pulse. The sampling interval for Doppler processing will be the pulse repetition interval (PRI). The shaded region in Fig. 9.13 shows the samples that will be used for Doppler processing at a given range. In the case of MTI, the samples are sent through an MTI filter. For pulsed Doppler, the samples are sent to an analysis algorithm to extract Doppler information and other attributes.

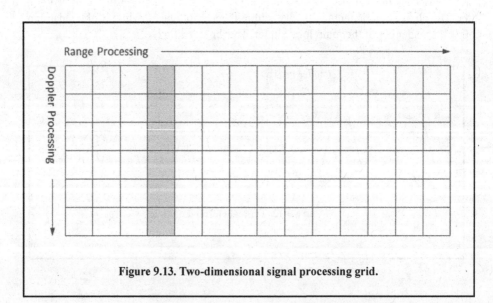

Figure 9.13. Two-dimensional signal processing grid.

9.8.2. Range and Doppler Ambiguity

Recall that the unambiguous range is

$$R_u = \frac{c}{2f_r}$$

Eq. (9.62)

where f_r is the PRF. Beyond R_u, it is ambiguous if the return was from a target within R_u or a different target beyond R_u. At the same time, the sampling rate for Doppler processing is f_r and the criteria for the sampling rate is the Nyquist rate in order to avoid aliasing that would lead to Doppler ambiguity. Recall that the Doppler frequency f_d is given by

$$f_d = \frac{2v_r}{\lambda}$$

Eq. (9.63)

where v_r is the radial velocity either approaching (positive) or receding (negative) from the radar. Therefore, the maximum radial velocity without aliasing is

$$v_{max} = \frac{f_r \lambda}{2}.$$

Eq. (9.64)

Solving Eq. (9.64) for f_r and equating with Eq. (9.63) at v_{max} yields

$$\frac{2v_{max}}{\lambda} = \frac{c}{2R_u}.$$

Eq. (9.65)

Eq. (9.65) describes the basic trade-off between unambiguous range and unambiguous Doppler. Figure 9.14 shows the unambiguous range versus the maximum radial velocity for several values of transmit frequency. Values beneath a given line are considered unambiguous. Clearly the situation becomes more difficult as the frequency is increased. The terms "low PRF" and "high PRF" do not apply to specific values of the f_r as these would be different for different frequencies. In general, low PRF indicates that range is unambiguous, but Doppler is not. High PRF indicates that the reverse is true. In medium PRF, both range and Doppler are ambiguous.

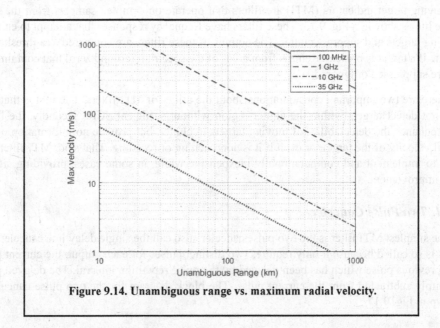

Figure 9.14. Unambiguous range vs. maximum radial velocity.

Another consideration for choice of PRF is the increase in average power brought on by additional pulses within a dwell. If the transmitter is coherent, this allows for coherent integration and the ability to improve signal-to-noise (SNR) ratio. Most modern radars have the ability to operate at numerous different PRFs, allowing the ability to adapt to different situations and environments. The limits of unambiguous range and Doppler are factors that are included in the radar designer's choice of transmit frequency.

9.8.3. Generalized Spectrum for Ground and Airborne Systems

Target returns must compete with noise and clutter, and in some cases, other forms of interference, for detection. In a clutter limited environment, Doppler processing allows for means to enhance detection for moving targets whose Doppler spectrum is sufficiently different than clutter. Figure 9.15 shows the spectra for a simple case which is, in general, enough to describe the case for ground-based systems. As can be seen in the figure, the clutter is assumed to be centered at zero Doppler with minimal extent. Although clutter does exist in the sidelobes, because the platform is not moving, there is no additional spectral spread. The noise is assumed to be "white" and hence exists throughout the spectrum at the same level. Included in the figure are the spectra of multiple moving targets. While these returns still compete with noise, their spectra are sufficiently removed from clutter.

The situation for a moving platform, such as an aircraft, is a bit more complicated. The Doppler frequency characteristics for the airborne radar are shown in Fig. 9.16. The entire spectrum is shifted (see Eq. (9.58)) and the main lobe clutter is centered at $(2v_r\cos\theta_e)/\lambda$. The main beam is also broadened as described by Eq. (9.59). Sidelobe clutter, although not as large as the main lobe, is also broadened and extends through large regions of the spectrum. Finally, there is a large return from nearly normal incidence called the "altitude line". If there is no vertical component of platform motion, the altitude line is at zero Doppler relative to moving targets.

9.9. Moving Target Indicator

Moving target indicators (MTI) are filters that operate on complex samples from the same range bin as shown in Fig. 9.13. These filters have frequency responses that attempt to enhance moving targets and suppress clutter. The outputs of these filters are compared to a threshold to decide if a target is present. Returns from areas of the spectrum (around zero) that contain clutter are suppressed or ignored.

There are two important considerations about the utility of MTI filters. The first is that they will not detect targets within the clutter region without sufficient SCR. Secondly, the filters only enhance the detectability of moving targets in clutter, but provide no information on the radial velocity of the target, or even if it is approaching or receding. That said, MTI filters are easy to implement and computationally inexpensive while, in some cases, providing significant improvement.

9.9.1. Two Pulse Canceler

The simplest MTI filter is the two pulse canceler, also call the single delay line canceler. The filter is so called because it only requires two distinct pulses for each output, the current pulse and previous pulse which has been delayed by the pulse repetition interval. The delayed pulse is simply subtracted from the current pulse. The block diagram for the two pulse canceler is shown in Fig. 9.17.

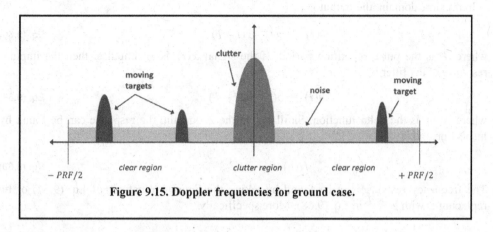

Figure 9.15. Doppler frequencies for ground case.

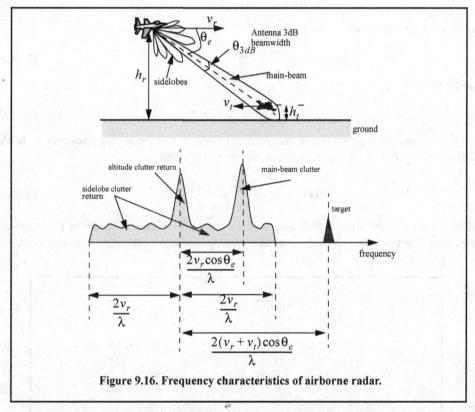

Figure 9.16. Frequency characteristics of airborne radar.

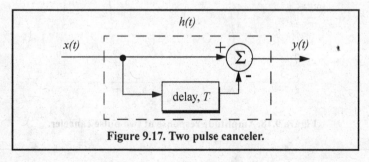

Figure 9.17. Two pulse canceler.

In the time domain, the output is

$$y(t) = x(t) - x(t-T),$$ Eq. (9.66)

where T is the pulse repetition period. If the signal $x(t)$ is an impulse, then the impulse response of the filter is

$$h(t) = \delta(t) - \delta(t-T)$$ Eq. (9.67)

where $\delta(\ )$ is the delta function. Similarly, in the Z-domain, the response can be found by inspection and is

$$H(z) = 1 - z^{-1}.$$ Eq. (9.68)

The frequency response can be found by taking the Fourier transform of Eq. (9.67) or by replacing z with $e^{j2\pi FT}$ in Eq. (9.68). More specifically,

$$H(F) = 1 - e^{-j2\pi FT}$$ Eq. (9.69)

which can be rewritten as

$$H(F) = e^{-j2\pi FT}(e^{j2\pi FT} - e^{-j\pi FT}),$$ Eq. (9.70)

and finally,

$$H(F) = 2je^{-j2\pi FT}\sin(\pi FT),$$ Eq. (9.71)

where F represents the continuous time (analog) frequency. If the analog frequency F is normalized to $f = FT$ and using the relationship $\omega = 2\pi f$, then

$$H(\omega) = 2je^{-j(\omega/2)}\sin\left(\frac{\omega}{2}\right)$$ Eq. (9.72)

where f unique from -0.5 to 0.5 and ω from $-\pi$ to π. Figure 9.18 shows the amplitude response of the two pulse canceler. Note that the response is periodic with f_r as expected.

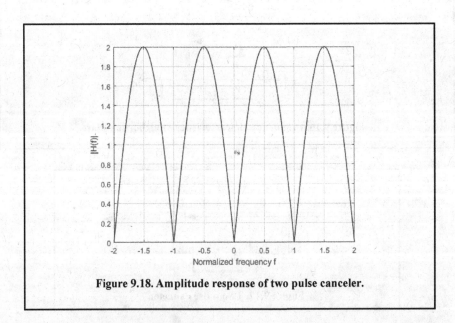

Figure 9.18. Amplitude response of two pulse canceler.

Consider the filter as a simple subtraction of complex samples from two distinct pulses at the same range. If the samples are identical, they would have the same amplitude and phase, or identically, no Doppler shift and hence would completely cancel. However, if there were a phase change between the two samples, this would indicate a Doppler shift and the samples would not cancel. From Fig. 9.18, the amount of cancellation or enhancement will be specific to the Doppler, i.e., the phase change. This is better shown in Fig. 9.19. The clutter and target spectra are shown in Fig. 9.19-a, and the two pulse canceler frequency response is shown in Fig. 9.19-b. Because of the response, the clutter is suppressed and the target retains the highest amplitude as shown in Fig. 9.19-c.

The power gain for the two pulse canceler as a function of normalized angular frequency ω is

$$|H(\omega)|^2 = H(\omega)H^*(\omega),$$

Eq. (9.73)

which can be expanded as

$$|H(\omega)|^2 = (1 - e^{-j\omega})(1 - e^{j\omega}),$$

Eq. (9.74)

and by using trigonometry identities, it can be written as,

$$|H(\omega)|^2 = 2(1 - \cos\omega) = 4\left(\sin\frac{\omega}{2}\right)^2.$$

Eq. (9.75)

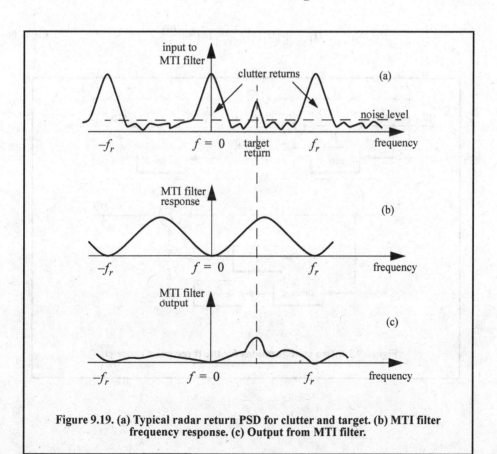

Figure 9.19. (a) Typical radar return PSD for clutter and target. (b) MTI filter frequency response. (c) Output from MTI filter.

9.9.2. Three Pulse Canceler

Only slightly more complicated in design than the two pulse canceler is the three pulse canceler, also referred to as a double delay line canceler. Two configurations for the three pulse canceler are shown in Fig. 9.20. The derivation of the response of the three pulse canceler follows that of the two pulse canceler. In the time domain, the output is

$$y(t) = x(t) - 2x(t-T) + x(t-2T). \qquad \textbf{Eq. (9.76)}$$

The impulse response of the filter is then

$$h(t) = \delta(t) - 2\delta(t-T) + \delta(t-2T). \qquad \textbf{Eq. (9.77)}$$

In the Z-domain, the response is

$$H(z) = 1 - 2z^{-1} + z^{-2}. \qquad \textbf{Eq. (9.78)}$$

The frequency response using normalized frequency is

$$H(\omega) = (1 - e^{-j\omega})^2 = 1 - 2e^{-j\omega} + e^{-2j\omega}. \qquad \textbf{Eq. (9.79)}$$

The amplitude responses for both the two and three pulse cancelers are shown in Fig. 9.21. Note that the gain for the three pulse canceler is higher than the two pulse, and that the stop band around zero is slightly larger. The power gain for the three pulse canceler in normalized frequency is

$$|H(\omega)|^2 = |H_1(\omega)|^2|H_1(\omega)|^2 = 16\left(\sin\frac{\omega}{2}\right)^4. \qquad \textbf{Eq. (9.80)}$$

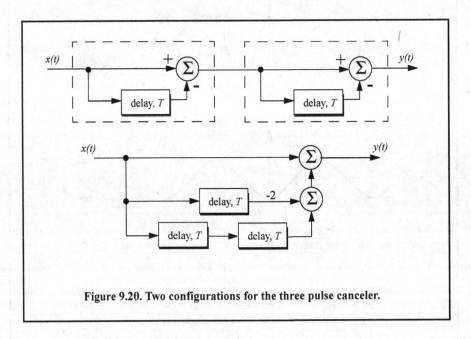

Figure 9.20. Two configurations for the three pulse canceler.

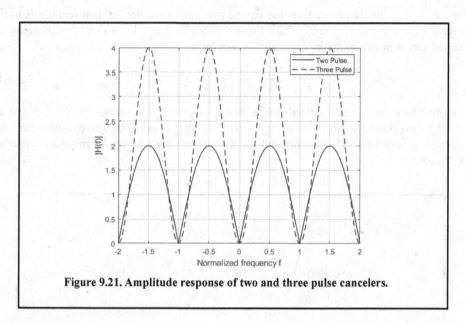

Figure 9.21. Amplitude response of two and three pulse cancelers.

9.9.3. The N+1 Pulse Canceler

It should be obvious at this point that the concept of a two or three pulse canceler can be extended to $N+1$ pulses and N delays. Regardless of the size of N, the implementation of the filter would be a finite impulse response (FIR) filter with "tapped" delay lines. The block diagram for the general filter is shown in Fig. 9.22. The frequency response of the general filter in normalized frequency is given by

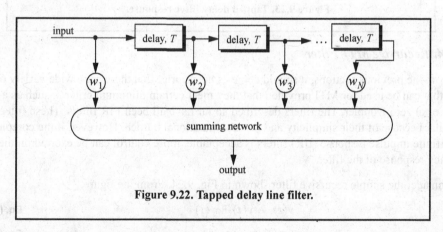

Figure 9.22. Tapped delay line filter.

$$H(\omega) = (1 - e^{-j\omega})^N,$$ **Eq. (9.81)**

The power gain is,

$$|H(\omega)|^2 = (|H_1(\omega)|^2)^N = \left(4\left(\sin\frac{\omega}{2}\right)^2\right)^N$$ **Eq. (9.82)**

where $H_1(\omega)$ is the frequency response for the two pulse canceler. All that remains is to find the required weights shown in Fig. 9.22. From Eq. (9.81), it may be obvious that these are just the coefficients from a binomial expansion, given by

$$w_i = (-1)^{i-1} \frac{N!}{(N-i+1)!(i-1)!} \; ; \; i = 1, ..., N+1 . \qquad \text{Eq. (9.83)}$$

Figure 9.23 shows the normalized amplitude response for three filters with $N = 2$, $N = 5$ and $N = 10$. As expected, the stop band increases with N, but the main lobe also becomes more narrow, meaning that target Doppler just outside the clutter zone may not be enhanced enough to get detected.

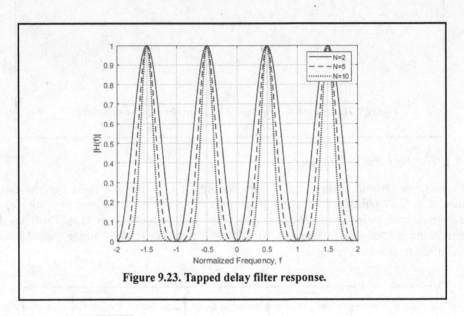

Figure 9.23. Tapped delay filter response.

9.9.4. Recursive MTI Filter

From the previous sections, it should come as no surprise that there are a wide variety of filters that can be used for MTI provided that they meet certain minimum criteria, such as a zero near or at zero Doppler. The filters described so far have all been FIR filters. These filters are popular because of their simplicity and low computational burden. However, if the complexity of infinite impulse response (IIR) filters is acceptable, more control can be exerted on the frequency response of the filter.

Consider the simple recursive filter shown in Fig. 9.24. From the figure,

$$v(t) = y(t) + w(t) \qquad \text{Eq. (9.84)}$$

$$w(t) = v(t-T) \qquad \text{Eq. (9.85)}$$

$$y(t) = x(t) - (1-K)w(t) . \qquad \text{Eq. (9.86)}$$

In the Z-domain

$$V(z) = Y(z) + W(z) \qquad \text{Eq. (9.87)}$$

$$W(z) = z^{-1}V(z) \qquad \text{Eq. (9.88)}$$

$$Y(z) = X(z) - (1-K)W(z) . \qquad \text{Eq. (9.89)}$$

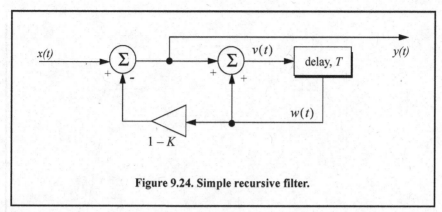

Figure 9.24. Simple recursive filter.

Placing Eqs. (9.87) and (9.88) into Eq. (9.89) and solving for $Y(z)$ provides

$$Y(z) = X(z) - (1-K)z^{-1}(Y(z) + W(z)).$$ **Eq. (9.90)**

Solving for $W(z)$ and inserting into Eq. (9.90) yields,

$$Y(z) = X(z) - Kz^{-1}Y(z) - z^{-1}X(z),$$ **Eq. (9.91)**

and finally

$$H(z) = \frac{X(z)}{Y(z)} = \frac{1 - z^{-1}}{1 - Kz^{-1}}.$$ **Eq. (9.92)**

Replacing z with $e^{j\omega}$ provides the frequency response

$$H(\omega) = \frac{X(z)}{Y(z)} = \frac{1 - e^{-j\omega}}{1 - Ke^{-j\omega}},$$ **Eq. (9.93)**

where ω is the normalized frequency and is periodic with period 2π. The frequency response for the recursive filter is shown in Fig. 9.25.

It is typical to set the value of $(1 - K)^{-1}$ to the number of pulses received during a dwell; therefore, the values for K in Fig. 9.25 represent *2, 5,* and *10* pulses respectively. Note from the figure that increasing K flattens the passband, but at the cost of reducing the stop band at zero. The power gain for the recursive

$$|H(\omega)|^2 = \frac{2(1 - \cos\omega)}{(1 + K^2) - 2K\cos\omega}.$$ **Eq. (9.94)**

9.9.5. Blind Speeds and PRF Staggering

Because MTI filters have a zero at zero Doppler, and because they have a frequency response that is periodic with period *PRF*, targets with radial velocities that correspond to multiples of the PRF will be suppressed by the filter. These speeds are called "blind" speeds and will preclude targets at these speeds from being detected.

One strategy to combat this problem is to choose a PRF that is high enough to move the blind speed to a value greater than the speeds of interest. This, however, is likely to make the unambiguous range too small to be tenable. The blind speeds are given by,

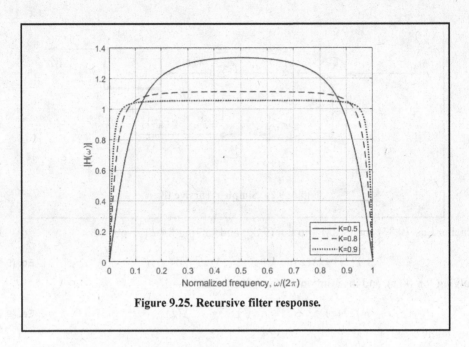

Figure 9.25. Recursive filter response.

$$v_b = \frac{m\lambda PRF}{2} \quad ;m = 1, 2, \ldots.$$

Eq. (9.95)

The first blind speed vs. unambiguous range can be found with Eq. (9.65). Because the MTI filter does not measure Doppler, there is no penalty for Doppler aliasing, i.e., a smaller unambiguous Doppler, provided there is a suitable solution for blind speeds.

The common method for dealing with blind speeds is to stagger the PRF. This can be done on either a pulse-to-pulse or dwell-to-dwell basis. Although dwell-to-dwell staggering can improve pulse Doppler performance, only pulse-to-pulse staggering can change the frequency response of the MTI filter in the inter-dwell period. This is not without penalties since staggering the PRF on a pulse-to-pulse complicates the coherent integration of pulses received during the dwell. Furthermore, clutter power that is folded into the receiver during the dwell can have very high dynamic range. For these reasons, pulse-to-pulse staggered is usually performed for low PRF.

Consider a system using two PRFs, f_{r1} and f_{r2}. These will have an inter-pulse period of T_1 and T_2, respectively. Assume that there exist two integers p_1 and p_2 such that

$$\frac{T_1}{T_2} = \frac{p_1}{p_2}$$

Eq. (9.96)

The first true blind speed will occur when

$$\frac{p_1}{T_1} = \frac{p_2}{T_2}$$

Eq. (9.97)

The ratio of p_1 to p_2 is known as the stagger ratio. If there are more than two PRFs, the first blind speed is at a PRF that is the least common multiple of all of the PRFs. For example, if there are three PRFs at $f_{r1} = 600Hz$, $f_{r2} = 800Hz$, and $f_{r3} = 1000Hz$, the blind speeds would be at multiples of $12kHz$ and the stagger ratio would be *12:15:20*.

Because the delays in the PRF staggered filters are time varying, the filters are, in general, not time invariant. Therefore, analysis of these filters using transform techniques becomes problematic. However, for monochromatic sinusoid, the output of these filters will be periodic. Therefore, analysis of the average power can be calculated using first principles.

Consider a two pulse canceler using at least two PRFs. The sampling times are given by

$$t_n = t_0 + \sum_{n=1}^{M} T_{(n \lozenge N)}$$ Eq. (9.98)

where T_n is one of the N inter-pulse periods of an N PRF stagger filter and $\lozenge$ symbolically indicates the modulo operation. The generalized sampling times for a multiple PRF stagger are shown in Fig. 9.26.

For a complex monochromatic input $ae^{j\Omega t}$, where a is the amplitude and Ω is the analog angular frequency. The input of the filter in discrete time is

$$x[n] = ae^{j\Omega t_n}.$$ Eq. (9.99)

The output of the filter would simply be

$$y[n] = a\exp(j\Omega t_n) - a\exp(j\Omega t_{n-1})$$ Eq. (9.100)

$$= a\exp\left(\frac{j\Omega(t_n - t_{n-1})}{2}\right)\left[\exp\left(\frac{j\Omega(t_n - t_{n-1})}{2}\right) - \exp\left(\frac{-j\Omega(t_n - t_{n-1})}{2}\right)\right]$$

$$= a\exp\left(\frac{j\Omega(t_n - t_{n-1})}{2}\right)\left[\exp\left(\frac{j\Omega T_n}{2}\right) - \exp\left(\frac{-j\Omega T_n}{2}\right)\right]$$

$$= 2ja\exp\left(\frac{j\Omega(t_n - t_{n-1})}{2}\right)\sin\left(\frac{\Omega T_n}{2}\right) = 2ja\exp(j\pi F(t_n - t_{n-1}))\sin(\pi F T_n)$$

where $F = \Omega/(2\pi)$ is the analog frequency. It is easy to show that the power of the output $(y[n])^2$ is periodic with period

$$T = \sum_{n=1}^{N} T_n$$ Eq. (9.101)

where N is the number of staggered PRFs. The average power gain of the filter is the ratio of the power at the output to the power at the input. The average power of the input is simply a^2. The average power at the output is the power of each output sample averaged over the period,

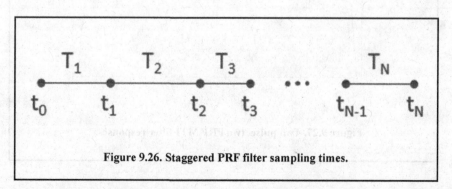

Figure 9.26. Staggered PRF filter sampling times.

$$|H(F)|^2 = \dfrac{\dfrac{1}{N}\sum_{n=1}^{N}(y[n])^2}{|x[n]|^2} = \dfrac{4a^2\sum_{n=1}^{N}\{\sin(\pi F T_n)\}^2}{Na^2} = \dfrac{4}{N}\sum_{n=1}^{N}\{\sin(\pi F T_n)\}^2. \qquad \textbf{Eq. (9.102)}$$

Consider a two pulse canceler with two PRFs, $f_{r1} = 400Hz$, and $f_{r2} = 600Hz$. Because $2 \times 600 = 3 \times 400$, this filter would employ a *2:3* stagger and the first true blind speed would be at *1200Hz*. Figure 9.27 shows the filter power gain. Note that the maximum power gain is decreased versus an un-staggered filter, but there is no blind speed until *1200 Hz*.

Now consider a two pulse canceler with three PRFs, $f_{r1} = 450Hz$, $f_{r2} = 600Hz$ and $f_{r3} = 750Hz$. The stagger ratio is now *12:15:20* and the first blind speed will be at *9 kHz*. The power gain for this filter is shown in Fig. 9.28.

This method may be extended to a three pulse canceler. Although the derivation is lengthy, it can be shown that the power gain for a three pulse canceler with N PRFs is

$$|H(F)|^2 = \frac{1}{N}\sum_{n=1}^{N}\{6 - 4\cos(2\pi F T_n) - 4\cos(2\pi F T_{(n \lozenge N)+1}) + \qquad \textbf{Eq. (9.103)}$$

$$2\cos[2\pi F(T_n + T_{(n \lozenge N)+1})]\}$$

where $\lozenge$ is the modulo operator. Figure 9.29 shows the power gain for a three pulse canceler and a *7:9:21* stagger ratio.

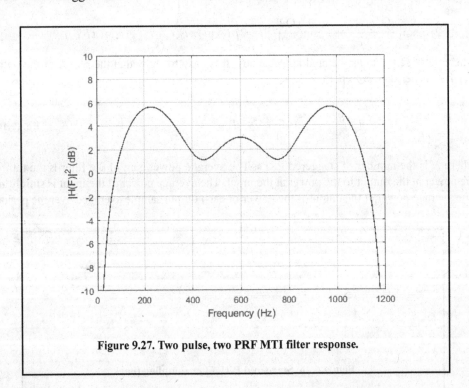

Figure 9.27. Two pulse, two PRF MTI filter response.

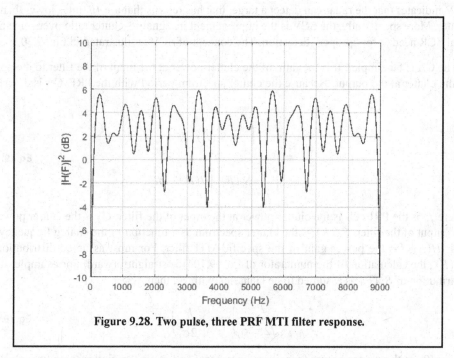

Figure 9.28. Two pulse, three PRF MTI filter response.

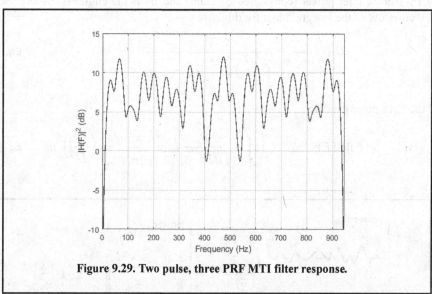

Figure 9.29. Two pulse, three PRF MTI filter response.

9.9.6. MTI Figures of Merit

There are three common figures of merit that are used to compare MTI filters. These are clutter attenuation (CA), the improvement factor (I), and sub-clutter visibility (SCV). Of these, SCV is the most complicated as it depends on the probability of detection, the probability of false alarm and other characteristics of the detector. Because of this, it is difficult to compare SCV in different radars and, as such, it is less used. However, the basic idea behind SCV is the radar's ability to detect a moving target in the presence of strong clutter. For example, *10dB*

SCV indicates that the radar can detect a target that has returns that are *10* times lower than the clutter. More specifically, the SCV is the improvement in signal-to-clutter ratio over some minimal SCR needed for "proper" detection. The concept of SCV is illustrated in Fig. 9.30.

The CA is far simpler. It is the ratio of the clutter power at the input of the filter to the power of the clutter at the output. Because the clutter spectrum period with the PRF, CA is described by

$$CA = \frac{C_i}{C_o} = \frac{\int_{-f_r/2}^{f_r/2} S_c(F) \; dF}{\int_{-f_r/2}^{f_r/2} S_c(F) \; |H(F)|^2 \; dF} \qquad \textbf{Eq. (9.104)}$$

where f_r is the PRF, C_i is the clutter power at the input of the filter, C_o is the clutter power at the output of the filter, $S_C(F)$ is the clutter spectrum as a function of the analog frequency F, and $|H(F)|^2$ is the power gain of the specific MTI filter. For most assumed distribution of $S_C(F)$, the calculation of the numerator of Eq. (9.104) is straightforward. For example, if the distribution of $S_C(F)$ is assumed to be Gaussian with F, then

$$C_i = \int_{-f_r/2}^{f_r/2} \left(\frac{P_c}{\sqrt{2\pi} \; \sigma_f}\right) \exp\left(-\frac{F^2}{2\sigma_f^2}\right) dF \qquad \textbf{Eq. (9.105)}$$

where P_c is the clutter power (considered constant) and σ_f is the clutter spreading. Because the P_c comes out of the integral, then for this case

$$CA = \frac{C_i}{C_o} = \frac{P_c}{\int_{-f_r/2}^{f_r/2} S_c(F) \; |H(F)|^2 \; dF}. \qquad \textbf{Eq. (9.106)}$$

For the three pulse canceler

$$C_o = \int_{-f_r/2}^{f_r/2} S_c(F)|H(F)|^2 \; dF = 16\int_{-f_r/2}^{f_r/2} \frac{P_c}{\sqrt{2\pi} \; \sigma_f} \exp\left(-\frac{F^2}{2\sigma_f^2}\right)\left(\sin\left(\frac{\pi F}{f_r}\right)\right)^4 dF. \qquad \textbf{Eq. (9.107)}$$

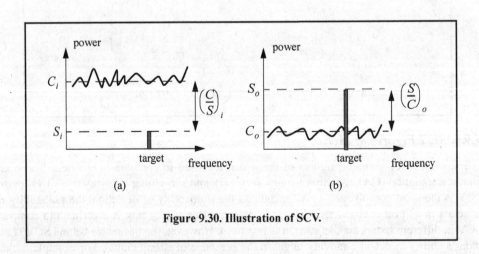

Figure 9.30. Illustration of SCV.

If it is assumed that the ratio of F/f_r is small, then Eq. (9.107) becomes

$$C_o = \int_{-f_r/2}^{f_r/2} S_c(F)|H(F)|^2 \, dF = 16 \int_{-f_r/2}^{f_r/2} \frac{P_c}{\sqrt{2\pi} \, \sigma_f} \exp\left(-\frac{F^2}{2\sigma_f^2}\right)\left(\frac{\pi F}{f_r}\right)^4 dF. \qquad \text{Eq. (9.108)}$$

Rearranging Eq. (9.108) yields,

$$C_o = \frac{16 P_c \pi^4}{f_r^4} \int_{-f_r/2}^{f_r/2} \frac{1}{\sqrt{2\pi} \, \sigma_f} \exp\left(-\frac{F^2}{2\sigma_f^2}\right) F^4 \, dF. \qquad \text{Eq. (9.109)}$$

The integral in Eq. (9.109) may be recognized as the fourth central moment of a Normal distribution with variance σ_f^2 whose value is $3\sigma_f^4$. Therefore

$$C_o = \frac{48 P_c \pi^4}{f_r^4} \sigma_f^4. \qquad \text{Eq. (9.110)}$$

The CA for this example

$$CA = \frac{C_i}{C_o} = \frac{f_r^4}{3(4\pi\sigma_f)^4}. \qquad \text{Eq. (9.111)}$$

The final figure of merit is the improvement factor, I. The improvement factor is the ratio of the signal to clutter at the output of the filter to the signal to clutter at the input of the filter. This can be written as

$$I = \left(\frac{S_o}{C_o}\right)\Big/\left(\frac{S_i}{C_i}\right), \qquad \text{Eq. (9.112)}$$

which can immediately be seen as

$$I = (S_o/S_i)(CA). \qquad \text{Eq. (9.113)}$$

The ratio in Eq. (9.113) is the average power gain, therefore

$$I = \frac{CA}{f_r} \int_{-f_r/2}^{f_r/2} |H(F)|^2 dF. \qquad \text{Eq. (9.114)}$$

Returning to the three pulse canceler example,

$$\frac{S_o}{S_i} = \frac{1}{f_r} \int_{-f_r/2}^{f_r/2} 16\left(\sin\frac{\pi F}{f_r}\right)^4 dF. \qquad \text{Eq. (9.115)}$$

Using the double angle trigonometric identity $(2 - 2\cos 2\vartheta) = 4(\sin\vartheta)^2$ results in

$$\begin{aligned} \frac{S_o}{S_i} &= \frac{1}{f_r} \int_{-f_r/2}^{f_r/2} \left(2 - 2\cos\left(\frac{2\pi F}{f_r}\right)\right)^2 dF \\ &= \frac{1}{f_r} \int_{-f_r/2}^{f_r/2} \left(4 - 8\cos\left(\frac{2\pi F}{f_r}\right) + 4\left[\cos\left(\frac{2\pi F}{f_r}\right)\right]^2\right) dF = 6 \end{aligned} \qquad \text{Eq. (9.116)}$$

Therefore, the improvement factor for clutter that is Normal distributed using a three pulse canceler is

$$I = \left(\frac{S_o}{S_i}\right)(CA) = \frac{f_r^{\ 4}}{2(4\pi\sigma_f)^4} . \qquad \text{Eq. (9.117)}$$

9.10. Pulse Doppler Processing

Unlike the MTI filter, pulse Doppler processing uses the samples from the range bins, taken at the sampling rate of the PRF, in order to determine the radial component of the target range rate. If the range measurements are sufficiently accurate and the range rate is stable over the dwell, the range rate could be determined by the ratio of the change in range to the change in time, that is

$$\dot{R} = (\delta R)/(\delta t) . \qquad \text{Eq. (9.118)}$$

However, it is more common to pass the samples through a bank of narrow band filters to extract the Doppler frequency. The resolution of the measurement will depend on the filters. The outputs of these filters are compared to a threshold, allowing for the detection of multiple moving targets, similar to the function of the MTI filter, but assigning a radial range rate and determining if the target is approaching or receding.

The type of waveform utilized by the radar at any given time will be dependent on several different parameters. The pulse width will determine the amount of energy placed on the target and, in the absence of pulse compression, the range resolution. But it is the PRF and dwell time that control many key aspects of Doppler processing and pulse Doppler processing, as was seen in the previous section. The choice of PRF will determine if the information that the radar is collecting on the target is range ambiguous, Doppler ambiguous, both, or neither. As we have seen, it is not always possible to be range and Doppler unambiguous at the same time. The next section describes how range and Doppler ambiguities are resolved. Another way of looking at pulse Doppler processing is that it is performing spectral analysis on the pulse-to-pulse samples. This is done with the use of the discrete time Fourier transform (DTFT).

9.10.1. Discrete Time Fourier Transform

The Fourier transform was introduced in Chapter 1 and is repeated here as Eq. (9.119). More precisely,

$$X(\omega) = \int_{-\infty}^{\infty} x(t)e^{-j\omega t} \ dt \qquad \text{Eq. (9.119)}$$

The DTFT operates on a discrete signal and is given by

$$X_d(\omega) = \sum_{m=-\infty}^{\infty} x(m)e^{-j\omega m} \qquad \text{Eq. (9.120)}$$

Like the Fourier transform, the DTFT is continuous with ω, but unlike the Fourier transform, it is periodic with period of 2π. In the continuous domain, an infinite *dc* signal can be seen as a rectangular pulse whose pulse width approaches infinity. Recall that the Fourier transform of an infinite *dc* signal would be a delta function at $f = 0$ and that the Fourier transform of a rectangular pulse is a *Sinc* function.

Consider samples of a *dc* signal with unit amplitude, the DTFT for *M* samples would be

$$X_d(\omega) = \sum_{m=-\infty}^{\infty} x(m)e^{-j\omega m} = \sum_{m=0}^{M} (1)e^{-j\omega m} \qquad \text{Eq. (9.121)}$$

Equation (9.121) can be simplified by recognizing the sum as a geometric series,

$$X_d(\omega) = \sum_{m=0}^{m} (1)e^{-j\omega m} = \frac{1 - e^{-j\omega M}}{1 - e^{-j\omega}} = \frac{e^{-j\pi f(M-1)}\sin(\pi f M)}{\sin(\pi f)} \qquad \text{Eq. (9.122)}$$

Note that both ω and f are the normalized frequency. Figure 9.31 shows the DTFT for the unit amplitude *dc* samples for different values of M. Because the samples are assumed to be zero for $m < 0$ and $m > M$, the processing is analogous to a rectangular pulse in the continuous domain. Note that as M is increased, the frequency response more closely resembles a delta function at $f = 0$, just as you would expect in the continuous domain. Thus, the finite "window" of samples acts as a rectangular pulse that tightens DTFT as M is increased. Now add a complex monochromatic sinusoid of the form

$$x[m] = ae^{j2\pi F_0 mT} \qquad \text{Eq. (9.123)}$$

where a is the amplitude of the signal, F_0 is the continuous time (analog) frequency shift, and T is the sampling period. It is straightforward to show that the DTFT for this signal is

$$X(F) = \frac{e^{-j\pi(F-F_0)(M-1)T}\sin[\pi(F-F_0)MT]}{\sin[\pi(F-F_0)T]}. \qquad \text{Eq. (9.124)}$$

From Eq. (9.124), it is clear that the transform is simply that of Eq. (9.122), shifted by F_0T. Figure 9.32 shows the DTFT for the signal of Eq. (9.124) with various numbers of samples with $F_0T = 0.3$. The choice of PRF, and hence T, determines the highest unambiguous Doppler frequency, which is $1/2T$. Figure 9.33 shows the DTFT of *50* samples of two complex sinusoids with unit amplitude and $F_0 = 200Hz$ and $F_0 = 400Hz$. The PRF is *500Hz*. The *200Hz* signal is centered at $F_0 = 200Hz$ as expected. However, the *400Hz* signal has been aliased to $-100Hz$ and would now appear as a receding target. Although the PRF controls the unambiguous Doppler, it is the number of samples that determines the Doppler resolution. Said another way, the resolution is a function of the integration time MT. Figure 9.34 shows the DTFT of a combination of two unit amplitude complex sinusoids at $F_0T = 0.3$ and $F_0T = 0.285$. When $M = 5$, the two signals are clearly unresolved, at $M = 50$ they are partially resolved and they are fully resolved at $M = 500$.

9.10.2. Discrete Fourier Transform

Once again, the discrete time Fourier transform (DTFT) of a discrete signal is continuous with frequency and periodic with a period equal to the PRF. Clearly the radar processor will not create a continuous DTFT, but will calculate samples of the DTFT. This calculation is called a discrete Fourier transform (DFT). Assume that the DFT will calculate N samples of the DFT and that, for now, the length of the discrete transform is finite, but unknown. The DTFT can be written as

$$X\left(\frac{2\pi}{N}k\right) = \sum_{m=-\infty}^{\infty} x(m)\exp\left(\frac{-j2\pi km}{N}\right) \quad ;k = 0, 1, ..., N-1. \qquad \text{Eq. (9.125)}$$

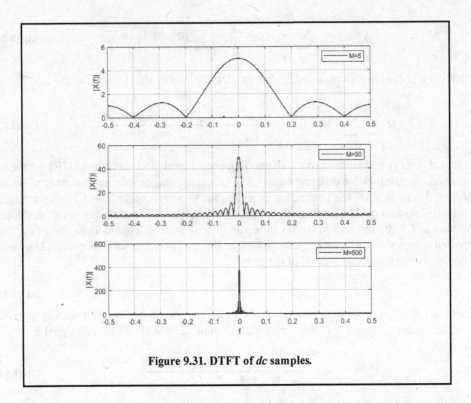

Figure 9.31. DTFT of *dc* samples.

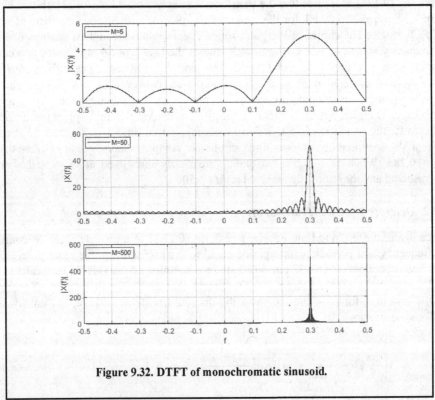

Figure 9.32. DTFT of monochromatic sinusoid.

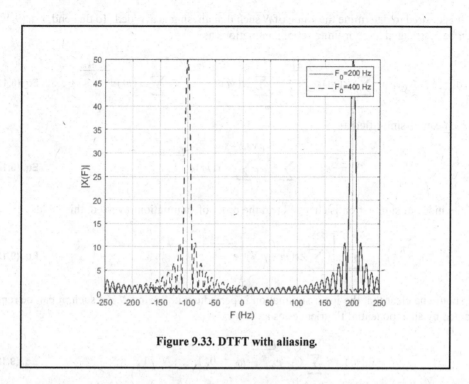

Figure 9.33. DTFT with aliasing.

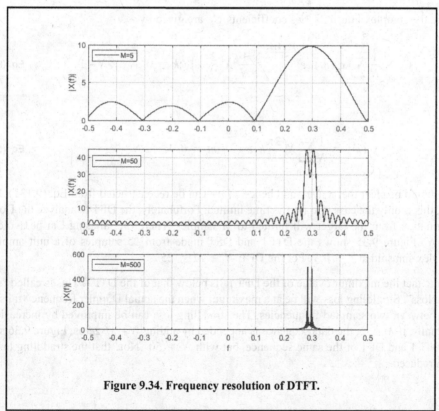

Figure 9.34. Frequency resolution of DTFT.

It is desired to determine the value of N such that aliasing is avoided. To that end, Eq. (9.125) can be rearranged as an infinite set of summations as

$$X\left(\frac{2\pi}{N}k\right) = \ldots + \sum_{m=-N}^{-1} x(m)e^{\frac{-j2\pi km}{N}} + \sum_{m=0}^{N-1} x(m)e^{\frac{-j2\pi km}{N}} + \sum_{m=N}^{2N-1} x(m)e^{\frac{-j2\pi km}{N}} + \ldots, \quad \text{Eq. (9.126)}$$

which can be simplified as

$$X\left(\frac{2\pi}{N}k\right) = \sum_{p=-\infty}^{\infty} \sum_{n=pN}^{pN+N-1} x(m)e^{\frac{-j2\pi km}{N}}. \quad \text{Eq. (9.127)}$$

If the index of summation is changed and the order of summation reversed, this yields

$$X\left(\frac{2\pi}{N}k\right) = \sum_{m=1}^{N-1} \left[\sum_{p=-\infty}^{\infty} x(m-pN)\right]e^{\frac{-j2\pi km}{N}} \quad ;k = 0, 1, \ldots, N-1. \quad \text{Eq. (9.128)}$$

It should be clear that the inner summation is periodic with period N. As such, it can be represented by an exponential Fourier series as

$$x_p(m) = \sum_{k=0}^{N-1} C_k\, e^{\frac{j2\pi km}{N}} \quad ;m = 0, 1, \ldots, N-1, \quad \text{Eq. (9.129)}$$

where the complex Fourier series coefficients C_k are given by

$$C_k = \frac{1}{N}\sum_{m=0}^{N-1} x_p(m)\, e^{\frac{-j2\pi km}{N}} = \frac{1}{N} X\left(\frac{2\pi}{N}k\right) \quad ;k = 0, 1, \ldots, N-1. \quad \text{Eq. (9.130)}$$

Finally,

$$x_p(m) = \frac{1}{N}\sum_{k=0}^{N-1} X\left(\frac{2\pi}{N}k\right)e^{\frac{j2\pi km}{N}} \quad ;m = 0, 1, \ldots, N-1. \quad \text{Eq. (9.131)}$$

It should be clear that $x_p(m)$ and hence $x(m)$ can be reconstructed from Eq. (9.131). However, this is only the case if $x_p(m)$ is time limited. Fortunately, the DFT to analyze the Doppler information from the target will limited to M samples. Therefore, aliasing can be avoided if $M \le N$. Figure 9.35 shows the DTFT and DFT made from 25 samples of a unit amplitude complex sinusoid at $f = 0.3$. For the DFT, $N = M = 25$.

Note that the maximum value of the DFT falls below that of the DTFT. This is called "straddling loss". Straddling loss will be at a maximum when the actual Doppler frequency falls halfway between two sampled frequencies. The straddling loss can be improved by increasing N. Normally, if $M \le N$, the data sequence is appended by adding $N - M$ zeros. Figure 9.36 shows the DTFT and DFT of the same sequence, but with $N = 50$. Note that the straddling loss has been reduced.

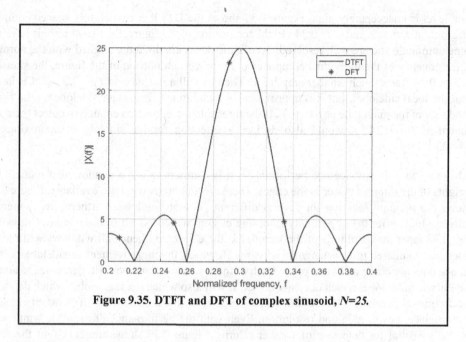

Figure 9.35. DTFT and DFT of complex sinusoid, *N=25*.

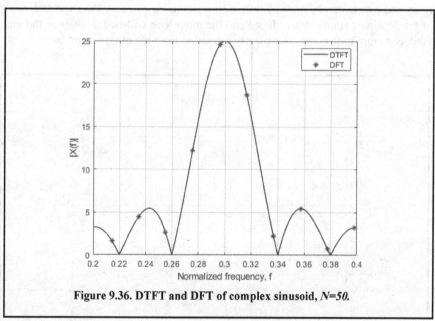

Figure 9.36. DTFT and DFT of complex sinusoid, *N=50*.

9.10.3. Windowing

It was seen from the previous section that the finite number of samples used to represent a sinusoid results in a *Sinc* function for the DFT of a complex sinusoid. This is equivalent to a "rectangular" window where all samples are treated equally. The effect of the rectangular window is that there are sidelobes present throughout the frequency span and are worse immediately adjacent to the main lobe of the DFT. In general, the first sidelobes of a rectangular window are about *13.4 dB* lower than the maximum value of the main lobe. Often, this sidelobe level is unacceptably high. Figure 9.37 shows the DTFT of two closely spaced complex sinusoids at $f = 0.3$ and $f = 0.24$. In the top portion of the figure, the two sinusoids have the same amplitude and are well resolved, even if the peaks are not quite aligned with the normalized frequency of the individual components. In the bottom portion of the figure, the sinusoid at $f = 0.24$ has a much smaller amplitude. There is still a rise around $f = 0.24$ that is larger than the local sidelobes, but it is approximately equal to the first major sidelobe on the right-hand side of the main lobe at $f = 0.3$. If the threshold were lowered enough to detect the component at $f = 0.24$, it would also declare a detection for the sidelobe at approximately $f = 0.3$.

In order to improve sidelobe performance, it is common to use a window that reduces the weights of the samples closer to the edges. There are numerous windows available. Figure 9.38 shows the window function for several different popular windows. Furthermore, numerous software tools offer the opportunity to design custom windows. All of the windows shown in Fig. 9.38 taper the amplitude of the samples at the edges, and hence all windows will reduce sidelobes compared to a rectangular window. However, this improvement in sidelobe performance does not come without a price. Each of these window functions will decrease the amplitude of the main lobe, which decreases SNR. It will also widen the main lobe, which degrades the frequency resolution. Therefore, windowing represents a basic tradeoff between sidelobe performance, power gain and resolution. Even with the performance drawbacks, windowing can be essential for detection of weaker returns. Figure 9.39 shows the DTFT of the same closely spaced sinusoids of Fig. 9.37, but with a Hamming window. As expected, the magnitude of the dominate sinusoid is reduced and the main lobe widened. However, the main lobe of the reduced amplitude sinusoid is clearly separated from the other sidelobes.

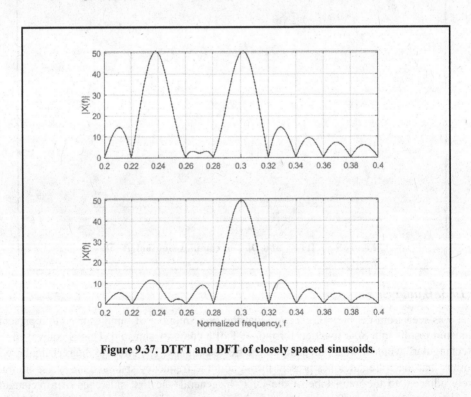

Figure 9.37. DTFT and DFT of closely spaced sinusoids.

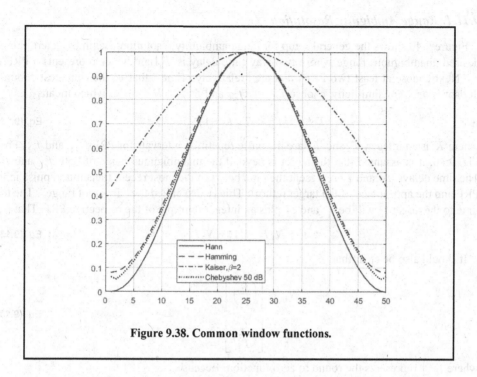

Figure 9.38. Common window functions.

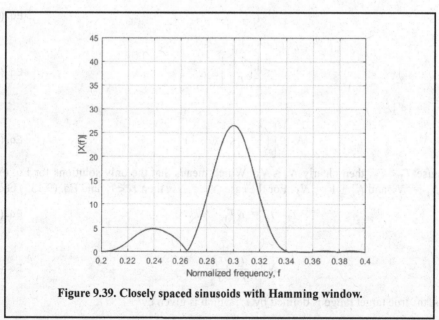

Figure 9.39. Closely spaced sinusoids with Hamming window.

9.11. Ambiguity Resolution

The measurement of unambiguous radial range rate requires a high PRF to avoid aliasing. Conversely, unambiguous range measurements require a low PRF. In the "medium" PRF regime, both range and Doppler can be ambiguous. At the cost of complexity and processing, both range and Doppler ambiguities can be resolved.

9.11.1. Range Ambiguity Resolution

Figure 9.40 shows the general setup for range ambiguity resolution. Begin by determining a desired unambiguous range whose two-way time delay is T_d and hence represents a PRF of f_d. Next choose at least two PRFs that are "relatively prime," that is, their greatest common divisor is one. For simplicity, choose $f_{r1} = Kf_{rd}$ and $f_{r2} = (K+1)f_{rd}$, which means

$$T_1 K = T_d = T_2(K+1)$$ Eq. (9.132)

where K is an integer, T_1 and T_2 are the pulse repetition intervals for PRFs f_{r1} and f_{r2}. From Fig. 9.40, it is assumed that the target is beyond the unambiguous range of both f_{r1} and f_{r2}. The time delays t_1 and t_2 represent the time between the most recent transmitted pulse in the PRF and the appearance of the target return[1]. This is also called the "apparent range". The true time to the target t_r will be t_1 and t_2 plus an integer multiple of the respective PRF. That is

$$t_r = t_1 + N_1 T_1 = t_2 + N_2 T_2$$ Eq. (9.133)

It should also be clear that

$$N_1 = \left\lfloor \left(\frac{t_r}{T_1} \right) \right\rfloor$$

$$N_2 = \left\lfloor \left(\frac{t_r}{T_2} \right) \right\rfloor$$ Eq. (9.134)

where $\lfloor \ \rfloor$ represents the round to zero function. Because

$$t_r \leq T_d$$ Eq. (9.135)

then

$$N_1 \leq \left\lfloor \left(\frac{T_d}{T_1} \right) \right\rfloor \leq K$$ Eq. (9.136)

and

$$N_2 \leq \left\lfloor \left(\frac{T_d}{T_2} \right) \right\rfloor \leq (K+1).$$ Eq. (9.137)

Because $T_2 < T_1$, then clearly $N_1 \leq N_2$. Which means that the only solutions for Eq. (9.133) are $N_1 = N_2$ and $N_1 + 1 = N_2$. For the case $N_1 = N_2$, then $t_2 < t_1$ and Eq. (9.133) becomes

$$t_2 - t_1 = NT_1 - NT_2$$ Eq. (9.138)

and

$$N = \frac{t_2 - t_1}{T_1 - T_2}.$$ Eq. (9.139)

Thus, the true target range is defined by t_r, which is given by

$$t_r = (NT_1 + t_1) = (NT_2 + t_2)$$ Eq. (9.140)

and the true range would be $R = ct_r/2$.

---

1. Note that the return is not from the most recently transmitted pulse, otherwise the target would be range unambiguous.

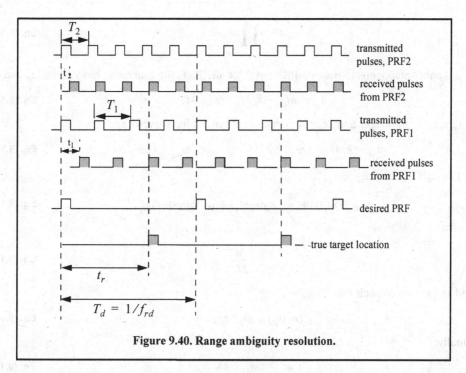

Figure 9.40. Range ambiguity resolution.

For the second case $N_1 + 1 = N_2$, Eq. (9.133) becomes

$$t_1 - t_2 = (N+1)T_2 - NT_1 \qquad \text{Eq. (9.141)}$$

which leads to

$$N = \frac{t_2 - t_1 + T_2}{T_1 - T_2}, \qquad \text{Eq. (9.142)}$$

and once again the true time delay is that of Eq. (9.140). Finally, if $t_1 = t_2$, then $t_r = t_1 = t_2$ and the target is unambiguous for both PRFs.

Although the two-PRF case is demonstrative, it cannot always be utilized in practice because the true time delays may occur at blind ranges, i.e., times when the receiver is off because the radar is transmitting. In these cases, the problem can be overcome by using an additional PRF. The generalized problem of resolving range ambiguities with three or more PRFs can be solved with the Chinese remainder theorem (CRT). In order to simplify the discussion, instead of time delay t_r, consider a range bin m_r. For a given PRF, there will be M unambiguous range bins where

$$M = \frac{R_u}{\Delta R} = \frac{T}{\Delta t} \qquad \text{Eq. (9.143)}$$

where R_u is the unambiguous range, ΔR is the size of the range bin, $T = 1/PRF$ is the interpulse period and $\Delta t = 2\Delta R/c$.

If there are P PRFs and it is required that the number of unambiguous range bins for each PRF, M_p are relatively prime, then there exists a set of M unambiguous range bins for the combination of PRFs such that

$$M = \prod_{p=1}^{P} M_p \qquad \text{Eq. (9.144)}$$

In a manner analogous to the two-PRF case, for any PRF, the true range bin will be located at

$$m_r = m_{ap} + k_p M_p \quad ; m_r \le M. \qquad \text{Eq. (9.145)}$$

where k_p is an integer and m_{ap} is the apparent range bin. Therefore,

$$m_{a1} + k_1 M_1 = m_{a2} + k_2 M_2 = \ldots = m_{ap} + k_p M_p. \qquad \text{Eq. (9.146)}$$

The CRT states that

$$m_M = n_1 \alpha_1 m_{a1} + n_2 \alpha_2 m_{a2} + \ldots + n_P \alpha_P m_{aP} \qquad \text{Eq. (9.147)}$$

where

$$n_p = \frac{M}{M_p} \qquad \text{Eq. (9.148)}$$

and α_p is chosen such that

$$(n_p \alpha_p) \lozenge M_p = 1. \qquad \text{Eq. (9.149)}$$

Finally,

$$m_r = m_M \lozenge M \qquad \text{Eq. (9.150)}$$

As an example, consider the simple (and not realistic) situation of $M_1 = 3$, $M_2 = 4$ and $M_3 = 5$. This creates a set of $M_1 M_2 M_3 = 60$ unambiguous range bins. Assume that the true target is located within range bin *22* of the unambiguous set. The apparent ranges would be

$$m_{a1} = 22 \lozenge M_1 = 1 \qquad \text{Eq. (9.151)}$$

$$m_{a2} = 22 \lozenge M_2 = 2 \qquad \text{Eq. (9.152)}$$

$$m_{a1} = 22 \lozenge M_3 = 2 \qquad \text{Eq. (9.153)}$$

and

$$n_1 = \frac{60}{3} = 20 \qquad \text{Eq. (9.154)}$$

$$n_2 = \frac{60}{4} = 15 \qquad \text{Eq. (9.155)}$$

$$n_3 = \frac{60}{5} = 12 \qquad \text{Eq. (9.156)}$$

To solve for α_p, recognize that

$$n_p \alpha_p = M_p i + 1, \qquad \text{Eq. (9.157)}$$

for some integer *i*. Solving for the lowest integer *i* leads to

$$\alpha_1 = 2 \qquad \text{Eq. (9.158)}$$

$$\alpha_2 = 3 \qquad \text{Eq. (9.159)}$$

$$\alpha_3 = 3.$$ **Eq. (9.160)**

Using all of these in Eq. (9.147) leads to

$$m_M = (20)(2)(1) + (15)(3)(2) + (12)(3)(2) = 202$$ **Eq. (9.161)**

and as expected, using this in Eq. (9.150) gives

$$m_r = m_M \lozenge M = 202 = 202 \lozenge 60 = 22.$$ **Eq. (9.162)**

Although the CRT algorithm provides a computationally tractable solution to ambiguity resolution, it lacks robustness. Errors of a single range bin due to straddling loss or quantization can lead to very large errors. In practice, the CRT will usually include enhancements designed to improve robustness.

9.11.2. Doppler Ambiguity Resolution

Range ambiguities exist when the true range is beyond the unambiguous range determined by the PRF. Returns from the target will appear at the apparent range and integer multiples of the unambiguous range.

The situation for Doppler ambiguity is completely analogous. Doppler ambiguities exist when the true Doppler is beyond the unambiguous Doppler determined by the PRF. Doppler frequencies from the target will appear at integer multiples of the PRF. Therefore, Doppler ambiguities are resolved in the same manner as range ambiguities.

Instead of measuring the apparent range, the radar will measure the apparent Doppler, which can be done with techniques outlined in the previous sections. Consider once again the two-PRF case, where the true Doppler is

$$f_d = f_1 + N_1 \, f_{r1} = f_2 + N_2 \, f_{r2}$$ **Eq. (9.163)**

where f_1 and f_2 are the apparent Doppler frequencies for f_{r1} and f_{r2} (the PRFs), respectively. As with range ambiguities, when $f_2 > f_1$,

$$N = \frac{f_2 - f_1}{f_{r1} - f_{r2}},$$ **Eq. (9.164)**

and when $f_1 > f_2$

$$N = \frac{f_2 - f_1 + f_2}{f_{r1} - f_{r2}}.$$ **Eq. (9.165)**

For either Eq. (9.164) or (9.165), once N has been determined, the true Doppler is found with Eq. (9.163). If $f_1 = f_2$, then the Doppler is unambiguous for both PRFs and $f_d = f_1 = f_2$. In the case of blind speeds, a third PRF is once again introduced.

9.11.3. Pulse Pair Processing

The techniques described so far are used to detect and track targets in the presence of clutter. Pulse pair processing (PPP) is often used to estimate parameters of volume clutter itself.

PPP derives its name from the utilization of two (or more) pulses to estimate frequency (and hence velocity) by comparing the phase of the pulses. The PPP is known for its use in weather radars, most notably for storm tracking or forecasting. There are several assumptions built into the use of PPP for weather. These include the assumption that ground clutter is negligible, and as such, the signals of interest are noise limited. This can be accomplished in ground systems simply by sufficient elevation angle. The generalized spectrum for PPP is shown of Fig. 9.41. Another assumption for PPP is that the power spectrum of the weather is Gaussian. The goal of PPP is then to estimate the power, mean Doppler shift and spread (variance) of the weather.

These estimates can clearly be made in the frequency domain by calculating the DFT of the pulse samples and performing various algorithms on them. What may be more interesting, and almost certainly less computationally expensive, is that these estimates can also be done in the time domain. An estimate of the power is particularly simple. The power can be estimated by

$$\hat{P}_x = \sum_{n=0}^{N-1} |x[n]|^2 \qquad\qquad \textbf{Eq. (9.166)}$$

where $x[n]$ is the vector representing the N samples of the returns. This is equivalent to the peak of the autocorrelation function $\mathcal{R}_x[n]$. The autocorrelation is defined as

$$\mathcal{R}_x[n] = \sum_{n=0}^{N-k-1} x[n] \otimes x^*[n+k] \quad ;k = 0, 1, \dots \qquad\qquad \textbf{Eq. (9.167)}$$

If $k = 0$, then Eq. (9.167) is

$$\mathcal{R}_x[n] = \sum_{n=0}^{N-1} x[n] \otimes x^*[n] = \sum_{n=0}^{N-1} |x[n]|^2 = \hat{P}_x \quad . \qquad\qquad \textbf{Eq. (9.168)}$$

An estimate of the mean Doppler shift can be found, once again, using the autocorrelation $\mathcal{R}_x[n]$,

$$\hat{F}_0 = \frac{-1}{2\pi T} \angle \mathcal{R}_x[1] . \qquad\qquad \textbf{Eq. (9.169)}$$

where $\angle$ symbolically indicates the argument of (i.e., angle).

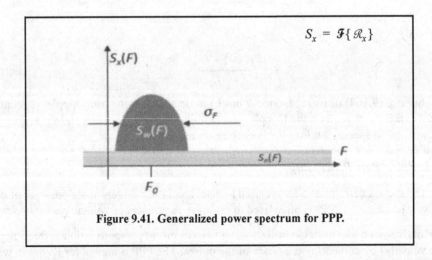

Figure 9.41. Generalized power spectrum for PPP.

To see that this is the case, consider a monochromatic sinusoid

$$x[n] = ae^{j2\pi nTF_0}$$

Eq. (9.170)

where a is the amplitude, F_0 is the analog monochromatic frequency and T is the PRI. The autocorrelation is defined in Eq. (9.167), and for $k = 1$,

$$\mathcal{R}_x[1] = \sum_{n=0}^{N-2} x[n] \otimes x^*[n+1] = \sum_{n=0}^{N-2} ae^{j2\pi nTF_0} \, a^* e^{-j2\pi nTF_0},$$

Eq. (9.171)

and after a few algebraic manipulations, we get

$$\mathcal{R}_x[1] = |a|^2 e^{-j2\pi TF_0} \sum_{n=0}^{N-2} 1 = |a|^2 (N-1) e^{-j2\pi TF_0},$$

Eq. (9.172)

Solving for the argument (angle) of Eq. (9.172) yields Eq. (9.169). While this has been derived for a monochromatic signal, Eq. (9.172) performs adequately for a wide variety of signals provided there is a dominant signal F_0.

Consider the noisy, normalized samples in Fig. 9.42. These samples are taken from a single range bin over several pulse repetition intervals. Figure 9.43 shows the normalized frequency content of the samples. Notice that the dominant frequency content is at *3kHz*. Calculation of Eq. (9.169) provides an estimate of *3014Hz*.

Finally, if the power spectrum of interest is assumed to Gaussian, it is of interest to determine the width of the power spectrum σ_f. If the spectrum is centered at zero, by removing the mean frequency, and band limited to $1/T$, then the autocorrelation function of the time domain samples will also be Gaussian. The discrete time autocorrelation function takes the form,

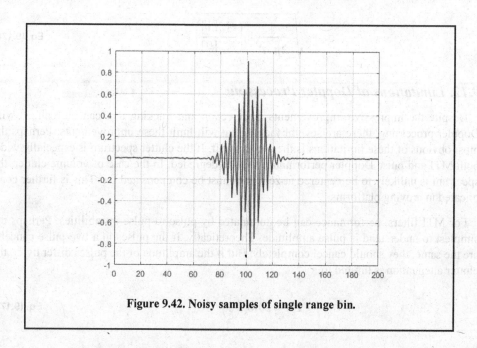

Figure 9.42. Noisy samples of single range bin.

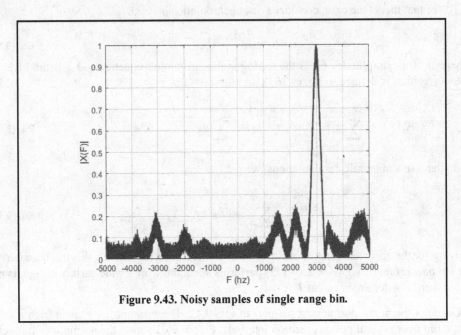

Figure 9.43. Noisy samples of single range bin.

$$\mathcal{R}_{x_1}[n] \;=\; |A|^2\, e^{-j2\pi^2 n^2 T^2 \sigma_f}, \qquad\qquad\qquad \textbf{Eq. (9.173)}$$

where $\mathcal{R}_{x_1}$ is the autocorrelation of the zero frequency centered samples. Because $x_{x1}[0] = |A|^2$, $\mathcal{R}_{x_1}[1]$ can be written as

$$\mathcal{R}_{x_1}[1] \;=\; \mathcal{R}_{x_1}[0]\; e^{-2\pi^2 T^2 \sigma_f^2}. \qquad\qquad \textbf{Eq. (9.174)}$$

Solving for σ_f^2 provides an estimate of σ_f using only $\mathcal{R}_{x_1}[0]$ and $\mathcal{R}_{x_1}[1]$,

$$\hat{\sigma}_f \;=\; \sqrt{-\frac{1}{2\pi^2 T^2}\ln\!\left(\frac{\mathcal{R}_{x_1}[1]}{\mathcal{R}_{x_1}[0]}\right)}. \qquad\qquad \textbf{Eq. (9.175)}$$

9.12. Limitations of Doppler Processing

Despite the impressive improvements in detection and tracking that can be realized with Doppler processing, there are several factors that will limit these improvements. Perhaps the most obvious of these limitations is the clutter itself. If the clutter spectrum is especially wide, both MTI and pulse Doppler performance will be degraded. In the case of volume clutter, the spectrum is unlikely to be centered at zero and must be compensated for. This is further complicated in moving platforms.

For MTI filters, performance can be dominated by pulse-to-pulse instabilities. Perhaps the simplest to understand is pulse amplitude. Theoretically, if the pulses in a two pulse canceler are the same, they should cancel completely. But if the amplitude of the pulses differ by ξ, the clutter attenuation is limited to

$$CA < 20\log\!\left(\frac{1}{\xi}\right) \qquad\qquad\qquad\qquad\qquad \textbf{Eq. (9.176)}$$

which in turn will limit the improvement factor for a given filter.

Timing-jitter, which are perturbations in the interpulse period, also can degrade performance. This can be illustrated by considering an analog implementation of a two pulse canceler. Consider two pulses, a_1 and a_2, both with amplitude a. If the start of two successive pulses each has an error ζ with respect to the desired start time, t_0, then subtraction of a_2 from a_1 results in an error signal a_r such that

$$a_r = a_1 - a_2 . \qquad \text{Eq. (9.177)}$$

This is illustrated in Fig. 9.44. Because the total nonzero time of the error signal a_r is

$$a_r = 2|\zeta_1 - \xi_2| , \qquad \text{Eq. (9.178)}$$

and the average power of the error signal is

$$\frac{2a^2(\zeta_1 - \xi_2)}{T} \qquad \text{Eq. (9.179)}$$

and the average power of the input is $(a^2\tau/T)$, where T is the period and τ is the pulse width. Therefore, if the pulses are otherwise identical, then the clutter attenuation would be

$$CA = \frac{\tau}{2|\zeta_1 - \xi_2|} . \qquad \text{Eq. (9.180)}$$

In general, the jitter will limit the CA to a value inversely proportional to the variance of the pulse start time error ζ. More specifically,

$$CA = \frac{\tau^2 a_r}{4\sigma_\xi^2} \qquad \text{Eq. (9.181)}$$

where σ_ξ^2 is the variance in the start time of the pulse.

Phase errors in the demodulation process can also limit performance. Instabilities in the local oscillator (LO) are called phase noise or flicker noise. These instabilities are manifested in random changes in the phase of the oscillator. In general, these changes are quite small, but can still have a significant impact on performance. Ideally, the frequency of the oscillator will be monochromatic. As such, it should be defined by a simple sinusoid, such as

$$x(t) = \sin(2\pi f_0 t) , \qquad \text{Eq. (9.182)}$$

where f_0 is the oscillator frequency. However, phase noise means that the signal is perturbed and includes a time-dependent phase term, such as

$$x(t) = a\sin(2\pi f_0 t + \varphi(t)) , \qquad \text{Eq. (9.183)}$$

where $\varphi(t)$ is the phase perturbation.

Because the instantaneous frequency is the derivative of the signal phase with respect to time, the oscillator frequency will include an offset due to the phase noise as

$$\delta f = \frac{1}{2\pi} \frac{d}{dt} \varphi(t) . \qquad \text{Eq. (9.184)}$$

For Doppler processing in particular, this will have the effect of spreading the spectrum of clutter returns, degrading the ability to detect and track moving targets, especially ones with smaller returns. This is shown in Fig. 9.45.

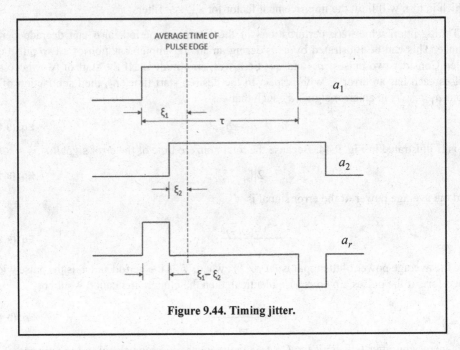

Figure 9.44. Timing jitter.

Single-sided phase noise is denoted as $\mathcal{L}(f)$ and defined as the ratio of power in a *1Hz* bandwidth, which is offset from the oscillator frequency by f to the total phase noise power in the side band. The unit for $\mathcal{L}(f)$ is dB_c/Hz. The phase noise power spectrum is simply

$$S_\varphi(f) = 2\mathcal{L}(f) \qquad\qquad \text{Eq. (9.185)}$$

where the *2* accounts for both side bands. The visualization of this definition is aided by Fig. 9.45. As a simple example, consider the two pulse canceler with two pulses return from clutter at the intermediate frequency. If the instabilities in oscillator impart a phase change, then the time domain output of the filter can be expressed as

$$A_0 = A\cos(2\pi f_{if}\ t) - A\cos(2\pi f_{if}\ (t+T)+\Delta\varphi) \qquad\qquad \text{Eq. (9.186)}$$

where A is the amplitude of the pulses, f_{if} is the intermediate frequency, and T is the PRI. Simplifying with trigonometric identities, Eq. (9.186) becomes

$$\frac{A_0}{A} = 2\sin\left(\frac{\Delta\varphi}{2}\right)\sin\left(2\pi f_{if}\ t+\frac{\Delta\varphi}{2}\right). \qquad\qquad \text{Eq. (9.187)}$$

If $\Delta\varphi$ is small, then

$$\sin\Delta\varphi \cong \Delta\varphi. \qquad\qquad \text{Eq. (9.188)}$$

Therefore,

$$CA = \frac{1}{(\Delta\bar{\varphi})^2} \qquad\qquad \text{Eq. (9.189)}$$

where $(\Delta\bar{\varphi})^2$ is the average change in phase. This limits the improvement factor I to

$$I = \frac{2}{\Delta\bar{\varphi}^2} \qquad\qquad \text{Eq. (9.190)}$$

Other instabilities include transmitter frequency and pulse width. Each of these pulse-to-pulse variations will impart limitations on the overall performance. These limitations may also be set by system parameters. For example, performance limitations due to pulse width instability are a function of the time-bandwidth product in pulse compression systems.

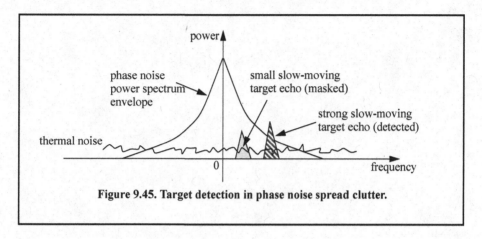

Figure 9.45. Target detection in phase noise spread clutter.

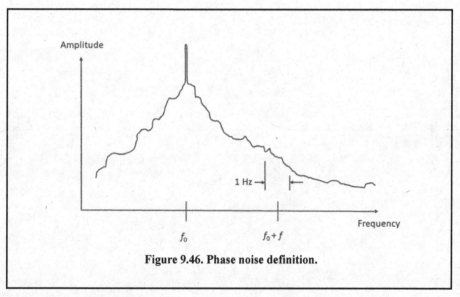

Figure 9.46. Phase noise definition.

Appendix 9-A

Fill Pulses in Pulse Doppler Radars

Herbert U. Fluhler

9.A.1. Range and Doppler Ambiguities

The unambiguous range formula was discussed in an earlier chapter. High PRF radar systems and/or pulse Doppler radars may exhibit severe range ambiguities because they use high PRF pulse streams. In order to resolve these ambiguities, pulse radar systems may utilize multiple high PRFs (PRF staggering) within each processing interval (dwell).

Remember that the line power spectrum for a train of pulses has a $|\sin(x)/x|$ envelope, and the line spectra are separated by the PRF, f_r, as illustrated in Fig. 9-A.1. A radar receiver Doppler filter bank is capable of resolving target Dopplers as long as the anticipated Doppler shift between adjacent targets is less than one-half the bandwidth of the individual Doppler filters (i.e., one-half the width of a frequency bin). Thus, pulsed radars are designed such that

$$f_r = 2f_{dmax} = \frac{(2v_{rmax})}{\lambda} \qquad \text{Eq. (9-A.1)}$$

where f_{dmax} is the maximum anticipated target Doppler frequency, v_{rmax} is the maximum anticipated target radial velocity, and λ is the radar wavelength.

9.A.2. Overview of Fill Pulses

As has been seen in the prior sections regarding range and Doppler ambiguities, the apparent (i.e. directly measured and not disambiguated) target location and target velocity in pulse Doppler radars is usually not where the target actually is in physical space, nor how fast the target is moving in reality. Both of these manifestations are examples of aliasing, where the radar is not sampling in an optimum manner: sampling too quickly in the case of range ambiguities, and sampling too slowly in the case of velocity ambiguities. In both cases, the suboptimal sampling rate (PRF) results in the well-known phenomena of aliasing result in fold-over of the detections from other ambiguous intervals, be they range intervals or Doppler intervals. In range measurement, the target shows up in some range bin whose range is designated B_i within the first range interval (called the unambiguous range interval, URI) defined within $(0, c/(2PRF))$ range, but one cannot tell for sure that it is really in the first range interval (the URI), or if it is in some other ambiguous range interval (ARI) that has folded into the URI because this range bin aliases with multiple corresponding bins at real ranges given by $(B_i + N \cdot c)/2PRF$ where N is the range interval count integer ($N=1$ for URI, $N > 1$ for all ARI).

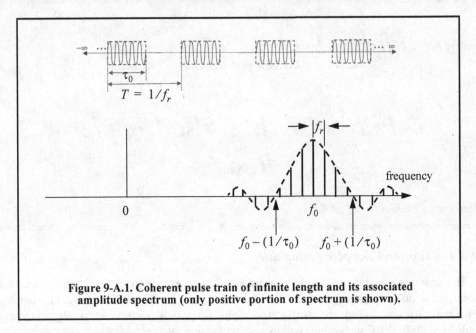

Figure 9-A.1. Coherent pulse train of infinite length and its associated amplitude spectrum (only positive portion of spectrum is shown).

This means that all these range bins all fold-over down into the first URI. In effect, a pulse Doppler radar only ever really measures the range bins in the URI, and all other range bins fold-over down into the URI. It is only with disambiguation employing multiple PRFs that one can solve the riddle (typically employing the Chinese remainder theorem) of which real range detection seen in an URI apparent range bin. A completely analogous situation exists for Doppler velocity.

A special situation occurs when a pulse Doppler radar operates with static (or for that matter slowly moving) scatters nearby within the field of regard, which is often the case. Examples of such static scatters include the ground clutter, vegetation swaying in the wind, the sea surface (sea clutter), clouds, rain and even the wind (which may carry dust particulates); all of these can cause extended reflections of pulse energy back to the radar (volume clutter). Because pulse Doppler radars are excellent at measuring and segregating targets based on their Doppler velocity, they can work well at identifying the above static or slow moving clutter returns, which are usually of disinterest, from the faster moving man made targets typically of interest. This is often achieved by employing special "notch filters" within the Doppler filter bank that are specifically designed to suppress the near stationary clutter so it will not compete with and mask the real (moving) targets of interest. This ability to discriminate static from moving targets suppresses the clutter which would otherwise do nothing more than desensitize the radar and thereby detect the real targets of interest, is one of the key reasons for the prevalence of pulse Doppler radars. However, as one strives to detect and track progressively smaller, and also progressively slower targets, imperfections in the most simple pulse Doppler radar operation accumulate to limit the sensitivity that might otherwise be theoretically achievable.

One of the more important of these imperfections relates to the fold-over property discussed above. Specifically, in addition to folding over targets from ARIs into the URI, a pulse Doppler radar will also fold-over any returns from clutter that exist in ARIs down into the URI. When one is looking for very weak return signals that have been depreciated by the $1/R^4$ SNR penalty of the radar range equation, suppressing that clutter almost perfectly becomes paramount. In order for the notch filter to ideally and near perfectly suppress the clutter so that maximum sensitivity can be achieved, it is imperative that all the clutter return energy in each URI range bin, including folded-over pulse return energy from clutter in corresponding ARI range bins, all be identical on every single pulse that is fed to the notch filter. If this is not the case, the filter will output a clutter residue response which is proportional to the difference between the returned energy between any pair of pulses in the Doppler waveform that are being integrated in the Doppler filter bank. The output clutter residue competes with the target sensitivity and desensitizes the radar. To address this problem, pulse Doppler radars often employ a number of additional pulses pre-pended to the main pulse waveform called "fill pulses."

Fill pulses are commonly used in pulse Doppler (PD) radars to mitigate filter transient response to received reflections from clutter in the range bins being interrogated. However, as typically implemented, this leads to dropping (not processing), and hence wasting the energy from, a number of the leading fill pulses transmitted in the PD waveform, thereby omitting their transmitted energy from the resultant Doppler filter response. This results in a net average power efficiency loss due to not processing these leading fill pulses, as well as producing other detriments. A straightforward non-linear processing approach is described which enables the coherent integration of the normally "lost" fill pulses typically employed in PD radar waveforms. The non-linear processing realizes a net improvement to SNR, signal-to-clutter ratio (SCR), velocity resolution, and velocity accuracy of targets detected and tracked by PD radars. A means approach for compensating for clutter phase migration induced by the rotation of a radar antenna is also presented. Finally, analog continuous wave (CW) radar is discussed as the dual to the time domain PD cast in the frequency domain.

Many radars (and other types of sensors) use PD type waveforms (PDW) wherein a series of time and phase coherent pulses of energy are transmitted into a directional beam for the detection of moving object reflections in the presence of other static background reflections comprising clutter interference. The PD radar type sensors are widely used for many purposes such as the military detection of space, sea, air, and ground targets; civil air traffic control; meteorology for detection of wind-driven rain; medical diagnosis and imaging; and perimeter security motion sensors to name a few. In many of these uses, the desired (usually small) signal may be obscured by sensor noise and/or clutter interference noise. Of the two, sensor noise, typically comprising at least thermal noise, is usually the smaller of the two, with clutter interference noise often being orders of magnitude larger. Clutter interference noise arises from imperfect cancellation of clutter, the undesired reflection of the transmitted energy from non-target scatterers residing somewhere within the interrogation beam. These non-target scatterers can be discrete (such as the face of a building) or distributed (such as reflections from the droplets in a cloud), and in reality, are usually a combination of both.

When the desired object's reflected signal is small and/or the clutter interference noise is large, PDW in conjunction with PD filters (PDF) provide a means to increase both the SNR and the signal-to-clutter ratio (SCR) (i.e., reducing the clutter interference noise). The PDW comprises a series of time and phase coherent pulses which are generally transmitted on short equal time intervals into a stationary or pseudo-stationary narrow beam. The time period between pulses need not be equal (although this greatly simplifies the implementation) but the timing must be known precisely, and all pulses must be phase coherent. The pulses are coherently integrated in a PDF comprising a linear time-invariant filter, usually implemented as a bank of Doppler filters (BDF or DFB), specifically designed to both increase the SNR and to suppress the clutter interference noise. The SNR is increased in a DFB because the coherently integrated signal energy increases as n_p^2 (with n_p being the number of received and coherently integrated pulses), whereas the thermal noise energy only increases nominally as n_p leading to an SNR increase of a factor of n_p. The clutter interference noise is significantly reduced, because the clutter return is coherently canceled in each Doppler filter by the substantially uniform phaser rotation of each pulse's clutter contribution around phaser diagram, thence summing to zero (at least ideally). Some residual clutter interference noise is always still present in the band pass of the Doppler filters because of imperfect coherence, often dominated by the system's phase noise and associated frequency spectrum. However, since there are usually about as many Doppler filters in the DFB as there are pulses, the total residual clutter interference and thermal noise is divided among the Doppler filters, thereby reducing the noises further. More specifically, the residual clutter interference noise can be derived from the frequency spectrum of the phase noise and the spectrum of the clutter interference noise within the band pass of each Doppler filter.

Linear time-invariant filters such as the Doppler filter generally require initialization at start-up in order to avoid undesirable transients which might tend to obscure the desired signal. For a scanning PD radar, each individual beam position comprises a new and independent dwell of a multiplicity of pulses and an associated instance of Doppler filtering, requiring its own transient start-up period. In this regard, infinite impulse response (IIR) filters require more careful treatment because the start-up transient can cause the filter to go unstable. This is not the case for finite impulse response (FIR) filters and why FIR filters predominate in PD radar implementations. The real world behavior of IIR filters is not nearly as dour as the theoreticians might lead one to believe, and successful IIR implementations can be achieved with great computational savings. However, both types of filters will manifest transient response to non-steady state inputs such as when the filter first starts up. Such filters are usually designed to operate in a steady-state mode substantially ignoring any transient response. However, steady-state operation implies that a transient start-up period occurred at a significant time prior to the start of the desired coherent integration period containing the pulses to be filtered so that the transients can settle out.

In non-continuously pulsing pulsed radars, this start-up period is implemented by preceding the desired coherently integrated pulses, called the "coherent integration period (CIP)" or alternatively the "coherent processing interval (CPI)," with a set of "fill pulses" of identical pulse width, pulse shape, pulse spectrum and nominally inter-pulse interval, as the pulses to be coherently integrated in the CPI. The presence of the fill pulses initializes the filter by filling the entire range extent of processed range bins, including both URI and ARI range bins, with coherent pulse energy. By filling the entire range extent with pulses, this entire filter and interrogated range extent system is primed (initialized) to achieve a steady state before the pulses to be coherently integrated are applied to the filter. As a result, the coherently integrated pulses will be filtered without significant debilitating transients. Note that the transients of concern here are those induced by reflections of the first few pulses from scatterers in the first ambiguous range intervals in the absence of reflections from further out ambiguous range intervals that the first pulses have not yet reached. Reflections from yet further out range intervals are usually not of consequence, since clutter rolls off with range due to the earth horizon (usually about *40 km* for a ground based radar at about *3 meters* altitude on flat terrain or ocean surface looking for targets at least *50 meters* above the surface).

The problem with the aforementioned fill pulses is that they consume radar energy and radiation on-time (i.e., occupancy time), but do not contribute to the coherent integration or thence do not contribute to the sensitivity of the radar because they are ignored, by design, since they contain undesired transient response (other than indirectly through the suppression of the aforementioned transients). Therefore, they are literally just wasted energy from a detection range perspective. However, although wasted, they are necessary, for without them the aforementioned transients desensitize and blind the radar.

Furthermore, the transmission of fill pulses can consume a significant fraction of the PDW dwell time, thereby robbing beam time from the surveillance raster of the radar as well. Since each beam dwell position requires a finite time period, longer dwell times incurred by the addition of fill pulses can increase the time needed to search a required solid angle volume. Additionally, track revisit rates are reduced by requiring fill pulses which degrades the potentially best tracking accuracy and robustness.

Finally, the need for fill pulses increases the prime power requirement of the radar and also forces the radar to emit more energy which can help attract anti-radiation missiles (a significant survivability threat to military radars). As a result of all these factors, there is a clear desire to either eliminate fill pulses altogether if possible, or at least to use their energy to contribute to the sensor's performance. The present technique focuses on recovering fill pulse energy to contribute to the sensor's performance. It can likewise be used to reduce the prime power requirement and the emitted radio frequency (RF) energy while retaining the same detection sensitivity.

9.A.3. Pulse Doppler Waveform with Fill Pulses

Figure 9-A.2 illustrates a traditional PDW comprising a number of fill pulses and a subsequent number of coherently integrated pulses collected and processed within the CPI, each separated from neighbors by the inter-pulse period (IPP). The fill pulses are used to fill up the range bins that have reflecting clutter scatterers in them, and these fill pulses are not processed for detection by the traditional PDW processing. These fill pulses therefore represent a waste of radar RF energy from a pure economics standpoint, although they are absolutely necessary to achieve good Doppler target detection performance in the presence of clutter.

Figure 9-A.3 shows what is effectively a space-time diagram of a 6-pulse CPI PDW with a fast time axis (vertical axis, proportional to Range) versus slow time axis (horizontal axis, proportional to dwell time) showing the pulse history of the 6-pulse coherently integrated pulsed Doppler radar waveform (8 pulses total) of Fig. 9-A.2.

Because the fast time axis is proportional to range, it can be further broken down into range intervals (RI), each corresponding to the furthest distance from a reflected pulse traveling the round trip distance to said furthest distance in the time between pulse transmissions, nominally the IPP. The first such R_{I_1} is called the "unambiguous range interval (URI)" equal in range to

$$R_{I_1} = \frac{1}{2} c \cdot IPP \qquad\qquad \textbf{Eq. (9-A.2)}$$

where c is the speed of light in the medium. The URI is characterized as starting at zero range at the antenna and not having any range ambiguity because it is the closest RI to the radar. The next RI is the first ambiguous range interval (ARI-1) characterized as starting at the end of the URI, and extending for a total of one RI further from the end of the URI. A range measured within the ARI-1 is ambiguous with a range measured from URI (hence its nomenclature of being "ambiguous"). That is, a pulse that is received during an IPP from the ARI-1, cannot be distinguished from a like pulse transmitted more recently if the more recent pulse is received at the same time as the prior transmitted pulse returning from a range in ARI-1. Since both more recent and less recent pulses in the pulse train of the PDW are temporally identical, there is no way to tell them apart except for maybe the signal strength appearing different due to the real and actual range difference when reflected from targets in different R_{I_s}. However, since one usually does not know a priori the radar cross-section (RCS) of the target, the signal strength cannot be used as a reliable indicator of the RI from which pulse reflection originated (although in a more advanced radar it might be used in a Bayesian probabilistic approach).

The PDW and associated dwell begin with the transmission and reception of the first pulse labeled by #1 as shown in Fig. 9-A.3. This first pulse is received by the end of the first IPP corresponding to the maximum range that may be registered unambiguously in URI. Immediately after completion of the reception of the first pulse, a second pulse labeled as #2 is transmitted. Note that while the second pulse #2 is transiting into the URI, the first pulse #1 is still traveling and transiting ARI-1, eventually arriving at and returning from the maximum range extent of the second range interval, ARI-1, one IPP later. Also at a time IPP later, the second pulse #2 of the PDW is received and registered similarly to the first pulse #1, returning from a farthest extent of the first range interval URI, but one IPP later in time which also corresponds to the maximum range that may be registered in URI. The timing is then such that the reception of a reflection of the first pulse #1 from a target at the furthest extent of ARI-1, coincides with the reception of a reflection of the second pulse #2 from a target at the furthest extent of the URI. Therefore, the range of the target in the ARI-1 is ambiguous with the range of a target in the URI, being separated by one range interval.

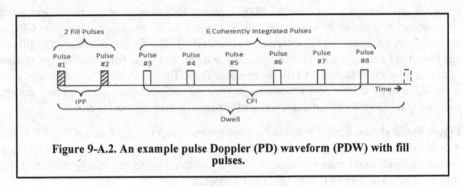

Figure 9-A.2. An example pulse Doppler (PD) waveform (PDW) with fill pulses.

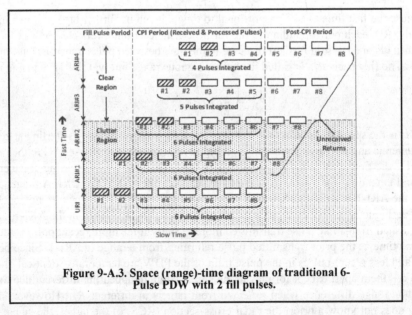

Figure 9-A.3. Space (range)-time diagram of traditional 6-Pulse PDW with 2 fill pulses.

As defined in this example, the clutter region (range extent that has clutter scatterers in it) extends across the URI and two range intervals, ARI-1 and ARI-2. Recalling the need for a time invariant filter to be initialized for maximum suppression of transient responses, the first two pulses of this PDW are assigned to be fill pulses. Their purpose is to fill with synchronous pulse energy, the two range intervals that contain clutter beyond the URI in the clutter Region, namely ARI-1 and ARI-2 of the ambiguous range intervals.

These first two pulses do not have any reflections returning from range intervals ARI-1 or ARI-2 from any prior pulses; they necessarily are transient in nature and are completely ignored in traditional PDW processing. Hence in traditional PDW processing the coherent integration of pulses does not begin until after the fill pulses in the fill pulse period have been transmitted. Therefore, in Fig. 9-A.3, coherent processing does not begin until the third pulse labeled #3 is transmitted as shown within the CPI period. All the pulses transmitted during the CPI period have reflections from the clutter in the clutter region from prior fill pulses #1 and #2, and / or subsequent pulses. Therefore, there will never be any transients induced by reflections from the clutter region. The PDW processing provides optimum results for the pulses that are coherently integrated within the CPI period in the different range intervals.

There are two problems with the above schema of PDW processing. First, although the use of fill pulses eliminates transient reflections from further out range intervals that would result in added clutter residue noise due to imbalanced clutter returns and thereby lower sensitivity, this scheme employs a total of 8 pulses, but only coherently integrates 6 pulses, thereby representing an excess expenditure of transmission energy which is not fully recovered in the reception and processing for the detection of targets. Stated more simply, the energy transmitted in fill pulses is lost for the detection of targets, as only the pulses in the CPI are coherently integrated for the reasons cited above. It is a first objective of the present approach to solve this problem and recover all the energy transmitted for all pulses toward the detection of targets.

A second problem with the traditional schema of PDW processing is that only the range intervals covered by the fill pulses (i.e., the URI, ARI-1 and ARI-2 in the example of Fig. 9-A.3) ever provide the full coherent integration of all the CPI number of pulses. Range intervals in the clear region, beyond the clutter region, do not contain any clutter reflections which could cause Doppler filter processing transients, but have a fewer number of pulses reflected to be integrated as illustrated at range intervals labeled for 5 and 4 pulses. The lost pulses are delayed past the CPI period into the post-CPI period where they are never received or sampled because they return after the CPI period. This is significantly detrimental to the detection of targets at far out ranges because there are literally fewer pulses in the CPI to integrate from range intervals in the clear region. Note that this loss of CPI pulses occurs at the farther ranges of detection which are already significantly challenged by the stressing $(1/R^4)$ free path loss. It is therefore a second objective of the present approach to provide more coherently integrated pulses in the clear region range intervals.

It is also interesting to note that if pulsed Doppler dwells were back-to-back (or nearly so, often with no more than one IPP separating them) and if they were on the same frequency, then the unreceived pulses from a first dwell could act as interfering signals to a second sequential dwell. This is more likely to be an issue if the first dwell employed a large number of fill pulses and the second dwell employed only a minimal number of fill pulses, or even no fill pulses, but regardless, depending on the number of fill pulses used and the extent of the clutter region it could be more or less of a problem. It is therefore a third objective of the approach to eliminate this possible source of interference between adjacent back-to-back dwells.

9.A.4. Recovery of Fill Pulses

Figure 9-A.4 illustrates a similar pulse train as Fig. 9-A.3 but shows how the above approach may be achieved. It is first assumed that the radar is a substantially digital sensor capable of recording real time in-phase and quadrature (I&Q) data for use in the signal data processor (SDP) and that the SDP has sufficient buffer size and computational resources to perform the required data and processing manipulations to be described. This is typically not a problem in most any modern SDP. The pulse transmission sequence in Fig. 9-A.4 is identical to the pulse transmission sequence of a traditional PDW radar in Fig. 9-A.3, with the exception of a delay in the transmission of the next subsequent dwell, as will become apparent very shortly. No additional pulses are transmitted or other wise modified.

The core of the approach is in the modification of the subsequent post-processing of the received and digitized pulses. The first step is to digitally record and store the I&Q data from all the pulses during each IPP in both the fill pulse period and the CPI period. This is almost the same process as is done in a traditional PDW processing, except that usually the fill pulse IPP data is not recorded, stored, nor used. Then, as shown in Fig. 9-A.4, instead of cutting off the CPI period after the transmission of pulse #8, the CPI period is extended for one additional (seventh) IPP. This makes the CPI period 7 IPPs in duration instead of only 6 IPPs. The I&Q data is collected for this *7th* IPP just like all the prior 6 period IPPs.

Upon completion of the original CPI period, the I&Q data for the first IPP that was recorded for the first fill pulse is copied and pasted over (added) to the first range intervals worth of fast time data in the I&Q data recorded for the *7th* IPP in the new CPI period as indicated by the large dark arrow. Note that all other things being equal, since all the pulses are assumed time and phase coherent, and identical, this transference of the first fill pulse data to the *7th* IPP (labeled #1') of the new CPI period is identically transparent. That is, after the copy and paste (add), the I&Q data will look absolutely identical to the data that had a pulse #9 transmitted at the end of the CPI period. The copy and paste (add) back fills a copy of what might have been the response of pulse #9 from the first URI interval using the first fill pulse to insert as a substitute. In the process of doing this, the data for the CPI in the first range interval of the *9th* pulse for the URI is flushed out, enabling a full 7 pulses of coherent integration in the first URI.

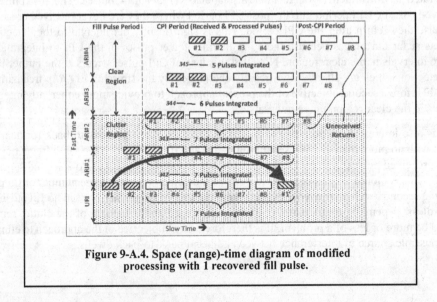

**Figure 9-A.4. Space (range)-time diagram of modified
processing with 1 recovered fill pulse.**

Similarly, the extended CPI period window now enables lengthening of the number of pulses in the CPI to a full seven IPPs farther down range intervals AR-1 and AR-2, with one extra pulse for each clear region RI, AR-3, and AR-4. This results in a direct improvement of both SNR and SCR proportional to the ratio of the number of coherently added pulses with the new method divided by the number of coherently added pulses in the traditional method, providing a corresponding improvement (after $(1/R^4)$) in detection range without the need to transmit additional RF power.

Note that as might be expected, the number of wasted unreceived pulses in the post-CPI period is now also reduced. In a completely analogous manner where the CPI was extended by one additional pulse as described above, the CPI may be increased by the same method to any maximum of the total number of pulses transmitted, including the fill pulses. Figure 9-A.5 illustrates the extension of the process shown in Fig. 9-A.4 to include all the fill pulses in the fill pulse period. In a like manner as before, the I&Q data from the second IPP of the fill pulse period is digitally recorded and stored. The CPI period is extended by two IPPs to include what might have been the *10th* pulse had that many pulses been transmitted for the CPI.

The process of Fig. 9-A.4 is performed for the first fill pulse as previously described. Then an essentially identical process is performed as indicated by the second large dark arrow for the second fill pulse and its two range intervals, copying that data and pasting (adding) is as shown over the corresponding range interval data in the *8th* IPP of the CPI period. This results in back filling the data for the range interval in the *8th* CPI period IPP as shown for pulse #2' and for pulse #1' which has propagated to the second range interval (ARI-1). Again, since the radar is assumed time and phase coherent, this copy and paste (add) operation provides an exact duplicate of the data that would have been received and recorded had a *7th* and *8th* CPI pulse (*9th* and *10th* total number of pulses in the PDW) actually been transmitted. Also, the further out range intervals 7 and 6 pulses respectively also have more pulses than before, thereby enhancing their SNR and SCR and hence sensitivity to targets at greater range. The number of unreceived pulses are further reduced because more transmitted energy is being used.

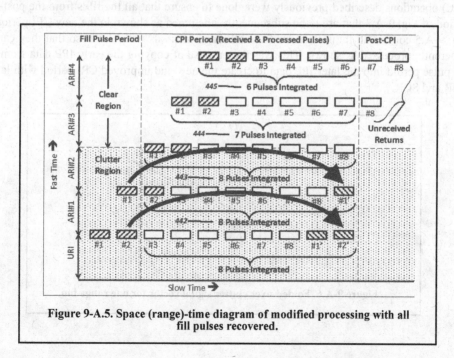

Figure 9-A.5. Space (range)-time diagram of modified processing with all fill pulses recovered.

The above process is obviously extensible to any number of fill pulses by one skilled in the art of radar PDW processing. The approach enables full recovery of all fill pulse energy through coherent addition of the fill pulses into the PDW processing for enhanced SNR and SCR. It also increases the length of the CPI to provide better Doppler resolution and hence better velocity measurement accuracy. The approach further increases the number of coherently integrated pulses in the farther out range intervals in the clear region to provide higher SNR and SCR at farther ranges. The approach also decreases the number of unreceived pulses, and helps avoid dwell-to-dwell interference. As a side benefit, it further enables detection and tracking of slower targets both because of the additional degrees of freedom afforded a PDW with more pulses and because the filter skirts can be steeper to get closer to the clutter ridge. By shortening the duration and increasing the range of the pulses that are unreceived, the potential for dwell-to-dwell interference is significantly reduced.

9.A.5. Doppler Filtering Fill Pulses

The means for Doppler processing the afore-described rearranged pulse data is discussed next. Figure 9-A.6 shows the composition of the received clutter signal vector (clutter vector or clutter) from one range bin collected during an IPP plotted on a I&Q graph. The clutter comprises the vector sum of all the clutter reflections from the clutter scatterers in a range bin folded in from all the range intervals within the clutter region filled by fill pulses. In keeping with the prior figures, this includes but is not limited to reflections from the aliased range bins in the URI, ARI-1, and ARI-2 range intervals. These aliased fold-overs of clutter from the farther range intervals comprise the "transients" that need to be removed by the initialization of the Doppler filter system with fill pulses in order to maximize Doppler filter performance. The copy and pasting (adding) of I&Q data described previously ensures that all the additional IPPs that are to be processed have these same clutter contributions in all IPPs processed.

In what follows they will no longer be shown explicitly but are known to be summed within the total clutter vector for each IPP. However, it is important to note that the copy and paste (add) operations described previously were done to ensure that all the IPPs from the post-IPP period of Fig. 9-A.3 that are to be subsequently integrated as shown in the new CPI period of Fig. 9-A.5 contain all the reflections from all range intervals with clutter so that they can be coherently processed as shown. This was the purpose of copying the early IPP data from the fill pulse period into the later IPP data to create the new and improved CPI period with larger SNR and SCR.

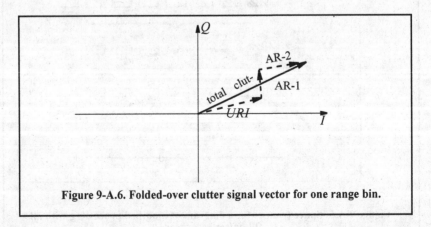

Figure 9-A.6. Folded-over clutter signal vector for one range bin.

Figure 9-A.7 shows illustrative I&Q measurement vectors for one folded-over range bin for each of the 8 IPPs in an 8 pulse PDW of clutter without any target. Note that the clutter measurement is (at least theoretically) identical for each IPP measurement because the clutter is stationary (obviously wind swept and volume clutter may not be completely stationary).

Figure 9-A.8 shows illustrative I&Q measurement vectors for one folded-over range bin for each of the 8 IPPs in an 8 pulse PDW for a radially moving target without any clutter present. Note that because the target is moving, the phase of the target signal vectors rotates in equal increments about the center of the I&Q axis. This is the important feature that makes it possible for Doppler filters to discriminate between clutter and moving targets. In this exemplary case, I&Q sample vectors rotate one full rotation in the time taken by the 8 IPP samples, but this is completely dependent on the velocity of the target. Each Doppler filter in a DFB will hypothesize a velocity of the target, and if the target matches that velocity, the Doppler filter will end up rotating all the signal vectors in Fig. 9-A.8 into the same direction. Then using complex addition, they will add up coherently. In contrast, all the clutter vectors of Fig. 9-A.7 are then rotated by the Doppler filter by rotations that appear random. When these are added coherently, they tend to cancel out, thereby canceling the clutter.

As shown in Figs. 9-A.7 and 9-A.8, and assuming equal I&Q axis scale in both figures, the target vector signal would appear to be about as large as the clutter vector signal in both figures. However, this is not usually the case in real applications, wherein the clutter vectors are normally much larger than the target vectors. This is not overtly germane to the application but prudent to point out for a realistic perspective toward the application. The objective of the Doppler filter then is to separate and cancel the large unchanging clutter vector signal of Fig. 9-A.7 from the potentially much smaller Doppler vector signal of Fig. 9-A.8 from the target.

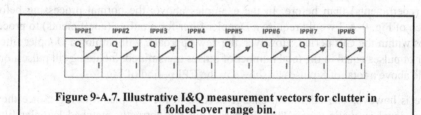

Figure 9-A.7. Illustrative I&Q measurement vectors for clutter in 1 folded-over range bin.

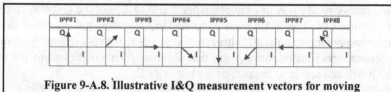

Figure 9-A.8. Illustrative I&Q measurement vectors for moving target in 1 folded-over bin.

In order to reveal the smaller target signal from the larger clutter signal, the Doppler filter must suppress the potentially larger clutter vector signal. This may be accomplished by rotating the I&Q data from each IPP by an angle $\pm k(360/n_p)$ degrees where n_p is the total number of pulses (alternatively total number of IPPs), and k is the specific sequential IPP count number (an integer). What this does is to spread each IPP's clutter signal vector in different directions evenly around the I&Q unit circle. When these IPP clutter vectors are added up, they will sum to zero because they are of equal magnitude and pointed evenly in different directions. Furthermore, there will be a band of target Doppler frequencies whose target complex signal phasers for each IPP start out pointing in different directions, but that will then be co-aligned by the same above-described rotations in the I&Q space. So, there will exist a Doppler frequency where the IPP target Doppler vectors become co-aligned, while at the same time the IPP clutter vectors become anti-aligned. The rotated IPP target Doppler vectors will then coherently add upon summation, and the rotated IPP clutter vectors will tend to cancel to zero upon summation. For different Doppler frequencies, different modulo 360° rotations are employed to ensure the clutter vectors always vector sum to zero.

With the fundamental operation of Doppler filters now reviewed, the modification needed to implement Doppler filtering with the modified I&Q data from Fig. 9-A.5 is now apparent. The copy and paste (add) operations leading up to Fig. 9-A.5 fills in missing clutter signal I&Q data for range intervals not filled with pulses within the post-CPI period, enabling those IPPs (specifically IPP #9 and #10 for the example given) to be coherently processed to create a larger CPI period with more than 8 coherently processed dwells as shown.

Note now that if a target is also present in any of the range intervals within the CPI region, and if the frequency of the target is not within the passband of a given Doppler filter within the Doppler filter bank, then those target Doppler vectors will be rotated into semi-random directions by the filter, and the vector sum will be some small residue which has a theoretical limit of zero. However, if the target Doppler frequency matches the frequency of the Doppler filter in the Doppler filter bank, then that means that the target Doppler frequency must be cyclical within the CPI Period. That is, the target Doppler frequency will complete an integral number of cycles within the CPI period for the case of 6 coherently processed pulses, or in the case of 8 coherently processed pulses as appropriate.

Obviously, the employment of the approach requires the use of a Doppler filter with more pulses (coefficients) than before. In the examples above, the normal processing before the approach of Fig. 9-A.3 would require a Doppler filter for 6 pulses (coefficients) to process the 6 pulses within the CPI period. However, the new approach will employ a Doppler filter for a number of pulses equal to the total number of pulses transmitted, including fill pulses, or in the example above a total of 8 pulses as shown in the CPI period of Fig. 9-A.3.

There is however one additional change needed to the Doppler filtering. Since the target Doppler signal is cyclic across the CPI period for the correctly matched Doppler filter, the Doppler filter must be modified to have a cyclic sequence of processing instead of a linear sequence of processing. By way of example, when the I&Q data of the first IPP, corresponding to the first fill pulse #1 in Fig. 9-A.4 is added to the I&Q data from the last IPP in the extended CPI period corresponding to pulse #1', this action requires a like re-sequencing of the Doppler filter coefficients, specifically, moving the first Doppler filter coefficient to the end of the sequence so it will be applied to the data of the last IPP #1'.

Mathematically, the Doppler filter for the traditional processing of Fig. 9-A.3 is

$$DF_i = \sum_{k=3}^{8} w_{i,k} \times x_k,$$

Eq. (9-A.3)

where DF_i is the output for the *ith* Doppler filter, $w_{i,k}$ is the filter coefficient for the *ith* Doppler filter and *kth* IPP, and x_k is the complex scalar I&Q measurement for a given range bin for the *kth* IPP, with k ranging from 3 to 8 corresponding to the CPI period in Fig. 9-A.3.

The new modified Doppler filter for the new approach after Fig. 9-A.5 may be expressed as

$$DF_i = \sum_{k=3}^{8} w_{i,k} \times x_k + w_{i,1} \times x'_1 \qquad \text{Eq. (9-A.4)}$$

where $x'_1 = x_1 + x_9$, the prime symbol denotes the modified I&Q data corresponding to the additional fill pulse IPPs recovered for the filter of this new approach. The new modified Doppler filter for this approach after Fig. 9-A.5 may be similarly expressed as

$$DF_i = \sum_{k=3}^{8} w_{i,k} \times x_k + w_{i,1} \times x'_1 + w_{i,2} \times x'_2 \qquad \text{Eq. (9-A.5)}$$

where $x'_2 = x_2 + x_{10}$. More generally and for arbitrary numbers of fill pulses and CPI pulses this can be expressed as

$$DF_i = \left[\sum_{k=n_{fp}}^{n_p} w_{i,k} \times x_k \right] + \left[\sum_{j=1}^{n_{fp}} w_{i,k} \times x'_{j+n_p} \right] \qquad \text{Eq. (9-A.6)}$$

where $x'_{j+n_p} = x_j + x_{j+n_p}$, n_{fp} is the number of fill pulses, and n_p is the total number of pulses transmitted.

The features and implications of the new approach are now summarized. The new approach seeks to recover the energy that is normally lost to fill pulses in PDW dwells and associated processing. The recovered energy is then used to increase SNR and SCR to what it would be if the fill pulses were regular CPI pulses. The method therefore does not require the addition of pulses to achieve higher SNR and SCR, but it does require passive collection of returning pulse energy from clutter within the clutter region for a short period of time after the last pulse has been transmitted. This requires extending the dwell by a time equal to the total number of IPPs times the number of what would have been fill pulses employed under the traditional processing paradigm. Therefore, the invention does not require the transmission of more power, but it does require extending the whole dwell by appending a subsequent reception-only period equal in time to the number of fill pulses times the IPP. This is usually an excellent trade because no additional RF power need be transmitted to achieve an increase in SNR and SCR.

It is noted that instead of using the new approach to seek and achieve an increase in SNR and SCR by increasing the dwell time over the traditional PDW processing, alternatively, the approach may be used to permit retention of the same SNR and SCR while reducing the number of pulses in the dwell, and hence reducing the dwell time. This can be of importance when it is desired to reduce the occupancy of a radar without reducing its performance. It should also be noted that since the approach essentially eliminates fill pulses as a separate modality in PDW processing. Because the effective number of Doppler filters are increased in the new approach, there is also a correspondingly higher Doppler resolution. This enables both more accurate tracking as well as additional degrees of freedom to create steeper nulls in the Doppler filters for better operation near the clutter lobe.

9.A.6. Caveats and Extension

There are two potential minor disadvantages to the approach which are generally of little consequence but may need to be accounted for. The first disadvantage is that the approach does require longer dwells as previously described. This is not really a disadvantage per se because one would have had to add more pulses and thereby extend the dwell anyway with the conventional PDW paradigm and processing to achieve the higher SNR and SCR provided by this approach. The advantage of the approach is that the increased SNR and SCR can be obtained without radiating additional energy, which is advantageous in most radar systems already operating at a maximum power output.

The second disadvantage applies only to rotating radars: stationary radars, or rotating radars that might back scan their beam while rotating on a pulse-to-pulse basis to compensate for motion, will not have this problem. For traditional rotating radars, the radar beam will be pointing at a slightly different position for the first fill pulse than it will be for the first extra IPP #1' after the traditional CPI period. By the time the radar is collecting I&Q on IPP #1', the antenna will have rotated to a slightly different azimuth, meaning that the clutter returns from the further out range intervals ARI-1 and ARI-2 (alternatively associated with pulses #7 and #8) will be from a slightly different azimuth than other pulses.

In a way, this may be inconsequential because in reality each and every IPP is taken at a different azimuth in a rotating radar anyway. However, whereas the I&Q data from all the range intervals in the CPI period are tightly correlated in time (having been taken only one or two IPPs apart), the I&Q data from the near-in range intervals of the extended IPPs may be temporally and spatially more correlated than the farther out range intervals by comparison. This could result in worse clutter suppression capability in some cases due to rotation, particularly at the farther ranges. However, given that the nearest range interval changes least in cross-range distance for a given azimuthal rotation than the far out range intervals, and because of the approach more pulses are being processed to smooth out and average unexpected deviations, it is likely that such degradations are relatively small or inconsequential.

Note further that if the rotational motion of an antenna unduly compromises the clutter suppression capability of the radar either in the absence of the presence of this new approach, there are means for dealing with this. For example, by measuring the phase angle of the clutter return at each beam position during each pulse for each unambiguous range bin and potentially for each pulse in each folded interval, the clutter phase migration rate from pulse-to-pulse during a dwell of Doppler pulses may be determined. With the antenna rotation modulation thereby removed from the I&Q data, the Doppler filtering operation, either with or without the present approach, may proceed with a resultant improvement in the low Doppler frequency and slow target motion sensitivity of the radar.

Finally, and to generalize further, it should be noted that due to Fourier time-frequency complementarity, there is a complementary frequency domain technique of radar for every time (pulse) domain technique. In that such domains are paired, there exists a dual in the frequency domain to the current time domain approach, and therefore the current approach also applies to frequency domain with suitable modifications.

Chapter 10

Radar Tracking

Scott C. Winton

10.1. Introduction

Because of technological advances in the last twenty or so years, most people are very familiar with the term "tracking," and they use it on an almost daily basis. For example, many people track packages from online retailers and use Global Positioning System (GPS) in their vehicles or on smartphones. Even with this in mind, if you were to ask individuals to define the term "tracking," they would likely say something like, "knowing where something is." While certainly this can be true, such a description would be insufficient, especially for radar systems. Without using any technical terms or rigid definitions, it would be more accurate to say that tracking comprises maintaining current estimates of useful information about *something*. From the radar point of view, this *something* is one or more targets of interest and the useful information will likely include the targets' location, velocity, and acceleration, in addition to a host of other information about the targets' kinematics. Actually, a radar tracker can accurately maintain estimates of many parameters or pieces of information about the targets in track. What makes the information useful depends on the application. Air surveillance radars, like the ones you would see at most major airports, track targets to ensure flight safety. A fire control radar, on the other hand, would implement the useful information to guide a weapon to an adversarial target.

Radars systems have been in the business of successfully tracking targets for over 70 years using specialized tracking filters. The Kalman filter, to which a good portion of this chapter is devoted, was first developed in the early 1960s. And because of the technological advancements since then, development of tracking approaches, algorithms, and architectures has been and continues to be a rich area of research that can (and does) produce numerous research articles and textbooks. While not one book on radar systems could be considered complete without at least one chapter devoted to tracking, it cannot be expected to be comprehensive in either breadth or depth. With this in mind, the primary purpose of this chapter is to provide the reader with sufficient understanding of radar tracking approaches and implementations as to lay the foundation for future learning of more specific topics. The focus of this chapter is on modern, multi-role radars that are capable of tracking numerous targets with sufficient signal and data processing and computing capabilities.

Based on these assumptions, this chapter focuses on the two major building blocks of modern tracking approaches: track filtering and data association. Of the two, data association is easier to describe. It is, in general, the assigning of detections (or measurements) to tracks.

Track filtering is an attempt to improve upon our "useful information" to something that has a better estimate of, or may not have been included in, the information in our measurements.

Section 10.2 provides a review of some basic concepts that will be useful, including state space and linear systems. It also introduces a simplified tracking architecture. Section 10.3 discusses the radar measurements, as every tracking system requires measurements to perform its intended purpose. For example, for a shipping firm, the measurement may comprise the scanning of a bar code of the packages being shipped. For GPS, the system will receive location measurements from several satellites in order to estimate its current position. For a radar system, the measurements are typically taken from detection of energy that has been reflected off the targets of interest, but may also include energy from unwanted sources, such as noise and clutter. This section will also take a look at some of the techniques employed to provide the best measurements possible. Section 10.4 deals with filtering, starting from the least squares and ending with the most sophisticated types. An in-depth analysis of batch processing and recursive least squares is presented. This will provide the necessary background for Kalman filtering, which is based on least squares.

Section 10.4.3 introduces the Kalman filter and its equations and provides examples of different variants of this tracking filter. The Kalman filter is considered to be an optimal estimator if the equations that define it are linear. Unfortunately, that is a difficult requirement for a radar system, simply because of how most radars make range and angle measurements. Section 10.4.4 describes the extended Kalman filter (EKF), which is used to deal with these non-linear relationships. Section 10.6 begins the discussion of data association. Section 10.6.1 describes the importance of gating to limit the number of data association hypotheses that must be considered. Sections 10.6.2 and 10.6.3 discuss the older, but still important, data association methods global nearest neighbor (GNN) and joint probabilistic data association (JPDA), respectively. The discussion of data association concludes in Section 10.6.4 with an introductory look at the multiple hypothesis tracker (MHT). Section 10.7 provides a description of techniques to track maneuvering targets. This includes adaptive single models and multiple models. The chapter concludes with an example of the interacting multiple filter (IMF).

10.2. Basic Concepts

10.2.1. Tracking Architecture

Figure 10.1 shows the functional components of a simplified radar tracking architecture. Starting on the left of the figure, the radar must establish where it is and a common time reference. This is particularly important if the radar is to interact with other systems. This is usually performed as part of a calibration and registration process. While operating, the radar will take measurements on targets. The tracker will then perform preprocessing gating in an attempt to simplify the data association process by eliminating unlikely detections from consideration to be associated with a given track. The correlation/association function then assigns measurements to specific tracks. The smoothing and prediction function attempts to remove measurement noise from the track estimate and predict where the target will be at the next measurement time. Finally, there must be rules with which to create or terminate tracks and a place to store the track information.

10.2.2. State Space Representation

In radar tracking, target tracking information is contained in what is referred to as a "state" of the target. It is therefore worthwhile to quickly review state space representation and how it relates to linear systems. Start by assuming that one can sufficiently describe a dynamic system, that is, a system that changes with time, by a set of n variables. It is then very convenient to group these variables into a vector called the "state vector" and represent it using the bold symbol $\mathbf{x}$. This dynamic system may have p inputs represented by the vector $\mathbf{u}$ and m outputs represented by the vector $\mathbf{y}$. The outputs are usually some form of observations of the states. A completely general system is shown in Figure 10.2.

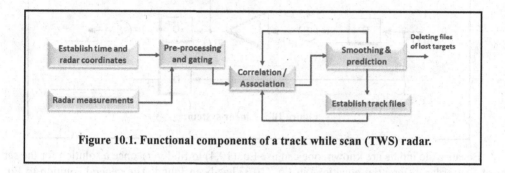

Figure 10.1. Functional components of a track while scan (TWS) radar.

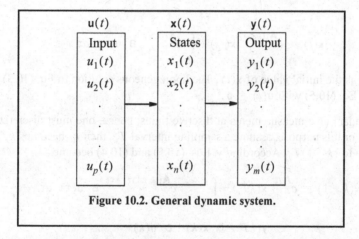

Figure 10.2. General dynamic system.

Typically, one needs to describe the relationship between the output, the input and the state variables, but because it is a dynamic system, one also needs to be able to describe how the state vector changes with time. So, for the general system, there are two sets of equations which describe the system. They are,

$$\dot{\mathbf{x}} = f_1(\mathbf{x}, \mathbf{u}, t) \qquad\qquad \text{Eq. (10.1)}$$

$$\mathbf{y} = f_2(\mathbf{x}, \mathbf{u}, t) \qquad\qquad \text{Eq. (10.2)}$$

where $\dot{\mathbf{x}}$ is the time derivative of the vector $\mathbf{x}$, f_1 f_2 are two general functions of $(\mathbf{x}, \mathbf{u}, t)$.

If the relationships between the inputs, state variables and outputs are linear (not necessarily in time), the set of equations take the form

$$\dot{\mathbf{x}}(t) = \mathbf{A}\ \mathbf{x}(t) + \mathbf{B}\ \mathbf{u}(t) \qquad\qquad \text{Eq. (10.3)}$$

$$\mathbf{y}(t) = \mathbf{C}\ \mathbf{x}(t) + \mathbf{D}\ \mathbf{u}(t) \qquad\qquad \text{Eq. (10.4)}$$

where $\mathbf{x}$ is the $n \times 1$ state vector; $\mathbf{y}$ is the $m \times 1$ output vector; $\mathbf{u}$ is the $p \times 1$ input vector; $\mathbf{A}$ is an $n \times n$ matrix; $\mathbf{B}$ is an $n \times p$ matrix; $\mathbf{C}$ is $m \times n$ matrix; and $\mathbf{D}$ is an $m \times p$ matrix. The block diagram for this linear system is shown in Figure 10.3.

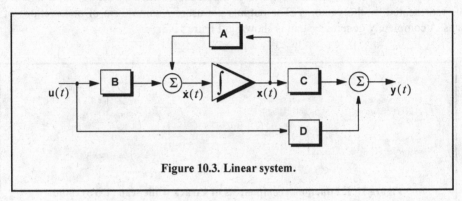

Figure 10.3. Linear system.

Because the inputs are known, one can use Eq. (10.4) to find $\mathbf{y}(t)$ once a solution for the set of first order differential equations in Eq. (10.3) has been found. The general solution to Eq. (10.3) is

$$\mathbf{x}(t) = e^{\mathbf{A}(t-t_0)} \mathbf{x}(t_0) + \int_{t_0}^{t} e^{\mathbf{A}(t-\tau)} \mathbf{B} \mathbf{u}(\tau) \, d\tau \qquad \text{Eq. (10.5)}$$

where $\mathbf{x}(t_0)$ is the initial value of $\mathbf{x}(t)$. The homogeneous solution to Eq. (10.3) is simply the first term of Eq. (10.5) with $\mathbf{u}(t) = \mathbf{0}$.

Modern radars take measurements at discrete times; hence, one must discretize Eqs. (10.4) and (10.5). For this purpose, assume a sampling interval T_s, then t_0 becomes kT_s, where k is the time step to $(k+1)T_s$. Accordingly, Eqs. (10.5) and (10.4) become

$$\mathbf{x}(k+1) = e^{\mathbf{A}T_s} \mathbf{x}(kT_s) + \int_{kT_s}^{(k+1)T_s} e^{\mathbf{A}((k+1)T_s - \tau)} \mathbf{B} \mathbf{u}(\tau) \, d\tau \qquad \text{Eq. (10.6)}$$

$$\mathbf{y}(k) = \mathbf{C} \mathbf{x}(k) + \mathbf{D} \mathbf{u}(k) \qquad \text{Eq. (10.7)}$$

In general, the integral in Eq. (10.6) must be solved at every time step. However, if one assumes the inputs $\mathbf{u}(t)$ are constant over the time interval $kT_s < t < (k+1)T_s$, then the function $\mathbf{u}(t)$ may be pulled out of the integral. After a change of variable of integration and some clean-up, Eq. (10.6) becomes

$$\mathbf{x}(k+1) = \Phi(k) \mathbf{x}(k) + \mathbf{u}(k) \int_0^{T_s} e^{\mathbf{A}\tau} \mathbf{B} \, d\tau \qquad \text{Eq. (10.8)}$$

where the matrix Φ is called the state transition matrix or the fundamental matrix and is given by,

$$\Phi(k) = e^{\mathbf{A}T_s}. \qquad \text{Eq. (10.9)}$$

The transition matrix describes the relationship between the current state and the previous state. The integral on the right-hand side of Eq. (10.8) now only requires to be solved once. The state transition matrix may be found in several different ways, including numerically. However, for many radar systems, the state will consist of a limited number of variables related by their derivatives. In this case, the state transition matrix can be found exactly using a Taylor expansion as

$$\Phi(k) = e^{\mathbf{A}T_s} = 1 + \mathbf{A}T_s + \frac{(\mathbf{A}T_s)^2}{2!} + \ldots + \frac{(\mathbf{A}T_s)^n}{n!} + \ldots. \qquad \text{Eq. (10.10)}$$

As an example, consider a radar target moving at constant velocity during the sampling interval. The state vector would be

$$\mathbf{x} = [x \;\; \dot{x}]^{\dagger} \qquad \text{Eq. (10.11)}$$

where the time dependence has been suppressed and symbol † indicates transpose. Assuming no inputs to the system, then the discrete time version of Eq. (10.3) for this system would be

$$\dot{\mathbf{x}} = \mathbf{A}\mathbf{x} = \begin{bmatrix} 0 & 1 \\ 0 & 0 \end{bmatrix} \mathbf{x}. \qquad \text{Eq. (10.12)}$$

Using this result in Eq. (10.10) shows that only the first two terms have non-zero components and therefore the state transition matrix is

$$\Phi(k) = \begin{bmatrix} 1 & T_s \\ 0 & 1 \end{bmatrix}. \qquad \text{Eq. (10.13)}$$

Finally, Eqs. (10.8) and (10.7) provide the current state and output of the system based only on the knowledge of the previous state.

10.3. Measurements

Types of radar system measurements may include target range, azimuth, elevation, range rate, and in some cases, some measure of the size of the target, such as radar cross-section (RCS). For single target tracking, the radar will keep its beam on the target while taking measurements. For track while scan radars, which is the focus of this chapter, the radar will track one or more targets while performing other functions, such as search. For these systems, the radar will move its beam off of any given target to service other functions, then return to take a measurement on that target. Radars normally have much better slant range resolution than cross-range.

10.3.1. Angle Measurements

There are multiple techniques available for angle measurements. In all cases, the goal is to provide an angle estimate that is improved over simply noting where the beam is pointed. Even for pencil beam antennas, the cross-range distance covered by a single beam will increase with range, therefore, accurate angle measurements will involve an understanding of where the target is in relation to where the radar antenna beam is pointing.

Sequential Lobing

Sequential lobing is an older angle measurement technique, but is simple to implement and serves as a foundation for understanding more complicated methods. Sequential lobing involves switching between two beam positions (in one dimension) that are symmetrically offset from what is believed to be the tracking axis. Returns from each beam position are then compared. If they are equal, the target is on the tracking axis, if not, the tracking axis; is adjusted. If the radar is to track two angles, two additional beam positions will be needed that are orthogonal to the first two. This method could also be implemented with two (or four) antennas that have offset beams. Figure 10.4 illustrates sequential lobing in one dimension. Sequential lobing has some significant drawbacks, including being resource intensive and susceptible to pulse-to-pulse changes such as those caused by target scintillation.

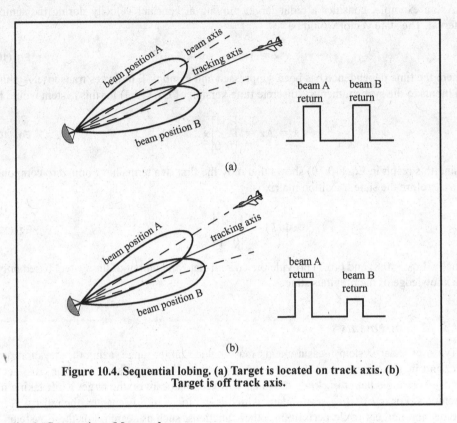

Figure 10.4. Sequential lobing. (a) Target is located on track axis. (b) Target is off track axis.

Amplitude Comparison Monopulse

Monopulse is similar to sequential lobing, but unlike sequential lobing, which requires two beam positions, monopulse is done with two receive channels simultaneously. Therefore, the measurement can be done in a single pulse. Originally dubbed simultaneous lobing, monopulse compares two channels to generate an error signal which can be used to adjust the angle measurement or, in the case of an antenna on a servo, create an error voltage that can be used to keep a single target on the tracking axis. This may be done by comparing amplitude or phase.

Monopulse begins by creating channels that form beams that are symmetric about the line of sight (LOS) axis of the antenna. For example, say we split a rectangular phased array antenna into element groups separated by the axes of the full array, say "left and right" or "up and down." Figure 10.5 shows the beams of these groups, labeled channels A through D. We can combine these channels in different ways through a comparator, as shown in Fig. 10.6. Using the output of the comparator, a difference channel can be created for two sets of orthogonal antenna measurements. The output of difference channels is dependent on the relative position of the target to the center axis of the antenna.

If the target is directly on the axis, the output will be zero. However, if the target is off the axis, the output of the difference channel is also dependent on other factors that impact all the channels, such as signal-to-noise ratio (SNR). To remove these dependencies and make the error signal only dependent on the target position relative to the axis, we normalize the difference signal by the sum signal.

As an example, consider channels with the familiar $\sin(\varphi)/\varphi$ pattern. The sum signal in one coordinate will be

$$S_\Sigma(\varphi) = \frac{\sin(\varphi - \varphi_0)}{(\varphi - \varphi_0)} + \frac{\sin(\varphi + \varphi_0)}{(\varphi + \varphi_0)}$$ Eq. (10.14)

and the difference signal will be

$$S_\Delta(\varphi) = \frac{\sin(\varphi - \varphi_0)}{(\varphi - \varphi_0)} - \frac{\sin(\varphi + \varphi_0)}{(\varphi + \varphi_0)}$$ Eq. (10.15)

where φ_0 is the angular offset of the individual beam pattern to the radar LOS (the squint angle).

Figure 10.7 shows the pattern for two channels with a squint angle of 0.25 radians. Figure 10.8 shows the sum pattern and Fig. 10.9 the difference pattern. Figure 10.10 shows the difference to sum ratio.

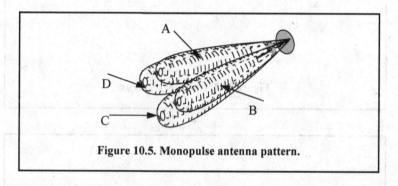

Figure 10.5. Monopulse antenna pattern.

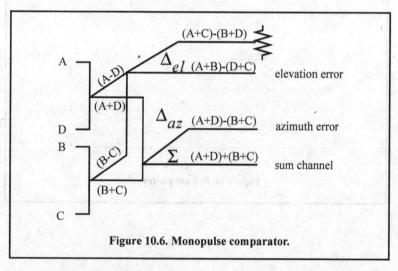

Figure 10.6. Monopulse comparator.

As we can see from the figures, the antenna pattern determines the shape of the sum and difference patterns. The slope of the linear region of the difference to sum ratio, often called the "error slope" determines the sensitivity of the measurement. If the slope is larger, the measurement will be more sensitive.

Development of the optimum monopulse design is a trade-off between design of the difference signal and the antenna sidelobe levels. In reflector antennas, the different receive channels are realized by offsetting feed antennas from the focal plane. As such, the sum and difference patterns are largely fixed and hence there is little ability to optimize both sidelobes and monopulse performance. However, in a phased array, the patterns can be synthesized independently, allowing for optimization.

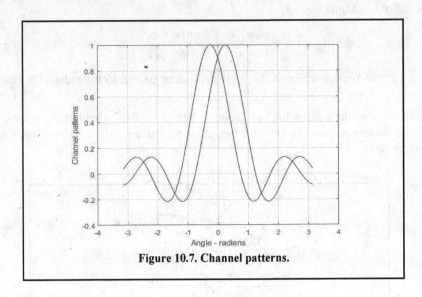

Figure 10.7. Channel patterns.

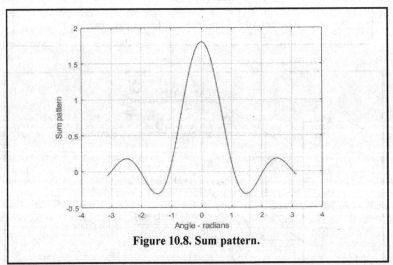

Figure 10.8. Sum pattern.

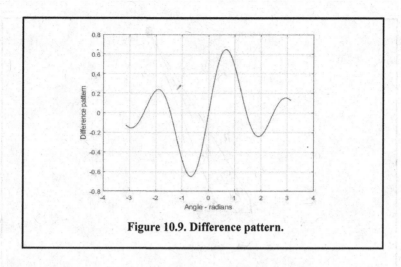

Figure 10.9. Difference pattern.

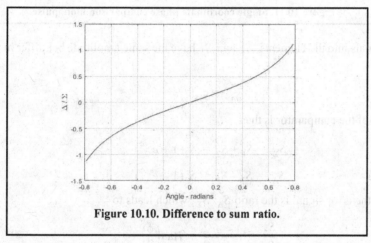

Figure 10.10. Difference to sum ratio.

Phase Comparison Monopulse

Phase comparison monopulse is similar to amplitude comparison, except the phase is now compared. From Fig. 10.11, one can see that phase length from the target to two offset antenna elements will only be the same if the target is on the antenna axis. If $d \ll R$, then

$$R_1 \approx R\left(1 + \frac{d}{2R}\sin\varphi\right)$$

Eq. (10.16)

and

$$R_2 \approx R\left(1 - \frac{d}{2R}\sin\varphi\right)$$

Eq. (10.17)

where d is the distance between the antenna elements and φ is the angle off the tracking axis. The phase length to the center of the elements is $(2\pi/\lambda R)$, where λ is the wavelength. It follows that the phase difference is simply

$$\phi = \frac{2\pi}{\lambda}(R_1 - R_2) = \frac{2\pi}{\lambda}\sin\varphi.$$

Eq. (10.18)

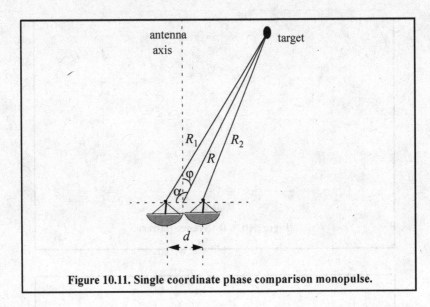

Figure 10.11. Single coordinate phase comparison monopulse.

If the signals into the elements, S_1 and S_2 have the same amplitude but differ in phase by ϕ, then,

$$S_1 = S_2 e^{-j\phi}.$$ **Eq. (10.19)**

The output of the comparator is then

$$S_\Sigma = S_1 + S_2 = S_2(1 + e^{-j\phi})$$
$$S_\Delta = S_1 - S_2 = S_2(1 - e^{-j\phi})$$ **Eq. (10.20)**

As before, the error signal is the ratio S_Δ / S_Σ, which leads to

$$\frac{S_\Delta}{S_\Sigma} = \frac{1 - e^{-j\phi}}{1 + e^{-j\phi}} = j\tan\left(\frac{\phi}{2}\right)$$ **Eq. (10.21)**

where clearly the magnitude of the error signal is

$$\left|\frac{S_\Delta}{S_\Sigma}\right| = \tan\left(\frac{\phi}{2}\right)$$ **Eq. (10.22)**

Again, the ratio S_Δ / S_Σ forms the error signal which is used to adjust the angle measurement.

Range Tracking and Measurements

True to its name, radio detection and ranging, the radar's measurement of range is fundamental. Electromagnetic waves travel at the speed of light, regardless of the wavelength. Therefore, the range of a target may be determined simply by the round trip time between the transmission and reception of a pulse. This time is

$$t_r = \frac{2R}{c}$$ **Eq. (10.23)**

where t_r is the round trip time, R is the range and c is the speed of light.

Modern digital radars sample the response of the system to the transmitted waveform. After the receive system has attempted to remove as much noise as possible, be this through matched filtering, or, in the case of pulse compressed waveforms, correlating the samples of the received waveform with stored samples of a "replica" of the transmitted waveform, the value of the samples represents the potential presence of a target at discrete points in time. Because of the relationship in Eq. (10.23), they also represent discrete points in range. Radars will collect samples from range windows, where the largest range window starts at the blind range and extends to the full range of the radar. Large range windows may be appropriate for some search functions, but typically tracking range windows are much smaller. A range cell is the smallest amount of range in which two targets are expected to be resolved. The range cell is determined by the bandwidth of the transmitted waveform and is usually reported as

$$\Delta R = c/2B \hspace{3cm} \textbf{Eq. (10.24)}$$

where B is the bandwidth of the transmitted waveform. One should note, however, that this value may increase (deteriorate) with the range sidelobe reduction techniques and other system factors. Radars will typically collect one or more samples per range cell. If the number is limited to one and the response of a point target is only in one range cell, then the target is located exactly at the center of the range cell. More typically, a point target will produce measurable responses in two adjacent cells, resulting in straddling loss. The situation is further complicated by the fact that nonpoint targets may produce detections in three or more bins.

Assuming a symmetrical pulse and at least one sample per resolution cell and that the return encompasses two or more consecutive cells, the range estimate can be improved upon by seeking the peak of the post-filtered (or compressed) pulse. If the number of samples is small, the simplest method would be a centroid tracker. The centroid is found in a region $p \in [R_1, R_2]$, for the sequence $x[p]$ by

$$C_x = \frac{\displaystyle\sum_{p=R_1}^{R_2} p\ x[p]}{\displaystyle\sum_{p=R_1}^{R_2} x[p]}. \hspace{3cm} \textbf{Eq. (10.25)}$$

If more samples or the entire envelope (in a digital or analog implementation) is available, then the range estimate may be improved by using a split gate system. In this scheme, two equally sized gates are switched at the expected maximum of the pulse envelope. The outputs of these gates are used to form sum and difference signals to create an error signal similar to that of monopulse. Figure 10.12 shows the block diagram for an analog implementation of split gate scheme. A digital implementation has more flexibility. Consider the noisy output of an envelope detected rectangular pulse as shown in Fig. 10.13 and having $20\,dB$ of SNR. The maximum of the "noiseless" pulse occurs at range sample 152. Now we convolve the noisy signal of pulse with the "early" and "late" gates which are superimposed in Fig. 10.14. Note that the late gate provides a negative signal. Figure 10.15 shows the output of the convolution. If we look for the zero crossing, we see that it is within a range cell of the true maximum. Now consider a detected pulse with only $6\,dB$ of SNR as shown in Fig. 10.16. The convolution of the noisy signal with the early and late gate shows a surprisingly clean signal. Despite a $14\,dB$ reduction in SNR, the zero crossing is within 2 range cells as shown in Fig. 10.17.

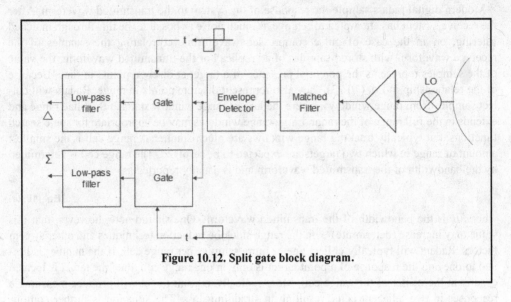

Figure 10.12. Split gate block diagram.

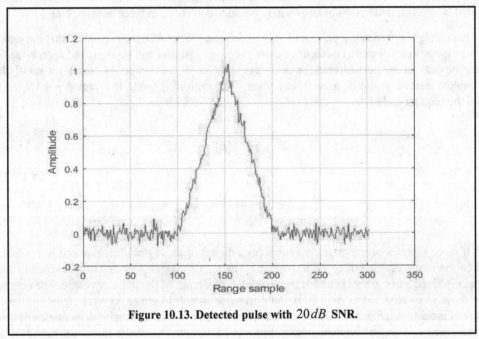

Figure 10.13. Detected pulse with $20\,dB$ SNR.

Measurement Accuracy

This section on measurements is concluded with a brief discussion of the accuracy of radar measurements. As observed in the previous example, the accuracy of the measurement is related to the SNR. Because noise is a random process, we can say that, in general, the standard deviation of the measurement follows the relationship

$$\sigma_m = \frac{\Delta_m}{k_m\sqrt{2SNR}},$$

Eq. (10.26)

where Δ_m is some form of the resolution of the measurement, such as the $3\,dB$ beamwidth of an antenna beam, or a range resolution cell. The factor k_m is a constant, but in the case of measurements that use the difference to sum error signal, k_m is related to the slope of the error signal in the linear region around the origin. The factor of 2 in the denominator is a recognition that most radar signals consist of 2 components, in-phase and quadrature, but only one of these affects the error signal.

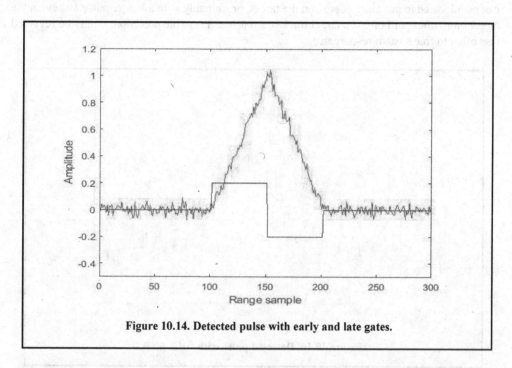

Figure 10.14. Detected pulse with early and late gates.

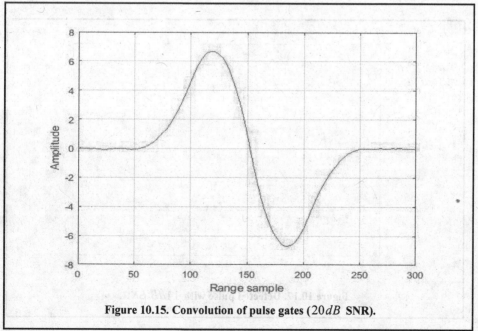

Figure 10.15. Convolution of pulse gates ($20\,dB$ SNR).

The resolution Δ_m is usually fixed by system design parameters, such as the size of the antenna or the maximum bandwidth of the receiver, but the SNR can be increased by placing more energy on the target. As we will see in subsequent sections, the other parameter that can be controlled dynamically and impacts tracking performance is the track revisit time, T_s. Therefore, the radar system can dynamically allocate resources to different tracks based on need and availability. If a track needs to have its state estimate error reduced quickly, resources can be allocated to put more energy on the target, presumably with a longer pulse, or revisit the target more often, or both. If a target track has reached a suitable precision, it may be revisited less often to free system resources.

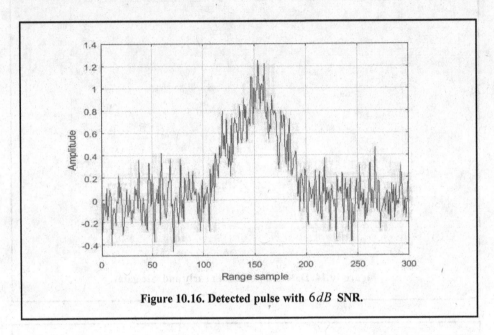

Figure 10.16. Detected pulse with $6\,dB$ SNR.

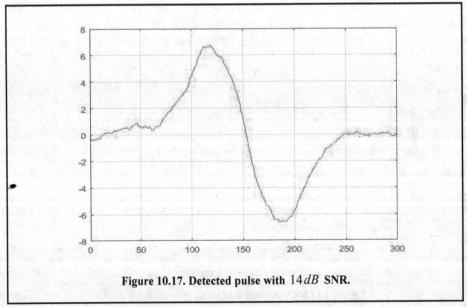

Figure 10.17. Detected pulse with $14\,dB$ SNR.

10.4. Filtering

After a measurement has been made, it must be associated with a track, or a new track can be started and the state estimate can be updated. A discussion of data association is provided later in this chapter. Once the measurements have been associated with a track, the track is "filtered" to remove the measurement noise. The workhorse of track filtering is the Kalman filter, which has its roots in least squares estimation. Least squares is examined first.

10.4.1. Least Squares

Assume that it is desired to estimate the value of a single parameter from several noisy measurements. If the estimate is made from all the measurements at one time, versus recursively, it is referred to as "batch processing". For demonstration, assume the parameter is the velocity of the target and that it stays constant over the course of N measurements and that we are measuring the velocity directly. The error would be $z_i - v$ for the ith measurement z_i, where v is the true target velocity. What is desired is to find an estimate of the velocity, $\hat{v}$, that minimizes the error in a least squares sense. That is, we want to minimize the value of the sum of the square of the errors the estimate incurs from the measurements, B, given by,

$$B = \sum_{i=1}^{N} (z_i - \hat{v})^2 .$$

Eq. (10.27)

Said another way, one wants to find the value $\hat{v}$ such that B is minimized over the measurements that have been taken. To find $\hat{v}$, take the derivative of B with respect to $\hat{v}$ and set it to zero. More specifically,

$$-N\hat{v} + \sum_{i=1}^{N} z_i = 0 .$$

Eq. (10.28)

Solving for $\hat{v}$, we obtain

$$\hat{v} = \frac{1}{N} \sum_{i=1}^{N} z_i .$$

Eq. (10.29)

Equation (10.29) provides the intuitive result that the estimate is the average value of the measurements. Now assume we want to solve for a multi-state vector instead of a scalar, but once again assume the vector is constant.

As an example, consider a target moving in one dimension with constant velocity. The measurements are both the position and the velocity of the target at various points in time. The constant vector is

$$\mathbf{x} = \begin{bmatrix} x_0 \\ v_0 \end{bmatrix} .$$

Eq. (10.30)

The relationship between the state vector and the measurements must be defined. If this relationship is linear, it may described in a matrix $\mathbf{H}$. For the two state constant vector of the example, both the position and the velocity of the target are measured, so

$$H = \begin{bmatrix} 1 & t_i \\ 0 & 1 \\ \cdot & \cdot \\ 1 & t_M \\ 0 & 1 \end{bmatrix}$$ **Eq. (10.31)**

where t_i is the time of the ith measurement and M is the total number of measurements. In general, if the size of the state vector is N and the number of measurements per observation (or "looks") is $p \leq N$, then the size of H is $N \times pM$.

The measurement model is

$$z = Hx + e$$ **Eq. (10.32)**

where z is the vector containing the actual measurements and e is the error vector, which we assume to be zero mean. Rearranging Eq. (10.32), the error vector is

$$e = z - Hx.$$ **Eq. (10.33)**

As it was for the scalar case, it is once again desired to find an estimate of x, $\hat{x}$ that minimizes, in the least square sense. More precisely,

$$B = (z-H\hat{x})^{\dagger}(z-H\hat{x}).$$ **Eq. (10.34)**

Note that the value B is a scalar. To minimize B, the properties of the derivative of a scalar with respect to a vector are utilized. Start by expanding B as

$$B = (z-H\hat{x})^{\dagger}(z-H\hat{x}) = z^{\dagger}z - (z^{\dagger}(H\hat{x})-(H\hat{x})^{\dagger}z + (H\hat{x})^{\dagger}(H\hat{x}))$$ **Eq. (10.35)**

Now take the partial derivative of B with respect to $\hat{x}$ and set it to zero,

$$\frac{\partial B}{\partial \hat{x}} = 0 - H^{\dagger}z - H^{\dagger}z + 2H^{\dagger}H\hat{x}$$ **Eq. (10.36)**

it follows that

$$0 = -H^{\dagger}z - H^{\dagger}z + 2H^{\dagger}H\hat{x}$$ **Eq. (10.37)**

and finally,

$$\hat{x} = (H^{\dagger}H)^{-1} H^{\dagger}z.$$ **Eq. (10.38)**

If the estimate $\hat{x}$ is unbiased, then the expected value of $\hat{x}$ is x. Using Eq. (10.32) in Eq. (10.38) yields,

$$E[\hat{x}] = E[(H^{\dagger}H)^{-1}H^{\dagger}(Hx + e)] = x + (H^{\dagger}H)^{-1}H^{\dagger}E[e] = x.$$ **Eq. (10.39)**

This is true because the error e is zero mean. The state estimate error is now given by

$$e_x = x - \hat{x}.$$ **Eq. (10.40)**

One can easily show that the expected value of the state estimate error is zero. But what about the covariance? Because our only assumption for e was that it was zero mean, we do not have enough information to obtain an accurate estimate of the state estimate error covariance. So far, all measurements have been treated equally, but what if each measurement was weighted, we now have the ability to obtain the state estimate error covariance.

If the measurements are to be weighted, then it can be shown that the equation to be minimized is

$$B = (z-H\hat{x})^\dagger W(z-H\hat{x})$$

Eq. (10.41)

where W is a square matrix that contains the weights of each measurement. If we assume that all the measurements are uncorrelated, then matrix W will be a diagonal matrix. Using the same procedure used in computing Eq. (10.38), the estimate is

$$\hat{x} = (H^\dagger WH)^{-1} H^\dagger Wz.$$

Eq. (10.42)

It follows that the covariance of the state estimate error is

$$P = E[e_x e_x^\dagger] = (H^\dagger WH)^{-1}(H^\dagger W)E[ee^\dagger](WH)(H^\dagger WH)^{-1}.$$

Eq. (10.43)

Define

$$R = E[ee^\dagger]$$

Eq. (10.44)

and let $W = R^{-1}$, then the state estimate error covariance becomes

$$P = (H^\dagger R^{-1}H)^{-1}.$$

Eq. (10.45)

Returning to the earlier example, assume that there are three "looks", each of which produces a position and·velocity measurement. Assume that these looks are 1 second apart. The measurement matrix H is

$$H = \begin{bmatrix} 1 & 1 \\ 0 & 1 \\ 1 & 2 \\ 0 & 1 \\ 1 & 3 \\ 0 & 1 \end{bmatrix}.$$

Eq. (10.46)

Assume the constant state vector to be estimated is $x = \begin{bmatrix} 5 & 2 \end{bmatrix}^\dagger$, which from Eq. (10.30) corresponds to the initial position and initial velocity. The measurement vector is $z = [Z_{x_1} \ Z_{v_1} ... Z_{x_3} \ Z_{v_3}]^\dagger$ where Z_{x_i} and Z_{v_i} are the ith measurements of position and velocity, respectively. From the truth model, measurements can be taken from

$$z = Hx + e.$$

Eq. (10.47)

The assumed position and velocity measurements are Gaussian distributed with $\sigma_p^2 = 2$ for the position measurement and $\sigma_v^2 = 3$ for the velocity measurement, the weights matrix is

$$R = W^{-1} = \begin{bmatrix} 2 & 0 & 0 & 0 & 0 & 0 \\ 0 & 3 & 0 & 0 & 0 & 0 \\ 0 & 0 & 2 & 0 & 0 & 0 \\ 0 & 0 & 0 & 3 & 0 & 0 \\ 0 & 0 & 0 & 0 & 2 & 0 \\ 0 & 0 & 0 & 0 & 0 & 3 \end{bmatrix}$$

Eq. (10.48)

Once again, the off diagonal terms indicate that the measurements are uncorrelated between position and velocity measurements and look to look. Also, because the measurements are Gaussian distributed, this ensures that the estimate is also Gaussian distributed. Using the measurement matrix **H** and measurement covariance matrix **R** from the example, Eq. (10.45) can be used to find the covariance matrix **P** of the estimate, which is

$$
\mathbf{P} = \begin{bmatrix} \dfrac{8}{3} & -1 \\ -1 & \dfrac{1}{2} \end{bmatrix}.
$$
                                                                                    Eq. (10.49)

The covariance matrix **P** describes the spread of the state estimate error based on the noisy measurements. If **H** and **R** from the example are utilized in Eq. (10.42) ten thousand times using sample measurements from Eq. (10.47) with variances described in the example, the distribution of the state estimate error $\mathbf{e_x}$ is shown Fig. 10.18. Also shown in Fig. 10.18 is a 99.9% confidence ellipse drawn from the eigenvalues of **P**. As expected, only about 0.1% of the ten thousand estimate errors falls outside the confidence ellipse. Clearly the spread of the estimate errors is related to the area of the ellipse. The volume of an ellipsoid is proportional to the product of the axes of the ellipse. This value is equal to the determinant of the covariance matrix **P**. Therefore, the determinant of **P** is commonly used as a single measure of the spread of the distribution.

Before leaving this example, we note that there are two parameters which impact the determinant of **P**, the number of measurements and span of time in which the measurements are taken. Assume that all measurements are equally spaced and that the only change is the number of measurements, N, or the time span, T. Figure 10.19 shows how the determinant of **P** decreases with an increasing N for $T = 20 \, \text{sec}$. This figure shows that the determinant of **P** will asymptotically approach zero as N is increased. A physical interpretation is that an increase of N drives down the variance of the estimate by averaging out the variations in the measurements (whose errors are zero mean), similar to improving the SNR by using coherent integration for a radar measurement.

Figure 10.19 also shows how the determinant of **P** decreases with increased T for $N = 20$. A physical interpretation is less intuitive. One such interpretation is that as the span of measurement time is increased, the model that has been utilized for the target motion, which is deterministic and represented in the measurement matrix **H**, reduces the variance of the estimate by limiting the "fit" of the model through the noisy measurements. This is more easily illustrated by considering the estimate of the slope of a line based on two noisy measurements. The slope would be calculated by the "rise over the run." As run is increased, the variance in the rise is of less importance to the fit, and the variance of the estimate is reduced. This can also be shown by taking the variance of the equation for the slope of the line and applying the properties of variance.

10.4.2. Recursive Least Squares

One problem with the procedure from the previous section is that if another measurement is received, Eq. (10.42) must be rerun. This can be computationally expensive, especially as the number of measurements becomes large. Assume that k measurements have been taken and that an estimate and a covariance matrix have been created using Eqs. (10.42) and (10.45), respectively. Call these $\hat{\mathbf{x}}(k)$ and $\mathbf{P}(k)$. Given one more measurement, it is desired to update the estimate and the covariance. The state equations are (see Section 10.5 for the derivation)

$$
\hat{\mathbf{x}}(k+1) = \hat{\mathbf{x}}(k) + \mathbf{K}(k+1)\{\mathbf{z}(k+1) - \mathbf{H}((k+1)\hat{\mathbf{x}}(k))\}
$$
                                                                                    Eq. (10.50)

$$K(k+1) = P(k)H^\dagger(k+1)C^{-1}(k+1) \qquad \text{Eq. (10.51)}$$

$$C(k+1) = H(k+1)P(k)H^\dagger(k+1) + R(k+1) \qquad \text{Eq. (10.52)}$$

$$P(k+1) = [I - K(k+1)H(k+1)]P(k). \qquad \text{Eq. (10.53)}$$

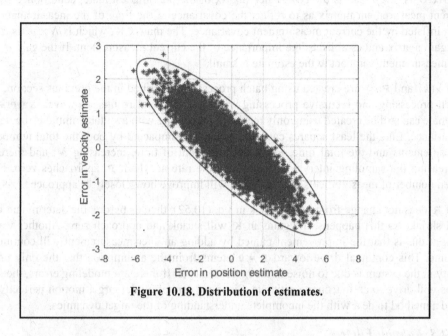

Figure 10.18. Distribution of estimates.

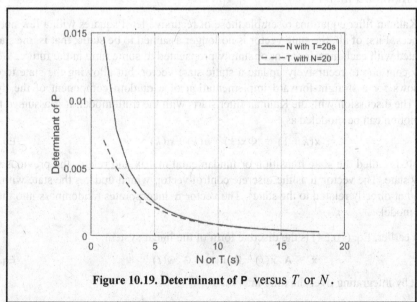

Figure 10.19. Determinant of P versus T or N.

Note that, aside from the additional equations, the formulation of Eqs. (10.50) through (10.53) are different than those of Eqs. (10.42) and (10.45) in that the vectors and matrices are on a "per look" basis, the vector z has a length of p and H is $N \times p$. The covariance matrix of the measurements, R, is still the inverse of W and is $p \times p$. As before, P is $N \times N$. While the matrix C is $p \times p$ and is the covariance matrix of the previous estimate, conditioned by the current measurement matrix as to reflect the covariance at the time of the measurement and then inflated by the current measurement covariance. The matrix K, which is $N \times p$, is called the gain matrix and establishes the importance of the current measurement. If the gain is low, the measurement's impact to the estimate is small.

If $\hat{x}(k)$ and $P(k)$ are created using batch processing described in the previous section, then batch processing and recursive processing will yield identical results. However, a workable estimate can still be created using only recursive processing with a suitable initial estimate and covariance. Like the least squares case, the estimate is impacted by both the total number of measurements and the total time. For a given amount of time, increasing N, and therefore decreasing the sampling interval, will increase the rate at which P approaches zero. For a given number of measurements, increasing T will improve how closely P approaches zero.

If R does not change from look to look in Eq. (10.52), then as before, the determinant of P will shrink. As this happens, the gains in K will shrink and approach zero. Another way to look at this is that the improvement gained by adding another measurement will continually decline. This continual drive toward $P = 0$ stems from the assumption that the only uncertainty in the system is due to noise in the measurements. If there are modeling errors, the solutions will drive to an inaccurate estimate. Since we cannot model target motion perfectly, we need a method to deal with the incomplete understanding of the target dynamics.

10.4.3. Kalman Filter

The Kalman filter equations resemble those of recursive least squares with a few noticeable differences. First of all, the state vector is no longer assumed to be static; that is, the state may be updated with each measurement or simply propagated to some time in the future. We could actually continue to recursively update a static state vector, but allowing the state to change also allows for a straight-forward implementation of a random component of the dynamic model. The discussion with the Kalman filter starts with the truth model. It is assumed that the target motion can be modeled as

$$x(k+1) = \Phi x(k) + u(k) + q(k) \qquad \text{Eq. (10.54)}$$

where Φ is called the state transition or fundamental matrix and relates the previous state to the new state. The vector u is the discrete control vector, which updates the state with effects that are not directly related to the state[1]. The vector q incorporates randomness into the target motion model.

From earlier, Eq. (10.54) is the discrete form of the linear system

$$\dot{x} = A\ x(t) + B\ u(t) + G\ w(t) \qquad \text{Eq. (10.55)}$$

and that by integrating over the time interval T_s

$$\Phi = e^{At} \qquad \text{Eq. (10.56)}$$

---

1. For example, for a target dynamics model that includes the impact of acceleration on a state vector that only includes position and velocity.

$$u(k) = \int_{(k-1)T_s}^{kT_s} e^{\mathbf{A}(kT-\tau)} \mathbf{B}\ u(\tau)\ d\tau.$$ Eq. (10.57)

The new term in Eq. (10.55) is $\mathbf{G}\ \mathbf{w}(t)$ where $\mathbf{w}(t)$ is a vector of zero mean white Gaussian random processes. This is what separates recursive least squares from the Kalman filter by allowing for randomness in the truth model. The discrete value $\mathbf{q}$ is found the same way as the discrete control vector, that is

$$\mathbf{q}(k) = \int_{(k-1)T_s}^{kT_s} e^{\mathbf{A}(kT_s-\tau)} \mathbf{G}\ \mathbf{w}(\tau)\ d\tau.$$ Eq. (10.58)

It is assumed that $E[\mathbf{w}] = \mathbf{0}$ and

$$E[\mathbf{w}(t)\mathbf{w}^{\dagger}(\tau)] = Q_s\delta(t-\tau)$$ Eq. (10.59)

where Q_s is the power spectral density, and since $E[\mathbf{q}] = \mathbf{0}$ then

$$E[\mathbf{q}(k)\mathbf{q}^{\dagger}(j)] = \mathbf{Q}(k)\delta_{kj} \qquad ;for\ any\ (k,j)$$ Eq. (10.60)

and δ_{kj} is the Kronecker delta function. Using Eq. (10.58) in Eq. (10.60) yields,

$$\mathbf{Q}(k) = E[\mathbf{q}(k)\mathbf{q}^{\dagger}(k)] = E\left[\int_{(k-1)T_s}^{kT_s} \Phi(\lambda)\mathbf{G}(\lambda)\mathbf{w}(\lambda)d\lambda \int_{(k-1)T_s}^{kT_s} \mathbf{w}^{\dagger}(\xi)\mathbf{G}^{\dagger}(\xi)\Phi^{\dagger}(\zeta)d\xi\right]$$ Eq. (10.61)

$$= E\left[\left(\int_{(k-1)T_s}^{kT_s} \Phi(\lambda)\mathbf{G}(\lambda)\mathbf{w}(\lambda)\right)\left(\int_{(k-1)T_s}^{kT_s} \mathbf{w}^{\dagger}(\xi)\mathbf{G}^{\dagger}(\xi)\Phi^{\dagger}(\xi)d\zeta\right)d\lambda\right]$$

but because $E[\mathbf{w}(t)\mathbf{w}^{\dagger}(\lambda)] = \mathbf{0}$, for $t \neq \lambda$, then Eq. (10.61) reduces to a single integral. More precisely,

$$\mathbf{Q}(k) = \int_{(k-1)T_s}^{kT_s} \Phi(\lambda)\mathbf{G}(\lambda)E[\mathbf{w}(\lambda)\mathbf{w}^{\dagger}(\lambda)]\mathbf{G}^{\dagger}(\lambda)\Phi^{\dagger}(\lambda)d\lambda = .$$ Eq. (10.62)

$$\int_{(k-1)T_s}^{kT_s} \Phi(\lambda)\mathbf{G}(\lambda)Q_s\mathbf{G}^{\dagger}(\lambda)\Phi^{\dagger}(\lambda)d\lambda$$

The Kalman filter will have the same measurement model as least squares, which is

$$\mathbf{z} = \mathbf{Hx} + \mathbf{e}.$$ Eq. (10.63)

where $\mathbf{e}$ is a zero mean Gaussian measurement noise that is assumed to have a known covariance matrix

$$R = E[\mathbf{ee}^{\dagger}].$$ Eq. (10.64)

There is also another difference in implementation versus the static state vector case. With the static state vector, the matrix $\mathbf{H}$ must account for the time variations of the dynamics model. With the dynamic state, these time variations are built into the fundamental matrix. The Kalman filtering is performed in three steps. These multiple steps require the introduction of additional notation. The first step is that a new state is predicted based solely on the transition matrix and control vector, if included in the model. This new state should be propagated to the time in which a measurement will be made. The notation for this propagated, but not "filtered" state estimate is $\hat{\mathbf{x}}(k+1|k)$. The covariance for this prediction is $\mathbf{P}(k+1|k)$. The equations for the prediction step are

$$\hat{x}(k+1|k) = \Phi x(k|k) + u(k) \qquad \text{Eq. (10.65)}$$

$$P(k+1|k) = \Phi P(k|k)\Phi^\dagger + Q(k). \qquad \text{Eq. (10.66)}$$

Since the process noise represents the uncertainty in our dynamics model, it is intuitive that the impact of the process noise is to inflate the covariance P by Q at each time step.

Before the next measurement is incorporated into the estimate of the state, the gain matrix K must be calculated using the relation

$$K(k+1) = P(k+1|k)H^\dagger(k+1)C^{-1}(k+1) \qquad \text{Eq. (10.67)}$$

where

$$C(k+1) = H(k+1)P(k+1|k)H^\dagger(k+1) + R(k+1). \qquad \text{Eq. (10.68)}$$

The filtered estimate, which would now include the impact of the latest measurement is

$$\hat{x}(k+1|k+1) = \hat{x}(k+1|k) + K(k)\{z(k+1) - H(k+1)\hat{x}(k+1|k)\} \qquad \text{Eq. (10.69)}$$

Finally, the covariance for the filtered estimate is

$$P(k+1|k+1) = \{I - K(k+1)H(k+1)\}P(k+1|k) \qquad \text{Eq. (10.70)}$$

where I is the identity matrix. Expanding Eq. (10.69) yields

$$\hat{x}(k+1|k+1) = \hat{x}(k+1|k) + K(k)z(k+1) - K(k)H(k+1)\hat{x}(k+1|k) \qquad \text{Eq. (10.71)}$$

The components of the matrix K will, at any time, be between zero and 1. If the gain is high, the propagated estimate will be largely removed and the new estimate will more closely resemble the measurement. Conversely, if the gain is very low, the measurement will be largely ignored and the new estimate will be calculated from the dynamics model.

Before walking through an example, it is worth noting that there may be conditions where the computational stability of Eq. (10.70) may become poor. In this case, an alternative version may be developed by recognizing that

$$P(k+1|k+1) = COV\{x(k+1) - \hat{x}(k+1|k+1)\} \qquad \text{Eq. (10.72)}$$

and inserting Eq. (10.69) yields,

$$P(k+1|k+1) = [I - K(k+1)H]P(k+1|k) \qquad \text{Eq. (10.73)}$$
$$[I - K(k+1)H]^\dagger + K(k+1)RK^\dagger(k+1)$$

For example, first consider the one-dimensional case (i.e., two state filter). The state elements will be position x and velocity v. The linear time domain expression for this system is

$$\dot{x} = Ax \qquad \text{Eq. (10.74)}$$

where

$$A = \begin{bmatrix} 0 & 1 \\ 0 & 0 \end{bmatrix}. \qquad \text{Eq. (10.75)}$$

The time domain state transition matrix is

$$\Phi(t) = e^{At} \qquad \text{Eq. (10.76)}$$

and the discrete state transition matrix can be found by taking the Taylor expansion of Eq. (10.76) for $t = T_s$; it follows,

$$\Phi(t) = e^{\mathbf{A}T_s} = I + \mathbf{A}T_s = \begin{bmatrix} 1 & T_s \\ 0 & 1 \end{bmatrix} \qquad \text{Eq. (10.77)}$$

which is the exact solution because all higher order terms are zero.

For this filter, we will only measure the position **x** of the target with a measurement variance of $\sigma_m = 1$. The process noise enters the state as

$$\frac{dv}{dt} = w(t) \qquad \text{Eq. (10.78)}$$

and the covariance matrix **Q** for **q** is (using Eq. (10.62))

$$\mathbf{Q}(k) = \int_0^{T_s} \begin{bmatrix} 0 & \lambda \\ 0 & 1 \end{bmatrix} \begin{bmatrix} 0 \\ 1 \end{bmatrix} Q_s \begin{bmatrix} 0 & 1 \end{bmatrix} \begin{bmatrix} 0 & 1 \\ \lambda & 0 \end{bmatrix} d\lambda = Q_s \begin{bmatrix} \dfrac{T_s^3}{3} & \dfrac{T_s^2}{2} \\ \dfrac{T_s^2}{2} & T_s \end{bmatrix}. \qquad \text{Eq. (10.79)}$$

Truth will be taken from Eq. (10.54) with $Q_s = [0, 0.1, 1, 10]$. The time step is *1 sec*. The initial state estimate error covariance **P** is greatly inflated to

$$\mathbf{P} = \begin{bmatrix} 100 & 0 \\ 0 & 10 \end{bmatrix} \qquad \text{Eq. (10.80)}$$

and for convenience, $\hat{\mathbf{x}}(0) = \mathbf{x}(0)$. Figure 10.20 shows the state estimate error for the first element of the state vector, the target position, with $Q_s = 10$. Figure 10.20 is not particularly useful except to show that indeed the state estimate error appears to have a zero mean and provides a qualitative view of the variance. Figure 10.21 shows the variance of the first element of the state estimate error, that is, $P(1, 1)$ for $Q_s = [0, 0.1, 1, 10]$. For the $Q_s = 0$ case, that is, no process noise and no randomness in the model, the variance approaches zero as time increases just as it does for the least squares approach. When randomness is introduced to the model, $P(1, 1)$ no longer approaches zero but achieves a steady state value that increases with increasing Q_s. If one were to increase Q_s further, it could see that $P(1, 1)$ would approach the measurement variance, σ_m^2.

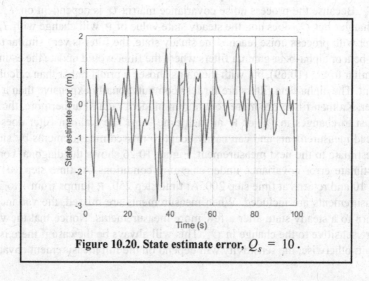

Figure 10.20. State estimate error, $Q_s = 10$.

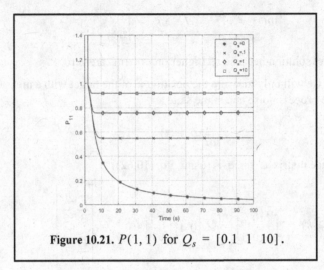

Figure 10.21. $P(1, 1)$ for $Q_S = [0.1 \quad 1 \quad 10]$.

If the uncertainty increases with Q_s, it would be understandable to ask the question, "why use process noise at all?" The problem is that the target dynamics cannot be modeled perfectly. Consider the case where the truth is taken from Eq. (10.54), but no process noise is included in the filter. Figure 10.22 shows the predicted error of the position state, $P(1, 1)$, as expected, approaches zero. However, we can see the actual state estimate error continues to increase as the filter diverges. Since we cannot create a fully deterministic model of the target motion, the inclusion of process noise allows us to account for this uncertainty and bound the error. Like the covariance, the Kalman gain will also no longer approach zero when process noise is included. Figure 10.23 shows the Kalman gain for the position state. As the process noise goes up, so does the steady state Kalman gain. With $Q_s = 10$, the filter is largely ignoring the model and updating the state based solely on the measurement. Figure 10.24 shows the Kalman gain for different values of the measurement covariance with $Q_s = 1$. As expected, the gain goes down with increasing **R** as the filter is putting less weight on the measurements.

As with RLS, increasing the sampling rate will increase the rate at which the estimate approaches steady state. However, unlike RLS, where the covariance approaches zero, the sampling rate will also impact the steady state value. Figure 10.25 shows $P(1, 1)$ for different values of T_s. Because the process noise covariance matrix **Q** is dependent on T_s, if the sampling rate changes but Q_s does not, the steady state value of **P** will change with T_s. When the Kalman filter with process noise reaches the steady state, the filter is very similar to that of the older alpha-beta or alpha-beta-gamma filters where the filter would update the estimate with an equation similar to Eq. (10.69), but with the gains chosen a priori rather than calculated at each measurement. The alpha-beta filters are far less computationally expensive than a Kalman filter. However, Kalman filters are more common in modern radar. Furthermore, the Kalman filter can adjust to changes in Q_s or **R** at each time step. The Kalman filter does not require evenly spaced measurements and can easily adapt to missed measurements by simply propagating the estimate to the next measurement. Figure 10.26 shows the diagonal components of the state estimate error covariance under changing conditions. At time step 101, Q_s jumps from 0.1 to 10 and returns at time step 200. At time step 250, **R** jumps from 1 to 2 and sets of missed measurements are included. When measurements are missed, the variance will jump up, but return to a steady state after a few more measurements. Notice that the velocity estimate is more sensitive to the change in Q_s. This will always be the case if there is no velocity measurement; otherwise, the sensitivity will depend on the full measurement covariance **R**.

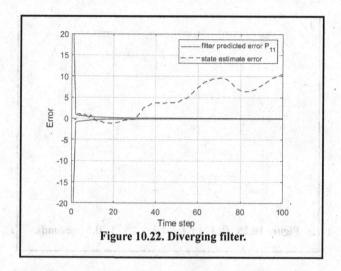

Figure 10.22. Diverging filter.

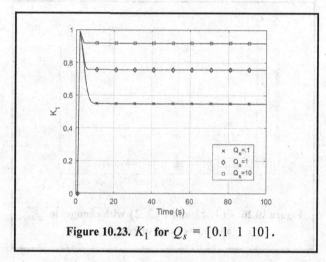

Figure 10.23. K_1 for $Q_s = [0.1 \ 1 \ 10]$.

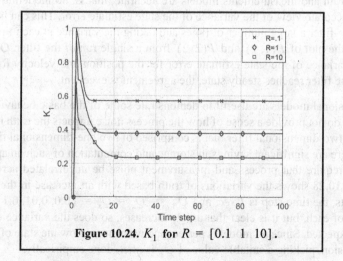

Figure 10.24. K_1 for $R = [0.1 \ 1 \ 10]$.

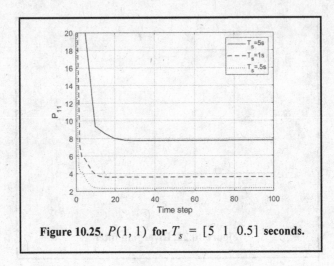

Figure 10.25. $P(1, 1)$ for $T_s = [5 \ 1 \ 0.5]$ seconds.

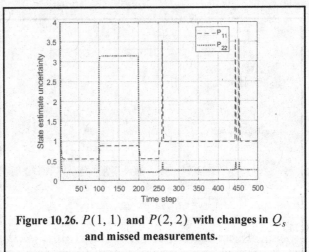

Figure 10.26. $P(1, 1)$ and $P(2, 2)$ with changes in Q_s and missed measurements.

When the truth and measurements models are accurate, that is, no modeling errors, **P** provides a very accurate view of the variance of the state estimate error. This can be easily shown by running the filter a large number of times and taking the variance at each time step. Figure 10.27 shows the plot of $P(1, 1)$ and $P(2, 2)$ from a single run of the filter. Overlaid are the plots of the variance of the state estimate error for the position and velocity for ten thousand runs. When the filter reaches steady state, the agreement is excellent.

One-dimensional models are useful to demonstrate some of the basic behaviors of the Kalman filter but do not provide a sense of how the process noise impacts the truth model. Now let us consider a two-dimensional filter that is comprised of two one-dimensional filters. It is easy to see that there are significant savings in storage and computation of such an approach. However, it does require that process and measurement noise be uncorrelated across the dimensions. Figure 10.28 shows the variations of truth based with an increase in the process noise. For these plots, the time step is *1 sec*, and $Q_{B's} = Q_x = Q_s = \{0.0, 0.01, 0.1\}$. This is only one instance of each, but it is clear that as Q_s increases, so does the variance of position and velocity, as expected. Since no model is perfect and we cannot know the state of the target with in finite precision, picking a suitable value of Q_s is often done empirically.

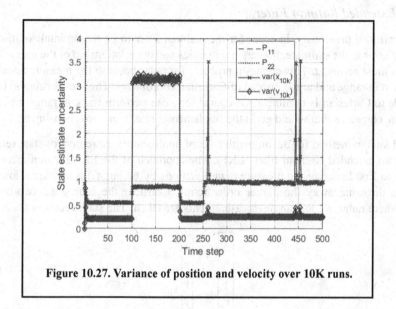

Figure 10.27. Variance of position and velocity over 10K runs.

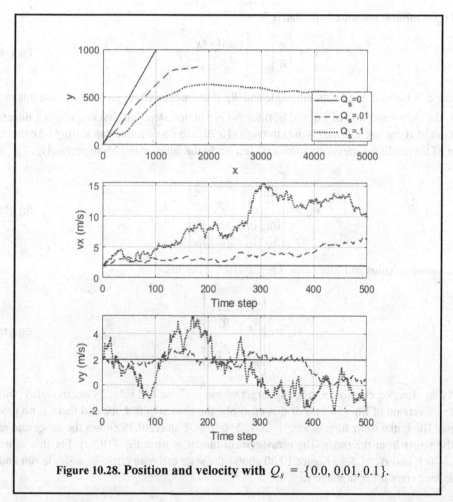

Figure 10.28. Position and velocity with $Q_s = \{0.0, 0.01, 0.1\}$.

10.4.4. Extended Kalman Filter

As mentioned previously, in order for the Kalman filter to be the optimal solution to drive down the error in the estimate, the target dynamics and the relationship of the measurements to the states must be linear. This creates a problem for radar because the measurements are most often taken in range and angle instead of Cartesian coordinates. The transformation from range and angle to Cartesian is nonlinear. Of course, one can perform track in range and angle, but the update equations that would go in the fundamental matrix are now non-linear.

A well-known method for dealing with a set of nonlinear measurement or state relationships is to use an extended Kalman filter (EKF). The approach of the EKF for nonlinear measurements is to first linearize the measurement equations by taking a Taylor expansion about the state and throwing away the higher order terms. Consider the four state, two-dimensional tracker where range R_r and angle measurements are taken. The state vector is

$$\mathbf{x} = \begin{bmatrix} x \\ v_x \\ y \\ v_y \end{bmatrix} = \begin{bmatrix} x \\ \dot{x} \\ y \\ \dot{y} \end{bmatrix}$$

Eq. (10.81)

and the nonlinear measurement matrix is

$$\mathbf{x} = \begin{bmatrix} \phi \\ R_r \end{bmatrix} = \begin{bmatrix} \mathrm{atan}(y/x) \\ \sqrt{x^2 + y^2} \end{bmatrix}$$

Eq. (10.82)

where ϕ is the measured azimuth angle and R_r is the measured range. One can use this matrix (i.e., the right-hand side of Eq. (10.82)) for the prediction step, but first one needs a linearized version of $\mathbf{H}$ for use in Eqs. (10.67) through (10.70). To do this, one can simply take the Jacobian of the nonlinear transformation with respect to the entire state. More precisely,

$$\mathbf{H_x} = \begin{bmatrix} \dfrac{\partial \phi}{\partial x} & \dfrac{\partial \phi}{\partial \dot{x}} & \dfrac{\partial \phi}{\partial y} & \dfrac{\partial \phi}{\partial \dot{y}} \\[2mm] \dfrac{\partial R_r}{\partial x} & \dfrac{\partial R_r}{\partial \dot{x}} & \dfrac{\partial R_r}{\partial y} & \dfrac{\partial R_r}{\partial \dot{y}} \end{bmatrix}.$$

Eq. (10.83)

After some calculus and some cleanup, Eq. (10.83) becomes

$$\mathbf{H_x} = \begin{bmatrix} \dfrac{-y}{R_r^2} & 0 & \dfrac{x}{R_r^2} & 0 \\[3mm] \dfrac{x}{R_r^2} & 0 & \dfrac{y}{R_r^2} & 0 \end{bmatrix}$$

Eq. (10.84)

As an example, consider a crossing target whose position and velocity are modeled with the discrete version of Eq. (10.1). For this example, the time step is *1 sec* and there is no process noise. The initial truth state is $\mathbf{x} = [-200 \ \ 2 \ \ 0 \ \ 0]^\dagger$. Figure 10.29 shows the range and angle to the target from the radar. The measurement model is from Eq. (10.32). For this example, $\sigma_\phi = 0.1$ and $\sigma_r = 5.5$. Figure 10.30 shows the state estimate error for a single run and the estimated error for both x and y.

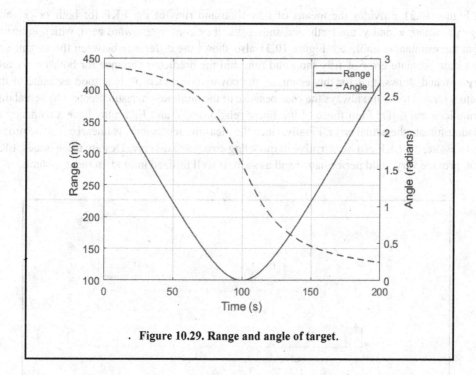

Figure 10.29. Range and angle of target.

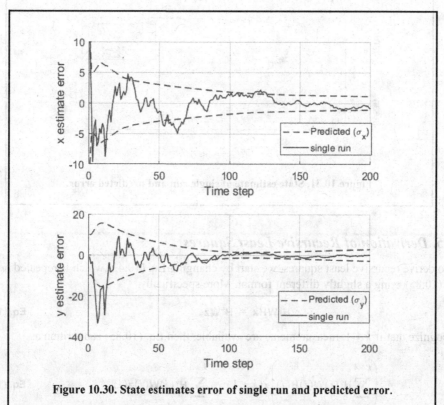

Figure 10.30. State estimates error of single run and predicted error.

Figure 10.31 provides the means of fifty thousand runs of the EKF for both $(\mathbf{x} - \hat{\mathbf{x}})$ and $(\mathbf{y} - \hat{\mathbf{y}})$, where $\mathbf{x}$ and $\mathbf{y}$ are truth, and shows that they converge toward zero, which indicates that the estimate is unbiased. Figure 10.31 also shows the difference between the variance of the state estimate error of fifty thousand runs and the predicted variance for both $(\mathbf{x} - \hat{\mathbf{x}})$ and $(\mathbf{y} - \hat{\mathbf{y}})$ and shows, that for this example, the covariance matrix $\mathbf{P}$ is a good estimate of the actual error. This is not always the case because of the nonlinear measurements. The actual distributions can differ from those of the linear relationships, and EKF may have a tendency to underestimate the actual error. Finally, since the measurement matrix is linearized at the propagated state, the EKF can be sensitive to modeling errors and diverge. Despite these issues, EKF can provide very good performance and as such, is well utilized in modern radar systems.

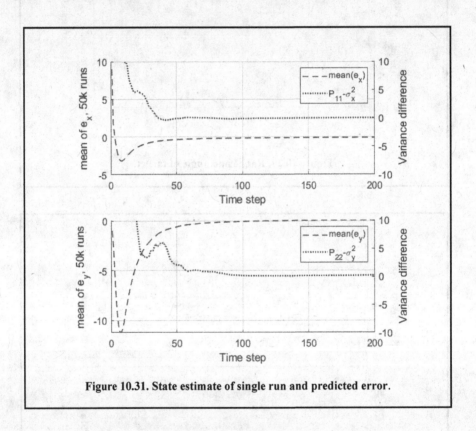

Figure 10.31. State estimate of single run and predicted error.

10.5. Derivation of Recursive Least Squares

To derive recursive least squares, we start by changing Eq. (10.42), which is repeated here as Eq. (10.85) using a slightly different format. More specifically,

$$\mathbf{H}^\dagger \mathbf{W} \mathbf{H} \hat{\mathbf{x}} = \mathbf{H}^\dagger \mathbf{W} \mathbf{z}. \qquad \text{Eq. (10.85)}$$

Recognize that if $k + 1$ measurements are available, then Eq. (10.85) can written as

$$\left(\sum_{i=1}^{k+1} \mathbf{H}^\dagger(i) \mathbf{W}(i) \mathbf{H}(i) \right) \hat{\mathbf{x}}(k+1) = \sum_{i=1}^{k+1} \mathbf{H}^\dagger(i) \mathbf{W}(i) \mathbf{z}(i) \qquad \text{Eq. (10.86)}$$

where the i denotes the portion of the **H** or **W** matrices for the measurement at $z(i)$. Expanding the right-hand side of Eq. (10.86) yields

$$\sum_{i=1}^{k+1} H^\dagger(i)W(i)z(i) = \sum_{i=1}^{k} H^\dagger(i)W(i)z(i) + H^\dagger(k+1)W(k+1)z(k+1).$$ **Eq. (10.87)**

Define[1]

$$Q(k+1) = \sum_{i=1}^{k+1} H^\dagger(i)W(i)H(i)$$ **Eq. (10.88)**

it follows that Eq. (10.86) is now

$$Q(k+1)\hat{x}(k+1) = \sum_{i=1}^{k+1} H^\dagger(i)W(i)z(i)$$ **Eq. (10.89)**

Now, inserting Eq. (10.87) into Eq. (10.89) yields

$$Q(k+1)\hat{x}(k+1) = \sum_{i=1}^{k} H^\dagger(i)W(i)z(i) + H^\dagger(k+1)W(k+1)z(k+1)$$ **Eq. (10.90)**

and it follows that

$$Q(k+1)\hat{x}(k+1) = \left(\sum_{i=1}^{k} H^\dagger(i)W(i)H(i)\right)\hat{x}(k) + H^\dagger(k+1)W(k+1)z(k+1).$$ **Eq. (10.91)**

By replacing the summation on the right hand side of Eq. (10.91) with $Q(k)$ and solving for $\hat{x}(k+1)$, yields

$$\hat{x}(k+1) = Q^{-1}(k+1)[Q(k)\hat{x}(k) + H^\dagger(k+1)W(k+1)z(k+1)].$$ **Eq. (10.92)**

Although **H** and **W** may change as time steps, one can assume them to be constant and accordingly, drop the index k.

Expanding Eq. (10.88) and solving for $Q(k)$ yields

$$Q(k) = Q(k+1) - H^\dagger WH$$ **Eq. (10.93)**

Substituting Eq. (10.93) in to Eq. (10.92) yields

$$\hat{x}(k+1) = Q^{-1}(k+1)[(Q(k+1) - H^\dagger WH)\hat{x}(k) + H^\dagger Wz(k+1)]$$ **Eq. (10.94)**

which can be rewritten as

$$\hat{x}(k+1) = \hat{x}(k+1) - Q^{-1}(k+1)[H^\dagger WH\hat{x}(k) - H^\dagger Wz(k+1)]$$ **Eq. (10.95)**

and finally,

$$\hat{x}(k+1) = \hat{x}(k+1) - (Q^{-1}(k+1)H^\dagger W)[z(k+1) - H\hat{x}(k)].$$ **Eq. (10.96)**

---

1. Not to be confused with the state estimate error covariance matrix.

Since one cannot use Eq. (10.96) to update the state until one has solved for Q^{-1}, and to do this use the matrix inversion lemma

$$(A + BCD)^{-1} = A^{-1} - A^{-1}B(DA^{-1}B + C^{-1})^{-1}DA^{-1}.$$ **Eq. (10.97)**

Using Eq. (10.97) into Eq. (10.93) yields,

$$Q^{-1}(k+1) = Q^{-1}(k) - Q^{-1}(k)H^\dagger(HQ^{-1}(k)H^\dagger + W^{-1})^{-1}HQ^{-1}(k).$$ **Eq. (10.98)**

Recognizing that $P = Q^{-1}$, then Eq. (10.98)

$$P(k+1) = P(k) - P(k)H^\dagger(HP(k)(k)H^\dagger + W^{-1})^{-1}HP(k).$$ **Eq. (10.99)**

Define the matrix C as

$$C(k+1) = HP(k)H^\dagger + W^{-1}.$$ **Eq. (10.100)**

Now, one can write the update equation for the covariance of the state estimate error as

$$P(k+1) = P(k) - P(k)H^\dagger C^{-1}(k+1)HP(k).$$ **Eq. (10.101)**

From Eq. (10.96) the current estimate is simply the old estimate plus a comparison of the current measurement at the old estimate propagated to the time of the new estimate. This term is called the "gain" and is defined as

$$K(k+1) = P(k+1)H^\dagger W.$$ **Eq. (10.102)**

The gain can simply be computed from Eq. (10.101), but this is not the form that is commonly used. Instead, one would seek an expression of the gain that uses only past values of P. To this end, insert Eq. (10.101) into Eq. (10.102) to get

$$K(k+1) = [P(k) - P(k)H^\dagger C^{-1}(k+1)HP(k)]H^\dagger W$$ **Eq. (10.103)**

which can be simplified to the form

$$K(k+1) = P(k)H^\dagger W - P(k)H^\dagger(W - C^{-1}(k+1)) = P(k)H^\dagger C^{-1}(k+1).$$ **Eq. (10.104)**

Substituting Eq. (10.104) into Eq. (10.101), then replacing W with R^{-1} and by adding the time dependence back into H and R for full generality, the results are then given below,

$$\hat{x}(k+1) = \hat{x}(k) + K(k+1)[z(k+1) - H(k+1)\hat{x}(k)]$$ **Eq. (10.105)**

$$K(k+1) = P(k)H^\dagger(k+1)C^{-1}(k+1)$$ **Eq. (10.106)**

$$C(k+1) = H(k+1)P(k)H^\dagger(k+1) + R(k+1)$$ **Eq. (10.107)**

$$P(k+1) = [I - K(k+1)H(k)]P(k).$$ **Eq. (10.108)**

10.6. Data Association

In the previous sections and examples, it was assumed that only measurements from the actual target were used by the filter. In practice, this is not always the case. In fact, even when tracking a single target in a noise limited environment, if nothing else is done, the sensor will pass a detection from noise (i.e., false alarm) to the tracker. The situation is further complicated by clutter detections and denser target environments. Modern radars can track hundreds, if not thousands, of targets at a time. Proper association of measurements to targets is not only essential, but surprisingly difficult. This can be illustrated with a simple example. The left-hand column of Fig. 10.32 shows three sets of detections from a single isolated target. In this case, it is simple to discern association of the detections into a track with the target moving to the right and slightly down as shown in the bottom left-hand frame. The right column shows three sets of detections for five targets. From the second frame, it is nearly impossible to determine which detections should go with the detections from the first frame. By the third frame, the picture is very cluttered and it may be that the sensor is not able to resolve the targets. Once again, the truth tracks are provided in the bottom frame. Figure 10.32 provides some insight into the complexity of the data association problem for a high resolution radar that can track many closely spaced targets. Data association continues to be a rich area of research for radars and other tracking sensors and systems.

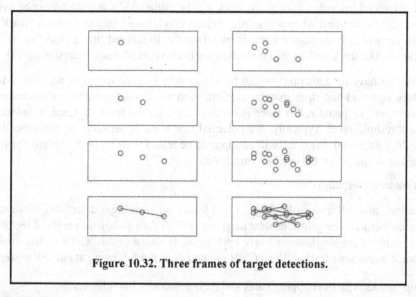

Figure 10.32. Three frames of target detections.

10.6.1. Gating

The first step in most data association techniques is gating. Used in many areas of engineering and science, gating is the process of trimming data sets that do not meet some minimum criteria. For radar tracking, gating is the process of removing unlikely hypotheses, i.e., particular track-detection pairings, from further considerations. Gating usually involves comparing the location of the detection to the propagated state estimate out of the Kalman filter. The Euclidean distance may make a suitable gate, but it is more common to use the square of the normalized residual. The track-detection pair will be retained for further consideration if

$$\varepsilon_{ij} = (\mathbf{z}_j(k) - \mathbf{H}\hat{\mathbf{x}}_i(k-1))^{\dagger} \, \mathbf{C}_{ij}^{-1} \, (\mathbf{z}_j(k) - \mathbf{H}\hat{\mathbf{x}}_i(k-1)) \leq G \qquad \textbf{Eq. (10.109)}$$

where $\mathbf{z}_j$ is the measurement from the detection j, $\mathbf{H}\hat{\mathbf{x}}_i(k-1)$ is the propagated estimate from the track i, and $\mathbf{C}_{ij}$ is the residuals covariance matrix calculated with the track-detection pair found in Eq. (10.68). Gating must consider every track-detection pair. If there are N detections and M tracks, there are NM track-detection pairs that must be considered. In a dense environment, this can lead to thousands, or even tens of thousands of combination. Because the actual data association method will be more computationally intensive, it highlights the need to perform gating. That said, even the gating step itself can become cumbersome. To combat this, coarse gating methods, such as dividing the tracking volume into grids or bins, may be employed. Computer science algorithms, such as binary search, may also reduce the computational burden.

The use of Eq. (10.109) results in an ellipsoidal gate. It should be noted that different shaped gates can also be constructed using other criteria. The value of G from Eq. (10.109) may be found empirically or through probabilities. Once the gating has been completed, there should be groups of:

1. Detections that did not fall into any gate
2. Tracks that had no detections within their gate
3. Detections that fall into one or more gates
4. Tracks with one or more detections in their gate

Detections that do not fall into any gate will be nominated for a new track. New tracks may be started with ad-hoc rules, such as the track will be initiated if N detections can be associated with the track in the first M opportunities. Tracks may also be initiated with a "track score." Track score, which is discussed later, is based on the likelihood that a detection is from an actual target. The track will be initiated when the track score reaches a threshold level.

Tracks that have no detections within their gate may be propagated or nominated for deletion. Once again ad-hoc rules may be applied, such as N updates without a detection, or the track score will be penalized if there is no detection and the track dropped if the score falls below a threshold level. Typically, if a potential new track is between the initiation threshold and the drop threshold, the track will continue to be tested until it either exceeds the initiation threshold or drops below the deletion threshold.

Global Nearest Neighbor

Detections that fall into multiple gates and tracks with multiple detections move on to the association method. The global nearest neighbor (GNN) data association method seeks to identify and maintain the single-most likely hypothesis. Because of this, GNN is often referred to as a "single hypothesis tracker." The GNN method does the following at each time step:

1. Groups tracks with overlapping gates and their detections into clusters
2. Creates a cost for each hypothesis within the cluster
3. Solves the assignment problem

Making assignments at the cluster level has the advantage that it avoids the potential contention for detections that might arise if assignments were made at the track level. Typically, clusters are overlapping gates that share, at least, some detections. For example, consider Fig. 10.33, if assignments were made at the track level and were based on the distance to the center of the gate, both tracks would contend for detection *D1* versus the detections at the edges of the gates.

The cost function normally utilized for GNN is

$$(\mathbf{z}_j(k) - \mathbf{H}\hat{\mathbf{x}}_i(k-1))^\dagger \; \mathbf{C}_{ij}^{-1} \; (\mathbf{z}_j(k) - \mathbf{H}\hat{\mathbf{x}}_i(k-1)) + \ln|\mathbf{C}_{ij}| \qquad \textbf{Eq. (10.110)}$$

where the natural log of the determinant of the residuals covariance matrix for track-detection combination ij is included to help ensure that poor quality tracks are less likely to be assigned detections that are due to higher quality tracks.

The cost values are now formed into a matrix, usually with the tracks as the rows and the detections as the columns. The goal of the assignment process is to maximize the number of assignments while minimizing the overall cost, i.e., sum of the individual costs. The assignment process can be performed by a wide variety of algorithms, but each is subject to the constraint that there can only be one assignment in each row or column. That is, only one detection can be assigned to a track and vice versa. Depending on the algorithm, detection that falls outside the gate of a given track can be assigned an arbitrarily high cost or simply marked as "not allowed."

Now consider track update with three overlapping gates and five detections as shown in Fig. 10.34. Using Eq. (10.110) and depending on the residuals and residuals covariance, the assignment matrix for the situation in Fig. 10.34 may look like

$$A = \begin{bmatrix} 6.24 & 100 & 5.37 & 7.64 & 3.57 \\ 9.00 & 10.61 & 9.61 & 100 & 100 \\ 6.08 & 6.09 & 100 & 6.52 & 8.95 \end{bmatrix} \cdot \qquad \text{Eq. (10.111)}$$

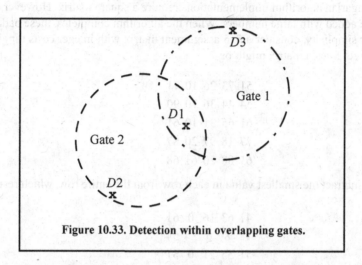

Figure 10.33. Detection within overlapping gates.

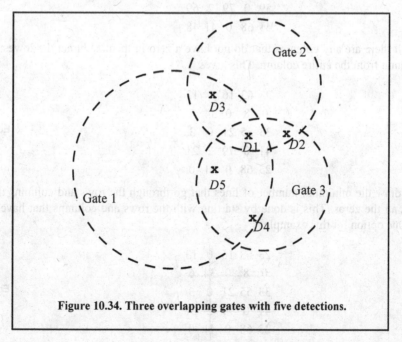

Figure 10.34. Three overlapping gates with five detections.

The object is now to find the combination of track-detection pairings that minimize the overall cost subject to the previously mentioned constraints. The value of *100* has been inserted for any detections that fall outside of the respective gates. The matrix in Eq. (10.111) is small enough that brute force may be used to find the combination with the minimum overall score. It turns out to be that *D5* is assigned to Track 1, *D1* is assigned to Track 2, and *D2* is assigned to Track 3. The brute force method requires that each combination of track-detection pairings, within the constraints, be considered and a total cost calculated. While this was simple enough for this example, the computational expense can become a burden as the clusters become larger. For this reason, there are numerous optimal, or nearly optimal, solutions to the assignment problem that do not require brute force. One of the more popular methods is the Hungarian method, which will be described briefly here.

Some Hungarian algorithm implementations require a square matrix. However, rows or columns can be added with large numbers. When the algorithm completes, these padded areas are ignored. For simplicity, consider a 5x5 assignment matrix with integer costs ranging from one to one hundred. Such a matrix might be

$$\begin{matrix} 51 & 73 & 26 & 10 & 71 \\ 54 & 44 & 36 & 70 & 90 \\ 61 & 65 & 31 & 10 & 61 \\ 77 & 18 & 97 & 20 & 87 \\ 61 & 88 & 20 & 61 & 68 \end{matrix} \quad \cdot \qquad \text{Eq. (10.112)}$$

Step 1 is to subtract the smallest value in each row from the entire row, which results in

$$\begin{matrix} 41 & 63 & 16 & 0 & 61 \\ 18 & 8 & 0 & 34 & 54 \\ 51 & 55 & 21 & 0 & 51 \\ 59 & 0 & 79 & 2 & 69 \\ 41 & 68 & 0 & 41 & 48 \end{matrix} \quad \cdot \qquad \text{Eq. (10.113)}$$

Step 2, if there are any columns that do not have a zero in them, subtract the lowest value in that column from the entire column. This gives

$$\begin{matrix} 23 & 63 & 16 & 0 & 13 \\ 0 & 8 & 0 & 34 & 6 \\ 33 & 55 & 21 & 0 & 3 \\ 41 & 0 & 79 & 2 & 21 \\ 23 & 68 & 0 & 41 & 0 \end{matrix} \quad \cdot \qquad \text{Eq. (10.114)}$$

Step 3, draw the minimum number of lines that go through the rows and columns that strike through all the zeros. This is done by starting with the rows and columns that have multiple zeros. One option for this example is

$$\begin{matrix} 23 & 63 & 16 & 0 & 13 \\ 0 & 8 & 0 & 34 & 6 \\ 33 & 55 & 21 & 0 & 3 \\ 41 & 0 & 79 & 2 & 21 \\ 23 & 68 & 0 & 41 & 0 \end{matrix} \quad \cdot \qquad \text{Eq. (10.115)}$$

If the number of lines equals the size of the matrix, in this case five, the algorithm stops. However, so far the number of lines is four, so the algorithm continues. Step 4, find the minimum value of the numbers that are not struck through, subtract that number from the numbers that are not struck through, and add it to the numbers that are struck through twice. This produces

$$
\begin{matrix}
20 & 60 & 13 & 0 & 10 \\
0 & 8 & 0 & 37 & 6 \\
30 & 52 & 18 & 0 & 0 \\
41 & 0 & 79 & 5 & 21 \\
23 & 68 & 0 & 44 & 0
\end{matrix}
\qquad \text{Eq. (10.116)}
$$

Return to Step 3 and find the minimum number of lines that strike through all zeros. This is

$$
\begin{matrix}
20 & 60 & 13 & 0 & 10 \\
0 & 8 & 0 & 37 & 6 \\
30 & 52 & 18 & 0 & 0 \\
41 & 0 & 79 & 5 & 21 \\
23 & 68 & 0 & 44 & 0
\end{matrix}
\qquad \text{Eq. (10.117)}
$$

Because the minimum number of lines matches the size of the matrix, the algorithm stops. It should now be possible to create a permutation matrix from the locations of the zeros. Said another way, there should be a zero in each row that allows for the constraint that there is only one zero in that column. For this example, that is

$$
\begin{matrix}
20 & 60 & 13 & \boxed{0} & 10 \\
\boxed{0} & 8 & 0 & 37 & 6 \\
30 & 52 & 18 & 0 & \boxed{0} \\
41 & \boxed{0} & 79 & 5 & 21 \\
23 & 68 & \boxed{0} & 44 & 0
\end{matrix}
\qquad \text{Eq. (10.118)}
$$

Using these values in the original assignment matrix

$$
\begin{matrix}
51 & 73 & 26 & \boxed{10} & 71 \\
\boxed{54} & 44 & 36 & 70 & 90 \\
61 & 65 & 31 & 10 & \boxed{61} \\
77 & \boxed{18} & 97 & 20 & 87 \\
61 & 88 & \boxed{20} & 61 & 68
\end{matrix}
\qquad \text{Eq. (10.119)}
$$

provides a score of 163, which matches the brute force solution. Because some other data association methods, besides GNN, require the first k best solutions to the assignment problem, additional solutions can be found with the Hungarian algorithm by making multiple sweeps. Each sweep has a number of runs equal to the size of the assignment matrix minus one. For this example, four. At each run, members of the "best" solution would be moved in and out. For example, the first run must not include the element (1,4), the second run must include the element (1,4), but not include element (2,1). The third must include (1,4) and (2,1) but not (3,5), etc., until all elements from the first solution have been removed. The best score from the full sweep is the second best solution. The second sweep proceeds as the first, but the first element from the best solution is omitted from all runs and the second best solution is moved in and out.

Joint Probabilistic Data Association

The joint probabilistic data association (JPDA) algorithm is an extension of the probabilistic data association (PDA) algorithm allowing for PDA to be utilized on multiple tracks. Like GNN, association for JPDA is usually done at the cluster level. However, unlike GNN, the algorithm attempts to calculate the association probabilities based on all possible measurements to all tracks within the cluster. The result is a mixture that is used in the Kalman filter equations. The algorithm also accounts for the probability that the detection is not from a target of interest. The Kalman state estimate update is modified as follows,

$$\hat{\mathbf{x}}_i(k+1|k+1) \;=\; \hat{\mathbf{x}}_i(k+1|k) + \mathbf{K}(k)\tilde{\mathbf{y}}_i \qquad\qquad \text{Eq. (10.120)}$$

where $\tilde{\mathbf{y}}_i$ is the mixed residual found by

$$\hat{\mathbf{y}}_i \;=\; \sum_{j=1}^{N} \beta_{ij}\tilde{\mathbf{y}}_{ij} \qquad\qquad \text{Eq. (10.121)}$$

where $\tilde{\mathbf{y}}_{ij}$ is the residual calculated for track i based on detection j, and β_{ij} is the probability of the hypothesis that detection j should be associated with track i. The value N is the total number of detections being considered for association within the cluster.

The state estimate error covariance update is

$$\mathbf{P}_i(k+1|k+1) \;=\; \beta_{i0}\mathbf{P}_i(k+1|k) + (1-\beta_{i0})\mathbf{P}^c(k+1|k+1) + \tilde{\mathbf{P}}(k+1) \qquad \text{Eq. (10.122)}$$

where β_{i0} is the probability that none of the detections should be associated with track i, the state estimate error is $\mathbf{P}^c(k+1|k+1)$ and it is calculated using the unmodified Kalman filter equations and

$$\tilde{\mathbf{P}}(k+1) \;=\; \mathbf{K}(k+1)\left[\sum_{j=1}^{N} \beta_{ij}\tilde{\mathbf{y}}_{ij}\tilde{\mathbf{y}}_{ij}^{\dagger} - \tilde{\mathbf{y}}_i\tilde{\mathbf{y}}_i^{\dagger}\right]\mathbf{K}^{\dagger}(k+1) \qquad \text{Eq. (10.123)}$$

where $\mathbf{K}(k+1)$ is the Kalman gain calculated with the unmodified Kalman equations. All that remains is to determine β_{ij}. This starts with the assumption that there are detections within the volume under consideration that are not due to the known targets. These may be thermal detection, clutter or new targets. It is assumed that these "false" detections are Poisson distributed with probability mass function

$$\mu_F(p) \;=\; e^{-\lambda V}\frac{(\lambda V)^p}{p!} \qquad\qquad \text{Eq. (10.124)}$$

where (λV) is the Poisson parameter, and λ is the density of the false detections within the volume V. In the nonparametric version of JPDA, λ becomes a constant.

It can be shown that the likelihood function for any cluster at any time k is the product of three hypotheses of a single track. That is,

1. There is no detection associated with the track
2. There is a detection, but it is not due to the target
3. There is a detection associated with the track

For the first case, the likelihood of a track with no detection is

$$\mathcal{L}_1 = (1 - P_D) \qquad\qquad \text{Eq. (10.125)}$$

where P_D is the probability of detection set by the sensor for the track update beam. For the second case, where there is a detection, but it is not due to the target, the likelihood is

$$\mathcal{L}_2 = \lambda^{-1} = V_g \qquad\qquad \text{Eq. (10.126)}$$

where V_g is the measurement volume under consideration. The assumption is that false detections are uniformly distributed within the volume. For the last case, a detection that is associated with the target, the likelihood is

$$\mathcal{L}_3(i,j) = P_D \, g_{ij} \qquad\qquad \text{Eq. (10.127)}$$

where g_{ij} is the Gaussian likelihood function, under the assumption that associated detections are Gaussian distributed, and is given by

$$g_{ij} = \frac{e^{-\varepsilon_{ij}/2}}{(2\pi)^{m/2} \sqrt{|C_{ij}|}} \qquad\qquad \text{Eq. (10.128)}$$

where ε is the square of the normalized residual found by Eq. (10.141) (from the maneuvering targets section), m is the size of the measurement vector and C_{ij} is the residual covariance for the track-detection pair.

For a given update within a cluster, the total combination of these three likelihoods will be the number of observations plus the number of tracks minus the number of associations. As an example, consider the case of Fig. 10.33, where the cluster has three detections and two gates. There are eight feasible hypotheses for this cluster. They are listed in Table 10.1. The first column of Table 10.1 is the hypothesis number and the second column is detection number associated with Track 1 for that hypothesis where a *0* indicates no detection associated with the track. The last column provides the likelihood for that hypothesis. Consider the first line, there are two tracks without associations and three observations; therefore, the likelihood should be a product of two $\mathcal{L}_1$ and three $\mathcal{L}_2$. In the second line, there is one association; therefore, the likelihood for that hypothesis is a product of one $\mathcal{L}_1$, two $\mathcal{L}_2$ and one $\mathcal{L}_3$.

Table 10.1. Feasible Cluster Hypothesis.

H	Track 1	Track 2	Likelihood
1	*0*	*0*	$\mathcal{L}_1^2 \mathcal{L}_2^3$
2	*0*	*1*	$\mathcal{L}_1 \mathcal{L}_2^2 \mathcal{L}_3(2,1)$
3	*0*	*2*	$\mathcal{L}_1 \mathcal{L}_2^2 \mathcal{L}_3(2,2)$
4	*1*	*0*	$\mathcal{L}_1 \mathcal{L}_2^2 \mathcal{L}_3(1,1)$
5	*3*	*0*	$\mathcal{L}_1 \mathcal{L}_2^2 \mathcal{L}_3(1,3)$
6	*1*	*2*	$\mathcal{L}_3(1,1) \mathcal{L}_2 \mathcal{L}_3(2,2)$
7	*3*	*1*	$\mathcal{L}_3(1,3) \mathcal{L}_2 \mathcal{L}_3(2,1)$
8	*3*	*2*	$\mathcal{L}_3(1,3) \mathcal{L}_2 \mathcal{L}_3(2,2)$

The joint probability of a given hypothesis is then the normalized likelihood. Finally, the probability β_{ij}, that is, the probability that track i is associated with detection j, is simply the sum of all hypothesis joint probabilities that include that association. For example, the probability of Track 1 being associated with detection 1 is the sum of the joint probabilities for *H4* and *H6*.

Multiple Hypothesis Tracker

The GNN method for association attempts to determine the best possible hypothesis for a given update and use that hypothesis for association. The JPDA associates data that is a weighted mix of the data from the update. In both cases, the hypotheses are only maintained for a single scan. The multiple hypothesis tracker (MHT) is a deferred logic approach that delays association in an attempt to resolve ambiguities. The MHT method comes in two main approaches: the original hypothesis oriented MHT (HOMHT), which was developed in 1979 and the track-oriented MHT (TOMHT) developed in 1990. It was clear early on that MHT was a dramatic departure from earlier data association methods and had the potential for significant improvements in dense and clutter environments. Before the development of TOMHT, there was significant research into the identification and mitigation of the challenges with HOMHT. Even today, MHT is, in itself, a popular topic within the literature. The MHT is a complicated approach. A full description of its implementations, challenges and performance could easily fill several chapters. Therefore, this discussion will introduce both HOMHT and TOMHT at a relatively high level. The goal will be to simply introduce the reader to the subject and provide the basis for continued exploration.

Before delving into the discussion of MHT, it is worthwhile to take a brief look at track scoring. Track scoring is a method for assigning a measure of quality to a track. It is convenient for the track score to use a log likelihood ratio (LLR) because it is dimensionless and can be converted to the probability of a true track with

$$P_T = \frac{e^{LLR}}{1 + e^{LLR}}.$$ Eq. (10.129)

Equally convenient is the fact that the track score $\mathscr{L}$ may be found recursively at each scan k as

$$\mathscr{L}(k+1) = \mathscr{L}(k) + \Delta\mathscr{L}(k+1).$$ Eq. (10.130)

There are different expressions that can be used for $\mathscr{L}$ available. One such expression is

$$\Delta\mathscr{L}(k+1) = \frac{\varepsilon_{ij}}{2} + \ln\left[\frac{\lambda_f\sqrt{|C_{ij}(k+1)|}}{P_d(k+1)}\right].$$ Eq. (10.131)

When a detection j is assigned to track i. Where λ_f is the density of detections not assigned to tracks (false alarms or new tracks) per unit volume, and P_d is the probability of detection for the sensor beam that produced the detection under consideration. If no track is assigned to the track, then

$$\Delta\mathscr{L}(k+1) = -\ln[1 - P_d(k+1)].$$ Eq. (10.132)

Track score is useful for evaluating hypothesis and tracks in the MHT framework, but may also be used for track creation and deletion.

For HOMHT, one possible basic architecture is shown in Fig. 10.35. As measurements from detections come in, gates are computed and clusters are developed, similar to that of Figs. 10.33 and 10.34. Clustering is a convenient way to divide the larger data association problem into smaller groups. Because of the dynamics of the tracks, at each scan it may be necessary to merge, separate or create new clusters. After gating and clustering, hypotheses are formed, which can be a difficult concept to visualize. Assume the cluster of Fig. 10.33. There are two tracks and three detections. The first detection can be associated with no track (designated *0*), either of the two established tracks, designated as *1* or *2*, or a new track, designated as *3*. The second detection can be associated with no tracks, Track 2 or a new track (designated as *4*). The third detection can be associated with no tracks, Track 1 or a new track (designated as *5*). This simple cluster creates *30* hypotheses.

Figure 10.36 shows the formation of hypotheses in a tree structure where each measurement forms a column of the tree. Each path from left to right represents a hypothesis. For implementation, these hypotheses can be enumerated into a matrix. At each scan, there will be a $M \times N$ matrix for the hypotheses. The number of columns N is the number of detections for that scan and the number of rows, M, will be equal to the surviving hypotheses. At each scan, each one of the hypotheses from the last scan will be expanded. This will include the hypothesis for no association and a new track for each measurement. This expansion will include M_n new rows depending on the number of tracks and measurements in the cluster and depending on the gating. This expansion will include N columns which correspond to the measurements for the scan within the cluster.

Returning to Fig. 10.35, the next step is to evaluate the hypotheses and delete unlikely ones. The evaluation may be done in many ways. In the original HOMHT, hypotheses probabilities were calculated by

$$P_l(k+1) = \frac{1}{p_0}\{P_d^{N_{DT}}(1-P_d)^{(N_{TGT}-N_{DT})}\beta_{FT}^{N_{FT}} \ \beta_{NT}^{N_{NT}}\}\left[\prod_{n=1}^{N_{DT}} \aleph(\mathbf{z}_i - \mathbf{H}\hat{\mathbf{x}}_j, C_{ij})\right]P_g(k) \quad \textbf{Eq. (10.133)}$$

where $P_l(k+1)$ is the probability of hypothesis l at $k+1$, p_0 is a normalization constant, P_d is the probability of detection, β_{FT} is the density of false targets, β_{NT} is the density of new targets, $\aleph$ is the Gaussian probability density function, N_{DT} is the number of measurements associated with tracks in hypothesis, N_{FT} is the number of false tracks in hypothesis, N_{NT} is the number of new tracks in hypothesis, N_{TGT} is the total tracks, and $P_g(k)$ is the probability of parent hypothesis at k. Other expressions for the hypothesis probabilities are available.

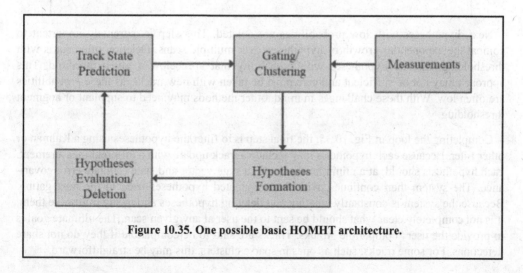

Figure 10.35. One possible basic HOMHT architecture.

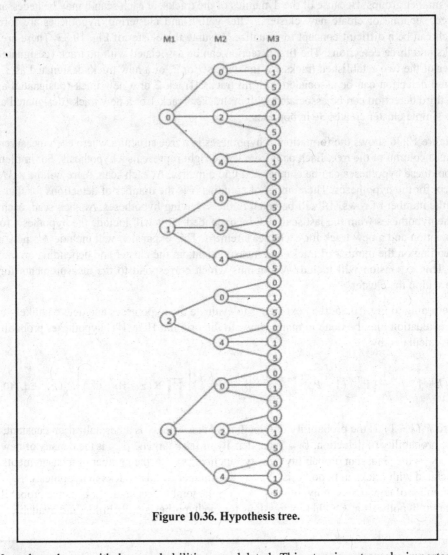

Figure 10.36. Hypothesis tree.

Next, hypotheses with low probabilities are deleted. This step is extremely important to combat the exponential growth of hypotheses over multiple scans. Deletion often starts with thresholding, that is, hypotheses with probability that are below a given threshold. This approach may not be sufficient and care must be taken with new tracks, as these probabilities are often low. With these challenges in mind, other methods may need to supplant or augment thresholding.

Completing the loop in Fig. 10.35, the final step is to filter the hypotheses using a Kalman or other filter. Because each hypothesis may include a track update with a different measurement, each hypothesis should, at a minimum, maintain a state vector and state estimate error covariance. The system then continues, with the propagated hypotheses used in the next gating. Because the system is constantly creating and deleting hypotheses and trying to resolve them, it is not completely clear what should be sent to the user at any given scan. The ultimate goal is to provide the user "compatible" tracks. Tracks are said to be compatible if they do not share detections. For some tracks, such as ones in sparse clusters, this may be straightforward.

The system will only retain hypotheses for a certain number of scans, called the window. One way to get a measure of what to send to the user is to look at the surviving hypotheses in the oldest scan. For example, if the entire column, meaning a detection, of the surviving hypothesis has the same track number, that track can be assumed to be confirmed and sent to the user. If not all, but most, of the columns have the same track number, it may also be appropriate to send to the user provided it passes some minimum quality test and perhaps may be mixed from the observations and probabilities. For others, it may be more appropriate to defer sending track information until the track can be further resolved. If it is determined that a track will be sent, the selection of state vector and state estimate covariance must be determined. It may be appropriate to send these from the hypothesis with the highest probability, or perhaps mix hypotheses in a method similar to that used in JPDA.

Perhaps the largest difference between HOMHT and TOMHT is how hypotheses are utilized. In TOMHT, hypotheses are not maintained scan to scan, only tracks. Hypotheses are then reformed at each scan. Figure 10.37 shows a possible data flow for TOMHT. As detections come in from a scan, gating and clustering is performed as usual. Track formation begins with updating each track in the cluster with one of the detections that falls inside the gate. New tracks are created from the parent track appended by every other detection inside the gate. A new track is also created from the parent track appended by the dummy assignment (no associated detection) and finally a new track is created under the assumption that each detection is the beginning of a new track. Obviously, this creates a large number of tracks and, by definition, each of these is incompatible. For efficiency, it is worth retaining a list of all tracks that are incompatible with the given track. All of these existing and newly formed tracks are then scored. The lowest scores are then dropped. Once again, thresholding is common, but other techniques may be used as well. One of the principal advantages of the TOMHT over HOMHT is that only the surviving, or even a subset of the surviving, tracks will be used to create hypotheses. In HOMHT, many of the created hypotheses are immediately dropped, wasting computational resources.

In TOMHT, hypotheses are sets of compatible tracks. There are several methods available for hypothesis formation. Many will include "track pruning." The idea behind track pruning is shown by an example. Consider a five-scan MHT window that started with two tracks. Figure 10.38 shows the surviving tracks spawned from the original two and the detection number from each scan for that track. Each branch, down to the bottom line, represents the ten surviving tracks. Note that all the tracks spawned from Track 1 or Track 2 are incompatible by definition. Therefore, a given tree can represent only one target. Notice that for both tracks, there are two branches at $N-3$. If it is determined that the true track is on one side of these two branches, the entire other side is dropped. In this example, it would result in the dropping of four tracks. Although not all tracks are compatible, multiple hypotheses of compatible tracks can be created. The actual pruning is performed by solving the multi-dimensional assignment problem, commonly by a Lagrangian relaxation algorithm; but other algorithms are available. A description of these methods is not provided here but is available in the Bibliography. It should be noted that pruning can also be used in HOMHT to reduce hypotheses.

There are also other techniques to limit the formation of low probability hypotheses. These include the use of the "N-best" assignments described for GNN. In the end, the most probable hypotheses are retained. Tracks that are not included in the most probable hypotheses are considered for deletion. The tracks that survive will be filtered, and state vectors and covariance matrices will be created or updated. After filtering, tracks that have very similar detection histories and/or state vectors are considered redundant and the two tracks are merged or the lower scoring track dropped.

Finally, tracks are stored in a database, and information is provided to the user. Because there may be multiple tracks that represent a single target, there must be a logic that is performed on the tracks and hypotheses to provide the user actionable information. That logic is dependent on the applications of the tracker. Whether it is HOMHT or TOMHT, MHT provides significant benefits in dense and cluttered environments. Research continues on MHT to improve performance while minimizing complexity and computational cost. The interested reader is encouraged to consult the bibliographic or other material on the subject.

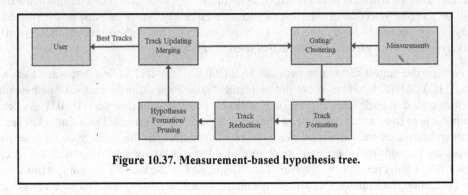

Figure 10.37. Measurement-based hypothesis tree.

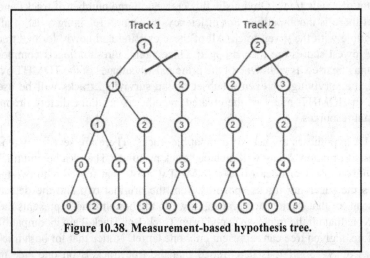

Figure 10.38. Measurement-based hypothesis tree.

10.7. Tracking Maneuvering Targets

In previous sections, it was shown how the Kalman filter provides for the uncertainty of the target dynamics model by including randomness within the model in the form of process noise. If there are no modeling errors, the Kalman filter solution is optimal, regardless of how much process noise. However, since the dynamics of the target cannot be known perfectly, the best performance will be achieved when the process noise can be kept small.

For the Kalman filters described so far, this means targets that essentially move in straight lines at a nearly constant velocity. Unfortunately, it is possible real targets will maneuver while being tracked. How to deal with maneuvering targets continues to be a consistent topic of research. Ways to group the different methods of dealing with maneuvering targets are the following: (1) single model whose parameters are sized for the expected maneuvers; (2) single model that adapts its parameters; and (3) multiple models.

10.7.1. *Field Parameter Filters*

The first method is obviously the most simple. Consider a target performing a coordinated turn as shown in Fig. 10.39. The target starts at $x_0 = \begin{bmatrix} 0 & -64 & 2 & 0 \end{bmatrix}^t$, moves at constant velocity until making a coordinated turn, and then once again moves at constant velocity. The total time in track is $300s$. Using a two decoupled two-state "constant velocity (CV)" Kalman filters as in the previous sections with very low process noise, Fig. 10.40 shows that estimate overshoots the turn and the filters diverge. However, if the process is raised high enough, the filter will once again track the target without diverging as shown in Fig. 10.41. Figure 10.42 shows the mean state estimate error for ten thousand runs of the CV filter for the x component. As Q_{sx} increases, the bias is removed. This is, of course, at the cost of the variance increasing. Another way to combat the bias in the estimate is to decrease the sampling time T_s.

Figure 10.43 once again shows the mean state estimate error for ten thousand runs of the CV filter with a decreasing time interval and $Q_{sx} = 1$. As expected, the bias decreases as the time interval decreased. However, unlike increasing Q_s, the variance of the state estimate error is also decreased as the time interval is decreased as shown in Fig. 10.44. Although decreasing the time interval will decrease both the bias of the estimate and the variance, it will obviously use more system resources.

Another method to track a maneuvering target with a single model and static parameters is to increase the order of the model. A similar model to the constant velocity model is the constant acceleration model. In this case, it is assumed that the acceleration is constant through the sampling interval. Using the methods applied to the CV model, the fundamental matrix is

$$\Phi = \begin{bmatrix} 1 & T_s & \dfrac{T_s^2}{2} \\ 0 & 1 & T_s \\ 0 & 0 & 1 \end{bmatrix}.$$

Eq. (10.134)

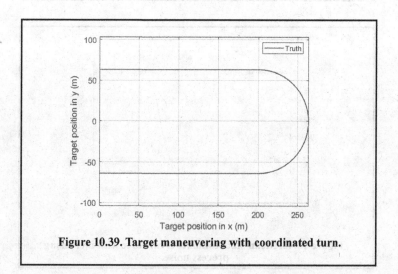

Figure 10.39. Target maneuvering with coordinated turn.

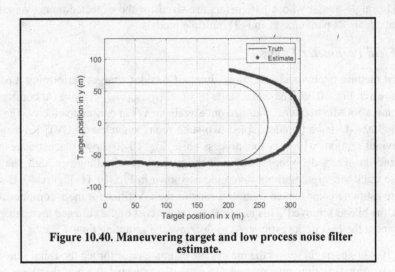

Figure 10.40. Maneuvering target and low process noise filter estimate.

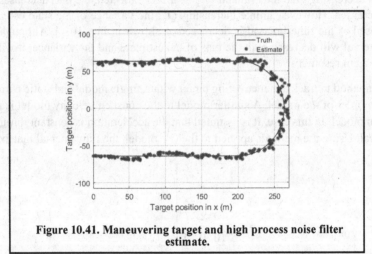

Figure 10.41. Maneuvering target and high process noise filter estimate.

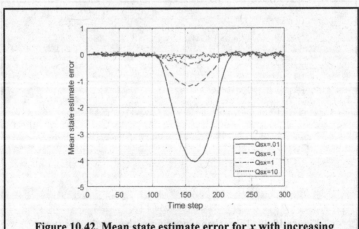

Figure 10.42. Mean state estimate error for *x* with increasing process noise.

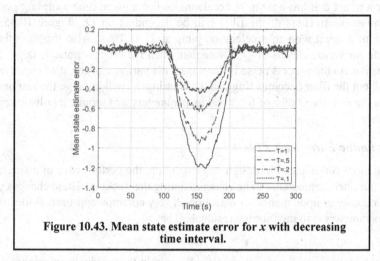

Figure 10.43. Mean state estimate error for *x* with decreasing time interval.

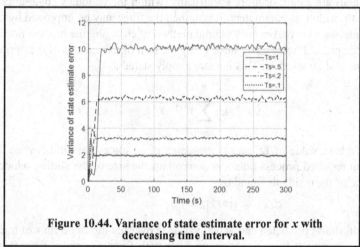

Figure 10.44. Variance of state estimate error for *x* with decreasing time interval.

For the CA filter, the process noise enters the system as the derivative of the acceleration, that is

$$\dot{a}(t) = w(t)$$ Eq. (10.135)

and

$$Q = Q_s \begin{bmatrix} \dfrac{T_s^5}{20} & \dfrac{T_s^4}{8} & \dfrac{T_s^3}{6} \\[2ex] \dfrac{T_s^4}{8} & \dfrac{T_s^3}{3} & \dfrac{T_s^2}{2} \\[2ex] \dfrac{T_s^3}{6} & \dfrac{T_s^2}{2} & T_s \end{bmatrix},$$ Eq. (10.136)

Whereas a CV filter will diverge during a sustained acceleration, the CA filter will easily track a sustained acceleration provided that the changes in acceleration are small compared to the ratio of Q_s to T_s. If not, then once again the filter may have trouble accurately predicting the state and the state error.

Consider a target that has a jump in acceleration. For a given time sampling period Ts, the variance and responsiveness of the filter will be dependent on Q_s. Figure 10.45 shows the acceleration of a target with an acceleration jump at $T_s = 100s$. Also shown is the acceleration estimate for various levels of Q_s. Note that when the process noise is large, the filter is very responsive. As the process noise is decreased, the variance of the state estimate decreases as expected, but the filter becomes sluggish. Decreasing T_s will improve the responsiveness of the filter. In the end, the choice of filter and its parameters will require a holistic approach and empirical data.

10.7.2. Dynamic Parameter Filters

Although more complicated in design and execution, the performance of a single filter will improve if the filter parameters can be changed during the tracking. These changes can be executed continuously or upon maneuver detection. A very common approach to identify the need to change parameters is to monitor the residuals. That is,

$$\tilde{y} = z - H\hat{x}. \qquad \text{Eq. (10.137)}$$

If the residuals are small, or more specifically, within the residuals covariance C, then the filter is working within its parameters. If not, then the filter may be improved by changing one or more parameters. One particularly simple method of changing the process noise continually is to modify the process noise covariance Q by the sum of the squares of the normalized residuals over some sliding window. This is more simply stated as

$$Q_i = Q_0 \sum_{j=0}^{m} \tilde{y}^\dagger C^{-1} \tilde{y} \qquad \text{Eq. (10.138)}$$

where Q_0 is a base value of Q_s and is presumed to be somewhere in between the minimum and maximum required process noise, m determines the size of the sliding window, and C is the covariance of the residuals found by

$$C(k) = HP(k|k-1)H^\dagger + R. \qquad \text{Eq. (10.139)}$$

Figure 10.46 shows predicted and actual variance over ten thousand runs of tracking the target for the x component for a nonadaptive filter with fixed Q_s and a filter that continually modifies Q_s according to Eq. (10.138). For the nonadaptive filter, Q_s was tuned to minimize the sum of the squares of the errors in the state estimate. For the adaptive filter, the predicted variance P_{11} will change for every run because Q_s is dependent on the residuals. In general, however, the adaptive filter will more closely follow the actual state estimate error variance and the variance will be lower.

If using a single filter, another option is to maintain low process noise until a maneuver has been detected and then increasing the process noise. This can have advantages over the continually changing filter if the target acceleration "jumps" and larger process noise is needed over a shorter time frame.

There are numerous maneuver detection tests available. Two of the more common ones are the chi-squared test and the generalized likelihood ratio (GLR) test. The chi-squared test, being the simpler of the two, will be discussed here, the interested reader is encouraged to seek out additional information of GLR. Under the assumption of bias-free operation and a Gaussian distributed measurement and process noise, the residuals will also be Gaussian distributed with zero mean and covariance C. If the normalized residual is defined as

$$\tilde{y}* = \tilde{y}/(\sqrt{c})$$

Eq. (10.140)

then it is easy to show that both the square of the normalized residuals,

$$\varepsilon = \tilde{y}^\dagger c^{-1} \tilde{y}$$

Eq. (10.141)

and the sum of a sliding window of the square of normalized residuals

$$\varepsilon^s(k) = \sum_{j=k-s+1} \varepsilon_j$$

Eq. (10.142)

are chi-squared distributed with $\{dim(\tilde{y})\}$ and $\{dim(\tilde{y}) \cdot s\}$ degrees-of-freedom, respectively, where s is the size of the sliding window.

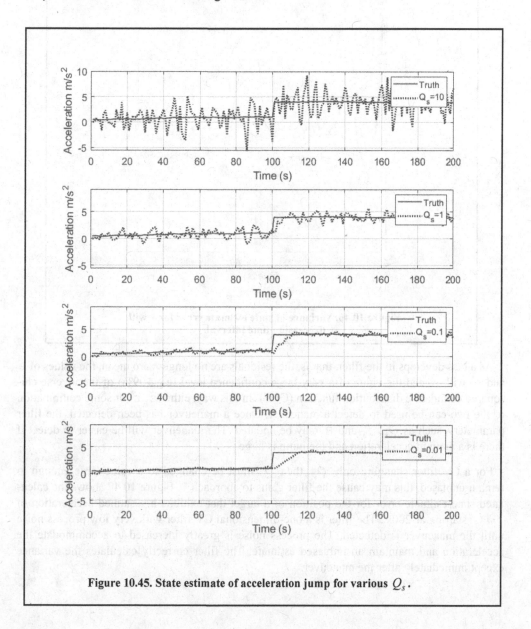

Figure 10.45. State estimate of acceleration jump for various Q_s.

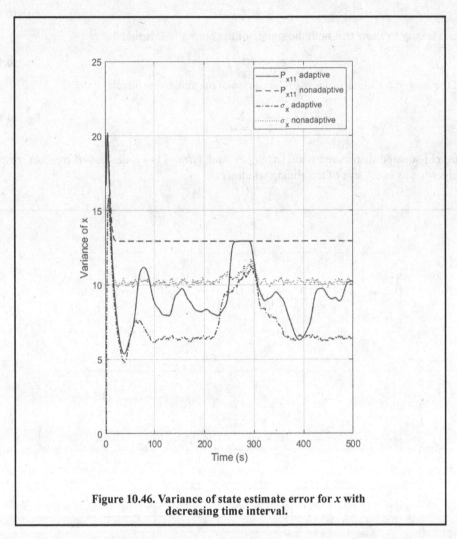

Figure 10.46. Variance of state estimate error for x with decreasing time interval.

As a bias develops in the filter, that is, the residuals are no longer zero mean, the values of ε and ε^s will exceed the value of a very large confidence level (e.g., 99%) of the inverse chi-squared cumulative distribution function (CDF). In this way, either ε, ε^s or some combination of the two can be used to detect a maneuver. Once a maneuver has been detected, the filter parameters, such as Q_s, T_s and $\mathbf{R}$ may be updated. The maneuver will be easier to detect if there is a jump in acceleration and the jump is large.

For a CV filter changing only Q_s, then Q_s must be changed to a value large enough to remain unbiased, this may cause the filter gains to approach 1. Figure 10.47 shows the calculated state estimate error for the position of a target that exhibits a sustained acceleration of $1\,m/s$ starting at $200s$. The filter is a one-dimensional CV filter with very low process noise until the maneuver is detected. The process noise is greatly increased to accommodate the acceleration and maintain an unbiased estimate. The filter correctly calculates the variance except immediately after the maneuver.

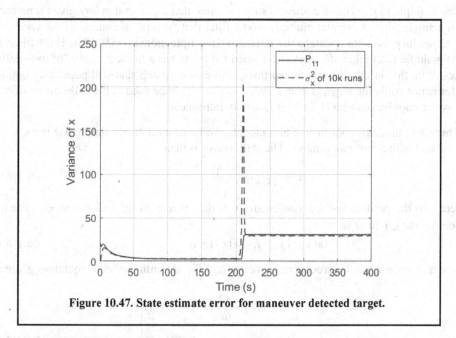

Figure 10.47. State estimate error for maneuver detected target.

10.7.3. Multiple Model Filters

Despite the increase in complexity and computation, there are advantages to moving to a multiple model approach. Among these are adaptability and the ability to maintain improved performance over a single model. As an example, if the process noise can be kept small, using a CV filter is preferred over a CA filter in order to keep the covariance low. However, a CA filter will readily adapt to changes in acceleration. If a CV and a CA filter are run in parallel, performance can be improved over either single model.

Similar to the previous example, consider a target moving at nearly constant velocity until there is a sustained acceleration of $2m/s$ starting at $400s$. Both a two-state CV filter and a three-state CA filter, with the same measurement variance, are run against the data. Figure 10.48 shows the position state estimate error for both the CV and the CA filter. Note that while the variance is clearly smaller for the CV filter, after the maneuver, with no parameter changes, the CV filter diverges, but the CA filter continues to track the target after a short lag.

Figure 10.49 shows that if Q_s is changed for the CV filter after the maneuver is detected, the filter will not diverge. But to keep the estimate unbiased, Q_s must be made quite large. In so doing, the variance becomes larger than that of the CA filter. Figure 10.50 shows the position state estimate error for the composite filter. Once again there is a lag in the filter after the jump. This may be improved by decreasing the sampling time, T_s or increasing the process noise to make the filter more responsive. Finally, Figure 10.51 shows the calculated variance of the state estimate error and the variance of the position state over then thousand runs. If the maneuver is detected successfully, the composite filter accurately represents the state error covariance. There are many combinations of multiple model filters. If running an entire CA filter in parallel with the CV is too computationally expensive, another option is to replace the CA filter with a filter that only calculates the acceleration and use this to adjust the output after maneuver detection. There are also many ways to determine which filter to use as the output of the combined filter, but it is common to pick the model with the highest likelihood that the data, and particularly the residuals, fit the model.

The multiple model filters discussed so far assume that the output at any given time comes from a single filter. A popular multiple model filter that "mixes" the output of the various filters to produce the state update is the interacting multiple model (IMM). The IMM filter, like most multiple filter methods, works best when the target has a limited number of well-defined states. With that in mind, it can be worthwhile to create models that will potentially optimize performance while the target is in that state. So that it may be used in the IMM discussion that follows, a coordinated turn (CT) filter is briefly introduced.

There are numerous coordinated turn models available; a relatively simple one is a CV filter augmented with a turn rate state ω. The state vector is then

$$\hat{\mathbf{x}} = \begin{bmatrix} x & \dot{x} & y & \dot{y} & \omega \end{bmatrix}^\dagger \qquad \text{Eq. (10.143)}$$

where x is the position in the x-coordinate, $\dot{x}$ is the velocity in the x-direction, etc. The truth model for the CT filter is

$$\mathbf{x}(k+1) = f_{CT}(\mathbf{x}(k)) + \mathbf{q} \qquad \text{Eq. (10.144)}$$

where $\mathbf{q}$ is once again the process noise vector and f_{CT} is nonlinear set of equations given as

$$f_{CT}(\mathbf{x}) = \begin{bmatrix} x + \dfrac{\dot{x}}{\omega}\sin(\omega T) - \dfrac{\dot{y}}{\omega}(1 - \cos(\omega T)) \\ y + \dfrac{\dot{x}}{\omega}(1 - \cos(\omega T)) + \dfrac{\dot{y}}{\omega}\sin(\omega T) \\ \dot{x}\cos(\omega T) - \dot{y}\sin(\omega T) \\ \dot{x}\sin(\omega T) - \dot{y}\cos(\omega T) \end{bmatrix}. \qquad \text{Eq. (10.145)}$$

The measurement model is the same as the CV filter.

Similar to nonlinear measurement equations discussed as part of the extended Kalman filter, the nonlinear update equations can be used directly to update the state; however, a linear matrix is required to update the covariance and calculate the gains. Once again, this is found by calculating the Jacobian matrix of f_{CT} and solving at the current state estimate. For this model, this becomes,

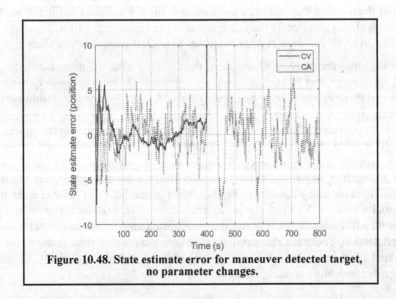

Figure 10.48. State estimate error for maneuver detected target, no parameter changes.

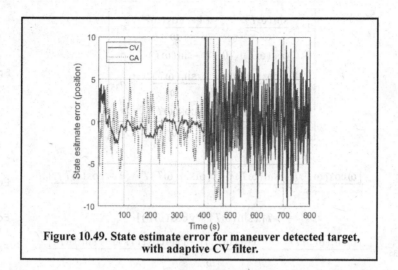

Figure 10.49. State estimate error for maneuver detected target, with adaptive CV filter.

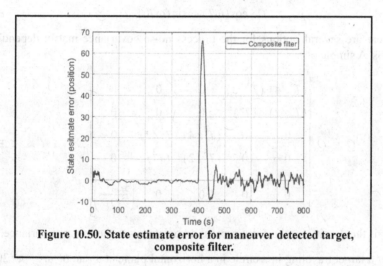

Figure 10.50. State estimate error for maneuver detected target, composite filter.

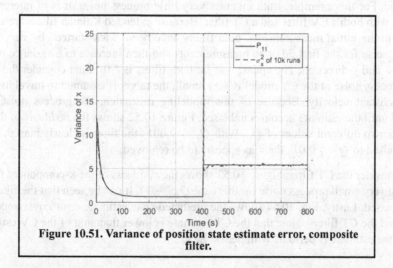

Figure 10.51. Variance of position state estimate error, composite filter.

$$\Phi = \begin{bmatrix} 1 & \dfrac{\sin(\omega T)}{\omega} & 0 & \dfrac{-(1-\cos(\omega T))}{\omega} & p_{15} \\ 0 & \cos(\omega T) & 0 & -\sin(\omega T) & p_{25} \\ 0 & \dfrac{1-\cos(\omega T)}{\omega} & 1 & \dfrac{\sin(\omega T)}{\omega} & p_{35} \\ 0 & \sin(\omega T) & 0 & \cos(\omega T) & p_{45} \\ 0 & 0 & 0 & 0 & 1 \end{bmatrix} \qquad \text{Eq. (10.146)}$$

where

$$p_{15} = \frac{\dot{x}[\omega\cos(\omega T)T - \sin(\omega T)] - \dot{y}[\omega\sin(\omega T)T - (1 - \cos(\omega T))]}{\omega^2} \qquad \text{Eq. (10.147)}$$

$$p_{25} = -T[\dot{x}\sin(\omega T) + \dot{y}\cos(\omega T)] \qquad \text{Eq. (10.148)}$$

$$p_{35} = \frac{\dot{x}[\omega\sin(\omega T)T - (1 - \cos(\omega T))] - \dot{y}[\omega\cos(\omega T)T - \sin(\omega T)]}{\omega^2} \qquad \text{Eq. (10.149)}$$

$$p_{45} = T[\dot{x}\cos(\omega T) - \dot{y}\sin(\omega T)] \qquad \text{Eq. (10.150)}$$

Finally, there are several options for the process noise covariance matrix depending on the assumptions. A simple one is

$$Q = Q_s \begin{bmatrix} (T^4/4) & (T^3/3) & 0 & 0 & 0 \\ (T^3/2) & (T^2) & 0 & 0 & 0 \\ 0 & 0 & (T^4/4) & (T^3/3) & 0 \\ 0 & 0 & (T^3/2) & (T^2) & 0 \\ 0 & 0 & 0 & 0 & \left(\dfrac{Q_\omega T^2}{Q_s}\right) \end{bmatrix} . \qquad \text{Eq. (10.151)}$$

where Q_ω is the density for the noise process associated with the turn rate variance.

Consider a target traveling in a circle in a horizontal plane at a rate of $\omega = \pi/200$ radians per second. For this example, truth includes very little process noise. It is of interest to track the target with both a CV filter and a CT filter. Because extended Kalman filters are vulnerable to errors in the initial measurements, both filters have been "kick-started" by very low measurement noise for the first *20* or so measurements and then increase to a variance of *25 m* in both the x- and y-direction. The update rate for both filters is *1.0s*. First consider the CV filter. As the process noise of the CV model is very small, the target is assumed to travel in a straight line at constant velocity. Because of this modeling mismatch, the process noise must be increased until the estimate becomes unbiased. Figure 10.52 shows the residuals of the x-component for two different values of Q_s. With $Q_s = 0.001$, the filter is clearly biased. However, if Q_s is raised to $Q_s = 0.01$, the bias appears to be removed.

Now consider the CT filter. Figure 10.53 shows the residuals of the x-component for the CT filter with very small process noise (in this case $Q_\omega = 0$). It can be seen that the filter appears to be unbiased. Lastly, Fig. 10.54 shows the predicted state estimate error covariance for both the CV and the CT filters. Note that the CT estimate is lower than that of the CV estimate, but also that the estimate is periodic with period π/ω.

Having described the CT filter, it is now time for a brief description of the IMM algorithm. An IMM can be built with any number of models, but three is common, each providing the model for one of the target assumed states. The algorithm starts with a matrix P_{ij}, known a priori, that defines the probability that at any given update, the target will transition from state i to state j, where i is the row of the matrix and j is the column. Because it is assumed that the target is in only one of these states, the rows of the P_{ij} matrix must sum to unity. If it is expected that the target will stay within a single state for an appreciable amount of time, the diagonals of the P_{ij} matrix will be large, and the off-diagonal terms small.

A convenient place to start the description is to assume that there are b models that have just completed a measurement update. This provides an estimate, $\hat{x}_i(k|k)$, a state estimate error covariance $\hat{P}_i(k|k)$, a probability that the target is in state i, $\lambda_i(k)$, where i is one of the b models. The initial probability $\lambda_i(0)$ may be set to $1/b$ for all i. First, the conditional probabilities, λ_{ij}, are calculated. These are the probabilities that, given the target is in state j, it transitioned from i. They are found by

$$\lambda_{ij}(k) = \frac{P_{ij}(k)\lambda_i(k)}{\bar{C}_j},$$

Eq. (10.152)

where $\bar{C}_j$ is the pre-measurement probability that the target is in state j and is calculated by

$$\bar{C}_j(k) = \sum_{i=1}^{b} P_{ij}(k)\lambda_i(k).$$

Eq. (10.153)

Note that $\sum_j \bar{C}_j(k) = 1$, then all the columns of $\lambda_{ij}(k)$ will also be equal to unity.

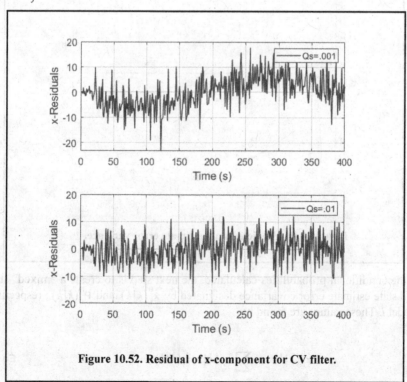

Figure 10.52. Residual of x-component for CV filter.

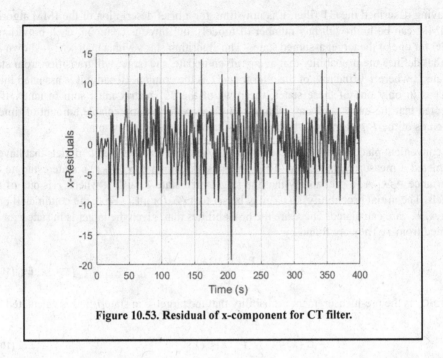

Figure 10.53. Residual of x-component for CT filter.

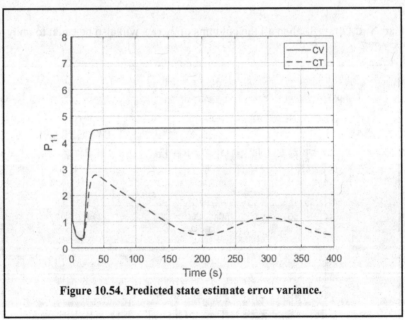

Figure 10.54. Predicted state estimate error variance.

With the conditional probabilities calculated, the next step is to create a "mixed" state estimate and state estimate error covariance designated by $\hat{\mathbf{x}}_i^0(k|k)$ and $\mathbf{P}_i^0(k|k)$, respectively, for each model i. These values are found by

$$\hat{\mathbf{x}}_i^0(k|k) = \sum_{i=1}^{b} \lambda_{ij}(k|k)\hat{\mathbf{x}}_i(k|k) \qquad \text{Eq. (10.154)}$$

and

$$P_j^0(k|k) = \sum_{i=1}^{b} \lambda_{ij}(k|k)[P_i(k|k) + (\hat{x}_i(k|k) - \hat{x}_i^0(k|k))(\hat{x}_i(k|k) - \hat{x}_i^0(k|k))^\dagger] \qquad \text{Eq. (10.155)}$$

where $\hat{x}_i(k|k)$ and $P_i(k|k)$ are the output from the current step of the "unmixed filters." The mixed estimate and covariance are used in the next time update for each model. That is

$$\hat{x}_j^0(k+1|k) = \Phi_j \hat{x}_j^0(k|k) \qquad \text{Eq. (10.156)}$$

$$P_j^0(k+1|k) = \Phi_j P_j^0(k|k)\Phi_j^\dagger + Q_j \qquad \text{Eq. (10.157)}$$

$$C_j(k) = H_j P_j^0(k+1|k)H_j^\dagger + R_j \qquad \text{Eq. (10.158)}$$

where H_j, Q_j, R_j are the measurement matrix, process noise covariance matrix and measurement noise covariance matrix, respectively, for each model. Note that the time dependence has been suppressed under the assumption that these are constant, but that is not required. As from the previous section, C_j is the residual covariance matrix for each filter.

The measurement update is taken using the propagated mixed state estimate

$$\tilde{y}_j(k) = z_j(k) - H_j \hat{x}_j^0(k+1). \qquad \text{Eq. (10.159)}$$

The output of the measurement update results in the update of the unmixed filters

$$K_j(k) = P_j^0(k+1|k)H_j^\dagger C_j^{-1} \qquad \text{Eq. (10.160)}$$

$$\hat{x}_j(k+1|k+1) = \hat{x}_j^0(k+1|k) + K_j(k)\tilde{y}_j(k) \qquad \text{Eq. (10.161)}$$

$$P_j(k+1|k+1) = P_j^0(k+1|k) - K_j(k)H_j P_j^0(k+1|k). \qquad \text{Eq. (10.162)}$$

In order to calculate an update for the model probabilities $\lambda_j(k+1)$, the likelihood that the measurement fits each of the given models is calculated by

$$L_j = \frac{1}{(2\pi)^{r/2} |C_j(k)|^{1/2}} \exp\left(\frac{-y_j^\dagger(k)C_j^{-1}\tilde{y}_j(k)}{2}\right) \qquad \text{Eq. (10.163)}$$

where r is the length of the measurement vector z, and $|C_j(k)|$ is the determinant of the residual covariance matrix at time k. The new model probabilities are simply the normalized likelihood times the pre-measurement probability

$$\lambda_j(k+1) = \frac{\bar{c}_j L_j}{\sum_{i=1}^{b} \bar{c}_i L_i}. \qquad \text{Eq. (10.164)}$$

If an output is required, the combined state estimate and state estimate error covariance can be calculated using the updated probabilities

$$\hat{x}_i(k+1|k+1) = \sum_{i=1}^{b} \lambda_i(k+1)\hat{x}_i(k+1|k+1) \qquad \text{Eq. (10.165)}$$

$$\mathbf{P}(k+1|k+1) = \sum_{i=1}^{b} \lambda_i(k+1)[\mathbf{P}_i(k+1|k+1) + \qquad\qquad \textbf{Eq. (10.166)}$$

$$\{\hat{\mathbf{x}}_i(k+1|k+1) - \hat{\mathbf{x}}(k+1|k+1)\}\{\hat{\mathbf{x}}_i(k+1|k+1) - \hat{\mathbf{x}}(k+1|k+1)\}^\dagger]$$

As an example, consider a three-model IMM filter that utilizes a 4-state CV filter, a 5-state CT filter and a 6-state CA filter. The measurement variance is *25 m*. To simplify the example, it is assumed the target is moving in a straight line at constant speed with very low process noise, making a coordinated turn with larger process noise, or making a sustained acceleration with intermediate process noise. It is also assumed that it is highly likely that the target will maintain its current state; however, it if does change, any other state is equally likely. These simplifications allow for the creation of truth with the target in each of the three states for equal lengths of time, with the appropriate process noise.

In the description of the IMM algorithm, it was assumed that all the filters had the same state. Since this is not the case for most problems, a suitable combined set of states must be created. Furthermore, the state estimate error covariance **P** must also be transformed to and from the combined state. For this example, the simplest combined state is that of the 6-state CA filter. More specifically, the combined state is

$$\hat{\mathbf{x}} = \begin{bmatrix} x \\ \dot{x} \\ \ddot{x} \\ y \\ \dot{y} \\ \ddot{y} \end{bmatrix}. \qquad\qquad \textbf{Eq. (10.167)}$$

The CV filter state can be transformed to be combined state simply by setting the acceleration components to zero. All that remains is to be able to move back and forth from the combined state to the CT state. The transformation from the combined state to the CT state can be accomplished simply by calculating

$$\omega = \frac{\dot{x}\ddot{y} - \dot{y}\ddot{x}}{\dot{x}^2 + \dot{y}^2}. \qquad\qquad \textbf{Eq. (10.168)}$$

The transformation of the covariance matrix is slightly more complicated. Here a 5×6 matrix must be calculated as

$$\mathbf{A}_{C2CT} = \frac{\partial \mathbf{x}_{CT}}{\partial \mathbf{x}_C}, \qquad\qquad \textbf{Eq. (10.169)}$$

taken at the current state, where $\mathbf{x}_{CT}$ is the CT state vector and $\mathbf{x}_C$ is the combined state vector. Fortunately, since the CT filter closely resembles the CV filter, the only non-zero entries of $\mathbf{A}_{C2CT}$ are

$$\mathbf{A}_{C2CT}(1,1) = \mathbf{A}_{C2CT}(2,2) = \mathbf{A}_{C2CT}(3,4) = \mathbf{A}_{C2CT}(4,5) = 1, \qquad \textbf{Eq. (10.170)}$$

and

$$\mathbf{A}_{C2CT}(5,3) = \frac{-\dot{y}}{\dot{x}^2 + \dot{y}^2}, \qquad\qquad \textbf{Eq. (10.171)}$$

$$A_{C2CT}(5, 6) = \frac{\dot{x}}{\dot{x}^2 + \dot{y}^2} . \qquad \text{Eq. (10.172)}$$

The state estimate error covariance matrix for the CT filter is now calculated by

$$P_{CT} = A_{C2CT} P_C (A_{C2CT})^\dagger . \qquad \text{Eq. (10.173)}$$

The process to convert back to the combined state and covariance is similar. The state is transformed simply by calculating

$$\ddot{x} = -\omega \dot{y} \qquad \text{Eq. (10.174)}$$

$$\ddot{y} = \omega \dot{x} , \qquad \text{Eq. (10.175)}$$

and calculating the A_{CT2C} matrix using Eq. (10.169) with different $(\partial x_C / \partial x_{CT})$ each time and solving at the current state. Once again, the only nonzero elements of the 6×5 A_{CT2C} matrix are

$$A_{CT2C}(1, 1) = A_{CT2C}(2, 2) = A_{CT2C}(4, 3) = A_{CT2C}(4, 5) = 1 , \qquad \text{Eq. (10.176)}$$

$$A_{CT2C}(3, 5) = -\dot{y} \qquad \text{Eq. (10.177)}$$

$$A_{CT2C}(6, 5) = \dot{x} \qquad \text{Eq. (10.178)}$$

with the combined covariance matrix P found using

$$P = A_{CT2C} P_{CT} (A_{CT2C})^\dagger . \qquad \text{Eq. (10.179)}$$

Returning to the example, Fig. 10.55 shows the truth state of the target and the average model probabilities for ten thousand runs. The target is traveling at nearly constant velocity for the first 400 s, executes a coordinated turn for the second $400s$, and executes a sustained acceleration in a straight line for the last $400s$. The figure indicates that the CV, CT and CA filters respectively dominate the time segments that the truth matches the model. However, this is noticeable mixing during the first $800s$. This should not be surprising because even though there is a difference in the process noise, the dynamics of both the CV and CT models can also be modeled with the CA filter. For the last $400s$ there is less mixing as neither the low process noise CV filter, nor the higher process noise CT filter can adequately model the sustained acceleration of the target during this period. Figure 10.56 shows the variance of the x-position for ten thousand runs of both the IMM filter and a CA filter whose process noise was chosen to keep the filter unbiased. The IMM filter clearly outperforms the CA filter. Note that these are still "bumps" in the variance, indicating that the change in the state was too abrupt to handle without a short bias in the filter.

Before leaving this section on filtering, it is worthwhile to review a few practical considerations. First, and perhaps foremost, any given filter implementation will likely require some level of "tuning" in order to best match the filter to the envelope of expected targets. Although it is worthwhile to decouple filters into Cartesian coordinate filters, this is difficult to do for radar tracking because almost all radars track in range and angle. That said, the extended Kalman filter, while not truly optimal, can provide robust performance. Most of the provided examples assumed that only the position of the target was measured. In fact, many radar systems can also measure velocity. It was shown that including acceleration into the filter can provide benefits. In practice, the improvements of filters that include acceleration, but only measure position, are quite limited.

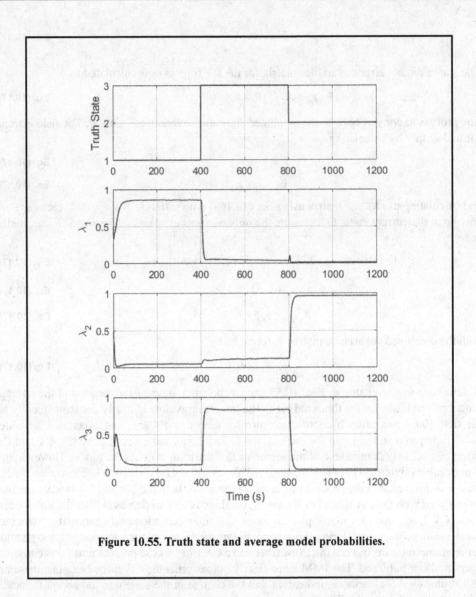

Figure 10.55. Truth state and average model probabilities.

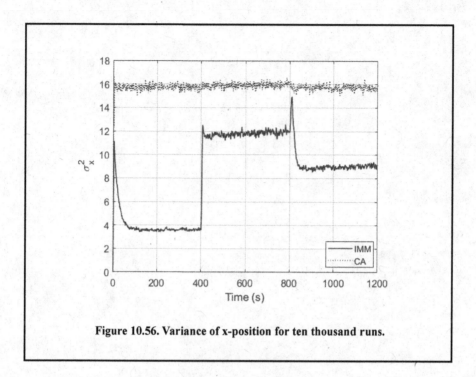

Figure 10.56. Variance of x-position for ten thousand runs.

Chapter 11

Canonical and Finite Difference Time Domain Methods for RCS Computation

Atef Z. Elsherbeni

In this chapter, the phenomenon of target scattering and methods of computing the radar cross-section (RCS) are introduced. Target RCS fluctuates a function of aspect angle, frequency, and polarization. Analytical expressions for RCS characteristics of canonical objects like are derived. Approximate expressions for RCS of simple shapes like finite length cylinders, circular, rectangular and triangular flat plates, and truncated cones (frustums) are presented. For more complex-shaped targets like rockets and airplanes, the finite difference time domain (FDTD) method is used to compute their RCS characteristics. Numerical examples are provided to show the salient RCS features of these targets and their combinations.

11.1. Radar Cross-Section Definition

In general, radar sensitivity is measured by the radar equation, where the signal-to-noise ratio (*SNR*), is the metric used for this measurement. More specifically,

$$SNR = \frac{P_t G^2 \lambda^2 \sigma}{(4\pi)^3 R^4 k T_s B L} ,$$

Eq. (11.1)

where P_t is the peak transmitted radar power, G is the antenna gain, λ is the wavelength, σ is the target radar cross-section (RCS), R is the range to the target, k is Boltzman's constant, T_s is the system effective temperature in degrees Kelvin, B is the bandwidth, and L is the total radar 2-way losses. The emphasis of this chapter is on the target RCS, σ, which can be very complicated to estimate. The RCS is primarily a function of the target size, shape, and its dielectric characteristic. Therefore, its value depends on many factors including the wavelength, polarization, direction and amount of incident energy on the target, as well as the size, complexity, and the target material and / or coating. Assume the power density of a wave incident on a target located at range R away from the radar is P_{Di}. The simplest representation of the target RCS is σ, is shown in the radar equation. In this context, the RCS is defined as the ratio of the power reflected back to the radar to the power density incident on the target,

$$\sigma = (P_r / P_{Di}) \ m^2 .$$

Eq. (11.2)

The units of the reflected power P_r is *Watts*, and the units for the incident power density P_{Di} is W/m^2, accordingly the units for the RCS is m^2 (i.e., *dBsm* when using decibel arithmetic). The power density of the scattered waves off the target at the receiving antenna is P_{Dr},

$$P_{Dr} = P_r / (4\pi R^2) .$$

Eq. (11.3)

Equating Eqs. (11.2) and (11.1) yields

$$\sigma = 4\pi R^2 (P_{Dr}/P_{Di}),$$
Eq. (11.4)

and in order to ensure that the radar receiving antenna is in the far field (i.e., scattered waves received by the antenna are planar), Eq. (11.4) is modified such that

$$\sigma = 4\pi \lim_{R \to \infty} R^2 \frac{\left|E^s\right|^2}{\left|E^i\right|^2} \qquad for\ 3D\ scatterers$$
Eq. (11.5)

$$\sigma = 2\pi \lim_{R \to \infty} R \frac{\left|E^s\right|^2}{\left|E^i\right|^2} \qquad for\ 2D\ scatterers$$

where E^i and E^s represent the incident and scattered field intensities on and off the target. The RCS defined by Eq. (11.5) is often referred to as either the monostatic RCS, the backscattered RCS, or simply target RCS. Bistatic RCS expression is the same; however, in this case, the radar receiving the signal is a different coordinates relative to the radar illuminating the target.

The analysis presented in this chapter mainly assumes far field monostatic RCS in the optical region. Near field RCS, bistatic RCS, and RCS measurements in the Rayleigh region will not be considered since their treatment falls beyond the scope of this book. Additionally, RCS treatment in this chapter is mainly concerned with narrow band (NB) frequency cases. In other words, the extent of the target under consideration falls within a single range bin of the radar. Wideband (WB) RCS measurements will be briefly addressed in other chapters of the book. Wideband radar range bins are small, typically in the order of *10 - 50 cm*. Hence, the target under consideration may cover many range bins. The RCS value in an individual range bin corresponds to the portion of the target falling within that bin.

11.2. RCS Dependency on Aspect Angle and Frequency

Radar cross-section fluctuates as a function of radar aspect angle and frequency. For the purpose of illustration, isotropic point scatterers are considered. An isotropic scatterer is one that scatters incident waves equally in all directions. Consider the geometry shown in Fig. 11.1. In this case, two unity ($1m^2$) isotropic scatterers are aligned and placed along the radar line of sight (zero aspect angle) at a far field range R. The spacing between the two scatterers is *1 m*. The radar aspect angle is then changed from zero to $180°$, and the composite RCS of the two scatterers measured by the radar is computed.

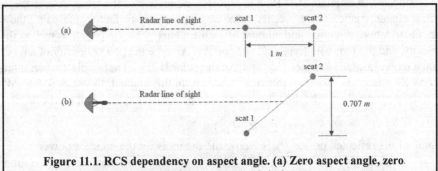

Figure 11.1. RCS dependency on aspect angle. (a) Zero aspect angle, zero electrical spacing. (b) $45°$ aspect angle, $1.414m$ electrical spacing.

This composite RCS consists of the superposition of the two individual radar cross-sections. Taking scatterer-1 as a phase reference, when the aspect angle is varied, the composite RCS is modified by the phase that corresponds to the electrical spacing between the two scatterers. For example, at an aspect angle $10°$, the electrical spacing between the two scatterers is

$$elec\text{-}spacing = \frac{2 \times (1.0 \times \cos(10°))}{\lambda} \qquad \textbf{Eq. (11.6)}$$

where λ is the radar operating wavelength.

Fig. 11.2 shows the composite RCS corresponding to this experiment where it is clearly evident that the RCS is dependent on the radar aspect angle and the spacing between the scatterers. Thus, knowledge of this constructive and destructive interference between the individual scatterers can be very critical when a radar tries to extract the RCS of complex or maneuvering targets. This is true because of two reasons. First, the aspect angle may be continuously changing. Second, the complex target RCS can be viewed as being made up from contributions of many individual scattering points distributed on the target surface. These scattering points are often called "scattering centers". Many approximate RCS prediction methods generate a set of scattering centers that define the backscattering characteristics of such complex targets.

Next, to demonstrate RCS dependency on frequency, consider the experiment shown in Fig. 11.3. In this case, two far field unity isotropic scatterers are aligned with radar line of sight, and the composite RCS measured by the radar as the frequency is varied from *8 GHz* to *12.5 GHz* (X-band). Figure 11.4 shows the composite RCS versus frequency for scatterer spacing of *0.25m* and *0.75m*.

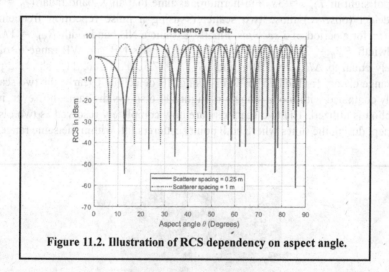

Figure 11.2. Illustration of RCS dependency on aspect angle.

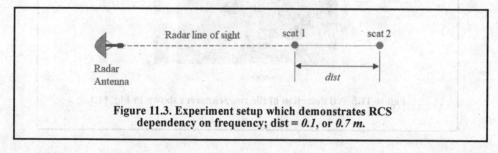

Figure 11.3. Experiment setup which demonstrates RCS dependency on frequency; dist = *0.1*, or *0.7 m*.

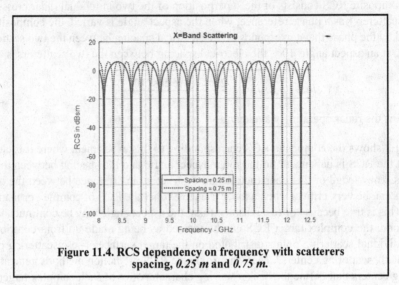

Figure 11.4. RCS dependency on frequency with scatterers spacing, *0.25 m* and *0.75 m*.

Observation of Fig. 11.4 clearly shows that the RCS is fluctuating as a function of frequency. Furthermore, little frequency change can cause serious RCS fluctuation when the scatterer spacing is large. Alternatively, when scattering centers are relatively close, it requires more frequency variation to produce significant RCS fluctuation.

Referring to Fig. 11.1, assume that the two scatterers complete a full revolution about the radar line of sight in $T_{rev} = 3s$. Furthermore, assume that an X-band radar ($f_0 = 9GHz$) is used to detect (observe) those two scatterers using a pulse repetition frequency (PRF), $f_r = 300Hz$ for a period of *3 seconds*. Finally, assume a NB bandwidth $B_{NB} = 1MHz$ and a WB bandwidth $B_{WB} = 2GHz$. It follows that the radar's NB and WB range resolutions are respectively equal to $\Delta R_{NB} = 150m$ and $\Delta R_{WB} = 7.5cm$. Figure 11.5 shows a plot of the detected range history for the two scatterers using NB detection. Clearly, the two scatterers are completely contained within one range bin. Figure 11.6 shows the same; however, in this case WB detection is utilized. The two scatterers are now completely resolved as two distinct scatterers, except during the times where both point scatterers fall within the same range bin.

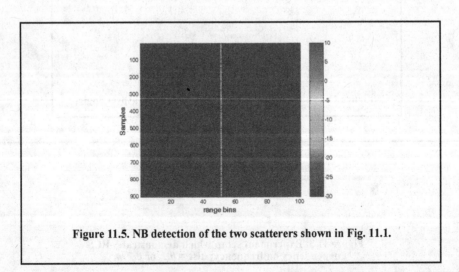

Figure 11.5. NB detection of the two scatterers shown in Fig. 11.1.

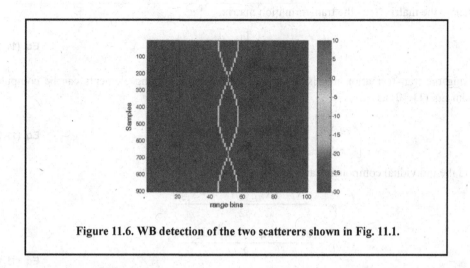

Figure 11.6. WB detection of the two scatterers shown in Fig. 11.1.

11.3. Target Scattering Matrix

Target backscattered RCS is commonly described by a matrix known as the scattering matrix, and is denoted by [$\mathbf{S}$]. When an arbitrarily linearly polarized wave is incident on a target, the backscattered field is then given by

$$\begin{bmatrix} E_1^s \\ E_2^s \end{bmatrix} = [\mathbf{S}] \begin{bmatrix} E_1^i \\ E_2^i \end{bmatrix} = \begin{bmatrix} s_{11} & s_{12} \\ s_{21} & s_{22} \end{bmatrix} \begin{bmatrix} E_1^i \\ E_2^i \end{bmatrix} .$$

Eq. (11.7)

The superscripts i and s denote incident and scattered fields. The quantities s_{ij} are in general complex, and the electric field subscripts 1 and 2 represent any combination of orthogonal polarizations. More precisely, $1 = H, R$, and $2 = V, L$, where H, R, V, L, respectively indicate horizontal, right circular, vertical, and left circular polarizations. From Eq. (11.4), the backscattered RCS is related to the scattering matrix components by the following relation:

$$\begin{bmatrix} \sigma_{11} & \sigma_{12} \\ \sigma_{21} & \sigma_{22} \end{bmatrix} = 4\pi R^2 \begin{bmatrix} |s_{11}|^2 & |s_{12}|^2 \\ |s_{21}|^2 & |s_{22}|^2 \end{bmatrix} .$$

Eq. (11.8)

It follows that once a scattering matrix is specified, the target backscattered RCS can be computed for any combination of transmitting and receiving polarizations. The reader is advised to see Ruck (1970, Vol. 1) for ways to calculate the scattering matrix [$\mathbf{S}$].

Rewriting Eq. (11.7) in terms of the different possible orthogonal polarizations yields

$$\begin{bmatrix} E_H^s \\ E_V^s \end{bmatrix} = \begin{bmatrix} s_{HH} & s_{HV} \\ s_{VH} & s_{VV} \end{bmatrix} \begin{bmatrix} E_H^i \\ E_V^i \end{bmatrix}$$

Eq. (11.9)

$$\begin{bmatrix} E_R^s \\ E_L^s \end{bmatrix} = \begin{bmatrix} s_{RR} & s_{RL} \\ s_{LR} & s_{LL} \end{bmatrix} \begin{bmatrix} E_R^i \\ E_L^i \end{bmatrix} .$$

Eq. (11.10)

Denote the matrix **T** as the transformation matrix,

$$[\mathbf{T}] = \frac{1}{\sqrt{2}}\begin{bmatrix} 1 & -j \\ 1 & j \end{bmatrix}.$$

Eq. (11.11)

Using the transformation matrix notation, the circular scattering elements can be computed from Eq. (11.10) as

$$\begin{bmatrix} s_{RR} & s_{RL} \\ s_{LR} & s_{LL} \end{bmatrix} = [\mathbf{T}]\begin{bmatrix} s_{HH} & s_{HV} \\ s_{VH} & s_{VV} \end{bmatrix}\begin{bmatrix} 1 & 0 \\ 0 & -1 \end{bmatrix}[\mathbf{T}]^{-1},$$

Eq. (11.12)

and the individual components are

$$s_{RR} = \frac{-s_{VV} + s_{HH} - j(s_{HV} + s_{VH})}{2}$$

$$s_{RL} = \frac{s_{VV} + s_{HH} + j(s_{HV} - s_{VH})}{2}$$

$$s_{LR} = \frac{s_{VV} + s_{HH} - j(s_{HV} - s_{VH})}{2}$$

$$s_{LL} = \frac{-s_{VV} + s_{HH} + j(s_{HV} + s_{VH})}{2}$$

Eq. (11.13)

Similarly, the linear scattering elements are given by

$$\begin{bmatrix} s_{HH} & s_{HV} \\ s_{VH} & s_{VV} \end{bmatrix} = [\mathbf{T}]^{-1}\begin{bmatrix} s_{RR} & s_{RL} \\ s_{LR} & s_{LL} \end{bmatrix}[\mathbf{T}]\begin{bmatrix} 1 & 0 \\ 0 & -1 \end{bmatrix}$$

Eq. (11.14)

and the individual components are

$$s_{HH} = \frac{s_{RR} + s_{RL} + s_{LR} + s_{LL}}{2}$$

$$s_{VH} = \frac{j(s_{RR} - s_{LR} + s_{RL} - s_{LL})}{2}$$

$$s_{HV} = \frac{j(s_{RR} + s_{LR} - s_{RL} - s_{LL})}{2}$$

$$s_{VV} = \frac{-s_{RR} - s_{LL} + s_{RL} + s_{LR}}{2}$$

Eq. (11.15)

11.4. Scattering off Basic Canonical Objects

In this section the scattering from some basic canonical objects such as cylinders, ellipsoids, spheres, and wedges is presented. All these objects have an exact analytical formulation for the scattering from known excitations, usually in a form of cylindrical or plane waves. The cylinders and the wedges are more common in shaping up radar targets, and hence a complete analytical formulation for their scattered near and far fields is presented here, and from the far field their RCS can be evaluated. The spheres and ellipsoids are less likely to be used for target construction, thus we will present here some approximate expressions for their RCS calculations without going through the details for their exact solutions as they are mathematically involved. Later in the chapter, a numerical simulation for combinations of these objects will be presented with some sample results.

11.4.1. Cylinder

In this section, scattering of a plane wave at oblique incidence on an infinite circular dielectric cylinder of radius a is considered. Expressions for the scattered and internal fields will be derived following the procedure presented in Wait (1955), Elsherbeni (1994), and Henin et al. (2007). Figure 11.7 depicts the problem geometry in three-dimensional space. A transverse magnetic to the z-axis (TM_z) plane wave is incident on an infinite dielectric cylinder, where the propagation vector makes an angle θ_0 with the negative z-axis. The incident electric field vector and the propagation vector lie in the plane $\varphi = \varphi_0$.

Mathematically, the electric field of a propagating plane wave may be written as

$$\mathbf{E}^i = \mathbf{E}_0 e^{-j\mathbf{k}\cdot\mathbf{r}},$$
Eq. (11.16)

where

$$\mathbf{E}_0 = E_0(-\cos\theta_0\cos\varphi_0\hat{\mathbf{x}} - \cos\theta_0\sin\varphi_0\hat{\mathbf{y}} + \sin\theta_0\hat{\mathbf{z}}),$$
Eq. (11.17)

$$\mathbf{k} = -k(\sin\theta_0\cos\varphi_0\hat{\mathbf{x}} + \sin\theta_0\sin\varphi_0\hat{\mathbf{y}} + \cos\theta_0\hat{\mathbf{z}}),$$
Eq. (11.18)

$$\mathbf{r} = x\,\hat{\mathbf{x}} + y\,\hat{\mathbf{y}} + z\,\hat{\mathbf{z}} = \rho\cos\varphi\hat{\mathbf{x}} + \rho\sin\varphi\hat{\mathbf{y}} + z\,\hat{\mathbf{z}}.$$
Eq. (11.19)

The vectors $\hat{\mathbf{x}}, \hat{\mathbf{y}}, \hat{\mathbf{z}}$ are respectively the unit vectors along the x, y, and z directions, and $k = 2\pi/\lambda$. The dot product in the exponential of equation (11.16) is then given by,

$$\mathbf{k}\cdot\mathbf{r} = -k(\rho\sin\theta_0\cos\varphi\cos\varphi_0 + \rho\sin\theta_0\sin\varphi\sin\varphi_0 + z\cos\theta_0),$$
Eq. (11.20)
$$= -k(\rho\sin\theta_0\cos(\varphi - \varphi_0) + z\cos\theta_0)$$

It follows that the components of the electric field may be written as,

$$E_z^i = E_0\sin\theta_0 e^{jkz\cos\theta_0}e^{jk\rho\sin\theta_0\cos(\varphi-\varphi_0)}$$

$$E_x^i = -E_0\cos\theta_0\cos\varphi_0 e^{jkz\cos\theta_0}e^{jk\rho\sin\theta_0\cos(\varphi-\varphi_0)}.$$
Eq. (11.21)

$$E_y^i = -E_0\cos\theta_0\sin\varphi_0 e^{jkz\cos\theta_0}e^{jk\rho\sin\theta_0\cos(\varphi-\varphi_0)}$$

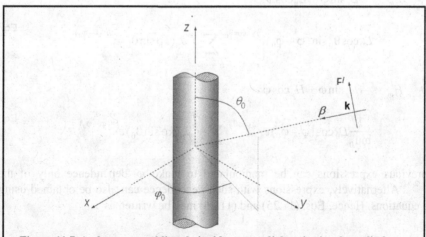

Figure 11.7. A plane wave obliquely incident on a dielectric circular cylinder.

Using cylindrical wave transformations, these components can be written as

$$E_z^i = E_0 \sin\theta_0 e^{jkz\cos\theta_0} \sum_{n=-\infty}^{\infty} j^n J_n(k\rho\sin\theta_0) e^{jn(\varphi-\varphi_0)}$$

$$E_x^i = -E_0 \cos\theta_0 \cos\varphi_0 e^{jkz\cos\theta_0} \sum_{n=-\infty}^{\infty} j^n J_n(k\rho\sin\theta_0) e^{jn(\varphi-\varphi_0)}.$$ **Eq. (11.22)**

$$E_y^i = -E_0 \cos\theta_0 \sin\varphi_0 e^{jkz\cos\theta_0} \sum_{n=-\infty}^{\infty} j^n J_n(k\rho\sin\theta_0) e^{jn(\varphi-\varphi_0)}$$

where $J_n(x)$ is the Bessel function of first kind of order n and argument x.

Assuming a plane wave, the magnetic field is related to the electric field by the relation,

$$\mathbf{H} = \frac{1}{\omega\mu}\mathbf{k} \times \mathbf{E},$$ **Eq. (11.23)**

where ω is the angular frequency of the incident wave. Using Eq. (11.22) in Eq. (11.23), the magnetic field components may be given by

$$H_x^i = -\frac{k}{\omega\mu_0}E_0 \sin\theta_0 e^{jkz\cos\theta_0} \sum_{n=-\infty}^{\infty} j^n J_n(k\rho\sin\theta_0) e^{jn(\varphi-\varphi_0)}$$

$$H_y^i = \frac{k}{\omega\mu_0}E_0 \cos\varphi_0 e^{jkz\cos\theta_0} \sum_{n=-\infty}^{\infty} j^n J_n(k\rho\sin\theta_0) e^{jn(\varphi-\varphi_0)}.$$ **Eq. (11.24)**

$$H_z^i = 0$$

The φ component of incident electric field and magnetic field may be found as

$$E_\varphi^i = -E_x^i \sin\varphi + E_y^i \cos\varphi$$

$$= E_0 \cos\theta_0 \sin(\varphi-\varphi_0) e^{jkz\cos\theta_0} \sum_{n=-\infty}^{\infty} j^n J_n(k\rho\sin\theta_0) e^{jn(\varphi-\varphi_0)}$$ **Eq. (11.25)**

$$H_\varphi^i = -H_x^i \sin\varphi + H_y^i \cos\varphi$$

$$= \frac{k}{\omega\mu_0}E_0 \cos(\varphi-\varphi_0) e^{jkz\cos\theta_0} \sum_{n=-\infty}^{\infty} j^n J_n(k\rho\sin\theta_0) e^{jn(\varphi-\varphi_0)}.$$ **Eq. (11.26)**

The previous expressions can be manipulated to make φ dependence only of the form $e^{jn(\varphi-\varphi_0)}$. Alternatively, expressions with such dependence can also be obtained using Maxwell's equations. Hence, Eqs. (11.25) and (11.26) may be written as

$$E_\varphi^i = -\frac{\cos\theta_0}{k\rho\sin\theta_0}E_0 e^{jkz\cos\theta_0}\sum_{n=-\infty}^{\infty}nj^n J_n(k\rho\sin\theta_0)e^{jn(\varphi-\varphi_0)}$$

Eq. (11.27)

$$H_\varphi^i = -\frac{jk}{\omega\mu_0}E_0 e^{jkz\cos\theta_0}\sum_{n=-\infty}^{\infty}j^n J_n'(k\rho\sin\theta_0)e^{jn(\varphi-\varphi_0)}.$$

Eq. (11.28)

For the scattered fields, the z-components may be written in the form,

$$E_z^s = \sum_{n=-\infty}^{\infty}a_n^s H_n^{(2)}(k\rho\sin\theta_0)e^{jn(\varphi-\varphi_0)}e^{jkz\cos\theta_0}$$

Eq. (11.29)

$$H_z^s = \sum_{n=-\infty}^{\infty}b_n^s H_n^{(2)}(k\rho\sin\theta_0)e^{jn(\varphi-\varphi_0)}e^{jkz\cos\theta_0}.$$

Eq. (11.30)

The prime indicates derivative with respect to the full argument of the function, $H_n^{(2)}$ is the Hankel function of the second kind of order n, and (a_n^s, b_n^s) are complex constants known as the electric and magnetic fields scattering coefficients, respectively. It follows that the z-components of the internal fields (i.e., the fields inside the dielectric cylinder) may be written as

$$E_z^d = \sum_{n=-\infty}^{\infty}a_n J_n(k_\rho\rho)e^{jn(\varphi-\varphi_0)}e^{jkz\cos\theta_0}$$

Eq. (11.31)

$$H_z^d = \sum_{n=-\infty}^{\infty}b_n J_n(k_\rho\rho)e^{jn(\varphi-\varphi_0)}e^{jkz\cos\theta_0}.$$

Eq. (11.32)

where the phase constant k_ρ may be determined using the fact that the field E_z^d satisfies the wave equation. It can be shown that the phase constant inside the dielectric is now given by,

$$k_d^2 = k_\rho^2 + k_z^2,$$

Eq. (11.33)

where $k_z = k\cos\theta_0$ and $k_d = \omega\sqrt{\mu_d\varepsilon_d}$. Even without the detailed solution of the wave equation, it is obvious the variation along the z-direction should be the same in the dielectric and free-space. Thus,

$$k_\rho = \sqrt{\omega^2\mu_d\varepsilon_d - k^2(\cos\theta_0)^2}.$$

Eq. (11.34)

The φ components of the scattered and internal fields may be determined using Maxwell's equations. For the scattered field components, we have

$$H_\varphi^s = -\frac{jk}{\omega\mu_0\sin\theta_0}e^{jkz\cos\theta_0}\sum_{n=-\infty}^{\infty}a_n^s H_n^{(2)\prime}(k\rho\sin\theta_0)e^{jn(\varphi-\varphi_0)}$$

Eq. (11.35)

$$-\frac{\cos\theta_0}{k\rho(\sin\theta_0)^2}e^{jkz\cos\theta_0}\sum_{n=-\infty}^{\infty}nb_n^s H_n^{(2)}(k\rho\sin\theta_0)e^{jn(\varphi-\varphi_0)}$$

$$E_\varphi^s = -\frac{\cos\theta_0}{k\rho(\sin\theta_0)^2}e^{jkz\cos\theta_0}\sum_{n=-\infty}^{\infty}na_n^s H_n^{(2)}(k\rho\sin\theta_0)e^{jn(\varphi-\varphi_0)} \quad , \qquad \text{Eq. (11.36)}$$

$$+\frac{jk}{\omega\varepsilon_0\sin\theta_0}e^{jkz\cos\theta_0}\sum_{n=-\infty}^{\infty}b_n^s H_n^{(2)\prime}(k\rho\sin\theta_0)e^{jn(\varphi-\varphi_0)}$$

and for the internal fields components, we have

$$H_\varphi^d = -\frac{jk_d^2}{\omega\mu_d k_\rho}e^{jkz\cos\theta_0}\sum_{n=-\infty}^{\infty}a_n J_n'(k_\rho\rho)e^{jn(\varphi-\varphi_0)} \qquad \text{Eq. (11.37)}$$

$$-\frac{k\cos\theta_0}{k_\rho^2\rho}e^{jkz\cos\theta_0}\sum_{n=-\infty}^{\infty}nb_n J_n(k_\rho\rho)e^{jn(\varphi-\varphi_0)}$$

$$E_\varphi^d = -\frac{k\cos\theta_0}{k_\rho^2\rho}e^{jk_0 z\cos\theta_0}\sum_{n=-\infty}^{\infty}na_n J_n(k_\rho\rho)e^{jn(\varphi-\varphi_0)} \qquad . \qquad \text{Eq. (11.38)}$$

$$-\frac{k_d^2}{j\omega\varepsilon_d k_\rho}e^{jkz\cos\theta_0}\sum_{n=-\infty}^{\infty}b_n J_n'(k\rho\sin\theta_0)e^{jn(\varphi-\varphi_0)}$$

Now, the boundary conditions require the continuity of the tangential electric and magnetic fields on the surface of the dielectric cylinder. More precisely at $\rho = a$ we have,

$$H_z^d = H_z^i + H_z^s, \qquad H_\varphi^d = H_\varphi^i + H_\varphi^s$$
$$E_z^d = E_z^i + E_z^s, \qquad E_\varphi^d = E_\varphi^i + E_\varphi^s \qquad \text{Eq. (11.39)}$$

Upon applying the boundary conditions, both sides of the equation are multiplied by the term $\exp\{jm(\varphi-\varphi_0)\}$ and integrating (with respect to φ) from 0 to 2π. This will lead to the equality of each term in the series in the right-hand side and left-hand side. Thus, from the continuity of the z-component, we have

$$j^n E_0\sin\theta_0 J_n(v) + a_n^s H_n^{(2)}(v) = a_n J_n(u) \qquad \text{Eq. (11.40)}$$

$$b_n^s H_n^{(2)}(v) = b_n J_n(u), \qquad \text{Eq. (11.41)}$$

where

$$u = k_\rho a$$
$$v = ka\ \sin\theta_0 \qquad \text{Eq. (11.42)}$$

Similarly, for the continuity of the φ component, we have

$$\frac{-j^n\cos\theta_0}{v}nE_0 J_n(v) - \frac{\cos\theta_0}{v\sin\theta_0}na_n^s H_n^{(2)}(v) + \frac{j\omega\mu_0 a}{v}b_n^s H_n^{(2)\prime}(v) = \qquad \text{Eq. (11.43)}$$

$$-\frac{v\cos\theta_0}{u^2\sin\theta_0}na_n J_n(u) - \frac{\omega\mu_d a}{ju}b_n J_n'(u)$$

$$\frac{-j^n v}{\omega\varepsilon_0 \sin\theta_0}E_0 J_n{}'(v) - \frac{j\omega\varepsilon_0 a}{v}a_n^s H_n^{(2)}{}'(v) + \frac{\cos\theta_0}{v\sin\theta_0}nb_n^s H_n^{(2)}(v) =$$

Eq. (11.44)

$$-\frac{j\omega\varepsilon_d a}{u}a_n J_n{}'(u) - \frac{v\cos\theta_0}{u^2\sin\theta_0}nb_n J_n(u)$$

where

$$\frac{\omega\mu_0}{k} = \frac{k}{\omega\varepsilon_0} = \sqrt{\frac{\mu_0}{\varepsilon_0}} \qquad , \frac{\omega\mu_d}{k_d} = \frac{k_d}{\omega\varepsilon_d} = \sqrt{\frac{\mu_d}{\varepsilon_d}},$$

Eq. (11.45)

where (ε_0, μ_0) and (ε_d, μ_d) are, respectively, the vacuum and dielectric permittivity and permeability constants.

From Eqs. (11.40) and (11.41) the internal field coefficients may be given in terms of the scattered field coefficient as

$$a_n = \frac{1}{J_n(u)}[j^n E_0 \sin\theta_0 J_n(v) + a_n^s H_n^{(2)}(v)]$$

Eq. (11.46)

$$b_n = b_n^s \frac{H_n^{(2)}(v)}{J_n(u)}.$$

Eq. (11.47)

Substituting Eqs. (11.46) and (11.47) into Eqs. (11.43) and (11.44), respectively yields

$$\frac{-j^n \cos\theta_0}{v}nE_0 J_n(v) - \frac{\cos\theta_0}{v\sin\theta_0}na_n^s H_n^{(2)}(v) + \frac{j\omega\mu_0 a}{v}b_n^s H_n^{(2)}{}'(v) =$$

Eq. (11.48)

$$-\frac{v\cos\theta_0}{u^2\sin\theta_0}n[j^n E_0 \sin\theta_0 J_n(v) + a_n^s H_n^{(2)}(v)] - \frac{\omega\mu_d a}{ju}b_n^s \frac{H_n^{(2)}(v)}{J_n(u)}J_n{}'(u)$$

$$\frac{-j\omega\varepsilon_0 a}{v}\frac{\sin\theta_0}{}E_0 J_n{}'(v) - \frac{j\omega\varepsilon_0 a}{v}a_n^s H_n^{(2)}{}'(v) + \frac{\cos\theta_0}{v\sin\theta_0}nb_n^s H_n^{(2)}(v) = \qquad .$$

Eq. (11.49)

$$-\frac{j\omega\varepsilon_d a}{u}\frac{J_n{}'(u)}{J_n(u)}[j^n E_0 \sin\theta_0 J_n(v) + a_n^s H_n^{(2)}(v)] - \frac{v\cos\theta_0}{u^2\sin\theta_0}nb_n^s H_n^{(2)}(v)$$

Equations (11.48) and (11.49) can be written in matrix form as

$$\begin{bmatrix} \left(\frac{1}{u^2} - \frac{1}{v^2}\right)\frac{v\cos\theta_0}{\sin\theta_0}nH_n^{(2)}(v) & \frac{j\omega\mu_0 a}{v}H_n^{(2)}{}'(v) + \frac{\omega\mu_d a}{ju}\frac{H_n^{(2)}(v)}{J_n(u)}J_n{}'(u) \\ \frac{\omega\varepsilon_0 a}{jv}H_n^{(2)}{}'(v) + \frac{j\omega\varepsilon_d a}{u}H_n^{(2)}{}'(v)\frac{J_n{}'(u)}{J_n(u)} & \left(\frac{1}{u^2} - \frac{1}{v^2}\right)\frac{v\cos\theta_0}{\sin\theta_0}nH_n^{(2)}(v) \end{bmatrix} \times$$

. Eq. (11.50)

$$\begin{bmatrix} a_n^s \\ b_n^s \end{bmatrix} = \begin{bmatrix} \frac{j^n \cos\theta_0}{v}nE_0 J_n(v) - \frac{j^n v\cos\theta_0}{u^2\sin\theta_0}nE_0 \sin\theta_0 J_n(v) \\ j^{(n+1)}\frac{\omega\varepsilon_0 a}{v}E_0 \sin\theta_0 J_n{}'(v) - j^{(n+1)}\frac{\omega\varepsilon_d a}{u}E_0 \sin\theta_0 J_n(v)\frac{J_n{}'(u)}{J_n(u)} \end{bmatrix}$$

Equation (11.50) can be simplified to

$$
\left[
\begin{array}{cc}
\dfrac{v\cos\theta_0}{\sin\theta_0}nH_n^{(2)}(v)\left(\dfrac{1}{u^2}-\dfrac{1}{v^2}\right) & j\omega\mu_0 aH_n^{(2)}(v)\left(\dfrac{H_n^{(2)\prime}(v)}{v(H_n^{(2)}(v))}-\dfrac{K J_n{}'(u)}{u\, J_n(u)}\right) \\[4mm]
-j\omega\varepsilon_0 aH_n^{(2)}(v)\left(\dfrac{H_n^{(2)\prime}(v)}{v(H_n^{(2)}(v))}-\dfrac{L J_n{}'(u)}{u\, J_n(u)}\right) & \dfrac{v\cos\theta_0}{\sin\theta_0}nH_n^{(2)}(v)\left(\dfrac{1}{u^2}-\dfrac{1}{v^2}\right)
\end{array}
\right] \times \qquad \textbf{Eq. (11.51)}
$$

$$
\begin{bmatrix} a_n^s \\[2mm] b_n^s \end{bmatrix}
=
\left[
\begin{array}{c}
j^n nE_0\cos\theta_0 J_n(v)\left(\dfrac{1}{v^2}-\dfrac{1}{u^2}\right) \\[4mm]
j^{(n+1)}\omega\varepsilon_0 aE_0\sin\theta_0 J_n(v)\left(\dfrac{J_n{}'(v)}{vJ_n(v)}-\dfrac{L}{u}\dfrac{J_n{}'(u)}{(J_n)(u)}\right)
\end{array}
\right]
$$

where $u = k_\rho a$, $v = ka\,\sin\theta_0$, $K = \mu_d/\mu_0$ and $L = \varepsilon_d/\varepsilon_0$. The system in Equation (11.51) can be solved using Kramer's method. After some mathematical manipulations, the expressions for the scattering coefficients, a_n^s and b_n^s are

$$
a_n^s = -j^n E_0\sin\theta_0\left[\frac{J_n(v)}{H_n^{(2)}(v)}+j\frac{2}{\pi v^2}\left(\frac{\dfrac{1}{v}\dfrac{H_n^{(2)\prime}(v)}{H_n^{(2)}(v)}-\dfrac{K J_n{}'(u)}{u\, J_n(u)}}{[H_n^{(2)}(v)]^2 D_n}\right)\right] \qquad \textbf{Eq. (11.52)}
$$

$$
b_n^s = j^n E_0\frac{k}{\omega\mu_0}\frac{2n\cos\theta_0}{\pi v^2}\left(\frac{1}{u^2}-\frac{1}{v^2}\right)\frac{1}{[H_n^{(2)}(v)]^2 D_n} \qquad \textbf{Eq. (11.53)}
$$

where

$$
D_n = \left(\frac{H_n^{(2)\prime}(v)}{v(H_n^{(2)}(v))}-\frac{K J_n{}'(u)}{u\, J_n(u)}\right)\left(\frac{H_n^{(2)\prime}(v)}{v(H_n^{(2)}(v))}-\frac{L J_n{}'(u)}{u\, J_n(u)}\right)-\left[\left(\frac{1}{v^2}-\frac{1}{u^2}\right)n\cos\theta_0\right]^2. \qquad \textbf{Eq. (11.54)}
$$

Finally, the internal coefficients for the cylinder are

$$
a_n = -j^{(n+1)}E_0\sin\theta_0\frac{2}{\pi v^2}\left\{\frac{\dfrac{1}{v}\dfrac{H_n^{(2)\prime}(v)}{H_n^{(2)}(v)}-\dfrac{K J_n{}'(u)}{u\, J_n(u)}}{J_n(u)H_n^{(2)}(v)D_n}\right\} \qquad \textbf{Eq. (11.55)}
$$

$$
b_n = j^n E_0\frac{k}{\omega\mu_0}\frac{2n\sin\theta_0\cos\theta_0}{\pi v^2}\left(\frac{1}{u^2}-\frac{1}{v^2}\right)\frac{1}{J_n(u)H_n^{(2)}(v)D_n}. \qquad \textbf{Eq. (11.56)}
$$

The RCS for the dielectric cylinder can then be evaluated using Eq. (11.5) with the z-component of the incident and scattered electric fields given as

$$
E_z^i = E_0\sin\theta_0 e^{jk\rho\sin\theta_0\cos(\varphi-\varphi_0)} \qquad \textbf{Eq. (11.57)}
$$

$$
E_z^s = a_0^s H_0^{(2)}(v_\rho)+2\sum_{n=1}^{\infty} a_n^s H_n^{(2)}(v_\rho)\cos[n(\varphi-\varphi_0)] \qquad \textbf{Eq. (11.58)}
$$

where $v_\rho = k\rho \sin\theta_0$. For the far scattered field, the following approximation for the Hankel function is to be used for large values of ρ;

$$H_n^{(2)}(k\rho \sin\theta_0) \cong \sqrt{\frac{2j}{\pi k\rho \sin\theta_0}} \; j^n e^{-j(k\rho \sin\theta_0)} \; .$$

Eq. (11.59)

With this approximation and the definition of the RCS in Eq. (11.5) the z-component of the RCS of the cylinder takes the form

$$\sigma_z = \frac{4}{k} \left| a_0^s + 2 \sum_{n=1}^{\infty} j^n a_n^s \cos[n(\varphi - \varphi_0)] \right|^2 .$$

Eq. (11.60)

The scattering from a conducting cylinder can easily be evaluated form the above analysis numerically by assuming large value for the relative dielectric material of the cylinder, or by deriving the proper expressions for the scattering coefficients, a_n^s and b_n^s using Eqs. (11.52) and (11.53) when ε_d approaches infinity.

The above analysis is for an oblique incident plane wave with arbitrary incident angles. For normal incidence on the cylinder, one has to set $\theta_0 = 90°$. The RCS for a perfectly conducting cylinder excited by a *2 GHz* incident plane wave at normal incidence and at oblique incidence are shown in Figs. 11.8 and 11.9, respectively. It is clearly visible that the oblique incidence alters the maximum value of the resulting RCS.

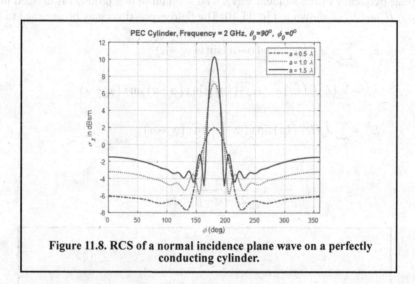

Figure 11.8. RCS of a normal incidence plane wave on a perfectly conducting cylinder.

11.4.2. Dielectric-Capped Wedge

The geometry of a dielectric-capped perfectly conducting (PEC) wedge is shown in Fig. 11.10. It is mathematically possible to find the exact scattered field expressions for this configuration of a 2-D wedge capped with a dielectric cylinder following the formulation presented in Elsherbeni and Hamid (1986). When this analytical solution is obtained, it can be reduced to several other configurations, such as wedge with conducting cap, wedge with sharp edge, half-plane with dielectric or conducting capped cylinder. Using the cylindrical coordinates system, the excitation due to an electric line current of complex amplitude I_e located at (ρ_0, φ_0) results in TM_z incident field with the electric field expression given by

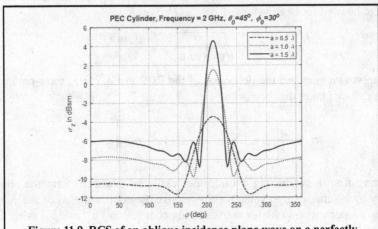

Figure 11.9. RCS of an oblique incidence plane wave on a perfectly conducting cylinder.

$$E_z^i = -I_e \frac{\omega\mu_0}{4} H_0^{(2)}(k|\rho - \rho_0|) \,, \qquad \text{Eq. (11.61)}$$

where $k = 2\pi/\lambda$, and $H_0^{(2)}$ is the Hankel function of the second kind of order zero, and ω is the angular frequency of the incident wave. The solution to this problem is divided into three regions, *I, II*, and *III* as shown in Fig. 11.10. The field expressions may be assumed to be

$$E_z^{\mathrm{I}} = \sum_{n=0}^{\infty} a_n J_v(k_1\rho)\sin v(\varphi - \alpha)\sin v(\varphi_0 - \alpha)$$

$$E_z^{\mathrm{II}} = \sum_{n=0}^{\infty} \left(b_n J_v(k\rho) + c_n H_v^{(2)}(k\rho)\right)\sin v(\varphi - \alpha)\sin v(\varphi_0 - \alpha) \qquad \text{Eq. (11.62)}$$

$$E_z^{\mathrm{III}} = \sum_{n=0}^{\infty} d_n H_v^{(2)}(k\rho)\sin v(\varphi - \alpha)\sin v(\varphi_0 - \alpha)$$

where

$$v = \frac{n\pi}{2\pi - \alpha - \beta} \qquad \text{Eq. (11.63)}$$

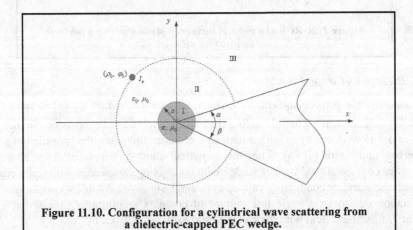

Figure 11.10. Configuration for a cylindrical wave scattering from a dielectric-capped PEC wedge.

while $J_\nu(x)$ is the Bessel function of order ν and argument x and $H_\nu^{(2)}$ is the Hankel function of the second kind of order ν and argument x. From Maxwell's equations, the magnetic field component H_φ is related to the electric field component E_z for a TM_z wave by

$$H_\varphi = \frac{1}{j\omega\mu}\frac{\partial E_z}{\partial \rho}.$$ Eq. (11.64)

Thus, the magnetic field component H_φ in the various regions may be written as

$$H_\varphi^{\mathrm{I}} = \frac{k_1}{j\omega\mu_0}\sum_{n=0}^{\infty} a_n J_\nu'(k_1\rho)\sin\nu(\varphi-\alpha)\sin\nu(\varphi_0-\alpha)$$

$$H_\varphi^{\mathrm{II}} = \frac{k}{j\omega\mu_0}\sum_{n=0}^{\infty}\left(b_n J_\nu'(k\rho)+c_n H_\nu^{(2)'}(k\rho)\right)\sin\nu(\varphi-\alpha)\sin\nu(\varphi_0-\alpha)$$ Eq. (11.65)

$$H_\varphi^{\mathrm{III}} = \frac{k}{j\omega\mu_0}\sum_{n=0}^{\infty} d_n H_\nu^{(2)'}(k\rho)\sin\nu(\varphi-\alpha)\sin\nu(\varphi_0-\alpha)$$

where the prime indicated derivatives with respect to the full argument of the function. The boundary conditions require that the tangential electric field component vanish at the PEC surface of the wedge. Also, the tangential field components should be continuous across the air-dielectric interface and the virtual boundary between regions *II* and *III*, except for the discontinuity of the magnetic field at the source point. Thus,

$$E_z = 0 \quad\text{at}\quad \varphi = \alpha, 2\pi - \beta$$ Eq. (11.66)

$$\left.\begin{array}{c} E_z^{\mathrm{I}} = E_z^{\mathrm{II}} \\ H_\varphi^{\mathrm{I}} = H_\varphi^{\mathrm{II}} \end{array}\right\} \quad\text{at}\quad \rho = a$$ Eq. (11.67)

$$\left.\begin{array}{c} E_z^{\mathrm{II}} = E_z^{\mathrm{III}} \\ H_\varphi^{\mathrm{II}} - H_\varphi^{\mathrm{III}} = -J_e \end{array}\right\} \quad\text{at}\quad \rho = \rho_0.$$ Eq. (11.68)

The current density J_e may be given in Fourier series expansion as

$$J_e = \frac{I_e}{\rho_0}\delta(\varphi-\varphi_0) = \frac{2}{2\pi-\alpha-\beta}\frac{I_e}{\rho_0}\sum_{n=0}^{\infty}\sin\nu(\varphi-\alpha)\sin\nu(\varphi_0-\alpha).$$ Eq. (11.69)

The boundary condition on the PEC surface is automatically satisfied by the φ dependence of the electric field Eq. (11.62). From the boundary conditions in Eq. (11.67), we get

$$\sum_{n=0}^{\infty} a_n J_\nu(k_1 a)\sin\nu(\varphi-\alpha)\sin\nu(\varphi_0-\alpha) =$$

$$\sum_{n=0}^{\infty}\left(b_n J_\nu(ka)+c_n H_\nu^{(2)}(ka)\right)\sin\nu(\varphi-\alpha)\sin\nu(\varphi_0-\alpha)$$ Eq. (11.70)

$$\frac{k_1}{j\omega\mu_0}\sum_{n=0}^{\infty} a_n J_\nu'(k_1 a)\sin\nu(\varphi-\alpha)\sin\nu(\varphi_0-\alpha) =$$

$$\frac{k}{j\omega\mu_0}\sum_{n=0}^{\infty}\left(b_n J_\nu'(ka)+c_n H_\nu^{(2)'}(ka)\right)\sin\nu(\varphi-\alpha)\sin\nu(\varphi_0-\alpha)$$ Eq. (11.71)

From the boundary conditions in Eq. (11.68), we have

$$\sum_{n=0}^{\infty}\left(b_n J_v\left(k\rho_0\right)+c_n H_v^{(2)}\left(k\rho_0\right)\right)\sin v(\varphi-\alpha)\sin v(\varphi_0-\alpha)=$$

Eq. (11.72)

$$\sum_{n=0}^{\infty} d_n H_v^{(2)}\left(k\rho_0\right)\sin v(\varphi-\alpha)\sin v(\varphi_0-\alpha)$$

$$\frac{k}{j\omega\mu_0}\sum_{n=0}^{\infty}\left(b_n J_v'\left(k\rho_0\right)+c_n H_v^{(2)'}\left(k\rho_0\right)\right)\sin v(\varphi-\alpha)\sin v(\varphi_0-\alpha)=$$

Eq. (11.73)

$$\frac{k}{j\omega\mu_0}\sum_{n=0}^{\infty} d_n H_v^{(2)'}\left(k\rho_0\right)\sin v(\varphi-\alpha)\sin v(\varphi_0-\alpha)$$

$$-\frac{2}{2\pi-\alpha-\beta}\frac{I_e}{\rho_0}\sum_{n=0}^{\infty}\sin v(\varphi-\alpha)\sin v(\varphi_0-\alpha)$$

Since Eqs. (11.69) and (11.73) hold for all φ, the series on the left- and right-hand sides should be equal term-by-term. More precisely, these equations reduce to

$$a_n J_v\left(k_1 a\right)=b_n J_v\left(ka\right)+c_n H_v^{(2)}\left(ka\right)$$

Eq. (11.74)

$$\frac{k_1}{\mu_0} a_n J_v'\left(k_1 a\right)=\frac{k}{\mu_0}\left(b_n J_v'\left(ka\right)+c_n H_v^{(2)'}\left(ka\right)\right)$$

Eq. (11.75)

$$b_n J_v\left(k\rho_0\right)+c_n H_v^{(2)}\left(k\rho_0\right)=d_n H_v^{(2)}\left(k\rho_0\right)$$

Eq. (11.76)

$$b_n J_v'\left(k\rho_0\right)+c_n H_v^{(2)'}\left(k\rho_0\right)=d_n H_v^{(2)'}\left(k\rho_0\right)-\frac{2j\eta_0}{2\pi-\alpha-\beta}\frac{I_e}{\rho_0}$$

Eq. (11.77)

From Eqs. (11.74) and (11.76), we have

$$a_n=\frac{1}{J_v\left(k_1 a\right)}\left[b_n J_v\left(ka\right)+c_n H_v^{(2)}\left(ka\right)\right]$$

Eq. (11.78)

$$d_n=c_n+b_n\frac{J_v\left(k\rho_0\right)}{H_v^{(2)}\left(k\rho_0\right)}.$$

Eq. (11.79)

Multiplying Eq. (11.78) by $H_v^{(2)'}$ and Eq. (11.79) by $H_v^{(2)}$, and by subtraction and using the Wronskian of the Bessel and Hankel functions, we get

$$b_n=-\frac{\pi\omega\mu_0 I_e}{2\pi-\alpha-\beta}H_v^{(2)}\left(k\rho_0\right).$$

Eq. (11.80)

Substituting b_n in Eqs. (11.74) and (11.75) and solving for c_n yield

$$c_n=\frac{\pi\omega\mu_0 I_e}{2\pi-\alpha-\beta}\left[H_v^{(2)}\left(k\rho_0\right)\frac{kJ_v'\left(ka\right)J_v\left(k_1 a\right)-k_1 J_v\left(ka\right)J_v'\left(k_1 a\right)}{kH_v^{(2)'}\left(ka\right)J_v\left(k_1 a\right)-k_1 H_v^{(2)}\left(ka\right)J_v'\left(k_1 a\right)}\right].$$

Eq. (11.81)

From Eqs. (11.79) through (11.80), d_n may be given by

$$d_n=\frac{\pi\omega\mu_0 I_e}{2\pi-\alpha-\beta}\left[H_v^{(2)}(k\rho_0)\frac{kJ_v'\left(ka\right)J_v(k_1 a)-k_1 J_v(ka)J_v'(k_1 a)}{kH_v^{(2)'}(ka)\,J_v(k_1 a)-k_1 H_v^{(2)}(ka)J_v'(k_1 a)}-J_v(k\rho_0)\right]$$

Eq. (11.82)

which can be written as

$$d_n = \frac{\pi \omega \mu_0 I_e}{2\pi - \alpha - \beta} \left\{ \frac{\begin{array}{c} kJ_v(k_1 a)\left[J_v'(ka) H_v^{(2)}(k\rho_0) - H_v^{(2)\prime}(ka) J_v(k\rho_0) \right] + \\ k_1 J_v'(k_1 a)\left[H_v^{(2)}(ka) J_v(k\rho_0) - J_v(ka) H_v^{(2)}(k\rho_0) \right] \end{array}}{kH_v^{(2)\prime}(ka) J_v(k_1 a) - k_1 H_v^{(2)}(ka) J_v'(k_1 a)} \right\} . \qquad \text{Eq. (11.83)}$$

Substituting for the Hankel function in terms of Bessel and Neumann functions, Eq. (11.83) reduces to

$$d_n = -j \frac{\pi \omega \mu_0 I_e}{2\pi - \alpha - \beta} \left\{ \frac{\begin{array}{c} kJ_v(k_1 a)\left[J_v'(ka) Y_v(k\rho_0) - Y_v'(ka) J_v(k\rho_0) \right] + \\ k_1 J_v'(k_1 a)\left[Y_v(ka) J_v(k\rho_0) - J_v(ka) Y_v(k\rho_0) \right] \end{array}}{kH_v^{(2)\prime}(ka) J_v(k_1 a) - k_1 H_v^{(2)}(ka) J_v'(k_1 a)} \right\} . \qquad \text{Eq. (11.84)}$$

With these closed-form expressions for the expansion coefficients a_n, b_n, c_n and d_n, the field components E_z and H_φ can be determined from Eq. (11.66) and Eq. (11.68), respectively. Alternatively, the magnetic field component H_ρ can be computed from

$$H_\rho = -\frac{1}{j\omega\mu} \frac{1}{\rho} \frac{\partial E_z}{\partial \phi} . \qquad \text{Eq. (11.85)}$$

Thus, the H_ρ expressions for the three regions defined in Fig. 11.10 become

$$H_\rho^{\mathrm{I}} = -\frac{1}{j\omega\mu\rho} \sum_{n=0}^{\infty} a_n \, J_v(k_1 \rho) \cos v(\varphi - \alpha) \sin v(\varphi_0 - \alpha)$$

$$H_\rho^{\mathrm{II}} = -\frac{1}{j\omega\mu\rho} \sum_{n=0}^{\infty} v\big(b_n J_v(k\rho) + c_n H_v^{(2)}(k\rho) \big) \cos v(\varphi - \alpha) \sin v(\varphi_0 - \alpha) \qquad \text{Eq. (11.86)}$$

$$H_\rho^{\mathrm{III}} = -\frac{1}{j\omega\mu\rho} \sum_{n=0}^{\infty} d_n \, H_v^{(2)}(k\rho) \cos v(\varphi - \alpha) \sin v(\varphi_0 - \alpha)$$

Far Scattered Field

In order to compute the wedge RCS, we consider the fields in region III. Therefore, the scattered field may be found as the difference between the total and incident fields. Hence, using Eq. (11.61) and E_z^{III} in Eq. (11.62) and considering the far field condition ($\rho \to \infty$) we get

$$E_z^{\mathrm{III}} = E_z^i + E_z^s = \sqrt{\frac{2j}{\pi k \rho}} e^{-jk\rho} \sum_{n=0}^{\infty} d_n j^v \sin v(\varphi - \alpha) \sin v(\varphi_0 - \alpha)$$

$$\qquad \text{Eq. (11.87)}$$

$$E_z^i = -I_e \frac{\omega \mu_0}{4} \sqrt{\frac{2j}{\pi k \rho}} e^{-jk\rho} e^{+jk\rho_0 \cos(\varphi - \varphi_0)}$$

Note that d_n can be written as

$$d_n = -\frac{\omega \mu_0 I_e}{4} \tilde{d}_n \qquad \text{Eq. (11.88)}$$

where

$$\tilde{d}_n = j\frac{4\pi}{2\pi-\alpha-\beta}\left\{ \begin{array}{l} kJ_v(k_1a)\left[J_v'(ka)Y_v(k\rho_0)-Y_v'(ka)J_v(k\rho_0)\right]+ \\ \qquad k_1J_v'(k_1a)\left[Y_v(ka)J_v(k\rho_0)-J_v(ka)Y_v(k\rho_0)\right] \\ \hline kH_v^{(2)'}(ka)J_v(k_1a)-k_1H_v^{(2)}(ka)J_v'(k_1a) \end{array} \right\} \qquad \text{Eq. (11.89)}$$

substituting Eq. (11.87) into Eq. (11.86), the scattered field $f(\varphi)$ may be found as

$$E_z^s = \underbrace{-\frac{\omega\mu_0 I_e}{4}\sqrt{\frac{2j}{\pi k\rho}}e^{-jk\rho}}_{g(\rho)}\underbrace{\left(\sum_{n=0}^{\infty}\tilde{d}_n j^v \sin v(\varphi-\alpha)\sin v(\varphi_0-\alpha)-e^{+jk\rho_0\cos(\varphi-\varphi_0)}\right)}_{f(\varphi)} \qquad \text{Eq. (11.90)}$$

Plane Wave Excitation

For plane wave excitation ($\rho_0 \to \infty$), the expression in Eqs. (11.80) reduce to

$$b_n = -\frac{\pi\omega\mu_0 I_e}{2\pi-\alpha-\beta}j^v = -\frac{\omega\mu_0 I_e}{4}\sqrt{\frac{2j}{\pi k\rho_0}}e^{-jk\rho_0}\tilde{b}_n \qquad \text{Eq. (11.91)}$$

where

$$\tilde{b}_n = \frac{4\pi}{2\pi-\alpha-\beta}j^v \qquad \text{Eq. (11.92)}$$

and the coefficient in Eq. (11.81) reduces to

$$c_n = \frac{\pi\omega\mu_0 I_e}{2\pi-\alpha-\beta}j^v\sqrt{\frac{2j}{\pi k\rho_0}}e^{-jk\rho_0}\frac{kJ_v'(ka)J_v(k_1a)-k_1J_v(ka)J_v'(k_1a)}{kH_v^{(2)'}(ka)J_v(k_1a)-k_1H_v^{(2)}(ka)J_v'(k_1a)} \qquad \text{Eq. (11.93)}$$

$$= -\frac{\omega\mu_0 I_e}{4}\sqrt{\frac{2j}{\pi k\rho_0}}e^{-jk\rho_0}\tilde{c}_n$$

where

$$\tilde{c}_n = -\frac{4\pi}{2\pi-\alpha-\beta}j^v\frac{kJ_v'(ka)J_v(k_1a)-k_1J_v(ka)J_v'(k_1a)}{kH_v^{(2)'}(ka)J_v(k_1a)-k_1H_v^{(2)}(ka)J_v'(k_1a)} , \qquad \text{Eq. (11.94)}$$

and the incident plane wave is now represented as

$$E_z^i = -I_e\frac{\omega\mu_0}{4}\sqrt{\frac{2j}{\pi k\rho_0}}e^{-jk\rho_0}e^{+jk\rho\,\cos(\varphi-\varphi_0)} . \qquad \text{Eq. (11.95)}$$

Finally, the complex amplitude of the incident plane wave, E_0, can be given by

$$E_0 = -I_e\frac{\omega\mu_0}{4}\sqrt{\frac{2j}{\pi k\rho_0}}e^{-jk\rho_0} . \qquad \text{Eq. (11.96)}$$

In this case, the field components can be evaluated in regions *I* and *II* only. As a result, the *z* component of total field in region *II* takes the form,

$$E_z^{II} = -I_e\frac{\omega\mu_0}{4}\sqrt{\frac{2j}{\pi k\rho_0}}e^{-jk\rho_0}\sum_{n=0}^{\infty}[\tilde{b}_n J_v(k\rho)+\tilde{c}_n H_v^{(2)}(k\rho)]\sin v(\varphi-\alpha)\sin v(\varphi_0-\alpha) . \qquad \text{Eq. (11.97)}$$

Hence, the corresponding scattered field is then represented as

$$E_z^s = E_z^{II} - E_z^i = -I_e \frac{\omega\mu_0}{4} \sqrt{\frac{2j}{\pi k \rho_0}} e^{-jk\rho_0}$$

$$\left[\sum_{n=0}^{\infty} [\tilde{b}_n J_v(k\rho) + \tilde{c}_n H_v^{(2)}(k\rho)] \sin v(\varphi - \alpha) \sin v(\varphi_0 - \alpha) - e^{+jk\rho \, \cos(\varphi-\varphi_0)} \right]$$

Eq. (11.98)

Equation (11.97) represents the scattered field from a capped wedge due to a plane wave incident. This scattered field, which is directly related to the corresponding RCS, can be evaluated at any cylindrical coordinates represented by (ρ, ϕ).

Special Cases

Case I: $\alpha = \beta$ (reference at bisector); the definition of v reduces to

$$v = \frac{n\pi}{2(\pi - \beta)}.$$

Eq. (11.99)

Case II: $\alpha = 0$ (reference at face); the definition of v takes on the form

$$v = \frac{n\pi}{2\pi - \beta}$$

Eq. (11.100)

Case III: $k_1 \to \infty$ (PEC cap); field expressions in region *I* will vanish, and the expansion coefficients in regions *II* and *III* will be given by

$$b_n = -\frac{\pi\omega\mu_0 I_e}{2\pi - \alpha - \beta} H_v^{(2)}(k\rho_0)$$

Eq. (11.101)

$$c_n = \frac{\pi\omega\mu_0 I_e}{2\pi - \alpha - \beta} H_v^{(2)}(k\rho_0) \frac{J_v(ka)}{H_v^{(2)}(ka)}$$

Eq. (11.102)

$$d_n = j \frac{\pi\omega\mu_0 I_e}{2\pi - \alpha - \beta} \frac{Y_v(ka)J_v(k\rho_0) - J_v(ka)Y_v(k\rho_0)}{H_v^{(2)}(ka)}$$

Eq. (11.103)

$$a_n = \frac{1}{J_v(k_1 a)} [b_n J_v(ka) + c_n H_v^{(2)}(ka)] = 0.$$

Eq. (11.104)

Note that the expressions of b_n and c_n will yield zero tangential electric field at $\rho = a$ when substituted in Eq. (11.62).

Case IV: $a \to 0$ (no cap); the expressions of the coefficients in this case may be obtained by setting $k_1 = k$, or by taking the limit as a approaches zero. Thus,

$$c_n = \frac{\pi\omega\mu_0 I_e}{2\pi - \alpha - \beta} [H_v^{(2)}(k\rho_0) \frac{kJ_v'(ka)J_v(ka) - kJ_v(ka)J_v'(ka)}{kH_v^{(2)'}(ka)J_v(ka) - kH_v^{(2)}(ka)J_v'(ka)}] = 0$$

Eq. (11.105)

$$b_n = -\frac{\pi\omega\mu_0 I_e}{2\pi - \alpha - \beta} H_v^{(2)}(k\rho_0)$$

Eq. (11.106)

$$a_n = \frac{1}{J_n(k_1 a)}[b_n J_v(ka) + c_n H_v^{(2)}(ka)] = b_n \qquad \text{Eq. (11.107)}$$

$$d_n = c_n + b_n \frac{J_v(k\rho_0)}{H_v^{(2)}(k\rho_0)} = -\frac{\pi\omega\mu_0 I_e}{2\pi - \alpha - \beta} J_v(k\rho_0) \qquad \text{Eq. (11.108)}$$

Case V: $a \to 0$ and $\alpha = \beta = 0$ (semi-infinite PEC plane); in this case, the coefficients in Eqs. (11.105) to (11.108) become valid with the exception that the values of v reduce to $n/2$. Once, the electric field component E_z in the different regions is computed, the corresponding magnetic field component H_φ can be computed as

$$H_\rho = -\frac{1}{j\omega\mu}\frac{1}{\rho}\frac{\partial E_z}{\partial \phi}. \qquad (11.109)$$

Sample Numerical Results

The far field patterns of the z-component of the electric field due to a line source excitation around a conducting wedge and a half-plane both with and without a capped cylinder are computed and displayed in Figs. 11.1 and 11.12, respectively. The common parameters used for these cases are: $f = 300 MHz$, $\alpha = \beta = 30°$, $a = 0.15\lambda$, $I_e = 1mA$, $\rho_0 = 0.5\lambda$, $\varepsilon_r = 3$, and $\varphi_0 = 180°$.

It is clearly shown that the maximum scattered field direction from a sharp wedge or a half-plane can be altered using a dielectric or a PEC capped cylinder. It is also shown that the conducting cap tends to smooth out the scattered field and does not produce sharp radiation. On the other hand, the dielectric cap can alter the main scattered radiation direction and produces an additional scattering direction, based on the cap relative permittivity, which can be as strong as the ones from the sharp edge.

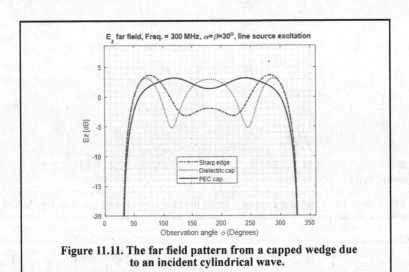

Figure 11.11. The far field pattern from a capped wedge due to an incident cylindrical wave.

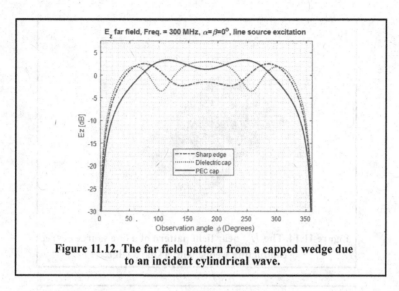

Figure 11.12. The far field pattern from a capped wedge due to an incident cylindrical wave.

The near field distribution around a conducting wedge with and without a capped cylinder in the presence of an electric line source or a plane wave excitation is also computed and displayed in Figs. 11.13 to 11.30. The common parameters in these figures are the same as for the far field pattern computations except for $\varepsilon_r = 5$. It is clear from these figures how the cap parameters affect the direction of the maximum radiation of the wedge (or the returned signal from the target) due to the cylindrical wave illumination. The near field distributions clearly demonstrated the effect of cap parameters in altering the sharp edge singular behavior which mainly contributes to a strong back RCS values. To further illustrate this sharp edge effect, Figs. (11.31) to (11.33) present the near field of the electric component of plane wave incident on a half-plane with a sharp edge, dielectric capped edge, and conducting capped edge with the same parameters listed above except that the wedge angles $\alpha = \beta = 0°$ or $\nu = n/2$.

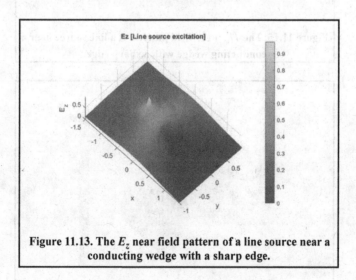

Figure 11.13. The E_z near field pattern of a line source near a conducting wedge with a sharp edge.

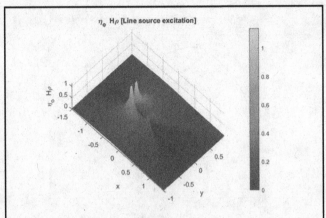

Figure 11.14. The H_ρ near field pattern of a line source near a
conducting wedge with a sharp edge.

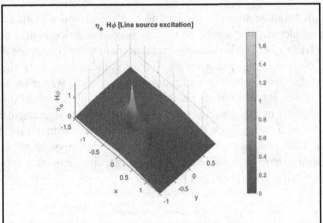

Figure 11.15. The H_φ near field pattern of a line source near a
conducting wedge with a sharp edge.

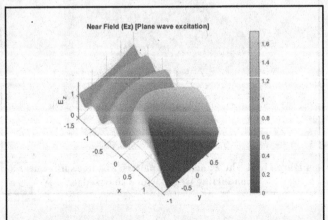

Figure 11.16. The E_z near field pattern of a line source near a
conducting wedge with a sharp edge.

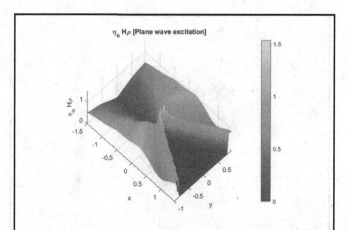

Figure 11.17. The H_ρ near field pattern of a line source near a conducting wedge with a sharp edge.

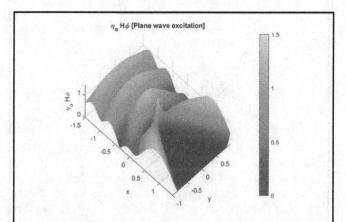

Figure 11.18. The H_φ near field pattern of a line source near a conducting wedge with a sharp edge.

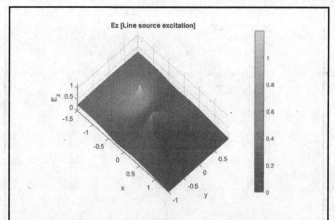

Figure 11.19. The E_z near field pattern of a line source near a conducting wedge with a dielectric cap edge.

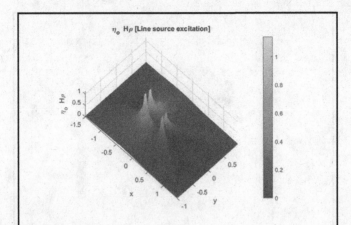

Figure 11.20. The H_ρ near field pattern of a line source near a conducting wedge with a dielectric cap edge.

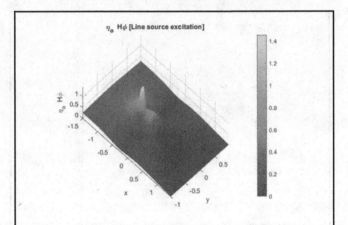

Figure 11.21. The H_φ near field pattern of a line source near a conducting wedge with a sharp edge.

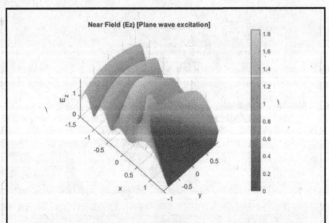

Figure 11.22. The E_z near field pattern of a plane wave excitation of a conducting wedge with a dielectric cap edge.

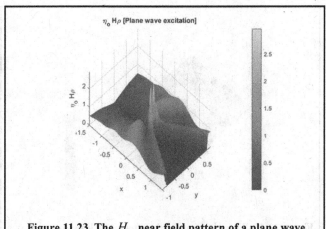

Figure 11.23. The H_ρ near field pattern of a plane wave excitation of a conducting wedge.

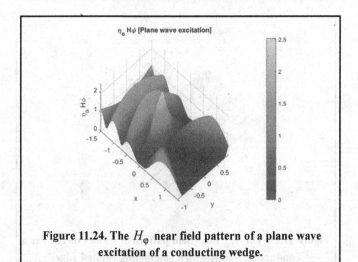

Figure 11.24. The H_φ near field pattern of a plane wave excitation of a conducting wedge.

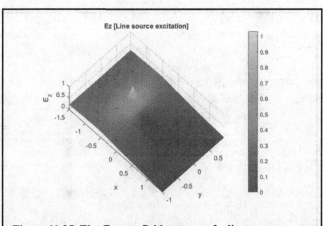

Figure 11.25. The E_z near field pattern of a line source near a conducting wedge with a conducting capped edge.

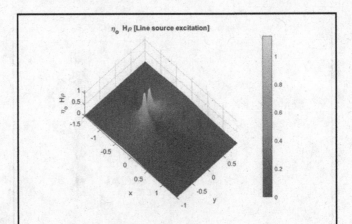

Figure 11.26. The H_ρ near field pattern of a line source near a conducting wedge with a conducting capped edge.

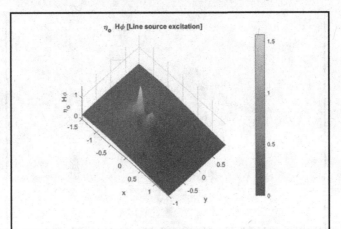

Figure 11.27. The H_φ near field pattern of a line source near a conducting wedge with a conducting capped edge.

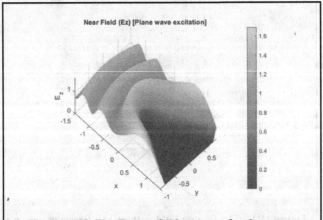

Figure 11.28. The E_z near field pattern of a plane wave incident on a conducting wedge with a conducting capped edge.

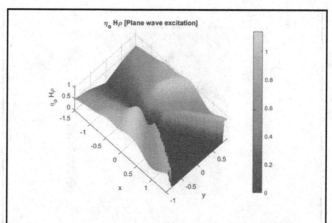

Figure 11.29. The H_ρ near field pattern of a line source near a conducting wedge with a conducting capped edge.

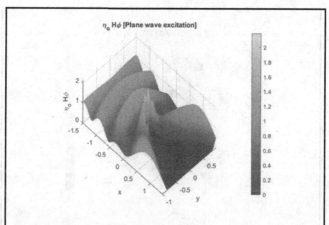

Figure 11.30. The H_ϕ near field pattern of a line source near a conducting wedge with a conducting capped edge.

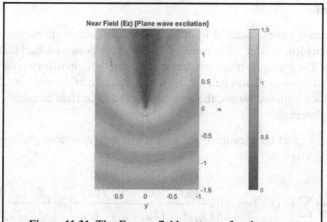

Figure 11.31. The E_z near field pattern of a plane wave incident on a half-plane with a sharp edge.

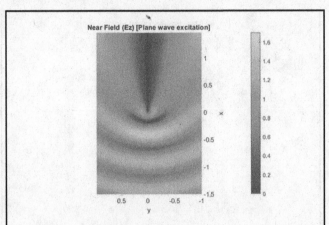

Figure 11.32. The E_z near field pattern of a plane wave incident on a half-plane with a dielectric capped edge.

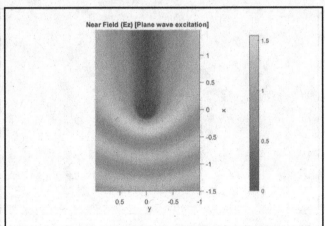

Figure 11.33. The E_z near field pattern of a plane wave incident on a half-plane with a conducting capped edge.

11.4.3. Spheres

Due to symmetry, waves scattered from a perfectly conducting sphere have the same polarization as the incident waves. This means that the cross-polarized backscattered waves are practically zero. For example, if the incident waves were left circularity polarized (LCP), then the backscattered waves will also be LCP. However, because of the opposite direction of propagation of the backscattered waves, they are considered to be right circularly polarized (RCP) by the receiving antenna.

The normalized exact backscattered RCS for a perfectly conducting sphere is a Mie series, after Mie (1908), given by

$$\frac{\sigma}{\pi a^2} = \left(\frac{j}{ka}\right) \sum_{n=1}^{\infty} (-1)^n (2n+1) \left[\left(\frac{ka J_{n-1}^o(ka) - n J_n^o(ka)}{ka H_{n-1}(ka) - n H_n^{(1)}(ka)} \right) - \left(\frac{J_n^o(ka)}{H_n^{(1)}(ka)} \right) \right] \qquad \textbf{Eq. (11.110)}$$

where a is the radius of the sphere, $k = 2\pi/\lambda$, λ is the wavelength, J_n^o is the spherical Bessel function of the first kind of order n, and $H_n^{(1)}$ is the spherical Hankel function of order n, and is given by

$$H_n^{(1)}(ka) = J_n^o(ka) + jY_n^o(ka).$$ Eq. (11.111)

Y_n^o is the spherical Bessel function of the second kind of order n. The normalized RCS $(\sigma/\pi a^2)$ of a perfectly conducting sphere as a function of its circumference relative to wavelength $(2\pi a/\lambda)$ is shown in Figs. 11.34-a and 11.34-b. In Fig. 11.34-b, three regions are identified. First is the optical region (corresponds to a large sphere). In this case,

$$\sigma = \pi a^2 \qquad a \gg \lambda.$$ Eq. (11.112)

Second is the Rayleigh region (small sphere). In this case,

$$\sigma \approx 9\pi a^2 (ka)^4 \qquad a \ll \lambda.$$ Eq. (11.113)

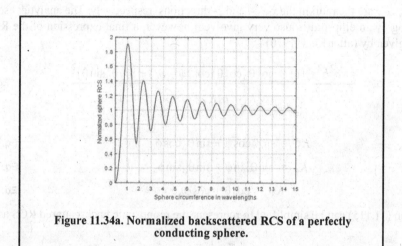

Figure 11.34a. Normalized backscattered RCS of a perfectly conducting sphere.

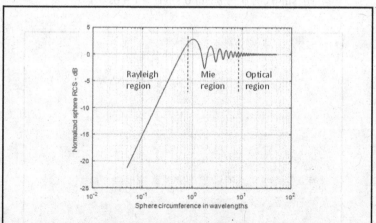

Figure 11.34b. Normalized backscattered RCS of a perfectly conducting sphere using semi-log scale showing three different regions.

The region between the optical and Rayleigh regions is oscillatory in nature and is called the Mie or resonance region. The backscattered RCS for a perfectly conducting sphere is constant in the optical region. For this reason, radar designers typically use spheres of known cross-sections to experimentally calibrate radar systems. For example, perfectly conducting spheres of known RCS are tethered to balloons and are flown in front of the radar as means to calibrate the system. In order to obtain Doppler shift, spheres of known RCS are also dropped from an airplane and towed behind it, where the airplane velocity is known to the radar.

11.4.4. Ellipsoids

An ellipsoid centered at *(0,0,0)* is shown in Fig. 11.35. It is defined mathematically by the following equation:

$$\left(\frac{x}{a}\right)^2 + \left(\frac{y}{b}\right)^2 + \left(\frac{z}{c}\right)^2 = 1 , \qquad \text{Eq. (11.114)}$$

where *a, b, c* are the radii in the *x*-, *y*-, and *z*- directions, respectively. The analytical solution of scattering by an ellipsoid is also very involved; however, a final expression of the RCS ellipsoid is given by (after Ruck 1970)

$$\sigma = \frac{4\pi a^2 b^2 c^2 [(1 + \cos\theta_0 \cos\theta)\cos(\phi - \phi_0) + \sin\theta_0 \sin\theta]^2}{[a^2 K_1^2 + b^2 K_2^2 + c^2 K_3^2]^2} . \qquad \text{Eq. (11.115)}$$

where

$$K_1 = \sin\theta\cos\phi + \sin\theta_0\cos\phi_0 \qquad \text{Eq. (11.116.a)}$$

$$K_2 = \sin\theta\sin\phi + \sin\theta_0\sin\phi_0 \qquad \text{Eq. (11.116.b)}$$

$$K_3 = \cos\theta + \cos\phi_0 . \qquad \text{Eq. (11.116.c)}$$

Equation (11.115) can be simplified to represent the monostatic backscattered RCS as

$$\sigma = \frac{\pi a^2 b^2 c^2}{[a^2 \sin^2\theta \cos^2\phi + b^2 \sin^2\theta \sin^2\phi + c^2 \cos^2\theta]^2} , \qquad \text{Eq. (11.117)}$$

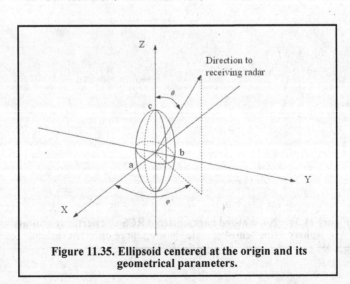

Figure 11.35. Ellipsoid centered at the origin and its geometrical parameters.

where the angles (θ, ϕ) represent the direction of backscattered RCS. When $a = b$, the ellipsoid becomes roll symmetric. Thus, the RCS is independent of ϕ, and Eq. (11.117) reduces to

$$\sigma = \frac{\pi b^4 c^2}{[a^2 \sin^2\theta + c^2 \cos^2\theta]^2},$$

Eq. (11.118)

and for the case when $a = b = c$,

$$\sigma = \pi c^2.$$

Eq. (11.119)

Note that Eq. (11.119) defines the backscattered RCS of a sphere in the optical region. This should be expected, since under the condition $a = b = c$ the ellipsoid becomes a sphere. Figure 11.36 shows the monostatic backscattered RCS for an ellipsoid versus θ in the plane defined by $\phi = 45°$. Note that at normal incidence ($\theta_0 = 90°$) the RCS corresponds to that of a sphere of radius c, and is often referred to as the broadside specular RCS value.

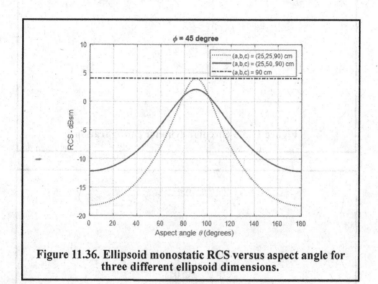

Figure 11.36. Ellipsoid monostatic RCS versus aspect angle for three different ellipsoid dimensions.

11.5. RCS Approximations of Simple Objects

This section presents examples of backscattered radar cross-section for a number of simple shaped objects. In all cases, only optical region approximations are presented. Most formulas presented are physical optics (PO) approximation for the backscattered RCS.

11.5.1. Finite Length Cylinder

For practical applications, the cylinder is usually of finite length as shown in Fig. 11.37 for a perfectly conducting cylinder. The approximation of the backscattered RCS due to a linearly polarized incident wave from a circular cylinder of radius, a, with normal incidence ($\theta_0 = 90°$) and non-normal incidence, is given, respectively, as (after Ruck 1970)

$$\sigma_{\theta_n} = \frac{2\pi H^2 a}{\lambda}$$

Eq. (11.120)

$$\sigma = \frac{a\lambda \sin\theta_0}{2\pi} \left[\frac{\sin(kH\cos\theta_0)}{\cos\theta_0} \right]^2.$$

Eq. (11.121)

Figure 11.38 shows the cylinder monostatic backscattered RCS for two values of H and $\lambda = 3.5\,GHz$. Note that the cylinder RCS is roll symmetric and accordingly it is independent of the angle ϕ.

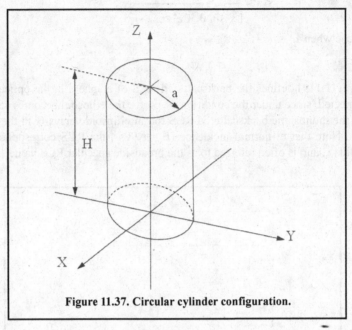

Figure 11.37. Circular cylinder configuration.

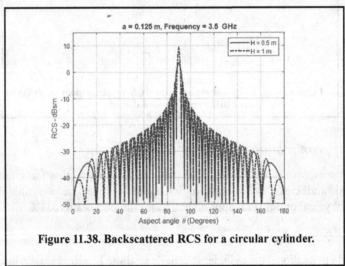

Figure 11.38. Backscattered RCS for a circular cylinder.

11.5.2. Circular Flat Plate

A flat circular plate of radius a placed in or parallel to the x-y plane is shown in Fig. 11.39 and is centered around the origin. Due to the circular symmetry, the backscattered RCS of a circular flat plate for normal incidence $\theta_0 = 0°$ has no dependency on ϕ and can be given as

$$\sigma = \frac{2\pi^3 a^4}{\lambda^2} \quad , \quad \theta_0 = 0°.$$

Eq. (11.122)

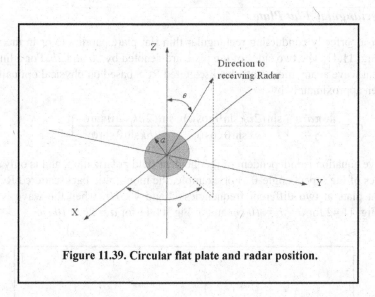

Figure 11.39. Circular flat plate and radar position.

However, for non-normal incidence, two approximations for the circular flat plate backscattered RCS for any linearly polarized incident wave are

$$\sigma = \frac{\lambda a}{8\pi \sin\theta \tan^2\theta} \qquad \text{Eq. (11.123)}$$

$$\sigma = 4\pi k^2 a^4 \left[\frac{J_1(2ak\sin\theta)}{2ak\sin\theta}\right] \cos^2\theta \qquad \text{Eq. (11.124)}$$

where $k = 2\pi/\lambda$ and J_1 is the spherical Bessel function of order one. The backscattered RCS corresponding to Eqs. (11.123) and (11.124) is shown in Fig. 11.40 below for $a = 40\ cm$, and a frequency of *10 GHz*.

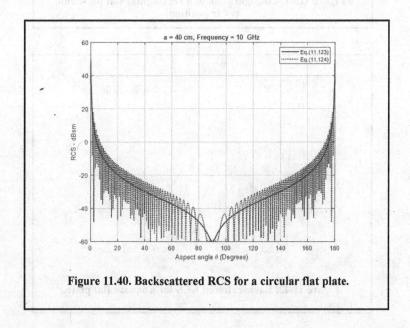

Figure 11.40. Backscattered RCS for a circular flat plate.

11.5.3. Rectangular Flat Plate

Consider a perfectly conducting rectangular thin flat plate parallel to or in the *x-y* plane as shown in Fig. 11.41. The two sides of the plate are denoted by *2a* and *2b*. For a linearly polarized incident wave at any monostatic backscattered RCS based on physical optical approximation is given approximately by

$$\sigma = \frac{46\pi a^2 b^2}{\lambda^2}\left[\frac{\sin(2ak\sin\theta\cos\phi)}{2ak\sin\theta\cos\phi}\;\frac{\sin(2ak\sin\theta\sin\phi)}{2bk\sin\theta\sin\phi}\right]^2 . \qquad \text{Eq. (11.125)}$$

The above equation is independent of the incident field polarization, and is only accurate for small values of the aspect angle θ. For example, the monostatic backscattered RCS of a rectangular flat plate at two different frequencies, *2* and *4 GHz*, when the wave is incident as shown in Fig. 11.42 for *a = b = 10 cm* and in Fig. 11.43 for *a = 2b = 10 cm*.

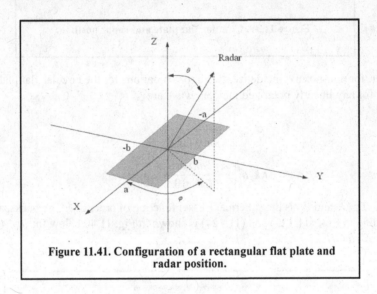

Figure 11.41. Configuration of a rectangular flat plate and radar position.

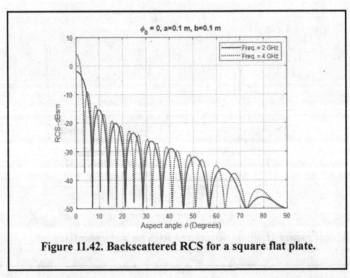

Figure 11.42. Backscattered RCS for a square flat plate.

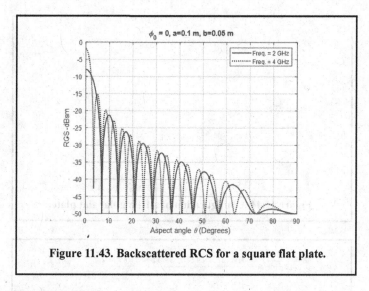

Figure 11.43. Backscattered RCS for a square flat plate.

11.5.4. Triangular Flat Plate

Consider the triangular flat plate defined by the isosceles triangle as oriented in Fig. 11.44. For a linearly polarized wave incident at any (θ, ϕ), the monostatic backscattered RCS can be approximated for small aspect angles $\theta \leq 30°$ by

$$\sigma = \frac{4\pi A^2}{\lambda^2} \cos^2\theta \, \sigma_0 \qquad\qquad \text{Eq. (11.126)}$$

$$\sigma_0 = \frac{[\sin^2\alpha - \sin^2(\beta/2)]^2 + \sigma_{01}}{\alpha^2 - (\beta/2)^2} \qquad\qquad \text{Eq. (11.127)}$$

$$\sigma_{01} = 0.25\sin^2\phi \left[\frac{2a}{b}\cos\phi\sin\beta - \sin\phi\sin2\alpha\right]^2 \qquad\qquad \text{Eq. (11.128)}$$

where $\alpha = ka\sin\theta\cos\phi$, $\beta = kb\sin\theta\sin\phi$, and $A = ab/2$. The monostatic RCS for waves incident in the plane $\phi = 0$, reduces to

$$\sigma = \frac{4\pi A^2}{\lambda^2}\cos^2\theta \left[\frac{\sin^4\alpha}{\alpha^2} + \frac{(\sin2\alpha - 2\alpha)^2}{4\alpha^2}\right] \qquad\qquad \text{Eq. (11.129)}$$

while for incidence in the plane $\phi = \pi/2$, the monostatic RCS becomes

$$\sigma = \frac{4\pi A^2}{\lambda^2}\cos^2\theta \left[\frac{\sin^4(\beta/2)}{(\beta/2)^4}\right] \qquad\qquad \text{Eq. (11.130)}$$

Fig. 11.45 shows the normalized backscattered RCS from a perfectly conducting isosceles triangular flat plate. In this example, $a = 0.2m$, $b = 0.4m$ for incidence in the planes $\phi = 0$ and $\phi = \pi/2$. Figure 11.46 shows the corresponding monostatic RCS for three different frequencies, *2*, *4*, and *8 GHz*.

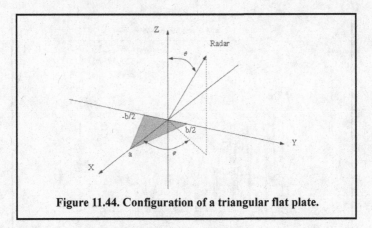

Figure 11.44. Configuration of a triangular flat plate.

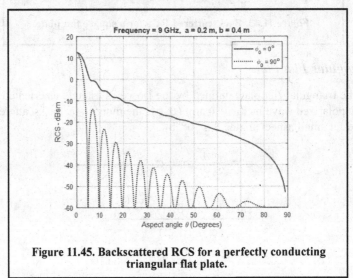

Figure 11.45. Backscattered RCS for a perfectly conducting triangular flat plate.

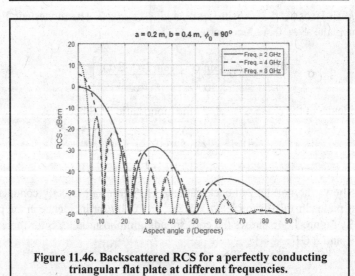

Figure 11.46. Backscattered RCS for a perfectly conducting triangular flat plate at different frequencies.

11.5.5. Truncated Cone (Frustum)

A frustum (truncated cone) geometry is shown in Figs. 11.47 and 11.48 where the half-cone angle α is given by

$$\tan\alpha = \frac{(r_2 - r_1)}{H} = \frac{r_2}{L}. \qquad \text{Eq. (11.131)}$$

The aspect angle at normal incidence with respect to the frustum's surface (broadside) is defined as θ_n. Thus, when a frustum is illuminated by a radar located at the same side as the cone's small end (i.e., $\theta = 180°$), the angle θ_n is

$$\theta_n = 90° - \alpha. \qquad \text{Eq. (11.132)}$$

Alternatively, for normal incidence of the radar signal defined as $\theta = 0°$, the corresponding angle θ_n is

$$\theta_n = 90° + \alpha. \qquad \text{Eq. (11.133)}$$

At normal incidence, one approximation for the backscattered RCS of a truncated cone due to a linearly polarized incident wave is

$$\sigma_{\theta_n} = \frac{8\pi(z_2^{3/2} - z_1^{3/2})^2}{9\lambda} \frac{\tan\alpha}{\sin\theta_n}(\sin\theta_n - \cos\theta_n \tan\alpha)^2 \qquad \text{Eq. (11.134)}$$

where λ is the wavelength, and z_1, z_2 are as defined in Fig. 11.47. Using trigonometric identities, Eq. (11.134) can be reduced to

$$\sigma_{\theta_n} = \frac{8\pi(z_2^{3/2} - z_1^{3/2})^2}{9\lambda} \frac{\sin\alpha}{(\cos\alpha)^4}. \qquad \text{Eq. (11.135)}$$

For non-normal incidence, the backscattered RCS due to a linearly polarized incident wave is

$$\sigma = \frac{\lambda z \tan\alpha}{8\pi \sin\theta}\left(\frac{\sin\theta - \cos\theta \tan\alpha}{\sin\theta \tan\alpha + \cos\theta}\right)^2, \qquad \text{Eq. (11.136)}$$

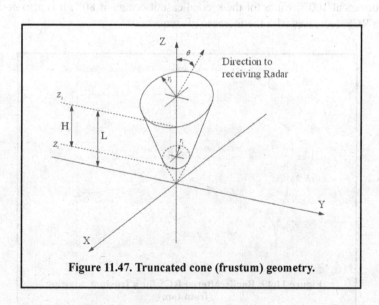

Figure 11.47. Truncated cone (frustum) geometry.

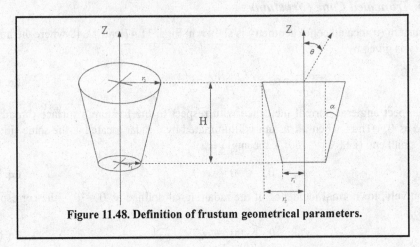

Figure 11.48. Definition of frustum geometrical parameters.

where z is equal to either z_1 or z_2, depending on whether the RCS contribution is from the small or the large end of the cone. Again, using trigonometric identities, Eq. (11.136) (assuming the radar illuminates the frustum starting from the large end) is reduced to

$$\sigma = \frac{\lambda z_2 \tan\alpha}{8\pi\sin\theta}\ (\tan(\theta - \alpha))^2.$$ **Eq. (11.137)**

When the radar illuminates the frustum starting from the small end, Eq. (11.137) should be modified to

$$\sigma = \frac{\lambda z_1 \tan\alpha}{8\pi\sin\theta}\ (\tan(\theta + \alpha))^2.$$ **Eq. (11.138)**

For example, consider a frustum defined by $H = 20.945\,cm$, $r_1 = 2.057\,cm$, and $r_2 = 5.753\,cm$. It follows that the half-cone angle is $10°$. Figure 11.49 shows its RCS when the frustum is illuminated by a radar in the positive z- direction. Figure 11.50 shows the RCS, except in this case, the radar is in the negative z- direction. Note that for the first case, normal incidence occurs at $100°$, while for the second case it occurs at $80°$. It is also noticeable that the frustum RCS decreases with the increase of frequency.

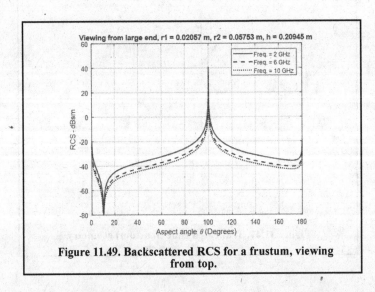

Figure 11.49. Backscattered RCS for a frustum, viewing from top.

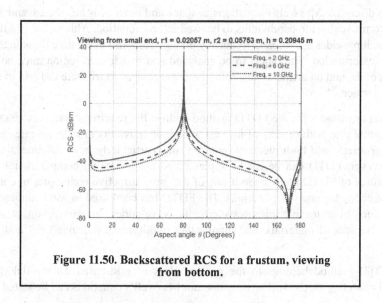

Figure 11.50. Backscattered RCS for a frustum, viewing from bottom.

11.6. RCS Using Computational Electromagnetics

Most scattering problems involve radar targets with very complicated shapes and composite materials. Among these are ground-based targets such as trucks, tanks, and artillery; air targets such as aircraft, helicopters, and missiles; and space-based targets, such as reentry vehicles and satellites. For such an object, there is generally no analytic method available to predict the radar cross-section. The field of computational electromagnetics (CEM) uses the growing power of computers to implement Maxwell's equations and solve these problems. The CEM has applications in other areas, too, such as antennas and waveguide design, wave propagation, and medical imaging. There are many CEM techniques to solve scattering problems, each employing different numerical approximations and analysis techniques. Among the most popular methods used are the finite difference time domain (FDTD) method, the finite element method (FE), integral equation methods such as the method of moments (MoM), and asymptotic techniques such as physical optics (PO), the physical theory of diffraction (PTD), and shooting and bouncing rays (SBR).

In this section we will focus on one of these CEM methods, namely, the FDTD method because of its popularity, flexibility, and ease of formulation and use in simulating composite and arbitrary shaped targets and the ability to produce multiple frequency domain bi-static RCS from a single time domain run (Elsherbeni, 2015). The FDTD method is one of the most adaptable methods for parallelization to run on multiple processors (Elsherbeni, 2014). This is a key feature of the method that reduces significantly the execution time, especially if the simulation is running on graphical processing units (GPU) (Elsherbeni, 2007).

11.6.1. The Standard Finite Difference Time Domain Method

The finite difference time domain (FDTD) method has gained great popularity as an effective tool for solving Maxwell's equations. The FDTD method can easily handle composite structure consisting of different types of materials. Thus, for the purpose of radar cross-section analysis the FDTD is useful for solving the scattering problems involving objects composed of complex, often inhomogeneous media. The FDTD method is based on a simple formulation that does not require complex asymptotic or Green's functions. It uses a finite difference scheme to discretize Maxwell's equations in space and time. This has the advantage of allowing waveforms with wide bandwidths to be used as an excitation. Although it is a time domain simulation, it provides a wideband frequency domain response using time domain to frequency domain transformation. The object to be analyzed and its adjacent region must be discretized into grid points, and an artificial absorbing layer is required to truncate the grid to simulate an unbounded space.

The main drawbacks for the FDTD method include the requirements for large grid size and non-conformal grid with objects of interest, which often results in less accurate discretization of target geometry and high memory requirements, particularly in three-dimensional simulations. However, FDTD can be easily implemented using parallel computational algorithms. These features of FDTD have made it one of the most attractive techniques in computational electromagnetics for many applications. The FDTD has been used to solve numerous types of problems such as scattering, microwave circuits, waveguides, antennas, propagation, non-linear and other special materials, and many other applications (Huang, 1999 and Elsherbeni, 2001).

The FDTD method belongs to the general class of grid-based differential time-domain numerical modeling methods. The time-domain Maxwell's equations can be stated as follows,

$$\nabla \times \mathbf{H} = \frac{\partial \mathbf{D}}{\partial t} + \mathbf{J} \qquad\qquad \text{Eq. (11.139)}$$

$$\nabla \times \mathbf{E} = -\frac{\partial \mathbf{B}}{\partial t} - \mathbf{M} \qquad\qquad \text{Eq. (11.140)}$$

$$\nabla \bullet \mathbf{D} = \rho_e \qquad\qquad \text{Eq. (11.141)}$$

$$\nabla \bullet \mathbf{B} = \rho_m, \qquad\qquad \text{Eq. (11.142)}$$

where $\mathbf{E}$ is the electric field intensity vector in units V/m, $\mathbf{D}$ is the electric displacement vector in units C/m^2, $\mathbf{H}$ is the magnetic field intensity vector in units A/m, $\mathbf{B}$ is the magnetic flux density vector in units $Weber/m^2$, $\mathbf{J}$ is the electric current density vector in units A/m^2, $\mathbf{M}$ is the magnetic current density vector in units V/m^2, ρ_e is the electric charge density in units C/m^3, and ρ_m is the magnetic charge density in units $Weber/m^3$. For linear, isotropic, and nondispersive materials, the electric displacement vector and the magnetic flux density vector can be written as

$$\mathbf{D} = \varepsilon \mathbf{E} \qquad\qquad \text{Eq. (11.143)}$$

$$\mathbf{B} = \mu \mathbf{H} \qquad\qquad \text{Eq. (11.144)}$$

where ε is permittivity and μ is permeability of the material. The electric current density $\mathbf{J}$ is the sum of the conduction current density $\mathbf{J}_C = \sigma^e \mathbf{E}$ and the impressed current density $\mathbf{J}_I$ as $\mathbf{J} = \mathbf{J}_C + \mathbf{J}_I$. Similarly, for the magnetic current density $\mathbf{M} = \mathbf{M}_C + \mathbf{M}_I$, where $\mathbf{M} = \sigma^m \mathbf{H}$. Here σ^e is the electric conductivity of the material in units S/m and σ^m is the magnetic conductivity of the material in units Ω/m. Using the two curl Eqs. (11.139) and (11.140) and Eqs. (11.143) and (11.144), Maxwell's curl equations can be rewritten as,

$$\nabla \times \mathbf{H} = \varepsilon \frac{\partial \mathbf{E}}{\partial t} + \sigma^e \mathbf{E} + \mathbf{J}_I \qquad\qquad \text{Eq. (11.145)}$$

$$\nabla \times \mathbf{E} = -\mu \frac{\partial \mathbf{H}}{\partial t} - \sigma^m \mathbf{H} - \mathbf{M}_I \qquad\qquad \text{Eq. (11.146)}$$

Equations (11.145) and (11.146) consist of two vector equations, and each vector equation can be decomposed into three scalar equations in the three-dimensional space. Therefore, Maxwell's curl equations can be represented with six scalar equations in a Cartesian coordinate system (x, y, z) as follows,

$$\frac{\partial E_x}{\partial t} = \frac{1}{\varepsilon_x}\left(\frac{\partial H_z}{\partial y} - \frac{\partial H_y}{\partial z} - \sigma_x^e E_x - J_{ix}\right)$$

Eq. (11.147)

$$\frac{\partial E_y}{\partial t} = \frac{1}{\varepsilon_y}\left(\frac{\partial H_x}{\partial z} - \frac{\partial H_z}{\partial x} - \sigma_y^e E_y - J_{iy}\right)$$

Eq. (11.148)

$$\frac{\partial E_z}{\partial t} = \frac{1}{\varepsilon_z}\left(\frac{\partial H_y}{\partial x} - \frac{\partial H_x}{\partial y} - \sigma_z^e E_z - J_{iz}\right)$$

Eq. (11.149)

$$\frac{\partial H_x}{\partial t} = \frac{1}{\mu_x}\left(\frac{\partial E_y}{\partial z} - \frac{\partial E_z}{\partial y} - \sigma_x^m H_x - M_{ix}\right)$$

Eq. (11.150)

$$\frac{\partial H_y}{\partial t} = \frac{1}{\mu_y}\left(\frac{\partial E_z}{\partial x} - \frac{\partial E_x}{\partial z} - \sigma_y^m H_y - M_{iy}\right)$$

Eq. (11.151)

$$\frac{\partial H_z}{\partial t} = \frac{1}{\mu_z}\left(\frac{\partial E_x}{\partial y} - \frac{\partial E_y}{\partial x} - \sigma_z^m H_z - M_{iz}\right)$$

Eq. (11.152)

The material parameters $(\varepsilon_x, \varepsilon_y, \varepsilon_z)$ are associated with electric field components E_x, E_y, and E_z, respectively. Similarly the material parameters (μ_x, μ_y, μ_z) are associated with magnetic field components H_x, H_y, and H_z, respectively.

The first step in the FDTD method is based on applying a finite-difference numerical approximation to the time and space derivatives appearing in Maxwell's equations (11.147) through (11.152). The central finite-difference scheme is used here as an approximation of the space and time derivatives of both the electric and magnetic fields. For example, the derivative of a function $f(x)$ at a point x_0 using central finite-difference can be written as

$$f'(x_0) = \frac{f(x_0 + \Delta x) - f(x_0 - \Delta x)}{2\Delta x}$$

Eq. (11.153)

where Δx is the sampling period. Secondly, the electric and the magnetic field components are assigned to certain positions in each grid or cell. In 1966, Yee was the first to set up the commonly used arrangement of these field components, as shown in Fig. 11.51, to solve both the electric and magnetic Maxwell's curl equations in an iterative time sequence (Yee, 1966).

Equations (11.147) through (11.153) are used to construct six scalar FDTD updating equations for the six components of electromagnetic fields by the introduction of respective coefficient terms as follows (Elsherbeni and Demir, 2016),

I. For the E_x component:

$$
\begin{aligned}
E_x^{n+1}(i,j,k) = {}& C_{exe}(i,j,k) \cdot E_x^n(i,j,k) \\
& + C_{exhz}(i,j,k) \cdot [H_z^{n+1/2}(i,j,k) - H_z^{n+1/2}(i,j-1,k)] \\
& + C_{exhy}(i,j,k) \cdot [H_y^{n+1/2}(i,j,k) - H_y^{n+1/2}(i,j,k-1)] \\
& + C_{exj}(i,j,k) \cdot J_{ix}^{n+1/2}(i,j,k)
\end{aligned}
$$

Eq. (11.154)

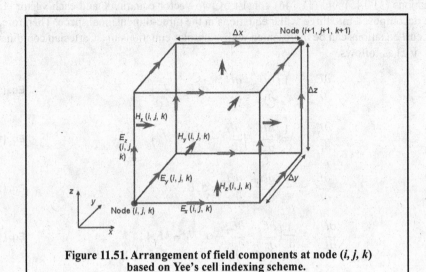

Figure 11.51. Arrangement of field components at node (i, j, k) based on Yee's cell indexing scheme.

where

$$C_{exe}(i,j,k) = \frac{2\varepsilon_x(i,j,k) - \Delta t \sigma_x^e(i,j,k)}{2\varepsilon_x(i,j,k) + \Delta t \sigma_x^e(i,j,k)}$$

$$C_{exhz}(i,j,k) = \frac{2\Delta t}{[2\varepsilon_x(i,j,k) + \Delta t \sigma_x^e(i,j,k)]\Delta y}$$

$$C_{exhy}(i,j,k) = \frac{-2\Delta t}{[2\varepsilon_x(i,j,k) + \Delta t \sigma_x^e(i,j,k)]\Delta z}$$

$$C_{exj}(i,j,k) = \frac{-2\Delta t}{2\varepsilon_x(i,j,k) + \Delta t \sigma_x^e(i,j,k)}$$

II. For the E_y component:

$$\begin{aligned}
E_y^{n+1}(i,j,k) = {} & C_{eye}(i,j,k) \cdot E_y^n(i,j,k) \\
& + C_{eyhx}(i,j,k) \cdot [H_x^{n+1/2}(i,j,k) - H_x^{n+1/2}(i,j,k-1)] \\
& + C_{eyhz}(i,j,k) \cdot [H_z^{n+1/2}(i,j,k) - H_z^{n+1/2}(i-1,j,k)] \\
& + C_{eyj}(i,j,k) \cdot J_{iy}^{n+1/2}(i,j,k)
\end{aligned}$$

Eq. (11.155)

where

$$C_{eye}(i,j,k) = \frac{2\varepsilon_y(i,j,k) - \Delta t \sigma_y^e(i,j,k)}{2\varepsilon_y(i,j,k) + \Delta t \sigma_y^e(i,j,k)}$$

$$C_{eyhx}(i,j,k) = \frac{2\Delta t}{[2\varepsilon_y(i,j,k) + \Delta t \sigma_y^e(i,j,k)]\Delta z}$$

$$C_{eyhz}(i,j,k) = \frac{-2\Delta t}{[2\varepsilon_y(i,j,k) + \Delta t \sigma_y^e(i,j,k)]\Delta x}$$

$$C_{eyj}(i, j, k) = \frac{-2\Delta t}{2\varepsilon_y(i, j, k) + \Delta t \sigma_y^e(i, j, k)}$$

III. For the E_z component:

$$\begin{aligned}
E_z^{n+1}(i, j, k) &= C_{eze}(i, j, k) \cdot E_z^n(i, j, k) \\
&+ C_{ezhy}(i, j, k) \cdot [H_y^{n+1/2}(i, j, k) - H_y^{n+1/2}(i-1, j, k)] \\
&+ C_{ezhx}(i, j, k) \cdot [H_x^{n+1/2}(i, j, k) - H_x^{n+1/2}(i, j-1, k)] \\
&+ C_{ezj}(i, j, k) \cdot J_{iz}^{n+1/2}(i, j, k)
\end{aligned}$$

Eq. (11.156)

where

$$C_{eze}(i, j, k) = \frac{2\varepsilon_z(i, j, k) - \Delta t \sigma_z^e(i, j, k)}{2\varepsilon_z(i, j, k) + \Delta t \sigma_z^e(i, j, k)}$$

$$C_{ezhy}(i, j, k) = \frac{2\Delta t}{[2\varepsilon_z(i, j, k) + \Delta t \sigma_z^e(i, j, k)]\Delta x}$$

$$C_{ezhx}(i, j, k) = \frac{-2\Delta t}{-[2\varepsilon_z(i, j, k) + \Delta t \sigma_z^e(i, j, k)]\Delta y}$$

$$C_{ezj}(i, j, k) = \frac{-2\Delta t}{2\varepsilon_z(i, j, k) + \Delta t \sigma_z^e(i, j, k)}.$$

IV. For the H_x component:

$$H_x^{\left(n+\frac{1}{2}\right)}(i, j, k) = C_{hxh}(i, j, k) \cdot H_x^{n-1/2}(i, j, k)$$

$$+ C_{hxey}(i, j, k) \cdot [E_y^n(i, j, k+1) - E_y^n(i, j, k)]$$

$$+ C_{hxez}(i, j, k) \cdot [E_z^n(i, j+1, k) - E_z^n(i, j, k)]$$

$$+ C_{hxm}(i, j, k) \cdot M_{ix}^n(i, j, k)$$

Eq. (11.157)

where

$$C_{hxh}(i, j, k) = \frac{2\mu_x(i, j, k) - \Delta t \sigma_x^m(i, j, k)}{2\mu_x(i, j, k) + \Delta t \sigma_x^m(i, j, k)}$$

$$C_{hxey}(i, j, k) = \frac{2\Delta t}{[2\mu_x(i, j, k) + \Delta t \sigma_x^m(i, j, k)]\Delta z}$$

$$C_{hxez}(i, j, k) = \frac{-2\Delta t}{[2\mu_x(i, j, k) + \Delta t \sigma_x^m(i, j, k)]\Delta y}$$

$$C_{hxm}(i, j, k) = \frac{-2\Delta t}{2\mu_x(i, j, k) + \Delta t \sigma_x^m(i, j, k)}.$$

V. For the H_y component:

$$H_y^{\left(n+\frac{1}{2}\right)}(i,j,k) = C_{hyh}(i,j,k) \cdot H_y^{n-1/2}(i,j,k) \qquad \text{Eq. (11.158)}$$

$$+ C_{hyez}(i,j,k) \cdot [E_z^n(i+1,j,k) - E_z^n(i,j,k)]$$

$$+ C_{hyex}(i,j,k) \cdot [E_x^n(i,j,k+1) - E_x^n(i,j,k)]$$

$$+ C_{hym}(i,j,k) \cdot M_{iy}^n(i,j,k)$$

where

$$C_{hyh}(i,j,k) = \frac{2\mu_y(i,j,k) - \Delta t\sigma_y^m(i,j,k)}{2\mu_y(i,j,k) + \Delta t\sigma_y^m(i,j,k)}$$

$$C_{hyez}(i,j,k) = \frac{2\Delta t}{[2\mu_y(i,j,k) + \Delta t\sigma_y^m(i,j,k)]\Delta x}$$

$$C_{hyex}(i,j,k) = \frac{-2\Delta t}{[2\mu_y(i,j,k) + \Delta t\sigma_y^m(i,j,k)]\Delta z}$$

$$C_{hxm}(i,j,k) = \frac{-2\Delta t}{2\mu_y(i,j,k) + \Delta t\sigma_y^m(i,j,k)}.$$

VI. For the H_z component:

$$H_z^{\left(n+\frac{1}{2}\right)}(i,j,k) = C_{hzh}(i,j,k) \cdot H_z^{n-1/2}(i,j,k) \qquad \text{Eq. (11.159)}$$

$$+ C_{hzex}(i,j,k) \cdot [E_x^n(i,j+1,k) - E_x^n(i,j,k)]$$

$$+ C_{hzey}(i,j,k) \cdot [E_y^n(i+1,j,k) - E_y^n(i,j,k)]$$

$$+ C_{hzm}(i,j,k) \cdot M_{iz}^n(i,j,k)$$

where

$$C_{hzh}(i,j,k) = \frac{2\mu_z(i,j,k) - \Delta t\sigma_z^m(i,j,k)}{2\mu_z(i,j,k) + \Delta t\sigma_z^m(i,j,k)}$$

$$C_{hzex}(i,j,k) = \frac{2\Delta t}{[2\mu_z(i,j,k) + \Delta t\sigma_z^m(i,j,k)]\Delta y}$$

$$C_{hzey}(i,j,k) = \frac{-2\Delta t}{[2\mu_z(i,j,k) + \Delta t\sigma_z^m(i,j,k)]\Delta x}$$

$$C_{hzm}(i,j,k) = \frac{-2\Delta t}{2\mu_z(i,j,k) + \Delta t\sigma_z^m(i,j,k)}.$$

After deriving the six FDTD updating Eqs. (11.154) through (11.159), a time-marching algorithm can be constructed, as shown in Fig. 11.52.

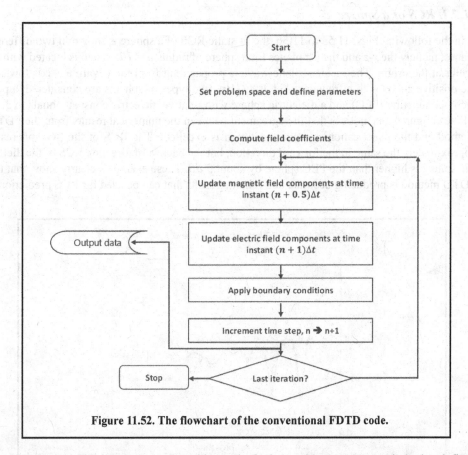

Figure 11.52. The flowchart of the conventional FDTD code.

In setting up the simulation using this method, the problem space needs to be defined, including boundaries, objects, material types, sources, etc., and defining any other parameters such as the excitation waveforms that will be used during the FDTD computation. The problem space usually has a finite size and specific boundary conditions that can be enforced on the boundaries. The most common and effective boundary is the one based on the convolutional perfectly matched layers (CPML). The FDTD simulation is processed through stepping in time with a specific time step. Based on the source waveform, type and composition of the object, and other simulation parameters, the number of time steps is determined. When the simulation is completed, the values of the desired field components are captured and stored as output data, and this data can be used for real time processing and/or post-processing in order to calculate other desired parameters such as the RCS in either time or frequency domains. The conversion to frequency is usually conducted using the discrete Fourier transform.

11.7. RCS Using the FDTD Method

In the following section, sample numerical simulations will be presented. These results show the capabilities of the FDTD method, with special emphasis on calculating the scattered fields or the RCS. First, we discuss the scattering from a sphere to show the validity and accuracy of the FDTD method when compared with the exact solution of a sphere, followed by the scattering from more composite structures that cannot be analyzed using other theoretical or canonical solutions.

11.7.1. RCS of a Sphere

In the following Figs. 11.53 to 11.56, the bi-static RCS of a sphere is shown in two different planes, namely the *x-z* and the *y-z* planes for a sphere of radius $a = 10\ cm$ and is located with its center at the origin. The incident plane wave is propagating from the negative *z*-axis towards the positive *z*-axis with a frequency set at *4 GHz*. Two types of spheres are considered, a perfectly conducting (PEC) and a dielectric sphere with relative dielectric constant equals to *3*. In all these figures, one notices that the agreement between the numerical results from the FDTD method and the exact canonical sphere solution is excellent. The RCS of the two spheres is approximately the same in the forward direction, but the backward direction RCS of the dielectric sphere is higher than the PEC sphere by about *5 dB*. These examples clearly show that the FDTD method is producing accurate and reliable results that can be used for RCS predictions.

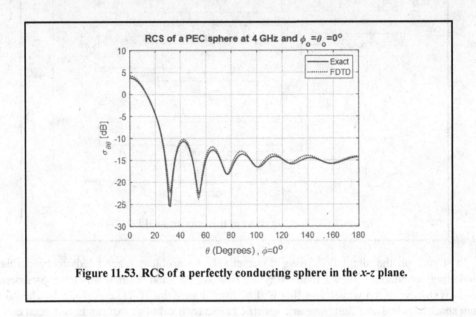

Figure 11.53. RCS of a perfectly conducting sphere in the *x-z* plane.

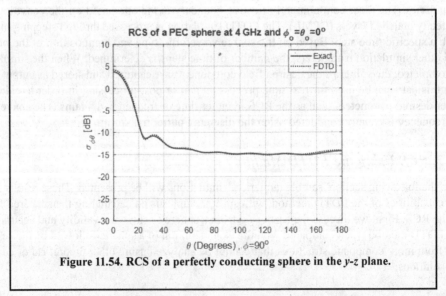

Figure 11.54. RCS of a perfectly conducting sphere in the *y-z* plane.

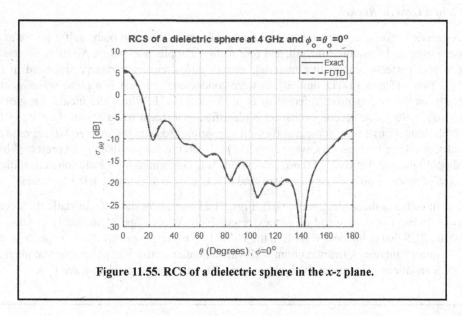

Figure 11.55. RCS of a dielectric sphere in the *x-z* plane.

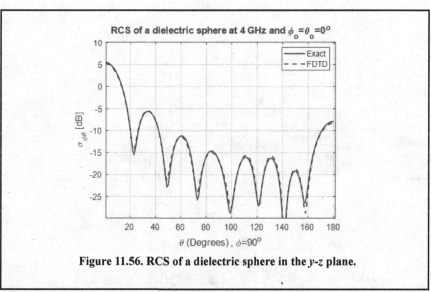

Figure 11.56. RCS of a dielectric sphere in the *y-z* plane.

11.7.2. RCS of Complex Objects

In the following two subsections, the bi-static RCS of complex shape objects will be evaluated using this full-time domain FDTD method. The results presented for multiple frequencies are obtained using a single FDTD simulation. Only different simulations are required when the source of the excitation is changed. These results were computed on a desktop computer housing NVIDIA Titan RTX GPU. The execution times and the memory requirements for each simulation will be documented to show the performance of the FDTD in predicting the RCS of such complex objects in a very reasonable time.

RCS of a Generic Rocket

A generic rocket is constructed from a finite cylinder as the main body, half a sphere as the nose, a truncated frustum as the tail, and four rectangular plates as wings. All these objects are made of a perfectly conducting material, and all geometrical parameters are listed in Fig. 11.57. Two different FDTD simulations were conducted. The first is a plane wave incident directly on the rocket nose, referred to as incident wave 1, where the incident angles are $\theta_0 = \phi_0 = 90°$. The second excitation is identified as incident wave 2 with $\theta_0 = \phi_0 = 0°$. In both simulations a time domain waveform supporting frequencies up to *10 GHz* is used and results, at selected frequencies, were extracted at the end of the simulation and presented here. It should be noted that each of these simulations was configured by 3.7 million cells utilizing *2.7 GB* of memory on a single GPU card, and execution was performed in *0.78 minutes*.

For three frequencies, *1*, *2*, and *4 GHz*, Figs. 11.58 and 11.59 show the bi-static RCS due to incident wave 1 in the *x-y* and *y-z* planes, respectively. While Figs. 11.60 and 11.61 show the bi-static RCS due to incident wave 2 in the *x-y* and *y-z* planes, respectively. As expected, when the frequency increases, the maximum RCS value increases. Also is it noticeable that the range of RCS variations is larger for the incident wave 2 relative to the incident wave 1.

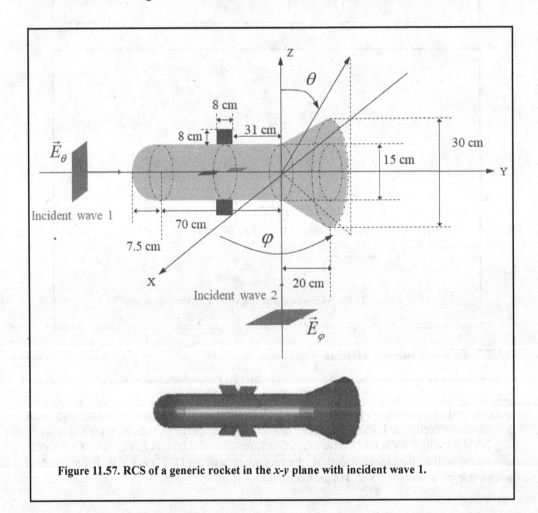

Figure 11.57. RCS of a generic rocket in the *x-y* plane with incident wave 1.

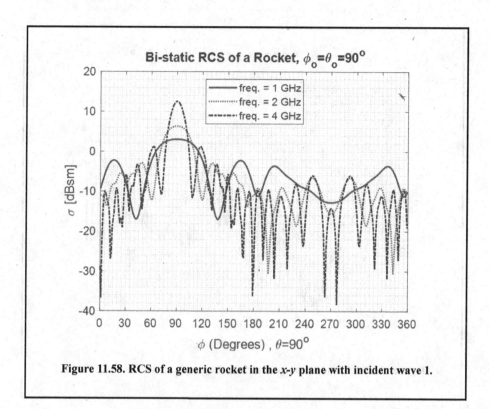

Figure 11.58. RCS of a generic rocket in the *x-y* plane with incident wave 1.

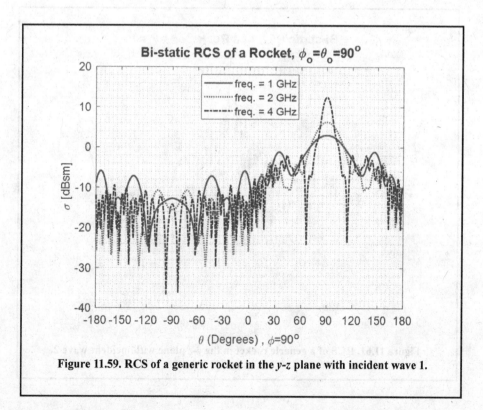

Figure 11.59. RCS of a generic rocket in the *y-z* plane with incident wave 1.

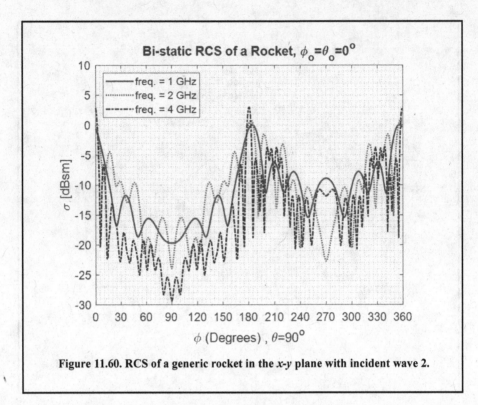

Figure 11.60. RCS of a generic rocket in the *x-y* plane with incident wave 2.

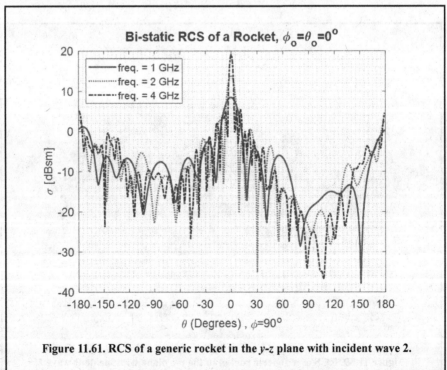

Figure 11.61. RCS of a generic rocket in the *y-z* plane with incident wave 2.

RCS of an Aircraft

Another very complex configuration can be presented by the generic fighter plane shown in Figs. 11.62 and 11.63. This configuration is composed of perfectly conducting material for most of the plane body, and dielectric material with relative dielectric constant of *4* representing the glass of the cockpit. The simulations conducted for two incident waves are similar to those described in the rocket simulation section. In both simulations a time domain waveform supporting frequencies up to *900 MHz* is used and results, at selected frequencies, were extracted at the end of the simulation and presented here. The approximate plane dimensions are: length = *15 m*, wing span = *9.74 m*, and height = *4.7 m*. The original raw data of the plane model was obtained from Professor Yasushi Kanai of Niigata Institute of Technology Kashiwazaki, Japan after his presentation at ACES 2019 conference (Ohtani et al., 2019). The current plane model is adapted for FDTD method and CEMS package by Prof. Veysel Demir of Northern Illinois University, Chicago, Illinois. In the current simulations, the plane is discretized with *2 cm* cell size in each direction making the FDTD domain size equal to *122.59 million* cells utilizing *4.6 GB* of GPU memory. The time domain iterative loop for each FDTD simulation associate with each excitation took approximately *4.6 minutes* while running on two parallel GPUs in a desktop computer. The FDTD computational electromagnetics simulator (CEMS) is used to perform the simulation (Demir, 2020), for incident waves with *300* and *600 MHz* operating frequencies.

Figures 11.64 and 11.65 show the RCS in the *x-y* when $\theta_0 = \phi_0 = 90°$ and in the *y-z* planes when $\theta_0 = \phi_0 = 0°$, respectively. Higher RCS values and more oscillations are observed for the *600 MHz* excitation relative to the *300 MHz*.

The above two examples clearly demonstrate the capability of the FDTD method in performing computational electromagnetics for complex configurations using moderate computer resources and within very reasonable execution times.

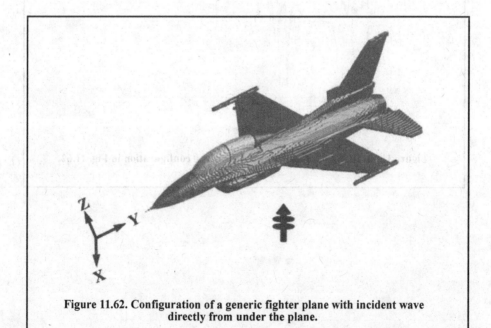

Figure 11.62. Configuration of a generic fighter plane with incident wave directly from under the plane.

**Figure 11.63. Configuration of a generic fighter plane with incident wave
directly on the nose.**

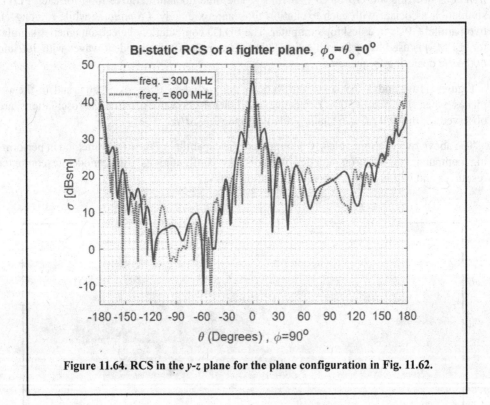

Figure 11.64. RCS in the *y-z* plane for the plane configuration in Fig. 11.62.

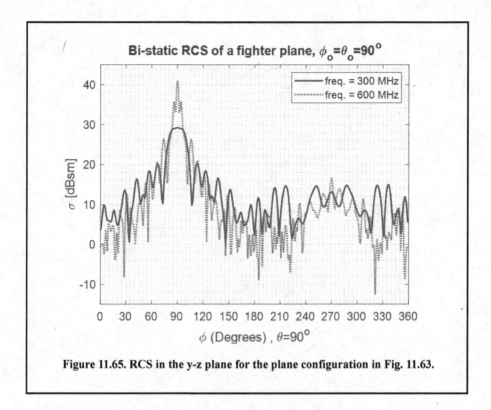

Figure 11.65. RCS in the y-z plane for the plane configuration in Fig. 11.63.

Chapter 12

Integral and Physical Optics Methods for RCS Computation

Walton C. Gibson

12.1. Introduction

In practice, radar engineers are most often concerned with the detection and tracking performance of a radar, where the radar cross-section (RCS) comprises only a number that goes into a Blake chart calculation. Or they may use a more complex digital simulation, where the radar signal processing and detection paths are modeled at the I, Q level. This requires a more complex representation of a target's RCS, which is often a function of aspect angle, frequency, and polarization. In each case, the engineer must have a source of RCS data, which may comprise real data obtained by measurement of a test article in a range, or synthetic data computed by various predictive codes.

In this chapter we will consider RCS prediction methods, commonly found in predictive codes, common types of RCS data products, and the RCS of complex objects. Although we will cover radiation and scattering problems at a high level, as well as several numerical solution methods, these are deeply complex topics that have been studied at length in the literature, and continue to receive significant academic attention. Therefore, this chapter is not intended to substitute for a course on electromagnetic theory or computational electro-magnetics (CEM).

12.2. Radiation and Scattering

In this section we will briefly review electromagnetic theory, discuss the Equivalence Theorem, and the equations of radiation and scattering. Our treatment will focus on the frequency domain version of Maxwell's Equations, as they are often the most appropriate approach when solving scattering problems. In contrast, the time domain version of Maxwell's Equations is often better suited at modeling wave propagation, field distributions, and transient responses in bounded nonlinear media.

12.2.1. Maxwell's Equations

In a homogeneous dielectric region having dielectric parameters, ε and μ, the electric and magnetic fields must satisfy Maxwell's Equations, which in the frequency domain

$$\nabla \times \mathbf{E} = -\mathbf{M} - j\omega\mu\mathbf{H},$$ **Eq. (12.1)**

$$\nabla \times \mathbf{H} = \mathbf{J} + j\omega\varepsilon\mathbf{E},$$ **Eq. (12.2)**

$$\nabla \bullet \mathbf{D} = q_e, \qquad \text{Eq. (12.3)}$$

$$\nabla \bullet \mathbf{B} = q_m, \qquad \text{Eq. (12.4)}$$

where $\mathbf{D} = \varepsilon \mathbf{E}$, $\mathbf{B} = \mu \mathbf{H}$, and the time dependence $\exp(j\omega t)$ is assumed and suppressed throughout this chapter. Though the magnetic current $\mathbf{M}$ and charge q_m are not physically realizable quantities, they are useful mathematical tools in solving radiation and scattering problems.

12.2.2. Boundary Conditions

At the interface between two regions, R_1 and R_2, each having different dielectric parameters, the generalized electromagnetic boundary conditions can be written as

$$\hat{n}_1 \times (\mathbf{E}_1 - \mathbf{E}_2) = -\mathbf{M} \qquad \text{Eq. (12.5)}$$

$$\hat{n}_1 \times (\mathbf{H}_1 - \mathbf{H}_2) = -\mathbf{J} \qquad \text{Eq. (12.6)}$$

$$\hat{n}_1 \bullet (\mathbf{D}_1 - \mathbf{D}_2) = q_e \qquad \text{Eq. (12.7)}$$

$$\hat{n}_1 \bullet (\mathbf{B}_1 - \mathbf{B}_2) = q_m \qquad \text{Eq. (12.8)}$$

where any of $\mathbf{M}$, $\mathbf{J}$, q_e, or q_m may be present, and $\hat{n}_1$ is the normal vector on the interface between R_1 and R_2 that points into R_1. At the interface between a dielectric (R_1) and a perfect electric conductor (PEC, R_2), the boundary conditions are

$$-\hat{n}_1 \times \mathbf{E}_1 = 0 \qquad \text{Eq. (12.9)}$$

$$\hat{n}_1 \times \mathbf{H}_1 = \mathbf{J} \qquad \text{Eq. (12.10)}$$

$$\hat{n}_1 \bullet \mathbf{D}_1 = q_e \qquad \text{Eq. (12.11)}$$

$$\hat{n}_1 \bullet \mathbf{B}_1 = q_m \qquad \text{Eq. (12.12)}$$

and between a dielectric (R_1) and perfect magnetic conductor (PMC, R_2), they are

$$-\hat{n}_1 \times \mathbf{E}_1 = \mathbf{M} \qquad \text{Eq. (12.13)}$$

$$\hat{n}_1 \times \mathbf{H}_1 = 0 \qquad \text{Eq. (12.14)}$$

$$\hat{n}_1 \bullet \mathbf{D}_1 = 0 \qquad \text{Eq. (12.15)}$$

$$\hat{n}_1 \bullet \mathbf{B}_1 = q_m \qquad \text{Eq. (12.16)}$$

In this chapter we will consider scattering by PEC objects only, thus $\mathbf{M} = 0$. The scattering by dielectric and composite PEC/dielectric objects is considered in Gibson (2014).

12.2.3. Formulations for Radiation

In general, they are different approaches to solving Maxwell's Eq. (12.1) through Eq. (12.4). Using the finite element method (FEM), they can be solved as presented in differential form, using variational techniques. However, FEM is a boundary-valued method that requires discretization of the entire solution domain, which becomes computationally expensive for three-dimensional (3-D) problems. In this way, the FEM is often better suited solving field distribution problems in bounded regions of smaller size, which may contain inhomogeneous materials.

In an unbounded dielectric region with wavenumber k, for an electric current $\mathbf{J(r)}$ the electric field everywhere can be written as

$$\mathbf{E(r)} = (-j\omega)\left[\mathbf{A(r)} + \frac{1}{k^2}\nabla\nabla\bullet\mathbf{A(r)}\right],$$ **Eq. (12.17)**

where $\mathbf{A(r)}$ is the magnetic vector potential given by

$$\mathbf{A(r)} = \mu\int_V G(\mathbf{r,r'})\mathbf{J(r')} \ dr'$$ **Eq. (12.18)**

and the 3-D Green's Function $G(\mathbf{r,r'})$ is

$$G(r) = \frac{e^{-jkr}}{4\pi r}.$$ **Eq. (12.19)**

where $r = |\mathbf{r-r'}|$. The corresponding magnetic field is

$$\mathbf{H(r)} = \frac{1}{\mu}\nabla\times\mathbf{A(r)}.$$ **Eq. (12.20)**

12.2.4. Near and Far Fields

The electric field given by Eq. (12.17) can be used to compute the field anywhere. Usually though, one is interested in the fields in one of two regions: the near field region or the far field region. The near field region is the area close to the source, where the fields comprise a super-position of stored (reactive) as well as radiated power. The region is of interest in the design of the radar antenna and mounting platform, as well as the nearby hardware and operating person-nel. It is also of interest in the design of proximity fuzes. The far field region is that which is far away from the source, where the fields have transitioned into purely radiative plane waves. It is the far field which is of most interest to radar engineers, as the target is typically located very far away from the radar. In this section we will derive expressions for both the near and far fields in three dimensions.

Three-Dimensional Far Field

When the field point is close to the source, as in Fig. 12.1-a, we must evaluate Eq. (12.17) directly to obtain the field. If instead it is located very far away from the source, the vectors $\mathbf{r}$ and $\mathbf{r-r'}$ are virtually parallel, as shown in Fig. 12.1-b. As a rule of thumb, this is typically satisfied when $kr \gg 1$. In this case, the fields are virtually planar, and under this assumption, we make the following approximations for r in the far field region,

$$r = \begin{cases} r-\mathbf{r}\bullet\mathbf{r'} & \textit{for phase variations} \\ r & \textit{for amplitude variations} \end{cases}.$$ **Eq. (12.21)**

Consider the radiated electric field in Eq. (12.17). The first term on the right-hand side results in fields that vary according to $1/r$, and the second term in fields that vary according to $1/r^2$, $1/r^3$ etc., due to the differential operators. In the far field, only those fields that vary as $1/r$ will have significant amplitude, and these fields are planar with no vector component along the direction of propagation. The far electric field $\mathbf{E}_{far}(r)$ is therefore simply

$$\mathbf{E}_{far}(r) = -j\omega\mathbf{A(r)}$$ **Eq. (12.22)**

where in the far field, $\mathbf{A(r)}$ becomes,

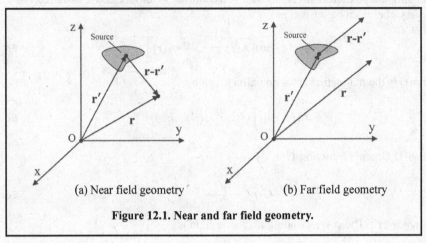

(a) Near field geometry   (b) Far field geometry

Figure 12.1. Near and far field geometry.

$$A(\mathbf{r}) = \mu \frac{e^{-jkr}}{4\pi r} \int_V J(\mathbf{r}') e^{-jk(\mathbf{r} \bullet \mathbf{r}')} d\mathbf{r}' . \qquad \text{Eq. (12.23)}$$

In spherical coordinates, the far electric field can be written in terms of its $\hat{\theta}$ and $\hat{\phi}$ components as

$$\mathbf{E}_{far}(\mathbf{r}) = -j\omega[A_\theta(\mathbf{r})\hat{\theta} - A_\phi(\mathbf{r})\hat{\phi}] \qquad \text{Eq. (12.24)}$$

and to obtain the far magnetic field $\mathbf{H}_{far}(\mathbf{r})$, we note that for plane waves in the far field, the electric and magnetic field are related via the relationship

$$\mathbf{H}_{far}(\mathbf{r}) = \frac{1}{\eta}\hat{\mathbf{r}} \times \mathbf{E}_{far}(\mathbf{r}) \qquad \text{Eq. (12.25)}$$

where $\eta = \sqrt{\mu/\varepsilon}$. For scattering problems, where R_1 is the unbounded exterior free space region R_0, $\mu = \mu_0$ and $\varepsilon = \varepsilon_0$. Given a scattered far field $\mathbf{E}^s$ due to an incident electric field $\mathbf{E}^i$, the radar cross-section, σ is defined as

$$\sigma = 4\pi r^2 \frac{|\mathbf{E}^s|^2}{|\mathbf{E}^i|^2} \qquad \text{Eq. (12.26)}$$

which has units of m^2. Note that the r^2 term in Eq. (12.26) cancels the $1/r^2$ term due to $\mathbf{A}$ in Eq. (12.23), so the RCS is not dependent on range. Also, many RCS prediction codes often assume the amplitude of the incident field to be unity, in which case the RCS is

$$\sigma = 4\pi r^2 |\mathbf{E}^s|^2 . \qquad \text{Eq. (12.27)}$$

It is also common to store the real and imaginary components of the scattered electric field amplitude instead of the RCS. This is highly desirable in digital simulations, where the *I, Q* components of a target's signature are needed to synthesize complex-valued pulse-compressed data versus range. Often what is stored is referred to as the *normalized* electric field $\mathbf{E}^s_{norm}$, given by

$$\mathbf{E}^s_{norm} = \sqrt{4\pi}\mathbf{E}^s \qquad \text{Eq. (12.28)}$$

where now, $\sigma = |\mathbf{E}^s_{norm}|^2$.

It is common in the literature to refer to $\hat{\theta}$ polarization as vertical polarization and $\hat{\phi}$ polarization as horizontal polarization. Note that these are not the same as the vertical and horizontal polarizations often seen in radar simulations, where those vectors are often defined in terms of the radar face coordinates.

12.2.5. Formulations for Scattering

Scattering problems can be treated as radiation problems where the radiating currents are generated by other currents or fields. For radar cross-section problems, these other sources comprise the fields radiated by the radar antenna and incident on the target. These induced currents then radiate the scattered field. As discussed in Section 12.2.3, radiation problems comprise the integration of a known current J to obtain the scattered field. However, for most practical problems, the current J has no analytic solution and must be determined numerically. Thus, scattering problems comprise three steps:

1. Formulating an integral equation for the unknown current J generated by the known incident field $\mathbf{E}^i$ (or $\mathbf{H}^i$)

2. Solving the integral equation

3. Integrating the current J to obtain the radiated or scattered fields $\mathbf{E}^s$

The last step is straightforward and can be carried out via Eq. (12.17) once J is known. However, the first two steps require more careful consideration. In this section, will first review the equivalence principle and use it to reformulate the scattering problem using equivalent surface currents. We will then develop surface integral equations of scattering. In a later section, we will then discuss several popular methods by which these equations are commonly solved.

Surface Equivalent

The radiated fields given by Eq. (12.17) assume the current J radiates in an unbounded, homogeneous dielectric region. If we introduce an obstacle with different material properties, we can no longer use that expression to compute the field. However, it is possible to formulate an equivalent problem that is more convenient to solve. To do so, we will use the surface equivalence theorem (also known as Huygen's Principle), which states that every point on an advancing wavefront is itself a source of radiated waves. Using this theorem, a radiating source can be replaced by a fictitious set of different but equivalent sources that lie on an arbitrary closed surface around the original source. By matching the boundary conditions, these currents generate the same radiated field outside the closed surface as the original sources. This will allow us to formulate an integral equation that can be solved for the currents induced on an object by an externally incident field.

To illustrate, consider the geometry of Fig. 12.2-a, where the electric and magnetic currents J and M generate known incident fields $\mathbf{E}_1$ and $\mathbf{H}_1$ in an unbounded region R_1 with dielectric parameters (μ_1, ε_1). A small, bounded region R_2 with parameters (μ_2, ε_2) is carved out inside R_1, where the interface between the two regions comprises the surface S with normal $\hat{n}_1$ that points into R_1, $\mu_1 = \mu_2$ and $\varepsilon_1 = \varepsilon_2$, the fields $\mathbf{E}_2$ and $\mathbf{H}_2$ inside R_2 are identical to $\mathbf{E}_1$ and $\mathbf{H}_1$, respectively. However, if either $\mu_1 \neq \mu_2$ or $\varepsilon_1 \neq \varepsilon_2$, region R_2 becomes an obstacle inside R_1 and the fields are no longer the same. The fields in R_1 now comprise as sum of incident and scattered fields, given by

$$\mathbf{E}_1 = \mathbf{E}_1^i + \mathbf{E}_1^s$$

Eq. (12.29)

$$\mathbf{H}_1 = \mathbf{H}_1^i + \mathbf{H}_1^s \qquad\qquad \text{Eq. (12.30)}$$

where $\mathbf{E}_1^i$ and $\mathbf{H}_1^i$ are the incident fields generated by $\mathbf{J}$ and $\mathbf{M}$, $\mathbf{E}_1^s$ and $\mathbf{H}_1^s$ are the fields scattered by the obstacle, and the fields E_2 and $\mathbf{H}_2$ inside R_2 are now referred to as *transmitted* fields.

Let us now remove $\mathbf{J}$ and $\mathbf{M}$ and replace them by fictitious but equivalent surface currents $\mathbf{J}_1$ and $\mathbf{M}_1$ on the outside of S, which we refer to as S^+. For the fields in R_1 and R_2 to remain unchanged, the boundary conditions on S^+ must satisfy the relationships

$$\mathbf{M}_1 = -\hat{\mathbf{n}}_1 \times (\mathbf{E}_1 - \mathbf{E}_2) \qquad\qquad \text{Eq. (12.31)}$$

$$\mathbf{J}_1 = \hat{\mathbf{n}}_1 \times (\mathbf{H}_1 - \mathbf{H}_2). \qquad\qquad \text{Eq. (12.32)}$$

Our goal is to now use Eq. (12.31) and Eq. (12.32) to obtain the equivalent currents, and use those to compute the scattered fields. However, there are two problems. First, while we know the incident fields $\mathbf{E}_1^i$ and $\mathbf{H}_1^i$, we do not know the scattered or transmitted fields. Second, even if we did know those fields, we still cannot use Eq. (12.17) and Eq. (12.20) to compute $\mathbf{E}_1^s$ and $\mathbf{H}_1^s$ due to the presence of the obstacle. However, for scattering problems, we are not interested in the transmitted fields. Thus, we can use the *extinction theorem,* see Chew (1995), assume those fields to be zero. Doing so, we can assign to R_2 the same dielectric parameters as R_1, and the boundary conditions on S^+ become

$$\mathbf{M}_1 = -\hat{\mathbf{n}}_1 \times \mathbf{E}_1 = -\hat{\mathbf{n}}_1 \times (\mathbf{E}_1^s + \mathbf{E}_1^i) \qquad\qquad \text{Eq. (12.33)}$$

$$\mathbf{J}_1 = \hat{\mathbf{n}}_1 \times \mathbf{H}_1 = \hat{\mathbf{n}}_1 \times (\mathbf{H}_1^s + \mathbf{H}_1^i). \qquad\qquad \text{Eq. (12.34)}$$

We now have an equivalent *exterior* problem, as illustrated in Fig. 12.2-b, where the fields outside S remain unchanged, and we only need to solve Eqs. (12.33) and (12.34).

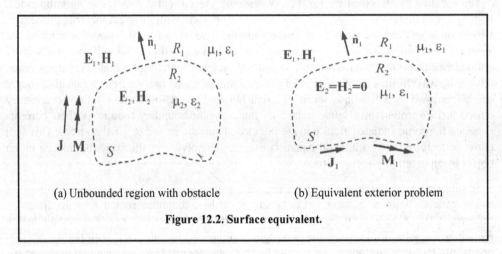

(a) Unbounded region with obstacle   (b) Equivalent exterior problem

Figure 12.2. Surface equivalent.

Surface Integral Equations

Let us now consider only the fields and currents of the exterior region R_1. Substitution of the unknown scattered electric field given by Eq. (12.17) into Eq. (12.33), and noting that $\mathbf{M} = \mathbf{0}$ on conductors, this yields

$$j\mu\omega(\mathcal{L}\mathbf{J})(\mathbf{r}) = \mathbf{E}^i(\mathbf{r}) \qquad\qquad \text{Eq. (12.35)}$$

where

$$(\pounds J)(\mathbf{r}) = \left[1 + \frac{1}{k^2}\nabla\nabla\bullet\right]\iint\limits_V G(\mathbf{r},\mathbf{r}')J(\mathbf{r}')\ d\mathbf{r}'\,. \qquad \text{Eq. (12.36)}$$

Similarly, substituting Eq. (12.20) into Eq. (12.34) yields

$$\mathbf{J}(\mathbf{r}) - \hat{n}(\mathbf{r})(\mathcal{K}J)(\mathbf{r}) = \hat{n}(\mathbf{r}) \times \mathbf{H}^i(\mathbf{r}) \qquad \text{Eq. (12.37)}$$

where

$$(\mathcal{K}J)(\mathbf{r}) = \nabla\times\int\limits_V G(\mathbf{r},\mathbf{r}')J(\mathbf{r}')\ d\mathbf{r}'\,. \qquad \text{Eq. (12.38)}$$

As $\mathbf{r}$ approaches $\mathbf{r}'$ on S^+, the $\pounds$ operator in Eq. (12.36) is well behaved; however, the $\mathcal{K}$ operator contains a singularity. This can be addressed using the limiting argument outlined in Gibson (2014), which yields

$$\frac{\mathbf{J}(\mathbf{r})}{2} - \hat{n}(\mathbf{r})(\mathcal{K}J)(\mathbf{r}) = \hat{n}(\mathbf{r}) \times \mathbf{H}^i(\mathbf{r})\,, \qquad \text{Eq. (12.39)}$$

for closed surfaces only, and for $\mathbf{r}$ not close to $\mathbf{r}'$. The expressions Eq. (12.35) and Eq. (12.39) comprise integral equations for the unknown current $\mathbf{J}(\mathbf{r})$ given a known incident electric or magnetic field. We refer to Eq. (12.35) as the electric field integral equation (EFIE), and Eq. (12.39) as the magnetic field integral equation (MFIE), respectively. These can be solved numerically, and once $\mathbf{J}(\mathbf{r})$ is known, the scattered field is computed via Eq. (12.17).

While both the EFIE or MFIE are valid, on closed conductors neither equation will produce a unique solution for all frequencies. This is due to the presence of spurious solutions that correspond to interior cavity (resonant) modes of the object itself, and radiate no field outside the object. The most popular and effective method for handling this problem is a linear combination of the EFIE and the MFIE. This enforces the boundary conditions on the electric and magnetic field simultaneously and will be free of spurious solutions. This is referred to as the combined field integral equation (CFIE), given by

$$\alpha EFIE + (1-\alpha)\eta MFIE \qquad \text{Eq. (12.40)}$$

where η is the impedance of the exterior region, and $0 \le \alpha \le 1$, where $\alpha = 0.5$ is commonly used. For thin, open conducting surfaces, the EFIE is used, as Eq. (12.39) is valid only on closed surfaces.

12.3. Numerical Methods

In this section we will discuss the more popular numerical methods used to solve the surface integral equations of scattering Eqs. (12.35) and (12.39) introduced in Section 12.2.5. These methods are categorized into two groups called "low-frequency" methods and "high-frequency" methods. The primary differences between these methods can be summarized as follows:

1. Low-frequency methods solve the integral equations directly with no implicit approximations; therefore, they model all the relevant physics and generate very accurate results. However, the computational and memory complexity of these methods often scale exponentially with the electrical size of the problem. Thus, run times may be very long, or some problems can be so large as to be unsolvable on the available computer system.

2. High-frequency methods make certain approximations to the integral equations that make the solution computationally tractable. Though they will cover radiation and scattering problems at a high level, and most often, these methods treat the scattering problem in the optical or asymptotic limit, and are sometimes also referred to as *asymptotic methods*. Most of these methods rely on a combination of ray optics, ray tracing, and edge diffraction, and generally omit other effects such as cavity resonances, and creeping and traveling waves, and often handle penetrable dielectrics poorly. As a result, the accuracy of their results is often poor to fair, though run times are often very short, making them very attractive for electrically large problems.

Historically, low-frequency methods were limited in their applicability due to the computing resources available at the time, so these methods were only applied to problems of very small electrical size. As a result, high-frequency methods were developed, making much larger problems numerically tractable, and much early research in the literature has focused on these asymptotic techniques. Deficiencies and inaccuracies in the results were understood and accepted, as in many cases these were the only methods that were applicable to certain problems. Almost all early radar cross-section solver codes implemented asymptotic methods, and many of them continue to be developed and used today. As computers have continued to improve and come down greatly in cost, there has been a resurgence in interest in low-frequency methods in the last *30* or so years. Several novel numerical algorithms have been developed that ameliorate greatly both the computational and memory complexity of these methods. Coupled with the astronomical increase in computing power, driven by large memory pools and multiple-core central processing units (CPUs), as well as graphics processing units (GPUs) that excel at massively parallel workloads, low-frequency methods continue to make a strong comeback.

12.3.1. Method of Moments

The method of moments (MoM) is a low-frequency method for accurately solving the integral Eqs. (12.35) and (12.39). In the MoM, the surface current **J** is first expanded using a sum of linearly independent basis functions with unknown coefficients, yielding

$$\mathbf{J}(\mathbf{r}) = \sum_{n=1}^{N} I_n \mathbf{f}_n(\mathbf{r}) \qquad \text{Eq. (12.41)}$$

where $\mathbf{f}_n$ and I_n comprise basis function n and its coefficient, respectively, and N is the total number of basis functions. Substitution of Eq. (12.41) into the CFIE Eq. (12.40) now yields a single equation with N unknowns. Using the MoM, we now apply a testing procedure where we form the inner product or moment between the discretized equation and N independent testing functions. Most often, a Galerkin-type testing is used, where the testing functions are the same as the basis functions. Doing this yields a $N \times N$ linear system, where the MoM-discretized CFIE has the form

$$\alpha \mathbf{z}^E + (1-\alpha)\eta \mathbf{z}^H = \alpha \mathbf{v}^E + (1-\alpha)\eta \mathbf{v}^H \qquad \text{Eq. (12.42)}$$

where the EFIE matrix elements $\mathbf{z}_{mn}^E$ are

$$\mathbf{z}_{mn}^E = j\omega\mu \underset{\mathbf{f}_m}{\int} \mathbf{f}_m(\mathbf{r}) \bullet \underset{\mathbf{f}_n}{\int} \mathbf{f}_n(\mathbf{r}') G(\mathbf{r},\mathbf{r}') d\mathbf{r}' d\mathbf{r} + \frac{j}{\omega\varepsilon} \underset{\mathbf{f}_m}{\int} \mathbf{f}_m(\mathbf{r}) \bullet \left[\nabla\nabla \bullet \underset{\mathbf{f}_n}{\int} \mathbf{f}_n(\mathbf{r}') G(\mathbf{r},\mathbf{r}') d\mathbf{r}' d\mathbf{r} \right], \text{Eq. (12.43)}$$

the MFIE matrix elements $\mathbf{z}_{mn}^H$ are

$$\mathbf{z}_{mn}^{H} = -\int_{\mathbf{f}_m}\mathbf{f}_m(\mathbf{r}) \bullet \left[\hat{\mathbf{n}}(\mathbf{r}) \times \int_{\mathbf{f}_n}\nabla G(\mathbf{r},\mathbf{r}') \times \mathbf{f}_n(\mathbf{r}')d\mathbf{r}'\right]d\mathbf{r} + \frac{1}{2}\int_{\mathbf{f}_m,\mathbf{f}n}\mathbf{f}_m(\mathbf{r}) \bullet \mathbf{f}_n(\mathbf{r})d\mathbf{r}. \qquad \text{Eq. (12.44)}$$

The right-hand side vector elements $\mathbf{v}_m^E$ are

$$\mathbf{v}_m^E = \int_{\mathbf{f}_m}\mathbf{f}_m(\mathbf{r}) \bullet \mathbf{E}^i(\mathbf{r})\ d\mathbf{r}, \qquad \text{Eq. (12.45)}$$

and the right-hand side vector elements $\mathbf{v}_m^H$ are

$$\mathbf{v}_m^H = \int_{\mathbf{f}_m}\mathbf{f}_m(\mathbf{r}) \times [\hat{\mathbf{n}} \times \mathbf{H}^i(\mathbf{r})]d\mathbf{r}. \qquad \text{Eq. (12.46)}$$

The expressions in Eqs. (12.43) to (12.46) can now be specialized, depending on the type of problem being considered. These can include thin wires, two-dimensional problems, 3-D bodies of revolution (BoRs), or 3-D surfaces of arbitrary shape. In each case, the surface geometry must be discretized, and appropriate basis functions chosen. As it is most applicable to the RCS of complex objects, we will briefly discuss the approach for 3-D surfaces of arbitrary shape, and common methods for solving the linear system.

It should be noted that the linear system resulting from the MoM discretization is full. This differs from other matrix-based techniques such as the FEM, which results in a sparse, banded matrix, with only a few nonzero entries per row.

MoM For 3-D Surfaces of Arbitrary Shape

For digital processing, a surface of arbitrary shape must first be reduced to a set of geometric primitives, and appropriate basis functions developed for those primitives. For 3-D surfaces, the most commonly used primitives are planar triangles (or facets), which are flexible and reasonably good at following the curvature of most realistic shapes. As a result, complex shapes such as ground and air vehicles can be represented with great precision by triangles, and most CAD programs can generate meshes of high quality. In addition, extensive numerical quadrature rules, as well as analytic solutions to the potential integrals encountered in Eqs. (12.43) to (12.44), have been developed for triangular subdomains. Figure 12.3 depicts a sphere, a reentry vehicle (RV), and a business jet, represented entirely by triangular facets.

For surfaces defined by flat, planar triangles, the most widely used basis function is the first-order Rao-Wilton-Glisson (RWG) basis function, defined as

$$\mathbf{f}_n(\mathbf{r}) = \frac{L_n}{2A_n^+}\rho_n^+(\mathbf{r}) \qquad \mathbf{r}\ in\ T_n^+ \qquad \text{Eq. (12.47)}$$

$$\mathbf{f}_n(\mathbf{r}) = \frac{L_n}{2A_n^-}\rho_n^-(\mathbf{r}) \qquad \mathbf{r}\ in\ T_n^- \qquad \text{Eq. (12.48)}$$

$$\mathbf{f}_n(\mathbf{r}) = 0 \qquad otherwise \qquad \text{Eq. (12.49)}$$

where T_n^+ and T_n^- are the two triangles that share edge e_n, and L_n is the length of the edge. On T_n^+, the vector $\rho_n^+(\mathbf{r})$ points toward the vertex $\mathbf{v}^+$ opposite the edge, and is

$$\rho_n^+(\mathbf{r}) = \mathbf{v}^+ - \mathbf{r} \qquad \mathbf{r}\ in\ T_n^+ \qquad \text{Eq. (12.50)}$$

and on the T_n^-, $\rho_n^-(\mathbf{r})$ points away from the opposite vertex $\mathbf{v}^-$, and is

$$\rho_n^-(\mathbf{r}) = \mathbf{r} - \mathbf{v}^- \qquad\qquad \mathbf{r} \; in \; T_n^- \,. \qquad\qquad\qquad \textbf{Eq. (12.51)}$$

These basis functions are assigned only to interior edges shared by two or more adjacent triangles. The RWG function is illustrated in Fig. 12.4.

Numerical results from the literature have shown that when using RWG basis functions, at least *10* edges per electrical wavelength ($100/\lambda^2$) are needed to yield reasonable accuracy. A higher number may also be needed in areas where variation in surface current is high, such as inside cavities and near sharp edges. Thus, the number of unknowns grows very quickly with the size of the problem, and for larger objects this may grow to tens of thousands or even millions. The solution of problems of such a large size presents us with several very significant problems:

1. The amount of memory needed to store the MoM matrix might range from several gigabytes (GB) to even terabytes (TB). This is a very large amount of random access memory (RAM), even by current computing standards, found only on high-end workstations, enterprise-class servers, and supercomputing systems

2. The CPU time needed to compute the MoM matrix elements scales as $O(N^2)$

3. The CPU time needed for a direct solution of the linear system via *LU* factorization scales as $O(N^3)$

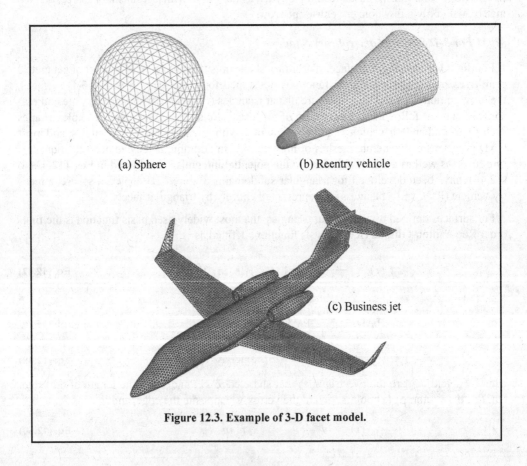

(a) Sphere

(b) Reentry vehicle

(c) Business jet

Figure 12.3. Example of 3-D facet model.

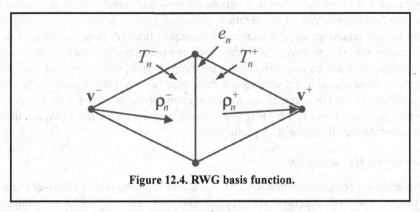

Figure 12.4. RWG basis function.

These issues clearly limit a direct application of the MoM to problems of very modest size. Indeed, all early MoM solver codes employed this direct approach, where the matrix is filled completely and LU factorization applied to solve the linear system.

Fortunately, novel compressive algorithms have been developed in the last 30 years that mitigate many of these difficulties. In general, these methods do the following, but in slightly different ways:

1. Some or all of the MoM matrix is stored, but in a compressed form that can be accessed quickly

2. Only a small fraction of the MoM matrix elements are actually computed

3. Solution of the linear system, via iterative or direct solution, is highly accelerated

We will now discuss two of the most popular methods, which are now commonly found in state-of-the-art MoM solver codes: the fast multipole method (FMM), and the adaptive cross-approximation (ACA). Both methods exploit the fact that the interactions between groups of basis functions separated by sufficient distance become effectively rank deficient and can be compressed. However, they solve the matrix system in very different ways.

Fast Multipole Method

In the fast multiple method (FMM), the bounding box of the object is carved up into many equally sized cubes, whose size is a fraction of a wavelength. By grouping basis functions into these cubes, the MoM system matrix becomes a block matrix. Only the diagonal blocks and off-diagonal blocks corresponding to cubes that are directly adjacent are filled and stored directly. Using multipole expansions, the remaining matrix elements are instead computed on the fly in aggregated form during the matrix-vector product step in an iterative solver. This achieves a computational complexity of $O(N^{1.5})$. The multilevel version, called the multilevel fast multipole algorithm (MLFMA), uses an octree to partition the geometry in a hierarchical way. It achieves a $O(N \log N)$ computational and storage complexity, greatly reduced from the $O(N^2)$ needed to computing the matrix-vector product and store the system matrix. The MLFMA makes it possible to solve problems with millions of unknowns on desktop workstations, and is in many commercial MoM solver codes.

The FMM does have limitations, which arise from its use of an iterative solver. It is well known that for many problems, the MoM matrix is often ill-conditioned, and this typically worsens as the problem size increases. Iterative solution of ill-conditioned problems may require many iterations per right-hand side (RHS) to converge, and in some cases the iteration may not converge at all. As a result, a secondary pre-conditioner matrix is often needed to improve the convergence rate of the iteration. However, pre-conditioners have their own setup time and storage requirements, and increase the compute time per iteration, which can significantly increase the total solution time. Also, for large problems, the time needed per matrix-vector product, and the corresponding iteration time, may be long. For radiation problems, such as those encountered in antenna design, there may be only a few RHSs, so the FMM may be the superior choice. However, as radar cross-section problems can have thou- sands of incident angles, this could lead to very long solve times. In these cases, the ACA, discussed next, is often the preferred choice for RCS problems.

Adaptive Cross-Approximation

In the adaptive cross-approximation (ACA), a similar approach is taken to partition the MoM matrix. The basis functions are grouped into many spatially localized groups using a clustering algorithm such as K-means, yielding a block matrix. The diagonal blocks are fully filled and stored directly; however, the off-diagonal blocks are compressed via a rank-revealing decomposition and stored in compressed form. To illustrate, consider an off-diagonal block Z_{mxn} having m rows and n columns. It can be decomposed via the singular-value decomposition (SVD) as

$$Z_{m \times n} = U_{m \times m} \Sigma_{m \times n} V^*_{n \times n} \qquad \text{Eq. (12.52)}$$

where the diagonals of Σ comprise the singular values, and U and V^* contain the left- and right-singular vectors, respectively. Now, for well-separated groups the interactions are rank-deficient, where the singular values in Σ decrease quickly below machine precision. Thus, $Z_{m \times n}$ can be approximated as

$$Z_{m \times n} \approx U_{m \times k} \Sigma_{k \times k} V^*_{k \times n} = Z_u^{m \times k} Z_v^{k \times n} \qquad \text{Eq. (12.53)}$$

where the *effective* rank k is chosen based on a threshold τ of largest to smallest singular values. Only Z_u and Z_v would be stored explicitly. Using the SVD in this way presents two problems, however. Each off-diagonal block must first be completely filled, and then SVD itself scales as $O(N^3)$, making the approach computationally infeasible for larger problems.

The ACA, as first applied to electromagnetic problems in Zhao et al. (2005), solves these problems. It is a simple, method-agnostic, low-overhead rank-revealing algorithm which iteratively constructs Z_u and Z_v in Eq. (12.53) by selecting only k rows and columns from Z, until the residual norm of the residual matrix falls below a chosen threshold. Therefore, to compute, compress and store the off-diagonal blocks, only a subset of their rows of columns need to be computed. As $k \ll m, n$ for most well-separated groups, matrix filling becomes efficient.

Though the ACA-compressed matrix system can be solved iteratively, a direct solution is preferred. It was found that if an LU factorization is performed, the off-diagonal blocks of the L and U matrix are also compressible. Following the right-looking block-LU factorization outlined in Gibson (2020), this factorization is very efficient, as the matrix products in the block updates involve blocks stored in rank-reduced form. These matrix products can be accelerated even further by an optimized level 3 BLAS, such as in the Intel math kernel library (MKL) for CPUs, or the NVIDIA cuBLAS for CUDA-capable GPUs. The use of the GPU is preferred in the LU factorization, as massively parallel GPUs excel at matrix operations and often yield much faster factorization times than if using the CPU alone.

For a problem with only a few RHSs, the ACA solution time may be longer than the MLFMA. However, RCS problems have a large number of RHS vectors corresponding to closely spaced incident angles. If these vectors are stacked together, they create a RHS matrix which is also in block form. It was also found in Shaeffer (2008) that these blocks, as well as the blocks of the solution matrix, are ACA-compressible. Thus, all RHSs can be solved for simultaneously via an efficient ACA-compressed *LU* back-substitution, where the blocks are again in rank-reduced form and matrix operation carried out via the Level 3 BLAS.

12.3.2. Physical Optics

Consider again the equivalent exterior problem in Fig. 12.2-b, where for a conducting surface, the surface current **J** is given by Eq. (12.34) and **M = 0**. Let us now make S very large compared to the wavelength, so that at every point on the surface, it can be treated as effectively flat and infinite in extent. On a conducting half-plane, the scattered magnetic field $\mathbf{H}^s$ is equal in phase and amplitude to the incident field $\mathbf{H}^i$. Thus, Eq. (12.34) becomes

$$\mathbf{J} = \hat{\mathbf{n}} \times (\mathbf{H}^s + \mathbf{H}^i) = 2\hat{\mathbf{n}} \times \mathbf{H}^i, \qquad \text{Eq. (12.54)}$$

which is known as the physical optics (PO) approximation for conductors. For an incident plane wave with θ^i and ϕ^i components, the incident electric field can be written as

$$\mathbf{E}^i(\mathbf{r}) = [E_\theta^i \hat{\theta}^i + E_\phi^i \hat{\phi}^i] e^{jk\hat{\mathbf{r}}^i \cdot \mathbf{r}} \qquad \text{Eq. (12.55)}$$

and the incident magnetic field as

$$\mathbf{H}^i(\mathbf{r}) = -\frac{1}{\eta}\hat{\mathbf{r}} \times \mathbf{E}^i(\mathbf{r}) = \frac{1}{\eta}[E_\theta^i \hat{\theta}^i - E_\phi^i \hat{\phi}^i] e^{jk\hat{\mathbf{r}}^i \cdot \mathbf{r}}. \qquad \text{Eq. (12.56)}$$

As the scattered electric field also has $\hat{\theta}^i$ and $\hat{\phi}^i$ components, its components can be obtained from the incident fields via the scattering matrix, written as

$$\begin{bmatrix} E_\theta^s \\ E_\phi^s \end{bmatrix} = \begin{bmatrix} S_{\theta\theta} & S_{\theta\phi} \\ S_{\phi\theta} & S_{\phi\phi} \end{bmatrix} \begin{bmatrix} E_\theta^i \\ E_\phi^i \end{bmatrix}, \qquad \text{Eq. (12.57)}$$

and using Eqs. (12.54) and (12.22), the scattering matrix elements are

$$S_{\theta\theta} = S_0[\hat{\theta}^i \times \hat{\phi}^s] \cdot \hat{\mathbf{n}}, \qquad \text{Eq. (12.58)}$$

$$S_{\phi\theta} = S_0[\hat{\phi}^i \times \hat{\phi}^s] \cdot \hat{\mathbf{n}}, \qquad \text{Eq. (12.59)}$$

$$S_{\theta\theta} = S_0[\hat{\theta}^s \times \hat{\theta}^i] \cdot \hat{\mathbf{n}}, \qquad \text{Eq. (12.60)}$$

$$S_{\theta\theta} = S_0[\hat{\phi}^s \times \hat{\theta}^i] \cdot \hat{\mathbf{n}}, \qquad \text{Eq. (12.61)}$$

where

$$S_0 = j\frac{k}{2\pi}\frac{e^{-jkr}}{r}\int_S e^{jk(\hat{\mathbf{r}}^i + \hat{\mathbf{r}}^s) \cdot \mathbf{r}'} \, d\mathbf{r}'. \qquad \text{Eq. (12.62)}$$

We note that in the monostatic case,

$$S_{\theta\theta} = S_{\phi\phi}, \qquad \text{Eq. (12.63)}$$

$$S_{\phi\theta} = S_{\theta\phi} = 0. \qquad \text{Eq. (12.64)}$$

As it assumes a locally infinite, flat surface, the PO integral is only performed over the directly illuminated portions of the surface S, and in general, it must be evaluated numerically. However, the integral can be evaluated analytically for planar triangles, making it ideal for analysis of surfaces described by facets. In PO-based software codes, a triangle ray tracer is used to determine the illumination function for individual triangles.

In general, the PO approximation is fairly accurate near specular angles, but performs poorly elsewhere. It does not include higher-order effects such as diffractions from edges, or multiple bounces. As such, it is often supplemented by other algorithms that approximate these, as discussed next.

12.3.3. Physical Theory of Diffraction

Near sharp edges, the surface current is not uniform and gives rise to diffracted fields which are scattered in nonspecular directions. Several different methods have been developed to approximate the nonuniform currents found near edges, and include these effects to augment the PO scattered field. One of the most widely used is the Mitzner incremental length diffraction coefficient (ILDC), which can be evaluated along the finite edge contours. Consider the geometry as defined in Fig. 12.5 for a wedge with external angle α, where $\mathbf{r}^i$ and $\mathbf{r}^s$ are the incident and scattering directions, ϕ^i and ϕ^s the corresponding local angles, respectively. The expression for the far scattered electric field E_s due to an incremental length edge is

$$\mathbf{E}_d^s = \frac{e^{-jkr}}{2\pi r}\left[(D_\perp - D'_\perp)\hat{\mathbf{e}}_\perp^i \cos\gamma - (D_{ll} - D'_{ll})\frac{\sin\beta^s}{\sin\beta^i}\hat{\mathbf{e}}_{ll}^i \sin\gamma\right.$$

$$\left.- (D_x - D'_x)\hat{\mathbf{e}}_\perp^i \frac{\sin\beta^s}{\sin\beta^i}\cos\gamma\right]$$

Eq. (12.65)

where $\hat{\mathbf{e}}_{ll}^{i,s}$ and $\hat{\mathbf{e}}_\perp^{i,s}$ are the unit vectors parallel and perpendicular to the plane of incidence and scattering, given by

$$\hat{\mathbf{e}}_\perp^i = \frac{\hat{\mathbf{t}} \times \hat{\mathbf{r}}^i}{|\hat{\mathbf{t}} \times \hat{\mathbf{r}}^i|}$$

$$\hat{\mathbf{e}}_{ll}^i = \hat{\mathbf{t}} \times \hat{\mathbf{e}}_\perp^i$$

$$\hat{\mathbf{e}}_\perp^s = \frac{\hat{\mathbf{t}} \times \hat{\mathbf{r}}^s}{|\hat{\mathbf{t}} \times \hat{\mathbf{r}}^s|}$$

Eq. (12.66)

$$\hat{\mathbf{e}}_{ll}^s = \hat{\mathbf{t}} \times \hat{\mathbf{e}}_\perp^s$$

and the polarization of the incident wave is along vector $\hat{\mathbf{p}}$ given by

$$\hat{\mathbf{p}} = \hat{\mathbf{e}}_\perp^i \cos\gamma + \hat{\mathbf{e}}_{ll}^i \sin\gamma$$

Eq. (12.67)

where γ is the angle between the incident electric field vector that is normal to the plane of incidence.

For triangular facet models, diffracting edges can be found by examining the angle between the two facets that share an edge. Wedges with small enough internal angles (often 120° or less) are retained for processing. For many PO and physical theory of diffraction (PTD) based software codes, these diffracting edge descriptions are often generated in external CAD programs, and cleaned up by hand manually to remove any "false" edges, or edges inside the model that are not visible to the exterior. For use in PO and PTD-based software codes, this data is typically saved to an *edge file* which is read in at run time.

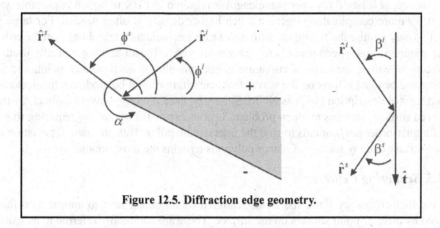

Figure 12.5. Diffraction edge geometry.

12.3.4. Shooting and Bouncing Rays

The PO and PTD approximations discussed thus far compute a first-order scattered field due to a directly incident electric field. Realistic targets, however, are very complex, and have cavities, wings, fins and other protrusions that give rise to secondary scattering due to multiple-bounce fields, as shown in Fig. 12.6-a. The shooting and bouncing ray (SBR) method is a very popular technique for predicting these higher-order scattered fields. In SBR, a very dense grid of finite ray tubes, representing the incident wavefront, is "shot" at the target, as shown in Fig. 12.6-b. The rays are traced according to the laws of geometrical optics (GO) as they bounce around on the target, where the phase, amplitude and polarization of the fields in each tube are maintained along the ray path. At each bounce point, the incident and reflected field is known, and a physical optics integral of the form in Eq. (12.62) is performed over the footprint of the ray tube on the scatterer's surface. This process is repeated until the ray exits the scene, or a maximum number of bounces has been reached. Note that if SBR is performed at the first bounce point, this effectively produces the first-order PO scattered field, so a separate PO calculation for all surface triangles is not necessary. This is a common option in SBR-based solver codes.

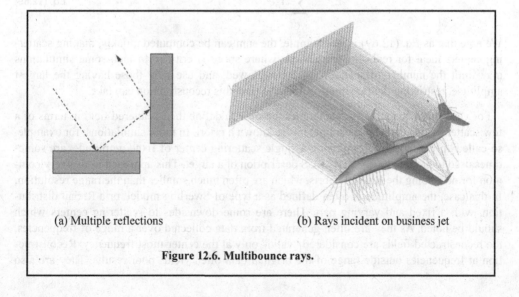

(a) Multiple reflections   (b) Rays incident on business jet

Figure 12.6. Multibounce rays.

In practice, at least *10* rays per wavelength is required in SBR to obtain reasonable results, though for more complicated targets, a much higher density is often needed. For large problems, this may require the tracing of millions of rays per incident angle. For target described by planar triangles, high-speed triangle ray tracers are very efficient and are typically used. With flat facets, however, the radii of curvature is not available at each bounce point, and so the twisting and bending effects on the wave- front curvature cannot be modeled. In some cases, a curved surface description (such as NURBS) may be used directly; however, direct ray tracing of curved surfaces remains an open problem. It is an expensive operation, requiring root-finding of higher-order polynomials to find the intersection point. Thus, to-date, tessellation of the curved surface and ray tracing of planar polygons remains the most popular approach.

12.3.5. Scattering Centers

In the high-frequency limit, the fields scattered by an object start to appear as if they are radiated by discrete point sources on the surface. These are commonly referred to as *scattering centers*. If the positions and amplitudes of these scattering centers can be isolated, the scattered field can be compressed, with some loss, and then reconstructed when needed. Thus, scattering centers are not an RCS prediction method per se. Instead, they are a product of reducing or distilling existing scattered field data, obtained from measurement or low and high-frequency codes, into a much smaller data product that allows for fast, real-time access and field reconstruction. Thus, they are commonly used in software drivers for real-time, hardware-in-the-loop (HWIL) operation, as well as purely software-based digital simulations.

Scattering Center Definition

Scattering centers comprise simple, point targets for a combination incident and scattered field polarization. For a single scattering center, the monostatic scattered field amplitude is

$$E^s = A e^{j2k\hat{\mathbf{r}}^i \cdot \mathbf{r}},$$

Eq. (12.68)

A is the scattering center amplitude, $\mathbf{r}$ is the three-dimensional location, and $\hat{\mathbf{r}}^i$ the direction of incidence and scattering. Given N scattering centers, the scattered field then comprises the sum

$$E^s = \sum_{n=1}^{N} A_n e^{j2k\hat{\mathbf{r}}^i \cdot \mathbf{r}_n}.$$

Eq. (12.69)

We note that as Eq. (12.69) is very simple, the sum can be computed quickly, making scattering centers ideal for real-time simulations where speed is critical. In fact, some simulations may limit the number of scattering centers allowed, and use only those having the largest amplitude, restricting the maximum amount of time this reconstruction can take.

For very simple targets, it is sometimes possible to define their scattered field in terms of a few scattering centers whose parameters are known a priori. In radar simulations, for example, so-called "point targets", comprising a single scattering center of fixed amplitude, are sometimes used to provide a very basic RCS description of a target. This approach is also very common for describing the RCS of debris, which are often much smaller than the range resolution. In this case, the amplitude is often defined as a type of Swerling model, or a Rician distribution, with a fixed and varying part. There are some downsides to scattering centers which should be noted. As they are often generated from data collected over a range of frequencies, the reconstructed fields are considered "valid" only at the center-most frequency. Reconstruction at frequencies outside range of the original data often yields poor results. They are also fairly poor at modeling non-point like and distributed scattering features, such as delayed returns and line scatterers.

Extraction

For targets of general configuration, scattering centers must be generated and extracted from data obtained from other sources. The most common method is through the use of an imaging/ CLEAN-based algorithm (Tsao and Steinberg, 1988), of which there are two versions. In the first version, complex-valued scattered field data is first collected versus frequency and number of incident angles θ^i, ϕ^i on the unit sphere. The angles chosen form a square "sector" on the sphere, centered around an incident angle pair θ_0, ϕ_0. This 3-D "data cube" is then converted to a volumetric inverse synthetic aperture radar (ISAR) image via the 3-D fast Fourier transform (FFT), yielding volumetric amplitude data versus down range (z), and cross-ranges x associated with ϕ, and y with θ. This image comprises the sum of the point-spread functions of all scattering centers, where the amplitude function $A(x, y, z)$ is

$$A(x, y, z) = \sum_{n=1}^{N} A_i h(x - x_n, y - y_n, z - z_n) \qquad \textbf{Eq. (12.70)}$$

and the point-spread function $h(x, y, z)$ is

$$h(x, y, z) = e^{j2kz} Sinc(\Delta_k z) Sinc(\Delta_\phi x) Sinc(\Delta_\theta y) \qquad \textbf{Eq. (12.71)}$$

where $\Delta_k = 2\pi B/c$, B is the bandwidth, Δ_ϕ and Δ_θ are the angular extents of the scattered field data versus ϕ and θ, respectively. More in-depth information on the synthetic aperture radar (SAR) imaging process can be found in Chapter 14.

Scattering centers can now be extracted from the image via the CLEAN algorithm, which is a simple, iterative process. In CLEAN, the voxel (image element) of largest amplitude in the image is located, and assumed to be the location of a scattering center. Its location and amplitude is recorded, and then its weighted point-spread function Eq. (12.71) is subtracted from all voxels in the image, effectively removing it. This process is then repeated for the next voxel of greatest amplitude, and so on, until the amplitude falls below some threshold or a maximum number of scattering centers has been found. To illustrate, in Fig. 12.7-a is shown an original two-dimensional ISAR image, obtained for an aircraft, and in Fig. 12.7-b the scattering center locations found by applying CLEAN to the image.

We note that the scattered field data must be sampled at a sufficient rate to avoid aliasing in each dimension. For targets that have significant multibounce returns, this can be problematic, as multibounce can result in off-body scattering locations that appear much further down-range than the actual target. Also, for very large targets, the number of samples in each dimension can be quite high, requiring significant amounts of random access memory (RAM) to store the image and an extended extraction time.

The second variant of this algorithm is a method described in Bhalla et al. (1989), based on the SBR technique. In this method, for an incident angle pair θ_0, ϕ_0, the SBR calculation is done normally; however, when doing the calculation at each bounce point, the scattered field is not computed and instead the amplitude and position is recorded. When the calculation is complete, Eq. (12.70) now comprises a sum over all these small "subscatterers," of which there may be millions. Because SBR is done for only a single incident direction, this is often referred to as a "one-look" algorithm. Since the positions of the sub-scatterers is known, a single large imaging volume is not needed. Instead, the volume can be partitioned into smaller subvolumes, and a fast image reconstruction used to generate the portion of the image comprising a sub-volume. The CLEAN algorithm is then applied to the each subvolume, as usual. In addition to reducing the memory footprint, this approach has the added benefit of avoiding the imaging of empty areas, where there are no subscatterers.

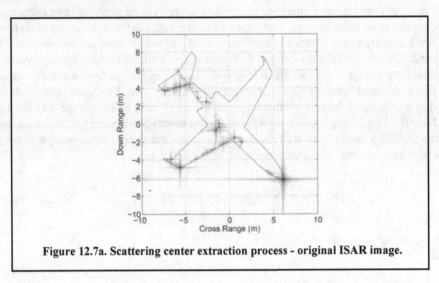

Figure 12.7a. Scattering center extraction process - original ISAR image.

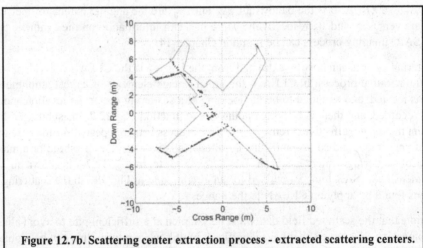

Figure 12.7b. Scattering center extraction process - extracted scattering centers.

Scattering Center Models

To describe completely the scattered field of an object over the unit sphere, for all θ and ϕ, the imaging and extraction process must be repeated for many different incident angles. Since this process can be computationally expensive, the most common approach is to perform the computation for a number of sectors on the sphere, each having a predefined extent in θ and ϕ. In reconstructing the field at some arbitrary θ^i, ϕ^i, the closest sector is then identified and the corresponding scattering centers used. This is fairly straightforward; however, the scattering centers are not continuous and can appear across sectors and may disappear across sector boundaries, an effect which is exacerbated by the one-look algorithm. As a result, the four closest sectors can be identified and a bilinear interpolation of the results applied.

12.4. RCS Data Products

In most cases, the radar engineers will not perform measurements or execute predictive codes, instead they will receive this data from other sources. These will comprise RCS data files often sourced from different test ranges or codes, they often vary widely in their fidelity, angle and frequency resolution, and file formats. The engineer must be cognizant of all these issues, as the data available may not be usable for their particular use case, may be in a different (and unknown) file format, scattering coordinate system, or it may be of dubious quality, all of which could adversely affect their analysis.

Data products typically comprise look-up tables of RCS or normalized scattered fields, versus angle and frequency, in various coordinate systems. Files may be in American Standard Code for Information Interchange (ASCII) or binary format. Scattering center files are similar. Some data products are provided with excellent documentation, detailing the coordinate systems used, target alignment, zero-roll convention, and sampling rates. On the other hand, documentation is often in error, and some data products may have no documentation at all. Thus, it is recommended that data products always be checked and scrutinized prior to use, so as to verify these details. Recommended steps include:

1. Check and verify the file format, ensuring that the data file can be loaded by existing tools and no loading errors are encountered.

2. Generate RCS versus aspect angle plots, at several roll angles. Cross-reference and check against similar plots in the documentation, if available.

3. Generate 2-D range-aspect intensity (RAI) plots via FFT in the frequency domain, if data permits. Verify data is not aliased in the range dimension, as this can negatively impact higher-fidelity simulations. Again, cross-reference against the documentation, if possible.

One topic that is often confusing is the scattering coordinates and target orientations used in computational codes, and how these relate to the coordinate systems found in data products, as they often differ. This is very important when looking up the RCS at the correct aspect and roll angle, and polarization. We will discuss coordinate systems in more detail in the next sections.

12.5. Scattering Coordinate System

In this section we discuss the coordinate system conventions used by virtually all industry standard RCS prediction software codes to specify target CAD geometry, scattering angles, and the scattering matrix.

12.5.1. Target Geometry Coordinate System

The standard Cartesian coordinate system (x, y, z) is used to describe all target CAD geometry (such as facet and edge files). Target geometry is treated as static, and the scattering angles are varied to obtain the scattered field at different incident angles θ^i, ϕ^i.

12.5.2. Spherical Coordinates

Consider the standard spherical coordinate system illustrated in Fig. 12.8, where at every angle pair (θ, ϕ) there exists the orthogonal linear basis vectors $\hat{\theta}$ and $\hat{\phi}$. These vectors are defined in terms of Cartesian coordinates as

$$\hat{\theta} = \cos\theta\cos\phi\hat{x} + \cos\theta\sin\phi\hat{y} - \sin\theta\hat{z}$$

Eq. (12.72)

$$\hat{\phi} = -\sin\phi\hat{\mathbf{x}} + \cos\phi\hat{\mathbf{y}}.$$

Eq. (12.73)

To fully characterize the far electric field scattered by a target, it is sufficient to determine the field scattered due to incident plane waves having orthogonal polarizations. As the scattered far field is planar and has only θ and ϕ components, scattering codes use these as the basis vectors for the incident and scattered field. Thus, given $\hat{\theta}^i$ and $\hat{\phi}^i$ polarized incident electric fields with amplitudes E_θ^i and E_ϕ^i, the $\hat{\theta}^s$ and $\hat{\phi}^s$ polarized scattered electric fields with amplitudes E_θ^s and E_ϕ^s can be written in terms of a scattering matrix [S] of the form in Eq. (12.57). For each polarization, there is a scattered field of the same polarization (co-polarization) and one of the opposite polarization (cross-polarization). Knowing all four components of the scattering matrix allows the reconstruction of the scattered field vector due to an incident wave of arbitrary polarization.

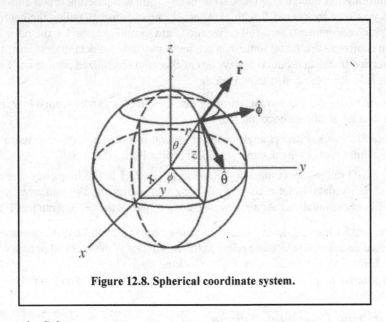

Figure 12.8. Spherical coordinate system.

Sampling on the Sphere

The scattered field is often needed over a wide range of θ and ϕ on the unit sphere. Scattering codes typically use a uniform spacing for both angles, resulting in the pattern depicted for the upper hemisphere in Fig. 12.9. Though this results in oversampling near $\theta = 0$ and $\theta = \pi$, it simplifies the implementation of scattering codes and their resulting output files, and most codes use this sampling convention.

Vertical and Horizontal Polarizations

The linear vectors $\hat{\theta}$ and $\hat{\phi}$ are often referred to as vertical and horizontal polarizations, respectively. Thus, the scattering matrix [S] is also commonly written as

$$\begin{bmatrix} E_v^s \\ E_h^s \end{bmatrix} = \begin{bmatrix} S_{vv} & S_{vh} \\ S_{hv} & S_{hh} \end{bmatrix} \begin{bmatrix} E_v^i \\ E_h^i \end{bmatrix}.$$

Eq. (12.74)

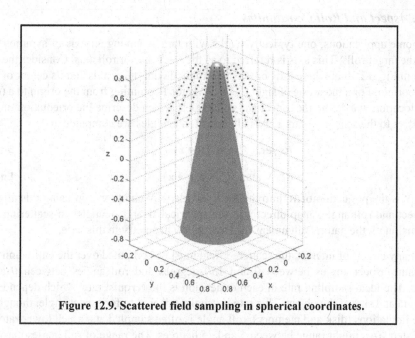

Figure 12.9. Scattered field sampling in spherical coordinates.

It is also common to refer to the scattering matrix elements by their subscripts. Therefore, instead of S_{vv}, S_{vh}, S_{hv} and S_{hh}, it is common to refer to them as vv, vh, hv and hh, respectively. There are many radars that use vertical and/or horizontal polarizations; however, these are in *radar coordinates* defined by the orientation of the radar antenna. Therefore, when using synthetic signature data in a radar simulation, conversion from scattering coordinates to radar coordinates is usually required. To illustrate, Let $\mathbf{E}^t$ comprise the components of far-zone electric field transmitted in the radar's reference frame, given by

$$\mathbf{E}^t = \begin{bmatrix} E_v^t \\ E_h^t \end{bmatrix}.$$

Eq. (12.75)

In target scattering coordinates, the components of the incident electric field $\mathbf{E}^i$ are then

$$\mathbf{E}^i = \mathbf{R}(\beta)\mathbf{E}^t.$$

Eq. (12.76)

where β is called the polarization angle, and $\mathbf{R}(\beta)$ is a rotation matrix given by

$$\mathbf{R}(\beta) = \begin{bmatrix} \cos\beta & -\sin\beta \\ \sin\beta & \cos\beta \end{bmatrix}.$$

Eq. (12.77)

The sign of β is such that E_v^t is rotated about the radar line of sight so that it is aligned with the vertical polarization vector in the target frame. The field components scattered by the target is then

$$\mathbf{E}^s = \mathbf{S}\mathbf{R}(\beta)\mathbf{E}^t.$$

Eq. (12.78)

and the electric field $\mathbf{E}^r$ received at the radar is in the radar's reference frame, so the inverse rotation $\mathbf{R}(-\beta)$ is applied, yielding

$$\mathbf{E}^r = \mathbf{R}(-\beta)\mathbf{E}^s = \mathbf{R}(-\beta)\mathbf{S}\mathbf{R}(-\beta)\mathbf{E}^t.$$

Eq. (12.79)

12.5.3. Aspect and Roll Coordinates

For some applications, one typically works with targets having an axis of symmetry about which the target rolls. This axis is referred to as the *body axis* or roll axis. Consider the reentry vehicle in Fig. 12.10-a, where the body axis is aligned with the $\hat{z}$ axis and its center of gravity is at the origin. For a radar line of sight (RLOS) vector $\hat{R}$ pointing from the origin to a (distant) sensor location, we define the aspect and roll angles, which describe the orientation of the target relative to the sensor. In this $\hat{z}$ axis alignment, the angles are computed as

$$aspect = \mathrm{acos}(\hat{R} \bullet \hat{z}) \qquad\qquad \textbf{Eq. (12.80)}$$

$$roll = \mathrm{atan2}(\hat{\rho} \bullet \hat{y}, \hat{\rho} \bullet \hat{x}) \qquad\qquad \textbf{Eq. (12.81)}$$

where $\hat{\rho}$ is the projection of $\hat{R}$ into the local *x-y* plane. We note that in using this alignment, the aspect and roll angles map directly to the spherical θ and ϕ angles in scattering coordinates, making it the natural alignment for target CAD geometry in this case.

For many targets of interest, the scattered field must be computed over the entire unit sphere, comprising aspect angles between *0* and *180* degrees and roll angles between *0* and *360* degrees. The ideal sampling rate in each dimension is the Nyquist rate, which depends on the waveband and size of the object. This rate is usually adhered to for aspect angle, though due to storage limitations (disk and memory), roll angle is often sampled at a much lower rate, where typical step sizes might range between *5* and *15* degrees. The range of roll angles may also be reduced due to roll symmetries in the target. Thus, the scattered field is sometimes computed over a small number of "roll cuts," with each cut comprising the field computed for aspect angles between *0* and *180* degrees at a single roll angle. Using the $\hat{z}$ axis alignment in Fig. 12.10-a, several roll cuts are illustrated in Fig. 12.10-b, where the roll angle increment is rather coarse.

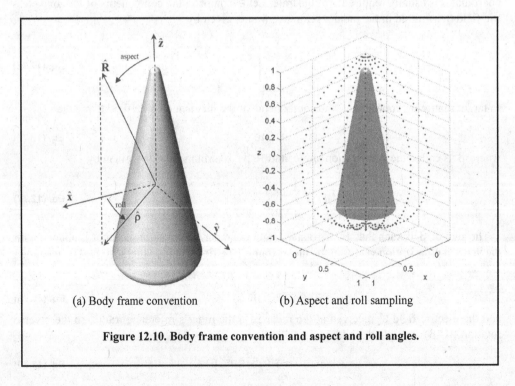

(a) Body frame convention   (b) Aspect and roll sampling

Figure 12.10. Body frame convention and aspect and roll angles.

12.5.4. Measurement Coordinate System

When there is a physical target available, it can be taken to a static range and its RCS measured. At most ranges, whether they are outdoor ranges or indoor anechoic rooms, it is practical for the transmit and receive antennas to remain static and the target to be moved to vary the incident angle. To do this, the target is placed on a pedestal which is rotated in the ground plane, as shown in Fig. 12.11-a. To obtain a roll cut, for example, the target roll axis is aligned with the transmitter, and the pedestal turned *180* degrees in small increments[1]. To obtain additional roll cuts, the target must be carefully lifted from the pedestal, turned about its roll axis to the desired position, and replaced on the pedestal. This process is then repeated for the required roll cuts.

Consider now the use of a scattering code to generate synthetic data for comparison against a measurement. One way to do this is to replicate the target alignment, rotation, and polarization vector conventions used at the range. In scattering codes, however, the target is fixed while the antenna moves, which is opposite the measurement range. However, as this rotation is relative, there is no problem having the target fixed and varying the incident angles, provided those angles are chosen correctly. One common target alignment used for this purpose is the $\hat{x}$ axis alignment of Fig. 12.11-b, which is an alignment commonly used for predicting the RCS of ground targets. As ground targets are typically seen by aerial platforms looking down, it is convenient to work with the local azimuth and elevation angles defined by the RLOS $\hat{R}$. Azimuth and elevation are related to the spherical angles θ and ϕ by the relationships

$$elevation = 90 - \theta \qquad \text{Eq. (12.82)}$$

$$azimuth = -\phi. \qquad \text{Eq. (12.83)}$$

To now reproduce the roll cuts generated in the range in the solver, we fix the elevation angle at zero degrees, and vary azimuth from *0* to *180* degrees. Most codes have an option for working directly with elevation and azimuth, though they are still converted to theta and phi internally. To obtain additional roll cuts, there are two possible options:

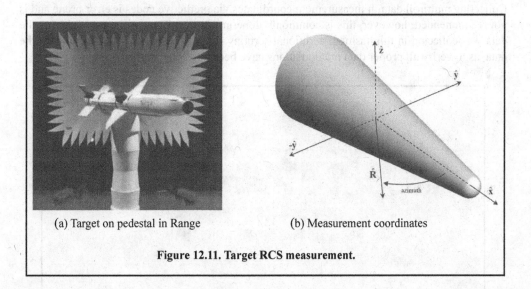

(a) Target on pedestal in Range   (b) Measurement coordinates

Figure 12.11. Target RCS measurement.

---

1. It can also be rotated *360* degrees, yielding two roll cuts offset by *180* degrees.

1. The user rotates the target CAD file about the $\hat{x}$ axis manually.

2. The signature code implements a mechanism for rotating the CAD file about the $\hat{x}$ axis between roll cuts automatically.

The resulting distribution of samples on the unit sphere relative to an $\hat{x}$ axis aligned target is illustrated in Fig. 12.12 for several roll cuts. This process is relatively straightforward as little to no manipulation of the angles or polarizations in the signature code output files is needed to compare the synthetic data against measurements.

However, this process is not ideal for generating scattered field over many roll cuts, as additional steps are needed to re-format and re-label the angles and polarizations to be consistent with the coordinate convention described earlier. If a single output file is generated for each roll cut, these files must be re-combined and re-ordered, and azimuth angle mapped to aspect angle. Additionally, the polarization vectors must be translated carefully during this conversion. To do so, we note that signature codes still operate in spherical coordinates when using the $\hat{x}$ axis based alignment, and the vertical and horizontal scattering vectors θ and ϕ remain unchanged. Therefore, these vectors must be rotated to yield their orientation relative to the target's roll axis as they would exist in a $\hat{x}$ axis configuration. This relationship is

$$\hat{\phi}_x = -\hat{\theta}_z \qquad\qquad \text{Eq. (12.84)}$$

$$\hat{\theta}_x = \hat{\phi}_z . \qquad\qquad \text{Eq. (12.85)}$$

The scattering matrix elements are then converted as

$$S_{vv,x} = S_{hh,z} \qquad\qquad \text{Eq. (12.86)}$$

$$S_{hv,x} = -S_{hv,z} \qquad\qquad \text{Eq. (12.87)}$$

$$S_{vh,x} = -S_{vh,z} \qquad\qquad \text{Eq. (12.88)}$$

$$S_{hh,x} = S_{hh,z} . \qquad\qquad \text{Eq. (12.89)}$$

Collecting multiroll data in measurement coordinates via predictive codes is error prone and is not recommended; however, this is commonly done in practice. Thus, if the user suspects the data was collected in this fashion, additional scrutiny should be applied when examining the data, as to verify all proper data manipulations have been correctly applied.

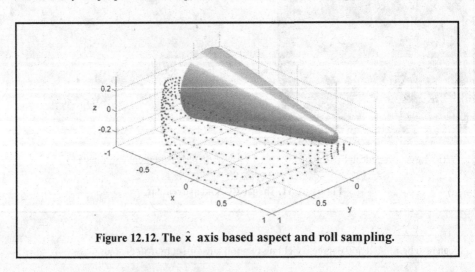

Figure 12.12. The $\hat{x}$ axis based aspect and roll sampling.

12.6. Examples

In this section, we will consider the monostatic RCS of several conducting, unclassified test articles of increasing complexity. In doing so, we will compare the accuracy of the method of moments (MoM) solution to the solution obtained via physical optics (PO) alone, as well as PO supplemented by edge diffracted fields via physical theory of diffraction and multibounce fields via shooting and bouncing rays. For our calculations, we use the industry-standard software code suite known as *lucernhammer*[1], which contains *Serenity*, a low-frequency MoM-based solver implementing an ACA-based direct solver and MLFMA-based iterative solver, as well as *lucernhammer MT*, a high-frequency tool that implements the PO, PTD and SBR methods. Both solver codes use facet-based target models and are highly optimized for parallel, multi-CPU shared memory systems, as well as distributed memory clusters.

12.6.1. Bodies of Revolution

First, we will consider the frustum and cone-sphere illustrated in Figs. 12.13-a and 12.13-b, respectively, where dimensions are in meters. These are bodies of revolution (BoRs) which are excellent test articles for computational codes. The RCS of the frustum should comprise primarily PO-type specular scattering, as well as single diffrations from the front and rear edges. The cone-sphere is a somewhat more challenging object, as the tip gives rise to tip diffractions, and the half-hemisphere in the rear supports creeping waves, neither of which are modeled by the high-frequency code. For both cases, zero incident angle is from the left side of the figure. For the MoM, we use the ACA-compressed matrix direct solver in *Serenity*.

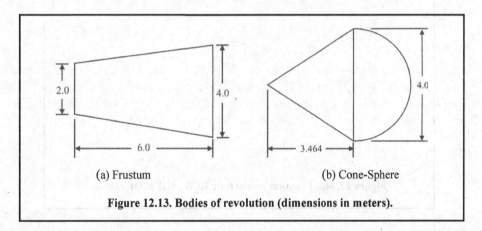

(a) Frustum   (b) Cone-Sphere

Figure 12.13. Bodies of revolution (dimensions in meters).

Frustum

The frustum is shown in Fig. 12.13-a, and the facet model constructed for this object comprises 28114 facets and 42171 edges. In Figs. 12.14-a and 12.14-b the RCS in vertical (VV) and horizontal (HH) polarizations, respectively, are compared and obtained from PO alone, PO+PTD, and the MoM. PO by itself does fairly well near specular angles, as expected, but is not as good at other angles, particular in horizontal polarization. Addition of the PTD corrections to the PO greatly improves the accuracy of the high-frequency solution in both polarizations, compared to the MoM, and the comparison is much better.

---

1. http://radarsoftware.com

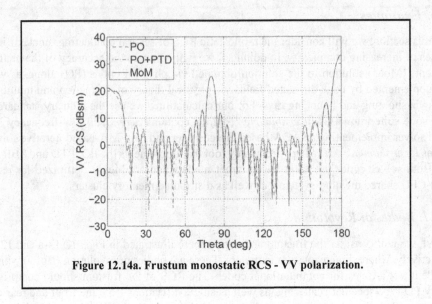

Figure 12.14a. Frustum monostatic RCS - VV polarization.

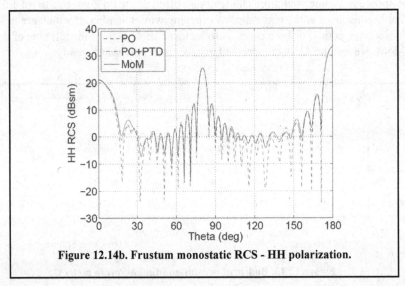

Figure 12.14b. Frustum monostatic RCS - HH polarization.

Cone-Sphere

The cone-sphere is shown in Fig. 12.13-b, and the facet model constructed for this object comprises *19176* facets and *28764* edges. In Figs. 12.15-a and 12.15-b are compared the RCS in vertical (VV) and horizontal (HH) polarizations, respectively, obtained from PO alone, PO+PTD, and the MoM. As with the frustum, PO alone compares fairly well to the MoM near specular angles, as expected, and fairly well at rear angles where the smooth hemisphere is visible, but poorly in the front where the tip is visible. Of particular note here is that the edge between the cone and sphere results in very little diffracted field, and the PTD corrections add very little to the PO solution. In this case, higher-order mechanisms, such as tip diffraction and creeping waves, are the likely cause of the differences between the PO/PTD and the MoM solutions at off-specular angles.

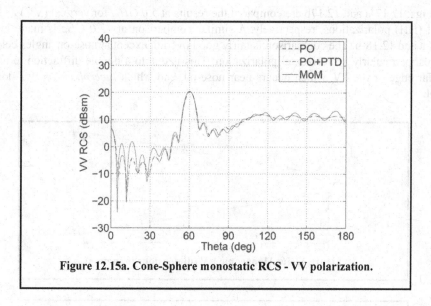

Figure 12.15a. Cone-Sphere monostatic RCS - VV polarization.

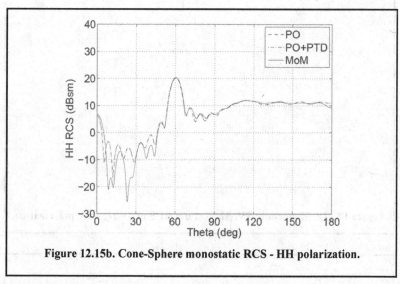

Figure 12.15b. Cone-Sphere monostatic RCS - HH polarization.

Monoconic Reentry Vehicle

Now, we consider the monoconic reentry vehicle (RV), whose dimensions are outlined in Fig. 12.16. This type of target is often encountered in ballistic missile related applications. Zero incident angle comprises nose-on incidence.

We compute the monostatic RCS for incident angles from 0 to 180 degrees, at frequencies of *5.0 GHz* (C-band) and *12.0 GHz* (X-band). At *5.0 GHz*, the RV is 17λ long, and at *12.0 GHz*, it is 40λ in length. Triangular facet models were constructed with *144592* and *781248* triangles, which resulted in *216888* and *1171872* unknowns, respectively, for the MoM solution. We again use the ACA-compressed direct solver in *Serenity*, and in *lucernhammer MT*, we use PO+PTD. As this is a purely convex target, with no protrusions, there are no multibounce fields, so SBR was not used.

In Figs. 12.17-a and 12.17b are compared the results at *5.0 GHz*, for vertical (VV) and horizontal (HH) polarizations, respectively. A similar comparison at *12.0 GHz* is made in Figs. 12.18-a and 12.18-b. The comparison is fairly good overall, except at nose-on angles below *30* degrees, particularly in horizontal polarization. This is due to a double-diffraction term from the rear edge of the RV, which occurs near nose-on, and which *lucernhammer MT* does not model.

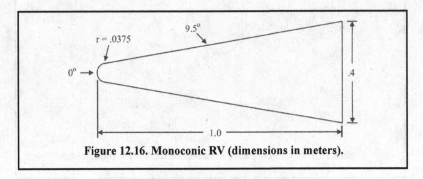

Figure 12.16. Monoconic RV (dimensions in meters).

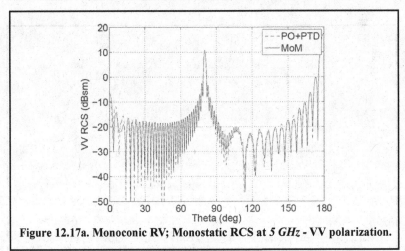

Figure 12.17a. Monoconic RV; Monostatic RCS at *5 GHz* - VV polarization.

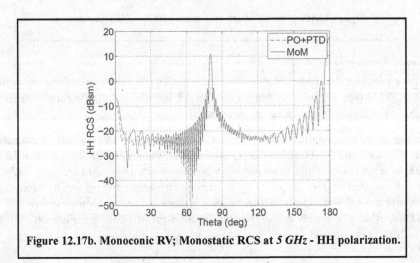

Figure 12.17b. Monoconic RV; Monostatic RCS at *5 GHz* - HH polarization.

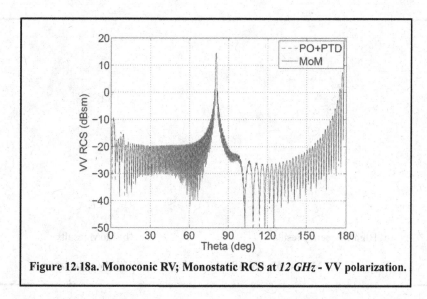

Figure 12.18a. Monoconic RV; Monostatic RCS at *12 GHz* - VV polarization.

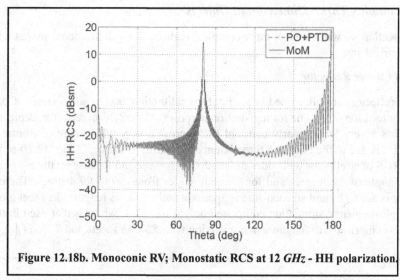

Figure 12.18b. Monoconic RV; Monostatic RCS at 12 *GHz* - HH polarization.

This double diffraction effect can be further visualized via a two-dimensional ISAR imaging of the RV. Using both signature codes, we generate scattered field data over a bandwidth of *1 GHz* centered at *12.0 GHz*, and over *6* degrees incident angle centered around nose-on. This will yield a down-range resolution of *~15 centimeters*, and a cross-range resolution of *~12 centimeters*.

The images generated from data generated by *lucernhammer MT* and *Serenity* are depicted in Figs. 12.19-a and 12.19-b, respectively, for vertical (VV) polarization. The scattering centers comprising the nose and base edge are almost identical between the two results. The additional scattering center visible in the MoM results, just behind the base edge, comprises the double diffraction.

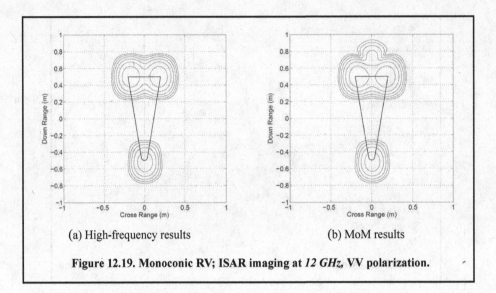

(a) High-frequency results   (b) MoM results

Figure 12.19. Monoconic RV; ISAR imaging at *12 GHz*, VV polarization.

12.6.2. Complex Three-Dimensional Objects

In this section we will consider more complex, realistic three-dimensional shapes with much larger electrical size.

Trihedral Corner Reflector

Corner reflectors are often used in the field for calibration, and to add a target of large RCS at a known location in a scene for registration purposes. The trihedral reflector, depicted in Fig. 12.20-a, has a very large, nearly constant RCS across a very wide range of frontal viewing angles. This is due to the two- and three-bounce ray paths, as shown in Fig. 12.20-b. We compute the RCS of a reflector with sides of length $a = 1$ *meter* and its base on the *x-y* plane, at an elevation angle of *45* degrees and for azimuth angles from *-90* to *90* degrees. The operating frequency is *5.0 GHz*, and so each side is approximately 17λ in length. The facet model used for the high-frequency simulation comprised only *6* triangles, whereas that used in the MoM simulation comprised a much more dense version with *524288* facets and *785664* edges.

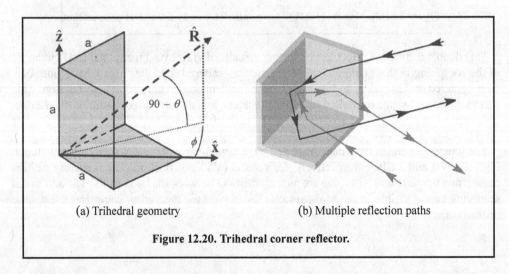

(a) Trihedral geometry   (b) Multiple reflection paths

Figure 12.20. Trihedral corner reflector.

In Figs. 12.21-a and 12.21-b the RCS in vertical (VV) and horizontal (HH) polarizations, respectively, are compared and obtained from the PO+PTD, PO+PTD+SBR, and the MoM. Multibounce effects clearly dominate the scattered field, as PO+PTD alone greatly under-predicts the RCS at all angles. The addition of multibounce fields via SBR greatly improves the high-frequency results at forward viewing angles. Compared to the MoM, however, SBR is observed to under-predict the RCS at these angles in both polarizations. This behavior of SBR is a deficiency that is frequently observed when compared to measurements or more accurate solver codes, particularly when the object has multibounce rich geometry such at jet inlets, or other types of cavities. We will observe this behavior again in the next section.

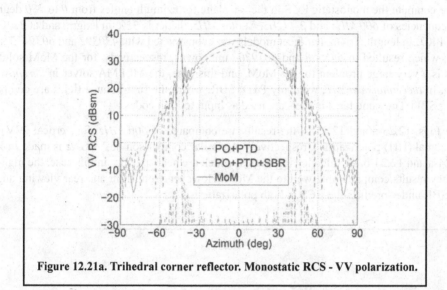

Figure 12.21a. Trihedral corner reflector. Monostatic RCS - VV polarization.

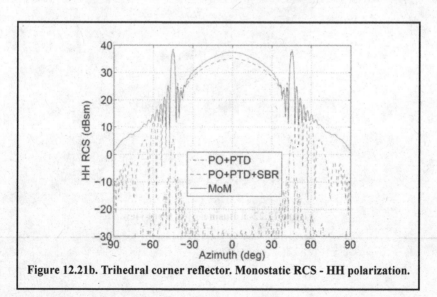

Figure 12.21b. Trihedral corner reflector. Monostatic RCS - HH polarization.

Business Jet

Finally, we will consider the business jet, illustrated previously in Fig. 12.3-c. This is a multibounce-rich target with very complex backscattering behavior, and comprises an excellent test for the methods outlined in this chapter. Renderings of the jet are shown in Figs. 12.22-a and 12.22-b from front and rear viewing angles, respectively. The jet has a length of *17.6 meters*, a wingspan of *16.2 meters*, and a height of *3.8 meters*. The original model was obtained from an Internet database of freely available 3-D models. To simplify the meshing process, the model was converted to a closed, conducting surface by removing features such as the windows and landing gear, and by closing off the engine nacelles. The model was then oriented in the *x-y* plane, with the nose aligned along the *+x* axis.

We compute the monostatic RCS in the *x-y* plane for azimuth angles from *0* to *180* degrees, at frequencies of *600 MHz* and *2.4 GHz*. At *600 MHz*, the jet is 35λ in length, and at 2.4 GHz, it is 140λ in length. Triangular facet models were constructed with *430392* and *6039472* triangles, which resulted in *645588* and *9059208* unknowns, respectively, for the MoM solution. This is a very large problem for the MoM, and this case, the MLFMA solver in *Serenity* was used. In *lucernhammer MT*, we apply PTD+SBR, where the first-bounce fields are computed using SBR. The same facet models are used as input to both codes.

In Figs. 12.23-a and 12.23-b the results are compared at *600 MHz*, for vertical (VV) and horizontal (HH) polarizations, respectively. A similar comparison at *2.4 GHz* is made in Figs. 12.24-a and 12.24-b. At side viewing angles, which are near specular in this case, the high-frequency results compare quite well to the MoM. However, from front and rear viewing angles, the SBR under-predicts the RCS in both polarizations.

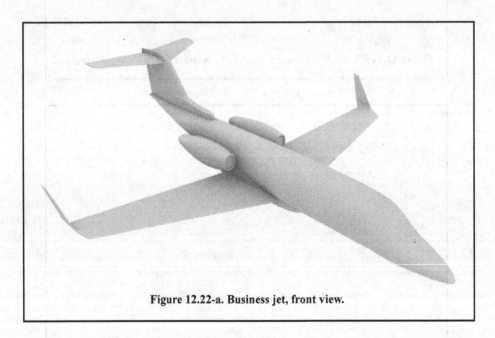

Figure 12.22-a. Business jet, front view.

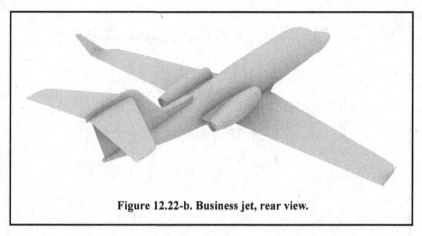

Figure 12.22-b. Business jet, rear view.

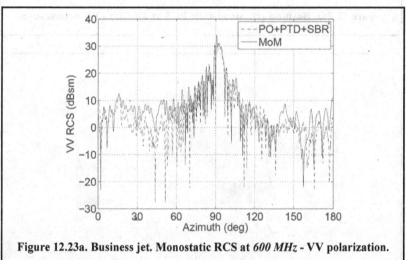

Figure 12.23a. Business jet. Monostatic RCS at *600 MHz* - VV polarization.

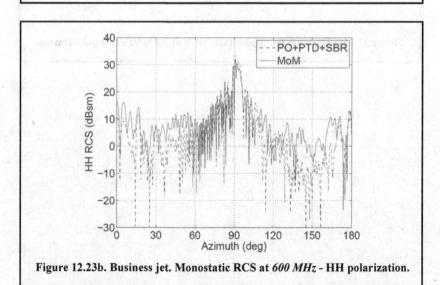

Figure 12.23b. Business jet. Monostatic RCS at *600 MHz* - HH polarization.

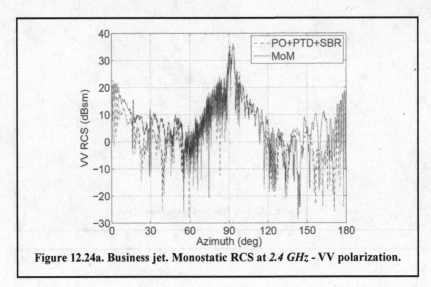

Figure 12.24a. Business jet. Monostatic RCS at *2.4 GHz* - VV polarization.

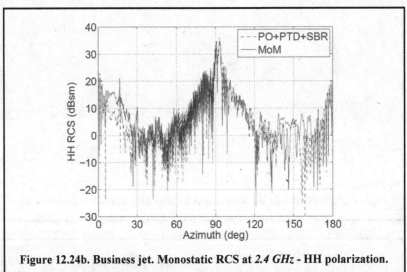

Figure 12.24b. Business jet. Monostatic RCS at *2.4 GHz* - HH polarization.

Chapter 13

Antennas for Radar Applications

Atef Z. Elsherbeni

An antenna is a structure that serves as an interface between any transmission line and free space whose purpose is to radiate or receive electromagnetic waves. The transmission line can be anything such as a simple wire, coaxial cable, or waveguide. As long as the transmission line can efficiently transfer electromagnetic energy to and from the antenna, the antenna can operate as the transitional device. Thus an antenna can act as a receiver for incoming energy from an electromagnetic field or as a radiator of electromagnetic waves. This chapter presents different types of antennas commonly used in radar systems.

13.1. Antenna Types

There are many types of antennas and their classifications can be related to their physical layout and construction or radiation characteristics. Based on the physical layout of antennas, the most common types of antennas are wire, aperture and slot-type, microstrip, helical, horn, lens, and reflector. When antennas are designed to achieve certain characteristics, they are labeled or assigned names related to these characteristics. Examples of such characterizations are low frequency antennas, high frequency antennas, radar antennas, tracking antennas, satellite antennas, earth station antennas, frequency-independent antennas, traveling wave antennas, etc. Antenna arrays are a group of individual elements of antennas arranged in pre-defined spatial positions where each element is fed according to a feeding topology to achieve certain radiation characteristics. This chapter will deal with different types of wire, aperture, helical and bi-conical antennas. Arrays of antenna elements arranged in one-dimensional (1-D), two-dimensional (2-D), and three-dimensional (3-D) space are also presented along with different types of feeding arrangements such as uniform, binomial, Dolph-Tschebyscheff, etc. Additionally, windowing techniques are available to further enhance the excitation amplitudes. Among these techniques are the Hamming window, Blackman window, and Kaiser window.

13.2. Antenna Basic Parameters

Antennas are usually designed to meet pre-specified radiation characteristics. These characteristics are defined in terms of parameters that in most cases are related to the radiated fields from the antenna itself. This section briefly lists the most common parameters such as radiation pattern lobes, radiation regions, directivity, radiation resistance, and gain. To easily define these parameters, let us assume that we have an antenna element located at the origin of a spherical coordinate system and that the radiation is to be measured at a spherical shell far

from the origin. The transmitted waves from the antenna are described by patterns and classified into three regions. The first being the reactive near-field region where no radiation is
detected. The second is the radiating near-field (Fresnel) region where the angular pattern
depends on the distance from the antenna. The third is the radiating far field (Fraunhofer)
region where the angular pattern does not depend on the distance from the antenna. These three
regions are described for a simple dipole antenna in Fig. 13.1. In the far field region, the radiation pattern takes one of three shapes based on the type of antenna. These three shapes can be
generated from antennas classified as: isotropic antenna, where the radiation is everywhere
with equal amplitudes; omni-directional antenna, where the antenna has a nondirectional pattern in one plane and a directional pattern in a perpendicular plane; and directional antenna
where the radiation is in specified directions more effectively than the others. These three types
of antenna radiation patterns are shown in Fig. 13.2.

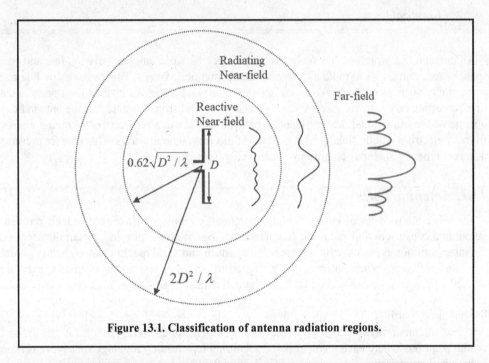

Figure 13.1. Classification of antenna radiation regions.

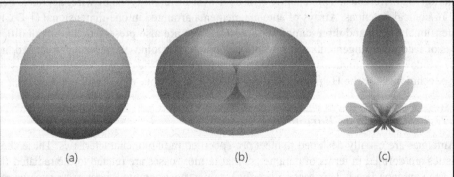

**Figure. 13.2. Common radiation pattern types: (a) isotropic, (b) omni-directional, and
(c) directional.**

Antennas can also be classified as broadside antennas when the main beam maximum is in a plane normal to the plane containing the antenna, or as endfire antenna when the main beam maximum is in the plane containing the antenna. Figure 13.3 shows examples of these antenna patterns. The principal planes of radiation for any antenna are defined as the E and H planes, where the E plane contains the electric field vector E and the direction of maximum radiation, and the H plane contains the magnetic field vector H and the direction of maximum radiation.

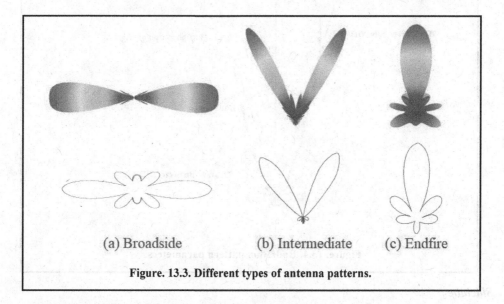

(a) Broadside   (b) Intermediate   (c) Endfire

Figure. 13.3. Different types of antenna patterns.

13.2.1. Radiation Pattern

The antenna pattern is a graphical representation of the spatial distribution of the radiated energy of an antenna in the far field. An antenna should only receive/transmit from/to a certain direction or from all possible directions depending on the type of the antenna and its intended application. The radiation pattern can be represented graphically in three dimension forms or in separate plane cuts using polar or rectangular 2-D graphs. Figure 13.2 represents the three main types of antenna's radiation patterns: isotropic when the radiated energy is distributed equally in all spherical directions, omni-directional where the radiated energy in one plane is invariant and have a directional patterns in a perpendicular plane, and directional where the radiated energy in a specific direction is more effective than in all other directions. The radiation patterns presented in graphical form are usually based on linear or logarithmic (dB) values. There are many parameters that describe the common beam radiation pattern. Among these are the main beam lobe (major lobe), sidelobes, half-power beamwidth, sidelobe levels, and backlobe level. These parameters are shown in Fig. 13.4.

Half-Power Beamwidth

The half-power beamwidth is the angular range of the antenna pattern main beam within which the radiated power level is higher or equal to half of its maximum.

Beam Solid Angle

A solid angle (Ω) is a two-dimensional angle defined as the solid angle through which all the power of the antenna would flow if its radiation intensity is constant. The solid angle unit of measurement is Steradian (*Sr*).

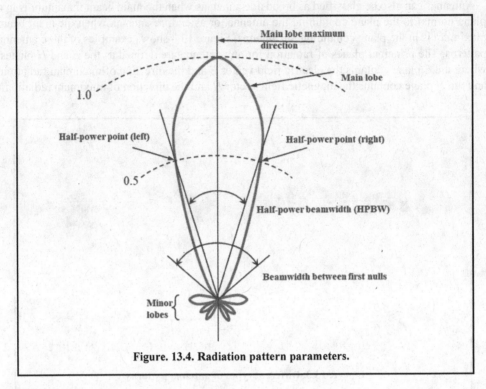

Figure. 13.4. Radiation pattern parameters.

Sidelobe

In addition to the main lobe, the radiation pattern of an antenna contains several sidelobes and a back lobe. These are undesirable lobes because they draw energy that could have been better supplied to the main lobe. The ratio between the largest sidelobe level to that of the main lobe is called "sidelobe level" which should be as low as possible for good antenna designs.

Forward / Backward Ratio

The forward/backward ratio represents the ratio of the magnitude of the main lobe at the maximum radiation direction to the magnitude of the back lobe at *180°* of the maximum radiation direction. It is desirable to have this ratio as large as possible.

Voltage Standing Wave Ratio

The voltage standing wave ratio (VSWR) value represents the transmission efficiency of the antenna in terms of the ratio of the transmitted power to the reflected power at the antenna input terminals with respect to a *50* Ohm impedance. A VSWR of *1.0*, *1.5*, and *2.0* represent *100*, *97*, and *89%* efficient antenna, respectively.

Antenna Bandwidth

Bandwidth of an antenna is the range of frequencies within which the antenna impedance, polarization, and radiation pattern are within an acceptable value of those at the antenna operating frequency (center frequency). For broadband antennas, the bandwidth is expressed as the ratio of the upper to lower frequency of acceptable operation. For narrowband antennas, the bandwidth is expressed as a percentage of the frequency difference (upper-lower) over the center frequency of the bandwidth.

13.2.2. Antenna Radiated Power

For time harmonic variations with the $e^{j\omega t}$ time dependence, the phasor or complex electric and magnetic fields are represented in terms of their instantaneous counterparts by

$$\tilde{E}(x, y, z;t) = Re\{E(x, y, z;t)e^{j\omega t}\}$$
$$\tilde{H}(x, y, z;t) = Re\{H(x, y, z;t)e^{j\omega t}\}$$

Eq. (13.1)

The instantaneous Poynting vector or power density can then be written as,

$$\tilde{W}(x, y, z;t) = \tilde{E} \times \tilde{H}$$

Eq. (13.2)

$$= [Re\{E(x, y, z;t)e^{j\omega t}\}] \times \left[\frac{1}{2}\{H(x, y, z;t)e^{j\omega t}\} + \frac{1}{2}\{H^*(x, y, z;t)e^{j\omega t}\}\right]$$

$$= \frac{1}{2}Re\{E \times H^*\} + \frac{1}{2}Re\{E \times He^{j2\omega t}\}$$

where after integrating over one period and dividing by the period, we obtain the average power density (W_{av}) or radiation density in the following form,

$$W_{av}(x, y, z) = W_{rad}(x, y, z) = \frac{1}{2}Re\{E \times H^*\} \qquad \left(\frac{Watts}{m^2}\right).$$

Eq. (13.3)

The expression in Eq. (13.3) leads to the average power radiated by the antenna or simply called the "antenna radiated power",

$$P_{rad} = P_{av} = \iint_S W_{rad} \bullet \ ds = \frac{1}{2}\iint_S \frac{1}{2}Re\{E \times H^*\} \bullet \ ds$$

Eq. (13.4)

where the operator $\bullet$ signifies the dot product.

13.2.3. Radiation Intensity

The radiation intensity, U, is a far field parameter and it is defined in a given direction as the power radiated by the antenna per solid angle and can be obtained by multiplying the radiation density by the square of the distance r^2. More precisely,

$$U = r^2 W_{rad}(x, y, z) = r^2 W_{av}(x, y, z) = \frac{r^2}{2}Re\{E \times H^*\} \qquad \left(\frac{Watts}{m^2}\right).$$

Eq. (13.5)

$$U(\theta, \phi) = \frac{r^2}{2\eta}|E(r, \theta, \phi)|^2 \cong \frac{r^2}{2\eta}[|E_\theta(r, \theta, \phi)|^2 + |E_\phi(r, \theta, \phi)|^2]$$

Eq. (13.6)

$$\cong \frac{1}{2\eta}[|E_\theta^o(\theta, \phi)|^2 + |E_\phi^o(\theta, \phi)|^2] = B_0 F(\theta, \phi)$$

where η is the intrinsic impedance of the medium, $E_{\theta, \phi}^o(\theta, \phi)(e^{-j\mathbf{k} \bullet \mathbf{r}}/r)$ is the far field intensity components corresponding to $E_{\theta, \phi}(r, \theta, \phi)$, the vectors E_θ, E_ϕ are the far field electric field components of the antenna, and $F(\theta, \phi)$ is the far field radiation intensity normalized to the constant B_0. Thus the average power radiated by the antenna or the antenna radiated power can now be written as,

$$P_{rad} = \iint_\Omega U(\theta, \phi) \ d\Omega = B_0 \int_0^{2\pi} \int_0^\pi F(\theta, \phi) \sin\theta \, d\theta \, d\phi.$$

Eq. (13.7)

13.2.4. Directivity

The Institute of Electrical and Electronics Engineers (IEEE) defines antenna directivity as: "the ratio of the radiation intensity in a given direction from the antenna to the radiation intensity averaged over all directions." This directivity definition translates, for non-isotropic antennas, as the ratio of the antenna radiation intensity in a given direction over that of an isotropic antenna. This leads to the following mathematical definition of the directivity,

$$D(\theta, \phi) = \frac{4\pi U(\theta, \phi)}{P_{rad}} = 4\pi \frac{F(\theta, \phi)}{\int_0^{2\pi} \int_0^{\pi} F(\theta, \phi) \sin\theta \, d\theta \, d\phi}. \qquad \text{Eq. (13.8)}$$

The directivity is a dimensionless function in terms of the far field angles and is usually represented in logarithmic scale.

13.2.5. Antenna Gain

Gain of an antenna is 4π times the radiation intensity in a given direction divided by the net power accepted by (or delivered to) the antenna from the connected transmitter. Considering that the total radiated power from an antenna is related to the total input power by the antenna radiation efficiency ε_{cd}, we then get the relationship between the gain and directivity as

$$P_{rad} = \varepsilon_{cd} P_{in} \qquad \text{Eq. (13.9)}$$

$$G(\theta, \phi) = \frac{4\pi U(\theta, \phi)}{P_{in}} = \varepsilon_{cd} \left[4\pi \frac{U(\theta, \phi)}{P_{rad}} \right] = \varepsilon_{cd} D(\theta, \phi). \qquad \text{Eq. (13.10)}$$

Therefore, the gain indicates the actual radiated power. This is usually smaller than the power provided by (or delivered to) the transmitter. However, since this power is easier to measure than the directivity, the antenna gain is used more often than the directivity. The gain is a dimensionless function in terms of the far field angles and is usually represented in logarithmic scale. The maximum gain is the gain in the direction of maximum radiation. When the gain is given by a single value, it is usually referring to the maximum gain.

13.2.6. Antenna Effective Aperture

An important parameter of antennas is the effective antenna area called A_e or "antenna aperture." Under the condition of optimal orientation and polarization, the maximum power that can be obtained from a receiving antenna is proportional to the power density of the plane wave incident at the receiving location. The radiation density of the wavefront is a power per unit area. The proportionality factor, therefore, has the dimension of an area represented by an antenna in an electromagnetic field. This area is called the effective antenna area A_e and is closely related to the directivity D of the antenna, which is also equal to the gain G for a lossless antenna. More specifically,

$$G = \frac{4\pi A_e}{\lambda^2} \qquad \text{Eq. (13.11)}$$

where λ is the wavelength. For nonlossless antennas, the gain G is equal to ρD, where the constant ρ is less than unity (i.e., $\rho < 1$). An effective antenna area can also be specified for linear antennas. It does not necessarily have to agree with the geometric extension of the antenna, which is particularly apparent with wire antennas. The ratio between the two quantities is called the "aperture efficiency of the antenna".

The effective antenna area depends on the radiation distribution over the geometric antenna area. If this radiation distribution is linear, then aperture efficiency is equal to one. However, this high aperture efficiency with a linear radiation distribution leads to large undesirable sidelobes. If the sidelobes are to be held below a specific small level, then the radiation distribution must be nonlinear, basically tapered towards the edges of the physical aperture. This distribution results in effective antenna area smaller than the actual geometric area of the antenna.

13.3. General Antenna Arrays

An array is a composite antenna formed from two or more basic radiators. Each radiator is denoted as an element. The elements forming an array could be dipoles, dish reflectors, slots in a wave guide, or any other type of radiator. Array antennas synthesize narrow directive beams that may be steered, mechanically or electronically, in many directions. Electronic steering can be achieved by controlling the amplitude and phase of the current feeding the array elements. However, for practical implementations, only the phase variations are commonly used. Arrays with electronic beam steering capability are called "phased arrays". Phased array antennas, when compared to other simple antennas, such as dish reflectors, are costly and complicated to design. However, the inherent flexibility of phased array antennas to steer the beam electronically and also the need for specialized multifunction radar systems have made phased array antennas attractive for radar applications.

In order to understand and develop the theory of radiation from antenna array, we should first define the basic parameters that characterize the radiation from a single element antenna located in an arbitrary position relative to the global coordinates. Figure 13.5 shows the geometrical fundamentals associated with a single radiating element.

Consider the radiation located at (x_1, y_1, z_1) with respect to a phase reference at $(0, 0, 0)$. The electric field measured at a far field point P is

$$E(\theta, \phi) = I_0 \frac{e^{-jkR_1}}{R_1} F(\theta, \phi) \qquad \text{Eq. (13.12)}$$

where I_0 is the complex amplitude, the wave number $k = 2\pi/\lambda$, and $F(\theta, \phi)$ is the element radiation pattern. Now, consider the case where the radiation source is an array made of many antenna elements, as shown in Fig. 13.6. The coordinates of each radiator with respect to the phase reference is (x_i, y_i, z_i), and the vector from the origin to the ith element is given by

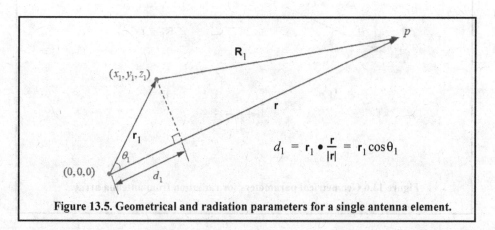

Figure 13.5. Geometrical and radiation parameters for a single antenna element.

$$\mathbf{r}_i = \hat{a}_x x_i + \hat{a}_y y_i + \hat{a}_z z_i \qquad \text{Eq. (13.13)}$$

where $(\hat{a}_x, \hat{a}_y, \hat{a}_z)$ are the unit vector components along the x-, y-, and z-axes. The expression of the far field component from an element i that adds to the total electric field is

$$\mathbf{E}_i = I_i \frac{e^{-j\mathbf{k} \cdot \mathbf{R}_i}}{|\mathbf{R}_i|} F(\theta_i, \phi_i) \qquad \text{Eq. (13.14)}$$

where

$$R_i = |\mathbf{R}_i| = |\mathbf{r} - \mathbf{r}_i| = \sqrt{(x-x_i)^2 + (y-y_i)^2 + (z-z_i)^2} \qquad \text{Eq. (13.15)}$$

$$= r\sqrt{1 + \frac{(x_i^2 + y_i^2 + z_i^2)}{r^2} - 2\frac{(xx_i + yy_i + zz_i)}{r^2}}$$

Using the spherical coordinates where $x = r\sin\theta\cos\phi$, $y = r\sin\theta\sin\phi$, and $z = r\cos\theta$, we get

$$\frac{(x_i^2 + y_i^2 + z_i^2)}{r^2} = \frac{|\mathbf{r}_i|}{r^2} \approx 1. \qquad \text{Eq. (13.16)}$$

Thus, a good approximation (using binomial expansion) for Eq. (13.15) is

$$R_i = r - (x_i\sin\theta\cos\phi + y_i\sin\theta\sin\phi + z_i\cos\theta). \qquad \text{Eq. (13.17)}$$

It follows that the phase contribution at the far field point from the *ith* radiator with respect to the phase reference $(0,0,0)$ is

$$e^{-j\mathbf{k} \cdot \mathbf{R}_i} = e^{-jkr} e^{jk(x_i\sin\theta\cos\phi + y_i\sin\theta\sin\phi + z_i\cos\theta)}. \qquad \text{Eq. (13.18)}$$

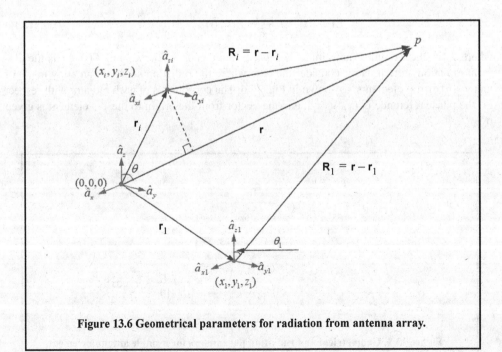

Figure 13.6 Geometrical parameters for radiation from antenna array.

Remember, however, that the unit vector $\mathbf{r}_0$ along the vector $\mathbf{r}$ is

$$\mathbf{r}_0 = \frac{\mathbf{r}}{|\mathbf{r}|} = \hat{a}_x \sin\theta\cos\phi + \hat{a}_y \sin\theta\sin\phi + \hat{a}_z \cos\theta.$$ **Eq. (13.19)**

Hence, we can rewrite Eq. (13.18) as

$$e^{-j\mathbf{k}\bullet\mathbf{R}_i} = e^{-jkr}e^{jk(\mathbf{r}_i\bullet\mathbf{r}_0)} = e^{-jkr}e^{j\psi_i(\theta,\phi)},$$ **Eq. (13.20)**

with

$$\psi_i(\theta,\phi) = k(x_i\sin\theta\cos\phi + y_i\sin\theta\sin\phi + z_i\cos\theta).$$ **Eq. (13.21)**

Finally, by virtue of superposition, the angular part of the total electric far field is given by

$$E(\theta,\phi) = \sum_{i=1}^{N} I_i e^{j\psi_i(\theta,\phi)}$$ **Eq. (13.22)**

which is widely known as the array factor (AF) for an array antenna where the complex current for the ith element is I_i.

In general, an array can be initially characterized by its array factor. This is true, since knowing the array factor provides the designer with knowledge of the array's (1) *3-dB* beamwidth; (2) null-to-null beamwidth; (3) distance from the main peak to the first sidelobe; (4) height of the first sidelobe as compared to the main beam; (5) location of the nulls; (6) rate of decrease of the sidelobes; and (7) location of grating lobes.

13.4. Linear Arrays

Consider a linear antenna array consisting of N identical elements with equal spacing as shown in Fig. 13.7. The element spacing is d (normally measured in wavelength units) and element #*1* is serving as a phase reference for the array. It is obvious that for this array configuration, the combined outgoing wave from all elements does not depend on the far observation angle ϕ. It is also clear that an outgoing wave from the ith element is leading the wave from the first element at the phase reference by $(i-1)kd\cos\theta$. This phase difference can be represented for the *ith* element as

$$\psi_i(\theta,\phi) = k(\mathbf{r}_i\bullet\mathbf{r}_0) = (i-1)kd\cos\theta.$$ **Eq. (13.23)**

Thus, from Eqs. (13.22) and (13.23), the electric field or the array factor at a far field observation point P with the assumption of isotropic elements is

$$E(\theta,\phi) = \sum_{i=1}^{N} e^{j(i-1)kd\cos\theta}.$$ **Eq. (13.24)**

Expanding the summation in Eq. (13.24) yields

$$E(\theta,\phi) = 1 + e^{jkd\cos\theta} + \dots + e^{j(N-1)kd\cos\theta}.$$ **Eq. (13.25)**

The right-hand side of Eq. (13.25) is a geometric series, which can be expressed in the form

$$1 + a + a^2 + \dots + a^{(N-1)} = \frac{1-a^N}{1-a}.$$ **Eq. (13.26)**

Replacing a by $e^{jkd\sin\psi}$ yields,

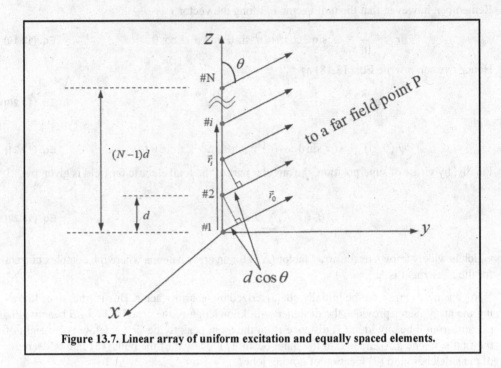

Figure 13.7. Linear array of uniform excitation and equally spaced elements.

$$E(\theta, \phi) = \frac{1 - e^{jNkd\cos\theta}}{1 - e^{jkd\cos\theta}} = \frac{1 - (\cos Nkd\cos\theta) - j(\sin Nkd\cos\theta)}{1 - (\cos kd\cos\theta) - j(\sin kd\cos\theta)}$$ Eq. (13.27)

The far field array intensity pattern is then given by

$$|E(\theta, \phi)| = \sqrt{E(\theta, \phi)E^*(\theta, \phi)}$$ Eq. (13.28)

Substituting Eq. (13.27) into Eq. (13.28) and collecting terms yield

$$|E(\theta, \phi)| = \sqrt{\frac{(1 - \cos Nkd\cos\theta)^2 + (\sin Nkd\cos\theta)^2}{(1 - \cos kd\cos\theta)^2 + (\sin kd\cos\theta)^2}}$$ Eq. (13.29)

$$= \sqrt{\frac{1 - \cos Nkd\cos\theta}{1 - \cos kd\cos\theta}}$$

and using the trigonometric identity $1 - \cos\theta = 2(\sin\theta/2)^2$ yields

$$|E(\theta, \phi)| = \left| \frac{\sin(Nkd\cos\theta/2)}{\sin(kd\cos\theta/2)} \right|$$ Eq. (13.30)

which is a periodic function of $kd\cos\theta$, with a period equal to 2π. The maximum value of $|E(\theta, \phi)|$, which occurs at $\theta = 0$, is equal to N. It follows that the normalized intensity pattern is equal to

$$|E_n(\theta, \phi)| = \frac{1}{N} \left| \frac{\sin((Nkd\cos\theta)/2)}{\sin((kd\cos\theta)/2)} \right|$$ Eq. (13.31)

The normalized two-way array pattern (radiation pattern) is given by

$$G(\theta, \phi) = \left|E_n(\theta, \phi)\right|^2 = \frac{1}{N^2} \left(\frac{\sin((Nkd\cos\theta)/2)}{\sin((kd\cos\theta)/2)}\right)^2 \qquad \text{Eq. (13.32)}$$

Figure 13.8-a shows the normalized gain pattern $G(\theta, \phi)$ versus θ for an *8* equally spaced with $d = \lambda$ and uniformly excited elements in linear array configuration along the *z*-axis. The radiation pattern has cylindrical symmetry about its *z*-axis and is independent of the azimuth angle ϕ. Thus, it is completely determined by its values within the interval ($0 < \theta < \pi$). In Fig. 13.8-b, the same pattern is shown in a polar format with relative and *dB* scales, while in Fig. 13.8-c the full 3-D pattern is shown.

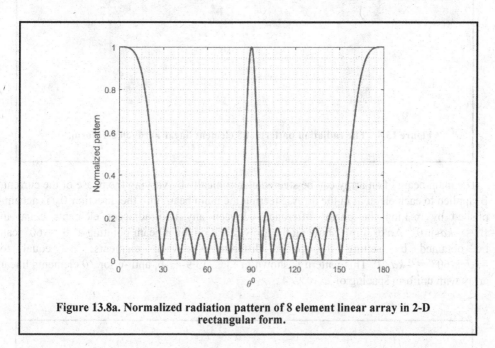

Figure 13.8a. Normalized radiation pattern of 8 element linear array in 2-D rectangular form.

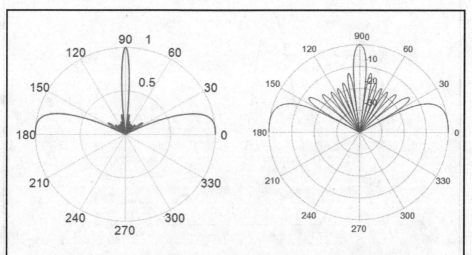

Figure 13.8b. Normalized radiation pattern of 8 element linear array in 2-D polar form, relative and dB amplitude.

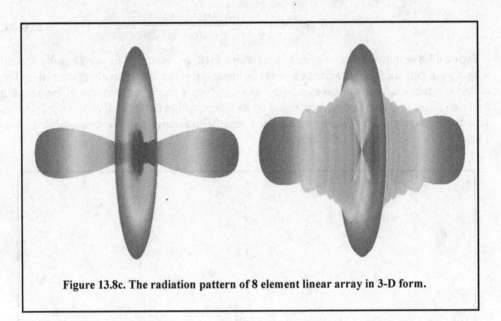

Figure 13.8c. The radiation pattern of 8 element linear array in 3-D form.

The main beam of an array can be steered electronically by varying the phase of the current, β applied to each element in the array. Steering the main beam into the direction θ_0 is accomplished by making the phase difference between any two adjacent elements equal to $\beta = -kd\sin\theta_0$. An example showing the array radiation main beam pointing at $\theta = 60°$ can be obtained by setting the phase difference between elements, β, equal to $-kd\sin 60° = -kd/2$. This pattern is shown in Figs. 13.9-a, -b, and -c for *10* elements linear array with uniform spacing of $d = \lambda/4$.

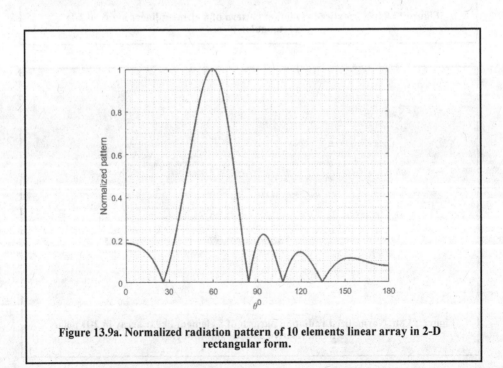

Figure 13.9a. Normalized radiation pattern of 10 elements linear array in 2-D rectangular form.

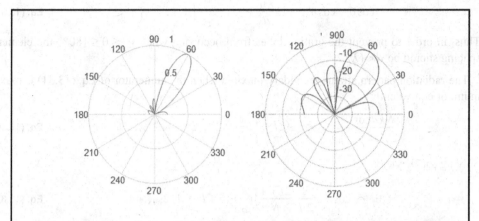

Figure 13.9b. Normalized radiation pattern of 10 elements linear array in 2-D polar form, relative and dB scales.

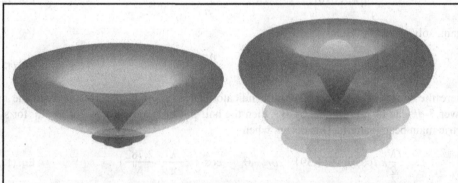

Figure 13.9c. The radiation pattern of 10 elements linear array in 3-D form with relative and dB scales.

When the main beam is perpendicular to the array axis, and the array is said to be a broadside array. Alternatively, the array is called an endfire array when the main beam points along the array axis. The radiation pattern maxima are computed using L'Hopital's rule when both the denominator and numerator of Eq. (13.31) are zeros. More precisely,

$$\frac{kd\cos\theta}{2}\bigg|_{\theta=\theta_m} = \pm m\pi \quad ; \quad m = 0, 1, 2, \dots . \qquad \text{Eq. (13.33)}$$

Solving for the maximum directions, θ_m, yields

$$\theta_m = \cos^{-1}\left(\pm\frac{\lambda m}{d}\right) \quad ; \quad m = 0, 1, 2, \dots \qquad \text{Eq. (13.34)}$$

where the subscript m is used as a maxima indicator. The first maximum occurs at $\theta = 90°$, and is denoted as the main beam (lobe). Other maxima occurring at $|m| \geq 1$ are called grating lobes. Grating lobes are undesirable and must be suppressed. The grating lobes occur at non-real angles when the absolute value of the arc-cos argument in Eq. (13.34) is greater than unity; it follows that $d < \lambda$. Under this condition, the main lobe is assumed to be at (broadside array). Alternatively, when electronic beam steering is considered, the grating lobes occur at

$$\left| \cos\theta - \cos\theta_0 \right| = \pm\frac{\lambda n}{d} \qquad ; \; n = 1, 2, \dots . \qquad \text{Eq. (13.35)}$$

Thus, in order to prevent the grating lobes from occurring when $0° \leq \theta \leq 180°$, the element spacing should be $d < (\lambda/2)$.

The radiation pattern attains secondary maxima when the numerator of Eq. (13.31) is maximum, or equivalently

$$\left. \frac{Nkd\cos\theta}{2} \right|_{\theta = \theta_l} = \pm(2l+1)\frac{\pi}{2} \qquad ; \; l = 1, 2, \dots . \qquad \text{Eq. (13.36)}$$

Solving for θ_l yields

$$\theta_l = \cos^{-1}\!\left(\pm\frac{\lambda}{2d} \frac{2l+1}{N} \right) \qquad ; \; l = 1, 2, \dots \qquad \text{Eq. (13.37)}$$

where the subscript l is used as an indication of sidelobe maxima. The nulls of the radiation pattern occur when only the numerator of Eq. (13.31) is zero. More precisely,

$$\left. \frac{N}{2}kd\cos\theta \right|_{\theta = \theta_n} = \pm n\pi \qquad ; \begin{array}{l} n = 1, 2, \dots \\ n \neq N, 2N, \dots \end{array} \qquad \text{Eq. (13.38)}$$

Again, solving for θ_n yields

$$\theta_n = \cos^{-1}\!\left(\pm\frac{\lambda}{d} \frac{n}{N} \right) \qquad ; \begin{array}{l} n = 1, 2, \dots \\ n \neq N, 2N, \dots \end{array} \qquad \text{Eq. (13.39)}$$

where the subscript n is used as a null indicator. The angle which corresponds to the half-power *3-dB* can be represented by θ_h, then the half-power beamwidth is $2\left| \theta_m - \theta_h \right|$ for symmetric main beam pattern. This occurs when

$$\frac{N}{2}kd\cos\theta_n = 1.391 \quad or \quad \theta_n = \cos^{-1}\!\left(\pm\frac{\lambda}{2\pi d} \frac{2.782}{N} \right) . \qquad \text{Eq. (13.40)}$$

13.5. Array Tapering

In the previous section, the 1-D array was considered for the simplest configuration of uniform spacing and equal amplitude excitation or amplitude excitation with the added phase shift β. This uniform configuration, however, is not suitable for most radar applications because the first sidelobe is always equal to *13.46dB* below the main lobe, as clearly shown in Figs. 13.8-a and 13.9-b. In order to reduce the sidelobe levels, the array must be designed to radiate more power towards the center, and much less at the edges. This can be achieved through tapering (windowing) the current distribution for the array elements. There are many possible tapering procedures that can be used for this purpose. In this section we will present sample results based on these windowing techniques and other based on binomial and Dolph-Tschebyscheff excitations. Furthermore, to provide a general linear array formulation, let us also consider arbitrarily positioned elements along the axis of the array.

The array factor or array pattern for any given linear array can be calculated by simply summing the phasor representation of the elements together. This requires the phases and amplitudes to be normalized with reference to the first element. In the case of nonuniform spacing and amplitudes, array factor pattern can be computed directly from Eqs. (13.22) and (13.23) while the excitation current amplitude and phase are determined according to the tapering or windowing procedures listed above. Windowing works by modifying the amplitudes of the elements from the center of the array to the elements at the edges of the array. For the case of no windowing (also referred to as a rectangular window) all elements are equal in amplitude. This configuration yields the reference beamwidth for the main lobe and the first sidelobe level at *13.46 dB* down as can be seen in Fig. 13.10 for a linear array. In this example, $N = 8$, $d = 0.5\lambda$ and the main lobe is scanned to $\theta_0 = 90°$.

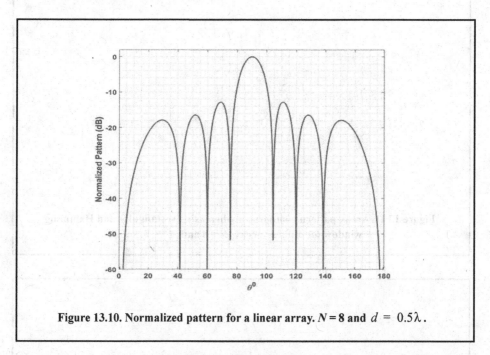

Figure 13.10. Normalized pattern for a linear array. $N = 8$ and $d = 0.5\lambda$.

The first windowing technique is known as the Hamming or raised cosine window. The amplitude of element n in the array is weighted by the following formula

$$I_n = 0.54 - 0.46\cos\left(\frac{2\pi n}{N-1}\right).$$

Eq. (13.41)

The Hamming window allows for the suppression of the first sidelobes down to near *-40dB* but doubles the beam width of the main lobe as can be seen in Fig. 13.11.

The Hanning window which is also a variant of the raised cosine window. Individual element amplitudes are weighted by the following formula

$$I_n = 0.5 - 0.5\cos\left(\frac{2\pi n}{N-1}\right).$$

Eq. (13.42)

The Hanning window allows for the suppression of the first sidelobes down to near *-32dB* but doubles the beam width of the main lobe as can be seen in Fig. 13.12. Another windowing technique available is the Blackman window. It is quite similar to the Hanning and Hamming windows but adds another cosine term to further reduce the sidelobes. Individual element amplitudes are weighted by the following formula

$$I_n = 0.42 - 0.5\cos\left(\frac{2\pi n}{N-1}\right) + 0.08\cos\left(\frac{2\pi n}{N-1}\right).$$

Eq. (13.43)

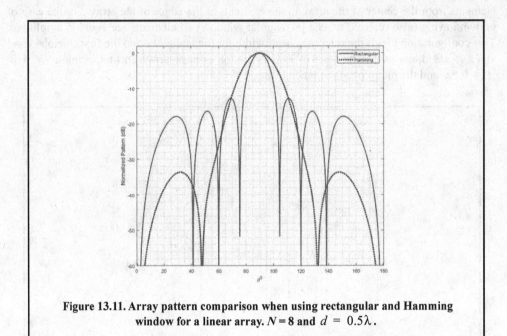

Figure 13.11. Array pattern comparison when using rectangular and Hamming window for a linear array. $N = 8$ and $d = 0.5\lambda$.

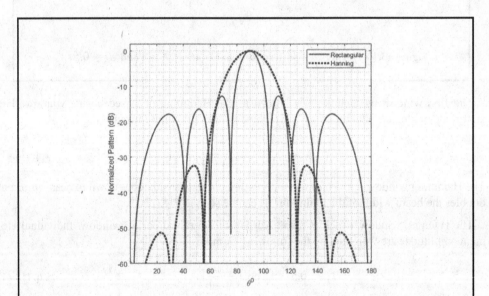

Figure 13.12. Array pattern comparison when using rectangular and Hanning window for a linear array. $N = 8$ and $d = 0.5\lambda$.

The Blackman window allows for the suppression of the first sidelobes down to near *-65 dB* but increases the beam width of the main lobe almost six times the size of the nonwindow case as can be seen in Fig. 13.13. The Kaiser window technique is quite different from the other windows listed above and is given by

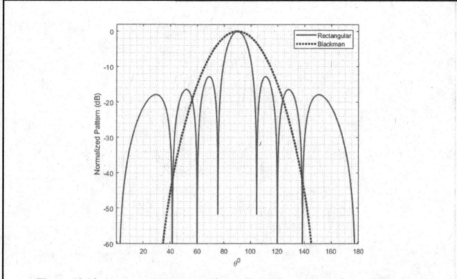

Figure 13.13. Array pattern comparison when using rectangular and Blackman window for a linear array. $N = 8$ and $d = 0.5\lambda$.

$$I_n = \frac{I_0\left(\beta\sqrt{1 - \left(\frac{2n}{N} - 1\right)^2}\right)}{I_0(\beta)}, \qquad \text{Eq. (13.44)}$$

where I_0 is the zero-order modified Bessel function of the first kind. This Kaiser window allows for the suppression of the first sidelobes down to near *-46 dB* but increases the beam width of the main lobe almost *2.3* times the size of the non-window (rectangular) case as can be seen in Fig. 13.14.

The binomial linear array, the amplitude coefficients for the antenna elements in the array are calculated using the binomial expansion of the function $(1 + x)^{m-1}$. This expansion is given for *m* elements by

$$(1 + x)^{m-1} = 1 + (m-1)x + \frac{(m-1)(m-2)}{2!}x^2 + \frac{(m-1)(m-2)(m-3)}{3!}x^3 + \dots . \quad \text{Eq. (13.45)}$$

The coefficients for the terms in the expansion are used as the amplitudes for the elements. When the element spacing is $d = 0.5\lambda$, the binomial array does not produce any sidelobes, but the main lobe beamwidth will be much larger compared to the uniform array as shown in Fig. 13.15 below for *N=8* and $\theta_0 = 90°$.

For the Dolph-Tschebyscheff linear array, the amplitude coefficients are calculated by determining the Tschebyscheff polynomial for the appropriate number of terms and using the coefficients terms as the amplitudes. The coefficients for the Tschebyscheff polynomial are calculated using an iterative procedure that first translates the target sidelobe levels, R_{dB}, into a voltage ratio, R_V by

$$R_V = 10^{(R_{dB}/20)}. \qquad \text{Eq. (13.46)}$$

Then an auxiliary variable z is determined from

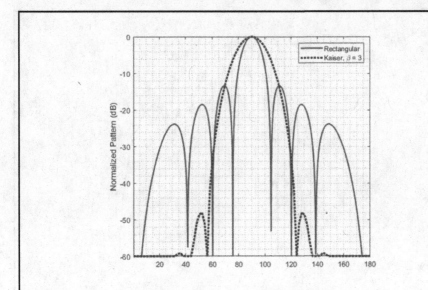

Figure 13.14. Array pattern comparison when using rectangular and Kaiser window for a linear array. $N = 8$ and $d = 0.5\lambda$.

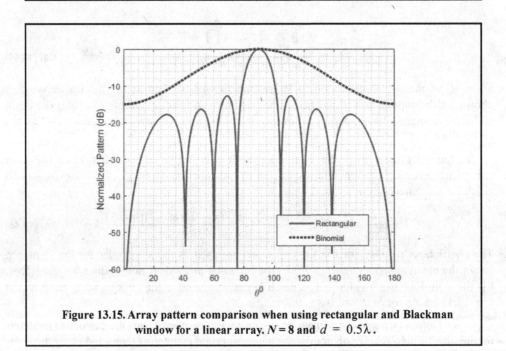

Figure 13.15. Array pattern comparison when using rectangular and Blackman window for a linear array. $N = 8$ and $d = 0.5\lambda$.

$$z = \cosh\left(\frac{1}{p}\cosh^{-1}(R_V)\right), \qquad\qquad \textbf{Eq. (13.47)}$$

where p is the order of the Tschebyscheff polynomial (one less than the number of elements in the array). Then the coefficients are determined by

$$a_n = \sum_{q=n}^{m} (-1)^{(m-q)} \; z^{(2q-1)} \; \frac{(q+m-2)!(2m-1)}{(q-n)!(q+n-1)!(m-q)!},$$ **Eq. (13.48)**

for an array of even number elements where $N=2m$. Whereas for an odd number of elements, $N=2m+1$, the coefficients are given by

$$a_n = \sum_{q=n}^{m} (-1)^{(m-q+1)} \; z^{2(q-1)} \; \frac{(q+m-2)!(2m)}{(q-n)!(q+n-2)!(m-q+1)!}.$$ **Eq. (13.49)**

In general, windowing reduces sidelobe levels at the expense of widening the main beam. Thus, for a given radar application, the choice of the tapering sequence must be based on the trade-off between sidelobe reduction and main beam widening.

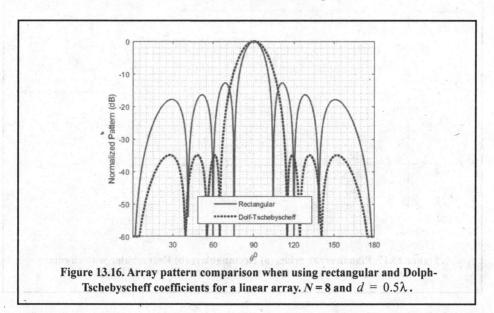

Figure 13.16. Array pattern comparison when using rectangular and Dolph-Tschebyscheff coefficients for a linear array. $N = 8$ and $d = 0.5\lambda$.

13.6. Planar Arrays

Planar arrays are some of the most commonly used arrays in real-world applications. They are a natural extension of linear arrays, and they allow for beam steering along both axes (elevation and azimuth when the array is located in the x-y plane) which gives these arrays a wide area to scan. Planar arrays can take on many configurations, depending on the element spacing and distribution defined by a "grid." Examples include rectangular, rectangular with circular boundary, hexagonal with circular boundary, circular, and concentric circular grids, as illustrated in Fig. 13.17. Planar arrays can be found in many applications from stationary radar systems to new adaptive cell phone towers.

13.6.1. Rectangular Grid Arrays

The planar rectangular 2-D arrays are usually composed by placing a number of elements in the x-y plane in a rectangular grid fashion similar to the geometry given in Fig. 13.18. The number of elements and spacing between adjacent elements can be defined in both the x and y directions independently. The progressive phase shift in each direction can be defined as well.

The array factor for a planar rectangular array with M elements in the x direction and N elements in the y direction can be found from an extension of the 1-D linear array formula. Uniform spacing and amplitudes are defined along both the x and y directions separately. This is because when the spacing is uniform in both directions, each row may be considered as a single element that is repeated along the other direction thus forming an array composed of elements that themselves are a linear array. Based on the arrangement in Fig. 13.18, it follows that the electric field component due to the elements distributed along the x-direction is given by,

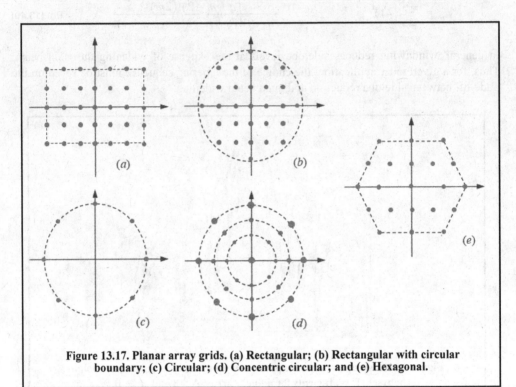

Figure 13.17. Planar array grids. (a) Rectangular; (b) Rectangular with circular boundary; (c) Circular; (d) Concentric circular; and (e) Hexagonal.

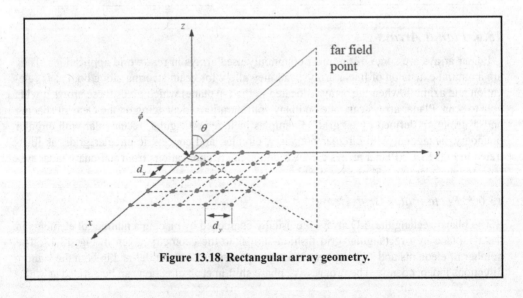

Figure 13.18. Rectangular array geometry.

$$E_x(\theta, \phi) = \sum_{m=1}^{M} I_{xm} e^{j(m-1)(kd_x \sin\theta\cos\phi + \beta_x)}$$

Eq. (13.50)

and the electric field component due to the elements distributed along the *y*- direction is

$$E_y(\theta, \phi) = \sum_{n=1}^{N} I_{yn} e^{j(n-1)(kd_y \sin\theta\sin\phi + \beta_y)} \quad .$$

Eq. (13.51)

The total electric field at the far field observation point is then given by

$$E(\theta, \phi) = \left[\sum_{m=1}^{M} I_{xm} e^{j(m-1)(kd_x \sin\theta\cos\phi + \beta_x)} \right] \left[\sum_{n=1}^{N} I_{yn} e^{j(n-1)(kd_y \sin\theta\sin\phi + \beta_y)} \right] ,$$

Eq. (13.52)

where

$$\beta_x = -kd_x \sin\theta_0 \cos\phi_0$$

Eq. (13.53)

$$\beta_y = -kd_x \sin\theta_0 \sin\phi_0 .$$

Eq. (13.54)

where the angles (θ_0, ϕ_0) point to the direction at which the beam is steered.

When the elements of the planar array are equally spaced and are assigned equal amplitudes $(I_{xm} = I_{yn} = I_t)$, where I_t is a constant, and a constant phase shift between columns and rows, the rectangular array intensity pattern can be reduced to

$$E(\theta, \phi) = \left[\frac{1}{M} \frac{\sin\left(\frac{M}{2}\psi_x\right)}{\sin\left(\frac{\psi_x}{2}\right)} \right] \left[\frac{1}{N} \frac{\sin\left(\frac{N}{2}\psi_y\right)}{\sin\left(\frac{\psi_y}{2}\right)} \right] ,$$

Eq. (13.55)

where $\psi_x = kd_x \sin\theta\cos\phi + \beta_x$ and $\psi_y = kd_y \sin\theta\sin\phi + \beta_y$. The radiation pattern maxima, nulls, sidelobes, and grating lobes in both the *x*- and *y*-axes are computed in a similar fashion to the linear array case. Additionally, the same conditions for grating lobe control are applicable.

Examples of field pattern for a planar rectangular arrays are presented in Fig. 13.19 and 13.20. In both figures the spacing between the elements in the *x* and *y* directions is $\lambda/4$ and the *M=N=20*. In Fig. 13.19, the progressive phase shifts in *x* and *y* directions are set to *0*, while in Fig. 13.20, the main beam is steered in the $\theta_0 = 30°$, $\phi_0 = 60°$.

13.6.2. Circular Grid Arrays

The circular 2-D array is formed by placing a number of elements spaced equally apart in the *x-y* plane along an imaginary circle as shown in Fig. 13.21. The uniform spacing between adjacent elements is controlled by both the radius of the circle and the number of elements in the array. In this case, *N* elements are distributed equally on the outer circle whose radius is *a*. For this geometry the *nth* element will be located at ϕ_n defined by

$$\phi_n = \frac{2\pi}{N}n \qquad ; \; n = 1, 2, ..., N.$$

Eq. (13.56)

The coordinates of the *nth* element in Cartesian coordinates are

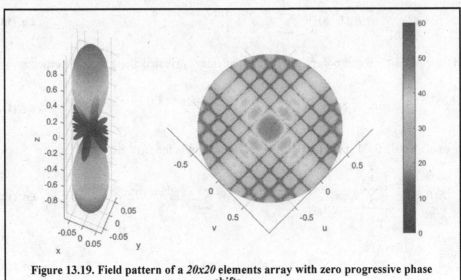

Figure 13.19. Field pattern of a *20x20* elements array with zero progressive phase shifts.

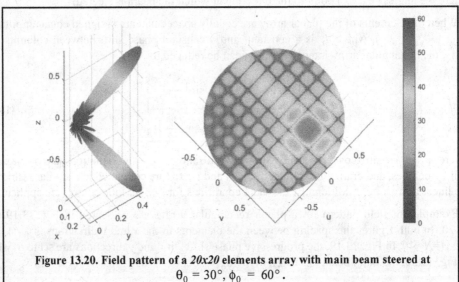

Figure 13.20. Field pattern of a *20x20* elements array with main beam steered at $\theta_0 = 30°$, $\phi_0 = 60°$.

$$x_n = a \cdot \cos\phi_n$$
$$y_n = a \cdot \sin\phi_n \, .$$
$$z_n = 0$$

Eq. (13.57)

The amplitude for each element can also be defined for each element. The array factor or field intensity for the circular array can be calculated using

$$E(r, \theta, \phi) = \sum_{n=1}^{N} a_n \frac{e^{-jkR_n}}{R_n},$$

Eq. (13.58)

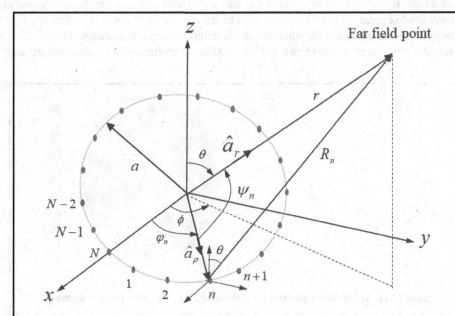

Figure 13.21. Configuration of a circular array centered around the origin in the *x-y* plane.

where

$$a_n = I_n e^{j\beta_n}$$

I_n is the amplitude excitation of element n

β_n is the phase excitation of element n relevant to the array center

$$R_n = \sqrt{r^2 + a^2 - 2ar\cos\psi_n} .$$

It follows that Eq. (13.58) can now be written as

$$E(r, \theta, \phi) = \frac{e^{-jkr}}{r} \sum_{n=1}^{N} a_n e^{jka \cdot \sin\theta\cos(\phi - \phi_n)} = \frac{e^{-jkr}}{r} E(\theta, \phi) , \qquad \textbf{Eq. (13.59)}$$

where

$$E(\theta, \phi) = \sum_{n=1}^{N} I_n e^{j[ka \cdot \sin\theta\cos(\phi - \phi_n) + \beta_n]} , \qquad \textbf{Eq. (13.60)}$$

and for the main beam to be in the direction θ_0, ϕ_0, the phase β_n takes on the form

$$\beta_n = -ka \cdot \sin\theta_0 \cos(\phi_0 - \phi_n) . \qquad \textbf{Eq. (13.61)}$$

Finally,

$$E(\theta, \phi) = \sum_{n=1}^{N} I_n e^{jka[\sin\theta\cos(\phi - \phi_n) - \sin\theta_0\cos(\phi_0 - \phi_n)]} . \qquad \textbf{Eq. (13.62)}$$

As an example, consider a *36* element circular array with uniform spacing and equal elements amplitude excitation but with phase shift to steer the beam towards $\theta_0 = 90°$, $\phi_0 = 0°$. The far field pattern for this array when the circle radius is 0.25λ is shown in Fig. 13.22. The pattern of the same array is also shown in Fig. 13.23 in 3-D format with relative and *dB* scales.

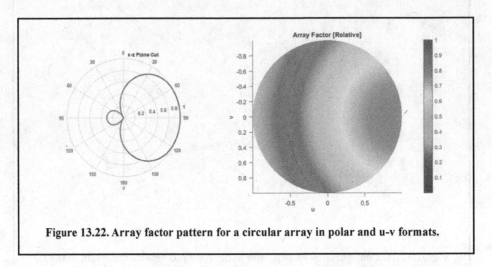

Figure 13.22. Array factor pattern for a circular array in polar and u-v formats.

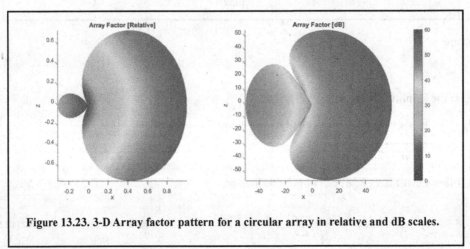

Figure 13.23. 3-D Array factor pattern for a circular array in relative and dB scales.

13.6.3. Concentric Grid Circular Arrays

One extension of the circular array is the concentric circular 2-D array which is composed by placing a number of elements spaced equally apart in the *x-y* plane along multiple concentric imaginary circles as shown in Fig. 13.24. The spacing between adjacent elements is controlled by both the radius of the circle and the number of elements in each circle. In the shown case with two concentric circles, N_2 elements are distributed equally on the outer circle whose radius is a_2, while other N_1 elements are linearly distributed on the inner circle whose radius is a_1. The center of both circles is considered the phase reference for the array. In this array configuration, there are $N_1 + N_2$ elements and the phases for each element are calculated to specify the main lobe direction. The array factor for a concentric circular array can be calculated by adding the array factors for each of the concentric rings as described in Section 13.6.2.

Consider two concentric circular arrays composed of 16 elements where $N_1 = N_2 = 8$, $a_1 = 2a_2 = 2\lambda$. Let the phase shift be set so that the main beam directed at $\theta_0 = 45°$, $\phi_0 = 90°$. Figure 13.25 shows the far field pattern using polar and u-v space, while Fig. 13.26 shows the same pattern in 3-D format in relative and dB scales.

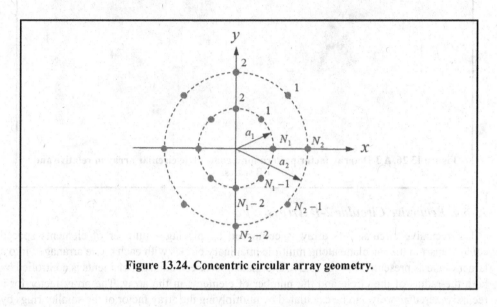

Figure 13.24. Concentric circular array geometry.

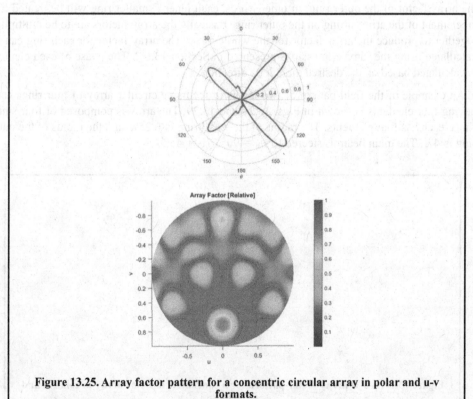

Figure 13.25. Array factor pattern for a concentric circular array in polar and u-v formats.

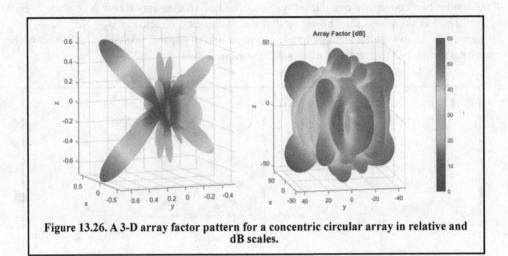

Figure 13.26. A 3-D array factor pattern for a concentric circular array in relative and dB scales.

13.6.4. Recursive Circular 2-D Arrays

The recursive circular 2-D array is composed by placing a number of elements spaced equally apart in the *x-y* plane along multiple imaginary circles with each circle arranaged into a larger circle as presented in Fig. 13.27. The spacing between adjacent elements is controlled by both the radius of the circle and the number of elements in the array. The array factor for a recursive circular array can be calculated by multiplying the array factor of the smaller rings by the array factor of the outer ring. In other words, each inner / smaller ring will be treated like an element of the array sitting on the outer ring. Basically the array factors are to be multiplied together to produce the array factor for the whole array. The array factor for each ring can be calculated using the same expressions presented in Section 13.6.2. The phase of each element is calculated based on the desired main lobe direction.

An example of the field pattern of two levels of recursive circular array of four rings each having four elements is shown in Figs. 13.28 and 13.29. The array is composed of four small rings, each has four elements. The radius of the small ring is 0.25λ and the radius of the outer ring is 4λ. The main beam is steered to $\theta_0 = 90°$, $\phi_0 = 45°$.

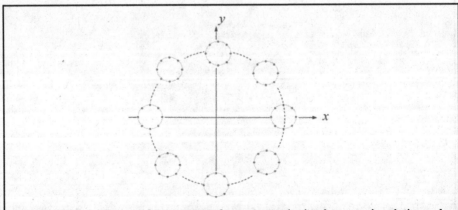

Figure 13.27. A 3-D array factor pattern for a concentric circular array in relative and dB scales.

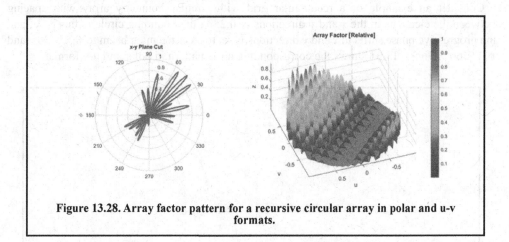

Figure 13.28. Array factor pattern for a recursive circular array in polar and u-v formats.

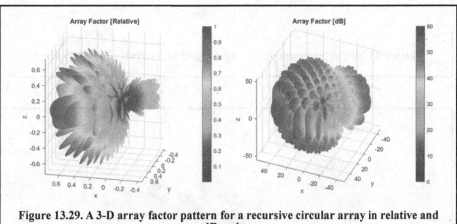

Figure 13.29. A 3-D array factor pattern for a recursive circular array in relative and dB scales.

13.6.5. Rectangular Grid with Circular Boundary Arrays

The circular bounded grid 2-D array is formed by defining a circular boundary along a rectangular grid as seen in Fig. 13.30. Each element lies upon the grid intersection and only elements inside the circular boundary are calculated.

The far field electric field associated with this array configuration can be easily obtained from that corresponding to a rectangular grid. In order to accomplish this task, one should follow these steps: First, select the desired maximum number of elements along the diameter of the circle and denote it by N_d. Also select the associated element spacings d_x and d_y. Define a rectangular array of size $(N_d.N_d)$. Draw a circle centered at $(x, y) = (0, 0)$ with radius r_d

$$r_d = \frac{N_d - 1}{2} + \Delta x,$$ **Eq. (13.63)**

where $\Delta x \le 0.25\lambda$. Finally, modify the weighting function across the rectangular array by multiplying it with the 2-D sequence $a(m, n)$ such that $a(m, n) = 1$ if the distance to the $(m,n)^{th}$ element is $< r_d$ and zero otherwise. The distance is measured from the center of the circle, as illustrated in Fig. 13.31.

Consider an example of a rectangular grid with circular boundary array with spacing between the elements in the x and y directions is 0.25λ, the bounding circle radius is λ, and the progressive phase shifts in x and y directions is set to steer the main beam to $\theta_0 = 30°$ and $\phi_0 = 60°$. Figure 13.31 shows the corresponding array pattern in polar and u-v format.

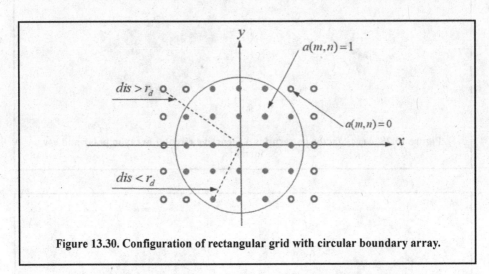

Figure 13.30. Configuration of rectangular grid with circular boundary array.

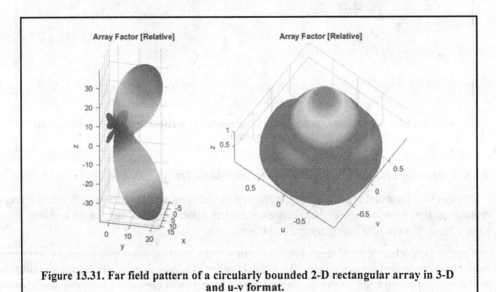

Figure 13.31. Far field pattern of a circularly bounded 2-D rectangular array in 3-D and u-v format.

13.7. Three-Dimensional Arrays

Three-dimensional (3-D) arrays are common in many radar applications. Here we will present basic formulations for two structured array configurations like rectangular parallelepiped and spherical arrays and then a generic formulation for arbitrary configuration of the array antenna elements.

13.7.1. Rectangular Parallelepiped 3-D Array

The rectangular parallelepiped 3-D array as shown in Fig. 13.32 is composed by placing a number of elements in the *x-y-z* space in a rectangular grid fashion. The spacing between adjacent elements in the *x*, *y*, and *z* directions can be arbitrary as well as the number of elements in each direction. The progressive phase shift in each direction can also be specified independently. The amplitudes of the element excitations in the following formulation are considered uniform.

For a 3-D rectangular array with uniformly separated number of elements in the *x*, *y*, and *z* directions and uniform amplitudes, the array factor can be calculated quite simply from an expansion of the 1-D or 2-D array formula. This is because when the spacing is made uniform in all directions, each row may be considered a single element that is repeated along the other direction, even though each direction may have different uniform spacings. Thus, forming an array composed of elements that themselves are an array. This leads to the following expression of the array factor that is composed of *M*, *N*, *P* elements in the *x*, *y*, *z* directions, respectively

$$E(\theta, \phi) = E_x(\theta, \phi)E_y(\theta, \phi)E_z(\theta, \phi) = \left[\sum_{m=1}^{M} I_{xm} e^{j(m-1)(kd_x \sin\theta \cos\phi + \beta_x)} \right]$$

Eq. (13.64)

$$\left[\sum_{n=1}^{N} I_{yn} e^{j(n-1)(kd_y \sin\theta \sin\phi + \beta_y)} \right] \left[\sum_{p=1}^{P} I_{zp} e^{j(p-1)(kd_z \cos\phi + \beta_z)} \right]$$

The above expression assumes that each element in the array has its own amplitude. However, when the planar array is equally spaced with all elements having equal amplitudes and a constant progressive phase shift between columns or rows, the expression for the array factor can be reduced to,

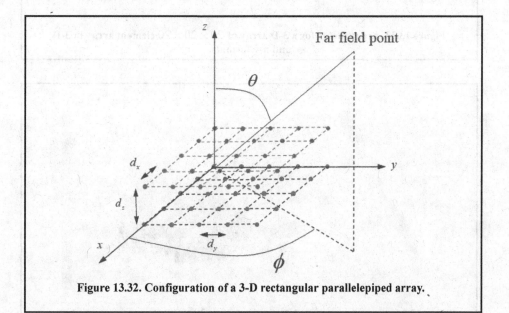

Figure 13.32. Configuration of a 3-D rectangular parallelepiped array.

$$E(\theta, \phi) = \left[\frac{1}{M} \frac{\sin\left(\frac{M}{2}\psi_x\right)}{\sin\left(\frac{\psi_x}{2}\right)} \right] \left[\frac{1}{N} \frac{\sin\left(\frac{N}{2}\psi_y\right)}{\sin\left(\frac{\psi_y}{2}\right)} \right] \left[\frac{1}{P} \frac{\sin\left(\frac{P}{2}\psi_z\right)}{\sin\left(\frac{\psi_z}{2}\right)} \right],$$ **Eq. (13.65)**

where $\psi_x = kd_x\sin\theta\cos\phi + \beta_x$, $\psi_y = kd_y\sin\theta\sin\phi + \beta_y$, $\psi_z = kd_z\cos\theta + \beta_x$, β_x is the element progressive phase shift along the x-axis, β_y is the element progressive phase shift along the y-axis, β_z is the element progressive phase shift along the z-axis, d_x is the element spacing along the x direction, d_y is the element spacing along the y direction, and d_z is the element spacing along the z direction.

Figure 13.33 shows the array factor for a 3-D array configuration of $20x20x20$ elements in x, y, z directions, respectively, and spacing between the elements in every row and between rows, and no progressive phase shift. The element spacing is 0.25λ. Similar array configuration is composed but with $\beta_x = -0.39$, $\beta_y = -0.68$, and $\beta_z = -1.36$ to produce a mainbeam at $\theta_0 = 30°$, $\phi_0 = 60°$. The corresponding array factor is shown in Fig. 13.34.

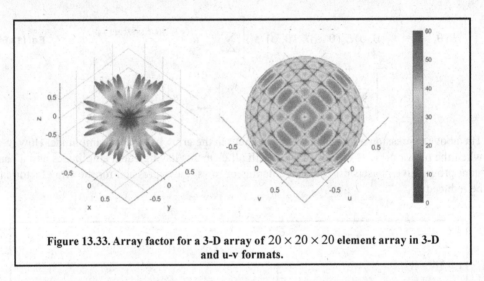

Figure 13.33. Array factor for a 3-D array of $20 \times 20 \times 20$ element array in 3-D and u-v formats.

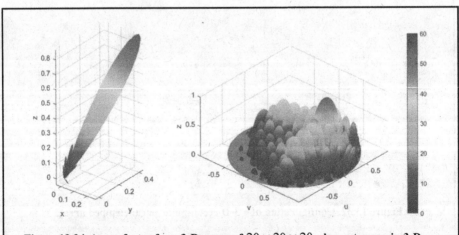

Figure 13.34. Array factor for a 3-D array of $20 \times 20 \times 20$ element array in 3-D and u-v formats.

13.7.2. Spherical 3-D Arrays

The 3-D spherical array is constructed by placing a number of elements in the *x-y-z* space along a series of imaginary circles forming a spherical boundary as shown in Fig. 13.35. The elements are spaced equally apart along each circle with the spacing between adjacent elements controlled by both the radius of the circle and the number of elements in the circular plane. The number of circular planes that create the sphere are to be specified together with the size of the sphere.

The array factor of a spherical array can be calculated from a two-step process. The first step is to calculate the array factor of the antenna elements in each circular plane of the sphere which is based on the formulas for a circular array using the same parameters as described in Section 13.6.2. The second step is to consider the circular planes as individual elements of a 1-D array with a nonuniform amplitude, nonuniformly spaced linear array. The phase of each antenna element is configured based on the specified main lobe direction. The final array factor of the entire spherical array is then represented by

$$E(\theta, \phi) = \sum_{n=1}^{N} I_n e^{jkR(\cos\zeta_n - \cos\zeta_{n0})}$$

Eq. (13.66)

where

$$\cos\zeta_n = \sin\theta\sin\theta_n\cos(\phi - \phi_n) + \cos\theta\cos\theta_n$$

$$\cos\zeta_{n0} = \sin\theta_0\sin\theta_n\cos(\phi_0 - \phi_n) + \cos\theta_0\cos\theta_n$$

R is the radius of the sphere

N is the number of total elements

I_n is the amplitude excitation of the nth element

(θ_n, ϕ_n) is the spherical angular position of the nth element

(θ_0, ϕ_0) is the spherical angular position of the far field mainbeam

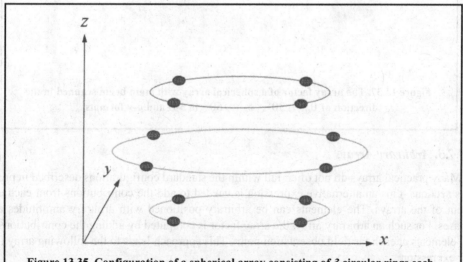

Figure 13.35. Configuration of a spherical array consisting of *3* circular rings each having *4* antenna elements.

An example of the array factor for a 3-D spherical array is shown in Fig. 13.36 for $R = \lambda/2$, and 6 circular rings with 15 elements in each ring. All elements have uniformly excited, and no phase difference is applied. The main beam of the array is then scanned in the direction of $\theta_0 = 30°$, $\phi_0 = 60°$ and the corresponding pattern is shown in Fig. 13.37.

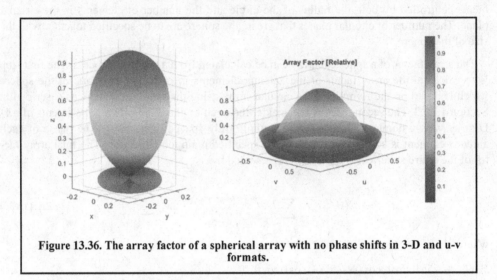

Figure 13.36. The array factor of a spherical array with no phase shifts in 3-D and u-v formats.

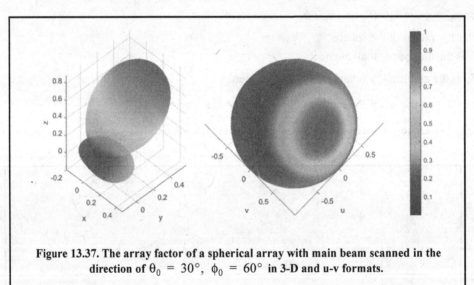

Figure 13.37. The array factor of a spherical array with main beam scanned in the direction of $\theta_0 = 30°$, $\phi_0 = 60°$ in 3-D and u-v formats.

13.7.3. Arbitrary Arrays

Many practical arrays do not often fall within the standard configurations described in previous sections, thus an alternative expression is needed to add the contributions from each element of the arrays. The elements can be arbitrary positioned with arbitrary amplitudes and phases. For such an arbitrary array, the array factor is computed by adding the contributions of all elements at each far field observation point. This approach leads to the following array factor expression

$$E(\theta, \phi) = \sum_{n=1}^{N} I_n e^{j(kd_n + \beta_n)} \qquad \text{Eq. (13.67)}$$

where

I_n is the amplitude excitation of the nth element

β_n is the phase excitation of the nth element

$d_n = x_n \sin\theta\cos\phi + y_n \sin\theta\sin\phi + z_n \cos\theta$

(x_n, y_n, z_n) is the coordinate of the nth element

The computation of the array factor for an arbitrary array configuration at all angles usually takes more time relative to the other structured array as their array factor expressions are mathematically developed in more closed form expressions.

13.8. Array Feeding and Beamforming Networks

Considering Eq. (13.22), it is obvious that the far field pattern of a linear array is a function of the complex current I_i which is applied to each element of the array. When an antenna array is implemented in hardware, the performance of the array is dependent on the ability to control the value of I_i for each antenna element. Transmission lines, phase shifters, time-delay networks, and other devices may be employed to accurately control the complex current at each element. The selection of an array feeding network is influenced by the complex current specified to each element and mechanical specifications of the array.

13.8.1. General Forms of Array Feeding Networks

An array feeding network comprises the transmission lines, phase shifters, couplers, or other RF components which convey an RF signal from a transmitter to the individual elements of an array (or in reverse, from the array elements to a receiver). Such a network is designed to have favorable RF characteristics (low insertion loss and good impedance matching), as well as to accurately control the complex current at each antenna element.

In Fig. 13.38, three array feeding network configurations are represented in schematic form. In the fixed phased array of Fig. 13.38-a, the quantity I_i is controlled by the selection and the design of the transmission lines connecting the array elements, power dividers, and other components can be parts of this type of feeding network. Steering of the fixed phased array is only possible by physically changing the hardware components of the feeding network, or by mechanically rotating the entire phased array. An example of the fixed phased array in a radar application is the slotted waveguide: in this design, the waveguide serves as a transmission line, and waveguide slits function as antenna elements. The slotted waveguide is typically mounted on a turntable, which enables beam steering through mechanical rotation of the entire antenna array. Another form of phased array is shown in Fig. 13.39 where the feeding network is based on microstrip line feeding network connecting all the radiation antenna elements with equal amplitude and phase of I_i.

Where it is not possible or practical to mechanically rotate the antenna array to achieve beam steering, it is possible to steer the array's beam by electronically changing the phase of the complex current at each antenna element. In the dynamic phased array of Fig. 13.38-b, each antenna is provided with an electronically controlled phase shifter. When an RF signal is applied to the network, a control computer individually alters the phase of the current arriving at each antenna. This enables the selection of arbitrary beam-steering angles, without any mechanical changes to the array. In some cases, the phase shifters are replaced by electronically-controlled time-delay networks. Another type of array feeding is an active electronically-scanned array (AESA) as shown in Fig. 13.38-c. In this configuration, each antenna element is provided with a separate transmit / receive (TR) module, and signals are conveyed to and from the individual TR modules in digital form. The AESA is the most flexible of the array feeding network configurations, because the amplitude and phase of the signal at each element may be individually and precisely controlled. In addition to steering the beam, tapering may be applied to an AESA with no changes to the array hardware.

One should point out that the feeding network topologies presented in Fig. 13.38 are not an exhaustive list. Numerous variations exist, including the inclusion of amplifiers within the network, or the division of antennas into sub-arrays. Indeed, an array may employ features derived from several of the network types shown, for example an AESA where each TR module is attached to a fixed-phase sub-array. The selection of an array feeding network is dictated by the design requirements of the array, as well as limitations of size, power consumption, and cost. Fixed arrays are a simple and robust design but are not feasible when electronic steering is desired. Conversely, the AESA topology provides flexibility and reconfigurability, but such designs can come at high cost, and require considerations of electronic, digital, and cooling connections at each TR module.

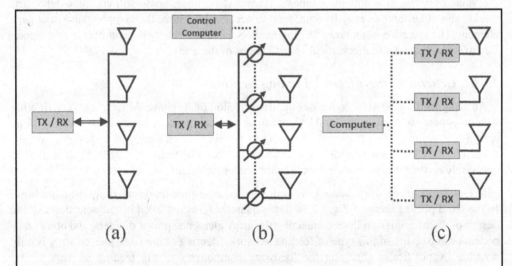

Figure 13.38. Schematic representation of three array feeding network configurations: (a) fixed phased array, (b) dynamic phased array, and (c) active electronically scanned array.

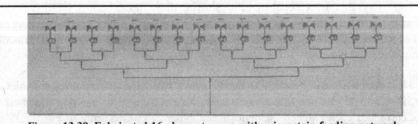

Figure 13.39. Fabricated 16-element array with microstrip feeding network.

13.8.2. Wideband Operation of Feeding Networks

In modern radar systems, to increase the time resolution is common to employ signals of significant bandwidth. The design of a wide band antenna element is not a difficult task, for example the lotus antenna in Fig. 13.40 supports operation for the entire X-band. However, for such wideband applications, the array feeding network should also support the required bandwidth which presents two challenges. First, the feeding network must be capable of consistent operation across a wide bandwidth. Second, the antenna array must be able to reliably form and scan the main beam at all desired operating frequencies. For this configuration, one would desire the array to operate from *8 GHz* to *12 GHz*. Thus if we consider $f = 8$ *GHz*, then *1.25f* and *1.5f* would correspond to *10* and *12 GHz*, respectively.

To demonstrate the operation of a phased array at different operating frequencies, consider the array factor of a linear array as described by Eq. (13.31) when the main beam is steered at specific angle using the pre-determined progressive phase shift at frequency *f*, and then the operating frequency would change within the operational wideband. Figure 13.41 represents the normalized array factor pattern for this linear array of 16 elements with $\lambda/2$ element spacing and excitations of equal amplitude and progressive phase shift computed at frequency *f* to steer the main beam at $\theta = 45°$ at frequency *f*. The effect of changing the operating frequency is demonstrated for a dynamic phased array which uses phase shifters in its feeding network. The figure clearly shows that when the frequency is shifted to *1.25f* and *2f*, the main beam does not stay as desired at $\theta = 45°$ and also the main beam beamwidth gets narrower. This effect is known as "beam squint," (Mailloux, 2005).

It is possible to construct a dynamic phased array which uses time-delay feeding network instead of phase shifters. The use of a time-delay provides a frequency dependent phase-shift, which creates a constant beam-angle over a range of frequencies. This effect is illustrated in Fig. 13.42 where an increase in frequency is accompanied by a decrease in main beam beamwidth, and a corresponding shift in the locations of the sidelobes but not the steered main beam.

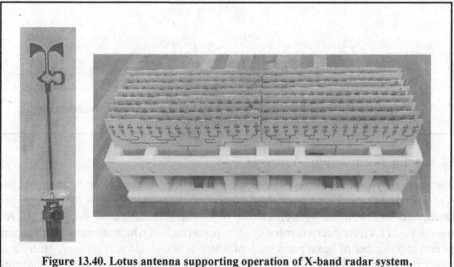

Figure 13.40. Lotus antenna supporting operation of X-band radar system, (left) single element, (right) array of 32x8 elements with fixed.

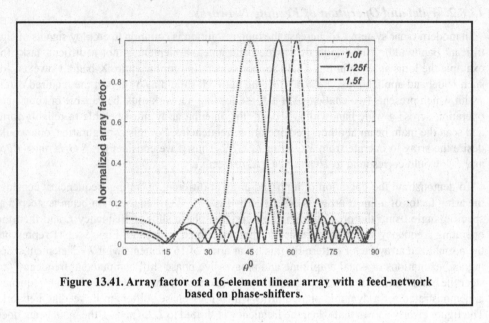

Figure 13.41. Array factor of a 16-element linear array with a feed-network based on phase-shifters.

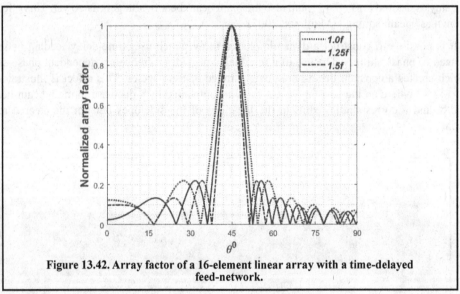

Figure 13.42. Array factor of a 16-element linear array with a time-delayed feed-network.

13.8.3. Array Beamforming Networks

The previously-described array feeding networks affect beam steering by changing properties of the network (for the dynamic phased array), or changing properties of the signal applied at each element (as in the AESA). On the other hand, beamforming networks (BFNs), as shown in Fig. 13.43, connect a number of array ports (each of which is connected to an antenna element) to a number of beam ports, each of which is associated with an array steering angle. To steer the beam of an array fed by a BFN, it is only necessary to connect the transmitter or receiver to a different beam port of the BFN. In this beamforming configuration, it is possible to simultaneously transmit or receive at multiple steering angles by attaching multiple transmitters or receivers to separate beam ports.

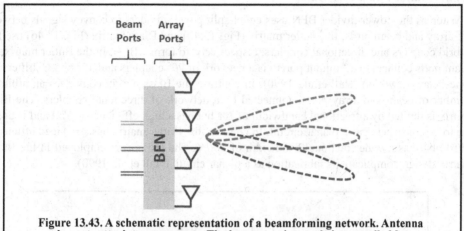

Figure 13.43. A schematic representation of a beamforming network. Antenna elements attach to array ports. The beam steering angle is controlled by connecting a transmitter or receiver to a specific beam port.

13.8.4. Power-Divider Beamforming Networks

A conceptually simple BFN topology is based on power dividers and phase shifters. It is a generalization of the fixed phased array feeding network of Fig. 13.38-a, with multiple beam ports. The power-divider BFN depicted in Fig. 13.44 incorporates equal-split power dividers to connect a beam-port to multiple array ports, and to connect array ports to multiple beam ports. To control beam steering, phase shifters are employed within the network. The values of these phase shifters are not dynamically changeable: they are specified based on the desired beam angles of the design. Beam steering is then controlled through selection of a beam port. While the design is somewhat cumbersome, it is robust, and such a design was employed on the Globalstar telecommunication satellites for *2.5 GHz* signals (Hansen, 2009).

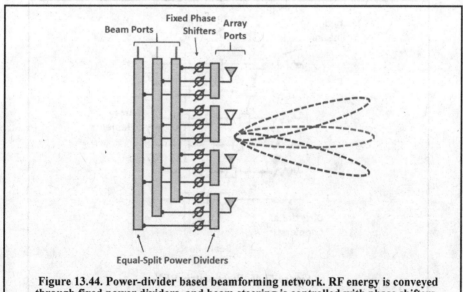

Figure 13.44. Power-divider based beamforming network. RF energy is conveyed through fixed power dividers, and beam steering is controlled with phase shifters.

13.8.5. Butler and Blass Matrix

Whereas the power-divider BFN uses equal-split power dividers to convey signals between the array and beam ports, the Butler matrix (Fig. 13.45) and Blass matrix (Fig. 13.46) use $90°$ hybrid couplers and directional couplers, respectively, to form a BFN. In the Butler matrix, 2^N beam ports connect to 2^N output ports via a network of $90°$ couplers and $45°$ phase shifters (or time-delay networks) (Hall et al., 1990). In contrast, the Blass matrix comprises an arbitrary number of beam and array ports, connected by a network of directional couplers. The Blass matrix is limited by a fractional bandwidth of 1% but has a high efficiency (75%) and is possible to be constructed as a planar circuit. In contrast, the Butler matrix has a reduced efficiency (40%) but has a wide fractional bandwidth of 200%. The crossovers employed in the Butler matrix design complicate its fabrication as a planar circuit (Hall et al., 1990).

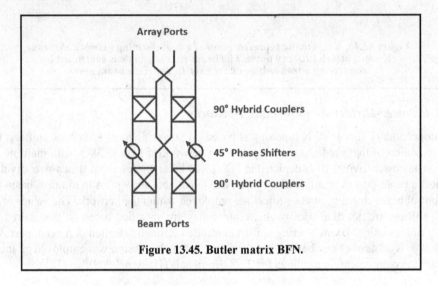

Figure 13.45. Butler matrix BFN.

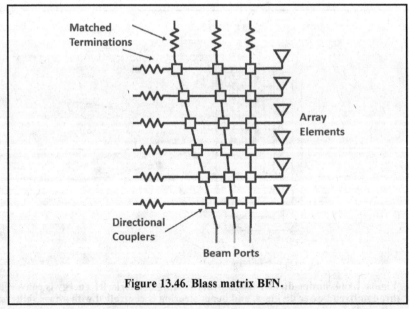

Figure 13.46. Blass matrix BFN.

13.8.6. Rotman Lens

The design which is now known as the "Rotman Lens" was published in 1963 by Rotman and Turner (1963), as an improvement upon other lens-based beamforming networks. The Rotman lens was designed to overcome weaknesses of previous designs, which created inconsistent beam-widths depending on the beam steering angle. By applying geometric optics principles, this design was optimized to reduce these aberrations. In contrast to the previously-described BFN designs, the Rotman lens does not comprise discrete couplers or phase shifters (Rappaport and Zaghloul, 2005). Instead, the geometry of the Rotman lens structure dictates its beam forming capability.

The original design concept for the Rotman lens is illustrated in Fig. 13.47. In this design, the lens region consists of a parallel-plate waveguide. To the left side, feed horns interface with the parallel plates to form beam ports. On the right side, coaxial probes enter the waveguide plates and serve as array ports. While this design was originally implemented in waveguide, it is possible to fabricate the Rotman lens using a variety of methods, including stripline, microstrip, and coplanar waveguide (Kilic and Dahlstrom, 2005). The possibility of fabricating the Rotman lens on a planar substrate without need for crossovers, and the low component count of the design, makes it attractive for a variety of applications. The Rotman lens achieves higher efficiencies (*53%*) and wider bandwidths (up to *400%*) than the Butler matrix.

An example of a Rotman lens implementation using microstrip fabrication is shown in Fig. 13.48 ((Hall and Vetterlein, 1990). Tapers are required to match the impedance of the microstrip to the impedance of the lens space: the actual lens is the space connected to all the tapers. In addition to the shown 5 beam ports and 5 array ports, tapers are connected to 4 "dummy ports," which attach to matched loads. The purpose of the dummy ports is to absorb reflecting waves, which would otherwise lead to undesired coupling between the beam ports.

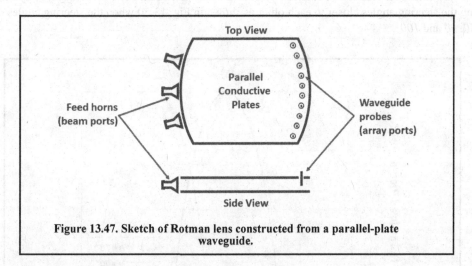

Figure 13.47. Sketch of Rotman lens constructed from a parallel-plate waveguide.

13.8.7. Design Considerations for Beamforming Networks

Array feeding networks, such as the dynamic phased array and AESA, allow for real-time variation of the phase of signals at the array ports, and therefore real-time steering of the array to arbitrary angles. In contrast, the beam angles of a BFN are predefined: they are a result of the BFN's component selection (for power-divider, Butler matrix, or Blass matrix designs), or the geometry (for the Rotman lens).

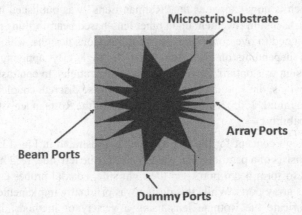

Figure 13.48. Rotman lens design implemented using microstrip construction. Black areas represent conductive microstrip material, and gray areas indicate where the conductor has been etched revealing substrate.

Selection of the beam steering angles for a BFN is informed by the application, but also constraints of the BFN itself. For example, if a BFN allows for the beam to be steered at *0* and *5°*, then it will not be possible to illuminate a target at *2.5°* with maximum energy. This effect is known as crossover loss, and its effect is illustrated in Fig. 13.49. In this example, a BFN is designed for three steering angles at *70, 90* and *110°* (Mailloux, 2005). The crossover loss represents the array factor value at the crossover between the steered beams which in this case is *-12 dB*. Crossover loss can be reduced by adding additional beam ports to the BFN, or by moving the steering angles closer to each other as shown in Fig. 13.50 when the steering angles are *80, 90* and *100°*.

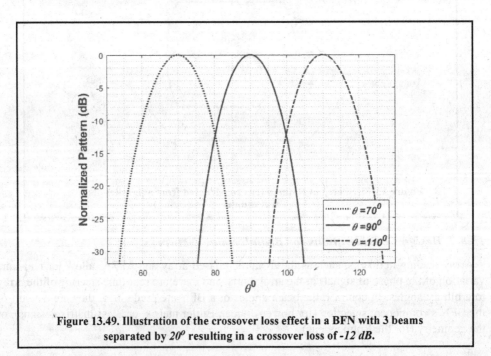

Figure 13.49. Illustration of the crossover loss effect in a BFN with 3 beams separated by *20°* resulting in a crossover loss of *-12 dB*.

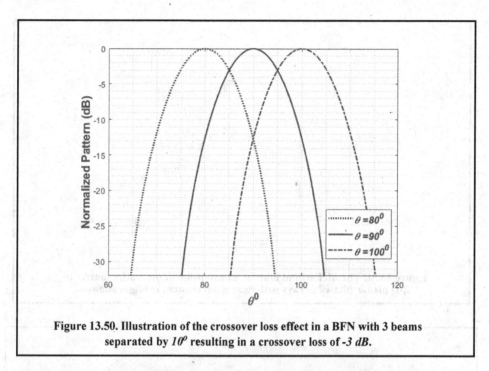

Figure 13.50. Illustration of the crossover loss effect in a BFN with 3 beams separated by *10⁰* resulting in a crossover loss of *-3 dB*.

13.8.8. Feeding and Beamforming Networks for Two-Dimensional Arrays

The previous discussion on beamforming focused on BFN designs for linear arrays. It is important to note, however, that these techniques are extensible to two-dimensional arrays as well. All of the phased array feeding network designs illustrated in Fig. 13.38 are applicable to 2-D array configurations. In addition, the power-divider BFN is readily extensible to 2-D array designs, when proper selections are made for the values of the fixed phase shifters.

It is possible to implement other BFN designs for 2-D arrays as well. The McFarland matrix in Fig. 13.51 is a modification of the Butler matrix for use with a planar array of antenna elements in a hexagonal pattern (Hansen, 2009). Extension of the Rotman lens has led to 2-D "bootlace" designs, wherein the planar 2-D "lens" region is changed to a 3-D lensing volume (McFarland, 1979). Such designs achieve many of the advantages of the Rotman lens, but they can be physically large and require a high quantity of components such as transmission lines and waveguide probes, making their fabrication impractical for many applications.

An alternative to fabricating specific 2-D BFNs is the interconnection of multiple planar 1-D BFNs, to comprise a 2-D BFN. Such a configuration is illustrated in Fig. 13.52 where a set of "X-Plane" BFNs accomplish beamforming along one axis (Hansen, 2009). A second set of BFNs is rotated *90°* with respect to the first set, and signals are transferred between the two sets via transmission line interconnects. The planar BFNs of this configuration may be Butler or Blass matrices, or Rotman lenses.

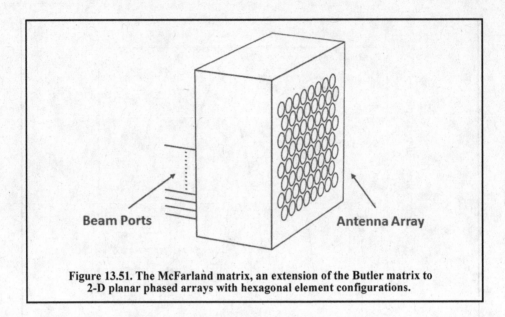

Figure 13.51. The McFarland matrix, an extension of the Butler matrix to 2-D planar phased arrays with hexagonal element configurations.

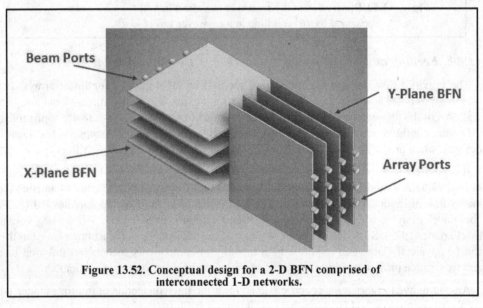

Figure 13.52. Conceptual design for a 2-D BFN comprised of interconnected 1-D networks.

Chapter 14

Synthetic Aperture Radar

Brian J. Smith

14.1. Basic Strip-Map Synthetic Aperture Radar Concept

Radars can be used in a ground mapping mode to make high resolution images showing terrain features and targets of interest. Synthetic aperture radar (SAR) imaging has the advantage of all weather, day-night operation and can be used in airborne and space based radar. SAR is an established technology that originated in the 1950s with some of the original work conducted by the Goodyear Aircraft Corporation. The key to today's high resolution widely proliferated SAR systems is the advancement of processing capability. The original SAR systems recorded the radar returns on film and optical processing used to form the resulting images. A key limitation of optical processing was there was no real time image formation, the aircraft had to land and have the film processed.

The fundamental concept of SAR is that an image can be formed using the motion of the radar to form a large synthetic array for cross-range resolution with down range resolution provided by the basic radar's fine range resolution. The large synthetic aperture results in a much narrower antenna beam width than the real beam of the radar. The basic concept of SAR image formation is simple; however, when high-resolution images are required, additional measurement and processing steps are necessary which will be covered in this chapter. It should be noted that SAR provides a plan view of the scene and tall objects will lay over and cast shadows in the resulting image.

14.1.1. Down Range Resolution

Assuming a two-dimensional (2-D) scenario and a pulsed radar with the antenna pointed $90°$ from the flight path is shown in Fig. 14.1. The down range resolution d_r is a function of the pulse bandwidth and is given by

$$d_r = K_r \frac{c}{2B}$$

Eq. (14.1)

where K_r is a broadening factor (~ 1.3 when using a Hamming window) due to pulse compression weighting, c is the speed of light in units m/sec, and B is the instantaneous pulse width bandwidth in Hz.

Figure 14.2 shows a plot of down range resolution as a function of signal bandwidth for $K_r = 1.3$. Image resolution is typically given as a requirement depending on the purpose of the SAR system. Typically, the required resolution is *1/5* to *1/20* of the major dimension of the smallest object to be recognized. To recognize city streets, buildings, waterways, and forested areas, a resolution of approximately *30* feet is required. This results in a *21 MHz* transmitted waveform bandwidth. For detecting vehicles, a resolution on the order of one foot is needed resulting in a required bandwidth of *640 MHz*. Linear frequency modulation (LFM) and non-linear frequency modulation (NLFM) are standard techniques used to obtain the required waveform bandwidths. The NLFM waveforms provide lower range sidelobes, and with the advent of direct digital synthesis (DDS) based radars, NLFM is readily implemented.

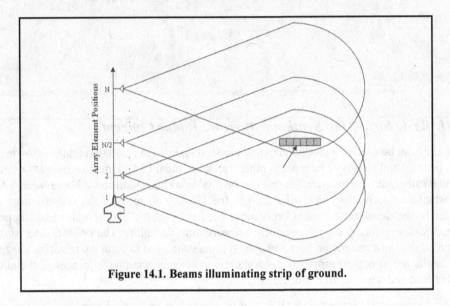

Figure 14.1. Beams illuminating strip of ground.

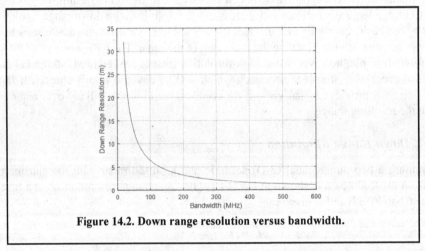

Figure 14.2. Down range resolution versus bandwidth.

14.1.2. Cross-Range Resolution

The azimuth resolution for a physical antenna of length L for a scene R meters from the radar is

$$d_a \cong \lambda R / L .$$

Eq. (14.2)

So, for a *1 m* array at X-band imaging an area *50 km* away the real antenna gives an azimuth resolution of *1500 m*. This resolution is too coarse for most ground mapping applications and is not viable for detecting ground targets.

The maximum azimuth resolution of strip-map SAR is limited by the amount of time a scatterer in the image stays in the antenna beam. The larger the real antenna, the smaller its beamwidth and hence the lower the maximum possible image resolution for a given operating frequency. So, unlike real beam operation, strip-map SAR is able to generate higher resolution images for smaller real antennas in the strip-map mode. It would seem that making the antenna very small would be the natural course of action for high resolution images. However, as maximum resolution increases, antenna gain and hence SNR decreases. Azimuth resolution of the SAR image is determined by the length of the synthetic array and is given by

$$d_a = K_a \frac{\lambda R_t}{2L_{array}\sin(\theta_{squint})} \qquad \text{Eq. (14.3)}$$

where d_a is the desired azimuth resolution, λ is the wavelength, R_t is range from the radar to the scene center, L_{array} is length of synthetic array, θ_{squint} is the squint angle to scene center (in radians), and K_a is a broadening factor due to windowing (~*1.3* for Hamming window).

The squint angle, θ_{squint}, is defined in Fig. 14.3. Figure 14.4 is a plot of the required synthetic array length versus desired azimuth resolution at S-band (*3 GHz*), X-band (*10 GHz*), and Ku-band (*16 GHz*) for θ_{squint} = *90* deg and the range to scene center of *50 km*. Figure 14.5 shows the impact on required array length as a function of squint angle at X-band. Equation (14.3) shows that as θ_{squint} approaches $0°$, the array length goes to infinity indicating SAR images cannot be formed looking straight along the flight path which is consistent with real arrays that cannot scan the beam parallel to the array face.

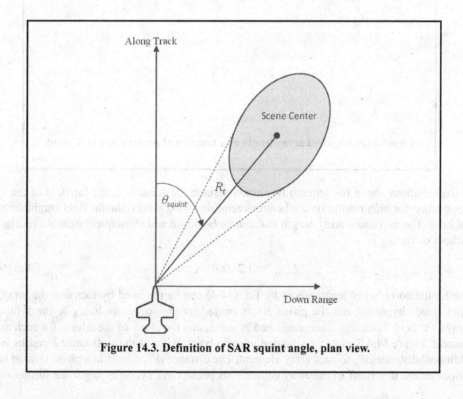

Figure 14.3. Definition of SAR squint angle, plan view.

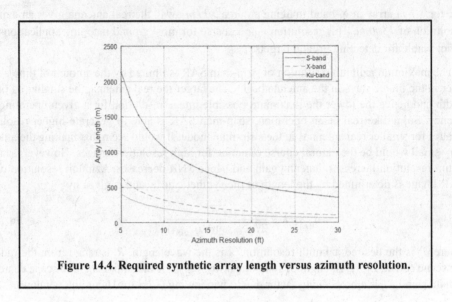

Figure 14.4. Required synthetic array length versus azimuth resolution.

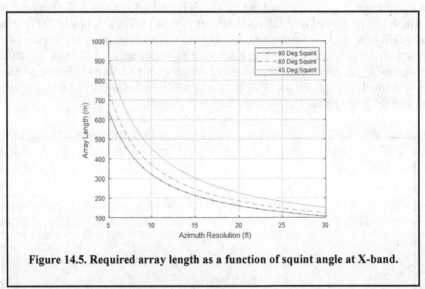

Figure 14.5. Required array length as a function of squint angle at X-band.

The equations above for azimuth resolution assume the scene is in the far field of the synthetic array, for high-resolution applications requiring long arrays, the far field condition may not hold. The maximum array length that can be achieved and subsequent azimuth resolution without correcting is

$$L_{max} = 1.2\sqrt{\lambda R}.$$ **Eq. (14.4)**

The limitation on array length given by Eq. (14.4) can be removed by focusing the array, in other words by taking out the phase errors caused by the scene not being in the synthetic arrays' far field. Focusing is accomplished by correcting the phase of the returns for each array element. Figure 14.6 depicts the situation where a point P, in a scene at distance R results in an additional distance ΔR_n to each array element. The distance ΔR_n results in a phase error at each array element that is off of the array center. This phase error becomes larger the further measurements are made away from the array center. The required phase corrections for each element can be found from the geometry of Fig. 14.6, more specifically,

$$R^2 + d_n^2 = (R + \Delta R_n)^2 \qquad\qquad \text{Eq. (14.5a)}$$

$$R^2 + d_n^2 = R^2 + 2R\Delta R_n + \Delta R_n^2 \qquad\qquad \text{Eq. (14.5b)}$$

$$d_n^2 = 2R\Delta R_n \left(1 + \frac{\Delta R_n}{2R}\right) \qquad\qquad \text{Eq. (14.5c)}$$

Assuming $\Delta R_n \ll 2R$, yields

$$\Delta R_n = \frac{d_n^2}{2R}. \qquad\qquad \text{Eq. (14.5d)}$$

The distance ΔR_n in meters can be converted to a phase angle in radians by multiplying by $2\pi/\lambda$ to give the required phase correction at each measurement location, n. To find the phase correction the distance ΔR_n must be multiplied by 2 to account for the round trip to point P. The resulting phase correction is given by:

$$\phi_n = -\frac{2\pi}{\lambda R}d_n^2. \qquad\qquad \text{Eq. (14.6)}$$

As an example, consider an X-band system ($\lambda = 3$ cm) with the scene center at 50 Km and a squint angle of 90°. From Eq. (14.4) the maximum unfocused array length is $L_{max} = 46.5\ m$ which results in an azimuth resolution of approximately *70 ft*. If a *5 foot* resolution is desired for this system, the array length would need to be *640 m*. Required phase corrections across the array are given in Fig. 14.7.

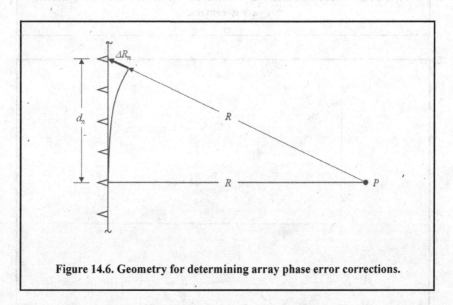

Figure 14.6. Geometry for determining array phase error corrections.

14.1.3. Pulse Repetition Frequency Considerations

To avoid range ambiguities, the return from pulse n must be received before the return from $n+1$. Figure 14.8 shows the range from the starting point (R_{start}) and end (R_{end}) of where the real antenna beam strikes the ground. The time it takes the pulse to return from the point where it initially strikes the ground is $T_S = 2R_S/c$, and from the end of the scene it is $T_E = 2R_E/c$. To avoid range ambiguities, the return from pulse $n+1$ cannot be received until after T_E from pulse n. So the time between pulses can be no less than $T_E - T_S$ $(T_{Sn+1} = T_{En})$ and in terms of PRF we have

$$PRF_{max} = \frac{1}{T_E - T_S} = \frac{c}{2(R_E - R_S)} \qquad \text{Eq. (14.7)}$$

In some high clutter scenarios R_S, is set to zero to ensure there are no unintended returns coming through the real antenna's sidelobes that can corrupt the SAR image.

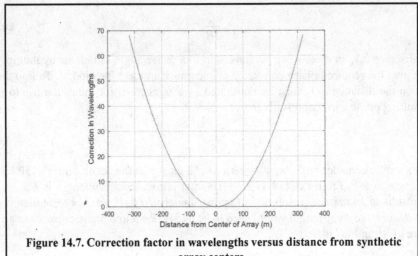

Figure 14.7. Correction factor in wavelengths versus distance from synthetic array centers.

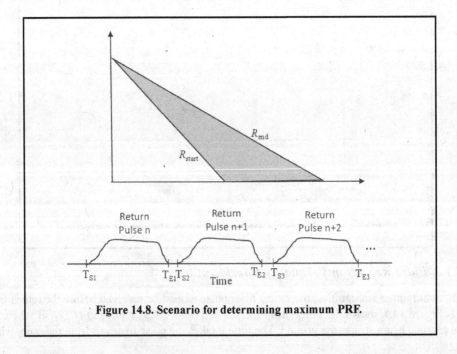

Figure 14.8. Scenario for determining maximum PRF.

Similar to real arrays, synthetic arrays will have grating lobes (multiple main beams) if the array measurements are too far part. For real arrays, the maximum distance between array elements to avoid grating lobes is $d = \lambda/2$. The distance between elements is the radar's speed times the pulse repetition interval (PRI) used. Figure 14.9 is a plot of the minimum required PRF needed at S-, X-, and Ku-bands versus radar velocity to ensure there are no grating lobes in the synthetic array. Due to limitation on platform speed and maximum PRF to avoid range ambiguities, frequently the requirement to make measurements half a wavelength apart cannot be met. Fortunately, the pattern of the real antenna can greatly reduce the size of the grating lobes in the synthetic array. One technique used to minimize the impact of grating lobes in the synthetic array when they cannot be avoided is to place them in a null of the real antenna pattern. For a real antenna of length l, the gain pattern is given by,

$$G = \left[\frac{\sin\left(\frac{\pi l}{\lambda}\sin\alpha\right)}{\frac{\pi l}{\lambda}\sin\alpha} \right]^2 . \qquad \text{Eq. (14.8)}$$

The nulls of the real antenna occur for

$$\alpha = \operatorname{asin}\left(\frac{n\lambda}{l}\right) \quad ; n = \ldots, -2, -1, 1, 2, \ldots . \qquad \text{Eq. (14.9)}$$

The grating lobes of the synthetic array occur at off-boresight angles given by

$$\alpha = \operatorname{asin}\left(\frac{n\lambda PRF}{2v}\right) \quad ; n = \ldots, -2, -1, 1, 2, \ldots \qquad \text{Eq. (14.10)}$$

where v is the radial velocity of the radar platform. Figure 14.10-a shows an example with the antenna pattern using a real antenna and the pattern of the synthetic array with grating lobes. Figure 14.10-b shows the resulting synthetic pattern when the two patterns are combined.

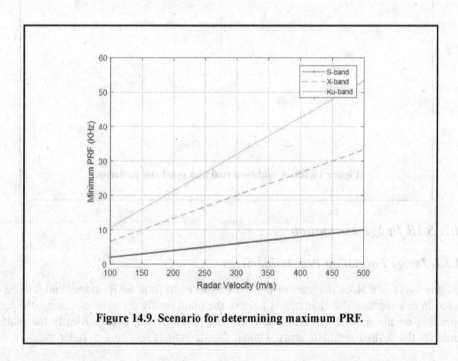

Figure 14.9. Scenario for determining maximum PRF.

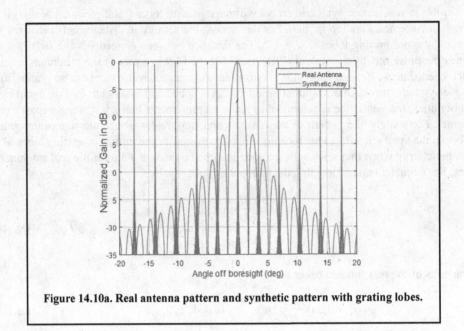

Figure 14.10a. Real antenna pattern and synthetic pattern with grating lobes.

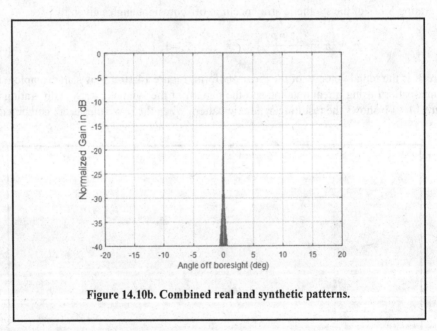

Figure 14.10b. Combined real and synthetic patterns.

14.2. SAR Image Formation

14.2.1. Image Formation Processing Steps

Figure 14.11 is a block diagram of the steps required to form SAR images and will be discussed in this section. The first step is to have the platform fly the synthetic array, the length depending on the desired azimuth resolution and given by Eq. (14.3). Ideally the platform would fly the desired synthetic array without any deviations resulting in radar measurements being made at the desired locations. Frequently the airborne platform deviates from the desired trajectory and an inertial measurement system (IMS) is used to measure the platform's actual position while the synthetic array is being flown. The IMS data are used to perform motion compensation for the raw radar measurements. Motion compensation can be performed after the radar data is collected or in real time on a pulse-to-pulse basis. Modern SAR systems frequently use real-time motion compensation.

The next step is to form the initial SAR image from the motion compensated radar data. For moderate resolution images, the process is to perform range compression and then track along for azimuth compression. Forming SAR images in this fashion is known as rectangular format processing. When forming high-resolution images, the radar data must first be reformatted to eliminate motion through resolution cells, then the down range and cross-range compressions can be conducted. Depending on the quality of the IMS and resolution of the SAR image, it may be necessary to process the initially formed SAR image with an auto-focus routine to eliminate any residual errors.

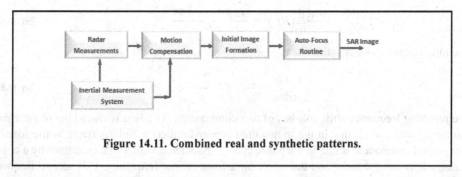

Figure 14.11. Combined real and synthetic patterns.

14.2.2. Motion Compensation

SAR imaging techniques assume the air platform is flying the desired flight path, typically a straight line or arc for circular SAR. The aircraft needs to maintain the ideal flight trajectory to within a fraction of a wavelength (typically $\lambda/8$) to avoid image degradation. For an X-band system, this would require not deviating by more than *4mm* from the ideal trajectory. This stringent requirement generally cannot be met in practice due to turbulence and vibration of the aircraft. Motion compensation is the process of correcting for the effect of this unintended motion on the radar signal processing. To compensate for these errors, the state of the platform/radar can be measured and used to adjust the radar returns.

An inertial measurement system is typically placed near or on the radar's antenna to measure accelerations. These measurements are then used to generate phase corrections to take out the undesired motion. The phase corrections can be applied to the radar data after the synthetic array has been flown or used in real time to adjust the phase of the waveforms. Generally, motion errors vary relatively smoothly in contrast to high frequency noise-like errors. This results in the uncompensated motion causing residual linear and quadratic phase errors in the radar returns. These errors, if large enough, will result in loss of image resolution, increased sidelobes, gain loss and shifts in range and azimuth.

14.2.3. Image Formation

After the radar data are motion compensated, down range and cross-range compression can be performed to yield the initial SAR image. Down range resolution is obtained through pulse compression of the transmitted pulse waveform. A standard technique is to use LFM wave-forms to increase the bandwidth and hence down range resolution in SAR images. The pulses in LFM are swept over a frequency range of ΔF and are given by,

$$s(t) = \cos[2\pi(f_c + \mu t^2)] \; ; \frac{-\tau}{2} \le t \le \frac{\tau}{2} \qquad \text{Eq. (14.11)}$$

where τ is the pulse width, f_c is the carrier frequency, and μ is the FM slope (i.e., $\mu = B/\tau$, where B is the bandwidth).

For a single point scatterer at range R, the phase response in radians is given by

$$\Phi = 2\pi\left(\frac{2R}{\lambda}\right) = 2\pi\left(\frac{2Rf_c}{c}\right). \qquad \text{Eq. (14.12)}$$

Differentiating Φ with respect to time results in a frequency shift, which is proportional to the time rate of change of the phase,

$$\frac{d\Phi}{dt} = \frac{4\pi}{c}\frac{d}{dt}(Rf_c) = \frac{4\pi R}{c}\dot{f_c} + \frac{4\pi f_c}{c}\dot{R}. \qquad \text{Eq. (14.13)}$$

The total frequency shift is then

$$f_t = \frac{1}{2\pi}\frac{d\Phi}{dt} = \frac{2R}{c}\dot{f_c} + \frac{2f_c}{c}\dot{R}. \qquad \text{Eq. (14.14)}$$

The resulting frequency shift consists of two components. The first is due to the phase change associated with the change in the transmitted carrier frequency and the range to the scatterer. The second component is due to the phase change associated with a change caused by a change in range between the radar and the target for a fixed carrier frequency. This second frequency shift component is the Doppler shift due to the relative velocity between the radar and the ground patch illuminated. From Fig. 14.12 the relative velocity $\dot{R}$ of a ground patch to the radar is

$$\dot{R} = f_d = v_r\cos\beta. \qquad \text{Eq. (14.15)}$$

Therefore, points at equal range will have differing Doppler shifts depending on the angle β. Down range resolution is typically obtained by matched filtering the radar returns using Fourier processing techniques as done in real beam radar systems. The result of down range compression is a 2-D matrix of complex values where the rows are range bins and the columns are synthetic array positions. Azimuth compression is formed on this matrix to yield the SAR image.

Synthetic aperture processing in azimuth exploits the linear FM modulation that the approximately quadratic variation in range to a scatterer introduces along the synthetic array. Azimuth compression can be performed by separating the points at equal range by filtering this difference in frequencies. Figure 14.13 shows the Doppler histories of evenly spaced points on the ground. So in each range bin, there is a difference in frequency for each azimuth bin, and the Fourier transform is used to filter or compress the image in cross-range to provide the desired azimuth resolution.

To help illustrate the image formation process, consider the following example: *10 ft* resolution in down and cross-range is desired, the radar platform is flying *300 m/s*, the squint angle is

$90°$, $\lambda = 3$ cm, range to scene center is *50 km* and a *5 km x 5 km* image is desired. From Eq. (14.1) the required transmit bandwidth to achieve *10 ft* down range resolution is

$$B = \frac{K_r c}{2 d_r} = 64 \, MHz .$$

Eq. (14.16)

For *10 ft* cross-range resolution requires the radar to fly a synthetic aperture of length

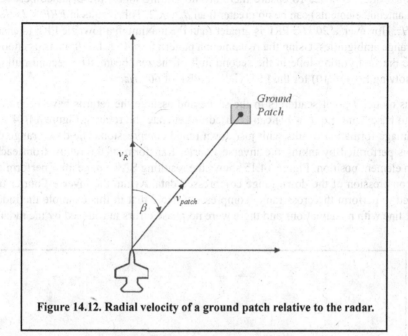

Figure 14.12. Radial velocity of a ground patch relative to the radar.

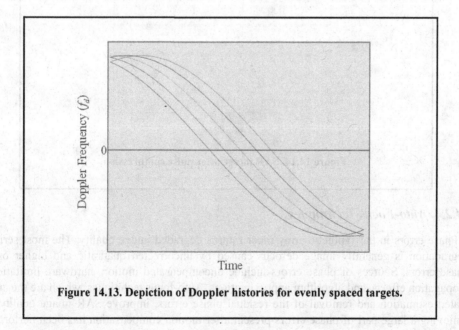

Figure 14.13. Depiction of Doppler histories for evenly spaced targets.

$$L = \frac{K_a R_t \lambda}{2 d_a} = 325 m\,.$$ **Eq. (14.17)**

The maximum array length without focusing from Eq. (14.4) is *41 m*, so the array will have to be focused using phase correction values from Eq. (14. 6). Let us assume we desire unambiguous range to the far end of the image, so this would set $R_S = 0$ in Eq. (14.7) resulting in a maximum PRF of *2.727 kHz*. To ensure there are no grating lobes, the distance between pulses (virtual antenna elements) can be no greater than $d_e = \lambda/2$. This results in $PRF = 1/PRI = V_r/d_e$ = *20 kHz*. However, a *20 kHz* PRF is greater than the maximum allowable PRF to ensure there are no range ambiguities. Using the real antenna pattern from Fig. 14.10-a lets us choose a PRF to place the first grating lobe in the second null of the real beam. The second null occurs at *3.44°*, solving Eq. (14.10) for the PRF yields a PRF of *600 Hz*.

Let us model *4* point scatterers in the scene and assume the returns have been down converted to base band. Eq. (14.14) can be used to generate the returns. Figure 14.14 shows the initial image formation results with just down range compression. The down range compression was performed by taking the inverse Fourier transform of the return from each virtual antenna element position. Figure 14.15 shows the resulting SAR image after performing cross-range compression of the down range compressed data. Again, the inverse Fourier transform was used to perform the cross-range compression. Note that in this example the radar flew a straight line with no deviations and there were no phase errors introduced by the radar.

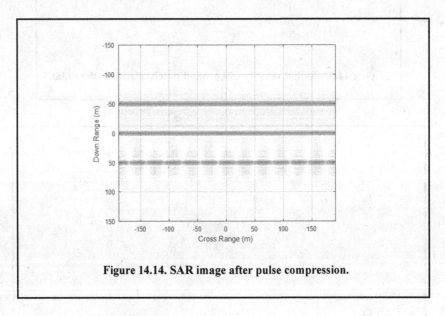

Figure 14.14. SAR image after pulse compression.

14.2.4. Auto-Focus Techniques

Phase errors in the synthetic array radar returns degraded image quality. The most serious degradation is generally image defocus caused by uncorrected quadratic and higher order phase errors. Sources of phase errors include uncompensated motion, hardware limitations, propagation effects, and algorithm approximations. Auto-focus techniques, which are the automated estimation and removal of the residual phase errors, improve SAR image quality by removing a large part of phase errors present after motion compensation has been performed on the radar returns.

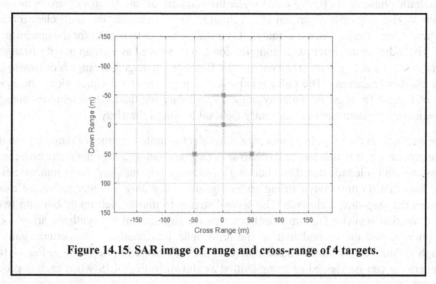

Figure 14.15. SAR image of range and cross-range of 4 targets.

Auto-focus algorithms use the radar data to aid in estimating the existing phase errors in the radar data. Once the phase errors are estimated, error compensation is performed on the radar data using these phase values. The process of error compensation involves three steps: (1) building a complex correction vector with phase equal to the negative of the estimated phase error, (2) multiplying the radar data by the correction vector, (3) re-forming the SAR image with the phase corrected data. One of the first auto-focus techniques developed in the 1970s is known as map-drift (MD). In MD two independent SAR images of a scene are cross-correlated. If the SAR images are well focused, the two images will register and the cross-correlation peak will occur at zero shift. If there are focusing errors, the cross-correlation peak will occur away from zero shift. The location of the correlation peak is used to estimate a phase correction to apply to the data. Typically several iterations are used.

The map-drift algorithm is based on assuming the phase errors across the synthetic aperture are quadratic in nature, as depicted in Fig. 14.16 where L is half of the synthetic array length (meters), y is the distance along array as measured from array center (meters), Φ is the maximum value of phase error at the ends of the array (rad), $\phi(y)$ is the phase error as a function of position along the array (rad), and a is a coefficient in the quadratic equation.

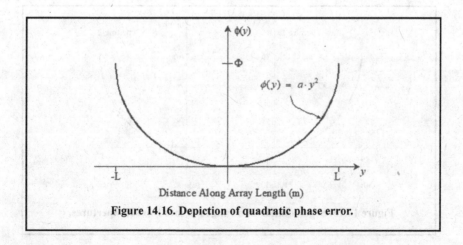

Figure 14.16. Depiction of quadratic phase error.

Quadratic phase errors (QPE) come under the category of low-frequency errors in SAR terminology. The map-drift algorithm is a technique for determining the coefficient a from the measured radar returns. Once a is found, it is a simple matter to correct for the quadratic phase error. The radar returns after range compression can be viewed as a group of data arranged in a matrix as shown in Fig. 14.17. The data in this figure are arranged in range bins (rows) and by pulse number (columns). The pulse number corresponds to the distance along the synthetic array of Fig. 14.16 where the velocity of the aircraft carrying the radar determines the spacing between array elements and subsequently the total length of the array.

The first step in the map-drift procedure is to select a limited number of range bins to use for future processing. It is standard practice to select approximately 5% of the range bins for future processing with selection based on choosing those range bins that have large returns. Selecting range bins that do not have a strong target signature, say only a clutter return for example, degrades the map-drift technique. The second step is to divide each range bin into two segments: the first segment (sub-aperture) contains the first half of the synthetic array, values *1* through *K/2*, and the second half of the array data into another sub-aperture, values *K/2* through *K*. So, we now have two sub-apertures for each range bin as shown in Fig.14.18. The sub-apertures can be viewed as being shifted as shown in Fig.14.19 when each is processed separately.

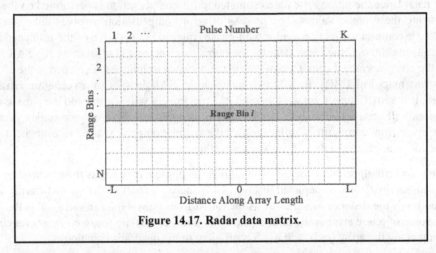

Figure 14.17. Radar data matrix.

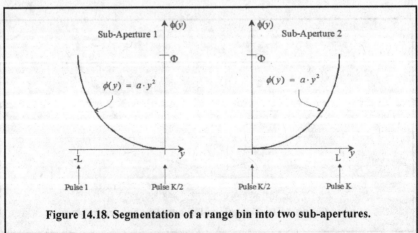

Figure 14.18. Segmentation of a range bin into two sub-apertures.

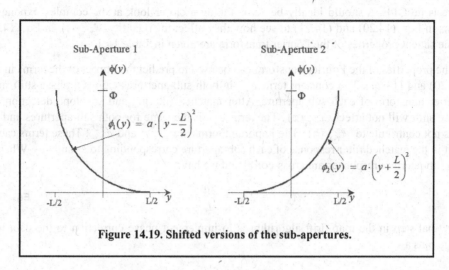

Figure 14.19. Shifted versions of the sub-apertures.

The sub-apertures can be expanded to yield

$$\phi_1(y) = \frac{\Phi}{4} - \frac{\Phi y}{L} + \frac{\Phi y^2}{L^2} \qquad\qquad \text{Eq. (14.18)}$$

$$\phi_2(y) = \frac{\Phi}{4} + \frac{\Phi y}{L} + \frac{\Phi y^2}{L^2}. \qquad\qquad \text{Eq. (14.19)}$$

It is clear from Eqs. (14.18) and (14.19) that each of the sub-apertures has the same constant and quadratic components, $\Phi/4$ and $\Phi y^2/L^2$, respectively. However, the linear component of each sub-aperture has opposite slopes. The different slopes of the linear components of the QPE are exploited in the map-drift algorithm to determine an estimate of a.

Azimuth compression in the SAR image is accomplished after range compression through a matched filtering process with a known reference signal $s_{ox}(y)$ for the range bin with signal $s_x(y)$. Let the quantity $f_x(y)$ denote one line in the SAR image corresponding to one range bin. The reference signal s_{ox} is generated with respect to scene center for each range bin. Let us denote the sub-aperture signals as s_{1x} and s_{2x}, respectively. The sub-aperture signals with QPE can be written as

$$\mathcal{F}\{s_{1x}(y)e^{j\phi(y)}\} = \mathcal{F}\left\{s_{1x}(y)e^{j(c_1 - c_2 y + c_3 y^2)}\right\} = \mathcal{F}\left\{s_{1x}(y)e^{jc_1}e^{-jc_2 y}e^{jc_3 y^2}\right\} \qquad \text{Eq. (14.20)}$$

where $\mathcal{F}$ is the Fourier transform operator, $c_1 = \Phi/4$, $c_2 = \Phi/L$, and $c_3 = \Phi/L^2$. Similarly,

$$\mathcal{F}\{s_{2x}(y)e^{j\phi(y)}\} = \mathcal{F}\left\{s_{2x}(y)e^{j(c_1 - c_2 y + c_3 y^2)}\right\} = \mathcal{F}\left\{s_{1x}(y)e^{jc_1}e^{-jc_2 y}e^{jc_3 y^2}\right\}. \qquad \text{Eq. (14.21)}$$

The map-drift algorithm is based on measuring the following quantity

$$\mathcal{R}_{x_2 x_1}(\tau) = f_{1x} \bullet f_{2x} \qquad\qquad \text{Eq. (14.22)}$$

where $\bullet$ symbolically denotes cross-correlation. The value $\mathcal{R}_{x_2 x_1}(\tau)$ is a measure of shift from aperture center when the responses from the two sub-apertures are cross-correlated. When there is no QPE, Δ should ideally be zero. Taking a closer look at the complex exponential terms in Eqs. (14.20) and (14.21) to see how they affect the quantity $\mathcal{R}_{x_2 x_1}(\tau)$ in Eq. (14.22). Some salient properties of the Fourier transform are given in Table 14.1.

The properties of the Fourier transform can be used to predict the impact of the terms in Eqs. (14.20) and (14.21). The constant term e^{jc_1} in both sub-apertures causes a phase shift in the Fourier transform of each sub-aperture. After matched filtering and envelope detection, this phase shift will not affect $\mathcal{R}_{x_2 x_1}(\tau)$. The term e^{jc_3} is the same for both sub-apertures and also does not contribute to $\mathcal{R}_{x_2 x_1}(\tau)$. The important terms are $e^{-jc_2 y}$ and $e^{jc_2 y}$. These terms cause a shift in the matched filter response of each sub-aperture corresponding to c_2 and $-c_2$. When the two sub-aperture responses are cross-correlated we have

$$\mathcal{R}_{x_2 x_1} = 2c_2 = \frac{2\Phi}{L}. \qquad \text{Eq. (14.23)}$$

The final step in the map-drift algorithm is to implement phase correction to the data in all range bins as

$$\phi(y) = e^{-j\hat{a}y^2} \qquad \text{Eq. (14.24)}$$

where $\hat{a}$ is an estimate of a obtained from the measurement of $\mathcal{R}_{x_2 x_1}$.

Another popular auto-focus technique is phase gradient auto-focus (PGA) developed in the late 1980s. This technique assumes the uncompensated phase effort is the same for each range bin. The phase effort is estimated by choosing the strongest scatter in each range bin of the SAR image, aligning each of them to a common azimuth location, and decompressing the image in azimuth. The phase error function is then estimated from the decompressed image and used to refocus the image. The process is repeated iteratively until the desired focusing is achieved.

Table 14.1. Relevant Properties of Fourier Transform.

Spacial Domain Function	Frequency Domain Equivalent
$f(y)e^{jc}$; constant phase shift	$e^{jc}F(\omega)$
$f(y)e^{jcy}$; phase shift	$F(\omega - c)$
$f(y)e^{jcy^2}$; frequency ramp	$F(\omega - cy)$

14.3. Image Quality Considerations

To obtain high quality SAR images, sidelobes in down- and cross-range must be controlled. Sidelobes are introduced by the Fourier processing used for range and azimuth compression, uncompensated non-linear aircraft motion, and phase variations of the transmitted and received signals. Peak sidelobe level (PSL) is the level of the first sidelobe peak relative to the main lobe peak. Integrated sidelobe level (ISL) is the total energy in the sidelobes relative to the main lobe. Generally accepted criteria for high quality images are PSL *35 dB* below the main lobe and ISL more than *25 dB* below the main lobe response. Integrated and peak sidelobes lead to different image artifacts. Peak sidelobes act as secondary main lobes and a strong return from the direction of a peak sidelobe is indistinguishable from the main lobe return and can produce a false return. Integrated sidelobes become important when imaging an evenly distributed weaker scene. In an application such as terrain mapping, a high ISL will degrade contract and fill in low return and shadow areas.

The signal strength of the returns from the scene depend on the type of terrain that is being imaged, radar band used, polarization, and grazing angle from the radar to the scene. Extensive analysis of terrain backscattering has been performed and is useful to simulate SAR systems and to predict performance. A standard technique is to determine the radar cross-section (RCS) per unit area and the associated statistics of the RCS fluctuations. The RCS per unit area is denoted as σ^0 with the units of *dBsm/m²*.

As an example, Table 14.2 (Ulaby and Dobson, 1989) provides the σ^0 values for short vegetation versus angle of incidence and radar frequency band utilizing horizontal polarization on transmit and horizontal polarization on receive (HH). The angle of incidence is defined as the angle from the scene center to the radar measured from the ground. For example a platform flying at *29,000 feet* imaging an area *50 km* away would have an angle of incidence of *10⁰*. Smooth road surfaces provide very little return at low grazing angles with σ^0 at X-band of approximately *-40 dBsm* which makes them very distinct in SAR images and can be used as reference points.

Resolution in SAR images is defined as the distance between point scatterers when a *3 dB* null occurs in the image. The standard test procedure is to use trihedral separated by the predicted resolution in the down range and cross-range directions. The sizes of the trihedrals required depend on the radar's operating band and should give a large return, typically around *30 dBsm* so that their returns do not compete with the scene background. The RCS for a trihedral with sides of length *l* is given by $\sigma = 4\pi l^4/(3\lambda^2)$.

When developing a SAR system, ground based testbeds can be used to verify system performance prior to expensive flight tests. Two typical types of testbeds are vehicle based and rail based. In vehicle based testbeds the radar, inertia measurement unit (IMU), and data recording equipment are mounted in the vehicle and the synthetic array formed by driving past the scene. In rail based testbeds the radar and IMU are mounted on a rail and travel along the length of the rail to form the synthetic aperture. The advantage of rail based systems is that precise known errors can be introduced which allows for the motion compensation and auto-focus algorithms to be accurately evaluated.

Table 14.2. Back Scattering Data, σ^0 for Short Vegetation HH Polarization.

Band	10⁰	30⁰	40⁰	45⁰	60⁰	80⁰
L	-26.1	-24.9	-15.5	-21.2	-17.6	-14.2
S	-20.2	-18.4	-15.9	-16.9	-14.2	-12.2
C	-17.6	-13.4	-13.7	-12.2	-10.0	-8.3
X	-15.3	-11.5	-10.6	-9.6	-7.8	-6.4
K_u	-14.9	-10.3	-9.0	-8.4	-7.0	-5.8
K_a	-15.4	-10.2	-8.6	-8.2	-6.6	-6.1

14.4. Spotlight SAR

There are many situations where a high-resolution image of a small area is desired and which the strip-map SAR mode is not suited. In these situations, the use of spotlight SAR is the preferred mode of operation. In spotlight SAR, the antenna beam is trained on a spot on the ground known as scene center, motion compensation point (MCP), and central reference point (CRP) as the radar platform flies the synthetic aperture. Spotlight SAR operation is depicted in Fig. 14.20. The maximum azimuth resolution of strip-map SAR is limited by the amount of time a scatter in the image stays in the antenna beam. The maximum resolution for a strip-map SAR using a real beam with a width of l is given by

$$d_a = \frac{l}{2}.$$ Eq. (14.25)

One popular method to increase resolution while maintaining good antenna gain is to utilize the spotlight SAR mode for the radar. In spotlight SAR, the limitation on azimuth resolution given by Eq. (14.25) is removed since the antenna beam is continuously repositioned to track the CRP.

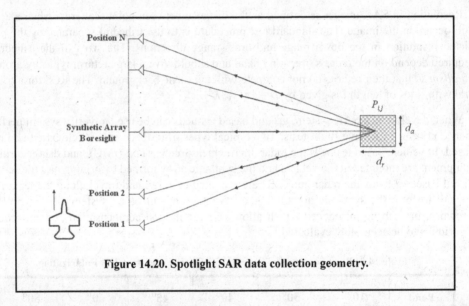

Figure 14.20. Spotlight SAR data collection geometry.

14.4.1. Motion through Resolution Cells

From the advent of the first SAR images in 1953, increase in image resolution has been a continual focus of SAR research. The initial SAR systems used analog optical processing techniques. The radar data were stored as shown in Fig.14.21 and this is known as rectangular format where the pulses are stored side-by-side and parallel to each other. The problem with the rectangular format, whether analog optical processing or digital processing is used, is the artifact known as motion through resolution cells (MTRC). Azimuth compression is accomplished in rectangular format processing by taking the inverse Fourier transform along the rows (range bins) of the resulting data matrix. The rectangular format algorithm fails when the range to scatterers and the range rate of scatterers vary over the synthetic aperture. For good quality images, the range to scatterers should not move by more than a resolution cell. The effects of MTRC become more severe, the further the scatterer becomes from scene center.

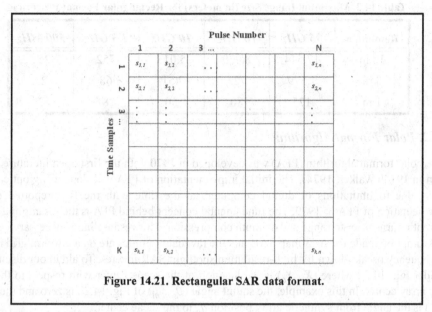

Figure 14.21. Rectangular SAR data format.

The MTRC effectively limits the size of the SAR image and can result in images that are intolerably small. The maximum scene radius of a SAR image when using the rectangular format algorithm is given by

$$r_0 < 2d^2/\lambda K \qquad \text{Eq. (14.26)}$$

where d is the desired cell resolution, $d_a = d_r$ and λ and K are as given in Eq. (14.3).

Consider the case where it is desired to have *1 m* azimuth, d_a, and range, d_r resolution using a *90°* squint angle, θ_{squint}. Let the range, R_t from synthetic array center to scene center be *10,000 m*. From Eq. (14.3) a *57 m* synthetic array will be required if a Ka-band (*35 GHz*) radar is used. The distance from the ends of the array to scene center is *10,000.041 m*. For good quality images, the range to scatterers in the scene should not differ by more than half a range cell, *1 m* in this example. In this example, no appreciable range migration occurs. Now consider the same example but with a desired resolution of *6 inches*. A synthetic array length of *374 m* is now required. The distance from the ends of the array to scene center is now *10,001.75 m*. The scatterers in the image are now migrating over *11* range bins as the synthetic array is formed. An actual SAR image formed using the rectangular format algorithm with this fine resolution would be very poor.

Table 14.3 provides the maximum image size when using the rectangular format algorithm for various resolution cell sizes and radar operating frequencies when using Eq. (14.26). Tactical SAR systems usually operate in K_a and K_u bands due to hardware component sizes and the requirement for relatively short range operation. It is clear from the table that high resolution tactical SAR (*>1 ft* resolution) cannot utilize the standard rectangular format algorithm. Fortunately, image formation algorithms have been developed to overcome the shortcomings of rectangular format processing. Some of these techniques are the polar format algorithm, range migration algorithm, chirp scaling algorithm, overlapped sub-aperture algorithm, and tomographic reconstruction. Of these techniques, the polar format algorithm is the oldest and is widely used. All other algorithms are typically compared to the polar format algorithm as a performance metric.

Table 14.3. Maximum Image Size (in meters) for Rectangular Format Processing.

Resolution	35 GHz	16 GHz	10 GHz	1.5 GHz	500 MHz
10 m	17,544	8,020	5,013	752	251
3 m	1,579	722	451	68	23
1 m	175	80	50	8	3

14.4.2. Polar Format Algorithm

The polar format algorithm (PFA) was developed in 1970 with the first open literature publication in 1974 (Walker, 1974). The initial implementation of PFA was done using optical processing due to limitations of digital computers at the time with the first reported digital implementation of PFA in 1979. The fundamental concept behind PFA is the resampling of the coherent returns prior to range and azimuth compression. This resampling is necessary because the assumption made for strip-map SAR that the raw data samples are on a uniform grid in spatial frequency breaks down for high-resolution spotlight SAR images. To aid in our discussion, consider Fig. 14.22 where (X_c, Y_c) is the location of the scene center with respect to the synthetic array center. In this example, the squint angle (θ_{squint}) of Fig. 14.22 is zero and the angle $\theta_0(d_n)$ is the angle from synthetic array position d_n to the scene center.

Define the transformation into wavenumber or k-space as

$$k = \frac{2\pi f_c}{c}.$$

Eq. (14.27)

The units of k are *radians/meter*. The orthogonal spatial frequency frame is (K_x, K_y). The radar returns for the synthetic aperture can be viewed in the (K_x, K_y) domain by the use of

$$k_x = 2k\cos(\theta(d_n))$$
$$k_y = 2k\sin(\theta(d_n))$$

Eq. (14.28)

where the aspect angle of the radar with respect to the center of the target area at radar position d_n is given by

$$\theta(d_n) = \text{atan}\left(\frac{Y_c - d_n}{X_c}\right).$$

Eq. (14.29)

To illustrate the issue with the radar returns, consider the desire to obtain *2 inch* resolution at X-band with the scene center *10 km* from the center of the synthetic array. Figure 14.23-a shows the resulting returns in k-space. As can be seen, the returns are not evenly spaced and applying Fourier processing directly on the data will result in a poor quality image. In PFA the raw data of Fig. 14.23-a are interpolated onto a rectangular grid as shown in Fig.14.23-b. Resampling can be performed using finite impulse response (FIR) filter techniques either as a two-step process by first performing down range interpolation and then azimuth interpolation or in one step using two-dimensional filtering. Once the interpolation is complete, the Fourier transform is used to perform range and cross-range compression resulting in the desired SAR image.

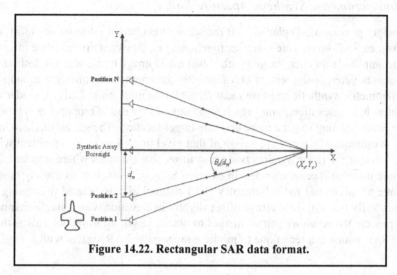

Figure 14.22. Rectangular SAR data format.

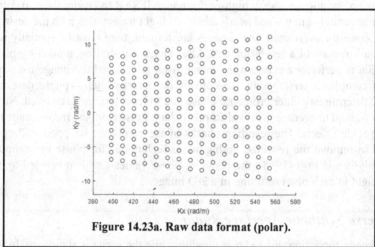

Figure 14.23a. Raw data format (polar).

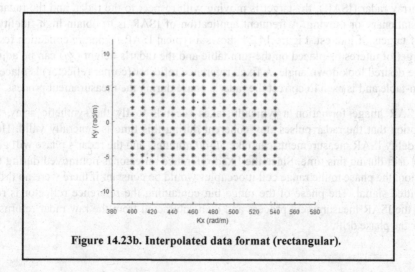

Figure 14.23b. Interpolated data format (rectangular).

14.4.3. Interferometric Synthetic Aperture Radar

SAR images provide a 2-D plan view if the scene direct height information is lost. However, the raw formed SAR images are complex functions, i.e., they contain the phase information as well as the amplitude for each image pixel. When a 3-D image of the scene is desired for applications such as determining terrain elevation, two common techniques are monopulse SAR and interferometric synthetic aperture radar (IFSAR). In monopulse SAR, the radar uses two-phase centers in the elevation plain, which is the same as the use of monopulse in ground based radars for beam splitting to get a more accurate target location. The sensed angle to image pixels gives an estimate of the relative height of that pixel in the image. The problem with monopulse SAR is that the radar requires two transmit/receive channels where standard SAR only requires one transmit/receive channel. In existing SAR systems, it is frequently cost-prohibitive to have an additional radio frequency (RF) channel and associated processing. Another approach is to fly two synthetic arrays offset slightly in elevation with a single channel system and then process the resulting pair of images to obtain height information. This is the process used in IFSAR which is a technique to mimic a monopulse SAR system with a single channel radar.

This technique requires a stable, high-performance IFSAR to ensure the two data collection passes have accurately known and nearly identical flight trajectories with the desired elevation separation. Once the individual SAR images are formed, they must be spatially registered to within a small fraction of a resolution cell. After image registration, a pixel-by-pixel complex multiplication is performed between the image from pass *1* and the image from pass *2*. This produces a complex interferogram. To convert the interferometric phase data into relative heights, the deterministic interferometric phase due to level terrain is removed. Next the interferogram is filtered to average the pixel-to-pixel phase noise from the radar, image misregistration, and speckle effects. The resulting phases of the pixels are wrapped at 2π and must be unwrapped to remove the resulting ambiguities. Techniques for phase unwrapping are provided in Ghiglia and Pritt (1998), the resulting phase values can then be used to estimate the scatterer height in each pixel resulting in a 3-D image.

14.5. Inverse Synthetic Aperture Radar

In SAR image formation, the radar is moving while the scene is stationary. In inverse synthetic array radar (ISAR), the target is moving with respect to the radar, and the radar can be either stationary or moving. A frequent application of ISAR is to obtain high-fidelity signatures of targets of interest. Figure 14.24 shows a typical ISAR signature collection test setup. The target of interest is placed on the turn table and the radar's height (Z_l) can be adjusted to give the desired look down angle. A fixed reference reflector (corner reflector) is placed off of the turn-table and is used to correct the radar's phase during the measurement process.

For SAR image formation it typically takes seconds to fly the synthetic array, and the assumption that the radar pulses stay coherent during this time is generally valid. However, high-fidelity ISAR measurements can take *30-60* minutes, and the radar's phase will generally start to drift during this time. Since the fixed reference reflector is not moved during the data collection, the phase to the range cell it occupies would be constant if there were no drift in the transmitted signal. The phase of the range bin containing the reference reflector is recorded during the ISAR measurement process and then subtracted from the raw radar returns to correct for the phase drift.

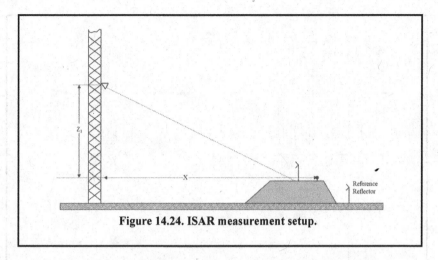

Figure 14.24. ISAR measurement setup.

As mentioned previously, SAR systems frequently use LFM coded pulses for down range resolution. High quality ISAR images can have resolutions on inches and typically use a discrete approximation to LFM, the stepped frequency waveform. The fundamental idea behind stepped frequency waveforms is to transmit multiple coherent pulses spaced Δf apart in frequency to cover the bandwidth of a single pulse, see Fig. 14.25. The use of stepped frequency waveforms greatly reduces the complexity and cost of the radar. The trade-off is time; it typically takes *64, 128*, etc. pulses to replace one LFM pulse. In addition, multiple polarization combinations (HH, HV, VH, VV) are generally desired which is accomplished by multiplexing the transmit and receive channels leading to additional pulses being required. However, this additional data collection time is small considering all factors.

In ISAR imaging the down range resolution is a function of the transmitted bandwidth as in SAR and is given by Eq. (14.1). In SAR imaging the azimuth resolution is determined by the synthetic array length flown by the radar platform. For ISAR the azimuth resolution is determined by the angle $\Delta\Omega$ through which the target rotates during the data collection as shown in Fig. 14.26-a. Cross-range resolution is obtained by using the Doppler frequency of the scatterers in a down range bin to separate them as shown in Fig.14.26-b. The instantaneous velocity of a scatterer at a range r_c from the center of rotation with respect to the radar is $v = \omega r_c$ resulting in a Doppler Frequency of

$$ f_d = 2\omega r_c \ (f_c/c) \qquad\qquad \textbf{Eq. (14.30)} $$

where f_c is the carrier frequency of the pulse. Two point scatterers in the same slant-range cell will have a difference in velocity of

$$ v_2 - v_1 = \omega r_2 - \omega r_1 = \omega r_c . \qquad\qquad \textbf{Eq. (14.31)} $$

This difference in velocity will result in a Doppler frequency difference between the *2* scatterers of

$$ \Delta f_d = 2\omega \ (c\Delta f_d/c) \qquad\qquad \textbf{Eq. (14.32)} $$

which results in a cross-range resolution of

$$ \Delta r_c = \frac{c\Delta f_d}{2\omega f_c} . \qquad\qquad \textbf{Eq. (14.33)} $$

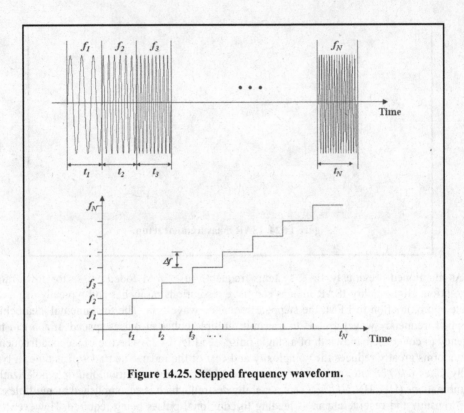

Figure 14.25. Stepped frequency waveform.

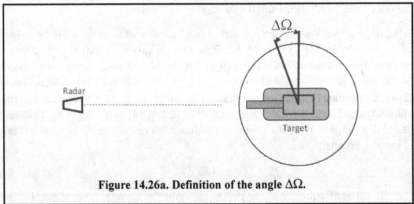

Figure 14.26a. Definition of the angle $\Delta\Omega$.

Noting that Doppler resolution is approximately equal to $1/T_i$, where T_i is the coherent integration time, substituting the value for Δf_d in Eq. (14.33) yields the cross-range resolution in terms of the angle of rotation as

$$\Delta r_c = \frac{c}{2\omega T_i f_c} = \frac{\lambda}{2\omega T_i} = K_a \frac{\lambda}{2\Delta\Omega}.$$ **Eq. (14.34)**

The factor K_a is added to take into account windowing to reduce azimuth sidelobes as in the case for SAR. Once the radar data are converted to baseband I&Q samples, the ISAR image is formed by taking the two-dimensional Fourier transform of the data. The first Fourier transform performs slant-range compression, and the second Fourier transform performs cross-range compression resulting in the desired ISAR image.

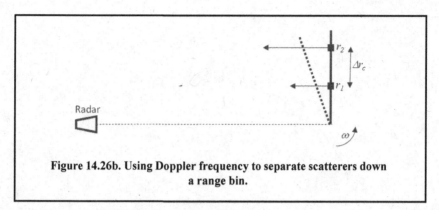

Figure 14.26b. Using Doppler frequency to separate scatterers down a range bin.

To avoid cross-range ambiguities, the cross-range signal must be sampled at least twice the highest expected frequency component. This requirement places restrictions on how fast the target can be rotated or how large a target can be imaged for a radar with a given effective PRF. Denoting the effective PRF as PRF', for an n pulse stepped-frequency waveform we have

$$PRF' = \frac{PRF}{n} \geq 2f_{d_{max}} = \frac{4f_c}{c}\omega r_{c_{max}}$$ **Eq. (14.35)**

where $r_{c_{max}}$ is the maximum cross-range dimension of the target. The number of the pulses n is determined by the desired down range resolution, f_c is the frequency band of interest, $r_{c_{max}}$ is determined by the target, and the PRF is set by the radar. With these parameters, given the maximum rate at which the target can be rotated is given by

$$\omega = \frac{cPRF}{4nf_c r_{c_{max}}}.$$ **Eq. (14.36)**

In SAR imaging there is a maximum synthetic array length beyond which the image degrades unless the radar data are focused to take out uncompensated quadratic phase terms. The same type of raw radar data correction (focusing) is also required in high-resolution ISAR images. The maximum integration angle without focusing is given by

$$\Delta\Omega_{max} = 1.2\sqrt{\frac{\lambda}{r_{c_{max}}}}$$ **Eq. (14.37)**

with a maximum resolution of

$$\Delta r_{c_{max}} = 0.5\sqrt{r\lambda}.$$ **Eq. (14.38)**

Focusing on ISAR data is achieved by subtracting the two-way phase deviation as done in SAR focusing.

Chapter 15

Wideband Radar Applications

Mark A. Barnes

15.1. Introduction

The radar operational bands are well defined, even though there are multiple standards, such as those by the Institute of Electrical and Electronics Engineers (IEEE) and North Atlantic Treaty Organization (NATO). However, the definition of the bandwidths of narrow band, medium band and wideband radars are poorly defined. This chapter discusses the definitions of various bandwidths; highlights the differences between radar bands and bandwidths; defines narrow band, medium band and wideband radar waveforms; and other wideband radar applications and analyses.

15.2. Band Versus Bandwidth

To better understand bandwidths, it is instrumental to review the differences between frequency bands, allocated bands and bandwidths. Figure 15.1 illustrates the differences, where each successive row represents a zoomed-in view of the row above. The top row corresponds to IEEE's ultra high frequency (UHF) band that spans from *0.3 GHz* to *1.0 GHz*. Within this band, the Federal Communications Commission (FCC) has allocated the UHF television broadcast band to *470* to *763*, *775* to *793* and *805* to *806 MHz* as illustrated on the second row. The UHF television broadcast band is broken into a series of channels that are licensed by geographic regions to avoid interference. The third row illustrates an example of one of the channel assignments to a station broadcast from *674* to *680 MHz*, thus the transmission occupies a *6 MHz* bandwidth. Hence, frequency bands are defined by wavelengths or other physical property, regulatory bands are defined by a service or purpose, and bandwidths are defined by specific systems. Many of the modern radars add an additional complexity by using different bandwidths depending upon the function being performed and, sometimes, by changing the carrier frequency to avoid detection and mitigate jamming.

15.2.1. Various Bandwidths

Another challenge is that bandwidth is defined in many ways. The definition is highly dependent upon textual modifiers and context. A common approach defines bandwidth by the frequency range where the power or energy spectral density, that is how the power/energy is spread as a function of frequency, is above a specified threshold. One of the most common and frequently assumed is the *3-dB* bandwidth (B_{3dB}). This is the frequency range where the spectral envelope is greater than *3-dB* below the spectral peak as shown in the bottom of Fig. 15.2.

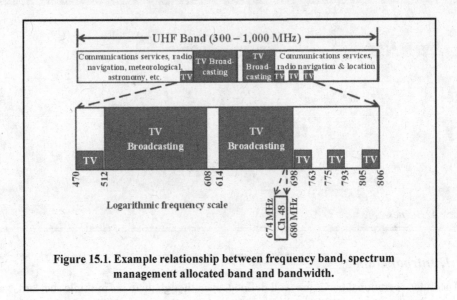

Figure 15.1. Example relationship between frequency band, spectrum management allocated band and bandwidth.

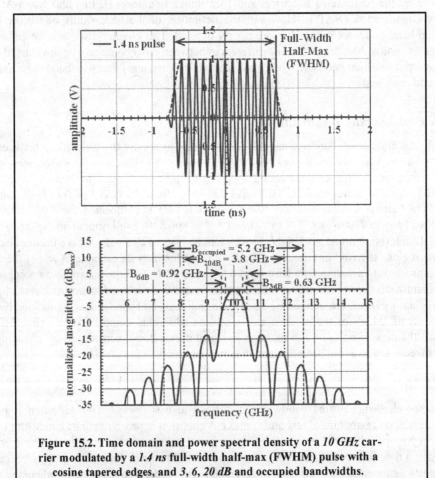

Figure 15.2. Time domain and power spectral density of a *10 GHz* carrier modulated by a *1.4 ns* full-width half-max (FWHM) pulse with a cosine tapered edges, and *3, 6, 20 dB* and occupied bandwidths.

The *3-dB* bandwidth tends to be very useful from a signal processing and radar performance standpoint, such as predicting the signal-to-noise ratio (SNR). A similar bandwidth is the *6 dB* bandwidth (B_{6dB}), which is useful in terms of processing signals and estimating performance. Another similarly defined bandwidth is the *20 dB* bandwidth (B_{20dB}). This is less common and is more likely to be used with respect to spectrum management and regulation to assess potential interference to other channels, receivers or devices.

Radar engineers often assume the inverse of bandwidth is equal to the pulse width or, when applicable, the compressed pulse width. The spectrum shown in Fig. 15.2 has a peak about the *10 GHz* carrier. Also shown are thresholds to highlight the *3-dB, 6 dB* and *20 dB* bandwidths. For the *1.4 ns* pulse sinewave, the inverses of these bandwidths are *1.6, 1.09* and *0.27 ns*, respectively. While the inverse of the *3-dB* bandwidth is close, it is not the exact inverse of pulse width for this modulation. The exact bandwidth is dependent upon the exact shape of the modulation or envelope; however, the pulse width-bandwidth approximation is extremely useful.

Figure 15.3 illustrates the amplitude as a function of time, also known as the time domain, of two theoretical pulse sinewaves from a *10 GHz* carrier modulated by pulses with cosine tapered edges with full-width half-max (FWHM) pulse widths of *2.8* and *0.7 ns*. These same waveforms can be represented by the combination of the magnitude and phase of the power spectral density as a function of frequency, also known as the frequency domain. Along with the spectrum for a *1.4 ns* pulse. Figure 15.4 shows the normalized magnitude of the associated power spectral density, where it is normalized by the maximum value of the spectrum for each pulse. As expected, the bandwidths are directly proportional to the width of the pulses, as long as the modulation's edge taper is scaled by the same proportion.

The occupied bandwidth requires context to interpret. The FCC defines the occupied bandwidth as the frequency range in which *5%* of the transmit power is below the lower frequency bound and *5%* is above the highest frequency bound. If the signals are weak or ambient signals are high, it becomes difficult to measure the total power and the occupied bandwidth's *5%* bounds. However, the occupied bandwidth is often close to the *20 dB* bandwidth, which is much easier to measure in a real-world environment.

Frequency agile transmissions precipitate the need for a couple more definitions of bandwidth. For example, a frequency agile (CW) pulsed-continuous wave radar may have the same pulse width for its transmission, but the carrier frequency for each pulse may hop to a different frequency as a function of time. Therefore, the instantaneous bandwidth corresponds to the single pulse of interest, which is approximately the inverse of the pulse width. The operational bandwidth that is much larger and contains the entire range of frequencies used operationally. The operational bandwidth must cover the widest instantaneous bandwidth, plus the difference between the highest and lowest carrier frequencies is

$$B_{operational} = f_{c_{max}} - f_{c_{min}} + B_{max_i}$$
Eq. (15.1)

where B_{max_i} is the maximum instantaneous bandwidth. The fractional bandwidth is the last covered and is used much less. The fractional bandwidth (B_{frac}) is the measured *3-dB* bandwidth normalized by the center frequency (f_c), more specifically,

$$B_{frac} = (B_{3dB})/f_c.$$
Eq. (15.2)

Fractional bandwidths have substantial meaning with respect to electromagnetic behavior. Antennas, waveguides and even pieces of chaff have resonant behaviors that are specific electrical dimensions, i.e., physical dimension divided by wavelength, of the devices, such as a half-wave dipole. Making devices operate at large fractional bandwidths often requires special techniques, which is why the original Department of Defense definition of ultra-wideband (UWB) was a fractional bandwidth greater than or equal to *25%*. However, in the FCC's first report and order for UWB devices of unlicensed operation, the bandwidth criteria changed to also include bandwidths greater than *1,500 MHz* to foster more competition in the industry.

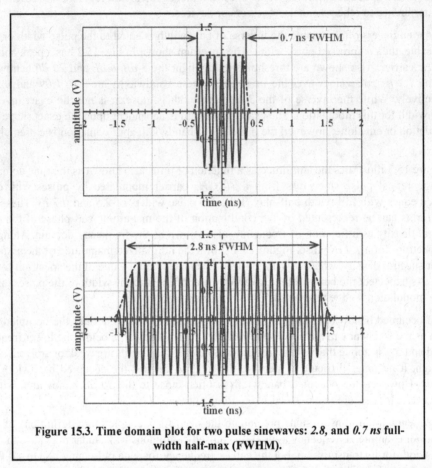

Figure 15.3. Time domain plot for two pulse sinewaves: *2.8*, and *0.7 ns* full-width half-max (FWHM).

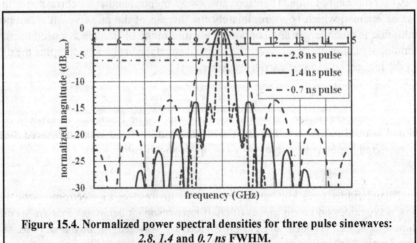

Figure 15.4. Normalized power spectral densities for three pulse sinewaves: *2.8, 1.4* and *0.7 ns* FWHM.

Systems with large fractional bandwidths become challenging to implement. It is easier to implement electronics with smaller fractional bandwidths (< *20%*) due to constraints, such as the gain and directivity flatness of realizable antennas. Therefore, designers often implement wideband radar in the high-frequency bands, such as S-band and higher. These high-frequency bands mean the systems operate with short wavelengths. The gain of an antenna is typically inversely proportional to the beam widths, and directly proportional to the antenna's electrical dimensions, which are the geometric dimensions divided by wavelength. The higher frequency bands often used by wideband radars result in smaller angle or cross-range resolution cells for the same physical size. The coupling of fine range resolution with high angle resolution is the cornerstone of a family of radars called high resolution radars.

For the remainder of this chapter, assume that bandwidth refers to the *3-dB* bandwidth of the data utilized by the signal processor unless specified otherwise. However, the bandwidths for the example systems might not be precisely the *3-dB* bandwidth due to limited available information.

15.2.2. Narrow Band, Medium Band and Wideband

Given the complexities of defining a bandwidth, there is a lack of precision in the radar field to define narrow band, medium band and wideband systems. For the context of this chapter, proceed with the guidelines of bandwidths, and the resulting monostatic radar range resolution shown in Table 15.1. The range resolution for a monostatic radar is a function of the speed of light, c and the compressed pulse width, τ_c, which is also related to the bandwidth, B. It is given by,

$$\Delta R = \frac{c\tau_c}{2} = \frac{c}{2B} \approx \frac{300(m/\mu\sec\ )}{2B}.$$

Eq. (15.3)

Note, the range resolution is independent of the range accuracy, which is a function of random errors such as jitter from circuit noise on digital edges, and biases such as unstable digital edge detection thresholds and variations in oscillator frequencies due to changes in temperature.

These guidelines are based on the range resolution required to complete various functions for objects of sizes for some common defense radar applications, such as detection, track and classification of aircraft, ships/boats and missiles. For example, an early warning air surveillance radar performing a broad search quickly for any single or formation of aircraft will likely use a narrow band waveform to utilize its large resolution cells that may be several times the size of a bomber to quickly cover a large search volume. Once the radar has detected and initiated a track, it may transition to a medium band waveform to improve its track quality while simultaneously isolating individual aircraft.

Table 15.1. Relationship between Bandwidth and Resolution.

Bandwidth Class	Bandwidth (*MHz*)	$\Delta R(m)$
Narrow band	0.03 – 3.0	50 – 5000
Medium band	3.0 – 300	0.5 – 50
Wideband	> 300	< 0.5

By transitioning to a medium band waveform, it fills the space in proximity of the track with resolution cells with a size comparable to a fighter aircraft. The higher quality track may then be handed off to a fire control radar in the form of search cues. The fire control radar will use wideband waveforms to produce small range resolution cells to distinguish individual reflective points or scattering centers along the aircraft to extract details and features of each aircraft. It will also refine the track quality to guide missiles to intercept the aircraft or specific part of the aircraft.

To illustrate this point, Fig. 15.5 depicts a notional missile complex and radar range profiles for three bandwidths. As the bandwidth increases, the range resolution becomes finer and the range profile gets distinct bumps as scattering centers along the missile resolve. Conversely, as the bandwidth decreases, the radar can sample less often to cover the entire range window. During surveillance and acquisition, narrow band waveforms with a range resolution comparable to the entire missile complex, as illustrated by the bottom row, rapidly search for signs of incoming threats. During the missile's phases of flight, various segments will separate, such as a spent boost stage or booster that has exhausted its fuel. The radar will use medium band waveforms with a range resolution nominally the size of a single segment, as shown in the middle range profile to enable precision tracks for critical objects, such as the warhead, the attitude control module (ACM) that orients and/or spin stabilizes the warhead, and the spent booster of the missile complex. Each separation produces debris objects, such as pieces of exploding bolts and bands that held the booster to the rest of the complex. The radar uses wideband waveforms to have fine range resolution to distinguish multiple scattering centers along the critical objects as depicted by the range profile in the top portion of the figure.

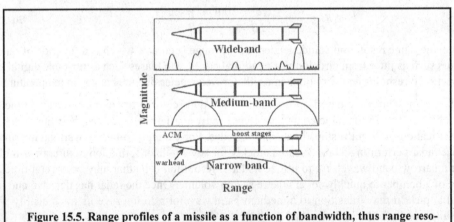

Figure 15.5. Range profiles of a missile as a function of bandwidth, thus range resolution, to search, track, and classify in addition to precision interceptor guidance.

Note that the terms classification, recognition, identification and discrimination are closely related to radar. The nuanced differences are even a function of the user community for a specific radar application. Typically, all of them require radar data from objects, where each object has a set of physical attributes, such as length, composite shape of various materials and locomotion. With the appropriate radar waveforms, which may be composed of more than one pulse, the radar can extract features, which are characteristics dependent on the attributes perceived by the radar, such as range extent, radar cross-section (RCS) and motion induced modulations. The radar compares the set of features to pre-computed feature sets associated with different groups or classes of objects with a means such as a Bayesian classifier. Often, the result is a declaration of the likely object class and an estimate of the probability that the class is correct. Wideband radars often provide a rich selection of candidate features, which may be necessary for robust, reliable algorithms.

Beyond fine range resolution and supporting classification, wideband radars benefit from other performance enhancements. By spreading transmit power over the large bandwidth, the systems have a relatively low power spectral density for low probability of intercept (LPI), non-interference for spectrum sharing or unlicensed operations and, sometimes, channelization. In a converse relationship, systems that use pulse compression can operate "below the noise floor", have increased jam resistance and, sometimes, are more difficult to spoof by an enemy attempting to jam via false target returns. Also, wideband radars often have small blind ranges, where some impulsive (a very short pulse) short-range systems will permit their receivers to enter nonlinear operations that range gating can reject. Finally, wideband radars help counter stealth techniques and chaff since they are a strong function of wavelength.

15.3. Wideband Radar Applications

There are numerous radar systems that require the benefits of wideband waveforms. The following lists wideband radar applications and the associated performance enabled by their bandwidths, where the systems are ordered by increasing bandwidth of the specific example application provided. This is a sampling, not an exhaustive list.

15.3.1. Foliage Penetrating Synthetic Array Radar

Foliage penetrating (FOPEN) radars can "see" (i.e., detect targets) through tree canopies, brush and other vegetation that obscure and conceal the ground surface and/or objects. Synthetic aperture radar (SAR) is a technique where usually either an aircraft or satellite passing an area of interest collects radar data that is processed to generate an image of the radar scatterers. Some uses of FOPEN SAR include terrain mapping, monitoring surface displacement, searching for archaeological structures, and monitoring changes to indicate vehicle movements or other intelligence information. Two primary challenges for this application are image resolution and attenuation, both of which are functions of frequency.

The finer range resolution enabled by the wide bandwidth provides finer image resolution, particularly for a system with a long range and path for a long SAR aperture. For SAR processing, the radar collects data for many transmissions along the path such as the depiction in Fig. 15.6, where the path is often a flight path or satellite trajectory. The voltage values for each range delay is attributed to the cell defined by the angle and range resolution, or resolution cell. As the amplitude from the radar returns from different viewing angles are attributed to the appropriate points in space, the summation will grow faster where objects are reflecting signal and a radar image will form.

One way to visualize the SAR imaging concept is to envision a string tied to an eye dropper and the other end tied to the location corresponding to the radar's antenna during a specific transmission, and an array of drinking glasses (with diameters proportional to the range resolution cells) corresponding to the region to be imaged. The length of the string is proportional to the range delay given by

$$t_{delay} = \frac{2R}{c} = \frac{2R}{300(m/\mu sec\ )}. \qquad \text{Eq. (15.4)}$$

The amount of water in the dropper corresponds to the amplitude at that range delay. Each glass within the antenna's half-power beamwidth (HPBW or θ_{3dB}) gets a deposit of water from the dropper, thus the glasses with water form an arc. Once the amplitude versus range is completed for one position, the exercise is repeated from the next position where the radar collected data. As the process is repeated for more and more antenna positions, the intersection of the arcs will accumulate water faster and indicate the positions of the brightest scatterers to create an image. The constructive and destructive interference of the returns will significantly improve the image when the radar retains coherency of the signal. Note that radars collect samples at fixed time intervals and the image will be in the form of Cartesian coordinates as opposed to spherical coordinates, thus the process will require using the closest sample or interpolating between samples. Backprojection is one name for this type of SAR image formation. There are many and sometimes more computationally efficient ways to generate SAR images, but the result will be similar.

As illustrated in Fig. 15.7, the image's resolution is primarily driven by the range resolution as the aspect angle approaches *90°*. The finer image resolution will aid in distinguishing and identifying targets from the clutter generated by the vegetation. Note that this resolution is two-dimensional, as the component coming out of the page is defined by the beamwidth of the antenna, which is usually much larger than the range resolution.

Larger bandwidths are easier to obtain within higher operational bands, but FOPEN is better at lower operational bands. Two mechanisms come into play when penetrating foliage, absorption and scattering. The radar's transmission will pass through the tree canopy, but the canopy absorbs some of the energy, converting it to heat. This process reduces or attenuates the signal incident to the earth's surface and/or surface targets, thus reducing the signal-to-noise ratio (SNR). Also, the leaves, branches and trunks reflect energy, thus even less energy reaches the intended targets. The SNR is also reduced by scattering, and is compounded by the undesired reflections from the canopy that form clutter, subsequently decreasing the signal-to-clutter ratio (SCR) and the clutter may even hide the signal of interest. Both the absorption and scattering by the foliage reduces the desired signal with a net result that is similar to the 1-way losses approximated by

$$L_{foliage}^{1way} = \begin{cases} 0.45\ f^{0.248}\ d_{tree} & ; 0 < d_{tree} < 14m \\ 0.45\ f^{0.248}\ d_{tree}^{0.588} & ; 14 < d_{tree} < 400m \end{cases} \qquad \text{Eq. (15.5)}$$

where f is the frequency in *GHz*, and d_{tree} is the tree depth in meters. This is illustrated in Fig. 15.8. The foliage attenuation dependency on frequency is why land-mobile voice-communication systems are often assigned to the UHF band to balance antenna size and range. The combination of wide bandwidth for finer SAR image resolution and foliage attenuation means FOPEN SARs typically have a large fractional bandwidth.

An example of a FOPEN SAR is the real-time, autonomous synthetic aperture radar built by SRC, Inc. This radar's intra-pulse frequency modulation waveform is several *MHz* in bandwidth and its center frequency is in the IEEE E-band (alternatively, the NATO D-band). This results in a system with a less than a meter range resolution. The tree depth, d_{tree} is bound as follows,

$$\frac{d_{so}h_{tree}}{h_a} < d_{tree} < \frac{d_{so}h_{tree}}{h_a\cos(\theta_{3dB}/2)} \qquad \text{Eq. (15.6)}$$

where d_{so} is the standoff distance of the radar, h_{tree} is the average tree height, h_a is the radar altitude, and θ_{3dB} is the antenna 3-*dB* beam width. Using Eq. (15.6) an unmanned aerial vehicle at an altitude of *2,000 m* and a standoff distance of *2,000* m, a forest *20 m* high will have a tree depth that varies from *20* to *26 m* across an $\theta_{3dB} = 80°$. The foliage will produce an $L_{foliage}^{1way}$ roughly from *8* to *10 dB*.

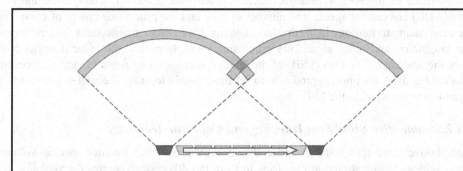

Figure 15.6. Synthetic aperture radars collect radar returns while the antenna is moving, and then process the data as if it were from a single array aperture.

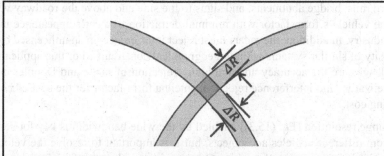

Figure 15.7. The resolution of a SAR image is defined primarily by the range resolution and the viewing geometry of viewing angles of the radar.

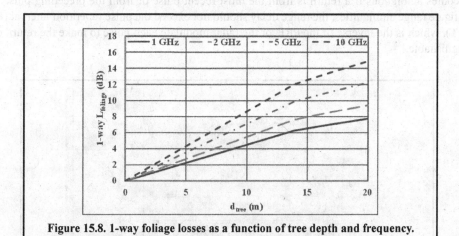

Figure 15.8. 1-way foliage losses as a function of tree depth and frequency.

To reconstruct the received signal, it must be sampled twice the bandwidth, and preferably higher for *2* to *4* oversampling, the ratio of the actual sampling rate to the minimum sampling rate. While oversampling should not introduce additional information, it has utility in analyzing the data and rejecting noise-like signals that are correlated across multiple returns. By collecting waveforms at a higher rate, the FOPEN radar may use a dozen or more returns to reject clutter outside of the HPBW through coherent processing. However, analog-to-digital converter (ADC) conversion speeds and number of bits, and the processing power of computers have been pacing technology items that have heavily driven radar architectures. To get the gain from integration and other algorithms processing multiple pulses, the radar designer must ensure the least significant bit (LSB) of the ADC is dominated by noise to get the necessary statistical trends. A common approach is to set the RF gain to make the root-mean-square of the random noise equal to the LSB.

15.3.2. Automotive Blind Spot Warning and Collision Avoidance

Automotive blind spot warning and collision avoidance radars monitor specific volumes around vehicles, as illustrated in Fig. 15.9, to warn the driver or to control the vehicle's systems to mitigate collisions. These applications require accurate measurements of relative distance and velocity to predict potential collisions. The radar may use Doppler processing to measure the range rate, which is related to velocity. Collision avoidance has the added complications in terms of rejecting vehicles in the opposite, adjacent and possibly curved lanes while rejecting guard rails, bridge abutments, and signs to the side and above the roadway while fitting within the vehicle's form factor with minimal detraction to a car's appearance in a very cost-driven industry. In addition, the radars must reject interference on an unlicensed basis due to a high density of similar systems without geographical constraints. For this application, the primary challenges are the accuracy and ambiguity rejection of range and Doppler measurements, channelization and interference rejection, antenna form factor for the desired coverage, and minimizing cost.

The fine range resolution (Eq. (15.3)) enabled by the wide bandwidth is key for separating the returns from different vehicles and objects, but it is important to resolve the velocity and reject ambiguities in both range and velocity. Often, a single radar waveform is composed of a sequence or train of pulses with the same center frequency and constant pulse repetition frequency (PRF) that enable the radar to measure Doppler shift and to improve SNR. However, it becomes ambiguous if a return is from the most recent pulse or from the preceding pulse. To mitigate range ambiguities, the range delay should not exceed the pulse repetition interval (PRI or T), which is the inverse of the PRF, or the radar modulate each pulse to make the return distinguishable.

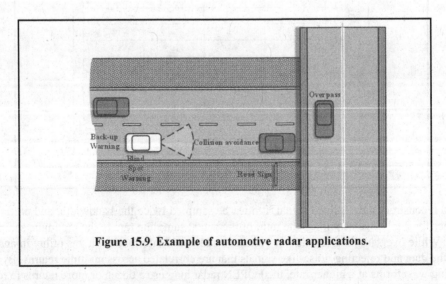

Figure 15.9. Example of automotive radar applications.

The relationship for the maximum unambiguous range, R_u, is

$$R_u < \frac{c}{2f_r} = \frac{cT}{2} \qquad \text{Eq. (15.7)}$$

where f_r is the pulse repetition frequency (PRF), and $T = 1/f_r$ is the period. As a target's range changes, there is a range rate that produces a shift in all the frequencies that compose the target's return. This is a Doppler shift, f_d, that is analogous to the shift in pitch a person hears as a race car speeds by, where the frequency is higher as it approaches or is closing, and the frequency is lower as it pulls away or is opening. The Fourier transform of the returns from a pulse train produces spectral lines at intervals of the PRF plus a Doppler shift. The radar can measure this Doppler shift and then convert it to the range rate $\dot{R}$ relative to a closing target defined by

$$\dot{R} < v \cos \alpha = \frac{cf_d}{2f_0} \qquad \text{Eq. (15.8)}$$

where f_0 is the radar operational frequency, the angle, α is the angle between the radial from the radar to the target, and the direction of the relative velocity, v. Since the spectral lines are periodic, the maximum unambiguous Doppler shift must be less than the PRF. Thus, the unambiguous range rate is,

$$\dot{R}_u < \frac{cf_r}{2f_0}. \qquad \text{Eq. (15.9)}$$

However, the Doppler and range rate ambiguities may be resolved by calculating the change in two position updates, thus retaining the accuracy of Doppler processing.

Electromagnetic compatibility is a key factor in automotive applications. The systems must be able to reject interference from an unusually high density of similar or identical radars without any geographic restrictions, and other ambient transmissions independent of national spectrum management. A dominant approach is to utilize frequency bands above X-band. These upper bands are less congested because time required for technological advances in radar RF components were necessary, thus the lower bands became congested with legacy systems. In addition, other radars and communication systems that require long range tend to avoid these higher frequencies, because of increased atmospheric attenuation by oxygen molecules and water vapor. These upper bands have the additional benefit of shorter wavelengths, which means smaller antennas to achieve the required HPBW as indicated by Eq. (15.10) and which are cosmetically less obtrusive. Additionally, modulating the pulses with channel encoding, such as phase or frequency shift keying, may provide interference rejection

$$\theta_{3dB} \approx \frac{\lambda}{D} \qquad \text{Eq. (15.10)}$$

where D is the maximum antenna dimension in the plane of θ.

For blind spot and back-up warning radars, short-pulse UWB systems are also applicable. The short-pulse systems typically have very low average transmit power. In addition, the short transmit pulse results in a small blind range in proximity of the radar, i.e., the radar is not transmitting while collecting data at very short ranges, which eases dynamic range requirements. The short-pulse radars may allow some receiver components to go into compression during transmission. The variety of automotive applications and the associated production volumes are major technology drivers. The industrial demand continues to reduce the cost, size, weight and power consumption. The roles of automotive radars are expanding with the evolution of autonomous vehicles. The automotive applications may become the most prolific radar indus-try, while making radar technology more accessible for other applications.

An example of an automotive radar is the AC100 by ZF TRW Automotive Holding Corp. with advertised applications for adaptive cruise control, pedestrian and vehicle collision warn-ing and emergency braking (ZF, 2020). This radar uses a frequency shift key (FSK) modulated waveform with a *400 MHz* bandwidth centered about *77 GHz* in the W-band (NATO M-band). This results in *37.5 cm* range resolution and a fractional bandwidth of *0.52%*. At *77 GHz*, the atmospheric attenuation is approximately *0.4 dB/km* at sea level, depending upon weather con-ditions. The AC100 supports two modes of dual low- and high-speed collision avoidance. The two modes allow the system to use different fields of view and ranges suited for the situations. In the low-speed mode, the radar has view of *70°*, and in high-speed mode it has a maximum range of *200 m*. Therefore, the attenuation due to oxygen and water vapor is less than *0.2 dB*.

15.3.3. Space Object Identification

Space object identification (SOI) radars observe and monitor man-made space-borne objects. While this application includes assessing the functions and capabilities of foreign sat-ellites, such radars also identify various objects and debris (space junk), and perform damage assessments of space vehicles. To support identifications, the systems typically require fine range resolution. Since the operational ranges are very large to observe exo-atmospheric objects from *100 km* to geosynchronous orbits at *35,800 km*, the angle resolution also must be fine to separate objects in cross-range and to focus the beams for high antenna gain. In addi-tion, a common technique employed is inverse synthetic aperture radar (ISAR), a sister tech-nique to SAR, except the image takes advantage of the object's rotation instead of antenna motion. The primary challenges for this application are fine resolution in terms of range, angle and Doppler, and receiving adequate signal at useful ranges. In this case, the angle resolution, ΔR_{cross}, is related to the antenna θ_{3dB} in radians by

$$\theta_{3dB} \approx \frac{\lambda}{2\Delta R_{cross}},$$ **Eq. (15.11)**

where $R \gg \Delta R_{cross}$ is assumed and λ is the wavelength.

Achieving adequate SNR is fundamental to all radar applications, and the single-pulse, monostatic radar SNR dependency on the range, R, due to spherical divergence is given by

$$SNR = \frac{P_t G A_e \sigma \tau}{(4\pi)^2 R^4 k T_0 FL} = \frac{P_t G^2 \lambda^2 \sigma \tau}{(4\pi)^3 R^4 k T_0 FL},$$ **Eq. (15.12)**

where P_t is the radar peak power, G is the antenna again, A_e is the antenna effective aperture, σ is the target RCS, τ is the pulse width, k is Boltzmann's constant, T_0 is the temperature and is equal to *290* Kelvin, F is the noise figure, and L is the total radar 2-way losses. The loss due to spherical divergence alone is *80* to*180* dB relative to *1 km*. Therefore, the SOI radars usually are high power. They may use an active steered array composed of separate transmitters to increase the total transmit power. They usually have large apertures such as par-abolic dishes or planar arrays with dimensions of hundreds of wavelengths that produce high gain and fine resolution angles. Also, they usually use relatively long pulse widths while retaining the bandwidth necessary for fine range resolution resulting in a high pulse compres-sion gain. Pulse compression gain, $G_{comp} = B\tau$, is achieved by distorting the transmit pulses phase in a manner that stretches the duration of the pulse and reduces the peak to prevent the power amplifier from compressing, and then correcting for the phase distortion to recover the pulse resolution and build up the signal's peak power comparable to a high-amplitude short pulse, where the effective increase in amplitude after signal processing, τ is the pulse width and B is the bandwidth of the transmitted pulse. The introduction of pulse compression was a key advancement for radars.

The ISAR images of space objects are a valuable tool for analysts. To generate an ISAR image, the radar's viewing or aspect angle must change over time. The relative rotation of the object produces Doppler shifts that are proportional to the cross-range offset of a scatterer from the center gravity of the object. It may be easier to envision the mechanism by thinking of a theoretical cone that is tumbling end-over-end and has a scatterer at its tip, see Fig. 15.10. When the cone is perpendicular to the radial, the Doppler shift, due to target's motion, reaches its maximum. If the angular velocity is constant, then the velocity is directly proportional to the distance from the center gravity (CG) and the tip of the cone. By transmitting uniform pulse trains, the radar collects a coherent time history of the returns with respect to range. After aligning the returns such that the range is relative to the object's center gravity, a Fourier transform across the time history for each range delay will generate a sequence of two-dimensional Doppler images of the object. The cross-range resolution of the image is defined by the object's rotation rate, the moment arm of the scatterer to the CG as,

$$f_d(t) = \frac{2\dot{R}(t)}{\lambda} = \frac{4\pi f_{rotation}}{\lambda} L\cos(2\pi f_{rotation})$$

Eq. (15.13)

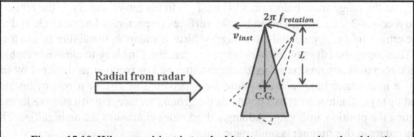

Figure 15.10. When an object is tracked by its center gravity, the object's rotation produces an instantaneous velocity that is proportional to the moment arm d, thus Doppler vs. range produces an ISAR image.

The radar's Doppler resolution is given by the time on target, T_{OT}, defined by the pulse repetition interval (PRI) and the number of pulses in the pulse train illuminating the object. An example of a low earth orbit (altitude between *160* to *2,000 km*) SOI radar is ARPA Lincoln C-band observables radar (ALCOR) (Mostly, 2012; Hall, 2012) that was manufactured by the Massachusetts Institute of Technology (MIT), Lincoln Lab for the U.S. Advanced Research Projects Agency, which was renamed to Defense Advanced Research Projects Agency (DARPA). In 1972, ALCOR became the first long-range, wideband radar. This radar's linear frequency modulation (LFM) waveform has a programmable bandwidth with a maximum of *512 MHz* centered about *5.7 GHz* in the C-band (NATO G-band). This results in a range resolution down to *30 cm* and a fractional bandwidth up to *9%*. The antenna's *12.2 m* diameter (i.e., parabolic dish antenna) provides approximate *0.3°* HPBW and *55 dBi* gain (i.e., G_{comp}). A maximum PRF of *323 Hz* yields an Ru of *464 km* and a compression gain roughly *35 dB*. In 1973, ALCOR assisted in repairing the U.S. Skylab by producing images aiding analysts to assess issues. ALCOR can generate roughly *200* images of space objects per year. The SOI mission at the Kwajalein Atoll is now augmented with a millimeter wave radar at Roi Namur (Stambaugh, 2012). After several technological advances and upgrades, the 2012 Roi Namur millimeter wave (MMW) radar's dual linear FM transmissions provide a *4 GHz* bandwidth centered about *35 GHz*, to produce a range resolution of 4 cm and images with 6 cm resolution.

15.3.4. Ground Perimeter Surveillance

Ground perimeter surveillance radars are a relatively new tool to assist with security of borders, military installations and sites with high-value assets, including airports and piers. The radars may need to operate in a variety of environments spanning urban areas, forests and waterways. These environments often have a large amount of clutter including sources that move, such as windblown trees. Trying to detect and distinguish slow moving targets that might have small RCS in or near high traffic areas, and of areas with wildlife complicate this application. For this application, the primary challenges are having adequate range and/or Doppler resolution to support algorithms to reduce the number of false alarms, whether due to clutter or undesired targets, while maintaining the required probability of detection and correct identification of the targets of interest, which may include inferring intent.

Ground perimeter surveillance lends itself to using monostatic, bistatic or multistatic radars, as illustrated in Fig. 15.11. A monostatic radar (e.g., $T_{x1} \rightarrow R_{x1}$) with an omni-directional antenna can determine the range to the target, but not bearing, hence forming a spherical ambiguity surface. A bistatic radar (e.g., $T_{x1} \rightarrow R_{x2}$) with omni-directional antennas has an ellipsoidal ambiguity surface with foci at the radar antenna locations and is defined by

$$\Delta t = \frac{(R_1 + R_2)}{c}$$

Eq. (15.14)

where R_1 is the range from transmitter-1 (i.e., T_{x1}) to the target and R_2 is the range from the target to receiver-2 (i.e., R_{x2}). The ambiguity surfaces respectively form a circle and an ellipse on the earth's surface. A potential advantage of bistatic radars is the ability to use the ellipses to only scan along the edges of the perimeter or fence line. One way to eliminate ambiguities is to use a directional antenna on either the transmitter and/or receiver as depicted by (a). Alternatively, a monostatic radar and a bistatic radar depicted by (b), or a pair of bistatic radars depicted by (c) will intersect at two points on the ground surface, significantly reducing but not eliminating the position ambiguity. Adding a third radar eliminates the ambiguities. The use of multiple radars in this manner is multistatic radar.

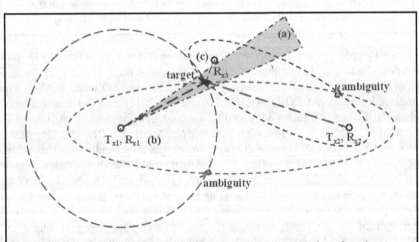

Figure 15.11. Perimeter surveillance may use monostatic radars (e.g.,
$T_{x1} \rightarrow R_{x1}$**), bistatic (e.g., $T_{x1} \rightarrow R_{x2}$), or multi-static, which is a combination**
of multiple radars, but direction antennas or multiple radars are needed to
eliminate position ambiguities.

The RCS of a target is a function of the bistatic angle. As illustrated in Fig. 15.12, there are three RCS regions: (1) backscattering, (2) bistatic scattering and (3) forward scattering. When the bistatic angle is very small, the entire backscattering region is comparable to a monostatic radar, which is typically what people mean by RCS without modifiers. When the bistatic angle is close to 180°, the forward scattering may be thought of as shadowing caused by the target blocking the energy directly from the transmitter to the receiver. The forward scattering of a target can be very dramatic and detectable, but the radar loses range information. The behavior of bistatic RCS is between forward and backscattering.

Ground perimeter surveillance radars operate in high clutter conditions, and may need to detect targets moving slowly, tolerate wind motion of foliage, and distinguish people and vehicles from wildlife. These typically rely on fine range resolution to support clutter rejection and identification. However, motion is an important distinguishing characteristic extracted by moving target indicator (MTI) or Doppler processing.

The MTI and Doppler algorithms are two different methods with the primary goal of rejecting near-stationary environment clutter. Both approaches use a time history of coherent radar returns from a train of pulses, where the amplitude of the returns is comprised of the signal, noise and clutter, as described for the ith pulse and j^{th} range bin by

$$v(i,j) = s(i,j) + w(i,j) + n(i,j) \qquad \text{Eq. (15.15)}$$

where s is the radar signal, w is the clutter signal, and n is the noise signal.

The MTI filters are often associated with low PRF systems. In this case, the radar takes the amplitude from a set of k prior pulses, calculates the average corresponding to each range cell, and then subtracts the average from the more recently received pulse ($v(i,j)$). More precisely,

$$v_{MTI}(i,j) = v(i,j) - \frac{1}{k} \sum_{m=i-k}^{i-1} v(m,j) . \qquad \text{Eq. (15.16)}$$

If the clutter is quasi-stationary during the time to collect $k+1$ pulses, then the clutter signal will be subtracted. Since the noise will be independent for each pulse, averaging reduces the noise power by a factor of k and becomes negligible even with a relatively small number of integrations, such as $k \geq 4$. The number of pulses integrated to make a background waveform and the subtraction effectively make a bandpass in terms of time variations at each range cell. If an MTI radar uses $k = 1$, then difference doubles the noise power. Note, the summation in this MTI equations is a form of finite impulse response filter, although a form of infinite impulse response filter can be effective.

Doppler processing is often associated with higher PRF radars and provides more flexibility in filtering motion. A fast Fourier transform (FFT) of each function of pulse number for each range cell generates a range-Doppler-intensity array. Then the radar can use bandpass filters to reject and select returns with specific range rates. After filtering, an inverse FFT (IFFT) of each function of Doppler frequency will produce a range-time-intensity array for return with the selected range rates. An additional advantage of Doppler processing is the possibility of extracting frequency features to distinguish the method of locomotion of vehicles, bipeds and quadrupeds.

An example of a ground perimeter surveillance is the monostatic Symphony Airfield Radar System (ARS) by Harris (L3Harris, n.d. a; L3Harris, n.d. b). This radar uses an FM continuous wave (FMCW) waveform with *600 Hz* bandwidth centered about *77 GHz* in the W-band (NATO M-band). This results in *25 cm* range resolution and a fractional bandwidth of *0.8%*.

The ARS scans the ground level *360°* at a rate of *216°/sec* with *1°* azimuth and *3°* elevation beamwidths. Harris advertises the ARS can detect a person at a range of *1,000 m* and a vehicle at *1,600 m*. Visible light and infrared cameras augment the radar by aiding identification up to *1,000 m*.

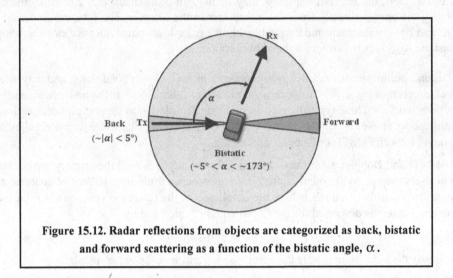

Figure 15.12. Radar reflections from objects are categorized as back, bistatic and forward scattering as a function of the bistatic angle, α.

15.3.5. Pavement Profiling and Inspection

One of the many applications of subsurface or ground penetrating radars (GPRs) is non-invasive inspection and profiling of roadways and runways to detect manufacturing defects, validate the layer thickness and search for structural degradation. These surfaces are under many different forms of stress, strain and wear. If they are not constructed correctly, they usually experience premature and costly failures. In some case, the failure has caused cave-in sickness, where there is erosion of the roadbed beneath the top surface and, over time, the upper layers collapse and may form a pothole. Filling potholes is problematic because the edges of the patch will not bond as well as the original asphalt, and the friction of tires will oblate the edges of the patch. The sooner and less intrusive a problem can be detected and addressed, the less expensive and more effective the repair. However, the layers of the roadbed and tell-tale voids beneath the surface are relatively small, thus requiring a wide bandwidth to achieve the necessary resolution, but at low frequencies that will penetrate the layers of different media. Table 15.2 provides notional layers of an asphalt roadway, along with ranges for the thicknesses and relative dielectric constants.

The range resolution, RCS and attenuation within materials are primarily dependent upon the electrical characteristics of the materials or media, specifically the permittivity, conductivity and, less often, the permeability. Note that the permeability of most nonferrous materials (ones without iron) are close to that of a vacuum, i.e., $\mu_0 = 4\pi \cdot 10^{-7} H/m$; therefore, it is often negligible. Although, occasionally assuming the relative permeability, μ_r, is *1* is a poor assumption given the numerous materials used as aggregate, including steel slag. The permittivity is often described as the relative dielectric, ε_r, which is the permittivity of the materials normalized by the permittivity of a vacuum or free space, $\varepsilon_0 = 8.85 \cdot 10^{-7} F/m$. In most cases, conductivity of earthen materials is dominated by aqueous solutions.

Table 15.2. Notional Layers of an Asphalt Roadway.

Thickness (mm)	Layer	Example Material	Relative Dielectric, ε_r
	air		*1*
75 - 150	*surface course*	*asphalt*	*4 - 8*
100 - 300	*base course*	*crushed aggregate*	*6 - 8*
100 - 300	*sub-base course*	*low cost crushed aggregate*	*6 - 8*
	subgrade	*earth fill*	*5 - 16*

In the case of roadways, the surface course should provide a layer that keeps water out, thus the lower layers tend to be dry, and conductivity is near *0 Mhos*. However, the surface may crack or segregate, allowing water into the other layers, which causes the dielectric constant and conductivity to increase, e.g., fresh water, (i.e., $\varepsilon_r = 80$, $\mu_r = 1$ and $\sigma \rightarrow 1mMho$). The conductivity results in increasing loss that grows with frequency. Using radars to estimate the relative dielectric constants of the layers may facilitate the assessment of the quality of a roadway structure (Saarenketo, 2006).

The electromagnetic plane wave propagation is dependent upon the exponent as a function of the electrical characteristics as given by

$$E_y = E_0 e^{j\omega t - (\alpha + j\beta)x} = E_0 e^{j\omega t - x\sqrt{j\omega\mu(\sigma + j\omega\varepsilon)}}, \qquad \text{Eq. (15.17)}$$

where

$$\alpha = Re\{\sqrt{j\omega\mu(\sigma + j\omega\varepsilon)}\} = Re\{\sqrt{j\omega\mu_0\mu_r(\sigma + j\omega\varepsilon_0\varepsilon_r)}\}. \qquad \text{Eq. (15.18)}$$

The real portion of the exponent, α, in the wave equation corresponds to loss per length or attenuation factor, and is usually dominated by the conductivity. The attenuation is the key limiting factor to how deep the radars can penetrate, where the losses usually decrease as the frequency decreases; thus, the motivation for GPRs to operate at lower frequencies. The imaginary portion of the exponent, β, is the phase constant, the inverse of which is the speed of electromagnetic plane waves through the media. This exponent effectively scales the electrical dimensions within the media

For low-loss, non-ferromagnetic dielectric media, the velocity is approximated by

$$v \approx \frac{1}{\sqrt{\mu\varepsilon}} = \frac{1}{\sqrt{\mu_0\mu_r\varepsilon_0\varepsilon_r}} = \frac{c}{\sqrt{\mu_r\varepsilon_r}}, \qquad \text{Eq. (15.19)}$$

and the monostatic radar range resolution changes

$$\Delta R_{media} \approx \frac{c}{2B\sqrt{\varepsilon_r}}. \qquad \text{Eq. (15.20)}$$

This also means techniques such as imaging become substantially more complicated, because variations in range delays are a function of the changing electrical property, where the dominant effect is due to the dielectric constant. The electrical scaling of objects also changes the RCS. In addition, the reflection from the interface of a pair of non-metallic media is related to the dielectric constants as approximated by Snell's Law for lossless dielectrics in accordance with

$$\rho_\perp = \frac{\cos\theta_i - \sqrt{(\varepsilon_2/\varepsilon_1) - (\sin\theta_i)^2}}{\cos\theta_i + \sqrt{(\varepsilon_2/\varepsilon_1) - (\sin\theta_i)^2}},$$ **Eq. (15.21)**

$$\rho_{ll} = \frac{-(\varepsilon_2/\varepsilon_1)\cos\theta_i + \sqrt{(\varepsilon_2/\varepsilon_1) - (\sin\theta_i)^2}}{(\varepsilon_2/\varepsilon_1)\cos\theta_i + \sqrt{(\varepsilon_2/\varepsilon_1) - (\sin\theta_i)^2}}.$$ **Eq. (15.22)**

All parameters in Eqs. (15.21) and (15.22) are shown in Fig. 15.13. The range and variability of relative permittivity of road construction materials usually produce discernible reflections at the layer interfaces, although some pairings of materials may result in subtle reflections. Voids filled with air or water, and metallic objects usually provide stronger reflections. The range and variability of relative permittivity of road construction materials usually produce discernible reflections at the layer interfaces, although some pairings of materials may result in subtle reflections. Voids filled with air or water, and metallic objects usually provide stronger reflections.

Typical pavement profiling and inspection radars use either short-pulse or LFM waveforms to achieve bandwidths in an excess of *700 MHz* often centered around *1 GHz* in the UHF/L-bands (NATO C/D-bands). Using fractional bandwidths of *70%* or greater introduces design challenges, such as low-loss and low-dispersion antennas, where dispersion in this context is a variation in group velocity across the bandwidth that produces a phase distortion. However, the need for high resolution at frequencies that can penetrate the media is necessary. While *700 MHz* corresponds to *21 cm* in the air, it will be approximately *10.5 cm* in a material with a dielectric constant of *4*. Profilers often collect a larger series of data as it travels along a roadway.

The returns collected during the radar's path may be processed with techniques such as 2-D deconvolution, which can be considered a cousin to SAR processing, to resolve the layer boundaries. However, the deconvolution process is complicated by the variations of electrical properties within a layer. Since these radars operate in a spectrum that is heavily occupied by legacy and often high-power systems, the pavement inspection radars often use very low average transmit power such as less than *1 mW*, and are shielded to prevent and reject above-ground emissions. Despite the wide, yet low, density of pavement inspection radars, the FCC rules implemented in 2002 significantly decreased the use of these devices (MDOT, 2006).

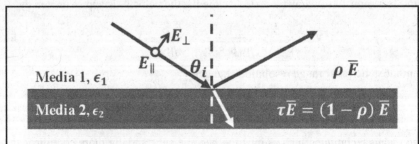

Figure 15.13. Incident vertical, $E_\perp$ and horizontal, $E_{||}$ electric field reflection, ρ and transmission at interface of a pair of lossless dielectric slabs.

15.3.6. Wall-Penetrating Radar for Detecting People

Wall-penetrating radars that are not used to inspect construction are primarily used by law enforcement and the military for situational awareness and for searching for people, although this application is not currently widespread. Walls, support structures, plumbing, furniture and so forth make a very congested radar environment. Not only do returns from these objects create clutter, but they also present returns associated with multipath and shadowing, where the radar senses the "disappearance" of clutter return due to blockage by a moving object. The multi-path and shadowing effects make it difficult to determine the number of people present. Fine range resolution is important to isolate returns from different objects while providing the additional benefit of covertness, as threatening entities may be scanning the RF bands for situational awareness. Like GPRs, these systems trend towards lower frequencies for better penetration. In addition, the lower frequencies also decrease the defocusing effects of some materials, such as that caused by the walls and ribs in cinder blocks, a commonly used building material worldwide. However, wall penetrating radar systems trend towards higher frequencies to reduce antenna size, increase gain and improve cross-range resolution. Selecting the operating bandwidth is performance balance.

The effects of various mechanisms on a wall-penetrating radar can be illustrated with short-pulse, UWB radars. The short-pulse system transmits a quasi-impulse, then samples the waveform directly without down conversion. The shortpulse provides fine range resolution and helps mitigate the close-in blind range, where the receiver cannot detect signals when the radar is transmitting, just like a person cannot hear when they are shouting. To resolve targets to a few centimeters requires a bandwidth exceeding *1 GHz*. As discovered by Nyquist, to capture all the information within a signal, the sampler and the associated analog-to-digital converter (ADC) must sample twice the bandwidth, thus a sampling rate in excess of *2 GHz*. The number of bits and sampling rates of ADCs is a historical limitation of radars. To operate with lower cost ADCs with slower sampling rates, the short-pulse radars rely on the target being quasi-stationary during a scan of the range swath, thus careful control of delays means multiple pulses can be used to artificially sample at a frequency beyond the ADC capabilities. This precision aliasing technique is also employed by many digital sampling oscilloscopes.

Figure 15.14 is an example of two such waveforms, a wall penetrating radar with and without a person in proximity, where the difference is almost imperceptible. Before the radar transmits, the receiver is only receiving noise. There is then a large clutter signal as energy is radiated directly from the transmit antenna into the receive antenna. This large signal is permitted to force the low noise amplifier on the receiver to go to compression, because it will be time gated out. As the operator holds this radar against a wall, returns from the wall, and potentially a person directly on the other side of the wall, arrive before the radar completes transmitting the shortpulse. There is also a tremendous amount of clutter generated due to returns from the building and its contents. Figure 15.15 shows the subtraction of the previous pair of waveforms. In this case, most of the clutter vanishes, although there is some residual. However, the return from the person next to the wall is clearly evident. Around the range of *2.7 m*, there is also another return that is either caused by multipath or shadowing. While that response appears small, it will become sizable when the radar corrects for R^4 due to spherical divergence, thus the return amplitude, *V*, at *3 m* is multiplied by *40 dB* or *10,000* relative to the return at *0.3 m*.

Figure 15.15 also illustrates the process of converting sample number to the range from the radar to the target. The radar is collecting samples at different range bins, consequently we can transform the sample number to sampling time, to range delay relative to the transmission and finally to range.

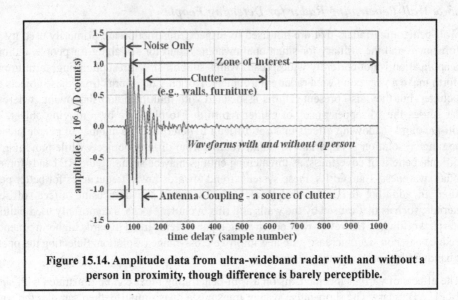

Figure 15.14. Amplitude data from ultra-wideband radar with and without a person in proximity, though difference is barely perceptible.

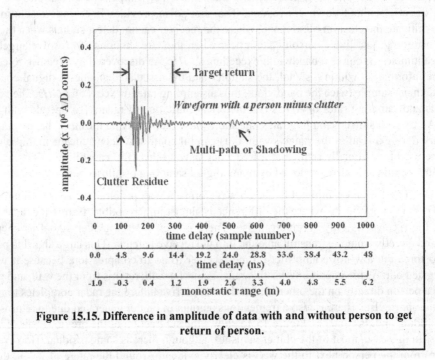

Figure 15.15. Difference in amplitude of data with and without person to get return of person.

The electromagnetic wave transmitted by radars does not propagate through metals. Therefore, wall-penetrating radars will not be effective with metal walled buildings. However, the radar should test to determine if it is being held against a metallic wall, and it should alert the operator, as needed.

Wall-penetrating radars often rely on motion to isolate the returns from people, subsequently the use of MTI and Doppler processing as described for perimeter surveillance radars. The motions that stand out the most are walking, running and crawling, as the reflection from the target's entire body is changing in range, providing more opportunities to detect the motion.

However, radars typically can detect breathing and postural sway, the body's natural, subtle but continuous position adjustments to maintain balance. Breathing when the chest is perpendicular to the radial is easier to detect because the rising and falling of the chest produces a discernible change in range hence phase, as opposed to the chest being parallel with the radial and detecting the subtle change in magnitude as the chest expands and contracts. Some systems go further and claim to be able to detect the very small changes associated with heartbeat, while others try to assess the position of the people, i.e., lying, sitting or standing, or carrying a weapon to distinguish threats from bystanders.

Note that radar operators holding the radars also have a postural sway and are breathing. If the radar is hand-held, it will appear as if its surroundings are moving; therefore, wall penetrating radars often are held against the wall, mounted on a tripod, or operated remotely. For hand-held units, the design must minimize the antenna back lobe to prevent false alarms caused by the operator's motions. Unfortunately, the operator may be detectable due to reflections from the wall immediately in front of the radar.

An example of a wall-penetrating radar is the RadarVision™ that was manufactured by Time Domain Corporation (Gauthier, 2002). This radar's impulsive waveform has a bandwidth of *1,400 MHz* centered around *2 GHz* within the L/S-bands (NATO D/E bands). This results in a *6.8 cm* range resolution and a fractional bandwidth of *70%*. The RadarVision for law enforcement was a product submitted under the first FCC waiver for unlicensed operation of UWB radars, the precursor to the FCC's first report and order on UWB devices. The radar also used pulse-to-pulse biphase modulation, i.e., the pulses were multiplied by *-1* or *+1*. This mitigated range ambiguities associated with its 10 MHz PRF, spread its emissions uniformly within its bandwidth to make it more noise-like and covert, and randomized ambient inference that was mitigated via coherent integration. While the initial radar of this product line only indicated motion within set ranges, the subsequent RadarVision 2000™ and its military variant, Soldier-Vision 2000™, cycled through an array of antennas and used SAR processing to generate an image after an MTI algorithm to provide the operator a floor plan view of moving and stationary people, such as the sample shown in Fig. 15.16.

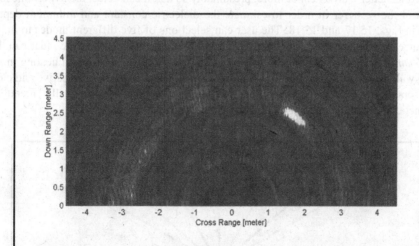

Figure 15.16. RadarVision 2000^{TM} image of a person walking behind a brick wall (Barnes, 2001).

15.3.7. Noninvasive Construction Scanning

Radars are also used to perform noninvasive construction scanning to detect various metallic and nonmetallic objects within walls and to aid in avoiding damaging items embedded within walls and floors. The simplest of these devices may be limited to stud finders that detect studs through thicker wall materials than competing sensor technologies. Some high-end devices provide more information about the object embedded within the wall, such as the number of objects and the precision of the information. Such devices often operate at very short ranges, from 0 to 20 cm, and may need to provide precision distance measurements, such as less than 1 cm. This helps to prevent damaging structures that are difficult to repair such as rebar, and hazards such as energized electrical wiring during activities like drilling and cutting.

Some of the techniques discussed in regards to GPR and wall-penetrating radars are applicable for this application as well. Compared to sensors that rely on inductance, radars have the advantage of being able to detect metallic and non-metallic objects, and some can even indicate whether a plastic pipe is filled with water or air. When the cost point allows, other sensors may be combined with the radar, such as a lower frequency inductive coil or an electromagnetic field sensor tuned for the local power grid for sensor fusion enhancement. The supply and demand for providing desired functionality for a price that the market will bear is very challenging, as the final cost of a simple stud finder for homeowners may need a cost point around *$10*, but precision piece for a specialty contractor may cost up to *$700*. Radars have been slowly but steadily increasing the number of applications around construction sites and home repair.

A sophisticated, non-invasive construction scanning radar is the D-tect^{TM} 150 by Bosch (Bosch, 2018). Its UWB waveform has a *3,300 MHz* bandwidth centered about *3.85 GHz* in the S-band (NATO F-band). The corresponding fractional bandwidth is *86%*. In air, the range resolution would be *4 cm*, although the resolution will be finer within a material. The user's manual lists an accuracy of *0.5* cm for both estimating the center of pipes and drilling depth. The device is mechanically scanned in a straight line, where it needs to scan a minimum of *10 cm* and works better with *60 cm* or more, presumably so that it can detect the hyperbolic migration path of the scatterer in order to estimate the dielectric constant and minimum depth, as depicted in Figs. 15.17 and 15.18. The user can select one of five different modes to improve performance based on the material being inspected. The manual indicates the radar can detect objects *6 cm* deep in universal mode, *15 cm* in concrete mode, *8 cm* in panel heating mode, *6 cm* in drywall mode and *6 cm* in hollow block mode. The device also has inductive and electric field sensors to provide a fused assessment on whether the object is non-metallic, metallic but not magnetic, or metallic and magnetic, and whether the object is electrified.

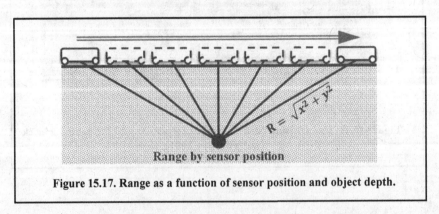

Figure 15.17. Range as a function of sensor position and object depth.

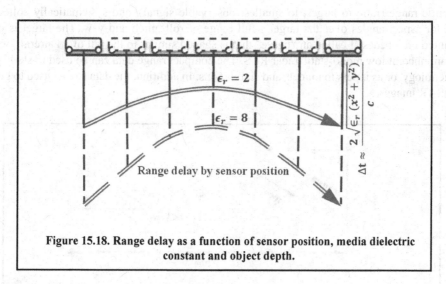

Figure 15.18. Range delay as a function of sensor position, media dielectric constant and object depth.

15.3.8. Industrial Robot Control

The number of industrial applications for wideband radar systems is growing rapidly as the cost, size and accuracy of the radars improve. Radars provide a distinct advantage in industrial settings where dust, fluids or other optical obscurants are present. Wideband radars can aid in precision and accuracy of position and velocity measurements for industrial robot control.

An example of an industrial robot control radar is the Omniradar RIC60A by Staal Technologies (Staal, 2020). The RIC60A uses a FMCW waveform to achieve a *7,000 MHz* bandwidth centered around *60.5 GHz* in the V-band (NATO M-band). By using the higher, less populated band, the radar has a fraction bandwidth of *12%*.

Radars employing FMCW waveforms usually modulate the frequency in a sinusoidal, linear sawtooth or, as shown in Fig. 15.19, a triangular manner. When the radar's returns are correlated with a replica of the transmitted waveform, the demodulated output's positive and negative frequency plateaus are proportional to the range. Thus, filters can be used to extract the range values. However, a moving target would inject a Doppler frequency shift that appears similar to a different range.

As shown in Fig. 15.20, the Doppler shift adds to both the demodulated output's lower and upper bounds. Therefore, the system can quickly measure both range and Doppler shift (thus range rate) by respectively measuring the difference and the sum of the demodulated frequencies. In a cluttered environment, a Fourier transformation of the demodulated output will produce a pulse compressed range profile, where the frequency corresponds to the radar's range.

15.3.9. Compact Radar Range

Compact radar ranges are test sites that collect RCS data from scale models of targets, such as spacecraft, aircraft, vehicles and ships. This is for when collecting data on full-sized targets is not desired or practical. Compact ranges can produce high-fidelity data over very wide bandwidth scaled directly with the model. That is, a *1:32* scale model fighter aircraft scanned at f_0 will be equivalent to a full-size fighter scanned at $f_0/32$. Some advantages of a compact range include independence of weather, high-quality calibration, very high SNR measurements, elimination of clutter due to walls covered with electromagnetic absorber material, high dynamic range (ratio to largest to smallest observable signal), and systematically collecting data for aspect angles over the target's full range of roll, pitch and yaw. The target is often mounted on a pedestal called an "ogive" that is shaped similar to the tail of an aircraft, which has an inherent low mono-static radar RCS. The compact range data can be used to study phenomenology, or as inputs to models and simulations. In addition, the data can be used to generate ISAR images.

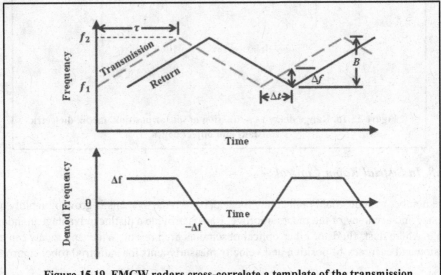

Figure 15.19. FMCW radars cross-correlate a template of the transmission with the radar returns (upper plot), and the resulting frequency offset (bottom plot) corresponds to the range delay.

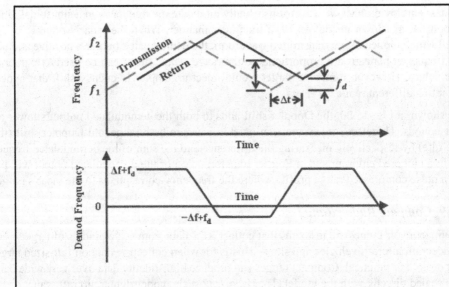

Figure 15.20. Linear FM modulation have range-Doppler coupling, but the demodulated frequencies of upchirp and downchirp waveforms can be used to solve both the frequency offset due to range and Doppler shift.

Many compact radar ranges use stepped frequency or synthetic wideband. The radar transmits and then receives a series of sinewave pulses where the carrier frequency systematically increments as depicted in Fig. 15.21. One way to think of how a stepped frequency radar works is to use an analogy with the FFT. The FFT takes a discrete sampled time domain waveform and converts it to a summation of a series of weighted sine and cosine functions, also known as the frequency domain. Fig. 15.22 shows how a triangular pulse in time domain is converted into the frequency domain, where this particular waveform has even symmetry thus the sine weightings are all zero, which is why they are not shown in the figure.

The FFT assumes the total time domain waveform is repeated over and over, thus the total time window T is analogous to a pulse train's PRI. The lowest frequency that can fit within the time window is the size of the frequency steps in the frequency domain, which is analogous to the PRF. The highest frequency that can be represented required two time samples, $f_{max} = 1/2\Delta t$, where Δt is the time between samples or sampling interval. A stepped frequency radar collects data in the frequency domain. It transmits a sinewave at each frequency on the left to get a quasi-steady state response, then steps to the next frequency. After collecting the response for each frequency and applying calibration corrections for each frequency, the radar uses an IFFT to transform the spectral components into the time domain.

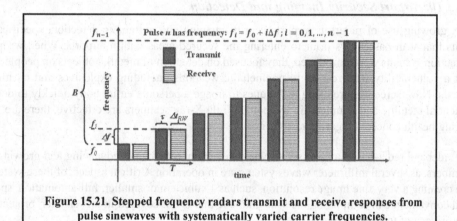

Figure 15.21. Stepped frequency radars transmit and receive responses from pulse sinewaves with systematically varied carrier frequencies.

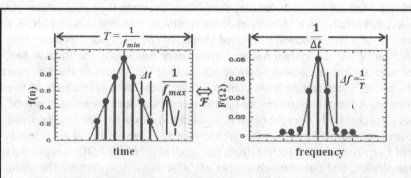

Figure 15.22. Relationship between sampling and time window in the time domain, and highest frequency and spectral lines in the frequency domain.

A significant constraint with stepped frequency radars is that the target needs to be quasi-stationary while the radar steps through the series of frequencies. Otherwise, accelerations will degrade the phase coherency across the bandwidth. Acceleration is not a problem for compact ranges because of the controlled motion of the target. An example of a compact radar range is the ElectroScience Laboratory's Compact Range at The Ohio State University (OSU, n.d.). This compact range is an anechoic design, where the ceiling, floor and walls are covered with pyramidal and wedge shaped, carbon-impregnated foam or radar absorbing material to minimize reflections. Its offset parabolic reflector has rolled edges to produce plane waves without blockage and to reduce the sidelobes, which enables data on targets as large as *2.4 m*. Combined with its precision positioning system, the radar can be configured to collect co-polarized or cross-polarized data for a complete scattering matrix, and with different horn antennas to enable wider bandwidths. While the range can collect data from *0.4* through *110 GHz* (Sandora, 2005), a common configuration is the step frequency radar using a feed stem with a ridge waveguide horn that spans *2* to *18 GHz,* or an *16,000 MHz* bandwidth center around *10 GHz* in the X-band (NATO I/J-bands). This single scan has a *1.88 cm* range resolution, and a fractional bandwidth of *80%*. Note that the fractional bandwidth will remain constant regardless of the model's scale.

15.3.10. Airport Security Imaging and Detection

A growing use of radars is airport security imaging and automatic detection, specifically units that scan passengers prior to entering the secured areas within airports. When weapon detection systems were introduced, they focused on detection of metallic objects on people and left a vulnerability with respect to nonmetallic weapons, including explosives and chemical agents. Now, screeners are using techniques to image a person's entire body quickly to detect potential metallic and nonmetallic weapons. While X-ray scanners are effective, there are lingering health concerns regarding exposure.

Wideband radar-based airport security and detection systems are advancing and growing in numbers, as several millimeter wave systems are in operation. Critical aspects of these systems are creating a very-fine image resolution, such as 1 cubic cm or smaller, full-automation, speed and convenience in completing the scan and, one that is not covered in this chapter, protecting the privacy of the passengers.

The European Union (EU) Seventh Framework Programme (SFP) jointly funded the concealed object stand-off real-time imaging for security to match their publications (CONSORTIS) project that resulted in a *16*-channel demonstration system that uses an FMCW waveform to generate *30,000 MHz* bandwidth centered about *340 GHz*. The corresponding range resolution is *0.5 cm*. While the system has an extraordinary bandwidth, the fraction bandwidth is *8.8%*, because the sub-millimeter wave operation is at the bottom of the far infrared band. While the system's architecture is the same as a radar, including a sparse array of fixed steered horn antennas, it benefits from electro-optical techniques, such as using "mirrors" or plate reflectors to mechanically steer the beam in azimuth and elevation. The *10 dB* azimuth and elevation beamwidths of *9.75°* enables the radar to scan a *~1 cm* spot size at *3.5 m* within the field of view of *1 m²*. To achieve a *10 Hz* refresh rate, each of its *16*-bit ADCs sample at a rate of *25 Mega samples/sec*, and cumulatively output of *147.4 Mega samples/sec*. The ability to adequately capture a 30,000 MHz bandwidth signal by sampling at *25 Mega samples/sec*, which is much lower than Nyquist sampling rate, highlights the power of LFM deramp processing.

This CONSORTIS demonstration system uses a direct digital synthesizer to generate fast chirp slopes, such as an uncompressed pulse width, $\tau_u = 40.96\,\mu$ sec. The resulting pulse compression gain is

$$G_{comp} = B\tau_u \qquad\qquad \textbf{Eq. (15.23)}$$

thus, the gain is *61 dB*. The radar performs the LFM pulse compression via deramp processing, specifically, the transmitter's LFM waveform is multiplied with the received signal. The output is a series of pulses with a duration equal to the pulse width at a frequency proportional to the range delay plus Doppler shift, where the range rate will be very small as people walk by the system. Taking a Fourier transform of the deramped output will compress the pulses, where frequency is proportional to range. The bandwidth is given by

$$\Delta f = \frac{2B\Delta R}{c\tau_u}, \qquad\qquad \textbf{Eq. (15.24)}$$

hence, a *1 m r*ange will result in *4.9 MHz* bandwidth.

15.3.11. Application Conclusions

Military radar systems continue to pave the way for future wideband advancements. The integration and complexity of modern military radars involve many of the aforementioned applications, functions and capabilities within a single system. Wideband airborne, shipborne and land-based defense radars have grown to support multiple functions that may include cued detection, quality track, data collection, classification, fire control, weapon guidance and hit assessment of simultaneous targets. In additional, the radars have requirements for covertness, jam resistance and integrating into a larger weapon system of systems that may include other radars/sensors. The multi-function capability drives the need for programmable medium band and wideband waveforms that include different modulation schemes simultaneously. This precipitates the need for a waveform scheduler to manage and balance the radar's resources and perform updates when given a set of priorities, particularly for the time-line associated with integrated air and missile defense systems.

A significant trend is the growing number of industrial and consumer products using wideband radars. Technology advancements in and the broad use of computers, video cameras, precision timing controls and telecommunication components make high-tech radars accessible, and the resulting increase in the number of applications and size of production volume is reducing the cost, size, weight and power consumption of the radars and associated processors. The ultimate limitation to radar applications may be management of the electromagnetic spectrum that is also being consumed with a rapidly growing wireless data communications demand.

Chapter 16

Modern Digital Array Antennas
for Radar Applications

Kenny D. Shrider

16.1. Introduction

A vast quantity of literature concerning array antennas is available for consumption. Many sources of this knowledge are available through textbooks and the Internet. Basic array antenna concepts are covered extensively within many of these sources. The development for array antenna principles typically starts with linear arrays and expands into planar array, describing the array factor and the array antenna pattern, the contribution to the antenna pattern by the individual element patterns, and then covers various array weighting techniques, such as Hamming, to control sidelobe levels. Rather than taking this typical approach to describe array antennas, the aim of this chapter is to discuss material that is not as widely covered by the bulk of the literature; and to focus on modern technology with only small mention of historical background. This is not to say that the material within this chapter is not covered within the available literature, however, much of the material is less common and may be harder to find. Also, there are opinions expressed by the author in various locations that may not be directly found within the literature but are fairly obvious deductions. The reader is encouraged to use the list of references and to search the Internet starting with the key words and acronyms used within this chapter for further reading. Finally, while many of the concepts discussed within this chapter can be applied to general array antennas, the intent is to focus on array antennas as they apply to radar.

Array antennas have been used since around the beginning of the 20th century. The earliest array antennas were used for radio frequency (RF) sinusoidal signal transmission using a radiated beam steered by the array. By World War II, array antennas were being used in radar applications. These early arrays are referred to as "passive arrays", as a single exciter and transmitter was used to provide power through the array network to each component (element) within the array. Varying signal phase or time delays (phase shifters or cable length) across the elements of the array was used to form and steer radar beams electronically. The same approach was used on receive where a single receiver would capture the signal after all of the phase shifted or time delayed signals from the elements within the arrays were combined. The process of applying this phase / time variation to the signals across the elements to steer the beam is called "beamforming". Passive electronically steered array (PESA) antennas are still in wide use in modern times. Figure 16.1 depicts, in a simplistic way, a PESA. There are also other techniques for steering array antenna beams such as frequency steering or through the use of a Butler matrix within the array network. Many arrays dynamically steer beams varying the profile of signal time delay, phase, or frequency variation across the array elements. For example, in a radar application, a beam can be steered in different directions on a pulse-by-pulse basis. Others statically steer beams. For example, a radar phased array antenna might transmit and receive search pulses, always in the same directions.

In coherent radars, most radars of the modern day, where the same stationary local oscillator (STALO) is used to drive the RF mixing on both transmit and receive, the exciter and receiver are together called the receiver-exciter (REX). Analog frequency up-conversion and down-conversion take place in the REX. The receiver typically includes superheterodyne mixing circuits, multiple stages to down-convert RF to an intermediate frequency (IF) and then to baseband. The exciter typically includes superheterodyne mixing circuits, multiple stages to up-convert baseband to IF and then to RF. Direct mixing to convert directly from RF to baseband and vice versa is called "homodyne mixing". See Figs. 16.2 and 16.3 for diagrams of the two REX types. Note that these figures include the entire circuit from RF to digital baseband for both transmit and receive. The REX is typically regarded as the part of the circuit that circulates IF and baseband signals but excludes the RF front-end. As can be seen in the figures, for transmit, the REX inputs digital baseband signals and outputs analog RF signals; and for receive, the REX inputs analog RF signals and outputs digital baseband signals. In Figs. 16.2 and 16.3, the transmitter is represented by the high-power amp within the RF front-end. Note that the splitter/combiner in the figures represents the PESA antenna and beamformer.

Technology innovations through the years since the war have paved the way for significant improvements for array antennas. These improvements include higher power, better efficiency, better accuracy and precision, more flexibility, better reliability, and the ability to perform multiple missions, all of this in many cases along with lower costs. Enablers include miniaturized and more capable electronics such as transmit receive modules (TRMs), microwave monolithic integrated circuits (MMICs), mixed signal (analog-digital) integrated circuit boards, and many more innovations and refinements. Since the earliest PESA antennas, major advancements include the active electronically steered array (AESA) and the digital array.

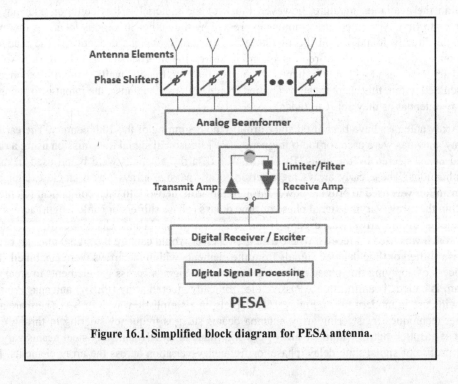

Figure 16.1. Simplified block diagram for PESA antenna.

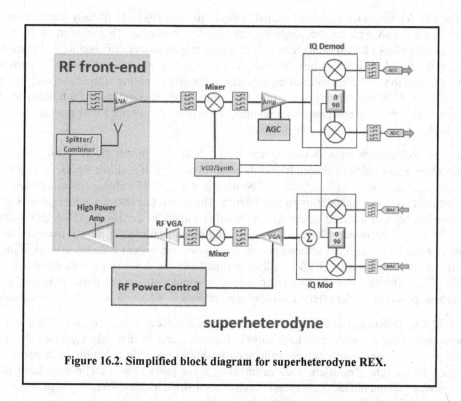

Figure 16.2. Simplified block diagram for superheterodyne REX.

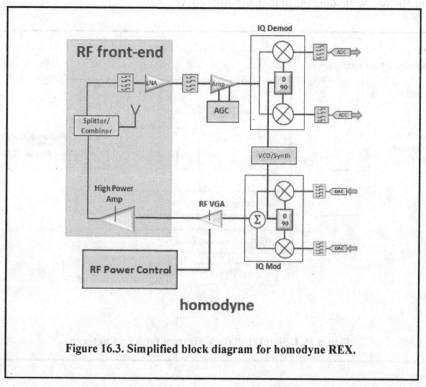

Figure 16.3. Simplified block diagram for homodyne REX.

The AESA antenna development started in the 1970s and 1980s. In its fully matured config-uration, the AESA replaces the single central transmitter/receiver RF front-end of the PESA with an individual TRM at each element. The AESA may still have only one REX. Figure 16.4 depicts the AESA. The AESA benefits over the PESA in that lower signal loss and distortion is achieved due to the replacement of high-power transmit RF cabling with low-power transmit cabling. For AESA employing sub-arrays (the entire array is composed of a number of sub-arrays, each sub-array composed of a number of elements), multiple REXs may be included, one REX for one or more sub-arrays.

Figure 16.5 depicts an AESA using sub-arrays. Note that in this figure, time delay units (TDUs) are also employed at each REX/sub-array. In the case of multiple REXs, cabling trans-porting signals at an IF or baseband will be used in place of RF cabling potentially lowering distortion, loss, and susceptibility to interference. The amount of circuitry with high-power RF signals has been minimized in the AESA. Another important benefit of AESA architectures over PESA architectures is the elimination of single-point failures. If the RF front-end trans-mitter or receiver in a PESA antenna system goes down, the system is nonfunctional. If one or more TRMs go down, the AESA is still operational and the degradation with number of lost TRMs is usually graceful. In parallel to AESA development was the development of solid-state high-power amplifiers (HPA), low-noise amplifiers (LNA), and other circuit components.

Solid state technology is what enabled AESA to be as successful as it is. Solid state transmit components contrast with their tube amplifier counterparts in that they typically use lower peak power / longer length pulses. Solid state is able to maintain much higher transmit duty factor than the tube amplifiers, such as traveling wave tubes (TWTs). The very latest HPAs incorporate gallium nitride (GaN) semi-conductor substrate which offers very high power den-sity and efficiency, yielding much higher-power HPAs.

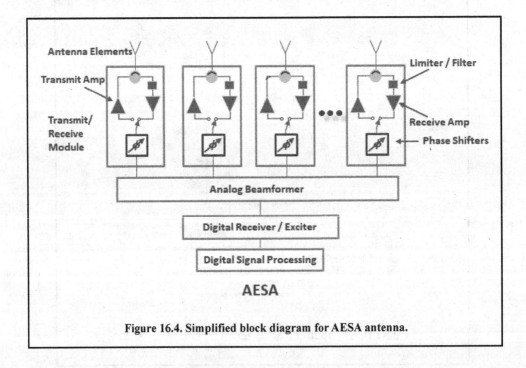

Figure 16.4. Simplified block diagram for AESA antenna.

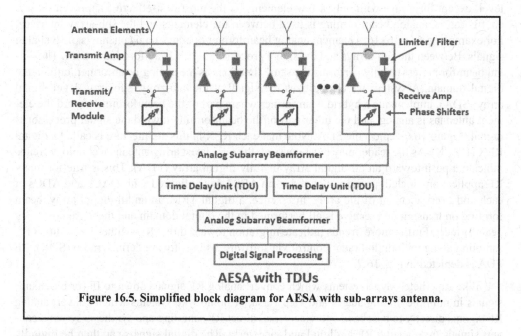

Figure 16.5. Simplified block diagram for AESA with sub-arrays antenna.

16.2. Introduction to Digital Arrays

A significant improvement over the all-analog AESA is the digital array. Digital array technology started around the beginning of the 21st century in parallel with the introduction of digital technology to many other areas. Benefiting from improvements within analog-to-digital converter (ADC) and digital-to-analog converter (DAC) and other components, digital technology has revolutionized electronics in just about every area. To name a few, photography, video playback, audio playback, and computational hardware have benefited tremendously from digital technology. The keys responsible for these benefits are smaller electronics, lower signal loss, lower noise, and lower distortion. Sensors, including radar, have also greatly benefited.

The earliest radars were all analog. A transmitter such as a magnetron, generated an RF pulsed signal that was routed to an antenna for transmission. Upon reception of the returned signal via the antenna, the signal was routed to the receiver, which performed signal envelope detection, generating a bipolar video signal that was routed to a cathode ray tube (CRT) which would display a trace or blip denoting a target (A-scope or plan position indicator). The higher the trace or brighter the blip, the larger/closer the target. The first digital technology introduced within radars was a computer which was used to control the radar and process a digitized form of the video signal, serving as the signal processor. Another digital innovation was using digital Doppler processing instead of an analog bank of Doppler filters. Eventually, everything in the back-end of the radar was replaced with digital technology. The only analog components remaining were within the front-end of the radar. Figures 16.1 through 16.8 represent more modern architectures which utilize digital signals.

Currently, there are array antenna radars and other devices in existence and under development that include signal digitization within the front-end at the sub-array level. A sub-array is a collection of elements into a super element, a term borrowed from finite element methodology, for example, 64 elements in the arrangement of *16* rows by *16* columns (16×16). Current technology dictates that, depending on frequency and application, digitizing at the sub-array level, except for arrays with only a few elements, is the most cost-effective approach. In this configuration, analog beamforming is used between the elements and the sub-array interface. For example, a *64* (16×16) element analog beamformer operates on *64* channels of IF analog signals. Between the sub-arrays and the signal processor, digital beamforming is used. The digital beamformer essentially performs the same functions as the analog beamformer, only in the digital domain. A system which digitizes the signal at the sub-array, sub-array level digital array (SDA), implements a hybrid beamformer where part of the beamforming toward the element antennas is analog, and the other part of the beamforming toward the signal processor is digital. Figure 16.6 depicts the SDA. Note that each REX in this architecture is called a digital REX (DREX). As the reader may have guessed, the very latest array antenna technology trends indicate a push toward an all-digital array or fully digital array (FDA). This is true for many RF applications including radar. For radar, an AESA is configured with DACs and ADCs at each and every element of the array, in essence, a digital TRM. In an all-digital array, beam forming on transmit and receive is all performed in the digital domain and there are no analog beamformers. Furthermore, trends indicate migration toward direct RF synthesis and direct RF sampling along with digital radar control via software, as in software defined radio (SDR). An FDA is depicted in Fig. 16.7.

Unlike superheterodyne systems which convert analog RF signals down to IF (or baseband) signals in multiple mixing stages and vice versa, or homodyne systems which convert analog RF signals directly to baseband and vice versa, direct RF sampling and synthesis systems convert signals from analog RF to digital and vice versa. The digital signals can then be digitally down-converted (frequency shifted) to a digital baseband signal via digital down-conversion (DDC) or up-converted from a digital baseband signal using digital up-conversion (DUC). Direct RF sampling/synthesis systems eliminate analog devices such as in phase/quadrature phase (IQ) modulator/demodulator, analog mixers, local oscillators, IF circuitry, etc. Many sources of error associated with the analog mixing process are avoided.

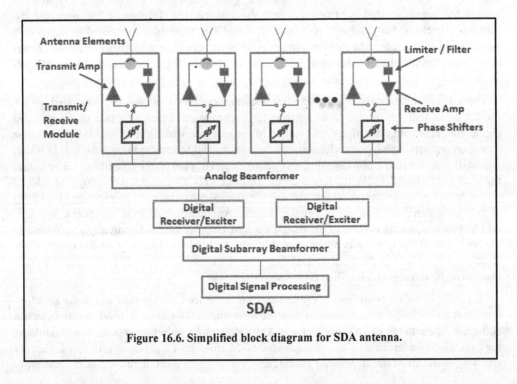

Figure 16.6. Simplified block diagram for SDA antenna.

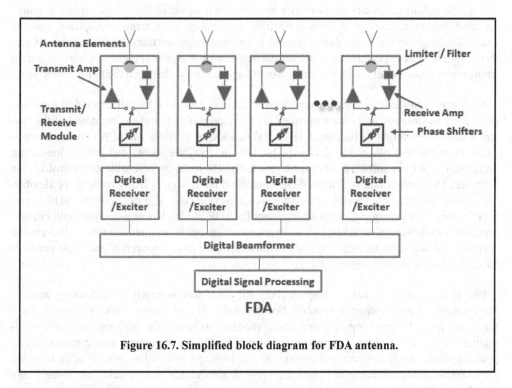

Figure 16.7. Simplified block diagram for FDA antenna.

Examples are IF circuitry 2nd and 3rd order harmonic distortion, passband ripple, group delay variation, quadrature matching, local oscillator (LO) leakage, and mixer products/harmonics (images). However, it should be noted that ADCs and DACs are themselves analog devices. Different types of errors may be introduced owing mainly to imperfections in the ADC and DAC devices, such as ADC/DAC device 2nd and 3rd order harmonic distortion, clock mixing spurs, and sampling frequency harmonics. In direct RF digital operation, the DAC and ADC time or phase jitter error must be extremely low to achieve errors in timing/phase by no more than a few percent of the wavelength.

The jitter error is related to the ADC/DAC device phase noise as its integration over the operational bandwidth. The higher the RF frequency, the better the jitter performance must be. The synthesis and sampling rates of modern DACs and ADCs can also be very high, enabling extremely wideband operation. Recall the Nyquist/Shannon sampling requirement that the sampling rate must be greater than or equal to two times the signal bandwidth. Figure 16.8 shows the direct RF digital architecture. Note that Figs. 16.2, 16.3, and 16.8, show only a single transmitter and receiver. For AESA, the RF front-end would be replicated many times, once for each TRM.

To reap the benefits of direct RF sampling / synthesis, careful frequency planning, cascade analysis, and circuit design/component selection must be conducted. As eluded to various types of spurious responses result from in-band and out-of-band excitation in both superheterodyne and direct RF digital architectures. However, the spectral spur amplitudes and frequency locations can be vastly different between the two architectures. The spurious response performance must be analyzed in regard to how it supports the requirements of the application. Since the architecture is significantly different between the two architectures, with the exception of possibly the RF front-end, components within the two architectures are different and therefore the system results for many performance metrics, such as noise figure and dynamic range, revealed through cascade analysis will be different. Finally, in an array architecture, cascade analysis throughout the array shows general improvement proportional to the number of elements for the system performance metrics where the improvement is related to the correlation from channel-to-channel which generally would vary somewhat between the two architectures.

SDR strives to facilitate flexible architecture radio (FAR). In FAR, all aspects of the radio system are flexible and software controlled. This includes digital and analog stages of the system whether they might be baseband, IF, or RF. In addition to radio, the SDR concept is applicable to radar and other RF devices. The benefits are the same, flexibility fine-tuning performance, all via software. Of course, the hardware must be amenable to control by the software. The bottom line is that the SDR controlled RF device is likely to be more flexible, more future proof, more capable, all at a lower life-cycle cost. The international SDR forum *http://www.sdrforum.org* is the governing body for SDR, which has now merged with citizens broadband radio service (CBRS) and software communication architecture (SCA) to form the wireless innovation forum *https://www.wirelessinnovation.org/*. Apparently, the latest vernacular uses software defined system (SDS).

Finally, another trend that has been ongoing for years now in nearly all technology areas is the tendency to use as many commercial-of-the-shelf (COTS) components as possible. Over the years, it has become apparent that this approach maximizes the performance while minimizing the life-cycle costs. This paradigm of using COTS components also means that one industry, for example defense and aerospace, can leverage innovation from another industry, for example telecommunication, and vice versa. It also means that systems are more future proof since COTS items are often designed, and have requirements, to be backward compatible. Improved components are often a "drop-in" replacement.

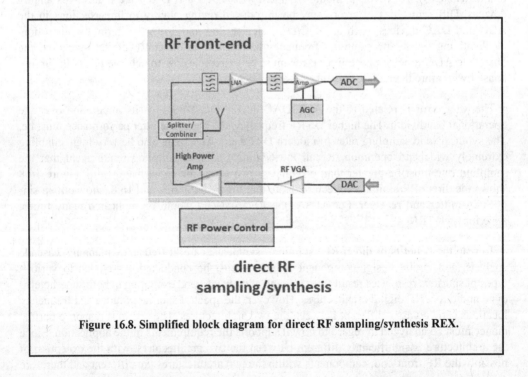

Figure 16.8. Simplified block diagram for direct RF sampling/synthesis REX.

16.3. Comparison of Array Antenna Architectures by Example

To illustrate performance levels of various array types, a simple radar example is offered. There are four array architectures being compared: PESA (Fig. 16.1), AESA (Fig. 16.4), SDA (Fig. 16.6), and FDA (Fig. 16.7). First, they will all be partially populated with elements. As mentioned earlier, it is well known that many error types improve in an array of channels relative to a single channel, as long as the error sources are not correlated from channel to channel. For example, many factors leading to the receive dynamic range (*DR*) of the system improve by the number of elements within the array, leading to a dynamic range improvement in decibels (*dB*) equal to $10log_{10}(N)$, where N is the number of elements. Without delving into the details of *DR*, such as its various definitions like spurious free dynamic range (SFDR), there are many non-ideal sources of the limitation to dynamic range from various devices within the receive chain, such as amplifiers, filters, and mixers. These limitations can be quantified with metrics such as *1 dB* compression point, third order intercept (related to 3rd order harmonic), etc. Suppose however, for the example, the limiting factor in *DR* is the ADC number of bits of resolution. The *DR* limit of an ADC is $6N_b$, where N_b is the number of ADC bits. The example will make a simple observation about *DR* in regard to the four array architectures.

In addition to *DR*, the example will also examine the effect on radar detection range. The signal-to-noise ratio (SNR) is proportional to the antenna gain on transmit and on receive and also proportional to the transmit power. The radar detection range is proportional to the fourth root of the SNR. Suppose the PESA radar has a transmitter capable of delivering *50 kW* power to the PESA which has $N = 2500$ *(50 × 50)* elements (partially populated). Also, suppose the PESA radar receiver contains an ADC with *16* bits of resolution. Now suppose the AESA radar has the same ADC after the analog beamformer; however, rather than the single transmitter, it has *10W* TRMs at each of its *2500* elements. The SDA is also an AESA; but rather than a single ADC processing the *2500* combined analog channels, it has $N_{SA} = 25$ ADCs each processing the signal from a sub-array composed of *100* elements (10 × 10). However, instead of *16*, the SDA ADCs each have *10* bits of resolution. Finally, suppose the FDA radar AESA antenna has *10-bit* ADCs behind each of the *2500* TRMs. Furthermore, in the example, the array antennas for all four radars will be transitioned from partially populated (designated as I) to fully populated (designated as II) $N = 10000$ (100×100) element array. For the SDR, this implies $N_{SA} = 100$ sub-arrays. Finally, the wavelength is assumed to *0.1 m* (S-band). Note that the examples throughout this chapter, including this example, assume that the element placement within the array uses a rectangular lattice. Many arrays employ a triangular lattice placement, which can achieve the desired antenna pattern characteristics with a slightly smaller element count. For a square aperture with equal horizontal and vertical element spacing, the fraction of elements required for triangular lattice versus rectangular lattice is equal to *sqrt(N)/ (sqrt(N) + 1)*.

For simplicity, the example ignores any performance improvements realized through the reduction of losses and distortion, due to digital instead of analog and / or IF low-voltage instead of RF high-voltage signals throughout the array network. Also, the system noise figure is assumed the same for all architectures. The results are summarized below. The values were chosen to illustrate the difference in the performance improvement as a function of *N*, the number of elements in the array. Note that the AESA, SDA, and FDA start out behind the PESA in both dynamic range and detection range performance. But when the arrays are fully populated, the AESA, SDA, and FDA achieve superior detection range, and the FDA achieves superior dynamic range.

The equations used for the example are

$$DR = \begin{cases} 6N_b & for PESA \ and \ AESA \\ 6N_b + 10\log_{10}(N_{SA}) & for \ SDA \\ 6N_b + 10\log_{10}(N) & for \ SDA \end{cases} \qquad \text{Eq. (16.1)}$$

$$G = \frac{4\pi A}{\lambda^2} \qquad \text{Eq. (16.2)}$$

$$P = \begin{cases} P_{Tx} & for \ PESA \\ NP_{TRM} & for \ AESA, \ SDA, \ and \ FDA \end{cases} \qquad \text{Eq. (16.3)}$$

$$R = R_0 \left(\frac{G^2 P}{G_0^2 P_0} \right)^{1/4}, \qquad \text{Eq. (16.4)}$$

where G_0, P_0, and R_0 are the antenna gain, transmit power, and detection range for the partially populated PESA radar. Also, A is the area of the antenna aperture, G is the antenna gain, R is the detection range, and P is the power. Table 16.1 shows different DR values under different conditions. The aperture area for the partially populated antenna, assuming half wavelength element separation is $A = 6.25 \ m^2$, and when fully populated, the area is $A = 25 \ m^2$.

Table 16.1. Dynamic Range, *DR*, under Different Conditions.

Array Type	DR	G, dB	P, kW	R (relative to R_0)
PESA I	96	39	50	R_0
AESA I	96	39	25	$0.84R_0$
SDA I	74	39	25	$0.84R_0$
FDA I	94	39	25	$0.84R_0$
PESA II	96	45	50	$2.38R_0$
AESA II	96	45	100	$2.83R_0$
SDA II	80	45	100	$2.83R_0$
FDA II	100	45	100	$2.83R_0$

16.4. Other Digital Array Advantages

Besides improving signal quality, partially and fully digital arrays will make other aspects of the system operation better and will enable some types of operation to become more practical to implement. Some of these capabilities are discussed below, as they generally apply to radar.

The capability to utilize simultaneous receive beams, which can and has been implemented in analog arrays, is more practically implemented with digital technology. This provides several benefits such as more efficiency in time management, for example search volume frame times can decrease, improved detection performance, and improved angle accuracy using algorithms such as maximum likelihood estimate (MLE) in place of monopulse processing.

Adaptive beamforming is certainly possible with arrays that are digitized at the sub-array level (SDA), and even possible with analog arrays; however, the full flexibility and number of degrees-of-freedom (DOF) is achieved with the FDA. Adaptive digital beam forming (ADBF) is used to dramatically reduce the level of RF interference that the system faces during operation. Essentially, ADBF takes samples at each sub-array or element, forms a covariance matrix characterizing the spatial stochastic behavior of the interference, and computes weighting (typically both amplitude and phase, but also phase only) in order to create antenna pattern nulls in the direction of interference sources. This is typically performed on receive to mitigate jamming effects but also can be implemented on transmit to reduce clutter interference resulting from reflections from high clutter regions. ADBF could also be extended to a technique called space time adaptive processing (STAP). In STAP, spatial DOF as well as temporal DOF are used to more effectively characterize, and therefore mitigate, the interference, specifically the non-stationary characteristics of the interference. For STAP, numerous time samples are collected at each sub-array or element. Both ADBF and STAP can be extremely computationally demanding for real-time processing.

For receive, in the absence of adaptive beamforming or to deal with residual interference signals while using adaptive beamforming, sidelobe cancellation and mainlobe cancellation can be employed. Again, analog versions are possible and do exist in the form of closed-loop cancellation; however, digital open-loop implementations are typically superior. In array radars, typically, a sidelobe canceler (SLC) uses auxiliary antennas; that is antennas that are not part of the main antenna array. However, sidelobe cancellation can also be performed using elements or sub-arrays that are also used by the main antenna. For this approach, however, there is the issue that the receiver noise in the SLC circuits is the same as (and therefore completely correlated with) the noise in the corresponding circuits in the main antenna (i.e., the circuits are one the same). This can cause the canceler to act on the receiver noise rather than the interference and the result is an elevation in effective antenna sidelobe levels, and therefore there is no improvement in interference rejection. This problem can be remedied by applying weighting to groups of SLC antennas that is orthogonal to the main array weighting of those same circuits. This weighting is in addition to the cancellation weighting. At the extreme, if using all of the sub-arrays or elements that the main antenna uses, this could be referred to as a general sidelobe canceler (GSC). A mainlobe canceler (MLC) implementation could use this approach. For digital implementation of SLC and MLC, signal samples are collected over time for each canceler antenna (element, sub-array, or group of sub-arrays) and for the main antenna after all beamforming. Since the number of canceler antennas plus the main antenna is generally much less (exception GSC) than the number of sub-arrays or elements that data is collected for implementing ADBF or STAP, SLC and MLC are typically much less computationally expensive than ADBF and STAP.

Multiple input multiple output (MIMO) operation via radar will be much more practical with all digital arrays. For example, enough flexibility in array control could exist to enable transmitting distinct frequencies, or orthogonal waveforms, from each element and then receiving all waveform returns at all elements, therefore achieving MIMO operation and benefiting from the resulting data rich in target information.

Since received digital signals can be easily stored in memory storage devices, it is conceptually possible to store the digitized received signals collected at each element or sub-array. If this could be accomplished, the element-level digital signal data could in essence be processed via algorithms that are designed to optimize performance. The algorithms could iterate using various weighting profiles over the element data. For example, for radar, this could potentially extract the very best performance possible from the radar in regard to target detection, clutter rejection, measurement accuracy, etc. By using this process, the optimal weighting profile could be found for each received pulse, further for each object detection.

A detail of the design for FDA or hybrid array that is digitized at the sub-array level (SDA), that should not be overlooked, is the vast quantities of data that must be moved through the digital portion of the array and into computational processing systems. As mentioned before, the current radar approach given the current cost-effective technology, on receive appears to be digitizing at the sub-array level, routing digital data from ADCs to further processing. This high-speed data transfer is typically done through transceivers containing multi-*Gbps* serializer / deserializer (SerDes) connections. From there, the data is sent to field programmable gate arrays (FPGAs) that perform operations such as DDC, digital quadrature demodulation, and ADC counts bit format to fixed point. The resulting digitized baseband IQ data from all of the sub-arrays is then sent via high speed network connections, such as Ethernet, to a digital beam forming computer that combines the sub-array data, while applying appropriate weighting, to form a beam. This computer may form several simultaneous receive beams and may also perform signal processing and other types of processing. But on transmit, the current approach is different. Rather than using the digital beam forming computer to generate and distribute a digital baseband IQ signals to all of the sub-arrays, instead a message is sent to the sub-array processing boards (FPGAs) indicating the waveform and amplitudes and phases (or time-delays) to use at each sub-array. The FPGA would have in its connected memory, a set of waveform data to use. The appropriate baseband waveform data consistent with the waveform indicated within the message would be fetched from the FPGA memory and passed through the FPGA to perform the appropriate quadrature modulation, DUC, and packaging for passing to the DAC through the SerDes and transceiver. This design just described is feasible and practical with current technology.

16.5. Extreme Data Rate Demands in Digital Arrays

To explore what would be needed for SDA and FDA in regard to data transfer in a radar, a parametric set of curves are presented in Figs. 16.9 through 16.13. There were several assumptions made in the generation of these plots:

1. Direct RF sampling is performed with an oversampling factor of two (twice Nyquist), four times the signal bandwidth. It is assumed that the maximum instantaneous waveform bandwidth is *20%* of the carrier frequency (*20%* percentage bandwidth), a lofty goal; however FDA is a lofty goal as well.
2. There is no DDC or DUC performed, as full bandwidth processing is desired.
3. The array is composed of elements that are half a wavelength apart.
4. For the SDA, each sub-array contains *16* (*4 × 4*) elements.
5. Each sample is represented with *16* bits.

The equations used to generate Figs. 16.9 through 16.13 are now presented. The number of sub-arrays is

$$N_{SA} = N_{SAy}M_{SAx} = \frac{A}{N_y \ M_x \ d_x \ d_y \ \lambda^2}, \qquad \text{Eq. (16.5)}$$

where A is the antenna area, $\lambda = c/f_c$ is the wavelength, c is the speed of light, f_c is the carrier frequency, M_x and N_y are, respectively, the number of elements in a row and in a column for the sub-array. For this example, $N_yM_x = 4 \times 4 = 16$. The total number of elements is

$$N = N_{SAy}M_{SAx}N_yM_x$$ **Eq. (16.6)**

where M_{SAx} and N_{SAy} are, respectively, the number of sub-arrays (super elements) in a row and in a column for the entire array. The maximum bandwidth is

$$B = \frac{P_B\, f_c}{100}$$ **Eq. (16.7)**

where P_B is the percentage bandwidth. For this example, $P_B = 20\%$. The sampling rate is

$$f_s = XB$$ **Eq. (16.8)**

where X is the oversampling factor. For this example, $X = 2$. The data rate for a single channel in bits per second is

$$R_{bch} = 2f_s\, N_b$$ **Eq. (16.9)**

where N_b is the number of bits representing a single value in a sample. For this example, $N_b = 16$. The factor two is to account for both real and imaginary components in the complex (IQ) sample. Note that some radars have two polarization channels (for example, vertical and horizontal). In this case, the factor two should be changed to four. The data rate for all of the sub-array channels for SDA, in bits per second, is

$$R_{bSAtot} = N_{SA}R_{bch}.$$ **Eq. (16.10)**

Finally, the data rate for all of the element channels for FDA, in bits per second, is

$$R_{belemtot} = NR_{bch}.$$ **Eq. (16.11)**

The left plot of Fig. 16.9 shows the parametric space, the x-axis representing the array antenna area in square meters, ranging from *0.01 m^2* to *100000 m^2*, and the y-axis and curve color representing the carrier frequency ranging from *100 MHz* to *100 GHz*. Note that the curves are limited in regard to minimum area being the area of a single sub-array. For reference, the right plot shows the data rate required for a single channel. This could also represent the data rate required for a single beam in a nondigital array radar (i.e., digitizing only after all of the analog beamforming takes place). Figure 16.10 shows on the left the number of sub-arrays in the SDA (assuming *16* elements per sub-array), and on the right the number of elements in the SDA and FDA. Figure 16.11 shows on the left the data rate required, given the above assumptions regarding the sampling rate's dependence on bandwidth and carrier frequency, for the sub-array architecture (SDA), and on the right the data rate required for the FDA. Note that the y-axis is given in *Gbps* units. In general, these data rates are extremely high and by observation, one can glean the dramatic increases in requirements as frequency and / or antenna area increase.

To put this in perspective regarding modern data link network technology, a typical high-speed data link has a rated capacity of *100 Gbps*. To match this, a typical data rate for computer buses is *100 Gbps* (for example using *PCIeV3.16* lanes). Note that PCIe version *4* and version *5* are promised to offer *200 Gbps* and *400 Gbps*, respectively. If the required data rate calculations in *Gbps* from above are divided by *100 Gbps*, then an estimate for the number of *100 Gbps* data links required can be computed. Not included here is the fact that the data link/bus specified max data rate is seldom reached continuously in practice (a maximum of *80%* the specified value may be more realistic); however, it is insightful to see the upper bound. The calculated number of links required is given for a single channel in Fig. 16.12 on the right, and for the SDA in Fig. 16.13 on the left, and finally for the FDA in Fig. 16.13 on the right.

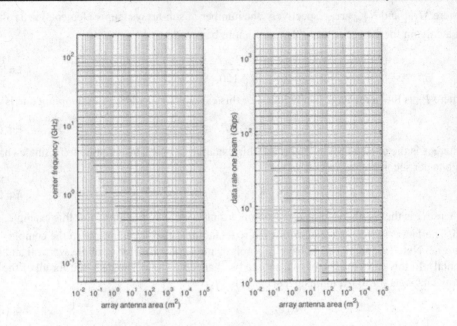

Figure 16.9. Parameter space, frequency versus array aperture size (left); data rate supporting maximum signal bandwidth required for single channel or one beam (right).

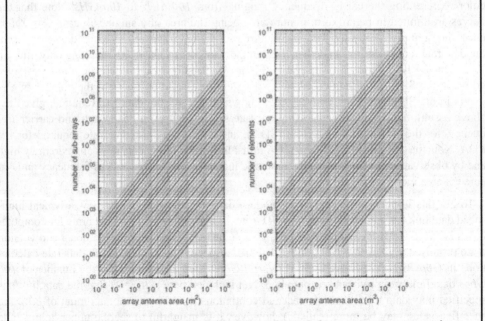

Figure 16.10. Number of sub-arrays in antenna for each frequency versus array size (left); number of elements in antenna for each frequency versus array size (right).

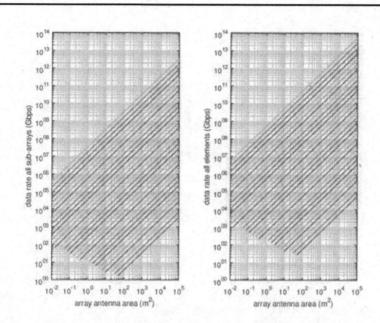

Figure 16.11. Data rate supporting maximum signal bandwidth required for all sub-array channels given frequency and antenna size (left); data rate supporting maximum signal bandwidth required for all element channels given frequency and antenna size (right).

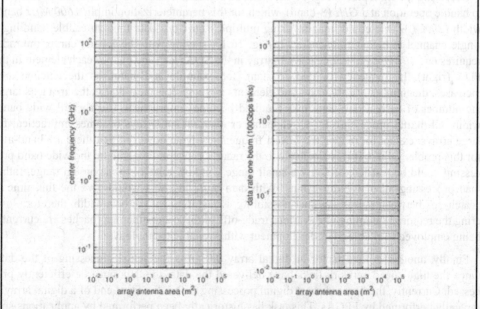

Figure 16.12. Parameter space, frequency versus array aperture size (left); number of *100 Gbps* data links supporting maximum signal bandwidth required for single channel or one beam (right).

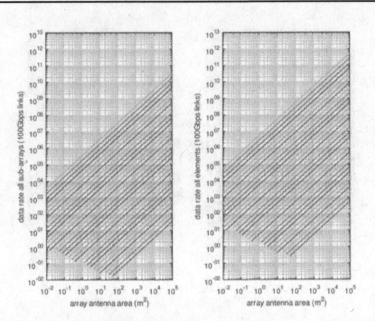

Figure 16.13. Number of *100 Gbps* data links supporting maximum signal bandwidth required for all sub-array channels given frequency and antenna size (left); number of *100 Gbps* data links supporting maximum signal bandwidth required for all element channels given frequency and antenna size (right).

Observing the right plot in Fig. 16.12, it can be seen that one *100 Gbps* data link is sufficient to handle operation at *3 GHz* (S-band), which for this parameterization implies *600 MHz* bandwidth (*20% f_c*). One could imagine using multiple *100 Gbps* data links to enable handling a single channel at higher frequencies. In Fig. 16.13, staying with the S-band curve, the radar requires one *100 Gbps* link for each sub-array in the SDA (left) and one for each element in the FDA (right). If frequency is held constant, for example at S-band, as the antenna area increases, the number of sub-arrays and elements increase. It is clear that as the area gets large, the number of current day data links required becomes impractical. Clearly full wide bandwidth, all digital processing for all elements or even all sub-arrays becomes impractical for large arrays, except for maybe the lowest frequencies. Note however, that there are band-aids for this problem. First, if it is amenable to the radar's concept of operation, the wide band processing could be restricted to only a small range window, relative to maximum range, rather than processing all of the range bins. With data buffering, this would give the link time to "catch-up" between pulses. Another possibility, is just to lower the bandwidth, therefore lowering the required sampling rate. Various trade-offs of these and other approaches are currently being employed to enable SDA development with available technology.

Finally, another critical factor in digital array design is the actual processing of the data. Once the high-speed network links have delivered the data, the data must be efficiently processed. Currently, the forward-most digital processing within the front-end of a digital array is typically performed by FPGAs. This task has historically been performed by applications specific integrated chips (ASICs), but the flexibility of FPGAs has prevailed in recent years. However, the latest trends show that general purpose graphics processor units (GPGPUs) are now beginning to replace FPGAs. This is being done for even greater flexibility, including on-the-fly processing changes, more floating-point operations per second (FLOPS) per dollar, and ease of programming (OpenCL or similar for GPGPUs versus VHDL or Verilog for FPGAs). For the radar application, the vast amount of data that needs to be processed seems to outweigh the amount of processing that needs to be performed on a given set of data. Therefore, it is really the bandwidth of processors and memory devices that limit the throughput rate of the processing, rather than the sheer processing speed of processors. Even so, it is typical for the bandwidth of these devices to significantly exceed the bandwidth of the previously mentioned high-speed data links. For example, typical computer memory bandwidth is around *150 GB/ sec* (*1200 Gbps*) and very high-end GPGPU devices can reach *900 GB/sec* (*7200 Gbps*). While careful consideration for the processing capability must and should be taken for digital arrays, it is apparent that with the current state of technology, the bottle-neck is the data link.

16.6. Digital Down-Conversion and Digital Up-Conversion

While the direct RF digital operation discussion below can be applied to analog array systems behind the analog beamformer (and non-array antenna systems as well), the capability is maturing with the latest and future technology in alignment with the maturation of digital arrays and therefore is expected to be more applicable to digital array systems. Direct RF sampling and synthesis typically includes digital down-conversion (DDC) and digital up-conversion (DUC) operations, respectively. In fact, these algorithms are often integrated within FPGAs supporting ADC/DAC on analog-to-digital and digital-to-analog boards. In its simplest form, DDC includes digital multiplication followed by quadrature demodulation, digital low pass filter (LPF), and decimation. The LPF can be implemented with a finite impulse response (FIR) filter or cascade integrator comb (CIC) filter. Generally, the quadrature demodulation can be accomplished with the use of the Hilbert transform which can be implemented within a FIR filter. In practical implementations, there can be multiple stages of down-conversions and also application of other operations to minimize distortions. FIR filter coefficients are typically computed using the Remez exchange algorithm, more specifically, the Parks-McClellan filter design algorithm. In the end, the signal is converted from a digital RF real signal straight from the output of the ADC, to a baseband IQ (complex) waveform. The resulting signal is then ready for further processing such as pulse compression.

Figure 16.14 is a simple demonstration of the DDC process. Octave (open-source programming language application for scientific programming) was used to generate and process an example signal, with the exception of computing LPF tap coefficients, as discussed below. A notional *1 μs* long, *600 MHz* bandwidth linear frequency modulation (LFM) pulse at *3 GHz* center frequency is used as the example waveform. Practically, there would also be noise contained in the signal, but this was omitted for clarity. The sampling rate f_s was chosen to be 10 GSPS, which does not have to be this high to support the bandwidth; but, this way, all of the interesting spectral information can be displayed in the *1st* Nyquist zone (*-f_s/2 to f_s/2*). Figure 16.14-A shows the energy spectral density (ESD) of the LFM signal. Note that since this signal is real, the spectrum is divided into half energy positive frequency and half energy negative frequency components. Note also that the width of the signal spectrum of each is *600 MHz*. The amplitude of the pulse was chosen such that the energy in the pulse is *1 Joule* (note that this is unrealistic, in an actual system a received signal energy is usually many orders of magnitude smaller).

Figure 16.14-B shows the power spectral density (PSD) of the digital *1W* LO sinusoid, which is at *3 GHz*. Figure 16.14-C shows the ESD of the signal after mixing the LFM pulse with the LO. From the mixing products, note that there is a baseband response, but there are also responses at negative and positive *4 GHz*. These are folded over (aliased) from *6 GHz* (f_{LO}

+/- f_s). The positive *6 GHz* response ends up at the negative *4 GHz* location, and vice versa. Figure 16.14-*D* shows the spectrum of the LPF. This filter was created using the web application at *http://t-filter.engineerjs.com*. The inputs to the filter tool were a sampling rate of *10 GSPS*, a passband from *0* to *600 MHz* with no more than *5 dB* ripple, a stop band from *12 GHz* to *5 GH,* and a stop band floor of *-40 dB*. The tool calculated a FIR filter with *23* taps, an actual ripple of *3.4 dB* and an actual floor of *-41.7 dB*. After using the filter tools generated *23* real filter coefficients and filtering the mixed signal with this LPF, the filtered signal has only baseband content and the energy has been halved (note that if noise were being included, this would not affect the SNR). This is shown in Fig. 16.14-E. At this point, decimation can be performed. The signal could be decimated by at least *8X*. The resulting sampling rate should be more than twice the signal bandwidth to meet the Nyquist criteria. Note that, up to this point, nothing has been done to introduce imaginary components into the signal (the filter coefficients are real). Figure 16.14-F shows this fact in that the phase of the filtered signal is either zero (positive real) or *180* degrees (negative real). A simple quadrature demodulation approach is to multiply the signal by a periodic signal [*1, 0, -1, 0*] to generate the real channel, and by a periodic signal [*0, -1, 0, -1*] to generate the imaginary channel. Using this simple sequence necessitates and effectively imparts another mixing of the signal with a sinusoid signal with frequency exactly *f_s*/4, *2.5 GHz* in this case. This was performed which resulted in a complex signal, whose ESD is shown in Fig. 16.14-G. Figure 16.14-H shows the phase for the quadrature signal which demonstrates that there are now real and imaginary components. Finally, the LPF in Fig. 16.14-D is again applied and the final baseband quadrature signal results. The resulting signal ESD is shown in Fig. 16.14-I. Three of the four signal spectral responses were removed by the final filtering resulting in only retaining *1/8* of the original energy. Again, this does not hurt the SNR because noise would have been filtered also.

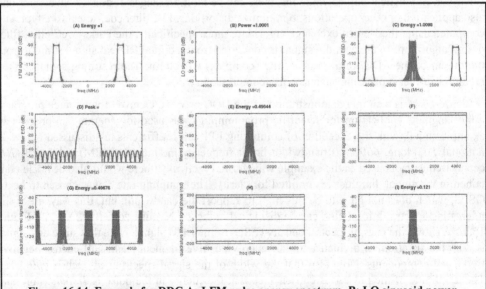

Figure 16.14. Example for DDC A: LFM pulse energy spectrum. B: LO sinusoid power spectrum. C: mixed signal energy spectrum. D: LPF spectrum. E: filtered signal energy spectrum. F: signal phase showing signal is real. G: energy spectrum of signal after quadrature demodulation. H: signal phase showing signal is complex. I: energy spectrum of final signal after second filtering.

The DUC is very similar to the DDC, essentially the inverse. Instead of quadrature demodulation, quadrature modulation is employed; instead of shifting the frequency down, the frequency is shifted up. Interpolation is used in place of decimation. These operations can be accomplished with digital multiplies and digital filters implemented with FIR or CIC. In the end, the signal is converted from a digital baseband IQ waveform to a digital RF real signal, ready for the DAC to convert to an analog RF signal.

16.7. Array Factor versus Huygens-Fresnel Principle

An industry-wide accepted approach to generating very good approximations of the far field antenna patterns for phased array antenna is the so-called array factor. The standard equation for the planar (2-D version of the 1-D linear) array factor assumes constant element separation in both horizontal d_x and vertical d_y directions. It assumes a rectangular sub-array shape with M_x number of elements in each row and N_y elements in each column. It also assumes a rectangular array shape with M_{SAx} number of sub-arrays in each row and N_{SAy} sub-arrays in each column. With beam steering of u_0 in the horizontal direction and v_0 in the vertical direction, $I_m I_n$ is the normalized excitation current at each element, and $k = 2\pi/\lambda$, the array factor is

$$AF = \sum_{n=1}^{N_y N_{SAy}} I_n \left[\sum_{m=1}^{M_x M_{SAx}} I_m e^{j(m-1)(kd_x(u-u_0))} \right] e^{j(n-1)(kd_y(v-v_0))}. \qquad \textbf{Eq. (16.12)}$$

Note that $I_m I_n$ can be used to apply any desired array weighting, real or complex. Assuming isotropic radiators, and with normalized excitation current distribution, the array factor can be used to compute the far field antenna gain ($|AF|^2$) in a given direction, defined by u and v. And the gain of an array with more realistic elements can be computed by multiplying the array factor by the element antenna pattern. The array factor is an approximation and does not account for element-to-element mutual coupling, edge diffraction and other second order pattern effects. As mentioned, the standard array factor assumes equally spaced elements arranged in a rectangular planar array; but the equation could be modified to allow for unequally spaced elements, triangular lattice, nonrectangular shape, and nonplanar arrays. The array factor, by definition, assumes array gain values are to be computed in the far field. In other words, the equation assumes a planar wavefront generated by the array.

An analogous but more general concept to the array factor is the Huygens-Fresnel principle which states that a given wavefront is essentially composed of the super-position of spherical wavefronts emitted by an array of infinitesimal sources, called Huygens' point sources. The use of Maxwell's equations via the field equivalence principle, most appropriately, Schelkunoff's formulation, provides the exact solution, which takes into account the full vector solution. However, the Huygens-Fresnel formulation treats the electric field as a scalar, rather than the more generalized field vector and therefore is approximated,

$$AF = \frac{1}{j\lambda} \iint \gamma E(x, y, 0) \frac{e^{-jkr}}{r} \, dx \, dy \qquad \textbf{Eq. (16.13)}$$

$$\gamma = \frac{1 + \cos\psi}{2} \qquad \textbf{Eq. (16.14)}$$

where E is the scalar component of the electric field complex amplitude for each Huygens point source at the antenna aperture. These electric fields are described for locations $(x, y, 0)$ across the aperture. The z-component is assumed zero, for planar array. The important attribute associated with Eq. (16.13) is that it contains calculations in Cartesian space rather than angle space, which is what Eq. (16.12) array factor uses. This will be taken advantage of in the following discussion. The obliquity factor given in Eq. (16.14) characterizes the angular spread of the radiation from each point source and as can be seen from Eq. (16.14), the directivity of the individual source slowly decreases with ψ. The obliquity factor is often omitted as it is often very close to unity for small ψ angles. The integrals in Eq. (16.13) imply a continuum of Huygens point sources across the antenna. Discretizing Eq. (16.13) around each element of an array, ignoring the obliquity factor, and adapting for planar array with steered beam yields the following equation

$$AF = \sum_{n=1}^{N_y N_{SAy} M_x M_{SAx}} \sum_{m=1}^{} I_n I_m e^{j(m-1)kd_x u_0} e^{j(n-1)kd_y v_0} e^{jkr_{mn}}. \qquad \text{Eq. (16.15)}$$

where

$$r_{mn} = \left| \vec{p} - a_{mn} \right| = \left| \vec{p} - [(m-1)d_x, (n-1)d_y, 0] \right| \qquad \text{Eq. (16.16)}$$

where $\vec{p}$ is the position in Cartesian coordinates for which the gain will be computed and a_{mn} is the location in Cartesian coordinates of each array element. Note that when $\vec{p}$ is in the far field, the array factor of Eq. (16.12) and the discrete Huygens-Fresnel principle of Eq. (16.15) give identical results. However, as the range decreases into the near field, the Huygens-Fresnel equation reveals the effect of spherical wavefronts, rather than the planar wavefront as assumed by the array factor. It is important to note that Eq. (16.15) assumes that the radar is optimizing its beam, for steering in the direction defined by u_0 and v_0, within the far field (Fraunhofer region) by setting element phases accordingly. Eq. (16.15) is a reasonable predictor of the resulting near field antenna pattern behavior while in the Fresnel (radiating) region of the near field. At closer ranges, in the reactive (non-radiating) region, other phenomena, the inductive fields and electrostatic fields, dominate the electric field behavior and the approximation becomes invalid. Finally, it should be noted that Eq. (16.15) has the same limitations as the array factor in regard to the second order pattern effects; and like the array factor in Eq. (16.12), Eq. (16.15) can be modified to allow for unequally spaced elements, triangular lattice, non-rectangular shape, and non-planar arrays.

The use of Eq. (16.15) will now be demonstrated with an example. Suppose the fully populated S-band planar array from above is steered to boresight ($u_0 = v_0 = 0$). This antenna has *100* row elements and *100* column elements. The element spacing is half of the wavelength, and the wavelength is *0.1 m*. An RF receiving device is placed at an elevation angle of zero and at various locations along an azimuthal arc around the radar at a range of *500, 200, 100, 50*, and *20 m*. This device is able to measure the gain of the radar's antenna at these locations. Equation (16.15) can predict the gain that the device will measure at the various locations. The normalized gain prediction is shown in Fig. 16.15. The normalization is with respect to the peak gain of the antenna pattern at *500 m*.

The horizontal and vertical dimension of the radar's square antenna array is $D = 100*0.1/2 = 5\ m$. While there is a continuum of electromagnetic (EM) field behavior as propagation expands throughout the three regions: non-radiating near field, radiating near field, and far field, there are generally accepted transition points between the regions. The transition range in the near field from the non-radiating to radiating region is $0.62\ Sqrt(D^3/\lambda)$, and the transition range between the near field and far field is $2D^2/\lambda$. For this antenna, these two ranges are *22 m* and *500 m*, respectively. The far field *500 m* curve in Fig. 16.15 is essentially the same (indistinguishable) result that would be obtained at any range greater than *500 m*. This is also the same result calculated for the array factor in Eq. (16.12). As the range decreases into the near field, it can be seen how the focus of the antenna pattern diminishes and the beam distorts. Predictions of this sort could help for various analyses including radiation hazard studies.

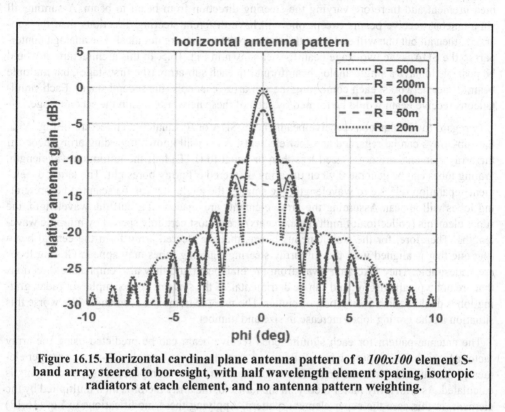

Figure 16.15. Horizontal cardinal plane antenna pattern of a *100x100* element S-band array steered to boresight, with half wavelength element spacing, isotropic radiators at each element, and no antenna pattern weighting.

16.8. Simultaneous Receive Beams

As with many of the other capabilities that are made practical with digital arrays, simultaneous receive beams are also possible with all-analog arrays. In order to do this, multiple analog beamforming networks, one for each receive beam, must be employed. As the frequency increases and the wavelength decreases, this becomes significantly more challenging to engineer. In the digital array, the task of forming simultaneous receive beams is limited only by the ability to efficiently perform digital beam forming. Presumably all simultaneous receive beams would be processed simultaneously in parallel; however, theoretically, the processing could be performed sequentially if the processing is fast enough to support operation. Where, in the analog case, the number of simultaneous beams is limited to the number of beamforming networks, in the digital case, the number is limited by the processing speed and throughput. At the upper bound, for either analog or digital, the number of useful beams is limited to the number of DOF.

For an FDA, there is maximum flexibility for forming high-quality beams. However, as described previously, with current technology, FDA architectures may not be practical yet. The SDA is more likely to be the architecture of choice at the current time. SDA architectures are certainly capable of supporting simultaneous receive beams; however, there are some limitations to be concerned with. In an SDA, since the phase variation profile within the sub-array is performed in the analog domain, this profile is locked-in to the signal at each sub-array. If in the digital beamformer portion of the SDA hybrid beamformer is steered to the same direction that each sub-array is steered, then the beam and antenna pattern will be as desired. However, the purpose of using simultaneous receive beams is to enable larger spatial coverage and angle measurement and therefore varying the steering direction from beam to beam. Assuming all simultaneous receive beams except one will have different steering directions than the sub-arrays, then all but one will end up with antenna patterns that are not ideal. The analog counterpart to the SDA is the two-stage beamformer shown in Fig. 16.5. In this architecture, it would be possible to have a single analog beamformer in each sub-array (the first stage), but multiple beamformer networks, each combining the sub-array channels (the second stage). Each simultaneous receive beam would be formed by each of these networks within the second stage.

In regard to simultaneous receive beams in an SDA or the analog architecture in Fig. 16.5, the sub-arrays can be regarded as super elements. As is well known regarding array theory, if the array elements are not spaced less than or equal to (LTE) half the minimum wavelength, grating lobes can be generated when the array is steered off array boresight. The larger the element separation relative to wavelength, the smaller the angle that can be scanned before grating lobes will appear. Assuming the array elements are spaced LTE half the wavelength, the super elements (collection of multiple elements) are almost certainly spaced by multiple wavelengths. Therefore, for the simultaneous beams that are steered array from the central beam (the one that is aligned with the sub-array steering), grating lobes may appear. Grating lobes are undesirable. They take gain away from the mainbeam and they also emphasize directions that are not typically useful, and can be detrimental, to the system. For example, for radar, grating lobes could be in the direction of clutter. The more extreme the scan angle, the worse this situation is; the grating lobes increase in size and number.

The antenna pattern for each simultaneous receive beam can be predicted using the array factor approach. The approach is as follows, an array factor for a single sub-array, or super element, is calculated. Next the array factor for the entire array composed of super elements is calculated. As with array factor theory, in the far field, the array factor is then multiplied by the element, in this case the super element, pattern. Applying these modifications to Eq. (16.12) yields the following,

$$AF = AF_{SA} \cdot AF_{SE}. \qquad \qquad \text{Eq. (16.17)}$$

$$AF_{SA} = \sum_{n=1}^{N_y} I_n \left[\sum_{m=1}^{M_x} I_m e^{j(m-1)(kd_x(u-u_0))} \right] e^{j(n-1)(kd_y(v-v_0))}. \qquad \text{Eq. (16.18)}$$

$$AF_{SE} = \sum_{n=1}^{N_{SAy}} I_n \left[\sum_{m=1}^{M_{SAx}} I_m e^{j(m-1)(kM_x d_x(u-u_0'))} \right] e^{j(n-1)(kN_y d_y(v-v_0'))}, \qquad \text{Eq. (16.19)}$$

where M_x and N_y are, respectively, the number of elements in a row and in a column for the sub-array. The M_{SAx} and N_{SAy} are, respectively, the number of sub-arrays (super elements) in a row and in a column for the entire array, so that $M_{SAx}M_x$ and $N_{SAy}N_y$ are, respectively, the number of elements in a row and in a column for the entire array. Equation (16.17) permits the phase steering at the element level (u_0, v_0) to be different from the phase steering at the sub-array level (u_0', v_0'). This feature of Eq. (16.17) makes it ideal for predicting simultaneous receive beam patterns where a set of receive beams is typically generated with slight variations in steering to result in a set of beams clustered closely but not aligned to the central beam. Note that when the steering angle at the element level and at the sub-array level are the same, Eq. (16.17) becomes Eq. (16.12).

Figures 16.16 through 16.18 illustrate the reason that simultaneous receive beams are usually clustered closely around the central beam, for which the elements within each sub-array are steered. These figures use the example S-band fully populated *10,000* element, *100* sub-array SDA from above. Each figure shows the central beam super-imposed with the sub-array steered beam. As the steering angle increases, the receive beam antenna pattern becomes less and less desirable. Note that for the illustration, no spatial sidelobe suppression weighting was used in the generation of these antenna patterns. Typically, sidelobe suppression weighting is used; however, it does not help the grating lobe problem.

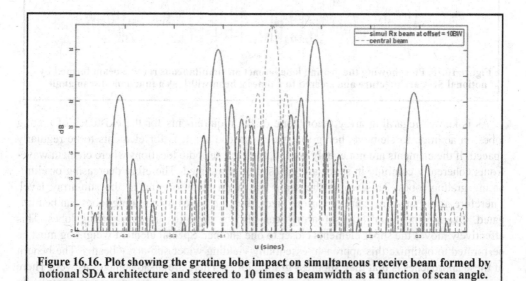

Figure 16.16. Plot showing the grating lobe impact on simultaneous receive beam formed by notional SDA architecture and steered to 10 times a beamwidth as a function of scan angle.

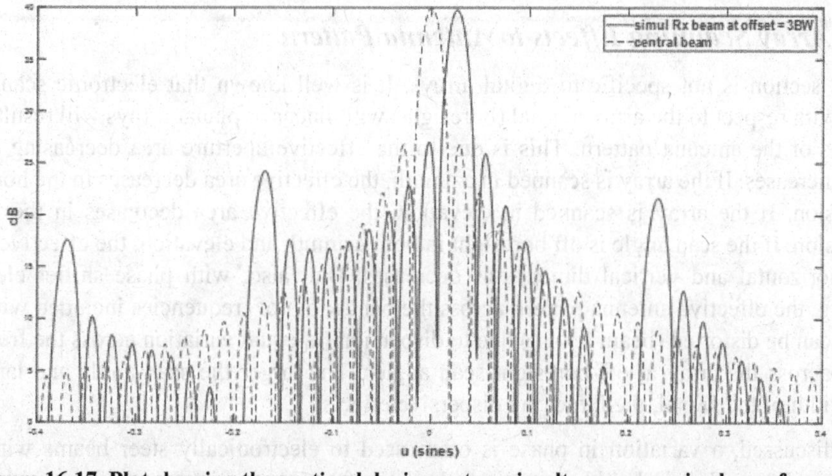

Figure 16.17. Plot showing the grating lobe impact on simultaneous receive beam formed by notional SDA architecture and steered to *3* times a beamwidth as a function of scan angle.

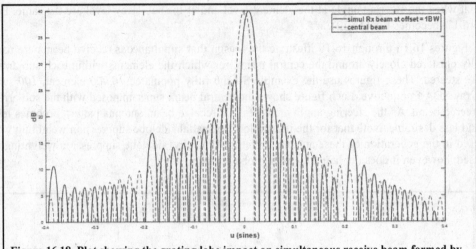

Figure 16.18. Plot showing the grating lobe impact on simultaneous receive beam formed by notional SDA architecture and steered to *1* times a beamwidth as a function of scan angle.

As is known regarding array theory, one of the requirements for the existence of grating lobes, in addition to elements being too widely spaced apart, is for elements to be regularly spaced. If the elements are not evenly spaced, then the periodic locations where element wavefronts coherently combine in space are diffused or eliminated. Therefore decreasing or eliminating grating lobes. This works the same way with beamforming at the sub-array level. Therefore, if the sub-arrays are of various sizes, then the issues with grating lobes can be mitigated. Overlapping equal size sub-arrays can also be done to suppress grating lobes. This effectively moves the super elements closer to one another. Special element weighting must be performed to optimize this approach, essentially yielding wider sub-array beams. The benefit of these approaches is that they suppress grating lobes. There are disadvantages as well. There is an increase in network complexity for analog beamformer, or digital processing complexity for digital beamforming. There is also a reduction in system dynamic range.

16.9. Array Scanning Effects to Antenna Pattern

This section is not specific to digital arrays. It is well known that electronic scanning in angle with respect to the array normal (boresight) with linear or planar arrays will result in distortions of the antenna pattern. This is due to the effective aperture area decreasing as scan angle increases. If the array is scanned in azimuth, the effective area decreases in the horizontal dimension. If the array is scanned in elevation, the effective area decreases in the vertical dimension. If the scan angle is off boresight in both azimuth and elevation, the effective area in both horizontal and vertical dimensions decreases. But, also, with phase shifter electronic steering, the effective antenna pattern across the bandwidth of frequencies included within the signal can be distorted (beam squint) due to dispersion (unequal variation across the frequency band) across the array at off-boresight scan angles. The larger the scan angle and larger the bandwidth of the signal, the larger the dispersive effects.

As discussed, a variation in phase is often used to electronically steer beams with array antennas. For wide bandwidth operation, the beamforming architectures often employ time delay at least at the sub-array level to limit the negative impacts of the dispersive effects resulting from large scan angles with wideband waveforms. For analog beamforming, approaches to applying time delays are to use photonic time shifters (if using optical fiber) or time delay units (TDUs). These devices can be tuned via digital control signal, similar to phase shifters. An all phase shifter array is undistorted as long as the phase changes across the array are within a wavelength. In this condition, the phase shifters are applying correct "time delay." compensation to the actual time delay in the signal across the array elements. As the beam is steered, as long as the signal is narrow band, when there are multiple wavelengths worth of time delay across the array, wrapping phase values (over $360°$) still satisfactorily provide compensation. When the signal is wideband, the wrapping phase cannot simultaneously provide satisfactory compensation across the band of frequencies. For this reason, a true time delay (or group delay) compensation is needed. Since this phenomenon is associated with the size of the array, good performance can be achieved using phase shifters on elements within sub-arrays and TDUs over sub-array signals (see the architecture in Fig. 16.5).

As discussed, for an array antenna that uses phase steering only, at non-zero scan angles, there is frequency steer across the spectrum of the waveform relative to the intended direction. This is referred to as squint angle and it is given by

$$\Delta\theta = \frac{\Delta f}{f_c}\tan\theta_s \qquad\qquad \text{Eq. (16.20)}$$

where f_c is the center frequency, Δf is the frequency offset $(f - f_c)$ from the center frequency, and θ_s is the scan angle. The array bandwidth is defined by industry to be the bandwidth that induces a squint angle equal to half the beamwidth of the antenna. The beamwidth at boresight and beamwidth at a non-zero scan angle can be, respectively, approximated by

$$\theta_{3dB0} = \frac{c}{f\,D} \qquad\qquad \text{Eq. (16.21)}$$

$$\theta_{3dB} = \frac{\theta_{3dB0}}{\cos\theta_s} \qquad\qquad \text{Eq. (16.22)}$$

where D is the antenna dimension and c is the speed of light. Setting Δf to $B/2$ and $\Delta\theta$ to $(\theta_{3dB})/2$, where B is bandwidth, yields the following

$$B = \frac{\theta_{3dB0}\, f_c}{\sin\theta_s} \qquad\qquad \text{Eq. (16.23)}$$

$$B = \frac{c\, f_c}{f\, D\sin\theta_s}. \qquad\qquad \text{Eq. (16.24)}$$

Note that if Eqs. (16.23) and (16.24) are divided by f_c, then they represent the ratio of bandwidth to center frequency. If those results are multiplied by *100*, then we have the percentage bandwidth.

$$P_B = 100\frac{B}{f_c} = 100\frac{\theta_{3dB0}}{\sin\theta_s}\% \qquad\qquad \text{Eq. (16.25)}$$

$$P_B = 100\frac{B}{f_c} = 100\frac{\lambda}{D\sin\theta_s}\%. \qquad\qquad \text{Eq. (16.26)}$$

If D/λ is the electrical dimension of the antenna, Eq. (16.26) indicates that the array bandwidth is inversely proportional to the electrical dimension of the antenna and also inversely proportional to the sine of the scan angle. This is intuitive given the discussion above. Note that there is no limitation on bandwidth when the scan angle is zero. A typical scan angle limit for an array radar, for various reasons such as scan loss and beam broadening, is $60°$. If the scan angle limit is set to $\theta_s = 60°$, then the percentage bandwidth is equal to twice the beamwidth where the beamwidth θ_{3dBdeg} is in units of degrees,

$$P_B = 100\frac{B}{f_c} = 100\frac{\theta_{3dB0}}{\sin 60} \approx 2\theta_{3dB0deg} \%. \qquad \text{Eq. (16.27)}$$

From the example described before, regarding data rate and throughput, *20%* bandwidth was assumed as the maximum. This is a lofty goal; however, according to Eq. (16.27), the size of the array to support $60°$ scan angles would have to be a size consistent with a $10°$ beamwidth. This size beamwidth may be too large for many applications, thus the need to use other than phase steering exclusively.

For digital arrays, wideband dispersion problems essentially go away. For SDA system, rather than using the analog TDUs, the signals out of each sub-array are digitized and time shifted (or phase ramp applied in frequency domain) relative to one another in the digital beam forming process. In an FDA system there are no phase shifters or TDUs. The elemental digital signals are all properly time shifted to steer the beam. Various forms of interpolation are used to apply low error time shifting.

As mentioned earlier, whether the array is analog, digital, or hybrid, it will suffer from antenna pattern distortion with increasing scan angle due to the decrease in effective aperture area. Usually, of most importance is the effect to the mainbeam. The mainbeam widens, or broadens, and loses gain as the scan angle increases. This can be visualized in Fig. 16.19, using the same example *10000* element antenna array. Here a beam is scanned using progressively larger scan angles.

It is clear that the beam widens and the gain decreases. For an array using isotropic radiators, the loss in gain due to scan loss is equal to the cosine of the scan angle (for two-way propagation in radar, it is the square of the cosine of the scan angle). The increase in scan loss is typically larger in actual systems due to the spatial multiplication with the individual radiator antenna pattern. Also note in Fig. 16.19 that the rest of the antenna pattern (the sidelobe structure) is affected by the scan also. This can potentially affect performance in regard to interference through sidelobes.

The beamwidth and gain are of critical importance in some applications. For example, in radar, the probability of detection (PD) across a search volume may not be constant due to the loss in gain. To compensate for this potential loss in PD, radar engineers sometimes design the radar operation to use more overlap in beam positions (recall also that beams are wider) in off boresight regions of the scan volume. Also, other approaches like longer pulse lengths or larger number of pulses could be used to compensate.

Array engineers often use an antenna coordinates system called "sine-space". In this system, the position of a point in space is described relative to the antenna with a value in the u dimension where $u = x/r$ and the v dimension where $v = y/r$, where x and y are the Cartesian horizontal and vertical locations with respect to the antenna boresight, respectively, and r is the range. This coordinate frame maintains the antenna pattern and beam shape, as it is scanned away from boresight. This coordinate system helps engineers analyze spatial coverage by the array. Figure 16.20 shows the same scanned beams from Fig. 16.19 but in sine-pace, clearly showing no beam broadening and antenna pattern distortion in sine-space.

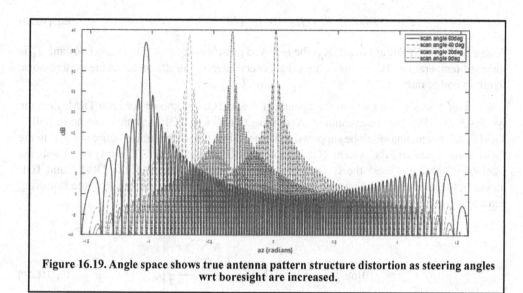

Figure 16.19. Angle space shows true antenna pattern structure distortion as steering angles wrt boresight are increased.

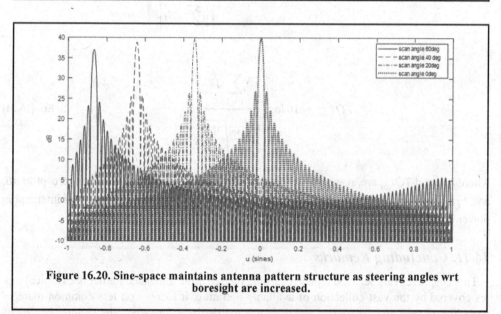

Figure 16.20. Sine-space maintains antenna pattern structure as steering angles wrt boresight are increased.

16.10. Noise Figure and Third Order Intercept in AESA

This section is not specific to digital arrays; but it is specific to AESA. Noise figure (NF) and third order intercept (TOI) are important measures of performance for RF systems. The second order intercept is also sometimes important, especially in homodyne receivers. They characterize in part the sensitivity and dynamic range of the system. The NF, expressed in *dB*, can be used to calculate SNR. The TOI, expressed in *dB* (sometimes *dB* milliwatts, *dBm*), can be used to calculate spur free dynamic range (SFDR).

$$ SNR = 10\log_{10}\left(\frac{E}{kT_0F}\right) $$

Eq. (16.28)

$$SFDR = \frac{2}{3}[TOI - 10\log_{10}(kT_0F)].$$ Eq. (16.29)

Where SNR and SFDR are in dB, E is the received pulse energy, k is Boltzmann constant, T_0 is standard temperature, TOI is the system third order intercept in dB, and F is the system noise figure in power ratio.

When an AESA is used within the system, if F and TOI are known for each TRM, then the system F and TOI can be computed. Assuming that F and TOI are consistent across all N TRMs, and no antenna sidelobe suppression is used, then the system noise figure is equal to the TRM noise figure and the system TOI is equal to N times the TRM TOI. However, if antenna sidelobe weighting is used, the system NF and TOI are still functions of the TRM F and TOI; however, they are also functions of summations over the weighting, as shown in the following equations,

$$F_{tot} = 10\log_{10}\left(\frac{SNR_{out}}{SNR_{in}}\right) = 10\log_{10}\left[\frac{N\displaystyle\sum_{i=1}^{N} g_i F_i}{\left(\displaystyle\sum_{i=1}^{N} \sqrt{g_i}\right)^2}\right].$$ Eq. (16.30)

$$TOI_{tot} = 10\log_{10}\left[\frac{N\displaystyle\sum_{i=1}^{N} \sqrt{g_i}}{\displaystyle\sum_{i=1}^{N} \sqrt{\frac{g_i}{toi_i^2}}}\right].$$ Eq. (16.31)

where F_{tot} and TOI_{tot} are, respectively, the system noise figure and third order intercept in dB, and F_i and toi_i are, respectively, the individual channel noise figure and third order intercept in power ratios.

16.11. Concluding Remarks

This chapter covers selected topics regarding phased array antennas. Rather than typical topics covered by the vast collection of available literature, it focuses on less common material regarding phased array antennas and their use, particularly for radar. The chapter begins by describing how phased array antenna technology has improved over the years and discusses the various types of electronic steering via radio frequency (RF) signal time, phase, and frequency. Also described are various architectures including passive electronically steered array (PESA) and active electronically steered array (AESA). Also discussed are arrays using analog beamforming, digital beamforming, and hybrid (analog and digital) beamforming. Sub-arrays are discussed and how the sub-array level is the natural division between analog and digital beamformers in hybrid systems. For all analog systems, the sub-array level is the natural division between phase steering and time delay steering. The architecture discussion concludes with a basic performance comparison, by way of example.

The chapter emphasizes the modern digital arrays and uses the terms sub-array level digital array (SDA) and fully digital array (FDA). The performance advantages of digital versus analog beamforming are discussed. Along with digitization of beamforming, receiver-exciter (REX) and digital receiver-exciter (DREX) are discussed. Also, direct RF sampling and synthesis is discussed including digital down-conversion (DDC) and digital up-conversion (DUC). This discussion includes performance metrics for analog-to-digital converter (ADC) and digital-to-analog converter (DAC). Direct RF digitization is contrasted with superheterodyne and homodyne systems, and performance advantages are discussed. Software defined radio (SDR) concepts are described as being a trend that is currently followed to enable the maximum flexibility in array antenna utilization. One of the chief challenges with moving digitization toward the array front-end is managing the required data rate and throughput of digital signals. An extensive example using modern network data link technology is provided to underline this area of concern. Another extensive example gives details of a notional DDC process using finite impulse response (FIR) filters. The digital array discussion completes with a description of capabilities that are exclusive to digital arrays, or much more practical to implement in digital arrays.

Array antenna patterns are discussed as the array factor (AF) is given, without derivation. The AF is discussed along with an adaptation of the Huygens-Fresnel principle of superposition of spherical wavefronts to array antenna. It is shown how the Huygens-Fresnel principle, in contrast to the AF, can be used to predict near field antenna patterns while illustrating with plots. Next, grating lobes are discussed in context with using simultaneous receive beams by sub-array antennas, either all-analog or hybrid analog-digital arrays. Plots are shown of grating lobes worsening, as simultaneous receive beams are steered away from the central beam. Techniques for mitigating the grating lobes are briefly described. Finally, off-boresight scanning effects in general are discussed in regard to mainbeam scan loss, beam broadening, and distortion of the sidelobe region, as the scan angle is increased. Plots are provided for this as well.

The chapter completes with a discussion of signal bandwidth limitations to scanning arrays using phase shifters only (array bandwidth) and signal quality performance metrics for the array system, such as signal-to-noise ratio (SNR), spur-free dynamic range (SFDR), noise figure (NF), and third order intercept (TOI). The derivation of AESA system NF and TOI given sidelobe suppression weighting and individual channel NF and TOI are included.

A list of references pertaining to this chapter, found in the bibliography at the back of the book, are as follows: Aliakbarian (2010), Asfour (2013), Budge (2015), Capps (2001), Dan (2011), Debatty (2010), Drabowich (1998), Headland (2018), Herd (2016), Holzman (996), Hu (2014), Kamoda (2011), Kenington (2005), Kester (2008), Kirk (2017), Lamontagne (2012), Lee (1993), Paul (1987), Rengarajan (2000), Sturdivant (2019), Syrjälä (2011), Talisa (2016), Taranovich (2016), Trinkle (undated), Tsui (2004), Unknown Author-1 (2019), Unknown Author-2 (2008), Unknown Author-3 (unknown date), Unknown Author-4 (2019), Ward (1989, 1990), Yu (2011), and Zatman (2001).

Bibliography

[1]   Abramowitz, M., and Stegun, I. A., Editors, *Handbook of Mathematical Functions, with Formulas, Graphs, and Mathematical Tables*, Dover Publications, New York, 1970.

[2]   Aliakbarian H, et al., Analogue versus Digital for Baseband Beam Steerable Array used for LEO Satellite Applications, *IEEE Conference*, May 2010.

[3]   Amditis, A., et el., *Multiple Hypothesis Tracking Implementation*. 2012. ISBN: 9789535102809. URL: *http://www.intechopen.com/books/laser-scannertechnology/ %20multiple- hypothesis- tracking-implementation*

[4]   Asfour, A., et al., Software Defined Radio (SDR) and Direct Digital Synthesizer (DDS) for NMR/MRI Instruments at Low-Field, *www.mdpi.com/journal/sensors*, 2013.

[5]   Balanis, C. A., *Advanced Engineering Electromagnetics*, John Wiley & Sons, 1989.

[6]   Balanis, C. A., *Antenna Theory, Analysis and Design*, 2nd Ed. John Wiley & Sons, 1996.

[7]   Balla, R. J., Belcher, M., Cosby, T., and Jones, G., Radar Requirements for Hit-to-Kill Fire Control, *1994 National Fire Control Symposium*, 2-4 Aug 1994, Boulder, CO.

[8]   Balla, R., Belcher, M., Holder, J., Levett, B., Waldbridge, W., Rickett, B., and Stafford, B., Collaborative ADBF Development for Missile Defense Radar, *11th AIAA Mulinational TMD Conference*, 1-4 June 1998, Monterey, CA.

[9]   Balla, R., Hennings, J., Aalfs, D., Belcher, M., Mitchell, M., and Ringheiser, D., Adaptive Digital Beamforming for Missile Defense Radar, *44th Annual Tri-Service Radar Symposium*, 23-25 June 1998, West Point, N.Y.

[10]   Balla, R., Krasnakevich, J, Burns, J., and Hart, W., THAAD Radar Design for Forward Based Radar, *2003 AIAA Multinational BMD Conference and Exhibition*, 9-12 June 2003, Koyoto, Japan.

[11]   Barkat, M., *Signal Detection and Estimation*, Artech House, Norwood, MA, 1991.

[12]   Barnes, M. A., Nag, S., Payment, T., Covert Situational Awareness with Handheld Ultra-Wideband Short Pulse Radar, *Proc. Society of Photo-optical Instrumentation Engineers (SPIE) 4374, Radar Sensor Technology VI.*, August 22, 2001.

[13]   Bar-Shalom, Y., and Fortmann, T. E., *Tracking and Data Association*. Orlando, FL: Academic Press, 1988.

[14]   Bar-Shalom, Y., Daum, F., and Huang, J., The Probabilistic Data Association Filter. Estimation in the Presence of Measurement Origin Uncertainty, *IEEE Control Systems Magazine,* Dec. 2009.

[15]   Barton, D. K., *Modern Radar System Analysis*, Artech House, Norwood, MA, 1988.

[16]   Bean, B. R., and Abbott, R., Oxygen and Water-Vapor Absorption of Radio Waves in the Atmosphere, *Review Geofisica Pura E Applicata (Milano)* 37:127, 1957.

[17]   Benedict, T., and Bordner, G., Synthesis of an Optimal Set of Radar Track-While-Scan Smoothing Equations, *IRE Transaction on Automatic Control, Ac-7*, July 1962, pp. 27-32.

[18]   Berkowitz, R. S., *Modern Radar: Analysis, Evaluation, and System Design*, John Wiley & Sons, Inc, New York, 1965.

[19]   Beyer, W. H., *CRC Standard Mathematical Tables*, 26th Edition, CRC Press, Boca Raton, FL, 1981.

[20]   Bhalla, R., Ling, H, Moore, J., Andersh, D. J., Lee, S. W., and Hughes, J., 3d scattering center representation of complex targets using the shooting and bouncing ray technique: A review, *IEEE Antennas Propagat. Magazine, vol. 40*, pp. 30–39, October 1998.

[21]   Bhalla, R., and Ling, H., Three-dimensional scattering center extraction using the shooting and bouncing ray technique, *IEEE Trans. Antennas Propagat., vol. 44*, pp. 1445–1453, November 1996.

[22]   Billetter, D. R., *Multifunction Array Radar*, Artech House, Norwood, MA, 1989.

[23]   Blackman, S. S., *Multiple-Target Tracking with Radar Application*, Artech House, Norwood, MA, 1986.

[24]   Blackman, S. S., and Popoli, R., *Design and Analysis of Modern Tracking Systems.* Norwood, MA: Artech House, 1999

[25]   Blake, L. V., *A Guide to Basic Pulse-Radar Maximum Range Calculation. Part-I: Equations, Definitions, and Aids to Calculation*, Naval Res. Lab. Report 5868, 1969.

[26]   Blake, L. V., *Curves of Atmospheric-Absorption Loss for Use in Radar Range Calculation*, NRL Report 5601, March 23, 1961.

[27]   Blake, L. V., *Radar / Radio Tropospheric Absorption and Noise Temperature*, NRL Report Ad-753 197, October 1972. Distributed by the National Technical Information Service (NTIS).

[28]   Blake, L. V., *Radar-Range Performance Analysis*, Lexington Books, Lexington, MA, 1986.

[29]   Boothe, R. R., *A Digital Computer Program for Determining the Performance of an Acquisition Radar through Application of Radar Detection Probability Theory*, U.S. Army Missile Command, Report No. RD-TR-64-2, Redstone Arsenal, Alabama, 1964.

[30]   Boothe, R. R., *The Weibull Distribution Applied to the Ground Clutter Backscatter Coefficient*, U.S. Army Missile Command, Report No. RE-TR-69-15, Redstone Arsenal, Alabama, 1969.

[31]   Bosch Power Tools. *Operating/Safety Instructions: Wall Scanned D-tectTM 150,* 28 August 2018. Retrieved May 14, 2020 from https://fccid.io/TXT-DTECT150A/User-Manual/User-Manual-1474376.iframe.

[32]   Bowman, J. J., Piergiorgio, L. U., and Senior, T. B., *Electromagnetic and Acoustic Scattering by Simple Shapes*, North-Holland Pub. Co, Amsterdam, 1969.

[33]   Brookner, E., Editor, *Aspects of Modern Radar*, Artech House, Norwood, MA, 1988.

[34] Brookner, E., Editor, *Practical Phased Array Antenna System*, Artech House, Norwood, MA, 1991.

[35] Brookner, E., *Radar Technology*, Lexington Books, Lexington, MA, 1996.

[36] Brookner, E., *Tracking and Kalman Filtering Made Easy*, John Wiley & Sons, New York, 1998.

[37] Budge, M., German, S., *Basic Radar Analysis*, Artech House, 2015.

[38] Burdic, W. S., *Radar Signal Analysis*, Prentice Hall, Englewood Cliffs, NJ, 1968.

[39] Capps, C., Near Field or Far Field, www.edn.com, 16 Aug 2001.

[40] Cadzow, J. A., *Discrete-Time Systems, An Introduction with Interdisciplinary Applications*, Prentice Hall, Englewood Cliffs, NJ, 1973.

[41] Carlson, A. B., *Communication Systems, An Introduction to Signals and Noise in Electrical Communication*, 3rd Edition, McGraw-Hill, New York, 1986.

[42] Carpentier, M. H., *Principles of Modern Radar Systems*, Artech House, Norwood, MA, 1988.

[43] Carrara, W.G., Goodman, R.S., Majewski, R.M., *Spotlight Synthetic Aperture Radar Signal Processing Algorithms*, Artech House, 1995.

[44] Chew, W. C., *Waves and Fields in Inhomogeneous Media*, IEEE Press, 1995.

[45] Compton, R. T., *Adaptive Antennas*, Prentice Hall, Englewood Cliffs, NJ, 1988.

[46] Cook, E. C., and Bernfeld, M., *Radar Signals: An Introduction to Theory and Application*, Artech House, Norwood, MA, 1993.

[47] Costas, J. P., A Study of a Class of Detection Waveforms Having Nearly Ideal Range-Doppler Ambiguity Properties, *Proc. IEEE 72*, 1984, pp. 996-1009.

[48] Crispin, J. W. Jr., and Siegel, K. M, Editors, *Methods of Radar Cross-Section Analysis*, Academic Press, New York, 1968.

[49] Curry, G. R., *Radar System Performance Modeling*, Artech House, Norwood, MA, 2001.

[50] Dan, W., et al., Space-Time Adaptive Processing Method at Subarray Level for Broadband Jammer Suppression, *IEEE Proceeding*, 2011.

[51] Davis, R., Fante, R., Crosby, W., and Balla, R., Maximum Likelihood Beamspace Processor, *IEEE International Radar Conference*, May 2000.

[52] Debatty, T., Software defined RADAR a state of the art, IEEE, 2010 *2nd International Workshop on Cognitive Information Processing*, 16 Jun 2010.

[53] DiFranco, J. V. and Rubin, W. L., *Radar Detection*. Artech House, Norwood, MA, 1980.

[54] Demir, V., and Elsherbeni, A. Z., Computational Electromagnetics Simulator Software (CEMS) Package, veysdemir@gamil.com, 2020.

[55] Dillard, R. A., and Dillard, G. M., *Detectability of Spread-Spectrum Signals*, Artech House, Norwood, MA, 1989.

[56] Drabowich, S., et al., *Modern Antennas*, Springer, Boston, MA, 1998.

[57] Edde, B., *Radar Principles, Technology, Applications*, Prentice Hall, Englewood Cliffs, NJ, 1993.

[58] Elsherbeni, A. Z., and Hamid, M., Diffraction by a Wide Double Wedge with Cylindrically Capped Edges, *IEEE Trans. Antennas Propagat., vol. AP-34, no. 7*, pp. 947-951, July 1986.

[59]   Elsherbeni, A. Z., A Comparative Study of Different Two-Dimensional Multiple Scattering Techniques, *Radio Science*, Vol. 29 No. 4, pp., 1023-1033, 1994.

[60]   Elsherbeni, A. Z., and Taylor, C. D. Jr, Interactive Visualization of Two and Three Dimensional Antenna Patterns. Software, Book II, Center on Computer Applications for Electromagnetic Education (CAEME), Sec. 4, Ch.8, 1995.

[61]   Elsherbeni, A. Z., and Ginn, P., Interactive Analysis of Antenna Arrays. Software, Book II, Center on Computer Applications for Electromagnetics Education (CAEME), Sec. 4, Ch. 7, 1995.

[62]   Elsherbeni, A.Z., Christodoulou, C. J., and Gomez-Tagle, J., The Finite Difference Time Domain Technique for Microstrip Antennas, *Handbook of Antennas in Wireless Communications*, Editor: Lal Godara, CRC Press, Boca Raton, FL, Ch. 7, 2001.

[63]   Elsherbeni, A., Inman, M. J., and Riley, C., Antenna Design and Radiation Pattern Visualization, *The 19th Annual Review of Progress in Applied Computational Electromagnetics*, ACES'03, Monterey, CA, March 2003.

[64]   Elsherbeni, A., Demir, V., *The Finite-Difference Time-Domain Method: Electromagnetics with MATLAB Simulations*, SciTech Publishing, Inc., second ed., 2016.

[65]   Ernst, R., Development of a Compact, Highly Integrated 60GHz FMCW Radar for Human Vital Sign Monitoring, Master's thesis, Halmstad University, June 29 2016.

[66]   Federal Communications Commission (FCC), The Office of Engineering and Technology Grants Waivers for Ultra-Wide Band Technologies, July 8 1999.

[67]   Federal Communications Commission (FCC), Revision of Part 15 of the Commission's Rules Regarding Ultra-Wideband Transmission Systems, 2002.

[68]   Fehlner, L. F., *Marcum's and Swerling's Data on Target Detection by a Pulsed Radar*, Johns Hopkins University, Applied Physics Lab. Rpt. # TG451, July 2, 1962, and Rpt. # TG451A, September 1964.

[69]   Fielding, J. E., and Reynolds, G. D., *VCCALC: Vertical Coverage Calculation Software and Users Manual*, Artech House, Norwood, MA, 1988.

[70]   Fluhler, H. U., Coherent Integration of Fill Pulses in Pulse Doppler Type Sensors, *U.S. Patent US10459070B2*, October 29, 2019.

[71]   Fowler, C., Entzminger, J., and Corum, J., Assessment of Ultra-Wideband (UWB) Technology, *IEEE Aerospace and Electronic Systems Magazine, 5(11), 45-49. DOI: 10.1109/ 62.63163*, 2012.

[72]   Gabriel, W. F., Spectral Analysis and Adaptive Array Superresolution Techniques, *Proc. IEEE*, Vol. 68, June 1980, pp. 654-666.

[73]   Gauthier, S., and Chamma, W., Through-the-Wall Surveillance. Retrieved May 14, 2020 from *https://apps.dtic.mil/ dtic/tr/fulltext/u2/a633865.pdf*, 2002.

[74]   Gelb, A., Editor, *Applied Optimal Estimation*, MIT Press, Cambridge, MA, 1974.

[75]   Gibson, W. C., *The Method of Moments in Electromagnetics*, Taylor & Francis/CRC Press, second ed., Boca Rato, FL, 2014.

[76]   Gibson, W. C., Efficient solution of electromagnetic scattering problems using multi-level adaptive cross approximation (MLACA) and LU factorization, *IEEE Trans. Antennas Propagat., vol. 68*, pp. 3815–3823, May 2020.

[77]   Ghiglia, D. C., Pritt, M. D., *Two-Dimensional Phase Unwrapping Theory, Algorithms and Software*, John Wiley & Sons, 1998.

[78] Goldman, S. J., *Phase Noise Analysis in Radar Systems, Using Personal Computers*, John Wiley & Sons, New York, NY, 1989.

[79] Grewal, M. S., and Andrews, A. P., *Kalman Filtering: Theory and Practice Using MATLAB*, 2nd Edition, Wiley & Sons Inc., New York, 2001.

[80] Hall, P. S., and Vetterlein, S. J., Review of radio frequency beamforming techniques for scanned and multiple beam antennas, *Antennas and Propagation IEE Proceedings H - Microwaves*, vol. 137, no. 5, pp. 293-303, Oct. 1990.

[81] Hall, T. D., Duff, G. F., Maciel, L. J, The Space Mission at Kwajalein, *Lincoln Laboratory Journal, 19(2), 48-63*, 2012.

[82] Hamlin, A., Balla, R., Cashion, R., and Tew, N., THAAD Radar Search and Acquisition, *2004 AIAA Multinational BMD Conference and Exhibition*, 19-22 July 2004, Berlin Germany.

[83] Hamming, R. W., *Digital Filters*, 2nd Edition, Prentice Hall, Englewood Cliffs, NJ, 1983.

[84] Hanselman, D., and Littlefield, B., *Mastering MATLAB 5: A Complete Tutorial and Reference*, MATLAB Curriculum Series, Prentice Hall, Englewood Cliffs, NJ, 1998.

[85] Hansen, R. C., *Phased Array Antennas. Vol. 213*. John Wiley & Sons, 2009.

[86] Headland, D., et al., Tutorial: Terahertz beamforming, from concepts to realizations, *APL Photonics*, 06 Feb 2018.

[87] Henin, B. H., Elsherbeni, A. Z., and Al Sharkawy, M. H., Oblique incidence plane wave scattering from an array of circular dielectric cylinders, *Progress in Electromagnetics Research, PIER, vol. 68*, 261-279, 2007.

[88] Herd, J., and Conway, D., The Evolution to Modern Phased Array Architectures, *Proceedings of the IEEE*, Vol. 104, No. 3, p 519-529, Mar 2016.

[89] Hirsch, H. L., and Grove, D. C., *Practical Simulation of Radar Antennas and Radomes*, Artech House, Norwood, MA, 1987.

[90] Holzman, E., Intercept Points of Active Phased Array Antennas, *IEEE MTT-S Digest*, 1996.

[91] Hovanessian, S. A., *Radar System Design and Analysis*, Artech House, Norwood, MA, 1984.

[92] Hu, H., Aspects of the Subarrayed Array Processing for the Phased Array Radar, *Hindawi Publishing Corporation International Journal of Antennas and Propagation*, Volume 2015, Article ID 797352, 25 Nov 2014.

[93] Huang, C. W., Chen, J. B., Elsherbeni, A. Z., and Smith, C. E., FDTD Characterization of Meander Line Antennas for RF and Wireless Communications, *Electromagnetic Wave Monograph Series, Progress in Electromagnetic Research (PIER 24)*, Chief Editor: J. A. Kong, vol. 24, Ch. 9, pp. 185-200, 1999.

[94] Inman, M. J., and Elsherbeni, A.Z., Programming video cards for computational electromagnetics applications, *IEEE Antennas Propagation Magazine*, Vol. 47, Issue 6, pp. 71-78, 2005.

[95] Inman, M. J., Elsherbeni, A. Z., Maloney, G. J., and Baker, B. N., Practical Implementation of a CPML Absorbing Boundary for GPU Accelerated FDTD Technique, *Journal of the Applied Computational Electromagnetics Society (ACES)*, vol. 23, no. 1, March 2008.

[96]   James, D. A., *Radar Homing Guidance for Tactical Missiles*, John Wiley & Sons, New York, 1986.

[97]   Jin, J., *The Finite Element Method in Electromagnetics*, John Wiley & Sons, New York, 2002.

[98]   Kamoda, H., et al., Reduction in quantization lobes due to digital phase shifters for phased array radars, *Proceedings of the Asia-Pacific Microwave Conference 2011*, pp. 1618-1621, Jan 2011.

[99]   Kanter, I., Exact Detection Probability for Partially Correlated Rayleigh Targets, *IEEE Trans, AES-22*, March 1986, pp. 184-196.

[100] Karels, S. N., Viggh, M. E., and Balla, R. J., Techniques to Achieve Ultra-Precise Attitude Determination for Range Baselines, Institute of Navigation (ION), GPS-94 Conference, Sept 1994, Salt Lake City, UT.

[101] Karels, S. N., Viggh, M. E., and Balla, R. J., Extending Narrow-Correlator Technology to P(Y) Code Receivers: Benefits and Issues, ION GPS-94 Conference, Sept 1994, Salt Lake City, UT.

[102] Karels, S. N., Viggh, M. E., and Balla, R. J., Applications of Global Positioning System (GPS) Attitude Determination to Weapon Systems Ballistics, *Joint Services Data Exchange for Guidance, Navigation, and Control*, Nov 1994.

[103] Kay, S. M., *Fundamentals of Statistical Signal Processing: Estimation Theory*, Volume I, Prentice Hall Signal Processing Series, Englewood Cliffs, NJ, 1993.

[104] Kay, S. M., *Fundamentals of Statistical Signal Processing: Detection Theory*, Volume II, Prentice Hall Signal Processing Series, Englewood Cliffs, NJ, 1993.

[105] Keller, J. B., Geometrical Theory of Diffraction, *Journal Opt. Soc. Amer.*, Vol. 52, February 1962, pp. 116-130.

[106] Kenington, P., *RF and Baseband Techniques for Software Defined Radio*, Artech House, 2005.

[107] Kester, W., *Converting Oscillator Phase Noise to Time Jitter, Analog Devices*, MT-008, Oct 2008.

[108] Kilic, O., and Dahlstrom, R., Rotman lens beam formers for Army multifunction RF antenna applications, *IEEE Antennas and Propagation Society International Symposium*, 2005, vol. 2B, pp. 43-46.

[109] Kirk, B., et al., Development of a Software-Defined Radar, *US Army Research Laboratory*, Oct 2017.

[110] Klauder, J. R., Price, A. C., Darlington, S., and Albershiem, W. J., The Theory and Design of Chirp Radars, *The Bell System Technical Journal*, Vol. 39, No. 4, 1960.

[111] Klemm, R., *Principles of Space-Time Adaptive Processing*, 3rd Edition, IET, London, UK, 2006.

[112] Knott, E. F., The relationship between mitzners ILDC and michaelis equivalent currents, *IEEE Trans. Antennas Propagat., vol. 33*, pp. 112–114, January 1985.

[113] Knott, E. F., Shaeffer, J. F., and Tuley, M. T., *Radar Cross Section*, 2nd Edition, Artech House, Norwood, MA, 1993.

[114] Kraus, J. D., and Marhefka, R. J., *Antennas for all Applications*, 3rd Ed, McGraw-Hill, New York, 2002.

[115] L3Harris. (n.d. a). Airfield Radar System (ARS) [Advertisement]. Retrieved from *https://www.harris.com/ solution/airfield-radar-system-ars*.

[116] L3Harris. (n.d. b). Symphony Airfield Radar System (ARS): Complete Solution for Security and Non-Cooperative Surveillance. Retrieved from *https://www.harris.com/ sites/default/files/downloads/ solutions/symphony-airfield-radar-system-ars-es.pdf*.

[117] Lamontagne, G., et al., Direct RF Sampling GNSS Receiver Design and Jitter Analysis, *http://www.SciRP.org/journal/pos*, 2012.

[118] Lathi, B. P., *Signals, Systems and Communication*, New York: John Wiley & Sons, 1965.

[119] Lativa, J., Low-Angle Tracking Using Multifrequency Sampled Aperture Radar, *IEEE-AES Trans.*, Vol. 27, No. 5, September 1991, pp. 797-805.

[120] Lee, S. W., and Mittra, R., Fourier Transform of a Polygonal Shape Function and Its Application in Electromagnetics, *IEEE Trans. Antennas and Propagation*, Vol. 31, January 1983, pp. 99-103.

[121] Lee, J., G/T and Noise Figure of Active Array Antennas, *IEEE Transactions on Antennas and Propagation*, Vol. 41. No. 2, p. 241-244, Feb 1993.

[122] LeFande, R. A., *Attenuation of Microwave Radiation for Paths through the Atmosphere*, NRL Report 6766, Nov. 1968.

[123] Lerro, D., and Bar-Shalom, Y., Tracking with Debiased Consistent Converted Measurements Versus EKF, *IEEE Trans. on Aerospace and Electronic Systems 29.3*, pp. 1015-1022, July 1993.

[124] Levanon, N., *Radar Principles*, John Wiley & Sons, New York, 1988.

[125] Levanon, N., and Mozeson, E., Nullifying ACF Grating Lobes in Stepped-Frequency Train of LFM Pulses, *IEEE-AES Trans.*, Vol. 39, No. 2, April 2003, pp. 694-703.

[126] Levanon, N., and Mozeson, E., *Radar Signals*, John Wiley-Interscience, Hoboken, NJ, 2004.

[127] Lewis, B. L., Kretschmer, Jr., F. F., and Shelton, W. W., *Aspects of Radar Signal Processing*, Artech House, Norwood, MA, 1986.

[128] Li, X. R., and Jikov, V. P., A Survey of Maneuvering Target Tracking. Part IV: Decision-Based Methods, *Proceedings of SPIE Conference on Signal and Data Processing of Small Targets*, Apr. 2002.

[129] Li, J., and Stoica, P., Editors, *MIMO Radar Signal Processing*, John Wiley & Sons Inc., New York, 2009.

[130] Liggins, M. E., Hall, D. J., and Llinas, J., *Handbook of Multisensor Data Fusion. Theory and Practice, 2nd ed.* The Electrical Engineering and Applied Signal Processing Series. Boca Raton, FL, CRC Press, 2009.

[131] Ling, H., Lee, S. W., and Chou, R., Shooting and bouncing rays: calculating the RCS of an arbitrarily shaped cavity, *IEEE Trans. Antennas Propagat.*, vol. 37, pp. 194–205, February 1989.

[132] Long, M. W., *Radar Reflectivity of Land and Sea*, Artech House, Norwood, MA, 1983.

[133] Lothes, R. N., Szymanski, M. B., and Wiley, R. G., *Radar Vulnerability to Jamming*, Artech House, Norwood, MA, 1990.

[134] McFarland, J. The RN 2 multiple beam array family and the beam forming matrix, *1979 Antennas and Propagation Society International Symposium. Vol. 17*. IEEE, 1979.

[135] Maffett, A. L., *Topics for a Statistical Description of Radar Cross Section*, John Wiley & Sons, New York, 1989.

[136] Mahafza, B. R., *Introduction to Radar Analysis*, CRC Press, Boca Raton, FL, 1998.

[137] Mahafza, B. R., *Radar Systems Analysis and Design Using MATLAB*, 2nd Edition, Taylor & Francis, Boca Raton, FL, 2005.

[138] Mahafza, B. R., *Radar Signal Analysis and Signal Processing Using MATLAB*, Chapman & Hall/CRC, Boca Raton, FL, 2008.

[139] Mahafza, B. R., and Polge, R. J., Multiple Target Detection Through DFT Processing in a Sequential Mode Operation of Real Two-Dimensional Arrays, *Proc. of the IEEE Southeast Conf. '90*, New Orleans, LA, April 1990, pp. 168-170.

[140] Mahafza, B. R., Heifner, L.A., and Gracchi, V. C., Multitarget Detection Using Synthetic Sampled Aperture Radars (SSAMAR), *IEEE-AES Trans.*, Vol. 31, No. 3, July 1995, pp. 1127-1132.

[141] Mahafza, B. R., and Sajjadi, M., Three-Dimensional SAR Imaging Using a Linear Array in Transverse Motion, *IEEE-AES Trans.*, Vol. 32, No. 1, January 1996, pp. 499-510.

[142] Mailloux, R. J., *Phased Array Antenna Handbook*, Artech House, 2005.

[143] Marchand, P., *Graphics and GUIs with MATLAB*, 2nd Edition, CRC Press, Boca Raton, FL, 1999.

[144] Marcum, J. I., A Statistical Theory of Target Detection by Pulsed Radar, Mathematical Appendix, *IRE Trans.*, Vol. IT-6, April 1960, pp. 259-267.

[145] Medgyesi-Mitschang, L. N., and Putnam, J. M., Electromagnetic Scattering from Axially Inhomogenous Bodies of Revolution, *IEEE Trans. Antennas and Propagation.*, Vol. 32, August 1984, pp. 797-806.

[146] Meeks, M. L., *Radar Propagation at Low Altitudes*, Artech House, Norwood, MA, 1982.

[147] Melsa, J. L., and Cohn, D. L., *Decision and Estimation Theory*, McGraw-Hill, New York, 1978.

[148] Mensa, D. L., *High Resolution Radar Imaging*, Artech House, Norwood, MA, 1984.

[149] Metzen, P. L., Globalstar satellite phased array antennas, *Proceedings 2000 IEEE International Conference on Phased Array Systems and Technology* (Cat. No. 00TH8510). IEEE, 2000.

[150] Meyer, D. P., and Mayer, H. A., *Radar Target Detection: Handbook of Theory and Practice*, Academic Press, New York, 1973.

[151] Mie, G., Beitrage zur optic truber medien, speziell kolloidaler metallosungen, *Annalen der Physik*, 25(330), pp. 377-445, 1908.

[152] Mississippi Department of Transportation (MDOT). (2006, August). Ground Penetrating Radar Study, Phase I Technology Review and Evaluation. Final Report, FHWA/MS-DOT-RD-06-182. Retrieved June 26, 2020 from *https://rosap.ntl.bts.gov*.

[153] Monzingo, R. A., and Miller, T. W., *Introduction to Adaptive Arrays*, John Wiley & Sons, New York, 1980.

[154] Morchin, W., *Radar Engineer's Sourcebook*, Artech House, Norwood, MA, 1993.

[155] Morris, G. V., *Airborne Pulsed Doppler Radar*, Artech House, Norwood, MA, 1988.

[156] Mostly Missile Defense. (2012, May 17). Space Surveillance Sensors: ALCOR Radar (May 17, 2012). Retrieved May 16, 2020 from *https://mostlymissiledefense.com/2012/05/17/space-surveillance-sensors-alcor-radar-may-17-2012*.

[157] Nathanson, F. E., *Radar Design Principles*, 2nd Edition, McGraw-Hill, New York, 1991.

[158] Navarro, Jr., A. M., *General Properties of Alpha Beta and Alpha Beta Gamma Tracking Filters*, Physics Laboratory of the National Defense Research Organization TNO, Report PHL 1977-92, January 1977.

[159] Neu, T., RF-sampling tool kit for system designers, *Texas Instruments Analog Design Journal*, 2018.

[160] North, D. O., An Analysis of the Factors Which Determine Signal/Noise Discrimination in Pulsed Carrier Systems, *Proc. IEEE 51*, No. 7, July 1963, pp. 1015-1027.

[161] Oppenheim, A. V., and Schafer, R. W., *Discrete-Time Signal Processing*, Prentice Hall, Englewood Cliffs, NJ, 1989.

[162] Oppenheim, A. V., Willsky, A. S., and Young, I. T., *Signals and Systems*, Prentice Hall, Englewood Cliffs, NJ, 1983.

[163] Orfanidis, S. J., *Optimum Signal Processing, an Introduction*, 2nd Edition, McGraw-Hill, New York, 1988.

[164] Ohtani, T., Kanai, Y., and Kantartzis, N. V., Efficient RCS Evaluation for the Conventional TF/SF Separation Model in the FDTD Technique, *Applied Computational Electromagnetics Society (ACES) Conference*, Miami, 2019.

[165] Papoulis, A., *Probability, Random Variables, and Stochastic Processes*, 2nd Edition, McGraw-Hill, New York, 1984.

[166] Parl, S. A., New Method of Calculating the Generalized Q Function, *IEEE Trans. Information Theory*, Vol. IT-26, No. 1, January 1980, pp. 121-124.

[167] Paul, C., Nasar, S., *Introduction to Electromagnetic Fields*, 2nd Ed., McGraw-Hill, 1987.

[168] Peebles, P. Z., Jr., *Probability, Random Variables, and Random Signal Principles*, McGraw-Hill, New York, 1987.

[169] Peebles, P. Z., Jr., *Radar Principles*, John Wiley & Sons, New York, 1998.

[170] Pettit, R. H., *ECM and ECCM Techniques for Digital Communication Systems*, Lifetime Learning Publications, New York, 1982.

[171] Polge, R. J., Mahafza, B. R., and Kim, J. G., *Extension and Updating of the Computer Simulation of Range Relative Doppler Processing for MM Wave Seekers*, Interim Technical Report, Vol. I, prepared for the U.S. Army Missile Command, Redstone Arsenal, Alabama, January 1989.

[172] Polge, R. J., Mahafza, B. R., and Kim, J. G., Multiple Target Detection through DFT Processing in a Sequential Mode Operation of Real or Synthetic Arrays, *IEEE 21st Southeastern Symposium on System Theory*, Tallahassee, FL, 1989, pp. 264-267.

[173] Poularikas, A., *Signals and Systems Primer with MATLAB*, Taylor & Francis, Boca Raton, FL, 2007.

[174] Poularikas, A., and Ramadan, Z. M., *Adaptive Filtering Primer with MATLAB*, Taylor & Francis, Boca Raton, FL, 2006.

[175] Poularikas, A., and Seely, S., *Signals and Systems*, PWS Publishers, Boston, MA, 1984.

[176] Putnam, J. N., and Gerdera, M. B., CARLOS TM: A General-Purpose Three-Dimensional Method of Moments Scattering Code, *IEEE Trans. Antennas and Propagation*, Vol. 35, April 1993, pp. 69-71.

[177] Rappaport, C. M., and Zaghloul, A. I., Multifocal bootlace lens design concepts: a review, *IEEE Antennas and Propagation Society International Symposium*, 2005, vol. 2B, pp. 39-42.

[178] Reed, H. R. and Russell, C. M., *Ultra High Frequency Propagation*, Boston Technical Publishers, Inc., Lexington, MA, 1964.

[179] Reid, D. B., An Algorithm for Tracking Multiple Targets, *IEEE Trans. on Automatic Control AC-24.6*, pp. 843-854, Dec. 1979.

[180] Rengarajan, S., The Field Equivalence Principle: Illustration of the Establisment or the Non-Intuitive Null Fields, *IEEE Antennas and Propagation Magazine*, Vol. 42, No. 4, Aug 2000.

[181] Resnick, J. B., *High Resolution Waveforms Suitable for a Multiple Target Environment*, MS thesis, MIT, Cambridge, MA, June 1962.

[182] Richards, M. A., *Fundamentals of Radar Signal Processing*, McGraw-Hill, New York, 2005.

[183] Richards, M. A., Scheer, J. A., and Holm, W. A., *Principles of Modern Radar. Basic Principles,* SciTech Publishing, Raleigh, NC, 2010.

[184] Rihaczek, A. W., *Principles of High Resolution Radars*, McGraw-Hill, New York, 1969.

[185] Robertson, G. H., Operating Characteristics for a Linear Detector of CW Signals in Narrow-Band Gaussian Noise, *Bell Sys. Tech. Journal*, Vol. 46 April 1967, pp. 755-774.

[186] Robertson et al.., A High Frame Rate, 340 GHz Imaging Radar for Security, *2018 IEEE Radar Conference. DOI: 10.1109/RADAR.2018.8378530*, 2018.

[187] Rosenbaum, B., *A Programmed Mathematical Model to Simulate the Bending of Radio Waves in the Atmospheric Propagation*, Goddard Space Flight Center Report X-551-68-367, Greenbelt, Maryland, 1968.

[188] Rotman, W., and Turner, R. Wide-angle microwave lens for line source applications, *IEEE Trans. Antennas Propag.*, vol. 11, no. 6, pp. 623-632, Nov. 1963.

[189] Ross, R. A., Radar Cross Section of Rectangular Flat Plate as a Function of Aspect Angle, *IEEE Trans*. AP-14, 1966, p. 320.

[190] Ruck, G. T., Barrick, D. E., Stuart, W. D., and Krichbaum, C. K., *Radar Cross Section Handbook*, Volume 1, Plenum Press, New York, 1970.

[191] Ruck, G. T., Barrick, D. E., Stuart, W. D., and Krichbaum, C. K., *Radar Cross Section Handbook*, Volume 2, Plenum Press, New York, 1970.

[192] Rulf, B., and Robertshaw, G. A., *Understanding Antennas for Radar, Communications, and Avionics*, Van Nostrand Reinhold, 1987.

[193] Ryan, COL W., Balla, R. J., and Lopez, F., Ground Based Radar Electronic Warfare Validation Test Program, *38th JEWC*, Norfolk, VA, May 1993.

[194] Ryan, COL W., Balla, R. J., and Cornwell, R. K., TMD-GBR Anti-Radiation Missile Countermeasures Program, *39th JEWC*, Colorado Springs, CO, May 1994.

[195] Ryan, COL W., Smith, B. J., and Balla, R. J., GBR ARM 6-DOF Simulation and Countermeasures Development, *39th Joint Electronic Warfare Conference (JEWC)*, Colorado Springs, CO, May 1994.

[196] Saarenketo, T., *Electrical Properties of Road Materials and Subgrade Soils and the Use of Ground Penetrating Radar in Traffic Infrastructure Surveys*, academic dissertation, University of Oulu, Finland, November 11, 2006.

[197] Sandora, J. S., *Design of the ElectroScience Lab's 0.4- 100 GHz Compact Range Radar System*, Master's thesis, The Ohio State University, 2005.

[198] Sanyal, P. K., Davis, R. M., and Balla, R. J., Spoofing Monopulse Seekers with Adaptive Phase Distortion, 1998 Fire Control Symposium, 3-6 Aug 1998, San Diego, CA.

[199] Scanlan, M. J., Editor, *Modern Radar Techniques*, Macmillan, New York, 1987.

[200] Shaeffer, J., Direct solve of electrically large integral equations for problem sizes to 1 M unknowns, *IEEE Trans. Antennas Propagation, vol. 56*, pp. 2306–2313, August 2008.

[201] Scheer, J. A., and Kurtz, J. L., Editor, *Coherent Radar Performance Estimation*, Artech House, Norwood, MA, 1993.

[202] Schelher, D. C., *MTI and Pulsed Doppler Radar with MATLAB*, 2nd Edition, Artech House, Norwood, MA, 2010.

[203] Shanmugan, K. S., and Breipohl, A. M., *Random Signals: Detection, Estimation and Data Analysis*, John Wiley & Sons, New York, 1988.

[204] Shatz, M. P., and Polychronopoulos, G. H., *An Algorithm for Evaluation of Radar Propagation in the Spherical Earth Diffraction Region*. IEEE Transactions on Antenna and Propagation, Vol. 38, No.8, August 1990, pp. 1249-1252.

[205] Sherman, S. M., *Monopulse Principles and Techniques*, Artech House, Norwood, MA, 2006.

[206] Singer, R. A., Estimating Optimal Tracking Filter Performance for Manned Maneuvering Targets, *IEEE Transaction on Aerospace and Electronics, AES-5*, July 1970, pp. 473-483.

[207] Shervin, C. W., Ruina, J., Rawcliffe, R. E., Some Early Developments in Synthetic Aperture Radar Systems, *IRE Trans. Military Electronics, Vo. MIL-6, No. 2*, April 1962, pp. 111-115.

[208] Skillman, W. A., *DETPROB: Probability of Detection Calculation Software and User's Manual*, Artech House, Norwood, MA, 1991.

[209] Skolnik, M. I., *Introduction to Radar Systems*, McGraw-Hill, New York, 1982.

[210] Skolnik, M. I., Editor, *Radar Handbook*, 2nd Edition, McGraw-Hill, New York, 1990.

[211] Smith, B. J., Garner, W., and Cannon, R., Precision Dynamic SAR Testbed for Tactical Missiles, *2004 IEEE Aerospace Conference*, 2004.

[212] Song, J. M., Lu, C. C., Chew, W. C., and Lee, S. W., Fast Illinois Solver Code (FISC), *IEEE Trans. Antennas and Propagation*, Vol. 40, June 1998, pp. 27-34.

[213] Song, J. M., Lu, C. C., and Chew, W. C., Multilevel fast multipole algorithm for electromagnetic scattering by large complex objects, *IEEE Trans. Antennas Propagat., vol. 45*, pp. 1488–1493, October 1997.

[214] Soumekh, M., *Synthetic Aperture Radar Signal Processing*, John Wiley & Sons, 1999.

[215] Staal Technologies. Robotics. Retrieved from *https://www.staaltechnologies.com/project/chemicals*, June 14 2020.

[216] Stambaugh, J. J., Lee, R. K., & Cantrell, W. H., The 4 GHz Bandwidth Millimeter-Wave Radar, *Lincoln Laboratory Journal, 19(2), 64-76*, 2012.

[217] Stearns, S. D., and David, R. A., *Signal Processing Algorithms*, Prentice Hall, Englewood Cliffs, NJ, 1988.

[218] Stimson, G. W., *Introduction to Airborne Radar*, Hughes Aircraft Company, El Segundo, CA, 1983.

[219] Stratton, J. A., *Electromagnetic Theory*, McGraw-Hill, New York, 1941.

[220] Stremler, F. G., *Introduction to Communication Systems*, 3rd Edition, Addison-Wesley, New York, 1990.

[221] Sturdivant, R., et al., *System Engineering of Phased Arrays*, Artech House, 2019.

[222] Stutzman, G. E., Estimating Directivity and Gain of Antennas, *IEEE Antennas and Propagation Magazine 40*, August 1998, pp. 7-11.

[223] Stutzman, W. L., *Antenna Theory and Design*, 2nd Ed. John Wiley & Sons, New York, 1997.

[224] Swerling, P., Probability of Detection for Fluctuating Targets, *IRE Transaction on Information Theory*, Vol. IT-6, April 1960, pp. 269-308.

[225] Syrjälä, V., et al., Design Considerations for Direct RF Sampling Receiver in GNSS Environment, Tampere University of Technology Institute of Communications Engineering, Finland, 2011.

[226] Taflove, A., *Computational Electromagnetics: The Finite-Difference Time-Domain Method*, Artech House, Norwood, MA, 1995.

[227] Talisa S, Benefits of Digital Phased Array Radars, *Proceedings of the IEEE,* Vol. 104, No. 3, p 530-543, March 2016.

[228] Taranovich S., A Technical View into Modern Mil/Aero Radar Systems, *www.edn.com*, 05 Jan 2016.

[229] The Ohio State University (OSU). (n.d.). Compact Range. Retrieved June 16, 2020 from https://electroscience.osu.edu/facilities/compact-range.

[230] Trinkle, M., SNR Considerations for RF Sampling Receivers for Phased Array Radars, University of Adelaide, Australia, undated.

[231] Trunck, G. V., *Automatic Detection, Tracking, and Senor Integration*, NRL Report 9110, June 1988.

[232] Tsao, J., and Steinberg, B., Reduction of sidelobe and speckle artifacts in microwave imaging: The CLEAN technique, *IEEE Trans. Antennas Propagat., vol. 36*, pp. 543–556, April 1988.

[233] Tsui J, *Digital Techniques for Wideband Receivers*, 2nd Ed., *SciTech Publishing*, 2004.

[234] Van Trees, H. L., *Detection, Estimation, and Modeling Theory*, Part I, Wiley & Sons, Inc., New York, 2001.

[235] Van Trees, H. L., *Detection, Estimation, and Modeling Theory*, Part III, Wiley & Sons, New York, 2001.

[236] Van Trees, H. L., *Optimum Array Processing*, Part IV of *Detection, Estimation, and Modeling Theory*, Wiley & Sons, New York, 2002.

[237] Tzannes, N. S., *Communication and Radar Systems*, Prentice Hall, Englewood Cliffs, NJ, 1985.

[238] Ulaby, F. T, Dobson, M. C., *Handbook of Radar Scattering Statistics for Terrain*, Artech House, Norwood, MA, 1989

[239] Unknown Author-1, Advantages of Direct RF Sampling Architectures, ROM Industries Corp., 05 Mar 2019.

[240] Unknown Author-2, Digital Up/Down Converter (DDC/DUC) for WiMAX Systems, Lattice Semiconductor Corp, May 2008.

[241] Unknown Author-3, Texas Instruments Introduction to Direct RF Sampling, version 1p0, RF Sampling Training Workshop Lecture Series.

[242] Unknown Author-4, Understanding Key Parameters for RF-Sampling Data Converters, www.xilinx.com, 20 Feb 2019.

[243] Urkowitz, H., *Decision and Detection Theory*, Unpublished Lecture Notes, Lockheed Martin Co., Moorestown, NJ, undated.

[244] Urkowtiz, H., *Signal Theory and Random Processes*, Artech House, Norwood, MA, 1983.

[245] Van Vleck, J. H., The Absorption of Microwaves by Oxygen, *Physical Review*, Vol. 71, 1947a.

[246] Van Vleck, J. H., The Absorption of Microwaves by Uncondensed Water Vapor, *Physical Review*, Vol. 71, 1947b.

[247] Vaughn, C. R., Birds and Insects as Radar Targets: A Review, *Proc. IEEE*, Vol. 73, No. 2, February 1985, pp. 205-227.

[248] Veysel, D., and Elsherbeni, A., Computational Electromagntics Simulator (CEMS), *software package version 4, veysdemir@gmail.com*, February 2020.

[249] Wait, J. R., Scattering of a plane wave from a circular dielectric cylinder at oblique incidence, *Can. J. Phys.*, Vol. 33, 189-195, 1955.

[250] Walker, J. L., *Range-Doppler Imaging of Rotating Objects*, Ph.D. dissertation, University of Michigan, 1974.

[251] Ward, J., Compton, R., Performance analysis of large adaptive sidelobe canceler arrays with reused elements, ElectroScience Laboratory Ohio State University, June 1989.

[252] Ward, J., Compton, R., Sidelobe Level Performance of Adaptive Sidelobe Canceler Arrays with Element Reuse, *IEEE Transactions on Antennas and Propagation*, Vol. 38. No. 10, Oct 1990.

[253] Wehner, D. R., *High Resolution Radar*, Artech House, Norwood, MA, 1987.

[254] Weiner, M. M., Editor, *Adaptive Antennas and Receivers*, Taylor & Francis, Boca Raton, FL, 2006.

[255] Weiss, A. J., Elsherbeni, A. Z., Demir, V., and Hadi, M. F., Using MATLAB's Parallel Processing Toolbox for Multi-CPU and multi-GPU Accelerated FDTD Simulations, Applied Computational Electromagnetics Society (ACES) Journal, vol. 34, no. 5, pp. 283-288, May 2019.

[256] Weissberger, M. A., An Initial Critical Summary of Models for Predicting the Attenuation of Radio Waves by Foliage. Electromagnetic Compatibility Analysis Center, Annapolis, Maryland. Retrieved from *https://apps.dtic.mil/dtic*, July 1982.

[257] White, J. E., Mueller, D. D., and Bate, R. R., *Fundamentals of Astrodynamics*, Dover Publications, New York, 1971.

[258] Wolff, E. A., *Antenna Analysis*, Artech House, Norwood, MA, 1988.

[259] Yee, K., Numerical solution of initial boundary value problems involving Maxwell's equations in isotropic media, *IEEE Transactions on Antennas and Propagation, vol. 14, no. 3*, pp. 302-307, 1966.

[260] Yu, Y., et al., Design and Simulation of a Fully Digitized GNSS Receiver Front-End, School of Electronic and Information Engineering, Beihang University, Beijing, China, 24 May 2011.

[261] Zarchan, P., and Muso, H., *Fundamentals of Kalman Filtering. A Practical Approach. 4th ed.* Progress in Aeronautics and Astronautics, American Institute of Aeronautics and Astronautics, 2013.

[262] Zatman, M., Digitization Requirements for Digital Radar Arrays, *IEEE Magazine*, 2001.

[263] ZF. Radarsystem AC 1000 T. Advertisement. Retrieved from *https://www.zf.com/prod-ucts/en/lcv/ products_51202.html*, May 16 2020.

[264] Ziemer, R. E., and Tranter, W. H., *Principles of Communications, Systems, Modulation, and Noise,* 2nd Edition, Houghton Mifflin, Boston, MA, 1985.

[265] Zierler, N., *Several Binary-Sequence Generators*, MIT Technical Report No. 95, Sept. 1955.

[266] Zhao, K., Vouvakis, M. N., and Lee, J. F., The adaptive cross approximation algorithm for accelerated method of moments computations of EMC problems, *IEEE Trans. Elec-tromagn. Compat., vol. 47*, pp. 763–773, Nov 2005.

Index

Printed in the United States
by Baker & Taylor Publisher Services